Serious Daring

WORDPLAY

foresight

imagination

CHALLENGE

JOY solitude

craft hilarity

discipline MYSTERY

inspiration

timing CLARITY

courage

Serious Daring

Creative Writing in Four Genres

Lisa Roney
University of Central Florida

New York   Oxford
Oxford University Press

Oxford University Press is a department of the University of Oxford.
It furthers the University's objective of excellence in research, scholarship,
and education by publishing worldwide.

Oxford   New York
Auckland   Cape Town   Dar es Salaam   Hong Kong   Karachi
Kuala Lumpur   Madrid   Melbourne   Mexico City   Nairobi
New Delhi   Shanghai   Taipei   Toronto

With offices in
Argentina   Austria   Brazil   Chile   Czech Republic   France   Greece
Guatemala   Hungary   Italy   Japan   Poland   Portugal   Singapore
South Korea   Switzerland   Thailand   Turkey   Ukraine   Vietnam

Published in the United States of America by
Oxford University Press
198 Madison Avenue, New York, NY 10016
http://www.oup.com

Library of Congress Cataloging-in-Publication Data
Roney, Lisa, author.
   Serious daring : creative writing in four genres / Lisa Roney, University
of Central Florida.
      pages cm
   ISBN 978-0-19-994162-9 (acid-free paper)
   1. Creative writing. 2. Authorship. I. Title.
   PN189.R66 2015
   808.02--dc23
                                                  2014009691

Printing number: 9 8 7 6 5 4 3 2 1

Printed in the United States of America
on acid-free paper

Contents in Brief

Contents

Preface

TO INSTRUCTORS

Serious Daring: Creative Writing in Four Genres features a flexible organization allowing for various course structures. It also combines a thorough and rigorous approach to craft with increased attention to close reading skills; an anthology that combines classic, contemporary, and newer readings; and an expansion beyond the how-to aspects of writing to contextual and practical issues.

Every term, when instructors of Creative Writing step into our classrooms, a world of surprises awaits us. This has always been true of the Creative Writing workshop—a place where individuality reigns and the approach is truly student-centered. However, over the past couple of decades, the study of Creative Writing has become increasingly popular, and we have seen our class sizes grow, our students become more diverse in experience and ability, the publishing world shift and splinter to both daunting and exciting effect, and the traditional modes of reading and writing compete and merge with other media. I sat down to compose *Serious Daring: Creative Writing in Four Genres* in response to these phenomena, and I hope that it will provide much-needed tools for instructors and students to embrace these new challenges, as well as support the enduring power of the craft-based workshop.

It takes serious daring for our students to do their best, impassioned writing, sometimes even for them to admit an interest in expressing themselves. It takes serious daring for us to try to guide our students through the vast, elusive task of producing good writing. And it takes plain old nerve to try to incorporate in one textbook the plethora of practical tips that writers have gleaned and the profound questions that they have wrestled with over the decades. Creative writers are as individualistic in how they teach as in how they write. No one pedagogy prevails—we don't even agree on exactly which genres should be included in a multi-genre introductory course, much less on whether we should separate the study of each genre and if so in what order they should come. I welcome this iconoclastic streak in my fellow writers and teachers, and acknowledge that each individual will find parts of this book more relevant than others. No doubt, you may want to teach the chapters in a far different order than they are given in the table of contents. However, unlike the other textbooks on the market—each one of which excels in its own way—this one is designed with variation in mind. Instead of locking you into a particular pattern for your course, *Serious Daring* allows you to choose your own structure and try different ones at different times, in other words, to be innovative with your own courses.

Another goal of *Serious Daring* is to add to the introductory material that will be familiar to experienced instructors by modeling and encouraging a sustained creative practice for students long after they have finished the introductory course. I hope to prepare students for the realities of a writer's life by acknowledging social and practical issues around writing, something that few courses and fewer texts address. I have encountered two extremes in my introductory students: those who believe it's completely unrealistic to hope of being a writer and those who think that they will easily become famous authors. Because I have seen both kinds of students in introductory courses, I believe we should raise such issues early. Whether they go on to become MFA graduates and published authors or write and read primarily for their personal pleasure, we owe them the guidance to continue and ourselves the practical honesty that makes that possible.

Key Features of the Book
Flexibility.

Serious Daring allows a syllabus to be structured either along craft elements with mixed-genre discussions or genre by genre. Each **Craft Matters** chapter except the first focuses examples on one genre, and the book can easily be taught one genre at a time. However, each chapter also acknowledges the use of that element in other genres, keeping the book from being divided into completely rigid and separate sections. Although readings are suggested that will complement the content of each chapter, and those works are often used as examples in those chapters, the readings themselves are included in the separate **Anthology** section to allow instructors to choose which and how many readings to assign at any given time. In addition, the chapters in the **Writing Life** section may be taught at different points in the semester. **Chapter 13: Reading as a Writer**, for instance, provides clear explication of two sample readings to demonstrate techniques students might use with other work, and I would recommend teaching it early in the semester. **Chapter 15: The Literary vs. Genre Debate** might be taught as part of a fiction or poetry unit.

Practicality.

Whether our students take an introductory Creative Writing course to fulfill a general education requirement or because they are already dedicated to pursuing writing long term, they usually lack a vocabulary for the "usefulness" of the course of study or realistic prospects for where it might take them. Both types of students benefit from some meta-discourse about what it means to be a writer, what skills the workshop and creative process foster within and beyond themselves, and the larger context of a writing life, whether amateur or professional. The **Guidepost** sidebars (see below) allow for occasional reflection on these matters, and **Chapter 16: The Writing Life** provides opportunity for lively discussion on how students might continue to benefit from this course of study and other writers' experiences.

Comprehensiveness.

As many of our courses move to the online arena or become populated by increasing numbers of students, instructors have the need for a textbook with a thorough approach and a narrative voice that supports the idea of the teacher as a fellow writer. Thorough explanations both allow for rigor (deeper understanding for students with some previous knowledge) and remediation (basic and complete coverage of issues for students new to writing creatively). The craft chapters, for instance, often include tables that clarify definitions and techniques. I also occasionally use a personal anecdote in order to emphasize that instructors are also writers and that we participate together in a community of readers and writers.

Organization

The book is arranged into four sections: **Craft Matters**, **Writing Life Matters**, **Anthology**, and **Appendices**.

The **Craft Matters** section provides discussions of the elements of craft and discussions of examples of how contemporary masters have managed those elements in their own work. Each chapter also contains numerous **Pathways** exercises to spur and refine student writing ideas and a **Guidepost** sidebar that shares general skills and traits that the field of Creative Writing can foster. Within this section, five short **Destination** mini-chapters are intermittently placed to focus briefly on the major features of each genre and provide students with tip lists for their own work in those genres. The **Craft Matters** section may be taught genre by genre, but if you choose to focus on each element and only then ask students to focus on particular genres, that framework is easily accommodated. Or if you include some genres and not others, the chapters can be assigned with a different unit. You could teach **Chapter 11: Action and Dialogue** easily as part of a fiction unit, for example. Instructors may easily teach any combination of genres using this book. Chapter 1 opens with getting-started exercises and discussions of motivations and sources for writing material. The eleven remaining chapters in this section move gradually from a focus on poetry (Chapters 2–4), through creative nonfiction (5–6), fiction (7–10), and drama (11–12), but each chapter addresses issues in the other genres and acknowledges that all the elements are relevant in each genre.

The **Writing Life Matters** section at the end of the book provides a selection of topics that might be assigned at the end, beginning, or at various times in the semester. These focus on the writing process (including workshopping and revising), the importance and development of close reading skills, the literature vs. genre debate that comes up for so many of us in classes today, and the practical aspects of how writers make a living. These chapters also provide a few **Pathways** to focus discussion.

The **Anthology** contains a combination of a few texts that are classically used in the Creative Writing classroom and other, newer ones that provide fresh perspectives; some are brief, but I include an array of lengths and styles to expose students to a range of creative possibilities. Specific texts are suggested to accompany particular chapters, but they could also easily be used in other contexts. Selections include **33 poems** (with 5 embedded in chapters), **14 pieces of fiction** (with 1 embedded), **9 pieces of creative nonfiction, 6 short plays, 6 short commentaries about writing**, and **1 example of graphic narrative**.

Two **Appendices** offer specific and detailed information about A) proper formatting of manuscripts, and B) verse forms. Appendix A addresses the need for students to have a ready reference for the technicalities of formatting their work professionally and consistently without major instructional time. Appendix B allows for expansion of the discussion of poetry in a course or as a reference for students wishing to experiment with more formal verse types.

Additional Resources

The **Instructor Resources website** found at www.oup.com/us/roney provides the following: alternative syllabi for different ways of organizing a course, potential "reading questions" that could accompany assignment of each piece in the **Anthology**, additional Pathways activities, including some designed for larger class sizes, and a Writing Life Plan assignment that I used in a Creative Writing lecture course of more than a hundred students, but that provides a useful tool for helping students in any setting work toward a future as writers.

TO STUDENTS

For an overview of all the features of this book, you might want to read the Organization section in "To Instructors" above. In any event, note that this book is not meant to be read necessarily straight through from beginning to end. Creative Writing is artisanal by nature, meaning that there is no one fixed way in which to learn. Your instructor may want to begin with fiction or with poetry or may want to delay the focus on any one form of writing and spend more time on the elements first. Any of these provides a legitimate beginning for the study of Creative Writing. Trust your instructor to create the roadmap. Here are a few tips for getting the most out of this book:

Keep two or three bookmarks in its pages.

You may be referring to more than one place in the book in a given class period. Bookmarks don't have to be fancy—they can be scraps of paper or Post-it notes, but if you use them you'll find it easier to focus on things you want to discuss rather than finding the exact page after the moment has passed.

Try out as many Pathways as you can.

The book contains more than a hundred writing exercises and prompts. Your instructor will assign you some of them, and these exercises make particular points about skills you need to acquire as a writer. However, remember that the Pathways should always serve you as a writer. Connect them to projects you're already working on or to subjects you already have in mind. Take off from them, twist them around, be opened not limited by them. They will help you surprise yourself.

Devote time to reading carefully.

Most of us can speed-read these days—it's what the Internet and our busy lives train us to do. Masterfully written work, however, often yields its layers of meanings and methods of production through only careful and multiple readings. To see what they can show you about your own writing, slow down and absorb each chapter and savor the mastery of each reading selection. Take notes, scrawl in the margins, dissect passages and stanzas, be ready to raise questions for discussion. Read actively, not passively.

Read beyond the borders.

Throughout this book, I reference numerous works that are not contained within its pages. I don't do this to drop names, but to encourage you to go out and find those works and others like them. Especially when something is mentioned on a topic that piques your interest, go look it up. Much of a writer's education is self-education.

Be prepared for a bit of terminology.

All fields, even many hobbies, have particular jargon that's used by insiders. Creative Writing is no different. You wouldn't expect to get much out of a tennis match with no idea what "love" means in that context, or enjoy a football game without knowing what a "first down" is. You don't need to memorize all the terms in this book, but the more you learn, the more you'll be able to discuss creative writing in a knowledgeable and accurate way. Test out these new words, feel them on your tongue, and enjoy the precision of this sometimes-new vocabulary. Don't let it intimidate you.

Keep an open mind.

To become a great or even good writer, you have to engage in lifelong reading, see the world with fresh eyes, and hold yourself open to new experiences and new ways of thinking. These are also attitudes and habits that can benefit you in many other professional and personal ways, as pointed out in the Guideposts throughout the book. Whether your goal is to become a professional writer, an avid amateur, or simply to gain communication and community-building skills, Creative Writing has much to offer you if you keep an open mind. As my mother used to say when I got stubborn, "Information cannot argue with a closed mind." Don't ever snap yours shut. Stay alert. Stay awake. Trust the process, even when it seems weird. Embrace your time here.

ACKNOWLEDGMENTS

As a not-for-profit educational publisher, OUP is indebted to all of the academics who participated in this peer-review process; it is a critical step in our publishing program that ensures we produce texts tailored to the needs of instructors and students: **Chris Anderson**, Pittsburg State University; **Kathleen Andersen-Wyman**, Brazosport College; **Rebecca Basham**, Rider University; **Kyle Beachy**, Roosevelt University; **Charmaine Cadeau**, High Point University; **Stephanie Carpenter**, University of Michigan—Flint; **Ken Chamlee**, Brevard College; **Aaron Clark**, Brookhaven College; **Claire Crabtree**, University of Detroit—Mercy; **Leila Crawford**, Atlantic Cape Community College; **Doug Davis**, Gordon State College; **Gary Eddy**, Winona State University; **Sally Emmons**, Rogers State University; **Kevin Ferns**, Woodland Community College—Yuba; **Jessica Flynn**, New York University; **Karen Golightly**, Christian Brothers University; **Chad Greene**, Cerritos College; **Carol Guerrero-Murphy**, Adams State University; **Leilani R Hall**, California State University—Northridge; **James Hannah**, Texas A & M University; **Joseph Haske**, South Texas Community College; **Alan Hines**, Kutztown University of Pennsylvania; **Cindy King**, University of North Texas—Dallas; **Laura Kopchick**, University of Texas—Arlington; **Deborah Landau**, New York University; **Ted Lardner**, Cleveland State University; **Carmen Livingston**, Community College of Allegheny County; **Donna Long**, Fairmont State University; **Megan Milks**, Illinois College; **Neli Moody**, San Jose State University; **Daniel Nester**, College of Saint Rose; **Lee Newton**, Bradley University; **Lisa Norris**, Central Washington University; **Martha Petry**, Jackson College; **Todd Pierce**, California Polytechnic University; **Pat Rushin**, University of Central Florida; **Anne Shaw**, Franklin Pierce University; **Bonnie Spears**, Chaffey College; **Jake Strautmann**, Boston University; **Tramble Turner**,

Penn State—Abington; **Brittany Vovan**, The City College of New York; **Gyorgyi Voros**, Virginia Tech; **Jack Wang**, Ithaca College; **Michelle Weisman**, College of the Ozarks; **Scott West**, Harford Community College; **Lex Williford**, University of Texas—El Paso; **Martha Witt**, William Paterson University; **Wayne Zade**, Westminster College.

I'd like to express my personal gratitude to my original editor, Frederick Speers, for his belief in and inspiration throughout this project. In addition, I would like to thank Wesley Hall for his unstinting efforts at negotiating permissions. Harold Schweizer, Bucknell University, and William Stull, University of Hartford, assisted me greatly in tracking down permission for a favorite piece for inclusion in the anthology.

Many of my students, colleagues, and teachers over the years have contributed directly and indirectly to this book, and to all of them I am grateful. To my own teachers—Paul West, Peter Schneeman, Charlotte Holmes, Bob Downs, and others—I owe an enormous debt. Special thanks go to John King, Don Stap, Terry Thaxton, Russ Kesler, James Campbell, Anna Jones, Tison Pugh, Peter Telep, Pat Rushin, Jamie Poissant, Steve Chicarel, and Barry Sandler at the University of Central Florida. Thanks to Catherine Carson, Genevieve Tyrrell, and Jeffrey Shuster for help with proofreading. In addition, my dear friends Ivonne Lamazares, Gigi Marino, Sally Pont, Holly Henry and Joann Leonard have provided listening ears and many suggestions. I also owe a debt of gratitude to my mother, Anne Meek, for her editorial expertise, as well as setting me on the writing path years ago. Alpha and omega, my personal thanks go to my husband, Bruce Janz, a gem of a man in all ways, whose support and intelligence I could not have done without.

Serious Daring

PART I

Craft Matters

Chapter 1

Serious Daring— The First Step on a Writer's Path

KEY ANTHOLOGY READINGS

Tess Gallagher, "Ode to My Father" (on writing, poetry)

Al Young, "A Little More Traveling Music" (poetry)

Craig Thompson, excerpt from *Carnet de Voyage* (graphic narrative)

Creative writing can be one of the most fulfilling, mind-expanding, rewarding, and fun activities on the planet, but it takes two things: boldness and passion, on the one hand, and the discipline to learn the craft, on the other. Usually we begin with the passion—the desire to write, a belief in a story we have to tell, and the nerve to tell it. As novelist Eudora Welty put it, "Serious daring starts from within."

However, for our daring to be serious (and therefore important), we have to buckle down and learn a few things, reading what masterful writers have done and learning techniques that can help our poems and stories come out the way we want them to. The nature of your own writing experience will depend in part on things outside your control—your compatibility with teachers and peers, support for the literary arts in your community, unexpected life events. In the long run, though, whether or not you will produce the best writing you are capable of and find the experience enthralling will depend largely upon you. No book can teach you how to write; what this book can do is provide a shortcut to many things that writers have learned over the years and to provide avenues into strategies and methods that will make you a stronger writer.

When you set out on the writer's path, be aware that it may wind, twist, turn, loop, and take all kinds of shapes and forms in both space and time. Argentinian writer Jorge Luis Borges imagines this path as "one sinuous spreading of labyrinth that would encompass the past and the future and in some way involve the stars." As writers, we continuously learn and find our way through this labyrinth of opportunities.

MOTIVATIONS

Perhaps you have been writing stories for as long as you can remember, or you're from a family that sits around the dinner table telling each other about the events of the day or about things that someone did a long time ago. Perhaps at school, your teacher praised you for an assignment you wrote, or you made your classmates laugh or gasp with your tales of magic or bravery. In this case, storytelling and thinking about language may feel like an inherent part of your personality, something you can't live without. You want to know how to do it better, how to make your way as a writer.

On the other hand, perhaps only recently you've encountered an overwhelming experience that you don't quite know what to do with, such as a clash in your family or an upheaval among your friends. Perhaps you have feelings inside that you burn to explore, to lay out in the light so that you can see them with more clarity. Or, perhaps you signed up for a Creative Writing course merely because you have to fulfill a curriculum requirement and this seemed like the most enjoyable option.

The specific reasons that we want to write are as varied as we are as people. Yet we know that storytelling has been around for a long, long time, and that it is almost instinctual for people to do it. It took perhaps hundreds of years for written stories to evolve after the invention of hieroglyphs, but *The Egyptian Book of the Dead* and the Sumerian *Epic of Gilgamesh* are two of the oldest. Their written versions date to 1250 BC and 2000 BC, respectively, but both were likely told orally well before being written down. The *Iliad* and *Odyssey* of Homer date back to the eighth century BC and represent the beginnings of literature in the Western world.

Even if you have an easy answer to the question of why you want to write—"I like to entertain people" or "I want to escape the humdrum life I live"—the first layer of reasons may not be all there is to it. I encourage you to dig deeper, to think about the important role that stories have played in your life.

Different writers recognize different motivations in their own lives. Tess Gallagher's "Ode to My Father" (p. 368) describes how in her family growing up, "We had no language between us." Her poems have been built on "the need to forge a language that would give these dead and living lives a way to speak." Al Young, on the other hand, mentions in his poem "A Little More Traveling Music" (p. 534) that he couldn't forget "all that motherly music, / those unwatered songs of my babe-in-the-wood days/until, committed to the power of the human voice, I turned to poetry & to singing by choice." As divergent as they may be, we can all benefit from starting to explore the sources of our desire to write. (See **Pathway 1.1.**)

On the other hand, defining motivations for writing is like trying to pin down the wagging tail of an enthusiastic dog. It's good to be aware of your passions, of the experiences that haunt you, of who you are or are beginning to be, but these things may shift and slide out of your grasp, especially at the beginning of your journey as a writer. Writing will define you as much as you define it. It is not a journey with a pre-defined ending any more than it has a clearly identifiable origin.

SOURCES OF MATERIAL

When you start writing down your own stories and ideas, you enter a long and vibrant tradition that exists in relation to your sense of personal exploration. You may be more or less aware of the particulars of this tradition through your education in literature and your own personal reading. You may also have different kinds of relationships to parts of this long tradition—some of it might seem out of touch with your modern-day concerns or stuffy in its presentation. On the other hand, you may wish that you could inhabit the life and writing style of an author you admire. Tradition is something that all writers greet with ambivalence, a combination of hostility and encouragement. At our best, we will learn from writers of the past while exploring our own pathways.

You might, then, think of your desire to write as a bicycle that you find leaning against the wall by your front door one day with a note that indicates it's yours. If you take care of it, occasionally oil the chain, put air in the tires, mostly follow a few rules of the road, and don't leave it out too long in the rain, there is no telling where it might take you.

Whether you feel like a writer already or are just figuring out what you might have to write about, you'll want to start thinking of your life as "material." To do this, you may need to look at your life in a new way and find the meaning in both where you've been before and where you are now. Appreciating the experiences you've had and pursuing new ones will augment and enrich your writing. Let's look at a few categories of experience to help raise your awareness of the material you have and can develop.

Childhood/Past Experiences

Novelist and short story writer Flannery O'Connor once said, "Anybody who has survived his childhood has enough information about life to last him the rest of his days." While we will continue to garner new experiences, O'Connor makes an important point about our ability to draw on our childhood and family life up to this point. We may also want to reconnect with the unfettered imagination we had as smaller children—children who were open and excited about everything they encountered and who often saw things going on around them that were curious and strange, even when the adults didn't admit it.

Both your childhood and your recent life can offer good sources of material for your writing. We will discuss in Chapter 5 more specifics about using memories in your writing, but early on you may want to start thinking about experiences you've had that have stayed with you over the years. What did these moments teach you about your friends or family members—or about strangers you met in the park? How did you come to learn what you know about life today? What events and moments still color your perceptions?

For instance, a personal example—I have a long-term interest in crime stories, and in my own writing I often focus on the issue of harmful secrets and the need for truth-telling. I realized a few years ago that this is tied to an event of my childhood, when a housewife who lived near my family was murdered in her home one afternoon right after she'd begun baking a cake. The neighborhood filled up with police cars, and eventually they found, abandoned in a ditch, a fake police officer's uniform, which the intruder had evidently used to get Rose Busch to let him in. This case was never solved, but people speculated that her murder had to do with her husband's secret affair. This haunting story has long affected my sense of dark, hidden secrets in seemingly ordinary people's lives. **Pathway 1.2** asks you to consider past events that haunt you.

You may also want to think about passions that you have and how they developed. Do you love music, surfing, Morocco, or spiders? Do you know more about them than the average person? If so, you may be able to draw on that knowledge in a variety of ways in your writing. That doesn't necessarily mean writing a memoir about your high school trip to Morocco or your family's emigration from there; rather, it might mean creating a fictional character in a story or play who dreams of living in Tangier though her parents forbid her to leave home, or writing a poem in which images of open-air souks contrast with images of American shopping malls.

Whatever your childhood was like, you can be sure that if you look hard enough at it that you will find aspects of it that bear exploring or that can inform your writing in every genre. In addition to the previous two, **Pathways 1.3, 1.4, 1.5, 1.6**, and several in Chapter 5 will help you think about the ways in which your own past provides a set of experiences for you to draw on.

Current Daily Life

Daily life forms the most common subject matter of creative writing, especially poetry and creative nonfiction. Even if you are interested in the most far-out, magical, and outlandish fictional universe, your own daily experiences will form the foundation of what you are interested in and how you construct that fictional world.

John Gardner, author of fourteen novels, including *Grendel*, a retelling of the Beowulf myth from the monster's perspective, notes in his book *The Art of Fiction* that

> the realistic writer may set out to conjure up the personality of his aunt, creating for her, or copying from life, some story through which her character is revealed, and thus he reveals his strong feelings for his aunt. . . . The fabulist—the writer of nonrealistic yarns, tales, or fables— may seem at first glance to be doing something quite different, but he is not. . . . [S]ince character can come only from one of two places, books or life, the writer's aunt is as likely to show up in a fable as in a realistic story. (21–22)

In other words, whatever form you're interested in using, inspiration will almost inevitably come from the world that surrounds you.

Writers tend to be highly observant people, sometimes even seeming to hover in the background taking mental notes. Everything that passes in front of our eyes and through our other senses is potential material for our writing, even though we may not always know it at first. **Pathway 1.7** will help you become aware of how interesting even commonplace events around you can be.

Writers also need to search for the *meaning* in their own and others' experiences. Sometimes this can feel at first like a bit of a stretch or an exaggeration, and we may sometimes question our own interpretations, but meaning-making is one of the central tasks of the writer. Writers make sense out of the same sensations, situations, events, and emotions that other people simply live through. Tess Gallagher, for instance, recognizes that the seemingly ordinary conversations she's had with her father and his friends at the Chinook Tavern reveal "a power and a beauty I did not want to see lost to the world." A writer's power involves finding the meaning in events both strange and ordinary, both recent and recalled. (See **Pathways 1.8 and 1.9**.)

In these two ways—unusually careful observation and meaning-making— you will be able to look anew at your daily life, past and present, and create from it writing that expresses important ideas and that has something worthwhile to convey beyond yourself and your immediate circle. This connection between the intimate and personal, on the one hand, and the wider world, on the other, is an unusual feature of Creative Writing as opposed to other areas of study— such as history or physics—and is one of its most rewarding aspects.

Adventures

We frequently encounter images of writers, such as Ernest Hemingway, who are known for their great adventures that became background or subjects of their work. Hemingway enrolled in the ambulance corps in World War I, at the age of seventeen, and was injured before returning home to recover. Later, he spent time traveling in Africa and went to Spain for the running of the bulls. Hemingway, however, is only one kind of writer, and many others lead quiet lives and travel mostly in their imaginations. In fact, many well-known writers maintain strict schedules for their work and live in one place for most of their lives—a diverse array of writers, from poets Wendell Berry and Scott Russell Sanders to science-fiction novelist Ursula Le Guin and horror master Stephen King, have commented on the value of, as Sanders puts it, "staying put" and focusing on a regular discipline of work.

In writers, there always exists a tension between the desire for stimulation, on the one hand, and the need for concentrated alone time with the pen or keyboard. Both of these needs of the writer are important for you to be aware of in your own life, and "adventure" can be found in a multitude of spaces, including local ones. In fact, in some ways adventure is an attitude, and there are opportunities to experience new things around every corner, even in the smallest of towns or the most remote of outposts. **Pathway 1.10** sends you out to find adventure, perhaps in seeing through new lenses.

However, you can also start thinking now about what travels and other pursuits might enrich your writing. Perhaps you have always had a travel bug and have wanted to visit certain places that now you can add to your list of goals with a purpose in mind and an awareness of how you need to pay attention in such situations. Or perhaps you grew up in Saudi Arabia or Peru (even if it's Peru, Nebraska) before you lived where you live now, and you believe that revisiting that place from your past will jog your memory and allow you to write more concretely about that place or your time there. You may want to work in a certain field—organic farming or taxi driving or personal training—in order to delve into a different realm more long-term. Even though many of these tasks take special training that you may not have at this point, your community, both inside and outside your college or university, no doubt offers many festivals, organizations, travel abroad programs, and other opportunities that can become part of your education as a writer.

Note that benefits accrue from thinking about these things now, as you start your work as a writer. You may need to work and save for travel or plan study abroad or semesters for internships around your course requirements. And it may simply take some imaginative thought for you to figure out what adventures will best augment your work as a writer. Stretch your imagination in this regard through **Pathways 1.11 and 1.12.**

Experience in the Community of Writers

You should take opportunities to participate in the community of writers, both local and more broad, by going to author readings, book signings, and conferences, and creating or joining writers' groups, either face-to-face or online. Most public author events include a time for question-and-answer with the audience, and you should be in that audience. There is no greater thing than for you to be able to see how the literary community works and how various writers talk about their work.

Some of these events will be electrifying and inspirational, giving you new ideas for your own work or giving you a thrill at hearing a writer's work in his or her own voice. Sometimes they can encourage you with insightful answers to your questions and tips on how to succeed or survive. On the other hand, writers, even well-known ones, are human and get tired on the lecture circuit. Even if a particular event lacks electricity, you will accumulate knowledge about what it means to be a published author. As Craig Thompson notes in the excerpt of his travel graphic memoir *Carnet de Voyage* (p. 528), even famous writers he's admired from afar deal with everyday mundane things like jobs and relationships. And yet, he takes comfort in meeting and sharing work with them, in being taken in as part of the writing world.

In addition, as we'll discuss in Chapter 13, reading and keeping up with what others are writing is vital to advancing your skills as a writer yourself and emphasizes that writers and readers are part of a large-scale, worldwide community of storytellers, language enthusiasts, and thinkers.

GETTING STARTED

Advice and formulas for success abound, but the truth is that there is no one correct method for producing great writing. This book will give you methods that have helped many writers over the years, but writers each have their own variations and particulars, from the time of day they like to write to whether or not they prefer silence or cacophony in the background and whether they plan each story before they write it or draft it fully before they really know where it's going.

The biggest two mistakes that beginning writers make are the polar opposites of each other. The first is to reject ideas too quickly, and the other is to think that the first words jotted down are so precious as to be perfect and immutable. Although they seem like opposites, either habit will paralyze your growth as a writer. Writers must work back and forth between spontaneous, nonjudgmental outpouring of words, on the one hand, and perfectionism and attention to craft and detail, on the other. These modes differ, and you likely prefer one aspect more than the other, but only in the space between them and in mastering both will you find your best work.

In the initial stages of writing, of course, getting stuff down on the page is the first order of business. To help you take your first steps, here we take a moment to consider a couple of fundamentals, strategies for finding and developing ideas.

Brainstorming

Brainstorming is any form of thinking that jolts us out of our usual ways of thinking. It will be a useful technique in your creative writing whether you come to the keyboard with myriad specific ideas that you're already fixated on or you have no idea where to begin. Throughout this book, many of the Pathways will help jump-start that part of the process or help you take steps beyond that initial daring idea. You might also simply start with a list of whatever is on your mind.

In brainstorming, of course, the idea is to take everything that comes through your mind without rejecting any of it—and even without particularly praising any one idea over another. Of course, at some point that pure brainstorming transmogrifies into a somewhat different process—that of getting excited about one idea or image over another.

That is the stage at which brainstorming helps even those who already have a good idea or ideas to pursue because with each original notion, you can then work the brainstorming process again. For any given germ of a poem or story, jot down a list of associated words, images, characters, specific actions your characters might take, and the like, that you might develop further. This can become an informal version of outlining, something that we usually do in more formal writing situations or once we start working on longer forms of creative writing—the novel as opposed to the short story, for instance. As with any brainstorming, not all of the items on your list will end up in your poem, essay, story, or play. But it is also a good habit to keep track of your brainstorming efforts, whether at the scale of grand ideas or at the smaller level of images and seemingly random observations. You never know when you will want to return to these and dig through them for more ideas. You can return over and over to old brainstorming ground, often finding new things there, buried just under the surface.

Keeping a Journal

Because brainstorming often provides such rich sources for larger works, and because writers so vitally need to constantly develop their observation skills, your teacher may assign you to keep a writer's journal, whether filled with responses to writing exercises from this book or with your own sketched-out perceptions about what you see around you, or some combination of the two. Having some method of keeping notes about ideas you have and people, places, interactions, and sensual stimuli you encounter will develop your confidence that you will never run out of material.

Your journal may take many forms—traditionally it would be a small notebook that you could carry in a purse or jacket pocket so as to always have it with you at a moment's notice. Many writers have been famous for their particular preferences—Ernest Hemingway for his many small blue-backed spiral-bound ones, Jennifer Egan for recording her newfound desire to become a writer in a leather-bound travel diary she took to Europe after college. Today, of course, we have electronic devices on which we can record our jottings, as well as taking hundreds of reminder photographs, and store whole libraries of reading. Even if you don't have a device or notebook with you, however, doesn't mean you can't keep track of images and thoughts that arise—many writers are famous for scribbling on bar napkins, placemats, receipts, and the like—anything to capture a vivid moment in order to preserve the memory for later conversion into art. You can scan things into PDF files or type them up into documents once home or keep an old-fashioned paper file. (See **Pathway 1.13**.)

Another great aspect of writers' journals is that they are low-stakes places to try things out. By their nature, they are modest in the attempts they make—acknowledged to be a space for rough impressions, trial runs, and even for mistakes that will never see print. They are a place where you don't have to worry about perfection—you can be as sloppy or precise as you want, you can cease to worry about your punctuation and spelling, and you can try things you know are risky—all of the judgment and sifting will come later. A journal is a free place to explore, its blank pages as open as the highway on the first day of a cross-country trip.

A Word about Genres

When you first sit down to write, you usually start with an idea of whether you're going to write a poem or a story or a play. These are what we usually refer to as genres of creative writing. It should be mentioned, however, that the term **genre** is used in two distinct but overlapping ways in the world of creative writing. A word still close to its original Latin roots (genus), "genre" most simply means type or sort. Most commonly, it's used to distinguish between poetry, fiction, creative nonfiction, drama, and other forms of writing. All of these genres share certain features and techniques that we will discuss in Chapters 2 through 12, but each genre also has particular issues that are more strongly associated with it than with other genres. We'll discuss a few of those differences and overlaps in the following craft chapters and in short mini-chapters called Destinations that will focus on qualities to watch for in your work in particular genres.

However, first I want to note the other common use of the word "genre"—usually in the phrase "genre fiction." Fiction is one genre, but "genre fiction" refers to various types of narrative that share specific conventions and sometimes even formulas for their production, such as science fiction, action/adventure, fantasy, romance, mystery, and numerous other sub-categories. Most of the work that we'll discuss in this book will not fall into those categories but will focus on settings and situations that are traditionally considered to contain more potential for literary value and originality. We will discuss the changing issues and debates surrounding work that is considered genre fiction or work that contains genre-fiction elements in Chapter 15.

The chapters in Part I, the Craft Matters section of this book, will take you step by step through a consideration of several issues of writing that we generally refer to when we speak about "craft"—imagery and figurative language, sound and rhythm, form, memory, research, description and setting, character, plot, point of view and voice, action and dialogue, and performance. These are the various elements of a literary work that in effect are never separated, but which we analyze and discuss separately to better learn how they work. Even though we may eat a dish and marvel at its unified flavor, back in the kitchen we need to know what separate ingredients go into making it.

Similarly, we often associate some craft elements with specific genres more than others, even though such elements are found in all of the genres. For instance, we may think about sound and rhythm most frequently in terms of poetry, which usually retains a closer connection to songs and song lyrics than prose and drama do, yet sound and rhythm are indeed important in those other genres as well. Sometimes, genres merge—one only has to think of Shakespeare, with his dramas written in verse, to see that genre boundaries are never too firm and that the elements commonly associated with one particular genre also are relevant in the others.

Because you have been a reader for quite some time, you may think that you know exactly what kind of writing you want to do, but I urge you to be open to all forms presented in this book. You may be right about where your talents and preferences lie, but fixation on one or the other genre may hamper you from discovering new modes and styles of writing you could ultimately come to love. It never hurts to try new things, and doing so often opens up whole new worlds.

PATHWAYS

Pathway 1.1. Motivations list. Make a list of factors that have brought you to this course or area of study. Include positive effects you hope to get out of writing. Be as specific to yourself as possible, and note any specific relevant incidents or anecdotes. In class, compare your list with others' and note the similarities and idiosyncrasies of lists. Keep your list for later writing ideas.

Pathway 1.2. Childhood hauntings. Jot down a list of a few events from childhood that haunt you. These may include traumas or celebrations within your family, but consider those that you only remember hearing about from the larger community, too—a favorite shop was robbed, a new bridge was built. After you've made a list, choose one to start writing about. What comes back to you? What do you wonder about? Do you understand completely why you remember this?

Pathway 1.3. Photo stories. Look through your old photo albums or pictures you have stored on your phone or computer. Pick one that you're in and start a poem or memoir based on what you see in the picture and what you remember from when it was taken.

Pathway 1.4. Influential people. What people have made you into who you are today? These can be your closest friends and relatives, but they can also include people who have hurt you or that you have been inspired by from afar. Write a few lines about each one, trying your best to avoid clichés. In just a couple of lines, go deep into how you feel about each person.

Pathway 1.5. Scar. Write about a scar on your body. Describe it, tell how you got it, and say what you think that scar says about you.

Pathway 1.6. Job experiences. Make a list of all the jobs (paid or volunteer) you've ever had. Think about each one—what you hated or liked about each job, what you remember about the tasks and people involved—and then write a paragraph about how each of those situations might show up in your writing— as a setting for a poem or story or play, as a character you might develop, or as a type of conflict that might form a plot. Give a whole new meaning to the label "job experience."

Pathway 1.7. Strangest things. Start with this phrase, "The other day, the strangest thing happened. . . ." Write for thirty minutes. If one anecdote runs dry, start again, and again.

Pathway 1.8. Idiosyncratic you. What do you know that no one else knows? What do you do or feel or think that's different from what most people do or feel or think? Do you have insight that is unusual or that few people share? Sometimes the most fascinating ideas come from these uncommon worlds we inhabit or perspectives we get from them. Write for a few minutes about what makes you unique as an individual. Jot down a list and expand into paragraphs a few that seem they might make for fruitful writing subjects or character traits.

Pathway 1.9. Desire. Write about the thing you want most in the world. Branch out beyond sexual desire to contemplate where you want to be, how you want to be, what gives you comfort, what you want to accomplish, what you hope happens for your loved ones, what you're nostalgic about but can't get back. Maybe it's something as simple as a bowl of potato soup or as complex as the opportunity to be a pilot. Describe it in loving detail, whether it actually exists in front of you or not.

Pathway 1.10. Space alien. Attend a large, public event, either of a type that you've attended many times before—such as a sporting event or a concert or a church or synagogue service—or one that perhaps is more unusual and perhaps new to you—a dog show, a tractor pull, a gallery opening—and pretend that you are a space alien who just landed there out of the blue. Try to observe things in a new way and focus on details that you might not otherwise notice. Turn this occasion into an emotional adventure. Imbue your writing about it with the intensity that would be there if you really were a space alien and this was your first day on Earth.

Pathway 1.11. Your future. Write a two-page futuristic story. However, instead of focusing on robots or space travel or the other trappings of the usual science fiction genre, write only a few years into the future, and write a story in which the main character is based on you. Try not to be grandiose or silly, but envision some real situation you might be in and how your personality might react. Keep the plot simple—you're eating in a restaurant five years from now when an ex-boyfriend from college walks in; you're applying for a job that you're desperate to get to feed your growing family; you get on the airplane to travel to Shanghai for the first time.

Pathway 1.12. Place list. Create a list of places you'd like to travel and that you think would influence your writing if you did. These can be relatively local and specific, such as "I'd like to go to spring break at Daytona Beach," or as far-off as a desire to live and work in Tibet. Think about how you're going to get there. If you take notes along the way, you will have a lot of material for a book or an essay about the process of getting there as well as about the place itself. Keep your list. Update it from time to time, from year to year.

Pathway 1.13. Get a journal. There are many ways to keep a journal—in a plain spiral-bound notebook of any size from small to large, in a fancy cloth or leather book with creamy, unlined pages, on a blog, or in a secret computer file. In whatever form, keep a journal. Make a conscious decision about what form will suit you best, keep you wanting to write, and suit the course you're in. You can create other journals later, but if you haven't already, get started on one now. Many of the other Pathways in this book can be recorded there.

FURTHER ANTHOLOGY READING

Frederick Smock, "A Poet's Education" (on writing)

GUIDEPOST: DIRECTIONS YOU MIGHT GO

Creative writing is a practice that develops many valuable habits of mind.

Creative Writing is a worthwhile end in itself—obviously I believe this passionately or I wouldn't have made it my life's work. Most writers feel a need to express what's inside us, to entertain ourselves and others, and to convey what we see and believe. Works of art and literature influence our society in endless ways, and writers retain an important role. But studying Creative Writing may also open doors in many other arenas. Each chapter in Part I: Craft Matters offers a Guidepost that will allow you to stop briefly and take account of broader values and habits of mind that we foster as we study language and story and the human factors that underpin our writing.

If you're interested in majoring in English or Creative Writing, you may have heard the question "What are you going to do with *that?*" and you may have concerns about where your major will take you. If you're a student who plans to follow one of the supposedly "more practical" courses of study, you may yourself think of Creative Writing as a mere break from your other studies, something peripheral. Whichever group you fall into, I hope that pointing out the complex array of human and intellectual skills that can be fostered in a Creative Writing workshop will raise your awareness of the myriad possibilities for you, and the value of participating in both the play and work of writing creatively.

There are many lists available on the Internet of the skills that employers find the most desirable in a job applicant. Take a look for yourself by searching some version of "most desired employment skills" or "skills employers want," and you will likely find "communication skills" at the very top. Communication includes writing skills but also the ability to speak and present your ideas verbally in a meeting or presentation. The practice that you will gain expressing your ideas about your peers' writing in workshops provides unparalleled experience in the tactful communication strategies most needed in many business and public-sector professions. One poll of hiring managers by the National Association of Colleges and Employers notes that communication skills are the ones deemed most vital in a job candidate, but they are also those most frequently *lacking*. Your abilities with writing, editing, and verbal communication should serve you well whatever path you follow.

In addition, the highly unusual workshop process will allow you to combine your personal interests and self-expression with your academic learning. Workshop methods foster both independence and teamwork, help you learn to take criticism of your work gracefully and use it productively, allow you to practice presenting and defending your ideas to a group, and teach a mastery of complex tasks when no formula exists. These are precisely the characteristics valued for professional and managerial positions. Among the other abilities that almost all employers seek are interpersonal skills, self-motivation, flexibility, leadership ability, creative problem-solving, and research strategies. This is one likely reason why, according to research by the National Center for Education Statistics, liberal arts graduates' salaries often catch up to or even surpass those in fields of a more technical nature by mid-career. As employment tasks become more complex and managerial, these human skills become more and more important. Although there are other ways to develop these values and abilities, Creative Writing courses cultivate them through the process of writing, critique, and workshop. You will use these strategies throughout your life, no matter where it takes you.

Destination: **POETRY**

We all know a poem when we see one, right? Most poems have the obviously distinguishing feature of being written in lines with breaks at places other than the ends of sentences or paragraphs. Yet, there are so-called **prose poems** that may not look like the usual poem, and other aspects of language and phrasing play vital roles, even perhaps more vital roles, than the line breaks.

MAIN FEATURES OF POETRY

Line breaks. The main thing to understand about line breaks in poetry is that they are not random, even when you create them intuitively rather than by a formal, predictable structure. You may choose where to break lines in a variety of ways—by a preset number of syllables (as in a Shakespearean sonnet, where each line is ten syllables), by a chosen emphasis on certain words or turning points in a sentence, and/or by the way the line looks in relation to other lines. Line breaks creates subtle emphases that help determine the meaning as well as the rhythm of a poem, and the last word in a line garners extra attention. The second stanza of Judith Ortiz Cofer's "The Changeling" (p. 307) begins:

> In my brother's closet, I'd change
> into his dungarees . . .

Clearly, Cofer wants us to pay close attention to that word "change." We see it in the title and again before this line break. It stands out.

Rhythm and sound. Although sound and rhythm are indeed elements of all spoken and written language, we pay special attention to them in poetry. For instance, take the following sentence, and read it aloud: "Not to close things, but to open them, is the line drawn ruthlessly the way mother drew her open sewing scissor over the swollen belly of the melon." Then read it as Lynn Emanuel wrote it in her poem "The Out-of-Body Experience":

> Not to close things, but to open them,
> is the line drawn
>   ruthlessly
> the way mother drew
>   her open sewing scissor
> over the swollen belly
>   of the melon.

The breaks create a rhythm within the poem of short, almost breathless lines that nonetheless flow in a rippling sensation from the opening line of the stanza.

Reliance on imagery and layers of meaning. Emanuel's poem (in its entirety on p. 344) also demonstrates another primary characteristic of poetry—its use of powerful imagery and figurative language that creates a density and multiplicity of meaning. The above stanza, second in the poem, takes what might otherwise be the simple slicing of fruit and shifts it to a more sinister sense of cutting into a human body (a "belly"), evoking the merciless nature of those who open up not only parts of the physical world, but minds as well. The entire poem goes on to characterize its narrator as "looking down on / (from a great distance, / dwarfed and vivid) / the Amazonian / wandering of the guts / exposed" and "a colder cold, a dark / dark," indicating perhaps the skill of detached observation that every writer must develop. In other words, because of the various associations of the specific words and images a poet chooses, the poem takes on layers of meaning that may be quite complex. Poetry, then, speaks both at the level of immediate emotional impact and at the level of intellect. It is simultaneously heart-wrenching and cerebral.

The writing elements associated most strongly in poetry, and the way they factor into the other genres, are discussed further in Chapters 2, 3, and 4. All the other elements of writing that we'll discuss in other chapters may also contribute to meaning and form in poetry. For instance, a narrative poem, which tells a story, might very well rely on character and setting, even a kind of plot. Some poems don't include those elements, hinging instead on the sense of an instant, or on language games or surrealistic, dreamlike, even nonsense images, but if your poems do tell a story, you might also want to look at the **Destination** questions for those genres.

QUESTIONS ABOUT YOUR POETRY

- **Have you started with a concrete image or a series of images rather than an abstract idea?** Doing so will bring your poem to life and make it vivid for you and your reader.
- **Have you chased out all the clichés?** Poems often focus on timeless emotions, but they need to find fresh ways to express feelings in order to be more than diary entries. Eliminating clichés at the level of idea and language use is a good start.
- **Have you chosen accurate words, beautiful words (or hideous ones if that's what's called for), splendid words, the perfect words for what you mean?** Playing with language, acquiring and using a larger, more expressive vocabulary, and arranging words in compelling or contrasting juxtapositions will make your poetry richer.
- **Have you put connotation, metaphor, and other figures of speech to good use in creating layers of meaning?** To make your poem worth reading over and over, pay attention to the complexity of connotations and figures of speech that create comparisons and allusions in your work.

- **How does your poetry sound?** You want to use hard and soft sounds to appropriate effect, and you want to create bridges of sounds that weave through a poem.
- **Do your line breaks contribute to nuances of meaning?** Attending to exactly where each line begins and ends will allow you to control where readers pause to savor and where they stop to pay attention.
- **Do your line breaks contribute to the rhythm of the poem?** Even starting with how quickly or slowly your lines progress provides a start to thinking about rhythm, and then you can think about variation versus regularity, punctuated versus run-on rhythms, and so on.
- **Have you used repetition of sounds and words and other patterns without going overboard and making your poem too predictable and sing-songy?** Rhythm can be powerful, but it's easy to edge over into a comic, nursery-rhyme feel.
- **If you've tried a named poetic form for a particular poem, have you allowed variations that keep the focus on the poem itself rather than the form?** Often, our earliest formal poems become slaves to the master of form rather than using the form to augment the meaning and development of the poem's content. This can be a tough balance, so be aware of it.
- **Have you kept a sense of play and fun in this poem, even if it evokes serious emotions? And vice versa?** Poetry exhibits language play, and even the most devastating poem to the reader constitutes a kind of playing or puzzle-solving to the writer. At the same time, even the seemingly most ribald and silly poems may be finely crafted. Pay attention to that balance in your poetry writing.

Chapter 2

Imagery and Figurative Language

READINGS WITHIN THIS CHAPTER

John Haines, "On the Mountain" (poetry)

Rae Armantrout, "Home Federal" (poetry)

KEY ANTHOLOGY READINGS

Larry Levis, "At the Grave of My Guardian Angel: St. Louis Cemetery, New Orleans" (poetry)

Julio Ortega, "Las Papas" (fiction)

Writing that transports and inspires us often makes us feel as though we are "there" and depends for its effectiveness on inventive use of language and powerful images that connect our senses with our minds. Sometimes fresh juxtapositions of words happen by accident—imagine, for instance, finding a strange grocery list left in a cart—grape juice, crackers, diapers, vodka. Is a young mother tempted to give her fussy child vodka in his grape juice? Or, perhaps, is a pastor picking up last-minute supplies for communion and daycare at her church, but feeling so stressed over declining tithes that she feels the need for a nip before services? The seeming contradictions make us take notice.

Most of the time, however, our daily use of language follows a regular course. We need this predictability—it makes the world run smoothly for us to agree on some basics of communication. Imagine the effect if every time you went into a shop to buy a cup of coffee and the barista greeted you with, "Are there green holes in the sky?" or "Where underneath the blanket is the insecurity?" instead of "What can I get you?"

Because we spend so much time with these routine uses of language, most people forget or never fully explore the parameters and edges of language—how far it may be stretched, what variety of feelings and thoughts it can express, and the ways that it can bring new ideas into the world and affirm our most complex humanity. You may or may not consider yourself a budding poet, but everyone who values language—whether in terms of writing a compelling novel, putting together accurate and easily understood technical documents, or motivating people about a certain good cause—will find the study of poetry beneficial. Poetry is language at its most intensified. Though most of the examples I use in these first few chapters come from poetry, the techniques described have everything to do with intensifying our prose and drama as well.

Through one of his characters in *The Satanic Verses*, novelist Salman Rushdie puts it this way: "A poet's work is to name the unnameable, to point at frauds, to take sides, start arguments, shape the world, and stop it going to sleep." Only in the freshest use of language can we hope to waken people with words and change the way they see the world.

CONCRETE AND ABSTRACT LANGUAGE

One of the first issues you'll grapple with as you begin to write is how to translate your feelings and ideas into compelling language. For starters, you can use words that evoke tangible things perceived through the senses—things that we can see, hear, smell, taste, and touch. To get a feel for the importance of this kind of specificity and tangibility, juxtapose the term "friendship" with a photo of a real friend. Neither of these things *is* your friend in the flesh, but one comes a lot closer to reminding you of him or her. The photo is more concrete and less abstract.

In its usual sense, the word "concrete" refers to a building material—heavy, coarse, and often ugly. We usually find wood and even steel more appealing. So its metaphorical use to describe language that is beautiful as well as centered in the real, sensual world may seem counterintuitive. However, if you think about what the term is used to counter—abstract—its use begins to make a lot more sense.

Justice and liberty, for instance, are **abstract** concepts. These can be useful, but they have no physical presence. They exist solely in our heads and sometimes in our hearts. Love, hate, fear, joy, lust, greed (and the other seven deadly sins)—these are all abstractions. Because these terms have no clear physical correspondences in the world, they do not evoke the senses the way we hope to do in most creative writing. **Concrete**, on the other hand, is of the earth. All of the materials used to make the building product—sand, gravel, slag—are mined from the ground. In this way, the term "concrete" makes a great metaphor for language that we want to be rooted in sensory experience, to partake of the messiness and inescapable physicality of life, and to evoke sensations in order to make a story or poem or play vivid. (See **Pathway 2.1.**)

The picture of your friend—whether it's an actual photograph or a picture created by your written words—is what we refer to as an **image** or **imagery**. Images are created by concrete language describing things that you can see, taste, touch, smell, or hear, and they are one of the prime ways in which we bring life to the page and layer multiple meanings into our work. Notice how this works in the following poem.

ON THE MOUNTAIN
John Haines

We climbed out of timber,
bending on the steep meadow
to look for berries,
then still in the reddening sunlight
went on up the windy shoulder.

A shadow followed us up the mountain
like a black moon rising.
Minute by minute the autumn lamps
on the slope burned out.

Around us the air and the rocks
whispered of night . . .

A great cloud blew from the north,
and the mountain vanished
in the rain and stormlit darkness.

On first reading, the poem simply describes in vivid detail the experience of being overtaken by a sudden storm while "we" are out hiking and picking berries. Certainly, if you've ever been overtaken by sudden severe weather, this poem will bring that sensation back, and if you haven't, you can still almost feel the wind and the change in mood that the heavy clouds bring. This imagery allows the poem to be more evocative than a simple statement about being out in a storm. Because the "we" is never defined, a reader might first interpret it to mean a couple—on a romantic outing—but then we become aware that it could also refer to a family outing, or any one of several kinds of pairings or groups—two friends, a man and dog, a school group. This pronoun begins to open the poem up, and then we see that the situation on the mountain may have many meanings and implications beyond itself, all still rooted in the concrete images.

If the "we" belongs to a couple, the storm's darkness might imply developing trouble in the relationship, or even the trajectory from youthful desire to old-age infirmity. If we imagine children along, we might find ourselves feeling protective, and see that the poem might imply even larger things about the sudden way that the future can change, the dangers that we are in from various kinds of "storms," whether natural or human-made. (See **Pathways 2.2** and **2.3**.)

Like many things in the practice of creative writing, these distinctions between abstract and concrete sometimes get complicated. Even some abstract terms may at times evoke in us such strong images that we sometimes confuse them with images themselves. Think of the term "home," for instance. We may be so familiar with the particulars of our own home that we feel as though the word is a specific place in the world. But it's important to realize that "home" may mean different things for the person sitting across the table than it does for you. Perhaps your home is filled with the scent of curry, whereas her home is filled with the

Two alternate terms are generally used to refer to the voice of a poem—the **narrator** or the **speaker**. In a poem that tells a story, it's common to refer to a "narrator," whereas the slightly more general term "speaker" also applies to a poem that is more surrealistic or language-oriented in nature. When we read a poem that speaks directly using "I" or "we," we sometimes assume that the voice represents the actual poet speaking directly to us. Many times this is so, and you'll often hear poets speak of themselves in their work. However, we should always keep in mind that, unlike with creative nonfiction and fiction, or with documentary film, we don't have a designation that tells us whether a poem is fiction, fact, or somewhere in between. Often, too, poets write what is called a **persona poem**, which is clearly written in the voice of another person. Tess Gallagher's "3 A.M. Kitchen: My Father Talking" (p. 370), the poem woven into her short essay "Ode to My Father" discussed in Chapter 1, is one example. Sometimes these characters are based on neighbors or family members, sometimes historical figures, sometimes on imagination, and sometimes they provide an alter ego for a writer, or draw on a combination of sources. It is always good to keep in mind that in poetry, we really don't know how close any narrative voice is to the author. We will talk more about various narrator types in Chapter 10. (See **Pathway 2.6**.)

aroma of baking bread. Or perhaps, in the experience of the guy next to you, home is not so sanguine—his home might have been filled with strife and short on home-cooked meals of any kind. (See **Pathways 2.4** and **2.5**.)

In other words, home—or any other idea—needs to be evoked in all its specificity, and only then can it become a vivid and definite image of a place that others can visit with you.

ACCURACY AND FRESHNESS

Akin to using concrete imagery, specifying precisely what we mean also increases the vividness of our writing. Say you begin to read a story that evokes a clearing in a foggy forest; you know something important is about to happen there, but as you try to envision it, you wonder what kinds of trees those are that surround the clearing. It matters whether they are dark hemlocks with tall, slender trunks, or a bramble of palms and saw palmettos with their thick, spiky undergrowth. Telling us the name of a tree may, in fact, tell us a good bit about where this story takes place—in one word, "hemlock" might indicate the colder climate of the northern United States, whereas palms and palmettos evoke tropical or sub-tropical regions. **Pathway 2.7** asks you to think about your favorite words, and often these words become our favorites because of their precision and rarity (as well as sound qualities that we'll discuss in Chapter 3).

Accurate use of language contributes to one of the main qualities associated with poetry—**density** of meaning. Imagine if John Haines had used the word "bank" or "mountainside" instead of "shoulder" in "On the Mountain." Haines describes the shoulder as "windy," reminding us that the people in the poem have risen above the tree line, exposed to the elements, but we also think of the human body and the vulnerability of having (or touching) a bare shoulder. We're also reminded of the physicality of these people by the words "climbed," "bending," and "reddening," yet such references disappear after the first stanza, as the mountain itself does in the storm cloud. The natural forces seem to take over all the action of the poem—at first it's the sunlight that reddens, and then suddenly the shadow follows, the lamps burn out, the air and rocks whisper, the cloud blows in. The poem's tone of awe and loss of control depends on the use of specific words like "shoulder" to create that movement from human desires to inevitable and threatening processes. "Bank" or "mountainside" would not have the same effect.

This economy of language—making words serve multiple meanings through their precise usage—goes by a number of different terms in the creative writing world. You may hear it referred to as **compression** or **condensation** as well as density. All of these imply how poetry takes advantage of the various meanings of words, as well as metaphors and other figures of speech (discussed below) in order to enrich and expand associations. In the ten short lines of Rae Armantrout's "Home Federal," for instance, we can see both a range of emotions and a plethora of connections that open the poem beyond its literal meaning.

HOME FEDERAL
Rae Armantrout

A merchant is
probing for us
with his chintz curtain
                effect.

       *

"Ha, ha, you missed me,"
a dead person says.

       *

There's the bank's
colonial balcony
where no one has
                ever stood.

The word choices in this poem have to be precisely what they are—"chintz" evokes "cheesy" and "cheap" and even "chintzy." The use of the latter term is ironic in many ways—banks are usually associated with wealth and money, so Armantrout points out that the homey chintz is purely for "effect"; it is faking something, perhaps that the owners and managers of this bank are more similar to their customers in taste and financial reach than they are. The "colonial balcony / where no one has / ever stood" evokes some ideal of the past and a vague nationalism that customers might value. The poem evokes both humor and bitterness in response to the marketing goals of even the architectural and interior decorating of a bank building. The middle couplet suggests the relentless pursuit of customers that businesses of all kinds do, to the extent that death is the only escape. That's a lot to say in a mere thirty-three words, and it doesn't end there. As you read over the poem again, think of how the images allow you to experience the narrator's moment of confrontation with this particular bank building and to also expand on the larger issues in our money-oriented culture.

Accuracy of language is important, but it is also key for us to explore new ways to use words to break out of habitual ways of seeing the world. Sometimes, as we'll discuss below, this has to do with unusual juxtapositions of ideas in metaphoric language. Sometimes, though, it is as seemingly simple as using a word in a fresh, distinctive way. In the following lines from Larry Levis's poem "At the Grave of My Guardian Angel: St. Louis Cemetery, New Orleans" (p. 402), the narrator contemplates his fear of death, the brutal results of war, and the ways that people have been forced to come to grips with violence, often by denying it. He notes:

> It's the extinct whistling of an infantry; it is all the faded rosettes of blood
> Turning into this amnesia of billboards & the ceaseless *hunh?* of traffic.

The use of "rosettes" to describe blood and "amnesia" to describe billboards makes us pay special attention because we do not usually associate flowers with blood or a neurological condition with the kinds of signage that we see along the highway every day. Not only do these descriptions feel accurate—we can certainly envision the circles that seeping blood might make and recall that numb sensation of driving through roadways littered with a stream of advertising—but at the same time, we appreciate these phenomena more acutely because the exact words point out aspects we usually don't focus on.

In heightening our sensitivity about what words we choose, we will make our writing more precise and truer to our own vision. We will also convey more intensity to our readers.

DENOTATION AND CONNOTATION

One of the main ways that we create layers of meanings and use language accurately in our writing is to become aware of the difference between denotation and connotation. **Denotation** simply means the basic dictionary definition of a word. This kind of definition suggests that words correspond in a neutral and one-on-one fashion with objects and gestures. A table is "just a table." **Connation** means the more complex range of associations and subtle implications of a word. If you use the word "sigh," for instance, you probably don't mean simply that a character in a story or a persona in a poem breathed out a little loudly through her nose. Probably you mean to also indicate something about that person's emotional state—her fatigue, impatience, or frustration. These emotional components form the connotation.

In the above lines from Larry Levis, the word "extinct" is a great example of a word chosen for its connotations as well as its denotation. At its most basic, of course, "extinct" simply means no longer existing. Juxtaposed in the poem with "whistling"—usually used for a person walking along making cheerful music—"extinct" here invokes a situation in which whistle instead refers to wind passing over an empty stretch of road where soldiers once fell in battle. That the soldiers are not simply dead, but a whole infantry is extinct underlines the desolation the narrator feels—extinction is often used to discuss the permanent destruction of an entire species. The narrator links his sense of history and his individual losses to the potential erasure of the whole human race.

The connotations of words often depend at least in part on their root language. Modern English has borrowed from many precursor languages, but two of the primary influences in its development have been Anglo-Saxon and Latin (the latter of which ultimately became languages such as French and Spanish). Historically, Latin was used primarily by the ruling classes and the royal courts, whereas Anglo-Saxon evolved among the lower classes as the language of commerce and everyday life. These two influences still often create two channels for our diction that are fairly easy to distinguish. "Diction," for instance, is the fancier Latinate word for "words."

Many synonyms in our language today can be contrasted in this fashion between the often more elegant, educated-sounding Latinate terms and the more "common," harsh-sounding, clipped, shorter, even perhaps crude Anglo-Saxon words. Feline or cat? Scarlet or red? Although our guesses will not always be correct in this regard, it's often a useful way of thinking about what kind of word you want to choose for a given character or situation.

Many words shift meaning over time, sometimes acquiring multiple meanings and sometimes seemingly switching denotations completely. Examples abound. Think of the word "concrete," which we discussed above, and which originally was used in verb form to mean the process of solidifying or congealing; in the 1800s, it's easy to see how this came to be applied to a new construction material, but then later it took on yet another meaning applied more generally to real things manifest in the physical world. Think also of words like run, process, hiccup, plateau, shrimp, and monster, all of which have multiple, though somewhat related meanings. Most words begin with one denotation, but then are used more widely and in different ways, thereby acquiring multiple denotations. We'll discuss in the next section how these changes in meaning often occur through the use of metaphor. These historical shifts in meaning keep language exciting, challenging, and vibrantly alive. (See **Pathways 2.8** and **2.9**.)

FIGURATIVE LANGUAGE

Figurative language is defined as words used in non-ordinary or non-literal ways for literary effect so that they mean more than apparent at first glance. The particular various methods for doing so are collectively referred to as **figures of speech** or **tropes**. No doubt, human beings began using figurative language as soon as their habits of speaking went beyond counting and basic communication and began to include storytelling, and for that reason, we have a host of terms to describe figures of speech that are linked to their roots in the ancient

Greek language. Most areas of expertise have such specialized vocabularies—musicians use Latin terms such as *vivace* or *lento* to describe upbeat or slow pieces and physicians refer to heart attacks as myocardial infarctions—and creative writing does too.

We're more familiar with some of this terminology than others. You may not know offhand what the term **meiosis** means, even though you might have noticed someone's use of deliberate understatement, as when a friend describes her new boyfriend by saying, "He's okay," when you know she's crazy about him. The Greek term **hyperbole**, on the other hand, has become commonplace. In daily life, when a friend says, "I thought I was going to die" in response to his embarrassment in an awkward social situation, we might tell him to cut the hyperbole. Reasons can vary for this kind of mismatch between statements and emotions—it could indicate an attempt to distance oneself, a kind of dishonesty or desire for protection from certain feelings, or simply a reserve in the face of certain listeners. Think of your hypothetical friend—she might not be sure how intensely the boyfriend feels, or she might not want other people to know because she doesn't want to be teased. Whether you use these strategies in your own voice or in dialogue in a piece of writing, they can become features of personality on the page.

Whether a particular term is familiar or not, it is helpful to have a sensitivity to and awareness of at least some of the dozens of tropes available to you so that you can draw on a larger range of these expressive tools yourself. Don't by any means limit yourself to the most common ones; use **Table 2.1** as a resource for trying a variety. (Also see **Pathways 2.10** and **2.11**.)

Metaphor and Simile

Metaphor and simile are the most common types of figurative language and are ones that you are likely already quite familiar with, though it bears taking a closer look at their rich effects and variations. Often, when the term "metaphoric language" is used, it refers to both metaphor and simile. **Metaphor** compares two different things by treating them as equivalents, as in *My uncle is a toad*. **Simile** makes the fact of comparison explicit by linking the terms with *like* or *as*, as in *My uncle is like a toad*. Although there are subtle differences between them, they both rely on similarities between different things.

Two helpful terms when discussing metaphor and simile are tenor and vehicle. The **tenor** is the subject of any metaphor or simile—in the statement *My uncle is a toad*, for instance, "my uncle" is the tenor; "toad" is the **vehicle**. The term "vehicle" reflects the fact that "toad" carries a whole host of associations back to the tenor of the statement in the same way a car carries people or a truck carries loads of various goods. In this case, for instance, toads are not only slimy, but we might also think of them as ugly and green (or greedy); we might think of them as floppy or squishy; we might think of them as making a chorus of trilling sounds every

Table 2.1

Tropes. There are many more kinds of tropes, but these are some of the most common and useful. The ones in boldface are further discussed in the chapter, but they are also listed here for ease of reference.

metaphor	comparison of two things that are not alike by treating them as equivalents *My uncle is a toad.*
simile	explicit comparison of two different things *My uncle is like a toad.*
irony	use of a word or phrase to imply something different from what is said on the surface *The largest dog at the show was named Tiny.*
sarcasm	a step beyond irony, where the complete opposite of what is said is meant; usually bitter in tone In the face of rain, noting to a co-worker, *"Beautiful day, eh?"*
metonymy	use of some aspect of or something closely associated with something to stand in for the whole *He's the worst kind of suit—boring and greedy.*
synecdoche	use of a part of something to stand in for the whole *Her parents bought her a new set of wheels for her sixteenth birthday.*
antanaclasis	repetition of the same word with different meanings or contexts (similar to syllepsis except the word is repeated) *It doubled me over to lose double the money.* *Live in peace, or rest in peace.*
syllepsis	when one word is used (one time) to modify or govern two other words but with two different meanings (similar to antanaclasis except the word is used only once) *By God, I'll run this marathon and the meeting afterward.* *PEACE: Live in it, or rest in it.*

paronomasia	use of two words alike in sound but different in meaning and spelling (sometimes more generally used to mean any type of pun) *She shows off her pearls until they become perils.* *The crazy dog barked til the bark fell from the tree.*
anthimeria	use of one part of speech as a different part of speech (a noun for a verb, an adjective for a noun, etc.) *We'll workshop your manuscript tomorrow.* Or *He needed a good cry after he lost his job.*
personification	giving human abilities or qualities to inanimate objects, plants, animals, or ideas *Trouble sought me out.*
rhetorical question	any question asked for a purpose other than receiving an answer, often to point something out emphatically *José asked George, "Why are you so stupid?"*
paradox	a statement that is contradictory but contains some element of the truth *I felt so alone in the crowd.*
oxymoron	the use of two opposite terms together; a compressed paradox *We had a working vacation.*
synaesthesia	mixing of the senses *The sight of her stabbed him between the eyes.*
meiosis	deliberate understatement *Usain Bolt is a pretty good runner.*
litotes	a form of understatement in which a directly negative statement is used *Usain Bolt is not a bad runner.*
hyperbole	exaggeration for effect *He's so funny, he kills me.*

evening. What's important about having an awareness of these two parts of a metaphor is that it will help you think about how to adapt or change either side of the equation to make your metaphors more powerful. Maybe, for instance, if you think more carefully about *toad*, you realize that it doesn't quite capture your uncle's desperation. With an awareness of how tenor and vehicle work, you might decide instead to say *My uncle is a snarling stray cat.*

You have likely already become familiar with this basic meaning of metaphor, but you may have thought less about the fact that metaphor relies on *both* the similarities and the differences between the two things compared. The startling freshness of a new metaphor emerges from this combination of similarity and difference. Consider the following list of statements:

> *I have a terrible headache.*
> *My head hurts like a bandage being torn off.*
> *My head is filled with stingrays.*
> *My head is a moon covered with craters full of rock shards.*

The latter three are all statements that bring the first one to life with more detail and specificity by using various vehicles for the tenor of "my head." Each of them might be effective in a particular context, but the statements by themselves demonstrate why some metaphors and similes work better than others. The first metaphor isn't really surprising—because a bandage being torn off is familiar bodily pain (and not severe), there's nothing particularly compelling about comparing one's headache to that sensation. The last one—about the craters full of rocks—may be, on the other hand too obscure for a reader to understand the full implications. Perhaps the moon image shows how the pain has created a sense of distance, but to understand that the rocks might create pain with their jagged edges asks a reader to make too big a leap (unless, of course, this forms part of an extended metaphor that is further clarified). *My head is full of stingrays*, however, combines similarity and difference succinctly. Whether we have been stung by a stingray ourselves, we know such wounds are extremely painful. And the image of stingrays swimming around in a person's head adds a sense of dizziness or wooziness—of being swarmed by multiple creatures—that adds to the symptoms being described. There's an unstated assumption that pain can take over and that one's head might seem like a lagoon or other body of water outside one's control. This metaphor suggests confusion and alienation as well as pain, and it is all the richer for these added associations.

This doubling up and layering of meaning is one of the things that gives metaphorical language its power. "On the Mountain" (above) provides a great example of an **extended metaphor**, also known as a **conceit**, and demonstrates how imagery and figurative language work together in poems. Images and figurative language may also combine in powerful ways in prose, and training in this feature of poetry helps create more richness in nonfiction and fiction as well. In Julio Ortega's "Las Papas" (p. 466), for instance, the potatoes of the title (*las papas* in Spanish) connect to a host of associations—the nurturance of cooking and of parenting, the heritage of the main character's native Peru, the adaptability and toughness it takes to thrive as an immigrant, and so on. These meanings embed themselves in the sensory and emotional responses of readers—evocative imagery recreates the flavorful and good-smelling meal the character creates while remembering his distant family in Peru and helping his own son with his homework.

If a metaphor or simile, whether extended or not, doesn't produce this layered effect, it may be weaker than it should be. In fact, our world is full of figurative language, and we are surrounded by its use. In the same way that shifts in meanings of a word can be taken for granted, so can the usually metaphorical process by which words so often take on new meanings. Even many clichés once must have seemed surprising and insightful in their comparison of one thing with another—happy as a pig in mud, sleep like a log, the moon is made of green cheese. There was a time, when someone first coined such phrases, that they probably had the power to reveal a new perspective. In fact, they seemed so apt that they became widely used and then their impact dulled.

This raises the issue of how closely connected words' connotations often are to metaphor. Many connotations of words are similarly the result of their metaphorical use in the past. Once a new meaning for a word comes into common use, then the metaphor becomes "dead" or "frozen" and no longer seems to us like a metaphor. The first time someone described encountering a minor setback as a "hiccup" must have seemed funny and creative, but today we take this use of the word for granted, and use it literally. This is one of the reasons that it can be a challenge to continue to make our language fresh and to find new, startling yet apt ways of describing the world around us: writers and speakers repeatedly come up with new ways of saying things, but they can ultimately become stale, and we have to think again.

One great example of this kind of **frozen** or **dead metaphor** is, "He's a real ham." Today, we go straight to the idea that a ham is a person who does exaggerated or silly things for attention, but it originated at a time when actors on stage applied a great deal of make-up so they could be seen even from the back of a large audience. They became known as "hams" because grease from pig carcasses was used as a make-up remover, and the more make-up they used the more they had to "ham it up" to remove it. Gradually, the word evolved to indicate the outsize drama of actors, no matter how they removed their make-up, and then more generally to any over-the-top behavior, especially of a comic sort. Clichés are often basically overused metaphors or similes, but ones for which a denotative switch has not yet occurred.

Another problem with metaphors that bears mention is the **mixed metaphor**, or one where two different metaphors are used at once, creating a kind of confusion or collision of meaning. "She has beat back every hurdle that was placed in front of her," for instance, creates a comic effect rather than a respect for the person working so hard. We *leap over* hurdles; we *beat back* enemies or attacks. What happens with a mixed metaphor is that neither implied metaphor is complete, and therefore the sense gets lost. The denotative and connotative meanings in our language so frequently merge and overlap that we're often unaware of mixing metaphors. (See **Pathway 2.12**.)

Irony

Another key trope is **irony**, where a word or phrase is used with two layers of meaning—its face value and a different, perhaps even an opposite, meaning underneath. Irony is associated with a humorous or gently mocking tone, and it depends on someone "getting it" when others may hear simply the face-value meaning. You might wink, for instance, at your brother across the table at a family holiday, as you tell your grandmother once again that her noodle kugel is the absolute best in the world, even though you and your brother would rather have spicy pad Thai. Your brother may see the irony, whereas your grandmother probably won't. Much of today's commentary on such television programs as *The Daily Show* and *The Colbert Report* depends on highlighting ironic comments not intended to be so by their original speakers.

Because the original meaning is not entirely abandoned, the user of irony is creating a comparison between the two interpretations of the statement, and that comparison function is akin to that of metaphor. You don't want to indicate that your grandmother's kugel is horrible, but you do want to compare it to the more tantalizing pad Thai. As in metaphor, both the similarities and differences of meaning are important.

One good example in poetry comes from Larry Levis:

> We'd better be getting on our way soon, sweet Nothing.
> I'll buy you something pretty from the store.

These lines use the trope of **personification**, a subset of metaphor—"Nothing" is spoken to, like a person that the narrator is driving with in a car, and stands in for what the narrator fears he will be left with in the relentlessness of passing time. But the lines also make the ironic assertion that "buying something pretty" will have the capacity to sooth the sense of emptiness, something the poem overall clearly does not mean.

Sarcasm, on the other hand, is generally understood to be a type of irony that is more direct—that means precisely the opposite of what is said and often points this out with some bitterness. If you did actually loathe your grandmother's casserole, telling her it was good would veer over into sarcasm. You would probably say it with some nasty affect, perhaps rolling your eyes, or shoving the plate away from you on the table. Your grandmother would be the butt of your resentment and there would be a real desire for her to hear that you mean the opposite of what you say. In contrast to Levis, consider Ann Hodgman's comic essay "No Wonder They Call Me a Bitch" (p. 387), in which she recounts trying various types of dog food to see how they stack up to advertisers' claims. At one point she notes "how pleasant it was to turn to *dry* dog food!" Though comparatively true, as the dry is not as disgusting as the canned, Hodgman clearly means us to understand that there is nothing at all tasty about dry dog food. While Hodgman's tone seems playful rather than angry, her essay makes a sharp commentary about our susceptibility to ridiculous advertising claims. This essay provides a good example of how irony and sarcasm form a continuum—while it is most certainly ironic, it might also be argued that it goes as far as to be sarcastic. But there is no hard and fast line between the two.

The above are examples of **verbal irony**, focused on the turn of a word or phrase, but in your work you may also want to think about **situational irony**, which has to do with the larger story being told or image being explored—certainly, Ann Hodgman's eating various types of dog food constitutes situational irony. Verbal and situational irony often build upon one another.

Metonymy

Metonymy is a figure of speech in which a substitution is made—in this case, some attribution or suggestive word for what is literally meant. You might say *I live off the sweat of my brow* or *Her bed is never empty*. People sweat when they work hard (at least when they do physical labor), and so the first statement indicates that its speaker is neither lazy nor independently wealthy. In the second instance, "bed" stands in for a sex life—and the fact that hers is never empty tells us that she keeps busy romantically. The negative in this statement, however, lets us know that more is implied than simply that this person is in a relationship; since it is *never* empty, we get the idea that perhaps she cheats or has multiple partners.

Metonymy functions similarly to a metaphor to point out a perhaps overlooked quality of an object or person, but its use creates a closer relationship between the two things compared. This is a figure of speech based on *continuity* or *contiguity* between two things rather than the similarity between two unlike things that creates strong metaphors. The poems already included in this chapter demonstrate the difference. The multiple possible meanings that I discussed for John Haines's "On the Mountain" rely on metaphorical connections—the comparison is never directly made, but the weather is being compared to a number of possible *very different* entities—aging, gradual loss of intimacy, and so on. On the other hand, Rae Armantrout's "Home Federal" relies instead on metonymic connections between a long-gone traditional idea of home and the fake chintz curtains and colonial balcony of commercial enterprises. By demonstrating that the latter is false, she indicates the former is similarly made up. This is a conclusion based on similarity rather than difference.

Synecdoche

Similar to metonymy, really a subset of that category, **synecdoche** is a figure of speech that uses a part of something to stand in for the whole thing. For instance, if we say, *Marika is the eyes of this organization*, we're using a structure seemingly like that of a metaphor, focusing on qualities we might otherwise not attend to. But because Marika does indeed have possession of those eyes she's using in her organizational role, the comparison narrows rather than enlarges our view of Marika. The effect of synecdoche, then, is one of focus, or intensification.

Take this statement: *Mr. Kleinman is no redneck.* "Redneck," a term first used in the late nineteenth century, refers to the fact that farmers typically got sunburned when working in the fields, and the term became a general stand-in for those who behaved in uneducated ways. We can assume that Mr. Kleinman has more sophistication than that, though this statement also raises the question of why the idea came up at all. Mr. Kleinman, then, may make a pretense of crudity, may pretend to have more of a rural background than he really does. There are many other instances of particular parts of the body standing in for entire personality types, but synecdoche also may be used for other objects and even actions. *Wave* may stand for ocean, as in Samuel Taylor Coleridge's line "The western wave was all a-flame," or it may stand for a hasty dismissal, as in *He gave us the wave.*

Synecdoche is useful in all genres of writing, but perhaps most particularly in film and screenplay. Whenever you see an extreme close-up in a movie, that is essentially a form of synecdoche—the part of a person's face or body or another object represents the entire person, a place, an emotion, or even a relationship—a man putting his hand in the curve of a woman's back might imply a romantic relationship or a growing sexual tension between them. In Alfred Hitchcock's classic *Psycho*, the stabbing murder of Janet Leigh's character Marion is filmed almost entirely in close-ups—the knife jerking, her hand grabbing the shower curtain, the shower curtain hooks popping loose as she falls, the shower head still running water, Marion's feet with water (and blood) coursing down the drain, and then finally a close-up of her eye, open and unblinking in death. Each of these focused images represents some important facet of the character's murder without showing a broad view of the scene. *Psycho*, of course, was released in 1960 when censorship would have prevented a full depiction, but the use of these close-up shots also increases the intimacy and chilling experience of Marion's fear during her murder. Sometimes, in other words, showing a part is more powerful than showing an overview.

The power of imagery and figurative language resides in vividness and compactness. The activities in this chapter focus on trying out various approaches in order to enrich and deepen your writing. In the next chapter we will discuss even more ways of using these tropes, as well as schemes of repetition and rhythm that augment the single phrase or figure of speech.

PATHWAYS

Pathway 2.1. Abstract to concrete. Take an abstraction (like friendship, love, justice) that's important to you and write a poem or passage of prose that substitutes a particular moment or person for the abstraction. Don't use the abstract word at all, not even in the title; let it arise in your concrete images.

Pathway 2.2. Descriptive poem. Write a poem that begins as a description of a simple object or event. Focus on accuracy and depth of detail. Avoid, at least at first, figures of speech, and see what you can convey with description alone.

Pathway 2.3. All your senses. We tend to rely on imagery that's visual. Try writing a poem or passage of prose that focuses on one of your other senses—hearing, smell, taste, or touch. Try writing two stanzas, one based in the present (the smell of bagels rising out of the shop you just passed by) and one from memory (the perfume your grandmother always wore).

Pathway 2.4. Group exercise: Shared subject, different poems. As an entire class or in small groups, agree upon a subject matter you will all write about, such as the common theme of trees in Fady Joudah's, Harryette Mullen's, and William Carlos Williams's poems recommended as supplemental reading for this chapter. Bring your different poems to class and discuss what different experiences and sensations led to your different interpretations of the subject.

Pathway 2.5. Group exercise: Exquisite Corpse. The "Exquisite Corpse" method began as a Surrealist strategy to free writers' imaginations, and by now there are many variations. In this version, choose an abstraction or idea as a theme that you all stick to. Then agree upon a sentence structure, or word type order with the same number as in your group. (One of the most common is Adjective Noun Verb Adjective Noun for groups of five.) Each person in your group then writes an assigned word type using concrete language on a piece of paper, which is folded to conceal the word, and then passed to the next person for the next word type. If you do this with four or five pieces of paper, you will have five sentences or lines. Open them up and read aloud, then write out each line. You may want to post typed versions on the class website or wiki and see how the imagery flows. What surprises did new writers introduce? How did different attitudes toward the abstraction emerge? What interesting elements emerged that might inspire a new direction for a subject you might have dealt with too predictably otherwise? Your group may want to "give" one line to each person who then works with the line in more personal ways.

Pathway 2.6. Persona poem. Write a persona poem or paragraph (in the voice of someone other than yourself). You might even want to do a series of three or more short ones. Use real people that are distinct—maybe someone older or of a different gender, someone who is from a different region and therefore has a way of speaking that you notice, perhaps someone in your family who holds very different religious or political views from you. See what you can capture and what insight you might gain from trying to spend a few moments in that person's voice.

Pathway 2.7. Group exercise: Word pleasure. Write down a list of favorite words. Discuss why you like these particular words and what they mean. (One of my favorites is "clowder," for instance, which means a large group of cats.) Then "borrow" a word from each other person in the group. At home, try writing a poem that starts on the theme of one of your favorites, but that also includes the ones you've borrowed from your group mates. See what new contrasts and ideas come up.

Pathway 2.8. New meanings. Choose a word you like and make up a new meaning for it. This new meaning should share some quality with the original meaning, but be a distinct usage, the way "hiccup" and "concrete" function. Write a short poem that makes use of both meanings of the word.

Pathway 2.9. Synonym play. Choose a common noun or adjective—such as "man" or "red"—and list as many synonyms as you can think of. (For red, for instance, you might list maroon, scarlet, crimson, cerise, blood, ruby, cherry, magenta, claret, vermillion, and so on.) Then write a sentence with one of these words; rewrite with a different word and note how each choice would influence the tone and meaning of the sentence. For instance, what's the difference between *That scrawny girl won the race* and *That slender girl won the race*?

Pathway 2.10. Shifting tropes. Choose a poem or passage of prose that you've written or that's in the book's anthology and that contains a metaphor or simile. Rewrite by changing the metaphor or simile to a different type of figure of speech from **Table 2.1**. Do this four or five times and see how the poem or passage changes.

Pathway 2.11. Emergency metonymy. Think of an emergency situation that you've observed or even been a part of (this might involve a medical emergency, a traffic accident, or some other high-stress event). First write a few lines describing what happened. Then, as you work to break this into the lines of a poem, or set it up as the start of a memoir, use metonymy or synecdoche to change the title or label of all the people on the scene. A nurse might become a stethoscope, for instance, or you might describe yourself as a broken collarbone.

Pathway 2.12. Dead metaphors. Keep a list of instances of language use that might once have seemed fresh and apt, but which have become clichéd. In other words, spend a week looking for dead metaphors. Note especially times when this watering down of the power of metaphor results in mixed metaphors that people may not notice.

FURTHER ANTHOLOGY READINGS

Fady Joudah, "Sleeping Trees" (poetry)
Harryette Mullen, "Tree" (poetry)
William Carlos Williams, "Young Sycamore" (poetry)

GUIDEPOST: RISK-TAKING

Language and the world are constantly remade.

Remaking language, as writers do, through vivid, fresh use of words and figures of speech, is a valuable endeavor in and of itself. Writing requires attention to the details of language in a way that might seem trivial from the outside—is "red" the right word, or should I use "scarlet" to convey a sense of threat? It's the back-and-forth experimentation required to get a passage or poem "just right" that demands open-mindedness and a skill with juggling that is useful in other spheres. As you learn what makes your literary choices effective, you are simultaneously learning an entire methodology for solving problems.

Taking a close look at the workings of metaphor also can remind us of why a pursuit such as poetry can help us in other walks of life. In the world of scientific discovery, for instance, metaphors often help to make possible the leaps in thinking that allow for new scientific theories to be pursued. Metaphors can explain new discoveries and clarify the communication of highly technical information to lay audiences. For instance, we still talk about electricity as having a flow or current like water, though we have known since the discovery of the electron in 1898 that electricity is the result of charged particles, not fluids. However, because electricity still behaves in ways similar to fluids, and because terms like "current" and "flow" took on new denotations over time, this fundamental metaphor is still in evidence in everyday language.

Whether metaphors are used to aid in important discoveries or need to be altered to include other perceptions, being aware of them will make you sensitive to their use and more able to understand how their use influences thinking all around you. Sometimes, creating a new metaphor is enough to unlock a whole new way of thinking about something, and sensitivity to metaphoric thinking is highly valued not only in the sciences and medicine, but in business and other professional endeavors as well.

Chapter 3

Sound and Rhythm

READING WITHIN THIS CHAPTER
Yusef Komunyakaa, "Salt" (poetry)

KEY ANTHOLOGY READINGS
Terrance Hayes, "The Golden Shovel" (poetry)
Sandra McPherson, "To a Penny Postcard, © 1911" (poetry)
Lisel Mueller, "Spell for a Traveler" (poetry)
Christopher Shannon, "Apollo (at) Eleven" (poetry)

Think about the way that your favorite song evokes emotion through its rhythm as well as the meaning of the lyrics. Poetry is another realm in which, through rhythm, we join our physicality with our emotions and mental impressions of the world. We also see this phenomenon in the practice of yoga and breath-based meditation, as well as in the increased mental focus often found in a variety of other athletic pursuits. The mind-body connection in all of these forms reminds us that we breathe and are physical, mortal beings as well as purveyors of thoughts and feelings.

Perhaps this helps to account for the reputation of writing, especially poetry, as being linked so strongly to our passionate emotions. As Lord Byron once noted, poetry remains "the lava of the imagination whose eruption prevents an earthquake." This connection between body and poetry remains all these centuries later. More recently, in a Chicago slam poetry competition, seventeen-year-old Adam Gottlieb chanted, "Poet breathe now because there's a fire inside you that needs oxygen to burn." (This competition is chronicled in the documentary

film *Louder Than a Bomb*.) "Breath," Gottlieb says, is "one poem we all share."
The physicality of language comes closer to the surface in poetry and drama,
which are more likely to be performed than prose forms. Prose writers, however,
can learn much about creating vibrant, living language through an understanding
of poetic rhythms. All writers should strive to keep alive this vital connection
between our human breathing and our words.

BREATH AND RHYTHM

Rhythm may seem like something that comes naturally, yet anyone who has tried at
some point to play the guitar or who has imagined singing on *American Idol* knows
that it can be more complex than it seems. The need for technical skill arises in both
music and poetry, and the rhythms of poetry are that much more subtle without the
regular guidance of a steady bass line or particular keys in which to be written. Although they share much, poetry does not use a system of pitches (melodies, harmonies, chords, etc.) found in music. So how do you establish rhythm in poetry?

Think about any poems that you may have remembered over the years, and
it's likely they will be quite regular in rhythm, even sound. All **limericks**, for
instance, are defined by a regular, even predictable rhythm and rhyme scheme,
which makes them easy to recall. In the following silly example, for instance, it
would be easy to guess the last word, even though the poem is nonsensical:

> There was an old gal in a boat,
> Whose stomach continued to bloat.
> She leaned on the rail
> And before we could yell,
> A dragon came out of her _____.

Much poetry, especially of the rhyming variety, is considered formal and
sophisticated, but the limerick takes those expectations and turns them on their
head. More complicated forms and limericks, however, still have in common
regularity of pattern. What we call "formal" poetry (which we'll discuss more
in Chapter 4), which uses rhyme, fixed numbers of syllables, and other patterns,
emerged before people wrote things down, when they depended on those patterns
to be able to remember the epic stories that poems told. Note, however, that all
defined forms allow for variation. Limericks, for instance, sometimes have eight
syllables in the first, second, and fifth lines, and sometimes nine, and the third
and fourth lines vary between five and six syllables. The number of syllables
should be consistent, but notice that a slight variation, such as the extra linking
syllable "And" in the above limerick, doesn't ruin the poem. Even the rhyme
doesn't remain all **true** or **perfect rhyme**—the slight variation in "rail" and
"yell," called **off rhyme, slant rhyme,** or **half rhyme,** works perfectly well, and
often works best in subtler work. In fact, poets often play with such variations.

As you write your own poems, pay attention to the sounds and rhythms that begin with our breathing and the formation of words in our mouths and lungs. Even though we think of poetry and prose existing today primarily in written form—in an almost disembodied state as marks on a piece of paper—we should remember that the rhythm of the human heartbeat and breath are always implied in every word we put down on the page or computer screen, even in prose and dramatic genres. Reading your own and others' work aloud helps you hear how the rhythms are working (or not), and also will give you insight into other qualities of your work, even sentence structure, gaps in information, and the flow of the work overall. (See **Pathway 3.1**.)

Also remember that our breathing is unconscious except when we are panting from physical exertion, emotion, or panic. As you begin to think about rhythm in your own poems, remember to become more conscious of it in the same way that you become more conscious of the work going on in your imagination. Melding ideas, images, and imagination with the technical aspects of rhythm can be a challenge. That's why exercises like **Pathways 3.2** and **3.3** try to engage both. The technical strategies you learn in this book should always serve your meaning. We concentrate on techniques so that they can become as easy as riding the proverbial bike to whatever destination you set.

Look for the two main methods writers use to create **rhythm**: repetition and accent. Repetition, of course, may refer to duplication of sounds, words, phrases, line lengths, and sentence structures, even of stanza, paragraph, section, and chapter lengths. And it may also refer to the reproduction of certain patterns of stressed and unstressed syllables or accents in words themselves. We'll discuss the issue of accent in Chapter 4, but here we'll discuss other types of repetition. Rhythm at its simplest refers to any pattern of sounds and silences; however, it also may indicate larger-scale issues of pacing through an entire piece of writing. As you write first drafts, you may pour out whatever words come into your head, but get in the habit of trying out different possibilities to find the sounds that work to support your meaning.

CHOOSING SOUNDS

Sound has many more varied and subtle options than those in the limerick above. We often will talk of sounds as augmenting certain emotional—and even intellectual—effects that we want to create through the meanings of the words we choose. In Terrance Hayes's poem "The Golden Shovel" (p. 383) we encounter these opening lines:

> When I am so small Da's sock covers my arm, we
> cruise at twilight until we find the place the real
>
> men lean, bloodshot and translucent with cool.

Even in these few short lines, we can hear that the long, slow "ooh" sounds reflect the languid evening activity and the relaxed demeanor of the men described, thus supporting the mood of the content. However, careful readers may also notice that the hard "k" sounds in "sock," "covers," "cruise," and "cool" contrast with the soft vowels, auguring, perhaps, that something not-so-simple co-exists with the fondness of the memory of Da. In other words, the sounds we choose in our writing can both support initial impressions and complicate them by foreshadowing changes that may come later.

At its most basic, paying attention to sound in your writing requires only that you be conscious of the qualities of various sounds and how we associate those sounds with other aspects of life. These are basic lessons that you may have learned when you studied phonics as a child, but we often forget about them as we become more fluent spellers and writers overall and cease to sit around a storytelling circle chanting rhymes. Even in our silent reading, however, we replay sounds in our minds, and the effects of varying sounds make a world of difference in the effects of our words—with short vowel sounds creating a more rapid pace, and longer ones a slower pace, and with hard consonants creating a clipped, sometimes harsh tone, whereas soft consonants are connected to easier flow of the words. One great way to increase your awareness of the role of pure sound can be found in **Pathway 3.4**.

This, of course, has causes in our biology and involves the breath—the soft consonants, also called **fricatives** after the friction they create, are produced when we don't fully stop the flow of air through the mouth, as in the sounds related to f, v, th, and the sibilants such as s, z, and sh. On the other hand, hard consonants are also referred to as **stops** or **plosives** (think implosion rather than explosion)—precisely because they are formed when the lips or tongue stops the flow of air, as when we use the letter sounds k, p. The letters t, b, d, and g technically form stops, but because of their somewhat less harsh sound are often described as soft consonants. Clearly, there is a range, depending on pronunciation and comparison to other nearby words. See if you can find any additional patterns (in addition to the k sounds and the long-sounding **diphthongs** of multiple vowels) in the lines from "The Golden Shovel" above. What is the effect of Hayes choosing to emphasize these particular sounds? Try working with sound variations yourself in **Pathway 3.5**.

An awareness of these phonetic issues at the level of each letter or diphthong is the place to begin being aware of how you are using sound in your writing, but the larger units of words, phrases, sentence structure, and even the way larger elements (such as long and short stanzas or paragraphs or units of dialogue) throughout whole pieces will also determine the rhythm of any poem, story, essay, or play that you write.

REPETITION AND SOUND PATTERNS

One of the major ways that we establish a rhythm is through repetition—and rhythms are created at multiple levels of every piece of art. In songs, for instance, we may have the regular pounding of a pedal on a bass drum, plus the repeated pattern of notes and time signature, and we may also have repeated words in a refrain or chorus. Similarly, in writing, in addition to apparent repetition of sounds, words, phrases, and syntax, we may have images and themes that crop up over again (called **motifs**), often with some variation. We may also use certain features of sentence and paragraph structure that create a rhythm even when the words are not the same. Lisel Mueller's "Spell for a Traveler" (p. 444) demonstrates the power of repetition to create rhythm. Even a few lines set up a strong rhythm through repetition:

> From the harbor of sleep bring me the milk of childhood,
> from the ocean of silence bring me a grain of salt . . .

The poem continues repeating the same sentence structure, using the words "from" and "bring" over and over, creating an obsessive quality that suits the poem. As with songs, we can create different kinds of rhythms in our prose and poetry—some with a strong, slow beat; some with quick, even frantic pacing; and others that are meandering and leisurely. Mueller's rhythm reflects the relentlessness and desperation of someone who has resorted to casting spells, as her title indicates. In the pairing of that rhythm with particular words and images, we see that her poem may be about more than simply someone who is away from home on a trip. (See **Pathways 3.6** and **3.7.** Look at Christopher Shannon's palindrome or mirror poem and **Pathway 3.8** to see yet another way to work with repetition.)

You can also affect the power of your poems through less obvious patterns of repetition called **schemes**, perhaps because they are not unlike those unstated plans of someone plotting to do another person in or get some advantage in business or politics. This use of the word has to do with a writer's ability to plan effects through a particular arrangement of letters, sounds, word order, and sentence structure. Just as with the tropes that we discussed in Chapter 2, there are many more types of schemes than we will discuss fully here, but an increased awareness of some of your options and the ways that these patterns have been used by other writers will better allow you to achieve your vision. We'll explore details about how and why some schemes work below via one poem. Once you've looked at Yusef Komunyakaa's poem, take a look at others in the anthology and see what schemes you can identify in them.

SALT
Yusef Komunyakaa

Lisa, Leona, Loretta?
She's sipping a milkshake
In Woolworths, dressed in
Chiffon & fat pearls.
She looks up at me,
Grabs her purse
& pulls at the hem
Of her skirt. I want to say
I'm just here to buy
A box of Epsom salt
For my grandmama's feet.
Lena, Lois? I feel her
Strain to not see me.
Lines are now etched
At the corners of her thin,
Pale mouth. Does she know
I know her grandfather
Rode a white horse
Through Poplas Quarters
Searching for black women,
How he killed Indians
& stole land with bribes
& fake deeds? I remember
She was seven & I was five
When she ran up to me like a cat
With a gypsy moth in its mouth
& we played doctor & house
Under the low branches of a raintree
Encircled with red rhododendrons.
We could pull back the leaves
& see grandmama ironing
At their wide window. Once
Her mother moved so close
To the yardman we thought they'd kiss.
What the children of housekeepers
& handymen knew was enough
To stop biological clocks,
& it's hard now not to walk over
& mention how her grandmother

Killed her idiot son
& salted him down
In a wooden barrel.

Letters and Words

You are no doubt familiar with **alliteration** by now, as it is the most familiar and easiest scheme to identify with its seemingly simple repetition of starting consonant sounds in a series of words. Alliteration has been painfully overused because it is so easy to use . . . and many times it produces a childish effect that we remember from grade school poems and tongue-twisters like "Peter Piper picked a peck of pickled peppers." Alliteration, however, can be subtly and well used and can form an underpinning to the meaning of a poem. Take a look at "Salt" above.

Several instances of alliteration point us to important facets of this poem's meaning. Most apparent, of course, is the use of the five names—three in the first line and two in the twelfth—all starting with the letter "L." The alliteration reflects a mind that has grown distant from certain details of childhood. Although the narrator of the poem had a close childhood relationship with the woman he now observes, he no longer can be sure of her name. Not only does the use of alliteration here mimic the way we comb through our memories, but it also perhaps reflects that the time of these two people's acquaintance was precisely when counting rhymes and tongue-twisters might have been a part of their playing. As you read this poem, see what other instances of alliteration you can find and what function you think they serve.

This poem also makes use of other letter- and word-level schemes: consonance and assonance. **Consonance**—repetition of consonant sounds in close proximity, whether at the beginnings or in the middle of words—is clearly in evidence in "Salt." If you trace the "s" sounds, starting with the title of the poem, you can see that there are more than average, even if you don't count the plurals at the ends of words—Lisa, sipping, shake, dressed, purse, skirt, say, Epsom, salt, and so on. In fact, these sibilant sounds give the poem a kind of hissing sound overall—perhaps hostile, but deceptively soft. You can trace other sound ladders in this poem as well—the many k sounds, and even the m's in grandmama, remember, moth, mouth, and so on.

The use of similar vowel sounds in the stressed syllables of adjacent words—or **assonance**—is trickier to find, and less strictly adhered to as a scheme in this poem. Assonance strictly defined means that the vowel sounds must be the same—not just the vowels themselves—and the o's in the examples below, for instance, don't always have precisely the same sounds. Komunyakaa allows the consonants to carry most of the rhythm. However, note points at which the vowel sounds stretch out—they are not in the moments when the narrator describes the woman in her current state, which mostly remain clipped, but you can see a few phrases slow with diphthongs and long vowels:

> buy box Epsom
> know know grandfather rode horse through Poplas Quarters searching
> [note that "know" and "rode" have the same vowel sound, but "horse"
>   and "Poplas" differ]
> moth mouth played doctor house
> down wooden barrel

These moments are distinct from the rest of the poem in their accusatory tone, and they slow readers down with longer, more drawn-out sounds. Even though Komunyakaa doesn't use strict assonance, he slows us down by using long vowel sounds, thus giving us a few more seconds for these particular negative images to sink in. (See **Pathway 3.9.**)

Although Komunyakaa's poem doesn't obviously use the word-level scheme of **onomatopoeia**—the use of words that sound like what they describe, such as *buzz*, *swoop*, *bump*, and so forth—we can find subtle traces of it here and there. Note, for instance, the way that words like "sipping" and "kiss" place the mouth in shapes more or less like what is required for the action described. Note also that Komunyakaa chooses such words when describing the actions of the white females in the poem—the woman sips her milkshake, and her mother before her nearly kissed the yardman, and in between these points at the beginning and end of the poem we also find attention brought to the daughter's lips when she was a child and ran up to the narrator "like a cat / with a gypsy moth in its mouth." The almost-onomatopoeia-like repeated images of these female lips give the poem an undercurrent of sexual intimacy that supports the direct mentions of the white man choosing black women for sexual purposes, the white and black children playing "doctor" and "house," and the white mother being physically drawn to the yardman. We see all the more clearly the dangers of feelings denied on racial grounds.

This kind of subtle use of effects characterizes excellent literary writing. Komunyakaa, for instance, does not overuse any of these strategies and so they do not become heavy-handed or unintentionally comic. Rather, he chooses carefully yet instinctively from an array of sounds that can support his meaning without overwhelming it or hitting readers over the head.

Take a close look at one or more of the other poems suggested for reading with this chapter and trace alliteration, consonance, and assonance in those poems. Also try going back to poems or prose that you have already drafted yourself and see how looking at these patterns of sound can help you clarify sensation, emotion, and even meaning.

Phrases and Sentences

In addition to the vast vocabulary of English, we have a language that is structurally flexible, and these myriad ways of putting together phrases and sentences prove to be the most powerful opportunities for us to fine-tune emotions and thoughts on the page. Most of the sentences we speak and write use the fundamental structure of first the subject, then the verb. Often these two crucial and basic parts of speech are followed by an object. The common subject-verb-object sentence is classic and all-pervasive in our daily lives.

> Alejandro drinks milk.
> I caught a cab.

Notice that both of these sentences could leave off the object at the end, but we would be missing important information—what Alejandro is drinking and whether you've caught a cab or a cold or a baseball. The subject-verb-object sentence contains a lot of information in all of its brevity. Sometimes a sentence will show a different pattern with something else following the subject and verb—an adjective, adverb, noun, or prepositional phrase—but in all of these common forms, even commonly in poetry, the subject and verb usually come first and order our way of thinking about the topic we're reading or hearing about. It's no coincidence that "subject" means either the main noun of a sentence or the overall topic of a piece of writing. The primacy of the subject (and whatever the subject is doing via the verb) affects how we think and how we interpret words. Even in Komunyakaa's "Salt," most of the sentences (as opposed to lines) begin with the subject: She's sipping, She looks, I want, I feel, I remember, We could pull.

Earlier in this chapter we've talked about how repetitions set up rhythms that guide us through a poem or prose work. That remains true at the sentence level as well. However, too much repetition leads to boredom, and writers tread the line between repetition and effective variations that add liveliness, change pace, and sometimes turn a story or poem in a new direction. Too many short subject-verb sentences lose their punch and grow dull. Komunyakaa varies the patterns with line breaks, prepositional phrases, and so on, but includes three sentences that begin differently—"Does she know . . .?," "Once", and one with the long compound noun "What the children of housekeepers / & handymen knew."

Schemes at the level of sentences are methods by which writers vary their sentence constructions while attending to rhythms as well. Because there are too many of these to discuss each in turn, I have included a list in **Table 3.1**. You may notice that while most of these schemes are patterns of repetition, some of them create instead interruptions or twists in the usual flow of thoughts in a sentence, or contrast a structure with an unusual meaning. As with the tropes described in Chapter 2, it's not so important that you know the Latin name of

Table 3.1
Sentence-Level Schemes.

isocolon	similarity of both structure and length
	I think, therefore I am. —Rene Descartes, *Discourse on the Method*
antithesis	contrasting ideas expressed in often parallel structure
	It was the best of times, it was the worst of times. —Charles Dickens, *A Tale of Two Cities*
anastrophe	inversion of the usual word order
	Now is the night one blue dew. —James Agee, "Knoxville: Summer, 1915" (p. 275)
parenthesis	insertion of some verbal unit in a position that interrupts the normal syntactical flow of a sentence, whether using parentheses or not
	They just lie there and groove, but after a while they start hearing— you won't believe this—they hear chamber music. —Tim O'Brien, "How to Tell a True War Story" (p. 447)
apposition	placing side by side two elements, the second of which serves as an explanation or modification of the first
	. . . this man was a prophet, a genius, a pioneer in the field of entertainment. —David Sedaris, "The Drama Bug" (p. 502)
ellipsis	deliberate omission of a word or words readily implied by the context
	I am the little girl she will someday tell, ". . . Be careful with marriage." Even though she is not [careful]. —Anne Panning, "Remembering, I Was Not There" (p. 473)
asyndeton	deliberate omission of conjunctions in a series
	My hands were blistered, my back was burned, my body ached. —J. M. Coetzee, *Foe* (excerpt p. 52)
polysyndeton	deliberate use of many conjunctions
	Gary was chuting away across space, moving and talking and catching my eye. —Annie Dillard, "Total Eclipse" (p. 325)

anaphora	repetition of the same word or group of words at the beginnings of successive clauses
	From the harbor of sleep bring me the milk of childhood, from the ocean of silence bring me a grain of salt . . . —Lisel Mueller, "Spell for a Traveler" (p. 444)
epistrophe	repetition of the same word or group of words at the ends of successive clauses
	A government of the people, by the people, for the people. —Abraham Lincoln, "The Gettysburg Address"
epanalepsis	repetition at the end of a clause of the word that opened the clause
	Swallow, my sister, O sister swallow, / How can thine heart be full of the spring? —Algernon Charles Swinburne, "Itylus"
anadiplosis	repetition of the last word or words of one clause at the beginning of the following clause
	All the willows weeping, / are not symbols for me / but symbols for me they stand . . . —Lynn Emanuel, "The Out-of-Body Experience" (p. 344)
antimetabole	repetition of words in successive clauses in reverse grammatical order
	We didn't land on Plymouth Rock; the rock was landed on us. —Malcolm X, speech in Washington Heights, NY
chiasmus	reversal of grammatical structure in successive clauses without repetition of exact words
	We thought her dying when she slept, / And sleeping when she died. —Thomas Hood, "The Deathbed"
polyptoton	repetition in the form of words from the same root but with different endings
	Child-as-heliostat fixed to reflect the sun's rays, continuously, even as the sun turns away. And heliotropes: any kind of small, reddish-purple flower from Heliopolis . . . —Lia Purpura, "On Looking Away" (p. 480)

(Continued)

Table 3.1   (Continued)

climax	arrangement of words, phrases, or clauses in an order of increasing importance, emphasis, or occurrence *We do not want to euthanize it, and dissect it, and leave its carcass on the seminar table.* —Frederick Smock, "A Poet's Education" (p. 510)
parallelism	similarity of syntax of a set of successive phrases, clauses, or sentences *I tried in vain to pick up all the hair that was ruining the rug, to smooth out the edges of the fabric they'd chewed on, to shut them up again in the wardrobe.* —Julio Cortazár, "Letter to a Young Lady in Paris" (p. 308)

each and every sentence-level scheme, but you be aware of the wide variety of choices you have in terms of sentence structure. **Table 3.1** provides a guide should you find that the quality of your sentences is either too chaotic or too predictable. Turn to it for inspiration to try something new, to change the pacing, or to make readers pay attention to a particular moment. (See **Pathways 3.10** and **3.11**.)

Notice that Komunyakaa has used a great many conscious sound effects at the level of letters and words, but few if any sentence-level schemes per se. This poem, after all, describes a chance encounter that brings back memories and knowledge of the past, and the directness of the speaker's voice carries a crucial part of its meaning. Take a look, however, at the way that Komunyakaa has emphasized his use of the word "and" by using instead the ampersand (&). We might consider this a form of **polysyndeton** or the deliberate use of many conjunctions, and it contributes here to a sense of the connections that exist even though often denied.

By contrast, take a look at the following opening paragraph from Nobel Prize winner J. M. Coetzee's novel *Foe*, a re-telling of the classic *Robinson Crusoe*. This story is narrated by a different—female—shipwreck survivor.

> At last I could row no further. My hands were blistered, my back was burned, my body ached. With a sigh, making barely a splash, I slipped overboard. With slow strokes, my long hair floating about me, like a flower of the sea, like an anemone, like a jellyfish of the kind you see in the waters of Brazil, I swam towards the strange island, for a while swimming as I had rowed, against the current, then all at once free of its grip, carried by the waves into the bay and on to the beach.

Read this paragraph aloud with your class and note the syntactical symbolism, the way the rhythms mimic the ocean waves. Several syntactical patterns are at play here, but none of them is rigid. Like the sea, each is forcefully but not mechanically rhythmic. That effect has as much to do with the variations as with the repetitions. (See **Pathway 3.12**.)

In the Coetzee paragraph, you will find an example of **asyndeton**, the elimination of a conjunction in a series. In this series the lack of a conjunction may itself signal the narrator's exhaustion—the narrator doesn't expend the energy to utter a word that she can do without. Coetzee also uses **anaphora** in the repetition of "like" at the beginning of three phrases in the last sentence. Anaphora is also used in discussions of poetry when the word or words are repeated specifically at the beginnings of lines as in Mueller's "Spell for a Traveler" (p. 444). As a reader, it's not likely that you noticed these per se as you first read this paragraph, but you probably noticed the effect of them on the tone. As you write, many of these effects will come to you "naturally," without your consciously naming them, and that is as it should be; however, it's also easy to see that Coetzee made choice after choice that wove together meaning with tone through sound and rhythm. As you strive to do the same, keep in mind that as you grow more familiar with these techniques, they will come to you with less conscious effort—in the same way that you may have to practice dance moves or chords before putting them together fluidly.

MUSICALITY

We started this chapter with the issue of breath, and we come back around to it at the end with a few thoughts about the quality of so-called musicality in poetry. It is something worth striving for, and we all recognize when we are reading poetry or prose that is beautiful-sounding or mellifluous as opposed to clunky or dull-sounding. The latter isn't always wrong—we might, in fact, choose awkward sounds in order to create consciously an experience of discomfort. In Sandra McPherson's "To a Penny Postcard, © 1911" (p. 419) a few of the sentence structures within the lines are a little bit off-kilter. The first lines begin with what seem like simply three descriptive phrases, but then, suddenly at the end of the stanza, the verb "sashes" appears, quite far from the noun to which it applies. This particular verb can also be used as a noun, forcing us to pay further attention in this moment. This kind of unusual **syntax**, or word order, produces its own kind of musicality, even if it is less obviously rhythmic than Mueller's "Spell for a Traveler."

Musicality as a term can apply to a number of aspects of poetry—the rhythms akin to those created in song, the lyric-like verse form, and so on—but around all of that it refers to the fact that of all types of writing, poetry is the one in which language itself is most emphasized, that is, language for its own sake. Poetry points out not only that we breathe, but it connects most clearly to the intellectual and emotional nature of language and to the fact that language is complex, richly layered, and dense with a variety of meanings. All literary writing does this, of course, but poetry points it out most clearly.

PATHWAYS

Pathway 3.1. Reading aloud. Choose two poems to read aloud, and record yourself doing so, then listen to yourself read. How would you describe the sounds and rhythms of each poem? For instance, does one feel fast and the other slow? Read aloud and record each poem a second time, emphasizing the characteristics you felt. Share these second recordings with someone—in class or at home—and ask what they hear. Identify how these rhythms were created.

Pathway 3.2. Gasping for air. Remember a time when something or someone took your breath away. This might be in a good or bad way, but usually we get breathless from awe, panic, surprise, shock, or some similar emotion. Write a poem that captures this loss of breath and perhaps your recovery.

Pathway 3.3. Person in motion. Choose a person you have strong feelings about and write a story or narrative poem about that person doing something. Capture the rhythm of that person or of how you feel about that person. Note that you might shift the rhythm over the course of the poem if something shifts in how you feel or what the person is doing. Avoid clichés such as the thumping of sex or the thwap of someone hitting tennis balls.

Pathway 3.4. Sound dominance. Find a paragraph of something written in another Indo-European language you don't know. Then translate it into English using words that sound like the original, foreign words rather than looking them up in a translation dictionary. You can keep this in prose or break it into the lines of a poem, but either way allow sound to dominate meaning. The piece may not make complete sense, but let yourself play and let go a bit of worrying about themes and clear connections. Let the paragraph or poem be surreal, let chance take over.

Pathway 3.5. Sound soup. Choose one of the poems in the anthology and write a poem that preserves nothing but the initial letter of each word and the number of words in a line. You may preserve the articles (a, an, the), prepositions (of, to), and conjunctions (and, or, but), but change the other words to suit your own meaning. See what effect it has on your subject that someone else and some other subject has determined these opening sounds.

Pathway 3.6. Obsession. Choose a word, phrase, or sentence structure that you will repeat over and over again in a poem about an obsession you have. You don't necessarily need to do this always at the beginning of each line, but set yourself a certain number of times you will use that word or phrase. Think about how and why you might vary it and how its meaning might evolve over the course of your poem.

Pathway 3.7. Group exercise: Almost obsessions. Agree on 1) a concern you all share—this might not rise to the level of obsession in 3.6, but it should be some issue that you all face to some degree (parents who don't understand, student loan debt, your school's bureaucracy, etc.)—and 2) on a word, phrase, or sentence structure that each of you will use repeatedly in a poem on that topic. Bring those poems back for comparison within your group. What do they share and how do they differ?

Pathway 3.8. Palindrome poem. Try writing a palindrome or mirror poem like Christopher Shannon's "Apollo (at) Eleven" (p. 509). First, make a list of words or phrases related to your topic, then reverse the list. Expand both lists into poetic lines. Make sure to write two stanzas, with each line containing the relevant word or phrase.

Pathway 3.9. Vowel sounds. Write two poems of five lines each on the same subject. In the first poem, use only (or mostly) long vowel and diphthong sounds—a as in babe, e as in weed, i as in bide, o as in boat, ou as in couch, and so on—and in the second use only (or mostly) short vowel sounds—a as in bat, e as in pet, i as in spiffy, o as in cot, u as in cut. Discuss which poem suits your subject better and why. You can also try this exercise with consonants, classifying them as hard and soft, or by trying one poem with mostly long vowels and soft consonants and the other with mostly short vowels and hard consonants.

Pathway 3.10. Scheming. Every day for a week, choose one of the schemes from **Table 3.1** and write a short paragraph or poem where you use that scheme repeatedly. Vary the content and vocabulary of each line, and perhaps establish a pattern whereby you alternate one scheme with another.

Pathway 3.11. Group exercise: Ten little rules. In your group or your class, make up ten rules, one for each line of a ten-line poem or ten-sentence story or memoir. At least five of these rules should have to do with a technical aspect of writing from Chapter 2 or this chapter, such as, "Include a metaphor or simile" or "Use personification." The other five rules should have to do with content, such as "Say something you don't mean" or "Contradict yourself." Once your group has set its ten rules, take them home and write a piece based on them, though you can use the rules in whatever order you want. (This exercise is adapted from "Twenty Little Poetry Projects" by Jim Simmerman in *The Practice of Poetry*, edited by Robin Behn and Chase Twichell.)

Pathway 3.12. Rhythms aloud. On your own or as a group, read aloud the paragraph above from J. M. Coetzee's *Foe*. Read it over and over again until you can virtually feel the ocean waves in the rhythm of your reading. Then jot a list of rhythms that you overhear in daily life and write your own paragraph that produces a similar syntactical symbolism based on a different rhythm of your own choosing.

FURTHER ANTHOLOGY READINGS

Michael Palmer, "The Cord" (poetry)

Al Zolynas, "Love in the Classroom" (poetry)

Lia Purpura, "On Looking Away: A Panorama" (creative nonfiction)

GUIDEPOST: TIMING

Timing, they say, is everything.

In this chapter, we've discussed sound and rhythm in various genres, especially poetry, but just about everything in the world is subject to issues of timing. Workshops, for instance, are not poems, but they rely on a rhythm of people taking turns to give comments to the author whose work is being discussed. You may have a particular piece of feedback in mind, but if your turn doesn't come up in a timely way, you may forget it and have to regroup before speaking. When one person talks too long or tries to dominate the discussion, or someone interrupts to interject a comment on a different tack, we all recognize that the rhythm and timing are off.

We recognize that some people just seem to have better timing than others in general. Maybe a friend always seems to be in the right place at the right time; perhaps another always knows exactly how to tell a joke. This kind of timing sometimes seems innate, but it is primarily a matter of practice and learning. Musicians, for example, often train with a metronome or play along with a previously recorded version of a song in order to master the beat. Anyone in any profession learns through experience how much time particular types of jobs will take and how to manage time for particular tasks.

That's not to say that timing is always predictable—there are forces beyond our knowledge, whether in our personal lives or in business or entertainment. However, studying the rhythm of language will help you remain sensitive to clues in your environment that affect your timing. In any conversation, careful listening—for changes in tone, for clipped and hurried diction, for stresses on particular words—will help you to be genuinely responsive and respectful. Your study of writing will serve you well to develop skill in hearing others and timing your own interventions more sensitively.

Chapter 4

Form

In creative writing, "form" is most often used to discuss particular types of verses structured according to fixed guidelines and principles of repetition and syllable emphasis, what we often refer to as **formal poetry**. Before going into formal—and less formal—poetry, however, I want to point out that *all* writing has some kind of structure or "shape." We might even start off describing the shape of a piece of work in almost human terms: Is this a slender, short book or a pleasingly plump tome? Even just glancing at a page or two of the writing, you can tell something about the internal structure—first, whether it follows the form of a poem, a piece of prose, or a script. Even with a page of prose, you can tell whether it is comprised of one long, continuous passage or short, rat-a-tat paragraphs or sections. Once you start to read, you can discern whether the overall shape is linear—following chronological order—or whether it jumps back and forth in time or seems to trace a convoluted loop-de-loop. With plays and screenplays, the term may simply indicate the formatting formulas commonly used to distinguish them from other genres, but we might also talk about how many acts and scenes there are, how many different settings, how many different costume changes. In film, think, for instance, of the difference between one long, continuous screenshot and a series of jump cuts. No matter the genre, form affects pacing and works with a host of other elements.

With a poem, of course, the shape confronts us directly. We know right away whether a poem is contained on one page or crosses over multiple ones, whether its lines are brief and pithy or long and winding, whether the lines are sober and evenly spaced or drunkenly shape-shifting throughout. We can tell without even reading the actual words whether the poet gives us time to breathe between stanzas or forges ahead relentlessly, carrying us across pages without even a pause. Poetry crystallizes the pacing of its writing and its reading in a visual way.

BREAKING LINES, MAKING STANZAS

If you have written poems in the past, you may have broken them into lines somewhat instinctively, using a combination of the usual prose grammatical units and a general feel for when a line is too short or too long. You probably have broken them where you might normally take a breath if reading aloud their phrases and sentences in prose. These often create perfectly appropriate pauses, but as you learn more about how line breaks work, you'll be able to try variations that will use them as a kind of revolutionary punctuation mark of their own. You'll find that one of the greatest pleasures of writing poetry is playing with where to put your line breaks, almost like those puzzles where you slide rectangles around until you can move one out of the opening on the side. (See **Pathway 4.1**.)

In poems, sentences often exist in tension with line breaks. You probably are used to the idea that a comma in a sentence creates a slight pause but less than that of a period or even a semicolon. In poetry, you have those differences plus the pauses caused by the line breaks. As poet Don Stap puts it, you might think of the pauses created by line breaks as mental pauses rather than physical ones. You need not stop dead at the end of each line, but hesitate only slightly, even internally, before you spill over to the next line. Line breaks, then, can sometimes reinforce the usual grammatical sense of sentences within poems, but they can also make the usual sense suspect or undermine it, thus creating subtle shifts and layers in meaning, as well as pacing that holds the potential for surprise.

More particularly, some lines end with the end of a sentence or clause or some shorter syntactic unit (such as a prepositional phrase), and we call these lines **end-stopped** because there is a kind of resolution at the end of the line itself. The pause at the end of such lines is greater than with lines where sentences and phrases carry over from line to line—or when even a basic syntactical unit will be split in ways that add to or even change the feeling, rhythm, or meaning of the sentence or phrase. The latter are referred to as **enjambed** lines (and the technique as **enjambment**), from the French word meaning "to straddle" or "to step across," as one would have to step over a door jamb. If the break between two lines of poetry is a door jamb, your enjambed lines cross it. Your end-stopped lines pause to knock.

There's debate about what precisely constitutes an enjambed line—some define it as any line that doesn't end at the end of a sentence, others as any line that doesn't end in some form of punctuation (period, semicolon, comma, etc.), still others note that enjambment requires the breakage of phrases, so, for instance, in the middle of a prepositional phrase as opposed to before or after one. Within your class, your teacher may want to indicate how you will use the term, but it may also be good to think of enjambment as variable—in other words, some lines are *strongly* enjambed, while others are only *moderately* or *weakly* enjambed.

Lynn Emanuel's "The Out-of-Body Experience" offers good examples of both end-stopped and various strengths of enjambed lines. Note in reading the full poem on page 344 that even her title ends with a comma and plays with the issue of enjambment. Usually, a noun is followed by a verb, and even a title that also functions as the first line of a poem would be enjambed in that case. But Emanuel modifies her title noun with an appositive phrase, "the extraterrestrial view," tipping us off from the outset that the poem may challenge our expectations. Let's also look at the lines of the last stanza in **Table 4.1**.

The first two lines of this stanza make the point well that end-stopped versus enjambed lines are not always signaled by punctuation; rather, enjambment is a matter of there being a strong impulse to read on to the next line to complete the image or idea. And describing a line as "weakly" enjambed does not imply the line isn't working—rather you have to decide which level of pause will work best in a particular poem at a particular point.

In this stanza of Emanuel's, we see the lines swing back and forth between stopping and surging forward. She adds a grammatically unnecessary comma at the end of the first line, which forces us to pause on the image of the willow tree—a stereotypical symbol of grief since Biblical times. The second line ends with a natural strong pause to emphasize her denial of the symbol, but the third line begins a tumble through several enjambed lines in which the grief reasserts itself. Finally, she comes back to the image of an aerial photograph that she had mentioned in the first stanza, and this different way of looking at things stops or at least momentarily slows the flow of grief. The last several lines of the poem change imagery to that of a river, which to the speaker's sense seems more akin to grief, and we have three lines in succession that are either end-stopped or barely enjambed, implying a halting progression even though a river is something that

Table 4.1
Enjambed and End-Stopped Lines in Lynn Emanuel's
"The Out-of-Body Experience."

All the willows weeping,	moderately enjambed (even though she uses a comma, the phrase is not complete without a verb)
are not symbols for me	end-stopped (even without punctuation, we feel a sense of resolution)
but symbols for me	strongly enjambed
they stand, staunchly	moderately enjambed
rooted in the black	strongly enjambed
rainy margin of this	strongly enjambed
aerial photograph:	end-stopped
I am the river	weakly enjambed/end-stopped
going over the spillway	weakly enjambed/end-stopped
like oiled bath water,	end-stopped
a colder cold, a dark	strongly enjambed
dark.	end-stopped

flows. The next to the last line, however, is starkly enjambed, pouring us over to the final one-word end-stopped moment. The finality of this last line is abrupt and harsh.

Two of the lines in this stanza may stand out to you for a different reason: they contain punctuation mid-line, creating a pause within the line in addition to the pauses at the ends of lines. This kind of mid-line break is called a **caesura**, related to the word "cease," and caesuras are another common technique that you'll want to master to control the pacing and emphasis in your poems. Emanuel's lines "they stand, staunchly" and "a colder cold, a dark" act in slightly different ways because of the lines' ends. The first one would make sense without the comma, and the line is only moderately enjambed, so the caesura slows us down. We pause to notice and wonder that not only do the trees stand but they do so staunchly and not in some other way before going on to find that they are "staunchly / rooted." The line break allows the fact that the trees both stand staunchly and are rooted staunchly to be succinctly condensed and connected; we might conclude that in order to stand strong, one must have good roots, whether a person or a tree. In the second instance, because the line is so strongly enjambed, the caesura creates a more dramatic, ominous effect. In general, caesuras create a more staccato rhythm or interrupt a set of smoothly flowing lines; sometimes they help vary rhythm slightly when it might otherwise become monotonous. (See **Pathway 4.2.**)

As with end-stops, however, caesuras are not necessarily marked by punctuation. Sometimes in poems with longer lines, a natural mid-line syntactic break occurs without punctuation. Take a look at Fady Joudah's "Sleeping Trees" (p. 391), a poem rife with both enjambment and caesura, though Joudah plays with the location of the mid-line pauses, varying them from the middle quite a lot. One example from this poem will show caesura without punctuation:

> My brother believed bad dreams could kill
> A man in his sleep, he insisted
> We wake my father from his muffled screams

All three of these lines use caesura, even though only the middle one marks the effect with punctuation. If you read the lines aloud, you will hear the pause between "believed" and "bad" and the one between "father" and "from." Because each phrase is strong on its own, there's a slight pause between them that allows these three lines to match each other rhythmically. The combination of mid-line pauses that shift slightly in location and the amount of enjambment in this poem help produce a sensation of instability and uncertainty.

As you read more poems and work with line breaks in your own poems, you will get a feel for the effects that different choices like this make. There are no hard and fast rules about how to decide where to break lines—sometimes breaks will come easily and other times you will move a word or two back and forth between lines for a while before deciding where they should be—or whether they belong at all. Any poem in this book or elsewhere can be examined for how the line breaks are working, and the more you read here and elsewhere, the more of a sense of the subtle effects of line breaks you'll have.

FREE VERSE

Compare Emanuel's and Joudah's poems with Robin Becker's "The Children's Concert" (p. 291). All of these poems are examples of what we call **free verse**; in other words, they follow no predetermined, set form, but rather have been constructed from an individual sense of pacing and rhythm. These three poems demonstrate how "free verse" doesn't mean free from *any* sense of pattern; rather, it means that the poet is free to choose from a range of possible patterns and to mix different ones. Notice how distinct the shapes of Emanuel's, Joudah's, and Becker's poems are on the page. Emanuel's establishes a sinuous pattern comprised of both uneven stanzas and uneven line lengths. All the stanzas in Joudah's poem, on the other hand, are comprised of stanzas of either six or two lines, though they do not alternate exactly. Instead, the longer stanzas provide paired narratives—one about the narrator's father, the other about a lover—and the **couplets** (two-line stanzas) compose pauses of strong, regret-filled images. While the stanzas are somewhat more predictable than Emanuel's, the line lengths remain fluid and variable, tenuous as dreams and memory.

When we turn to Becker's poem, we can easily see that she has set up an even more regular pattern than Joudah. She writes in **quatrains** (four-line stanzas) with the second and fourth lines of each shortened and indented. In some ways, this has, then, stepped over the line into formal poetry, even though the poem doesn't rhyme or follow a strict number of syllables per line. This poem begins innocently telling the tale of two sisters attending a musical concert, but between the second and third stanzas an enormous emotional shift occurs with the child's whisper changing into something threatening, almost sinister, as she tells her sister that they will be abandoned. Every other line is indented, also adding to the see-saw, back-and-forth feeling of tension between the two sisters and the ultimately different things that happen to them. The use of lines weakly enjambed across the second and third stanzas creates a flow, but the simultaneous line and stanza break creates the effect of a slight hesitation, a preparation for the argument that ensues between the sisters. The regularity of the quatrains contrasts sharply with the one-line stanza that ends the poem and that suits the finality and shock of the sister's death. Christopher Shannon's palindrome poem "Apollo (at) "Eleven" (p. 509), mentioned" in Chapter 3, also demonstrates a combination of free verse lines with attention to a pattern that borders on formal. (See **Pathway 4.3** and **4.4**.)

We might think of formal poetry as similar to using bodybuilding machines, whereas free verse is akin to using free weights. While you will find fanatics in both camps, either method can help you build muscle and tone, just as poetic structures help you express your emotions. Although the analogy isn't perfect, neither type ignores training altogether; free verse, like free weights, implies that you will still be paying attention to your poetic muscles. Anyone who doesn't isn't working out at all. You can see in these examples how even if you are drawn primarily to free verse, you can benefit from an understanding of more formal structures.

METER

In many ways, meter goes back to the source of rhythm that we discussed in Chapter 3—breathing. There, however, we focused on only one of the two major aspects of rhythm—the repetition of sounds, words, phrases, line lengths, and sentence structures. The other element most commonly used is the stress we place on certain syllables as we pronounce them either out loud or in our heads as we read silently. Although there are other sound elements that also contribute to rhythm—duration, pitch, tone, loudness, timbre—poets (at least in contemporary Western languages) attend to the stressed and unstressed syllables more than any other aspect of rhythm.

Meter refers most simply to the rhythmic structure of a poem, **prosody** to the detailed study of meter and other aspects of putting words into verse. There are three main types of meter used in English-language poetry: accentual-syllabic, accentual, and syllabic. These names make complete and obvious sense—syllabic meter attends to the exact number of syllables, accentual only to the number of stressed syllables, and accentual-syllabic to both total syllables and patterns of syllable emphasis.

However, meter is where our passion for poetry may begin to founder, not because it is as difficult and cold as vector calculus, but because we expect our feelings to come first. We are used to stepping back and learning specialized terms in other fields—no one expects to do vector calculus without knowing the contextual meanings of field, potential, and curl—but in writing poetry, the terminology can seem cumbersome. And it is true, as poet Hayden Carruth says, that the "substance of serious poetry is never at the service of prosody. It is the other way around: prosody is a tool, a technique, at the service of substance."

There are nonetheless myriad fixed forms of poetry that have served poets well for millennia or have been developed in recent years. Each one has its uses, and each one has created an emotional tradition that adds further richness to an individual poem. Some of these are explained and exemplified in Appendix B: Verse Forms, but in this chapter we will focus on a few key issues and examples to give you a feel for the possibilities.

Feet

Even our daily, spoken language has rhythm based on stressed and unstressed syllables. If you can get into a ridiculous enough mood, it can be fun to prance around your room in your pajamas declaiming words and phrases aloud and paying attention to the fact that some syllables come out of your mouth and lungs more forcefully than others. If you can't achieve the silliness, just sit somewhere and listen to the conversations around you—the ubiquitously varying emphases will be there for you to hear. Even deaf poets writing in American Sign Language create syllabic variations in rhythm—by adjusting the speed of the movements they make, repeating them, or pausing and holding them for different lengths of time.

Before literacy became the norm, of course, poems were memorized and repeated orally rather than written down. Because poets in an oral culture had to pay careful attention to the beats of the stressed syllables, often tapping them out with their feet as a memory aid, the various patterns of accented and unaccented syllables became known as **feet**. Today, this oral poetry tradition continues in slam and spoken-word poetry, as well as in other kinds of poetry readings.

As you may have heard before, the most common metrical unit is the **iamb**, or two syllables of which the second is more heavily stressed: at HOME, reJOICE, my DEAR, carTOON. Also common is the pattern of iambs in longer sentences, when the pattern plays out across several words. **Iambic pentameter**, that oft dreaded term in English classes, consists simply of five feet in an iambic stress pattern: U/U/U/U/U/, with U standing for an unstressed syllable and / for a stressed one. (These symbols are commonly used, both in print and written by hand over the syllables when someone is trying to indicate or figure out the pattern.) A line of iambic pentameter will, then, consist of ten syllables. Unrhymed iambic pentameter is called **blank verse**. A few examples from everyday language:

> *I'd like to introduce a friend of mine.*
> *For sale: a pair of skis, with boots and wax.*
> *The job requires a lot of work and thought.*

In fact, iambic pentameter is common enough that one collaborative poet and conceptual artist, Ranjit Bhatnagar, created a Twitter bot, Pentametron, that uses an algorithm to find rhyming iambic pentameter lines on Twitter and re-Tweet them as whimsical couplets. These couplets are then combined into fourteen-line sonnets on the Pentametron website.

Bhatnagar uses a program and an online pronunciation dictionary to identify the stresses in ten-syllable Tweeted lines, but the practice of **scansion**, or reading poetry for its particular metrical stresses, is complicated by the fact that different people speak with a variety of accents, and in different regions of the world even the same language may be spoken with distinct inflections. Depending on voice and accent, one reader may stress slightly different syllables than another. And some words are pronounced differently depending on which of various meanings is in play—think of words like "content," "complex," and "convict."

Metric designations are also complicated by the fact that not all feet are two syllables; some consist of three syllables (see **Table 4.2**). So, not only can the

Table 4.2
Metrical Feet. Note that because any multiple-syllable word will have at least one syllable accented, the pyrrhic must combine with other types of feet.

iamb	U/	for RENT, upSTAIRS
trochee	/U	MEMphis, SLEEPy
anapest	UU/	on the TOWN, paraCHUTE
dactyl	/UU	BASketball
spondee (less common)	//	SLOW DOWN
pyrrhic (less common)	UU	to a GREEN THOUGHT in a GREEN SHADE (Andrew Marvell) (two pyrrhics and two spondees)

number of feet in a line vary, but the number of syllables in a foot may also vary. This may at first seem overly mathematical for the subject of writing, but remember, first, that it's not calculus—only counting—and, also, that the main point is for you to develop your sensitivity to sound, both in terms of repetition and in terms of stressed versus unstressed syllables. Certainly, scansion is not an exact science, and most poets use any patterns organically rather than rigidly. (See **Pathway 4.5.**)

Syllabic Meter

Poems using **syllabic meter** may be the simplest formal poems to write because they don't count stresses at all, but rather attend only to the number of syllables in a line. This can be much easier for those of us who don't have much of a musical ear and have a hard time hearing exactly where the strongest beats are in a line. Syllabic poems may be part of more specific forms, such as the three-line, seventeen-syllable **haiku**, or might simply involve a poet saying, "I'm going to include x many syllables in each line." In the hands of a skilled writer, syllabic poems develop their own distinct rhythms and make use of stressed syllables, but they are defined much more simply than many other kinds of formal verse. Both the process and the result are described in this poem.

MISS CHO COMPOSES IN THE CAFETERIA
James Tate

You are so small, I
am not even sure
that you are at all.

To you, I know I
am not here: you are
rapt in writing a

syllabic poem
about gigantic,
gaudy Christmas trees.

You will send it home
to China, and they
will worry about

you alone amid
such strange customs. You
count on your tiny

bamboo fingers; one,
two, three—up to five,
and, oh, you have one

syllable too much.
You shake your head in
dismay, look back up

to the tree to see
if, perhaps, there might
exist another

word that would describe
the horror of this
towering, tinselled

symbol. And . . . now
you've got it! You jot
it down, jump up, look

at me and giggle.

This poem shows, both narratively and artistically, what can be gained by working within a formal structure. Because she has to find a word with a different number of syllables, Miss Cho thinks more carefully about language and word choice. The syllabic structure is related to the story the poem tells, but it also allows Tate to capture in a few short lines the chaos—as well as the ultimate human sharing—of cross-cultural experience. Tate also uses other techniques we've discussed—the repetition of certain sounds; a balance of end-stopped and enjambed lines; and even an occasional buried rhyme—to set up a rhythm that captures both the lightness of the moment in which the student is having fun with her poem and also the narrator's more self-conscious recognition of the "horror" of the "gaudy" holiday season. Miss Cho provides a great image for you to hold onto as you try a variety of forms and techniques both in your poetry and in other writing. (See **Pathways 4.6** and **4.7**.)

Accentual Meter

Another way that poets often work with stressed and unstressed syllables is to simply keep track of the stressed ones. This is called **strong-stress poetry** or **accentual meter**, and these forms disregard the total number of syllables to attend only to the ones that take emphasis. In other words, all the lines of a poem might have four stressed syllables, with an uncounted and varying number of unstressed ones in between. This technique was often used by modern poets such as e. e. cummings and T. S. Eliot, for instance, to give seemingly formless poems a strong but subtle pattern. The method goes back to the ancient Anglo-Saxons of Germany, and can be illustrated, for instance, by the opening lines of *Beowulf*:

> **Famed** was this Beowulf: **far** flew the **boast** of him,
> **son** of **Scyld**, in the **Scan**dian **lands**.

One of these two lines has twelve syllables, the other nine, but each has four accented syllables. The strong-stress method allows for a great deal of flexibility while at the same time maintaining a powerful drumbeat rhythm.

One use that contemporary authors have made of this strategy is to set up serious commentary contrasted by a loose, comfortable rhythm of strong-stress lines. You'll find this pattern, for instance, in Alicia Suskin Ostriker's "The Orange Cat" (p. 471), which balances the lightness of short, half-rhyming lines and strong-stress rhythm with a keen social observation about various kinds of hunger and desire. With or without rhyme, strong-stress is another fun and approachable way to begin working with meter. (See **Pathway 4.8**.)

Accentual-Syllabic Meter

In **accentual-syllabic meter**, the arrangements of stressed and unstressed syllables in lines of poetry are precise and, to a greater or lesser extent, fixed. It is rhythm formalized into regular patterns that attend to both the number of syllables and the number of accented and unaccented syllables. Sonnets, discussed more fully below, provide the most common type.

When a poet is working with regular rhythmic patterns, it is helpful to be able to know how many feet a line contains, and so it is common to see Latin numerical terms combined with the suffix -meter: monometer (meaning one foot), di- (meaning two feet), tri- (meaning three), tetra- (four), penta- (five), hexa- (six), hepta- (seven), and octameter (eight feet). Poems with one foot to the line (monometer) are rare, but two (dimeter), three (trimeter), and four (tetrameter) are fairly common. Here is the first stanza of one of several poems William Blake titled "Song" and wrote in trimeter:

> I **love** the **jo**cund **dance**,
>   The **soft**ly **breath**ing **song**,
> Where **inn**ocent **eyes** do **glance**,
>   And where **lisps** the **maid**en's **tongue**.

Notice that even here, in a poem that begins with (and continues on from here with) iambic tetrameter, the third and fourth lines each contain seven syllables. That's our first signal that the feet in those lines aren't all iambic, and in fact the third line contains a different kind of foot—an anapest between two iambs—and the fourth begins with an anapest. The UU/ adds a bit of jiggle to the rhythm, perhaps reflecting the shuffling of dancing feet or the flirtatious attitude that would have been risqué for dancers of that time.

You may not see immediately why such details are relevant to you as a poet when today poets aren't expected to write in formal verse. However, it can only help you to understand traditions as well as the direct effects of particular rhythms. Knowing about such traditions gives you a range of options, either for emulating a particular tradition or for poking fun at or altering them.

POETIC FORMS

Most of the poetry you have written is likely in **free verse**, that is, without a set pattern of meter and rhythm. Many great poems are written this way, and it's fine if that is your inclination. However, most poets before the twentieth century worked in set forms like the sonnet, villanelle, and sestina, or, in non-Western cultures, the haiku (Japanese), ghazal (Arab), and pantoum (Malaysian), and in recent years, there has been a resurgence of interest in writing in these forms. Writers have acknowledged that their understanding of rhythm is aided by at least some experimentation with traditional structures. After all, when Ezra Pound called for the poets of the early twentieth century to "make it new" in part by turning away from these forms, they had a solid background in and knowledge of them.

Today you have the opportunity to choose whether a formal or free structure is more appropriate for a given poem, and you may fear that imposing rhythmical structures on your lines of poetry will cramp the free flow of emotions through the writing. Nothing could be further from the truth—but the word "impose" holds a key to how we often go wrong in our thinking about formal metrical elements of poetry. Although it's true that this book and your instructor may ask you to try out a particular form of poem, you as the writer should think of choosing a form and subject matter that go together. Particular forms have recognized effects that can help you achieve a desired emotional impact.

For instance, poets often find that working within the confines of a sonnet helps give uncontrolled emotions a framework. In Richard Frost's poem below, the occasional elevated word and the sonnet form—with its long history that might be considered predictable and old-fashioned—contrasts with the crude behavior of the narrator's brother.

FOR A BROTHER
Richard Frost

> When I was young, there was a song that went,
> "I told you that I love you, now get out."
> Last night, drunk at my party, you knocked over
> the gas grill and blackened swordfish, you lout,
> then tried to feel up my neighbor's daughter.
> You sick rantallion, you phone at four a.m.
> with a new joke, or to brag, or to beg for a loan.
>   Young, I didn't know what that song meant.
> It just seemed funny. Today I am
> bone tired of the crude fraternal weight
> of your old bullying, you jackalone,
> you sack of black rats' balls, you tank of piss.
> And yet I love you, and so I must wait
> until you're dead before I publish this.

We can imagine that this brother might call the narrator boring or dull for not participating in such bad behavior himself, and we see in the form the contrast between the two brothers. In addition, the poet allows the form to fray around the edges a bit—not all the lines rhyme exactly as the sonnet form demands, nor is the meter strictly iambic pentameter. In this way, Frost puts us on notice that this is not the usual sweet or celebratory love sonnet like those written by Andrew Marvell or Elizabeth Barrett Browning. Yet the poem relies on the tradition of the Shakespearean sonnet in which the last two lines form a couplet that turns to a concluding remark or even a turn-around of the previous lines. (This shift is called, simply enough, the **turn** or **volta**, and is discussed further in Appendix B.) With the last two lines of Frost's poem, we are informed not only that the narrator loves his brother in spite of his problems, but indirectly that the narrator's brother must have died since the poem has indeed been published. This forces us to reconsider every interaction described, and to see the brother perhaps as desperate and troubled rather than simply obnoxious. The sonnet form itself helps deepen our understanding of the situation.

There are a variety of sonnet types, but they are generally all fourteen lines long and written in iambic pentameter. Different types of sonnets use different rhyme schemes, and the turn occurs at different locations. There are, of course, as many variations as there are poets who write in the form, and many contemporary poets play with the form quite a lot. Take a look at Adrienne Su's "Four Sonnets about Food" (p. 520), for example. Each of this sequence of poems follows the traditional sonnet form by being fourteen lines long, and they even echo the Shakespearean form with a turn in the last two lines. However, the poems are written in lines that are unmistakably shorter than iambic pentameter, and while there is quite a bit of rhyming ("do" and "stew," "nourishes" and "flourishes") the rhyme is much looser than in many sonnets. The content of the poems themselves reflects some uneasiness or tension around traditional gendered domestic arrangements, and so this tension within the sonnet form is itself a clever aspect of the poems.

The sonnet is perhaps the most well-known of all the traditional styles, but there are myriad fixed forms, and I encourage you to seek them out, especially when the shape of a given poem you are working on doesn't seem to be coming together or when you are looking for a different avenue into writing a poem. Appendix B: Verse Forms defines a few more, and the anthology includes some examples. (See **Pathway 4.9.**)

PROSE FORMS

When we talk about form in prose and plays, we may be referring to length (Is something a novel or short story, a full-length play in three acts or a short one-act, etc.?), to genre (Is it fiction, nonfiction, play, or screenplay?), or to subgenre (If it's nonfiction, is it memoir or literary journalism?). Today, we may even be referring to the delivery mode, whether in a paper book or magazine or via electronic media. However, often when we discuss form in prose, and even in plays, we may also focus on the conscious stylistic elements of our writing.

Formalism refers to attention to the grammar, syntax, diction, and other choices a writer has made on the page, especially ones related to structure and method of composing. All writers, of course, are formalists to a certain degree, as we all choose our words carefully and make a million sub-conscious as well as conscious choices about the way we write. In some writing, however, these non-content aspects are used as a starting point or as a method for augmenting the subject or story in some particular way.

One example can be found in Dinty W. Moore's essay "Son of Mr. Green Jeans" (p. 430) which follows the form of an *abecedarian*. That is, Moore has written the piece in short segments sub-titled in alphabetical order. The essay can't easily be summarized, but all the various sections have something to do with fatherhood, and so the abecedarian form makes sense with its allusions to how parents teach their children their ABCs. What, we might ask about this or any work with such a distinct form, does the form of the work say about its content? (See **Pathways 4.10** and **4.11**.)

There are many other ways that writers refocus themselves on structural aspects of their work, and the French group OuLiPo is famous for stretching these methods to the limit. They suggest game-like strategies, such as following mathematical or logical structures, or omitting a particular letter (such as "a" or "e") from an entire work. Chapter 3 notes the use of a palindromic or mirror structure, and this is another formalist technique that can be used quite literally (with every letter in reverse) in short works and more loosely in longer ones.

Many of these formal concerns show up in our work in the form of experiments, and the literary world today welcomes such experiments at all levels of form. The twentieth century saw the beginning of much of this spirit of change in particular poetic and prose forms and in such moves as the importation of non-Western forms such as the pantoum, the radical opening up of concrete poetry and other forms of language poetry that focuses on the outer edges of language, the invention of the "plotless" story, and so on. This fascination with form continues. A few such experiments have been performed by writers such as Italo Calvino (see p. 303), with his fantastical stories based on scientific theories; Julio Cortázar, with novels such as *Hopscotch*, designed so the chapters can be read in any order; David Foster Wallace, who often uses footnotes as a main part of a story rather than for citing obscure sources; Jonathan Safran Foer, who sometimes includes typographical symbols as substitutes for words; and Giannina Braschi, who defies English-only rules in a radical assertion of her mixed-language heritage.

This book touches on the many hybrid forms of prose writing in **Destination: Hybrid Forms and Emerging Media**, as well as common prose structures in Chapters 7 and 9. In the meantime, two of the very short forms that blend poetry and prose are as follows:

The prose poem. A prose poem is exactly what it sounds like: a hybrid between poetry and prose that is usually short (one page or less). They may look like prose but are imbued with poetic characteristics such as reliance on intense imagery, careful arrangement of sound and rhythm, even a consideration of line breaks (though that becomes more difficult as poems are frequently reproduced in multiple formats today).

Postcard stories may be on the decline since so few people send things via snail mail anymore and thus there are fewer sources for the cards on which these micro-stories are written. There are occasionally still writers and artists who set up special projects, handing out postcards on the street and asking strangers to send them in, or writing a series and sending them out. However, under the new name of **micro-fiction** these very short stories have proliferated in our time-stressed and distracted age. Micro-fiction goes by many names: **short-shorts, flash fiction, sudden fiction,** and their nonfiction cousins. Both online and print publications now frequently support these abbreviated works. Two that publish online are *Brevity*, which publishes creative nonfiction under 750 words, and *Smokelong Quarterly*, which publishes flash fiction up to 1000 words. *NANO Fiction* is a print magazine that publishes stories up to 300 words long. But there are also many other places where you can find this kind of epigrammatic, intensified writing, and it is definitely one of the trends of our times.

PATHWAYS

Pathway 4.1. Rebreaking lines. Choose a short poem you have written before. Rewrite it five different times with different punctuation and line breaks, sometimes making small changes, other times radical changes. You may find that these changes make you want to change some of your word choices as well. Bring the five poems to class and trade with a classmate. Without telling which poem came first or which version is your favorite, discuss with your classmate what his or her impressions are.

Pathway 4.2. Group exercise: Lineation play. As a group, choose one of the prose pieces in the Anthology for you all to work with. Each go home and write a version of the first paragraph (or a set number of sentences if the first paragraph is too long or too short) that turns it into poetry. Think about where to break lines and alter punctuation or words to augment rhythm. Bring them back and compare the choices that you made.

Pathway 4.3. Conflicting feelings poem. Write a poem about an event about which you feel great conflict or mixed feelings. Remember to use concrete and specific imagery. But also consciously use your punctuation, line breaks, and caesuras to reflect your mixed feelings or hesitations.

Pathway 4.4. Love-hate poem. Write a love poem, or at least a poem of admiration, to someone you don't like or have misgivings about. Though you shouldn't become sarcastic, a bit of irony might work well. Think how your line breaks and punctuation can help you destabilize the surface emotions.

Pathway 4.5. Scanning poems. Turn to any of the poems listed at the end of this chapter and try to identify the accented syllables. At first just mark each accented one with a diagonal line above it, but then you might want also to count the unstressed syllables with a small U above them. Read the lines aloud to help you hear where the accents fall. Think about how this pattern relates to the meaning of the poem. Try writing two lines of iambic pentameter yourself.

Pathway 4.6. Syllabic poem. Choose a recent moment in your life that might connect to a larger issue, and then write a good first line. Now write the rest of the poem, but with all the lines using the same number of syllables as the first.

Pathway 4.7. Group activity: Syllabic variations. Divide into groups of three to five students with each group assigned to write poems with lines that have a certain number of syllables. It might be fun to count up by twos or threes, so that some are working with quite long lines while others are working with extremely short lines. Share and/or discuss the process and its challenges in class. What differences in tone are there in poems with short lines and those with longer ones?

Pathway 4.8. Accentual poem. Think of a relentless situation in your life—this might be as simple as the inevitable alarm going off in the morning or it could be as complex as a boss who regularly chastises you. Write a ten-line poem that captures that regular drumbeat in your life by using four strong stresses in each line. The total number of syllables doesn't matter, but emphasize the regularity through the beats.

Pathway 4.9. Formal poem. Choose one of the formal types of poems discussed in this chapter or in Appendix B and try writing one. It's fine if you are not up for the complications of a sestina or a sonnet, but try writing a poem in heroic couplets or writing a short poem in blank verse. Think ahead of time about what subject matter will benefit from this form.

Pathway 4.10. Abecedarian. Write a poem or piece of short prose about your childhood in the form of an abecedarian.

Pathway 4.11. Formal limits. Write a descriptive poem or prose piece without using any adjectives or adverbs. Or try one where you don't use the verb "to be" (is, are, etc.) at all.

FURTHER ANTHOLOGY READINGS

Agha Shahid Ali, "Stars" (poetry)

Mary Block, "Moving Song" (poetry)

James Byrne, "Sestina for R" (poetry)

Sherine Gilmour, "Little Boys" (poetry)

Amber West, "Pirate's Admonition" (poetry)

Dinty W. Moore, "Son of Mr. Green Jeans" (creative nonfiction)

GUIDEPOST: ADAPTABILITY

All creative acts balance between originality and convention.

Form makes you aware of parameters. When we talk about form—especially the guiding limitations of formal poems such as the sonnet or villanelle, which are written by a set of rules—the last concept we think about is "adaptability." Yet if you envision yourself writing a terrific poem—putting together vivid images, evoking sensations and emotions through words—no matter what the boundaries of the form are, you will see how adaptable you become as you learn these forms.

In the seemingly simple act of writing, you can discover how restrictions sometimes assist us in achieving heights. Imagine a person standing in an open field, wishing to be ten feet up in the air. Impossible. But if you add to the vision a ten-foot high scaffold, that person can climb way up and look out across the landscape. Learning to write poetry—and to think carefully and creatively about form in prose and dramatic writing—can be similar to building a scaffold to climb on.

In 2008, author Daniel Pink stated that "the MFA is the new MBA," and went on to note that the flexibility and adaptability of those trained in creative arts has become more and more valuable in the business world. Further, a recent study by professor and researcher Vivek Wadhwa, released in 2011, showed that, of 652 Silicon Valley leaders, fewer than 40 percent had backgrounds in science, engineering, and math, whereas 60 percent had diverse backgrounds, including those in arts and humanities. After all, arts and humanities students learn the critical thinking skills that allow them to approach a broad array of issues flexibly. You learn to analyze what is possible and to adapt your ideas, your words, your actions to situations that seem limiting. No matter the realm in which you put this ability to play, by identifying boundaries and accepting their reality, you learn to exceed them. Adaptability is a requirement of innovation.

Destination: **CREATIVE NONFICTION**

You may not think that you're as familiar with the genre of creative nonfiction as you are with fiction, or even poetry and plays. However, in some form or another, you've probably encountered it—this might have been in the stories your raconteur uncle tells about his exploits at holiday time or in personal testimonials given at church or synagogue or mosque or on someone's blog; you might have written oral histories at school or enjoyed an in-depth article about the struggles of an Olympic athlete. All of these partake of aspects of the genre now most commonly referred to as creative nonfiction. We define this wide-ranging genre as any prose grounded in fact, but which also uses writing techniques more commonly associated with literature rather than straight journalism.

MAIN FEATURES OF CREATIVE NONFICTION

Literary technique. Creative nonfiction differs from other forms of nonfiction like news reporting, research papers, technical writing, business writing, and so forth. Although much work in the genre is informative, it uses literary methods to bring fact-based stories to life—strong personal voice and perspective, rich description and characterization, intense imagery, well-thought-out structure, and attention to rhythm and word choice. The main features described in **Destination: Fiction** also apply to creative nonfiction, but this genre has a few additional special concerns.

The term "creative nonfiction" comes under fire because it can be taken to imply that those other forms of nonfiction don't involve any creativity at all, which, of course, they do. Others believe that the use of "creative" implies that the nonfiction isn't really nonfiction—that it's at least partly made up in the way that the word might be used popularly as a euphemism for a lie: "That was a really *creative* excuse." For another thing, "creative nonfiction" defines the genre by what it is not. Whereas fiction and poetry and drama all have their own words, creative nonfiction stakes its identity merely on not being fiction. That's a little bit akin to a situation where your sister is born before you, your parents name her Susie, but when you come along, they just call you Not Susie. My family, in fact, once named a dog Not Spot, but that got old so we resorted to calling her Notty or Naughty. Some people wish we could find a unique name for creative nonfiction, but so far nothing has stuck.

However, you will occasionally hear creative nonfiction called by other names, such as literary nonfiction or narrative nonfiction. Also be aware that creative nonfiction is often divided into subgenres that can overlap considerably—not only memoir, literary journalism, and personal essays, but diaries and journals, travel writing, nature writing, cultural criticism, belles-lettres, and so on. The umbrella term most simply refers to nonfiction writing that aspires to go beyond "just the facts" via literary techniques. (In this book, I use the term "creative nonfiction" for any literary writing grounded in fact, and the term "essay" for an individual piece of creative nonfiction.)

Grounding in fact and memory. When you begin to write creative nonfiction, you may have questions about what to do if you don't remember the particular color of your shirt on an important day or the exact words your friend used in a given conversation. In part, this depends on the type of creative nonfiction you're writing, and we'll discuss a few distinctions between **memoir, personal essay, and literary journalism** in Chapters 5 and 6. However, always remember that the goals of creative nonfiction focus on making sense of and interpreting real events and people, not making things up. Writing of any kind is an act of the imagination, and sometimes even nonfiction writers put a spin on things. David Sedaris, for instance, in "The Drama Bug" (p. 502), quotes himself as a teenager speaking in pseudo-Shakespearean fashion, such as "Perchance, fair lady, thou dost think me unduly vexed by the sorrowful state of thine quarters." Whether he spoke those exact words can't be determined unless he carried a tape recorder his entire life, but he captures an honest memory of an obnoxious phase he went through.

Distinctive voice. Exceptions exist, but almost always creative nonfiction uses the "I" pronoun clearly representing the author's experiences. Even when creative nonfiction writers write about others rather than themselves, even when they keep themselves in the background as subjects and narrators, they usually have a distinctive voice and personality that allows readers to develop a sense of relationship with them. They share personal concerns and obsessions, and through their voices they establish trust and/or fascination.

Self-examination and discovery. Creative nonfiction, particularly the memoir, finds its appeal to readers in honest self-examination and a sense of the author gaining as well as sharing insight. The narrator's personality must shine, but not in the sense of self-serving, bragging, or exaggerated bravado. Often we write creative nonfiction to examine difficult experiences we've had, and a good rule of thumb is to treat others with respect on our pages and to balance criticism of them with self-examination.

Showing *and* telling. Reflection forms one of the major features of much creative nonfiction. Although the form may be somewhat limited in terms of your choices about plot, one of its appealing features is that it allows you to reflect directly on situations in addition to creating compelling scenes.

QUESTIONS ABOUT YOUR CREATIVE NONFICTION

- **Have you created a strong, distinctive voice?** With memoir in particular, it can be effective to "write like you talk." You would pay attention to trying to capture other people's or characters' personalities in the particular ways they speak, so remember to do so with your own narrating voice.

- **Have you remembered to fill in details that may seem obvious to you but won't be to readers?** One of the most common problems in first drafts of creative nonfiction comes when there are gaps that the author automatically fills in for him- or herself. Remember that you may have a strong sense of how close together the houses are in your neighborhood, but a reader won't have the same background.
- **Have you avoided making yourself look unbelievably good?** Honesty plays a significant role in most creative nonfiction, and usually we find it easy to be honest about others. But we need to also be honest about ourselves. In fact, when you try to make yourself look too good, you may come off as unbelievable, a braggart, or worse. Instead, be vulnerable, be tough, be real.
- **Are any factual claims defendable?** Do any research that will augment any factual claims you make, including asking others who were present and using more traditional resources of background information.
- **Will anyone potentially be hurt by your writing?** Sometimes we find it necessary to risk emotional offense to tell our stories, but this should never be done in cavalier fashion, and you should remember at this stage in your writing life to avoid anything potentially libelous or with other legal ramifications, not to mention anything that might alienate those you care about.
- **Do you understand how your writing connects to the larger world around you?** Sometimes this takes a while to emerge, but remember to think about why your story does have value and importance, what it can offer in the way of insight, comfort, or challenge.
- **Have you made best use of literary methods?** Think about imagery, figures of speech, word choice, sentence structure, rhythm, sound, characterization, setting, structure, and point of view.

Chapter **5**

Memory

KEY ANTHOLOGY READINGS
David Sedaris, "The Drama Bug" (creative nonfiction)
Ann Hodgman, "No Wonder They Call Me a Bitch" (creative nonfiction)
Anne Panning, "Remembering, I Was Not There" (creative nonfiction)

Memory can be both a rich and tricky resource for writers, and this chapter tries to alert you to both its strengths and potential pitfalls. Memory is most often associated with the genre named after it—that of **memoir**. Memoir, most simply, consists of true life stories, but unlike more formal biographies and auto-biographies, it's written from memory more than facts that could be confirmed in school reports or family documents.

Though our discussion here will focus on memoir, this chapter will help you to work productively with your memory in all genres. You may notice that most of the Pathways in Chapter 1 and at least one in every other chapter of this book ask you to retrieve some feeling or detail from your past, from experiences and sensations that you recall. As the narrator of Marcel Proust's famously long novel *Remembrance of Things Past* notes, the entire story he tells has been brought out by the simple flood of sensory memory that occurred when he drank a cup of tea and ate a cookie that reminded him of his aunt's tea from years before. Such sensual memories—almost hard-wired into our bodies—are often the starting point for writing. The hallmark of memoir, memory also forms the ground for much fiction, drama, and poetry. The short passages in the Anthology from E. L. Doctorow (p. 337) and James Agee (p. 275) demonstrate how valuable early memories can be in our writing, whether fictionalized or not. (See **Pathway 5.1**.)

CHANGING VIEWS OF MEMOIR

When you think of memoir, you may think of an elderly gentleman of a previous century sitting down with a quill pen and scratching out the story of his long life. So much the better if he has been witness to famous events—floods, famines, wars, riots, the crowning of kings, the overthrow of queens, or the discovery of continents (or planets) previously unknown to his people. You may think that you are not experienced enough or involved enough in world-changing events to write a memoir.

Views of memoir have changed, however, and we have come to understand that all kinds of people's experiences have value and reflect on the wider cultures of which we are a part. David Sedaris, in "The Drama Bug" (p. 502), shares implications about high school and the exasperated wisdom of parents, as well as the challenges of not quite fitting in. We write memoir out of individual memory and experience, but it also reflects cultural memory.

We have also come to understand that memoir does not always depend on high drama per se. The interpretation of meaning informs each human's life, and the ordinary is often fascinating in its own right. In recent decades, readers have hungered for insight about other people's search for meaning, to share on the page stories about people not so different from them who have dealt with an array of challenges. Sedaris's recounting of being a misfit student in his high school drama club doesn't involve murder or mayhem, but everyone who has been to high school can appreciate the humor of looking back on that awkward stage of life, even if not all of us are like Sedaris in every aspect.

This memoir and many others also focus on adolescence and demonstrate clearly that plenty of predicaments worth exploring happen before someone turns twenty or thirty. Just as you need not be famous, you need not be elderly to look back on your life in compelling ways. Try **Pathway 5.2, 5.3**, or **5.4** to access some personal stories that might make good memoirs. In the next section, we're going to discuss why it's worth telling these private stories.

THE RISE OF MEMOIR

Often it seems that memoir has taken the literary world by storm in the past few decades, and the media has made much of its increased popularity over the past thirty or so years. People give a multitude of answers when trying to explain why this shift in reading and publishing habits might be so. Some people bemoan the rise of memoir—they see it as a sign of cultural voyeurism akin to reality television or they believe that writers undertake the form out of self-indulgence and a desire to make themselves look good. They believe that a reliance on "facts" sacrifices the ultimate dedication to the artistry of fiction. On the other hand, others, myself included, celebrate the memoir form for its attention to the value of people's lives and its emphasis on self-reflection; they point out that good and bad writing exist in all genres and that memoir and personal essay forms actually have a long and distinguished history, including such writers as St. Augustine (354–430), Michel de Montaigne (1533–1592), Charles Lamb (1775–1834), and

Henry David Thoreau (1817–1862). It's worth noting that the novel, particularly in its early instances, focused on personal lives, as opposed to major historical events; that the novel was itself considered an inferior form perpetuated by "a damned mob of scribbling women," as Nathaniel Hawthorne put it in 1855; and that the novel arose over the course of the sixteenth and seventeenth centuries as an alternative to literary works written as factual histories. In other words, various literary forms rise and fall in popularity and vitality according to ongoing social changes.

This may matter less to you if you are interested primarily in poetry, fiction, or drama as a form, but at this stage of your writing life, I urge you to stay open to the entire range of forms and genres possible. Understanding these shifting trends can help you figure out your place in them.

How Memoir Got Where It Is Today

The rise of memoir followed in the footsteps of a similar rise in the study of Creative Writing as an academic subject of its own. While philosophy, rhetoric, history, the natural sciences, and mathematics have all been subjects of college and university study since at least the 1300s, Creative Writing only entered the academic scene in the late 1800s. This trend also coincides roughly with the rising status of women and minorities in our society. One aspect of the increased opportunities for people of all backgrounds is an acknowledgment that all people have a right (and perhaps a need) to express themselves, and this includes the self-examination inherent in any memoir.

In the nineteenth century, for instance, abolitionists relied on personal accounts by slaves in order to discount pro-slavery assumptions about black people's supposed inability to be educated. In non-literary arenas, media specialists and pundits acknowledge that a personal story can bring to life many a situation that mere statistics don't fully reveal; thus, individuals testify before Congress about the need for funding for cancer research or about the impact of policies and rules that have affected them. The intimate details of a person's life connect to us emotionally, whether they are told in fiction, poetry, nonfiction, or on stage or screen. But particularly during times of social change, many writers have felt it necessary to assert the veracity of their stories, to stand up and note that their personal experiences are worthwhile and valuable.

In the twentieth century and continuing today, many of the most influential memoirs are those written by people struggling for rights, struggling to be acknowledged as full-fledged citizens and human beings with their own set of interests and priorities. Most of these writers are authors of other forms of writing as well as memoir, and the same social issues can be seen, of course, in both fiction and poetry and other art of the recent decades as well. Tony Kushner's 1993 play *Angels in America*, for instance, galvanized public sympathy for gay men in the face of the AIDS crisis. Some fiction writers and poets included in this book whose work has focused on social transformations that have also been part of their own personal lives are Agha Shahid Ali, Robin Becker, Junot Díaz, Louise Erdrich, Terrance Hayes, Fady Joudah, Yusef Komunyakaa, Toni Morrison, Gary Soto, and Al Young.

In certain situations, some writers have felt that it made sense to honor the personal sources of their insights directly through memoir. Such memoirists see in their own struggles the kind of social importance mentioned earlier in the chapter, and they choose to raise awareness head-on. These writers represent widely divergent attitudes about the issues they address, but they all demonstrate how the chance factors of their backgrounds influenced their thinking and writing. Social struggles have changed and shifted over time, but writing from experience continues to be one of the major ways that writers produce social changes in prevailing attitudes. Perhaps David Sedaris's *Me Talk Pretty One Day* (2000) and Dan Savage's *The Commitment* (2005), by putting faces on the issues, have done as much to help foster understanding of homosexuality as anti-discrimination protests and lawsuits. Novels, plays, films, and poems can certainly do this, too, but sometimes authors feel a need to say clearly, "This is my experience. I did not make this up." By helping to start the online It Gets Better Project, which includes support for LGBT teens in video testimonials by adults about how their LGBT lives have improved over time in spite of a sometimes hostile society, Dan Savage has recently demonstrated again the ongoing power of public stories that are "real." (See **Pathway 5.5**.)

Much of this writing comes out of a tradition of "witnessing," a term originally used in a religious context, but later adapted by those who felt a need to testify about crimes of war and other human atrocities. Because such uses and abuses of power have often been covered up with more violence as well as secretive practices, certain people felt a need to come forward and assert the truth of such events as the Holocaust. "I was there, it really happened" provides powerful testimony when world events are called into question or need to be uncovered and brought to public attention. Silence in such circumstances can be seen as a result of oppression or cooperation with oppression. This impetus was shared by those subject to the more daily violence of racism and sexism, and became one of the major impulses behind the rise of memoir that continues today. As author Carol Hanish noted during the rise of women's rights, "It is . . . a political action to tell it like it is, to say what I really believe about my life instead of what I've always been told to say."

Your Own Social Moment

When you write down your own story, you assert the validity and importance of your own individual experience and implicitly make an argument for the ideals of democracy. Just as we grant political legitimacy to each person rather than only those in a pre-determined aristocracy, memoir and other literature isn't just about "important" or "famous" people's individual lives. Yes, details about celebrities and people of great accomplishment or genius may inspire us, and such people sometimes deserve special recognition, but there's a legitimate alternating interest in other kinds of lives, including yours. Your stories can illuminate struggles with life experiences that many share—divorce, illness, death of a loved one, closeness of family, or value of friendship—any number of events and ways of being that make up the fabric of our lives and our wider society.

It remains true, however, that our individual experience may not be important in and of itself, only for its own sake. While historians rely on traces of such minute personal experiences to understand the cultures of the past—whether in the shards of pottery at Vesuvius or in the meticulous recordings of daily events in a nineteenth-century farmer's diary—the demands of any literary genre also require a narrative that goes beyond just the "facts" of someone's or a culture's existence. As a writer interpreting your own life and emotions, no matter the genre, you must make a connection to the larger world, either explicitly or implicitly. You must go beyond "what I did on my summer vacation." Ann Hodgman's "No Wonder They Call Me a Bitch" (p. 387), which describes an experimental tasting of dog foods, goes beyond the gross-out factor to critique the world of advertising. Anne Panning's "Remembering, I Was Not There" (p. 473) moves beyond her complaints about her parents to implicit wider questions about pressures to marry and have children early, about whether women's sacrifices are worth it. (See **Pathway 5.6** and search for such connections in your own life.)

Your responsibility as a writer of memoir includes not only describing the ordinary but lending *insight* into the ordinary; the events may be usual, but the mind behind the story must see importance in the mundane, make connections and see patterns, and find the fascinating in the blade of grass. Otherwise, you might create a historical document, but there's little sense of discovery in contemporaneous readers. While you may look back at memoirs of the past and say, "But I'm not involved in social issues as exciting as the Civil Rights movement," just know that current trends may not have been labeled as such, or you may be too caught up in the experiences to know exactly what they mean on that larger scale. That doesn't mean that you should turn your life stories into sociological tracts—quite the contrary—but one of the keys to writing resonant memoirs is to be aware of how you fit into the world.

PERSONAL MEMORY AS A LITERARY TOOL

Much of our writing in any genre emerges out of our memories and concerns about the past as well as the present and future. It may seem obvious to say that the view of the world that shows up in our writing connects to how we grew up, what type of family we have, what experiences we had in school and on the playground. Yet we know better than to say that a writer's biography supplies the main lens through which we should view a piece of writing. The writing, we say, must stand—or fall—on its own. We compensate, much of the time, by ignoring this feature in ourselves and in other writers. However, while it is true that once a piece of writing goes out into the world, it must go on its own, it can also be helpful for you to explore your own memories and attitudes in a conscious way even if you don't intend to write memoir. Some mythologies to the contrary, writing is not a purely instinctual act, and exploring your memory is not only the place to start writing memoirs but fiction, poetry, and plays as well.

Memory as a Starting Point

You may think in response to all these social and cultural issues that you simply want to tell a story of something disturbing that really happened to you or to put down an account of the beautiful person that your aunt is. This is a good instinct, and it usually works well, in fact, to start your own writing from memory with whatever events or experiences stand out in your mind rather than front-loading larger concerns. At first you may not even be sure why they stand out for you. You don't want to impose interpretations on them, especially not at first. You want instead to see what comes to you. Eventually you will discover what social and larger human issues your experience connects to.

If you're a person eager to tell some stories from your life, you will likely take easily to writing memoir or nonfictional narrative poetry. However, if you are a person who isn't sure what to write about, or if you are shy about revealing details of your life, you may need to spend some time revisiting memories to see what stands out or emerges from your past. You may need to use some writing prompts to joggle your memory, such as ones included in the Pathways in this chapter. You may need some patience, as memory doesn't usually come to heel like a well-trained dog. Sometimes it can help to temporarily shift to doing something else, and then the memories will find you. Sometimes they respond to coaxing or concentration over time. It may be helpful to think of this process metaphorically and the memory as though it were a muscle you need to exercise or an archaeological site you need to excavate. It might be fun to think of your memory as a not-so-well-trained dog—you might have to bring it to you by acting playfully, by offering treats, or simply by being patient. (See **Pathway 5.7.**)

Often when you first start working on a memoir, it's a good idea to set aside a little time every day to go back to relevant times in your life, to the bits and pieces you remember, and those times will become clearer. Sometimes photographs or objects from your life can help. Sometimes working with words in the process of writing a memoir will crystallize moments in your mind. Many different paths lead into our memories, and if you keep trying them you will ultimately find the details you need or at the least you will have been on a fascinating journey.

Yourself as a Narrator

One of the most important tasks for you as you write memoir has to do with the fact that what ends up on the page does not equate exactly with the entirety of you. It is a written version of you. That doesn't mean that you shouldn't be truthful about who you are—or were—but try to hold yourself distinct from the stories you write about yourself. David Sedaris, in "The Drama Bug," for instance, has chosen to emphasize his naïve side in a kid who behaves in ridiculous ways, and while that humorous self-deprecation shows up in his other work and may be part of his personality in general, we are probably aware that he exhibits other qualities as well—drive, intelligence, insight, and so on.

When writing in first-person in memoir, you will be both "author" and "narrator." A first-person narrator in fiction may be a different gender or age from you, may live in a different town (or in a far-off land), or be distinct from you-the-author in many other ways. You can even create a persona in first-person fiction that you despise, which, in spite of any insecurities you may have, isn't usually how we feel about ourselves. However, in some ways, it can be useful when you write about yourself to consider yourself a **character** or **persona** as opposed to the whole real person you are. (Try **Pathway 5.8** or **5.9**.)

This becomes crucial when it comes time to present your memoir for workshop. One of the unique challenges of doing so is that you may feel that it is *you* being discussed as opposed to *your manuscript*. Often "you" on the page will come across in ways that you didn't anticipate and that don't reflect either your personality or your intended characterization of yourself. To remember that it's a representation of you that is being discussed will allow you to hear the criticism of your writing more clearly and without feeling personally misunderstood.

The voice that you establish for your persona on the page constitutes one of the primary ways that you will communicate artistically in a memoir. This may be a voice close to how you speak, or it may be different—more formal or more brassy or more gentle—but one of the most important aspects of a memoir's success is finding a voice and style that convey personality and distinction. We take this subject up in detail in Chapter 10. Remember, this may constitute your *written* personality as opposed to your whole personality, but paying attention to the consistency and uniqueness of your voice and vision will help you write a memoir that will engage its readers.

Time in Your Memoir

You won't likely be able to write about your entire life in one short piece of memoir. Even if you are only twenty years old, if you are working on a roughly twenty-page memoir, that would be one year a page. There are some fine memoirs that manage to move around over years of time, drawing together, for instance, thematic memories from a number of situations, but especially when you're first starting out, you might want to choose some particular incident or limited period of time to focus on. In this way, you can achieve a vivid level of detail and scene rather than writing only in summary. The same holds true in fiction, and its importance is inescapable in drama.

Remember also that other people do not have the memories you have. For you, the phrase "that time we went to Los Angeles" may evoke a whole range of sensations, sounds, sights, and tastes, but for someone reading your memoir, you have to recreate all that, whether it is the Los Angeles of dangerous and down-trodden Watts or the glitz of Beverly Hills or the artsy Venice Beach. These sensations come through in details, and details take space on the page and time to develop. Don't make the mistake of using too much shorthand or exposition to cover more time in your memoir. Instead, try letting one or a few moments imply the larger picture, just as your experience may say something important about larger social phenomena. (See **Pathway 5.10.**)

Reflection

As memoirist Patricia Hampl notes, "The appeal of memoir . . . is that you get to tell your story and you get to talk about it. Not 'Show, Don't Tell,' but 'Show and Tell.'" In memoir, then, readers usually ask for some interpretation of the events going on. **Reflection** on what has gone before becomes crucial to demonstrating the development of your own narrative persona in a piece of writing. Toward the end of "The Drama Bug," Sedaris notes, "I finally saw Hamlet for who he really was and recognized myself as the witless Yorick who had blindly followed along behind him." This short paragraph marks the turning point for the naïve boy and allows him to appreciate the mother who he felt thwarted him before. This kind of distinction between "what I understood then" and "what I understand now" points out why we as readers should care about a personal situation.

MEMORY AND IMAGINATION

Memory often gets targeted as the opposite of imagination, and the little, factual "truth" of memoir targeted as the opposite of the big, spirit-based "Truth" of fiction. In fact, of course, memoir and fiction have more in common than not. There are profound memoirs and there are shallow novels, just as there are the opposite. However, the status of memoir in the literary world remains somewhat controversial. There are many facets of this conversation, but at the least you should be fully aware that:

- memory is unreliable;
- even though creative nonfiction is distinct from journalism in its methods, this does not excuse out-and-out deceit in memoir any more than its factual base should excuse poor storytelling; and
- memory and imagination are not enemies but collaborators in all genres.

Working with Fickle Memory

Because of the notorious unreliability and variability of memory, memoir itself may take on these qualities. You probably have heard about studies that have demonstrated that when a group of individuals witnesses a traffic accident, they all report different "facts." In recent years with the advent of DNA testing, many people convicted of crimes based on eyewitness testimony have been proven innocent. "There are some things one remembers even though they may never have happened," notes playwright and novelist Harold Pinter.

If you write a memoir about your family, and you share it with them, no doubt you will find that not everyone remembers events the same way you do. Even when families tell stories around the Thanksgiving dinner table, they invariably argue. Such discussions are not necessarily violent or heated, but involve chewing over and lifting moments to the light for everyone's examination. "Really?" "What did you see that I didn't see?" "Why is your memory so different from mine?" While you may feel devoted to your own particular version of past events, you may also find it useful when writing a memoir to think of your family members as sources of information and subjects of research, which we discuss more in Chapter 6.

No one person has the exclusive right to define the truth. The best memoirs acknowledge this, and that uncertainty can become a feature by which memoirs examine the very nature of memory, knowledge, and selfhood. Keep in mind when writing a memoir that you are indeed writing one version of events. Someone else would write it differently, and if you write about it at two different times in your life you may write it differently each time. Anyone writing—or reading—a memoir should also understand this, though it's no excuse for a memoirist committing an outright lie or knowing exaggeration, especially not one designed mainly to make him- or herself look good or for sensationalist purposes.

Distinguishing Fickle from Fake

Creative nonfiction is fundamentally *interpretive*. Just as a poem or a novel or a play evokes emotion and creates an experiential effect, memoir does the same. The particular consciousness behind a piece of literature—whether poetry, creative nonfiction, fiction, or drama—is paramount. Every piece of creative writing reflects its author in some way and the nature of language, as well as the subject of the writing, whether that subject is a colony on Mars or how you brush your teeth. Because of this different emphasis, memoirists don't always follow the practices of journalism that include checking each "fact" with three sources, nor do they strive for journalistic "objectivity."

In recent years, however, there have been a number of scandals involving memoirs that were intentionally falsified by their authors. James Frey, perhaps the most notorious because his scandal erupted after an appearance on *The Oprah*

Winfrey Show, acknowledged that he had tried for some time to sell his book, *A Million Little Pieces*, as the semi-autobiographical novel it was, but that memoir was more popular with publishers so he finally lied about its nature. This differs from someone writing honestly from memory even though that memory may not be as verifiable as a journalistic report. James Frey provides a prime example of someone who purposefully confused the difference between creative nonfiction and journalism to sell work that had neither the literary truth of one nor the factual truth of the other.

In fact, there always have been false memoirs, and the history of novels published under the imprimatur of "true story" goes at least as far back as Daniel Defoe's *A Journal of a Plague Year*, published in 1722 as a factual account of the bubonic plague in London by an adult firsthand witness. It wasn't until the 1780s that someone figured out that Defoe was only five years old at the time of the plague in 1655 and *A Journal of the Plague Year* was just as fictional as his more famous novel *Robinson Crusoe*.

Poets and fiction writers have also relied upon false claims of experience or biography to promote their work. In the 1990s, for instance, numerous top poetry journals began publishing the work of a survivor of the Hiroshima bombs of World War II by the name of Araki Yasusada, but shortly rumors began circulating that he had not died of cancer in 1972, as the story claimed, but had been the invention of Kent Johnson, a still-living white college professor in Illinois.

Writing memoir takes a particular kind of integrity related to memory. It is tempting to change facts to make yourself look better or to make someone else look worse or to make your story more superficially exciting. Thinking of memoir writing as a form of exploration may help you avoid trying to exaggerate your perfection and develop standards of truth for yourself. If you are on an expedition of discovery, then you might envision your job as digging out whatever you find, whether it is pretty or not, and sharing it with your readers. There is a responsibility to be as faithful to the world as possible, understanding all the while its complications and uncertainties. You may devote yourself to the truth, knowing all the while that some elements of it may be elusive. (**Pathway 5.11** can help you test your own boundaries.)

Melding Memory and Imagination

British fiction and nonfiction author Julian Barnes, in *Nothing to Be Frightened Of*, notes that as writers grow older, "memory and the imagination begin to seem less and less distinguishable." He goes on: "My brother distrusts most memories. I do not mistrust them, rather I trust them as workings of the imagination, as containing imaginative as opposed to naturalistic truth."

Barnes points out that whenever you write down a life story, you are, in fact, changing what happened. By shaping the memories, you are changing the events from mere experience into a meaningful narrative. Even though you are writing a "true story," you must make decisions based on issues of writing as much as on "what really happened." You must focus on selecting the most revealing details (and leaving out the rest), on choosing words that convey appropriate emotions, on structuring the story for dramatic impact by its own logic (not simply chronologically). Perhaps more than any other genre, creative nonfiction illuminates how writing can change the past, for purposes good or ill.

Thus, there's a way in which the meaning of events is something that we create. Just as we do so while they are going on, we can do so again later, sometimes more clearly or in a way more narratively "true" or satisfying. Today it may be important that your mother betrayed you by grounding you; at another time it may be important that your so-called friends encouraged you to leap from a moving car and risk injuring yourself. In writing about your marriage today, you may feel you must start at the moment you first met your husband, but in ten years, you might decide that the moment when he held your hand in the hospital ER after a sudden illness is a more fitting opening to the memoir because it reveals the depth of marriage as opposed to other kinds of relationships.

It's even possible to include in a memoir moments that occurred before you were born or when you weren't present. In *The Bishop's Daughter* by Honor Moore, for instance, her father is a main subject of the book and only on page 93, after she has treated his early life, does she note, "And so I have come into the story." If such moments before your birth resonate in your life, you shouldn't hesitate to try describing them imaginatively, though there are challenges in doing so. It is entirely possible to do so honestly and to indicate in your writing that you are speculating or patching together family stories that have surrounded you. In "Remembering, I Was Not There," for instance, Panning tells us a lot about her own life, although she is focused on the time in her parents' lives before she was even born. She manages to make this honest by emphasizing her method rather than pretending somehow that she could have witnessed these events. They are nonfictional events, and no doubt she heard stories about them, but she has had to imagine them as well.

Writing a memoir in this way can perhaps be compared to writing formal poetry with a rhyme scheme or metrical pattern. There are accepted parameters for using the facts, but they in no way should limit the imagination that you bring to bear on the story.

Remember, also, that much fiction begins in our experiences. To help you think about when memoir begins to shade into fiction, try **Pathway 5.12**. We may choose fiction for a variety of reasons—to protect someone else's privacy, to avoid confrontation with those we depict, or because we find ourselves varying from the facts—but we should never turn our backs on the origins of our stories.

PATHWAYS

Pathway 5.1. Early memory. Describe your earliest (or one of your early) memories or fears. First, simply describe what comes to mind. Then ask yourself which sense seems most prominent, and try to recall your other senses at the time. Then try another paragraph in which you note anything potentially emotional, important, or telling in the memory. Did you feel particularly alone or crowded by others? Do you remember crying or laughing, being hungry or sleepy, hurting or feeling pleasure? Try to connect that early memory with your life today. Compare yours with the early memories by James Agee (p. 275) and E. L. Doctorow (p. 337).

Pathway 5.2. Body memory. Most of us have strong feelings about our bodies, and they often connect to other aspects of our lives—sports, illness or disability, sexuality, ethnicity, religious practices. We exist in the same body over time, but it also changes. Write about some aspect of your body, starting with an early memory and moving forward to near today. Concentrate on your senses.

Pathway 5.3. Parent memory. Write about a time you saw one of your parents cry.

Pathway 5.4. Memoir list exercise.
A. When you think about writing about your own memories and experiences, what topics come to mind? Make a list of several.
B. List at least five things you've done in the past six months (or one month, or week; your instructor may want to set time parameters). These don't need to be dramatically "important" events, just ways that you have spent your time.
C. Choose a category of nouns, a set of related items of some interest to you. List six to ten items in this category. Example: flowers in your parents' garden (fuschia, gardenia, peony, tulip, daffodil, iris).
D. Once you have these three lists, brainstorm about connections between them and about their wider importance beyond your life. What themes emerge among each list or among more than one? If there's good overlap, you may see that the items in List B could be specific scenes for writing about one of your topics in List A. List C could become a way of organizing your essay or provide related images for you to use.

Pathway 5.5. Social power. Write about a situation in which you have seen social power exhibited, where you observed or experienced an episode of racism, sexism, gay-bashing, or some other negative treatment of someone based on a group they belong to. This might be one of the more common unfortunate situations already mentioned, but you might also think about immigrant ancestry of a variety of types, Jewish or Muslim or Catholic heritage, or stigma that arose for you or a family member or someone else based on illness, disability, addiction, poverty, lack of education, or association with a crime another person committed. In your writing, don't preach about the situation, but describe its harsh reality based on a particular moment in time.

Pathway 5.6. Nested identities. Draw a series of at least five nested circles with yourself and your innermost self in the middle. Then, as suggested by Judith Barrington (see the Guidepost: Self-Awareness in this chapter), fill out each circle with groups that you are part of somehow, starting with 1) your closest family and friends, 2) your wider social set of friends and school/job, 3) your community, whether town or city or part of a city, and other similar identities such as groups you belong to, 4) your country or other parts of the world or groups you identify with even if you don't know most of the individuals in them. Think of one thing you've done recently that reflects your association or membership in your family or a larger group. Write two pages where you never mention the larger group but feel that your story represents it or contradicts expectations for it.

Pathway 5.7. Daily memories. Take a week and every day as soon as you wake up, write down a memory. It doesn't matter how far in the past or how recent, try to recall a variety of types of moments—intensely emotional, quiet, when you were alone and with others, what time of year or day it was. (Of course, you can do this for longer than a week, and you can also do it just before you go to sleep. The point is to make contact with your memories a regular thing. If you do so, more will tend to emerge.)

Pathway 5.8. Self character sketch. As you work on a memoir piece for workshop, write a separate one-page "character sketch" of yourself. Be true, but decide which aspects of your personality to emphasize in this piece, which are more relevant and which less so. This works best with work you've already defined in terms of subject matter; otherwise, you'll have no way to decide which traits resonate with your material.

Pathway 5.9. Self in third person. Try taking one of the earlier memories you've already written about, but use the third person to describe yourself rather than the first person. Pretend that you are a fictional character and that you are observing from your imagination. If you find that you begin to fictionalize, draw a line and start over with a new memory. Think about what you might find out about yourself (and your imagination) by writing about yourself in the third person. Which of these memories might become memoir, which fiction or a play, and which have the rhythm of poetry?

Pathway 5.10. Self in scene. Choose one moment in your life that is typical of something larger. Write a scene of that one incident or time, all in real time without any commentary. Just describe the setting, people, and actions. Think about two other scenes that relate to this theme but that show some important difference. Write those two scenes. How much like a complete memoir does this feel? What else must you add to make it complete?

Pathway 5.11. Confessional. Write a two-page confession about something not-so-nice that you or another family member has done in a way that you would be happy to show your strictest and most judgmental family member. Then rewrite it as though no one but you will ever see it. You may not feel comfortable sharing it with classmates or your instructor, but be prepared to at least discuss the process.

Pathway 5.12. Fictionalizing self. Take any of the memories from Pathway 5.1 or any of the other memory-based exercises you have done so far and try giving that memory to a character you've made up who is distinctly not like you. If you're twenty and female, give the memory to a seventy-five-year-old man. Even if it's nonsensical for that person (getting your first bra, for example), see where the combination takes you in a story or play.

FURTHER ANTHOLOGY READINGS

Andre Dubus III, "Tracks and Ties" (creative nonfiction)
E. L. Doctorow, excerpt from *World's Fair* (fiction)
James Agee, "Knoxville: Summer, 1915" (fiction)

GUIDEPOST: SELF-AWARENESS

The merely personal can take on larger meaning.

As we discuss in this chapter, it may help you at some point to think about how your own personal life stories are connected to the larger social and cultural moment in which you live. Judith Barrington, in her book *Writing the Memoir*, describes this process as a series of nested circles, with the center being your "inner life" and successive circles moving outward to "intimate" relationships such as those with your family, then a "neighborhood" including friends and school, further out to "communities" of work, subcultures, and acquaintances, then beyond to the mass culture of your country and the world. She notes that a memoir usually moves among these different strata, but that what makes a memoir successful is the "personal voice" that a reader comes to trust or be intrigued by.

In some ways this idea is a simplification; still, it can be helpful in your writing—especially nonfiction writing—for you to become aware of yourself within your context. In fact, the success of your writing depends on it. Just as it's possible to turn off another person in a social situation, it's possible to turn people away from what you have to say in print. The ability to pay careful attention to the way that language works and the effect it has on other people is one of the greatest skills that a writer can develop.

Of course, this skill goes well beyond the workshop atmosphere or even beyond the world of creative writing itself. If you think of great speech-writers of history—from Socrates and Demosthenes on through Sojourner Truth, Abraham Lincoln, Martin Luther King, Jr., Mahatma Gandhi, Winston Churchill, Eleanor Roosevelt, John F. Kennedy—you understand how the power of words becomes clear, even before the effects of heartfelt and well-timed delivery. This level of effectiveness requires an understanding of what you want to say and a certainty that you have both a right and a need to say it.

In addition, self-awareness that will help you as a writer and in many other kinds of employment exhibits an awareness of other people in relation to you, an understanding that you are not an island. Workshops foster this per-spective as students work together to improve each other's work as well as their own, and as you examine your creative nonfiction, fiction, plays, and poems for qualities that go beyond immediate self-expression. There is a lovely circular fashion in which your own self-exploration will reveal to you more about others and the world we all live in, and that understanding will in turn enrich what you know about yourself. The more clearly you are able to see yourself—and the immediate milieu you're in—the more realistic an understanding you'll have of the particular contributions you can make.

Chapter **6**

Research

According to novelist Zora Neale Hurston, "Research is formalized curiosity. It is poking and prying with a purpose." As you work on your creative writing, try to think of **research** as anything you do to find out what you need to know to write about a particular subject or setting, or about a particular person or kind of person. This can both overlap with and differ significantly from the research you do in other kinds of courses, whether focused on lab experiments or on reading scholarly works. We might think of its most obvious instances, such as looking into details to fill out the world in historical fiction and research-based essays, but you may also end up wanting confirmation of your own memories when you write even the most personal, intimate kinds of memoir and poetry.

MOVING OUT FROM AUTOBIOGRAPHICAL MATERIAL

You may have heard the common creative writing adage "Write what you know." Indeed, when you describe worlds and feelings with which you are familiar, you will have at your fingertips the details and authenticity that will bring them alive and make them believable. But what if you are fascinated with the life of someone you haven't met or with a different era—past or future—or a hypothetical other world entirely? What if you have stumbled into an experience that has frightened you or intrigued you but that you've never encountered before? Perhaps, for instance, your family took you on a trip to Italy to meet long-lost relatives, and you became fascinated by an old family vineyard or by the stories exchanged around the dinner table of a great-grandfather you never even met.

Travel writing offers a clear, fairly straightforward example of how you might want to combine your own personal experiences with places, people, and subjects on which you are not an expert. Setting a fictional work, whether in prose or drama, in a far-off location or time works similarly. Start thinking of research as anything that will make it possible for you to "know what you write about" even if you don't start off "writing what you know." If you have tried your hand at Pathway 1.9 or 1.12, you already may have an idea of where to begin exploring new interests through your writing and research, but **Pathway 6.1** will help in generating further ideas.

We often think of our reading as a way to escape our daily lives, to travel to far-off worlds, and to see even familiar realms in whole new lights through the eyes of a character or the powerful direction an author takes us. Sometimes, however, we forget to incorporate that same sense of exploration in our own writing or don't realize the digging and exploring those other authors had to do to create mind-expanding experiences. Even the most personal experiences you may write about deserve that spirit of exploration and open-mindedness.

Notice in the following passage from Annie Dillard's "Total Eclipse" (the entire essay starts on page 325) what a sharp lens she uses to convey the sensations she has endured:

> The second before the sun went out we saw a wall of dark shadow come speeding at us. We no sooner saw it than it was upon us, like thunder. It roared up the valley. It slammed our hill and knocked us out. It was the monstrous swift shadow cone of the moon. I have since read that this wave of shadow moves 1,800 miles an hour. Language can give no sense of this sort of speed—1,800 miles an hour. It was 195 miles wide. No end was in sight—you saw only the edge. It rolled at you across the land at 1,800 miles an hour, hauling darkness like plague behind it. Seeing it, and knowing it was coming straight for you, was like feeling a slug of anesthetic shoot up your arm. If you think very fast, you may have time to think, "Soon it will hit my brain." You can feel the deadness race up your arm; you can feel the appalling, inhuman speed of your own blood. We saw the wall of shadow coming, and screamed before it hit.

Dillard puts us in the scene with her and the several hundred others gathered on the hillside to watch this particular eclipse. She does this not only by describing what she saw in great detail and using metaphors that give us some more tangible glimpse into the situation, but she also adds a couple of startling facts that she has garnered from her reading. She even repeats three times the rate at which the shadow moves—perhaps because it is a fact hard to fully grasp.

Unlike most general descriptions of total eclipses—"it was astounding" or "it was scary"—Dillard's passage challenges us to relive her discomfort with her.

The essay as a whole also takes on more depth and resonance by the inclusion of her learning about the wider phenomenon. She has combined library research with reporting on an experience she sought out. Seek to make your own research serve your writing in these ways.

METHODS AND MEANS

Though in some contexts you may think of research as a kind of drudgery, if you link it to what fascinates you, what you would love to learn more about, you will find it one of the most rewarding aspects of becoming a writer. In research for our creative writing, we are not often limited—we can choose where to go. Our writing can open doors and provide a reason to learn whatever we want to learn. When you hear the word "research," keep in mind it means any method of gathering information. Writers are some of the most curious people in the world, and we use almost any means necessary to find out what we feel we need to know to make our writing compelling and convincing.

Library and Online Sources

Although you may have never visited the stacks at your university library, much research today can be done with the convenient click of your keyboard through databases and the Internet. There still may be treasures in the stacks, and I encourage you to delve into them from time to time, but the Internet has made even much textual research a lot less physically taxing—a host of information, including images, is at your fingertips on your computer. There are new challenges with this kind of research, of course. For one thing, it's sometimes difficult to tell what is a good source of information and what is merely junk that some random person has uploaded to the Web. As long as you have learned through your more scholarly or English composition courses how to assess these online sources, however, you have a wealth of information available as a creative writer. One story I wrote and published, "Nothing by Comparison," demanded a setting in Dubrovnik, a city in Croatia on the Adriatic Sea. I had never been there, and so I based my descriptions of the city on two research sources: a friend of mine who had been there and vast numbers of maps and photographs that I scrutinized in books and online. I read about the weather there, I perused travel books and travelogues, and I was able through my imagination to create a connection to a place I had never been. After it was published I received a letter from a reader extolling the city's historic beauty and thanking me for bringing it back so strongly to his memory after many years away.

You may also want to write with fulfilling detail about places and people distant in time or place. Louise Erdrich's short story "Saint Marie" (p. 346), for instance, takes place in the 1930s, decades before the author was born, and every year numerous novels with historical settings, as well as books of actual history, hit the book lists. Just a few recent ones are Hilary Mantel's *Bring Up the*

Bodies, set in Tudor England; T. C. Boyle's *San Miguel*, at the turn of the twentieth century; and Alice Hoffman's *The Dovekeepers*, during the Roman Empire. Denis Johnson's 2002 novella *Train Dreams* follows the rough life of a character born and orphaned in the late 1800s who becomes part of the Westward expansion. These works, of course, exhibit contemporary characteristics—they don't sound as though they were written at the times of their settings—however, the authors use authentic detail. We talk more about the importance of such details in Chapter 7, but often they take some research. (See **Pathway 6.2.**)

Travel, Talking, and Experience

Reading and perusing photos, is only one kind of research. If I had been able, financially and time-wise, I could also have visited Dubrovnik myself to experience the actual sensations of the place—the sound of the language spoken in the streets, the scent of the ocean air, and the pervading sense of history in a city vital since the sixteenth century and threatened with military destruction when the former republic of Yugoslavia split apart. Though traveling halfway across the world may seem more difficult than clicking through screens at the computer, it would have been a way for me to make sure, for instance, that the picture I composed took into account the bombings that had damaged the historical architecture in the old city.

Getting out in the world, then, is one primary source of research that we don't often think of under that label. It forms an invaluable practice for any writer, no matter the genre. Although you can do much useful research sitting at home at the computer, that isn't always enough to bring life to your writing or to give you new sensations and experiences to write about. This is at least partly the reason that Ernest Hemingway volunteered for the ambulance corps during World War I, ventured to Pamplona for the running of the bulls, and later took off to Africa on safari. Even though we can't always make room in our day-to-day lives for such extreme adventures, there are always ones closer to home, worlds that you haven't yet explored just out your back door, so to speak. (See **Pathways 6.3** and **6.4.**)

Talking with other people may be a part of traveling to new realms, or it may be a part of getting to know better the people in your own vicinity, but either way it can be another vital research technique in all genres. Interviewing is a skill most commonly taught in reporting spheres, but all writers should make listening carefully to others a lifelong habit. Doing so can inform your work in myriad ways. You may want to write about a conflict that has fractured your family for many decades, and to do so you'd need to hear from various people involved. Or in order to create the right atmosphere for a story set in a hospital, you may want to capture the strange combination of complicated medical terminology and gossip that characterizes nurses as they chit-chat at their station. Certainly, if you are writing plays for either stage or screen, where dialogue forms the core of how you present characters and situations, then you must be able to distinguish one character from another by their speech habits and quirks and be sensitive to how emotion is conveyed with something other than exclamation points. You'll need to understand how gestures and facial expressions contribute to what we gather about a person's motivations and personality. (See **Pathway 6.5**.)

Self-Research

Socrates famously said, "The unexamined life is not worth living," and that may be true within the realm of memoir writing as well. You may be motivated to write a memoir out of some immediate experience that affected you in some way, but consider how many memories slip away from us or remain tucked away unconsidered. We take them for granted as part of our lives, but we don't give them much thought. Some of them we forget entirely until something jogs a memory awake. If we take a step back and look at such vague or partial memories again, especially if we explore aspects that remain unexplained, then we may find out something new about ourselves. Of course, all of the Pathways in Chapter 5 are designed to try to get you to look at your memories and experiences in new ways, but some of the ones in this chapter might be applied to yourself as well. If you can informally interview family members, you can sometimes learn about whole parts of your own history you had no idea about before. Think about your own life as a locus for research and exploration, and you will uncover new truths about yourself. (Try **Pathway 6.6** for one way to think of even yourself as deserving of study.)

PERSONAL ESSAYS

In Chapter 5, we focused on the memoir, but there are two other subgenres of creative nonfiction that more often combine personal experience with research. One of these, the **personal essay**, may start with your own personal musings about a given subject, but it makes an outward reach to what others have thought or how others have experienced the same issue. This form may make use of the same kind of fact-based research that you have used in more formal kinds of essays that you have written with clear thesis statements, persuasive arguments, objective or impersonal perspectives, and analysis of ideas. Personal essays, however, defy fixed formulas (such as the five-paragraph presentation of evidence) and tend to follow their own provisional, conversational tone and structure.

As with all these genres and subgenres, of course, the personal essay mixes and merges with other kinds of nonfiction writing. It might best be distinguished by the idea that in a personal essay as opposed to a memoir the experience of the author is not exactly the main point. If you write a personal essay, your voice and personality will still be prominent, and you will likely use your own experiences, but your focus will be broader. Stephen Kuusisto's "Letter from Venice" (p. 393), for example, goes beyond his story to a contemplation of blindness and more generally to what assistance we need to appreciate places we travel to. Lia Purpura's "On Looking Away" (p. 480) likewise weaves her insistent personality into a manifesto-like response to public and private forms of violence. Unlike in literary journalism, here you will more likely focus on the local, the familiar, the daily—aspects of life we think of as common but that may bear a closer look. Subjects such as friendship, marriage, food, nature (discussed above), subways, fashion, travel—even sleeping or bathing or walking—can be explored in original ways that help us understand our world better.

You may find the personal essay form attractive because in it you may feel free to express an opinion as an opinion in addition to demonstrating your attitude toward the world through the actions and words of your real or imagined characters. The personal essay follows the writer's mind, even perhaps as it wanders on a quest to figure out a particular phenomenon. Personal essays are strong for the same reasons other writing is strong, of course—vivid scene and compelling characters still have a central role to play—but it allows you to occasionally step in and offer an interpretation, to say, "Here is how I feel," or "Here is what I think." The form encourages rumination and contemplation.

In general, form in these creative nonfiction genres is extremely flexible. As a beginning creative writer, you don't need to be overly obsessed with exactly whether you are writing a memoir or a personal essay. Over time, you will become more comfortable with classifications, or at least with the various issues that go into discussions of these classifications. They only should concern you right now, however, as long as they help you to distinguish a particular direction a piece of your own writing might go. You may, for instance, be struggling to write a memoir about your relationship with your mother, but find that no matter how many scenes you write, you can't escape stereotypes. In that case, you might find that thinking a little more widely—reading material from psychology to great novels that include the mother-daughter or mother-son relationship, talking to friends or relatives about motherhood, even something like examining works of art over the ages that show mothers and their children—will help you leap forth. Perhaps, if you get insights from talking to others or you end up working in a day care or school setting where you observe parents and children, you will conceive of an entire literary journalism project along these lines. In the meantime, you may find that the personal or lyric essay form allows you to open up your own experience, ask questions, and connect the dots in different ways. Merely by thinking about the frame of your subject a little differently, it may fall into the right shape. Otherwise, don't worry too much about distinguishing the types of creative nonfiction; instead, focus on finding the right combination of elements for the piece you are writing. (See **Pathways 6.7** and **6.8**.)

LITERARY JOURNALISM AND IMMERSION

If you lean toward an interest in the news or simply toward stories other than your own, you may want to pursue the field of literary journalism. **Literary journalism**, a subgenre of creative nonfiction, involves a range of techniques for writing about others. It began in the world of traditional journalism, but it differs in that its authors don't attempt objectivity, but instead go into their subject matter in deep and personal ways.

One of the main accusations targeting the entire genre of memoir is that it can be self-indulgent or narcissistic. We deal with that accusation in some ways in Chapter 5, but also always remember that there are others out there who have interesting lives but who aren't necessarily writers themselves, people whose stories you might want to illuminate. There are major historical events—both past and present—that impact our lives but also call for thoughtful examination in literary in addition to journalistic form. The creative nonfiction writer is often called upon to interpret these experiences, events, and people in ways that will make them more vivid than simple statements of fact and statistics, to remind us that large-scale phenomena happen at a human scale.

In 1959, Truman Capote, a staff writer at the *New Yorker* magazine, saw a small item in the newspaper about a Kansas family—a husband and wife and the two youngest of their four children—brutally murdered in their rural home. The book that he finally published in 1966, *In Cold Blood*, marked a turning point in the general depiction of such crime stories. Up to that time, such crimes had not been treated with literary care or even much detail—they were news items and nothing more. Capote, however, saw a deeply human story meriting profound examination, and spent months—eventually years—interviewing and befriending the killers, as well as the people of the nearby town, and writing about them. When *In Cold Blood* was published, Capote referred to it as the first "nonfiction novel" because he had relied on techniques usually associated with fiction—complex characterization, detailed descriptions of people and places, the creation of scenes rather than summaries, and non-chronological plotting that revealed the tragic set of circumstances that led to the violence in that family farmhouse.

Today, you will hear this kind of writing referred to by a number of names and its practice varied from writer to writer, but it still often keeps one foot in the world of straight reporting and another in the personal perspectives of its authors. The best-known literary journalists exhibit a wider interest in culture and the human side of stories than do typical newspaper reporters, and their work aims to be not only written from a personal perspective but stylistically the finest its authors can make it. Some of the best-known early practitioners, such as Norman Mailer, Joan Didion, Tom Wolfe, and Terry Southern, also wrote fiction and/or screenplays. One well-known subset, gonzo journalism, with its emphasis on often wild adventures and the impossibility of objectivity, was practiced by the likes of Hunter S. Thompson and P. J. O'Rourke.

Immersion journalism provides one working method in which a writer sets out to experience a certain situation, often over months or years, in order to write with deeper understanding about it, though this research takes them outside their own daily lives. George Plimpton, one of the earliest practitioners, became known for training and competing with professional athletes and recording the experiences in such books as *Out of My League, Paper Lion,* and *Open Net.* More recently, Ted Conover, became a guard at Sing Sing in order to uncover the details of life in prison and Barbara Ehrenreich left her upper-middle-class life with minimal resources and set out to live on a minimum-wage job in order to explore the traps of poverty.

Not all literary journalism requires full immersion; for instance, Rebecca Skloot's recent best-seller, *The Immortal Life of Henrietta Lacks*—which chronicles the case of a woman whose cell samples formed the basis for much cancer research, though she herself was never told—is a fine example of literary journalism based on extensive documents and interviews, but not an infiltration of another life; Skloot worked as a university professor while she researched and wrote the book.

Whether fully immersive or not, much literary journalism research often demands large investments in both time and money. For this reason, you may need to prepare more gradually for this kind of writing than for memoir, poetry, or even fiction. Just remember that projects closer to home can be a good starting place. You don't have to travel to the other side of the world—or even of town—but just keep an eye open for interesting events and people and be willing to pursue them until you find the story in them. Lee Gutkind's essay "Teeth" (p. 373), for instance, stemmed from a series of motorcycle rides he took through an area near his home in Pittsburgh during which he would stop and talk with people. He found these individuals and their community worth contemplation. (See **Pathway 6.9.**)

This may be a good way for you to take your own writing if you have a penchant for talking with people and an interest in the larger social trends of which you are a part. In addition, although you may not have the resources to put your regular life on hold for a year or more in order to fully research a different path than your own, you may find the concept of immersion helpful in less stringent ways. Immersion requires that you suspend your usual expectations and be open to new experiences and new mindsets. It puts you in a mode that both allows for and requires careful observation and attention to the new. Too often, we try to start off with an already determined conclusion for a piece of writing we've just begun. Whether you embed yourself in a real-world experience in order to observe something new, or in a fictional world you've created, that open-minded concept of immersion clears your vision for surprises.

ETHICS

As you develop as a writer and make decisions about what to write about, you'll encounter the issue of who inhabits your pages and how much those characters resemble actual people. In memoir and literary journalism, in particular, you will be faced with the possibility that your words—even if they are intended to explore your own emotional reality or do good by revealing poignant or previously unheralded lives—might hurt someone. It is a complex task to figure out when that might happen and in which particular instances it might be worth the risk of doing so. You will make your own choices and find your own particular moral compass, but it's important to at least be aware from the beginning that you have others' emotions and public identities in your hands. While some satire written with an intention of revenge can be successful, most of the time human caring and compassion provide a more compelling and worthwhile base. Even things written with a certain amount of bitterness often stem from a desire to protect or an expression of disappointment in someone for whom we had high hopes. As writers, we balance concern for our own self-expression with the right of others to control the stories of their own lives.

Until you begin publishing your work, you need not worry about legal issues, but be aware of the dilemmas you will face when depicting other people, whether well-known figures or ordinary people. We all write with hope that our words will have an impact on the world, and yet we often forget small-scale effects close to home, especially effects that might be negative. Perhaps sometimes it's easier to be conscious of this when writing nonfiction that's admittedly about "real people" and situations. It's good, however, to keep this in mind in all genres.

Just think of how your own mother might view the way you write about mothers, even in your fiction or poetry. She may believe that every mother you pen somehow represents her, and if you write a story in which the mother is cruel or crazy, she may take it personally. Whether there's a shadow of your own mother in your story or not, she may recognize something about herself and feel maligned. Now imagine if that story becomes a novel and is published and read—not only by people in far-off places, but by your neighbors and family friends. People may wonder how much your mother character is based on your actual mother, and your own mother may be embarrassed or angry. (**Pathway 6.10** asks that you and your class discuss such potential issues.)

Sometimes, however, you will find that it's worth taking the risk. In addition to being social beings who want to respect others, as writers we often have to fight self-censorship that might stem from fear of hurting someone's feelings. Sometimes the important issues that need to be brought to light take on a greater weight than the feelings of one individual. As discussed in Chapter 5, sometimes speaking out about hard things feels necessary to us, and our best stories, images, and insights may come in relation to the darker, more harmful side of human life—things that are not polite dinner conversation.

In fact, it's impossible for a writer to work without delving into the lives of other people and encroaching upon others' experiences. Try imagining work in any genre in which you didn't create a portrait of anyone but yourself. No more absurd idea exists. What you are charged with as a writer is determining when possible alienation is worth it and devising emotional means of coping with it if and when it happens.

RESEARCH IN POETRY, FICTION, AND DRAMA

Throughout this chapter, I have mentioned that research can be important in all genres. Research can ground the work, provide evocative detail, and simultaneously set your writing free from smallness. It can also help you avoid errors that might otherwise undermine your work.

There are many examples—we've already discussed the historical aspects of stories like Louise Erdrich's "Saint Marie" above. If you're going to poison a character, then you'd better know how different poisons work; if a dog is going to bite someone and set off a lawsuit, then you should know what breeds would do so and why; if a character on stage is going to perform a tae kwon do tornado kick, you need to know exactly how much space will be required. You will want to learn to recognize what I call *knowledge gaps* in all of your writing. Sometimes as we write, in the flow of ideas we may insert a placeholder—a street name that might reveal to a Philadelphia native that we haven't been there, the name of a fabric or color that may not be just what we mean—and that is fine as long as we recognize that these small gaps may also imply a larger missing link. We may go back later with Google maps and figure out a real street name.

Not all creative nonfiction, fiction, poetry, and drama needs to be researched. Sometimes we write from a moment of observation coupled instantly to our imagination. But research in all the genres is more common than you may think, and you should never hesitate to do it when it will benefit your work. Most good writing, we must keep in mind, requires incoming information as well as outgoing self-expression. It's best to write with an open mind rather than a predetermined message. There is nothing like new information, people, and experiences to remind us of that.

PATHWAYS

Pathway 6.1. Curiosity. Make a list of things/places/people/phenomena that you are curious about or things that mystify you. Why are stop signs octagonal in shape? Why do people get insomnia? How did the Loch Ness myth get started? What's the most beautiful butterfly in the world and where does it live? Why did my grandmother marry my grandfather? Then jot ideas for what methods you might use to find out more.

Pathway 6.2. Past object. Choose a year at least ten years in the past, and look up a little about life then. As soon as you encounter in descriptions of that time an object no longer in common use, focus on that kind of object—a horse-drawn buggy, a black-and-white TV, a straight razor. Look up some pictures and do a bit more reading about that object. Then write a short poem, essay, or story that uses the object in some way.

Pathway 6.3. Active object. Choose one item that you keep in your room, apartment, or house that you associate with a particular event or some meaningful activity that you have participated in as you wore or acquired this item. The snow globe you bought when you visited London? Your last Halloween costume? The trophy you won as a basketball player? Write about the event you most remember as connected to that item.

Pathway 6.4. Travel writing. Write a poem or essay about a place you have traveled recently. This works for relatively local places as well as exotic ones on the other side of the world. In either case, try to capture your sense of exploration and the most interesting aspects of your experience there.

Pathway 6.5. Family mysteries. Make a list of family mysteries or things you feel uncertain about in your family history. Interview someone in your family who might be willing to fill you in.

Pathway 6.6. Your name. Write about your name. You may know some history of your family name already, and your parents may have told you if you're named after a relative or why they picked your given name. But go beyond that. Find out historical meanings and associations, other people with your name, how far back your given name goes in your family, what other options your parents thought about, or whether your name was changed if you were adopted. Write a short essay about the importance of your name to you.

Pathway 6.7. Manifesto. Write a paragraph about something in your life that you'd like to change. Write with resolution, even anger if that seems appropriate. Then, in your second paragraph, connect this personal issue to a larger societal problem. Continue writing, combining your own personal experience to large changes you would like to see.

Pathway 6.8. "On X." Many classic personal essays have simple titles—"On Friendship," "On Marriage," "On the Pleasures of Bathing." Decide on your own more contemporary topic and write "On X." Use your own opinions, ruminations, and examples of X, but also take a look at what great writers and thinkers have said on the matter. Search out quotes and ideas on the Internet or recall them and bring them back from books you've read. If you've heard about relevant studies recently in the news (a certain percentage of the population prefers beer over wine, or the number of households with cats outnumbers the number of households with dogs, or whatever), make use of those, or seek them out if they will add to your ideas. Ask friends and family members what they think. Weave together a few of these facets, all the time keeping your thoughts and speculations primary.

Pathway 6.9. Exploring subcultures. Attend an event in your community that you would not normally attend. Maybe it's a club that features a different kind of music than you like. Or a cat or dog show when you are into strays (or a shelter if you are into purebreds). Or a church different from yours. There are myriad choices—garden clubs, casinos, knitting circles, boxing or car racing events, community theaters, political meetings. Use this event as a setting for an essay, story, poem, or play.

Pathway 6.10. Is it okay if I say that? Write down one hypothetical situation involved in writing about another person that you would like to discuss in terms of the potential ethical problems it raises. This might be something that you've thought about writing about but held back because you weren't sure, or it might be something you've seen or heard about someone else writing about. What questions do you have about these issues?

FURTHER ANTHOLOGY READINGS

Lee Gutkind, "Teeth" (creative nonfiction)

Larry Levis, "At the Grave of My Guardian Angel: St. Louis Cemetery, New Orleans" (poetry)

GUIDEPOST: CURIOSITY

Natural curiosity will introduce you to worlds outside yourself.

We live in a time when self-indulgence and narcissism are perceived to be dominant forces in our culture. Whether or not that's true is widely debated, but it's enough to know that an ability to understand the world beyond your own narrow concerns is highly valued in personal and work settings. You can achieve and demonstrate such outward focus by joining clubs, working in a local business or charity office, volunteering and participating in service learning, or studying fields that focus your attention outward.

However, your ability to communicate what you learn in these realms may be closely tied to thinking of your writing as a way in which you can connect your own personal views and experiences with those of the wider world. If you are an environmental sciences major, for instance, you may be learning a lot about soil and water, chemistry and toxicology, even economics; but ultimately you will need to be able to communicate that knowledge beyond other scientists to the general public. The skills gained in your creative writing study can help you understand how to do so through sensitivity to story and image.

If you're a Creative Writing major, you may use the research skills you gain in working on your essays, stories, poems, and plays to help you find work in a variety of walks of life. You will be trained in conducting research that has a personal and often impassioned purpose, and you'll learn to bring that mindset to any kind of research you do. We commonly approach creative writing as the process of bringing to the surface our own personalities, experiences, and points of view, but we also inevitably encounter our responsibilities to people and issues outside ourselves.

One of the most enjoyable aspects of being a writer is that no matter what you write about, it is always an occasion to learn—maybe your main character flies airplanes, perhaps you want to write a series of poems about your family history, or perhaps you are intent on creating a screenplay set in Shanghai, where you have only visited once. All of these occasions enrich and expand your mind, and this habit of self-directed learning can be carried into every realm of your life, whether it's figuring out what used car to buy or analyzing whether a business should open a branch in Poughkeepsie.

Destination: **FICTION**

Fiction usually swoops into our lives from early in our days on earth. Humans, and many animals, seem wired for imagination. Even a cat can turn a scrap of paper into pretend prey, and by age two or three babies seem to use imagination and fantasy to begin to fit together the pieces of reality in ever-larger circles around them. Studies show that children who participate in dramatic forms of play—dressing up, acting out their fantasies—grow up with better vocabularies, more flexibility, and an ability to adapt to changing circumstances.

Everyone in the room, then, will be more than passingly familiar with the genre of fiction. The first stories read to us by our parents, grandparents, baby-sitters, and other guardians may be based on true stories but are presented to us as fiction. We are encouraged from a young age to explore imaginative worlds, even though the ultimate goal often focuses on our learning about the real world this way. From the beginning, realistic fiction and creative nonfiction can be hard to tell apart, and the same remains true for the more sophisticated versions we encounter as adults. A poem (usually) looks like a poem, a script like a script, but both fiction and nonfiction use narrative forms and are written in prose. They also have a lot in common in terms of their use of basic narrative elements—setting, character, plot, voice, dialogue, scene, exposition, conflict, theme, and so on. Therefore, many of the features of fiction discussed below also apply to creative nonfiction, and some to dramatic forms and narrative poetry as well. Pay attention to both similarities and distinctions.

MAIN FEATURES OF FICTION

Creation of a coherent world. Some fiction is set in actual places—Baltimore or Nairobi, in an existing cathedral or a living room much like yours at home—and some is set in a place no one has ever been—a combination of features of houses the author has visited or an imaginary conception of a future or past world. Settings may also vary in how explicit they are—sometimes they are rendered in extensive detail and other times function more like a gesture drawing that captures only essential aspects. In all of these variations, the world of a story should hold together and operate consistently, allowing us to enter into that world.

Rich and complex characterization. The hallmark of literary fiction, rich and complex characters saunter, burst, or edge nervously onto the page in keeping with real people's behavior. No matter how bizarre or even fantastical the environment of a story, the characters who inhabit it should not usually fall into simple hero and villain categories, but struggle within themselves as much as against other people and forces.

Conflict. Tension arises in almost all human situations, and stories without any usually fall flat. Leo Tolstoy famously asserts, in *Anna Karenina*, that "all happy families are alike; each unhappy family is unhappy in its own way." Bliss, in other words, is boring. Some kind of desire and the obstacles that interfere with characters achieving their desires propel characters and events. This can be subtle rather than fist fights, but conflict drives stories.

Structural cohesion. Each story—even novel-length ones—has a shape. The shape and structure serve the story and influence readers' reactions as much as the literal meaning of the words on the page.

Consciously chosen point of view. One main difference between fiction and creative nonfiction revolves around point of view (or what some call narrative stance). Typically, creative nonfiction is written in first-person point of view, that is, directly in the voice of the author using the primary pronoun "I." Exceptions do exist—and both fiction and nonfiction can be written in an objective point of view that emphasizes only external appearances or in second person using "you" to address someone or substitute "you" for "I." In most cases, though, fiction writers have a much wider range of choices in terms of which character's perspective they will tell a story from, whether in first or third person, or whether they may even adopt a God-like omniscient point of view that allows them to move into and out of various characters' thoughts and motivations.

Stylistic excellence. Well-wrought fiction uses language more carefully, beautifully, innovatively than your average memo or news article. It aspires to use images, word choices, sentence and paragraph structures, and variations on pacing to make us see anew.

QUESTIONS ABOUT YOUR FICTION

- **Does the opening of the story pull you in?** Often we have to "warm up" as writers, but the first opening we jot down may not end up being the most intriguing or inviting moment for readers. Look throughout your story for what should become the starting point—something that will virtually drag busy readers' attention away from everything else and focus it on your tale.
- **Do you drop readers off where you want to at the end?** Too often, we just stop writing without figuring out the impact of the ending, but even worse we sometimes have an urge to wrap the moral of the story up at the end and put a tidy bow on it, even when a messier ending or a harsher or more mysterious ending would compel readers to keep thinking about our story.

- **Are your main characters compelling?** Have you avoided clichéd types of people and developed complexity in your view of humanity? Are your characters believable, sympathetic, and/or fascinating?
- **Do your main characters balance between believable consistency and growth?** Remember that a sudden turnaround in your character can often seem unbelievable. Radical change can sometimes be appropriate, but try smaller realizations, too.
- **Have you focused on an appropriate cast of characters?** Remember not to clutter your short story with too many characters. Allow us to get to know fewer characters well rather than parading a confusing array across a few short pages.
- **Is there a tension or conflict that drives the story forward?** Note any points in your story that seem to sag, and see if they're necessary. Does the story's tension rise to a climactic moment? Can you identify your own main plot points? Is the shape serving the ultimate goals of the story?
- **How does your story's organization work?** Does it flow? Does it make sense? Look at where you reveal basic background information or aspects of character, and make sure that you're providing it when it will be relevant to readers. Are transitions clear and coherent?
- **Have you found the most effective point of view from which to tell your story?** It's often good to try the opening of your story from a couple of different viewpoints or to try changing the point of view if something seems to not quite be clicking. But remember that changing the point of view involves much more than just switching pronouns. The entire worldview may change as well.
- **How would you describe the tone of the story?** Note particular passages where that tone is communicated and any others where you think it's not strong or consistent.
- **Does the setting support the story?** The role of setting and description varies from story to story, but make sure that the details you include, whether plentiful or more limited, serve the story.
- **How are you using stylistic elements?** Have you taken advantage of appropriate diction, a range of sentence types, a variety of paragraph lengths and densities for varied pacing, enriching figures of speech, and other elements to create a distinctive style?
- **Remember**, you may also want to look at **Destination: Plays** as well, in order to think carefully about action and dialogue in your story.

Chapter 7

Description and Setting

KEY ANTHOLOGY READINGS

Julio Cortázar, "Letter to a Young Lady in Paris" (fiction)
Stephen Kuusisto, "Letter from Venice" (creative nonfiction)

Other elements often get credit for being more fundamental in writing than setting—character and plot, for instance, often launch our discussions of fiction. These elements, of course, are crucial to any successful story, whether fictional or nonfictional. However, without your being able to bring readers into the world you create on the page, your characters and plots won't come to life. Just as a child must take a first breath when entering the world, your prose and poetry must pulse with life from the first word on the page if you are to compel readers to follow further down the page and on to the next one. Your work, after all, always competes with other, more tangible things that demand attention. Specific, compelling details and vivid description create the very worlds your characters act in. The strength of your imagery, as discussed in Chapter 2, begins this process, and this chapter will give you more methods and practice in bringing life to your fiction and nonfiction, even poetry, as well as touching on special setting concerns in writing for the stage.

WORLDS ON PAGES

Often we go through life on automatic pilot, not really seeing the details all around us, at least not consciously. We may be in a hurry or focused on tasks or personal relationships or preoccupied by myriad other concerns. We may have our eyes and ears stuck to our electronic devices. However, if we write while in this mind-set, the world we create on the page may come across as dull or flat, even abstract, almost as though our characters are separate from it. As writers, we need to approach our surroundings in an exploratory way, to see what speaks to us in the physical world, and then to bring the appropriate level of compelling and revealing description to the page. "The writer should never be ashamed of staring," said fiction writer Flannery O'Connor. "There is nothing that does not require his attention." (Try **Pathway 7.1** or **7.2**.)

Effective setting becomes a part of any story or other piece of writing, not tacked on or separated from the characters and action. We can see this principle in action in the first paragraph of Julio Cortázar's story "Letter to a Young Lady in Paris":

> Andrea, I didn't want to come live in your apartment in the calle Suipacha. Not so much because of the bunnies, but rather that it offends me to intrude on a compact order, built even to the finest nets of air, networks that in your environment conserve the music in the lavender, the heavy fluff of the powder puff in the talcum, the play between the violin and the viola in Ravel's quartet. It hurts me to come into an ambience where someone who lives beautifully has arranged everything like a visible affirmation of her soul, here the books (Spanish on one side, French and English on the other), the large green cushions there, the crystal ashtray that looks like a soap-bubble that's been cut open on this exact spot on the little table. . . .

The story is addressed to a particular character, Andrea, and what follows is a specific description of her apartment, down to the fact that she keeps her Spanish books "on one side" and the "French and English on the other," and an assertion about its "compact order." Strangely, however, this rather quiet litany of a seemingly peaceful setting is interrupted by the unexplained mention of "the bunnies" and the narrator's saying he didn't want to come and live there. Right away we wonder why not, and sense that something is amiss. The order of Andrea's apartment will not last, and Cortázar's rich description sets up the perfect atmosphere to be disrupted by chaos. This richly described setting defines both the main characters and the forthcoming action before anything even happens.

Not every writer's style is as maximalist as Cortázar's; each must find his or her own apt level of language. Both those who write with sparingly few and carefully chosen details and those who write with a profusion, even a cacophony of sensory information, may achieve great work. We may prefer one over the other as a matter of taste, but each of them accomplishes a style of description appropriate to the story told. Ernest Hemingway's more minimalist "Hills Like White Elephants" is discussed in detail in Chapter 14. Although this story contains little description, Hemingway nonetheless uses the opening paragraph to create both physical and emotional setting. The train, his narrator notes, "stops at this junction for two minutes" before going on to Madrid. Even in that one detail, Hemingway foreshadows the attitude that the man has toward his relationship with the "girl" by emphasizing the temporary nature of their surroundings.

Cortázar's and Hemingway's writing styles and their depictions of the main male characters differ dramatically, though the stories have some things in common—both are relatively short in length and feature two main characters—male and female—and a situation in which the woman is or is likely to be upset. Also in both cases, their respective authors have created environments that do more than merely display the characters' personalities and concerns; rather, they help to constitute those personalities. Neither of these stories leaps immediately into action or dialogue, but both draw us in with the strength of the worlds they create on the page. (See **Pathway 7.3.**)

The originality of your voice and vision can be greatly strengthened by your descriptive powers. This entails your continuing to expand your repertoire in terms of vocabulary, sentence structure, and large-scale ways of shaping a piece. It involves your willingness to experiment with imagery and searching for just the right word, and, perhaps most of all, it requires openness to playing with language, from the streamlined to the profuse. (See **Pathway 7.4.**)

SETTING AS CHARACTER

Sometimes places take on almost the personality of a person, and keeping in mind that setting can itself sometimes achieve the level of character will help you circumvent the tendency to consider it as mere backdrop. Extreme instances of this are perhaps most obvious in certain films where a part of the surroundings takes on unexpected life—Hal, the murderous computer in *2001: A Space Odyssey*; the seedy, oozing Hotel Earle in *Barton Fink*; the living, speaking trees in *Avatar*; or the elaborate, threatening yet protective train station in *Hugo*. In fiction, too, we might think of Edgar Allan Poe's "The Fall of the House of Usher," with the mansion's "vacant eye-like windows" and the nearby "sullen waters of the tarn." But your work needn't be in the science fiction or horror genre in order for your settings to play an active role in your work. In Tim O'Brien's "How to Tell a True War Story" (p. 447), for example:

> I still remember that trail junction and those giant trees and a soft dripping sound somewhere beyond the trees. I remember the smell of moss. Up in the canopy there were tiny white blossoms, but no sunlight at all, and I remember the shadows spreading out under the trees where Curt Lemon and Rat Kiley were playing catch with smoke grenades. . . . [W]hen he [Lemon] died it was almost beautiful, the way the sunlight came around him and lifted him up and sucked him high into a tree full of moss and vines and white blossoms.

This story is discussed more fully in Chapter 9, but it is also worth noting that, here, the place goes beyond *reflecting* the soul of its inhabitants, as Andrea's apartment does above. Instead, the setting seemingly becomes active—O'Brien notes that it was the sunlight itself that lifted Curt Lemon's body. In the atmosphere of the Vietnam War, the dense jungle full of unseen threats, the muddy rivers, the canopy of flowering trees that lets in no light, the mountain fog that prevents the men from seeing even themselves, the strange hallucinatory music they hear—these combine to become an antagonist to the soldiers just as much as the vague and faceless Vietnamese enemies. (**Pathway 7.5** suggests you try working with a particular setting as a character. While not always appropriate to go this far, this strategy can remind you of the potential power of setting in your work.)

In your nonfiction or fiction set close to home, bringing setting to life can be an even greater challenge than far-off or imaginary settings. Ironically, the settings that we hold most clearly in our own minds frequently fall flat in our writing because we take them for granted and forget the need to illuminate them for readers. When writing in the first-person voice of nonfiction and some fiction, we tend to take on a casual or intimate acquaintance with our readers and feel as though they can see what we see in our mind's eye. So, it's good to practice the memory exercises of Chapter 5 and the get-out-in-the-world-and-open-your-eyes ones of Chapter 6. However, it also helps to contemplate how these memories and descriptions form who you are, perhaps even to think of the world around you as something that has shaped and continues to influence your opinions, passions, and personality. The river and the canoeist are mutually dependent.

Those who write about nature are often particularly good at this, perhaps because they are so attuned to their own relationship to and place in the world around them. The settings in Annie Dillard's "Total Eclipse" (p. 325)—both the exterior hillside where people gather and the contrasting interior of the cheesy hotel where she stays—are key to the insights she shares about the place of humans on the planet. Other writers pay special attention to their surroundings for other reasons and thereby learn the importance of sensory detail—Stephen Kuusisto, for example, was born with a form of blindness that allows him to see only vague colors and shapes, and his "Letter from Venice" examines the careful experience of tourism without eyesight—the sounds and smells, he finds, must be supplemented with the visual interpretations of his wife and friends. At one point, he notes, "As long as my companion is a talkative enthusiast of the odd apparition, everything will be okay. I can know the world by proxy." But we all know the world by proxy—that's what reading gives us—and as writers we always need to be able to create the gift of attention and observation that Kuusisto's essay testifies to. (See **Pathways 7.6** and **7.7**.)

Even if setting plays a less central role than in these examples, thinking of place and time as vibrant parts of your story or essay will give your prose and even poetry and drama a base, an atmosphere, a mood. As with all the elements discussed in this book, setting can be examined in any piece of writing for the way in which the author has treated the space around the characters. Sometimes clues may be sparse, indicating perhaps a sense of isolation or a dream-like quality, sometimes they border on taking over from the people depicted, almost as if to enrich our view of the world in which we live so often with our eyes half-closed. Most of the time, you will want your settings and the descriptions that are woven throughout your work to be somewhere in between these two extremes. Whatever the level, however, you will face the challenge of deciding just which details, described in how much specificity, will create the illusion of experience. The next section outlines one important aspect of this decision-making.

SCENE, SUMMARY, AND EXPOSITION

Chapter 2 features numerous ways to enhance the descriptions that you write through inventive use of language and imagery. The way you balance scene, narrative summary, and exposition will be just as crucial to creating a vivid impression. Poetry relies less on these distinctions, unless it's narrative poetry, and obviously plays and screenplays are written almost entirely in scene, so the balance is different in those two genres. In fact, thinking about movies can provide a simple litmus test when you analyze your own prose in terms of the scenes it contains. If you can imagine a passage of your prose in movie form, then usually it constitutes scene; if not, then you have written summary or exposition.

Scene

Scene refers to any passage of your writing that seems to happen in "real time." Obviously, it's not real time, but a scene is designed to give the illusion that readers are right there with the characters observing what's happening in front of them. This is true whether the scene is written in present or past tense, and it's true whether the point of view is first person or third. (Chapters 9 and 10 contain more information on these aspects.) Scenes focus on what particular characters do and say, on the dialogue and action that *show* us their personalities, dilemmas, conflicts, and motivations. Of course, on stage or screen, scenes unfold in actual time right in front of us.

Most of the important moments in a story or essay should be written in scene because scene allows readers the most intimate connection with characters and events. Scene is also what opens up a story or essay to readers' own reactions and interpretations and thereby allows for more subtlety than if you just *tell* the reader what to think. As Flannery O'Connor notes, "A story is a way to say something that can't be said any other way, and it takes every word in the story to say what the meaning is." Fiction and creative nonfiction, that is, do not proceed in thesis statements, but rather in the illusion of experience.

Summary and Exposition

Scene, however, is not efficient. It takes up a lot of space to report line by line every word a character says and to describe every gesture and facial expression, every stride across the room or leap into the ocean off the side of a boat. Sometimes you need to give readers a certain amount of background material (also sometimes referred to as **backstory**), and this material would only get in the way of the main events of the story or essay if you tried to show exactly how it all happened over perhaps even years of time.

For such situations, you can call on narrative summary and exposition, two closely related modes of writing that contrast with scene. **Narrative summary**, or simply **summary**, refers to condensed description of events that continue to move a story forward though it is not opened out into full scene. You might think of its qualities as lying somewhere between those of scene and those of **exposition**, or passages of writing that do not include any action, only description of people and places, historical or contextual information, and anything else that is eternal or separated from the main moments presented in your story. See **Table 7.1** for comparison of the three modes.

There are no exact formulas or rules about how much scene versus how much exposition or summary is appropriate in any given piece of writing, though it is a commonplace of introductory workshops to hear the comment, "Don't forget to write in scene!" or "Show! Don't tell!" Most of the time, scene, summary, and exposition merge and overlap. Even the most scene-oriented writer will include, seemingly in passing, details or descriptions that bring to readers' minds a specific place, the time of year or the time of day, a character's past, or the narrator's attitude. Depending on the precise mood and tone of any given piece of writing, you will need to examine the balance among all three, asking yourself whether you might need a bit more description here or a line of specific dialogue there.

In the Cortázar story, for example, the first two paragraphs consist largely of background information, or exposition, though it is touched by the occasional reference to the narrator's current activity of writing a letter, which we might think of as narrative summary—it describes something happening, but not in detail. Cortázar keeps this passage of exposition and summary alive with its strange sense of foreboding and eccentric details and images—"as if suddenly the strings of the double basses snapped at the same time with the same dreadful whiplash at the most hushed instant in a Mozart symphony," for example. In the third paragraph, however, Cortázar shifts to scene—"I was going up in the elevator and just between the first and second floors I felt that I was going to vomit up a little rabbit." He has set this moment up by mentioning "the bunnies" in the first paragraph and by easing us into the elevator with summary and exposition about his general "weariness" and habit of moving his

Table 7.1
Scene, Summary, and Exposition. Order in the original is indicated by the numerals.

	Exposition	Summary	Scene
from Tim O'Brien's "How to Tell a True War Story" (p. 447). The passages of scene and exposition are more separated in this story, so the quotes taken here are not continuous.	1. The dead guy's name was Curt Lemon.	2. What happened was, we crossed a muddy river and marched west into the mountains, and on the third day we took a break along a trail junction in deep jungle. . . .	3. Except for the laughter things were quiet. At one point, I remember Mitchell Sanders turned and looked at me, not quite nodding, as if to warn me about something, as if he already *knew*, then after a while he rolled up his yo-yo and moved away.
from Stephen Kuusisto's "Letter from Venice" (p. 393). These all come from one paragraph, which begins with a summary, shifts for two sentences to backstory exposition, and then dives into the scene.	2. Corky was companionable, and unfazed by strange cities. She was also large and handsome with a noble head.	1. After finding our hotel I made a solo foray into the Venetian alleys. I wasn't exclusively alone since I was accompanied by Corky.	3. Before I'd gone two steps a passing woman remarked: "Cane guida! Bellissima!" I nodded on Corky's behalf and then we sailed up a causeway—man and dog pushed by wind, each of us taking in the aromatic salts and musk of this place we'd never seen before. We turned left and Corky guided me through a medieval warren of slippery paving stones and jutting shops. She hugged the walls, evading a pack of schoolchildren shouting in French. I heard bells from a door, tourists speaking Japanese, and something heavy rolling on casters.

Often essays or stories use a verb formulation that you may find particularly useful to think consciously about—the **iterative**, which indicates the repetition of an action, behavior, or situation over and over again. (It's related to the word "reiterate.") It's the way we describe the usual state of affairs or things that happen habitually, and in writing it often prepares us for the moment when something different occurs and a worthwhile tale begins. It forms the basis of much narrative summary.

The fourth paragraph of Julio Cortázar's "Letter to a Young Lady in Paris" (p. 308), for instance, describes what happens and how the narrator handles it *every time* he vomits up a rabbit. He does this during the story, but he has also been doing it before the action of the story. This is a common method for setting up conflict or change— think, especially, of memoir, in which you might write about your family going to church every Sunday you can remember, until . . . , until that one day when something else happened and your entire life turned upside down. The iterative often *feels* like scene—as in Cortázar's story, it may be invested with striking details and specifics. However, it tends to be slightly less active than actual scene by sheer fact of its repetitive nature. We may date repeatedly, but something changes when we meet someone we want to stay with—we pay more attention, we remember more clearly, and we alter our own behavior to accommodate something new.

The iterative is considered an "aspect" of verbs—unlike verb tenses, which indicate the exact location of events in the past, present, or future, aspects indicate how the events occurred—all at once, recently as opposed to long ago, or continuously in either the past, present, or future. In other words, when you use the iterative it won't be identifiable by a particular tense, but by the phrases that surround and support it—"we used to," "she always," "again and again." Sometimes it's appropriate to use, but often you'll want to watch that you aren't relying on it too much in lieu of depicting specific moments in time.

belongings, but he waits to focus his scenic action on what will become the major problem of the story—the little rabbits. The action is buried—perhaps because this narrator is ashamed of it—but the main events of this story connect to its most active moments.

In this kind of choice, creative nonfiction becomes just as "creative" as fiction, and the selection of scene and detail—telescoping, arranging and rearranging, zooming in and out, and so forth—contribute to the overall artistry of a piece of writing in terms of its structure. **Pathway 7.8** asks you to try out these techniques so that you will have a firm understanding of how to distinguish and use these three modes. They not only are keys to revealing your characters, but balance with the basic points of plot discussed in Chapter 9.

SPECIAL CONCERNS IN SCRIPTS

In this chapter, I haven't referred much to the subject of setting in drama and screenwriting. Obviously, settings are major elements of both stage plays and films, but they become in those venues less under control of the writer and more of the set designer and/or the director (as well as costume, lighting, and sound designers). In thinking about set design in your plays or screenplays, it's important to remember that a writer shares the creative tasks with a host of others. Drama and screenplay, then, take a team approach, and setting demonstrates this as much as or more than other aspects. (See Chapter 12.)

Even so, the way that plays and screenplays get to stage and screen is by their being read by people who have the means and power to produce them—theater and film directors, producers, script development executives, and sometimes by actors. You still have to create, albeit in a usually small amount of isolated space, a sense of the world in which the action and dialogue take place. You have to make that setting convincing and compelling, even though someone else is likely to determine its exact details. In the script of *Barton Fink*, for instance, here is how the infamous Hotel Earle is introduced:

> A high wide shot from the front door, looking down across wilting potted palms, brass cuspidors turning green, ratty wing chairs; the fading décor is deco-gone-to-seed.
> Amber light, afternoon turning to evening, slopes in from behind us, washing the derelict lobby with golden highlights.

That's all, but it carries with it a specific mood to be interpreted by set designers and a rich vocabulary, effective in spite of its brevity. In this regard, the writing of plays and screenplays might be said to take a hint from poetry—you may need to evoke certain crucial elements of the setting but do so in a condensed and abbreviated way that allows for multiple interpretations. (See **Pathway 7.9**.)

In playwriting, "setting" and "at rise" are the terms used to describe what an audience will see on the stage when the curtain rises. Though they are sometimes labeled and presented separately, usually they come together at the beginning of each scene. Scenes, of course, are easy to determine in drama because they are designated as such in every script and because they are marked by the falling and rising of the curtain.

Their collaborative nature does not mean that scene-setting is unimportant in scripts, though its nature is different in plays and screenplays. The limitations of the stage provide one set of parameters—where symbolic props produce the illusion of various spaces. With television and film, the inverse is true since they can be filmed almost anywhere—on a set or in a location that is a physical stand-in for another or in the actual location of the scene. No matter where filming takes place, a whole range of tools are used to result in the settings movie audiences take for granted.

For further insight into the frequent difficulties that producers, directors, and set designers encounter with on-scene locations, you might be interested in some documentaries that chronicle the successful and failed attempts to film certain pictures: *Burden of Dreams*, which follows the more than strenuous efforts required to haul a steamship over a mountain during the filming of *Fitzcarraldo* by Werner Herzog; *Hearts of Darkness: A Filmmaker's Apocalypse*, which chronicles the near destruction of director Francis Ford Coppola's career during the making of *Apocalypse Now* in the late 1970s; and *Lost in La Mancha*, about the failure in 2000 of Terry Gilliam to complete a film called *The Man Who Killed Don Quixote*, leading to a $15 million insurance claim due in part to interfering noise from a nearby military air target practice range and from bad weather, including flash floods. Though the script is still viable and the movie may yet be made, it's unlikely that the same shooting location will be used to bring the script's setting to life a second time around. However, neither the privilege of selecting such details, nor the expense and trauma of the failure of these choices, belongs to the writer of a script. In drama, those details must be imagined and evoked, but ultimately they must be filled out by producers, directors, and set designers.

PATHWAYS

Pathway 7.1. Radical attention. This can be done alone at home or in class as a group. Write about what is around you for exactly ten minutes. Be as focused as you can be on the moment and the place where you are, even if it doesn't seem interesting at first. If outside thoughts come in, put them down, but come back to your current place right away. Look at the furniture, the paint, the stains on the floor, the faces of nearby people. Notice the quality of the air, the hum of a heater or air conditioner, distant voices. Share these and compare how other people have perceived the task differently. Think about how personality, vantage point, mood, obsessions, and other factors have influenced the way you describe a current moment and ordinary place.

Pathway 7.2. Outside observation. Find a place to sit and watch. First, sit for a solid ten minutes just looking around you. Then begin to write and describe everything you can about what you see. Write quickly. Don't limit your senses to the visual; include what you can hear, smell, or feel around you in the air. After you spend a while writing from direct observation, turn to reflecting. Does anything seem more important than other aspects of what you've observed? What takes on meaning for you or reminds you of something?

Pathway 7.3. Intimate spaces. Write a one-paragraph description of a space in your home associated with one or the other of your parents. (This might be in memory if you no longer live with them or if they are no longer around.) This might be the kitchen, a workshop or studio, a "man cave," a bedroom, a garden, or another zone that one of your parents claims. Try to make this description reflect your parent's personality, even think of what story you would begin with the next sentence, but don't yet go beyond the setting. Share this with a group of classmates and see what they can anticipate from what you have written.

Pathway 7.4. Firsts. I've adapted this exercise from Natalie Goldberg's book of writing prompts, *Wild Mind*, and it's great at forcing you to push your descriptions away from cliché. Across the page, write down the name of a river you know, a color, a city, a street, a fruit, a month, a job, and a secret fear. Now spend ten minutes writing about your first kiss (or your first fight or any other "first" your group or instructor wants to choose), including all the items in your list.

Pathway 7.5. Living place. Start a poem, essay, or story in which the setting functions as a character. Write one to two pages where the main human character interacts with the setting rather than another human.

Pathway 7.6. Before it vanishes. Start with a place you know well. Describe it as though it will be destroyed or altered radically tomorrow—obliterated by a tornado or bomb, cut in half by a new highway, bull-dozed for a new development. What will you want to remember about that place after it is changed or gone? What would you want others to know if they had never been there? Weave in memories if that seems important, but concentrate on the place itself.

Pathway 7.7. House or shop observation. Start by taking a walk around your neighborhood—or another location nearby that interests you. When you come across a house or shop/business that looks interesting to you, observe as much as you can, and by implication about the people who live there or own the business. (Please note: this should not be a chain business where there would be rules against displays of individual personality.) Take notes. See all you can see (but remember not to trespass; if you bother anyone, leave and try elsewhere). Use the following questions to get you started, but don't be limited by them.

How big and what type is the house/building? How many people might live or work there? What can you tell about materials and construction? How old and what kind of shape is it in? Are there any clues about its history? What are the porches or external spaces used for? Are there flowers, trees, shrubs, vegetable gardens? How private is the space? What kinds of vehicles are nearby? Are the curtains/blinds open or closed? Can you tell what color they are? Can you see objects through the windows? If so, what? If you're writing about a shop, what does it sell? What kinds of displays does it have in the windows? Anything unusual?

Choose some adjectives for the building/shop. Does it look busy, quiet, happy, sad, bored, stiff, open, shut, comfortable (or not), clean, dirty, neat, squalid, sloppy, young, old, eccentric, ultra-normal, desperate, thriving, etc.? What can you tell about the people who use or own this space without ever seeing the people themselves?

Pathway 7.8. Scene practice. Write five paragraphs, each one containing one sentence each of exposition, summary, and scene. In the first one, follow the order of starting with exposition, moving to summary, and then starting a scene, but in the others vary the order of the sentence types. Refer to **Table 7.1** if needed.

Pathway 7.9. Stage setting. Write a description of a stage set for one of the essays or stories you have already written. What are the most vital elements of that prose setting? Consider what can be left to someone else's discretion and what is necessary for you to convey. This is a great exercise even if you don't go on to write a play because it helps you think about what's most important about your setting. Sometimes details can become extraneous and get in the way of the story. This will help you make sure that even rich description is not superfluous.

FURTHER ANTHOLOGY READINGS

Stuart Dischell, "She Put on Her Lipstick in the Dark" (poetry)

Tim O'Brien, "How to Tell a True War Story" (fiction)

Lia Purpura, "On Looking Away: A Panoramic" (creative nonfiction)

GUIDEPOST: ATTENTIVENESS

Paying close attention plays a crucial role in safety, accuracy, and good relationships.

Attention to detail is an end in itself in many work situations. Complex tasks with multiple layers and technological aspects require a huge amount of paying attention to detail. If we get distracted—texting while driving in traffic, for instance—we risk disaster. Creative writing is an activity in which you may cultivate the habit of paying close attention, focusing on what's important, and letting go of things that aren't. We are always working to get the balance right both in life and on the page, and if you cultivate this attentive attitude through your writing, you will be more likely to practice it in a variety of life situations as well.

Similarly, you may have heard about or experienced the benefits of meditation—increased focus, calmed feelings, and lowered stress. Meditation may begin specifically with attention to our own breath and body. As Rob Nairn notes in *What Is Meditation?*, "it requires one to remain psychologically present and 'with' whatever happens in and around one without adding to or subtracting from it in any way." Those skilled in meditation report an awareness of connection to the world around them, and, in fact, this is one of the major aspects of such practices as *zazen* or "just sitting," the key of Zen Buddhist meditation. Creative writers do not necessarily achieve a meditative kind of enlightenment, yet nonetheless find in their deep observations of the world around them a form of truth that they attempt to convey in their art.

Either way, care and focus in your work life make you competent and insightful; in your personal life they can add richness and understanding to your relationships with yourself, other people, and the environment. Whether you are dealing with a world-saving task or a mundane one, whether with the love of your life or the man who bags your groceries, cultivate perceptive attention for a satisfying way of approaching it all.

Chapter **8**

Character

Stories begin in different ways—sometimes a writer gets inspiration based on an overheard conversation or an observation of an argument on the sidewalk. Sometimes we start with family conflicts of our own, or traumas our friends have been through. "It begins with a character, usually, and once he stands up on his feet and begins to move," William Faulkner once said, "all I can do is trot along behind him with a paper and pencil trying to keep up long enough to put down what he says and does."

Even Faulkner, a character-driven author, uses the term "usually" in describing how he begins. Sometimes instead of a character, authors begin with an idea about events. Sometimes we will start with a plot predicament and a method we hope will get our character out of that hot spot. Once, for instance, a friend of mine handed me a small item from a local newspaper about a tattooed roughneck who had disappeared with his Harley and hadn't been seen by his family in more than a week. "Write that story," she said. "See where that takes you." There were, of course, numerous possibilities, but all methods of starting a story illustrate the inextricable tie between plot and character. Most writers vary their starting points depending on the inspiration for that particular story.

It is, then, somewhat arbitrary for this book to put the chapter on character before the chapter on plot. Your instructor may be justified in choosing to teach them in the opposite order. It is difficult, for instance, to set characters loose if you've no idea what they are going to do. On the other hand, conflict and situations emerge from personalities, and without some understanding of who you're dealing with, it's hard to know how they would react to what you might throw at them. Ultimately, both of these elements of story develop in tandem. We just initially separate them to focus on issues that will help you succeed in bringing them together in your work. As you begin focusing on character, **Pathway 8.1** will help you remember the connections between character and other aspects of your writing.

METHODS OF CHARACTERIZATION

Character in fiction refers to the portrayal of the personalities that take part in a story. Character in real life is observed; on the page it must be created, and sometimes it includes inner thoughts and feelings that we never truly know about another actual person. There are many sources for characters—and we have already discussed in this book various methods of getting out into the world and observing. You may want to create a fictional or dramatic character based on yourself, your friends, family members, or those you observe even briefly in casual settings—on the subway, at a sporting event, out shopping, or any one of a million other places. You may want to combine traits from a number of different people, or you may want to take one aspect of a loved one that bothers you intensely and examine it through a character that otherwise does not resemble that person you've started with. You might even want to begin with secret feelings or traits of your own that you don't normally express and give them to a character to explore on the page instead of doing so in your own life. (See **Pathways 8.2** and **8.3**.)

Pathway 8.3 demonstrates one of the main differences between writing fiction and nonfiction (and between writing fictional and documentary film scripts). Although much of this chapter can also help you bring to life the personalities of real people in creative nonfiction, in fiction you will be able to change people's behavior to suit the story you want to tell or as it evolves on the page. This seems at first convenient, but has its own set of challenges. For one, will your character retain verisimilitude and believability, or will you make your character bow to your intended plot in a way that breaks your readers' credulity? Will the vast options lead you on many false starts? Will you make it too easy for yourself and too tidy to be interesting? Keep in mind that to be effective your characters need to be more than puppets. Many writers speak of their characters as though they are real people because that helps keep us from feeling as though we can make them do anything we wish based on a whim. Obviously, in one sense, we can, but in another sense, our characters will be ruined if we don't treat them as having free will and being able to surprise even us.

Writers vary in their attitudes about this issue—some speak of their characters as having lives of their own and being beyond the control of the author. Truly, this is a bit of a pose—as John Banville puts it, "Fictional characters are made of words, not flesh; they do not have free will, they do not exercise volition. They are easily born, and as easily killed off." Yet, as we work to develop stories with fictional characters, we need to keep an open mind. In this way, we allow for fresh possibilities in our fiction and keep from getting bogged down in predictable stories and stereotyped characters. (See **Pathway 8.4**.)

Generally, we speak of a few main ways of developing character: how they look, what they say, what they do, and what and how they think. We'll examine each of these in turn.

How Characters Look

We might think of our characters as people that we meet at a party—when we first meet someone, we judge them based on their physical appearance—whether they smile or frown; whether they are clean and well-dressed, sloppy and unkempt, in the latest fashions or somewhat frumpish; whether they're obsessively in shape or have let themselves go. Right away, a person's appearance may raise questions and create tension in a story. Think, for instance, about why Sister Leopolda in Louise Erdrich's "Saint Marie" (p. 346) has fingers "thin and dry" as "a bundle of broom straws," but with "unnatural" strength. Or why the "sly expression" of the beggar boy makes Han so uncomfortable in Yiyun Li's "Son" (p. 405). In both stories, descriptions contribute to our sense of the main characters. Even in a play like Simon Fill's "Night Visits" (p. 357), where directors must be free to cast a variety of actors, when Emily enters, her "bruised face and arms" tell us she has been through something violent. (See **Pathway 8.5**.)

How Characters Speak and What They Say

We begin to get to know people at a party by chatting with them. We move from one knot of people to another, dipping into various conversations before we find one we want to jump into ourselves. Perhaps we're drawn in by a familiar topic that we feel passionate and confident about—we have found like-minded people in the room. Or perhaps we hear someone saying something we think is wrong-headed and long to correct. Perhaps one person is just plain old fascinating. We'll talk more about creating effective dialogue in Chapter 11, but the first thing to know about it is that what people say in fiction and on stage should not really imitate actual spoken conversation. In reality, much of the conversation that you overhear at a party is banal. When you think about dialogue as a force of character, it becomes much more pungent and idiosyncratic. Contrast the gentle but persistent nagging of Han's mother with the tone of Leopolda's words to Marie, such as, "You have two choices. One, you can marry a no-good Indian, bear his brats, die like a dog. Or two, you can give yourself to God." In both instances, the dialogue simultaneously reveals character and moves the actions of the story forward. (See **Pathway 8.6**.)

How Characters Act

Similarly, when you think about your characters' behavior and actions, think about how you pick up sometimes on little details that give subtle aspects of a personality away. Back in our hypothetical party, you may notice that one girl constantly curls her long hair around her forefinger, or that someone else has the habit of staring over the head of the person he's speaking to. At the party, you might not think too much about each of these individual quirks—for one thing, there are too many in the room for you to take account of all of them—but in fiction any trait you mention is part of building a character's uniqueness. In both Erdrich's and Li's stories, the secondary main characters exhibit some desperation—but each in her own way. Han's mother persists in pushing notebooks of potential wives and pamphlets about her church at him; Leopolda makes dramatic displays of her power to Marie by spearing the "devil" with her pole. As with description of surroundings, you want to find the right balance so that every trait you emphasize adds to the picture we get of the character and helps prepare us for actions and reactions of that character in the story. (Try **Pathway 8.7** or combine it with **8.6**.)

What Characters Think

Another common way of characterizing is directly through a character's thoughts. However, even after you've been at a party for a few hours, you don't really know what is in any of these people's minds. Someone may give you a funny look and you may feel unwelcome. Another may sidle up and touch your arm, and you feel you're being hit on. The friend who invited you may seem to be avoiding you, and you wonder what the heck is going on. You can't be sure. Even if people tell you in so many words how they feel, you are trusting rather than knowing for sure. In much fiction, we can, however, go into our characters' minds and know precisely what they are thinking. This depends somewhat on what point of view we are writing from in a story (see Chapter 10), but note that this God-like ability varies. In nonfiction, for example, we can only ever truly know what someone *says* he or she is thinking, though we can sometimes come to near-conclusions based on extensive interviews or observations. And because they are primarily visual and aural media, in drama and screenplays, what a character is thinking becomes directly available to us only through an aside, monologue, or voice-over. Even then, a character could be lying.

It is for these reasons that one of the most common creative writing adages in the world is "Show; don't tell." If we see a character doing things that conflict with his words, we know we are encountering a liar. If we see a person who speaks cheerfully on the phone with her mother about how well she's doing at school, yet the dorm room or apartment that she never leaves, even to go to classes, smells of rotten pizza and mildew, we know that something is amiss. This is more convincing to us than if a narrator just tells us that someone is a liar or is retreating from life. On a daily basis, we experience this—when a friend or acquaintance tells us, "Oh, that guy is full of garbage," or, "I heard she's really losing it," we can be skeptical unless we see the evidence for ourselves. Relying too much on a character's thoughts can even make us feel alienated from that character, especially if there's no backup for what he or she thinks. You'll find that if you don't show what you mean, your readers may question you instead of someone else you've tried to characterize. (**Pathways 8.8** and **8.9** get at these distinctions.)

Note that the various methods of characterization frequently coincide. You need not (and, in fact, it's usually preferable not to) write a separate long chunk of physical description, for instance, but rather allow details to emerge alongside the actions, words, and thoughts of a character. Sometimes a writer will foreground or overload us on physical and behavioral details that never really seem to have mattered, or that point out, "I'm describing this person." Note instead how the authors referenced in this book weave descriptive elements into the action, allowing our understanding to build gradually even across a short work.

DEPTH OF CHARACTER

In the hypothetical party I described above, you'll notice that I began with the first impressions gained by people's appearances. We often judge people this way, and people's appearances do usually have something to tell us about each person's personality. However, we all know that appearances can be deceiving, as explored in **Pathway 8.5**. Even beyond someone not looking stereotypical, however, the initial ways that someone behaves in front of us also sometimes prove to be part of a mask disguising hidden aspects of personality, buried dreams, ulterior motives, and haunted pasts. Sociopaths demonstrate this most clearly in real life: when you first meet one, he or she may seem the most engaging, exciting, fun, intelligent person you've ever met; but if you let such people into your life, you'll find a host of lies, back-stabbing, desperate need, and an incapacity for empathy. However, people who seem at first pathologically quiet or shy can reveal themselves to be loquacious, loving, and hilarious in their own comfort zones. Even if a person's personality isn't deceptive, it will have depths not immediately apparent—the difficulties that led to a reliance on humor, or a work ethic that extends back into a family's past.

Wherever your ideas for main characters come from, they will need to have driving force or **motivation** within the story you are about to tell. The progression of plot is almost always necessary to move a story forward, but the character's desire propels a story, no matter which form or genre it is in. It can be helpful to ask: What does your character *want*? This will influence all your character does and says in the pages of your story or play. In Erdrich's "Saint Marie," for example, the title character, who has lived in poverty and cultural confusion on the Indian reservation her whole life, sees that the local nuns have a better life materially; although she doesn't fully understand their Catholic faith, she sets out to join them. Her desire in the story is palpable throughout and sets off the entire series of events recounted, though it changes when she encounters the nuns' corruption.

Secondly, your main characters—or **protagonists**—must be developed, and your readers must care about them. Whatever the extent that you are fictionalizing (or not) a real person, you'll want your characters to be three-dimensional and well-rounded. Characters are most interesting when they have both strengths and weaknesses, flaws that complement their likeable qualities, and individual quirks that make them memorable. In the most compelling fiction, the line between heroes and villains is often not at all clear, reflecting the complicated reality in which we live and the difficulty we often have telling good choices from bad. Novels, stories, and plays provide excellent ground for us to examine subtleties and nuances of good and evil, not just oversimplified examples. Compelling characters can make us laugh and cry and spit with anger even though they exist only on the page and even though most of their desires are not easily or predictably met. They must be fully formed to engage us in this way.

Occupations and Preoccupations

One helpful way to think about developing your own characters is to think of them as having both what one writing teacher of mine, Paul West, called **occupations** and **preoccupations**. In other words, there is more than one level on which a character is acting, even in terms of his or her desires and motivations. In a simple demonstration, take a look around any class you might attend this week, or any gathering of people. In class, everyone is occupied by the lesson that is going on—this may consist of listening to the professor, taking notes, participating in group work or discussions, taking a quiz or test, or any of a number of other tasks. But, as you look around at your classmates and become more aware even of yourself, you realize that every person in the room also has preoccupations—things beyond the surface of attending class. It may be that you have a crush on another student and are paying closer attention to what he or she says than anyone else. It may be that you are worried about your next class, where a test is coming up, or about a friend outside of class who hasn't called or texted you when you expected it. There are a million other things that may be on your mind and your classmates' minds even as you participate heartily or try to pay attention. Some of these preoccupations will reveal themselves if we pay close attention—the glances that people exchange, the nervous touching and retouching of a cell phone, the jiggling of a foot.

So, we may be able to see easily some of a main (or even a secondary) character's motivations and desires, but some of them reveal themselves only gradually. Say your main character (let's call her Tia) walks into the restaurant where she works and says to a fellow waitress, "I just met my long-lost grandmother for the first time, and I'm hoping I can get to know her better," we can already see that her job (or occupation) may take second place to her preoccupation—how she will try to fulfill her wish. Though Tia greets patrons and distributes plates of food, we may also see her making phone calls or asking for the next weekend off.

Even what starts off as a preoccupation can mask deeper ones. Tia, for instance, may have preoccupations that are further buried, ones she doesn't reveal to her coworkers and friends until later in the story. She may desire to get to know her grandmother because her own father is alienated from his mother and she wants to know what happened to cause this rift. If her father has been remote and estranged from his own mother, and it's Tia's desire to understand why, she may encounter enormous conflict with her grandmother.

As readers, we may or may not know about a main character's ultimate preoccupations from the beginning of the story. For instance, in Li's "Son" we learn right away that the main character argues with his Chinese mother about her newfound Christian faith, but we don't learn until several pages into the story that he still nurtures hurt from when she burned the Bible a childhood friend gave him. As writers, we need to know and explore such preoccupations. (See **Pathway 8.10**.)

Consistency and Change

The two short stories that I've mentioned in this chapter differ widely in tone and mood. Erdrich's story is horrifying and intense with an eccentric first-person narrator who excels in almost hallucinatory descriptions; Li's third-person narrator and main character are both restrained, cold, and duty-bound. Yet, both have one thing in common: the main characters in the stories—and we as readers experiencing the characters' emotions with them—come to new understandings by the end.

By no means will you find this universally true. There are stories where the point may be that any change at all is difficult or impossible. There are essays and stories where a writer depicts an ugly and unchanging situation—so that readers' awareness changes perhaps more than a narrator's or other fictional characters'. In a novel such as Toni Morrison's *The Bluest Eye*, as readers we see a child rapist who is never regretful and a young black girl who never gets over her desire to be white, but we as readers are moved to examine our own beliefs closely and change them if they are cold or uncaring. Samuel Beckett's plays, such as *Waiting for Godot*, often show characters simply surviving, struggling to go on, but trapped in a seemingly hopeless landscape that mirrors the brutal truths of the larger human condition as Beckett saw it.

This line between characters who change and those who don't is a blurry one, but most of the time we find some kind of change satisfying as readers. The changes that characters go through in the course of a story, essay, or play may not be enormous. In fact, in the few pages of a short piece (whether a story, essay, or one-act or ten-minute play), there isn't usually time for a character to go from rags to riches or from a completely lonely state to being the life of the party. Yes, sometimes dramatic events occur in short works—certainly the accident at the middle of "Son" constitutes an extreme moment, though, like so much in Han's life, he covers it over, attempts to hide or erase it. And Sister Leopolda's actions in "Saint Marie" constitute dramatic violence, though the important changes are the ones that take place in Marie's consciousness as she comes to realize the falsity of the promises made on the reservation by the Catholic church. Even in these instances, the internal realizations—the almost unseen emotional shifts—take on the most importance.

If a character makes too sudden or dramatic a change, you will lose believability. A character may change, but not outside the bounds of the personality you have defined. As a storyteller, you will work with this tension between the desire for change or impact and the necessity that your characters demonstrate believable consistency as well. It is unlikely that someone who hates dogs, for instance, will suddenly realize how much pets can alleviate loneliness and give unconditional love. However, it might be interesting to write a story in which a series of steps brings him closer to understanding. Perhaps, for instance, he might get interested in spending time with a girl who loves her dog. You can see the potential for both conflict and growth—within the parameters of this character's history and personality—in such a scenario. Wrapping this up with a bow at the end and making the guy a total convert, while it might even happen in real life, may feel false and oversimplified on the page. You could leave such a tale with a sense of small acceptance on his part or with an ongoing tension that threatens not only the dog but the fledgling relationship, and either would feel more realistic.

You'll notice in the fuller discussion of drama in Chapters 11 and 12 that, of course, on stage and screen these moments must be converted into action or dialogue (or voice-over). In Fill's "Night Visits," Tom's shift from defeat to acceptance must be articulated in words and in the actions of his rising at Liz's insistence and his opening the window at the very end.

Sometimes characters will use a voice in which it's clear they are looking back, and they may even point this out from the beginning. Isabel Allende, for instance, begins her novel *The House of the Spirits* like so:

> *Barrabás came to us by sea*, the child Clara wrote in her delicate calligraphy. She was already in the habit of writing down important matters, and afterward, when she was mute, she also recorded trivialities, never suspecting that fifty years later I would use her notebooks to reclaim the past and overcome terrors of my own.

These "reminiscent narrators," as novelist Ellen Lesser calls them, draw attention to the process of change that has occurred already when the narrator begins speaking. The story will share with us how these changes have unfolded, but admitting that they are coming right away adds a reflective tone—and such hints are common in memoir, where it's so clear that the narrator already knows what he or she is about to tell us. Acknowledging in a given scene that you know now you were being foolish then, or that although you didn't realize it at the time this moment would change something significant, allows readers to trust you even more as a nonfiction writer.

In all the genres, however, it may be useful to remember the distinction between what I call *me-then versus me-now* (or *your-character-then versus your-character-now*). If you define in your head somewhere along the way of drafting a piece who your character was to begin with and who he or she will be by the end of the story, or from a more distant vantage point from which the story is told, that can help you keep in mind the kind of change that feels both important and possible. We will take up the issue of narrative distance implicit in various points of view in Chapter 10, but remember that each character and each human being may also grow and change within. (See **Pathway 8.11**.)

SECONDARY CHARACTERS

We've discussed to this point mostly how to bring your main protagonist into focus and help readers believe in and care about the fate of that main character. Here we'll turn to the other important personas that your stories involve.

Loving Even Your Villains

Most conflict stems from much more complex feelings than simple hate. Which are the conflicts you've had that affect you the most? They are not the run-ins with terrible drivers, nor with the crazy roommate you took an instant dislike to, nor even the ugly boss who seems stupid and mean. Instead, the conflicts that stick with us, that haunt us and make for great stories, are the ones where something more is at stake than merely wanting to escape someone we dislike intensely. The most compelling stories involve our protagonists in conflicts with people they—and we—care about.

Of course, we must primarily care about our protagonists, but, whatever you call them—**antagonists**, villains, adversaries, enemies, frenemies—these other main characters deserve our respect, and we should remember that somewhere, in someone's mind (even if just their own), they are the good ones. In Erdrich's and Li's stories, we can see this principle in action.

In Li's story, we see two mixed main characters. Han, our protagonist, in fact, is in many respects mean to his mother. We understand his frustration at having to conceal his sexual identity, but we also feel sympathy for her. As old-fashioned and in the way as she seems, even Han feels some love and respect for her, or tries to. The conflict in this story is as much within Han as it is between him and his mother. Erdrich's "Saint Marie" contains something of a more delineated antagonist in Sister Leopolda, the nun who mistreats Marie, but even in that story, we come to see, through Marie's eyes, the sad, human side of Leopolda by the story's end.

It can be difficult not to write out of a sense of pure revenge, especially when we're writing memoir in which we want to examine wrongs we feel have been done to us—perhaps a romantic love that has gone sour or parents who have abandoned or misunderstood us—but whether in fiction or nonfiction, it is imperative that you find a way to understand even your most heinous characters as human and therefore deserving of some sympathy. I call this "love," the kind of love the Greeks referred to as **agapē** (pronounced ah-gah-pay), the spiritual love of our fellow humans. It differs from erotic love and brotherly love, and the term was taken up in early Christianity to refer to God's love for humankind. When you take on the God-like role of controlling everything in a piece of writing, it seems fitting that you ask this of yourself.

That is not to say that there are not humans and characters deserving of deeply negative feelings. We see extremes of such people in the news every day—bombers, child molesters, murderers, embezzlers. And it is also more important that your characters be interesting, fascinating, enthralling people than that they be likeable, good, or "relatable." Just keep in mind the larger purpose in your writing. You may exhibit toughness, boundary-pushing, confrontation with the vile, and so on, but without a consciousness of the trials and woes of all people, your work will be hollow. If you can achieve this attitude, this will be one of the greatest skills you can attain from practicing creative writing that will inform how you see the world and your interaction with other people in all walks of life.

The Supporting Cast

Most short fiction and creative nonfiction cannot accommodate more than a handful of central characters. There are only so many people you will remember meeting for the first time in any given evening. Novels, on the other hand, we live with for days, weeks, or even months, and so they often merit not only more than one plot line but more characters, especially of a secondary, intermediate level of importance. A novel may still have one or two main characters, but it can sustain a larger fleet of supporting actors and actresses, so to speak.

I use stage and film terms here because they provide an easy way to envision the effect of trying to incorporate too many characters into a short story. Any story on stage or screen must focus on only a small number of characters at any given time because otherwise we would have a cacophony of characters speaking at cross-purposes. This might be appropriate in certain moments, but a narrative cannot be sustained in chaos. In any single scene, there may be walk-ons (serving a beer at the bar or saying good morning in the hallway) and there may be crowd scenes (a group gathering around a street fight or a mass of students hustling between classes on a campus). On stage, the latter are frequently represented by recorded noise and voices in the background rather than actual crowds, and on screen these groups become almost faceless. No one wins an Academy Award for Best Crowd Member. These are what I refer to as **tertiary characters**.

On the other hand, the Best Supporting Actresses and Actors, or **secondary characters**, often play a vital role in a story and getting them to just the right level of development is a bit tricky. As with so many aspects of creative writing, no hard and fast rules apply. Be aware, however, that the friend who answers the door to your character's apartment can choose to either let the boyfriend enter or tell him your main character is not at home. In other words, she can have an impact on how the story develops.

We often refer to these background characters as **flat**, because they aren't fully developed or well-rounded, and that term can sometimes be used as a negative description of a main character. Really, though, flat characters have their role to play. Take a look at the other nuns in "Saint Marie"—the description of them, though brief—"wide women with hands like paddles," "mild and sturdy French who did not understand Leopolda's twisted jokes"—contrast effectively with Leopolda. Though they border on a stereotype of what nuns *should* be like, and they remain nameless and barely distinct, they provide a vital threat to Leopolda, for if they found out what she was doing to Marie, Leopolda's game would be finished.

It's also true that in creative nonfiction—especially if you're writing about a family situation or something along those lines—it may be difficult to narrow the story down to a reasonable number of characters. We often feel as though we should describe "everyone who was there at Thanksgiving dinner" or the like. *How can I leave out Uncle Achmed?* we wonder, but if he played little role in the drama that unfolded, we might need to merely mention "an uncle" or even leave him out entirely. This is not to say that multiple characters won't ever work. Sometimes these walk-ons form in a sense part of the setting that allows the main characters to stand out all the more clearly. Whether in fiction or nonfiction and whether on the page or stage, we need to create a cast that includes only so many primary and secondary characters that are necessary for the story and that we can make vivid. Tertiary characters may remain part of the setting.

Keep in mind, however, that behind the scenes of your current story, these secondary, even tertiary characters have lives and rich personalities. They may even provide fodder for entirely new stories where the main character trades places with secondary ones. Erdrich's "Saint Marie," for instance, serves as the opening chapter in a set of related stories called *Love Medicine*, in which Marie is not always the main character. **Pathway 8.12** will help you think about the possibilities of your secondary characters. As short story master Grace Paley once said, "Everyone, real or invented, deserves the open destiny of life."

PATHWAYS

Pathway 8.1. Group exercise: Great fiction. In small groups (three to five students), each of you should think for a moment and write down one quality or craft element that makes your favorite fiction great other than terrific characters. Within your group, try to select one aspect as the one you'll share with the class and discuss several books that illustrate this quality. Try to focus on books that are as much literary as popular—not series books, for example. As a class, discuss the various points from each group and how character interacts with that other aspect of fiction.

Pathway 8.2. Observation vs. memory. Write one paragraph of description about a person you don't know but observe somewhere in public. Then write a second paragraph of description from a memory of someone you know well but who is not with you at the time. In each one, start with physical description, then move on to gestures, tics, expressions, spoken words, and so on. Finally, conclude with your impression or knowledge of each person's personality. How is it different writing from observation versus prior knowledge and memory?

Pathway 8.3. Transferred traits. Take a person you know and change one or more significant details about that person—change his or her gender, appearance, profession. Allow the fictional character to change from the real person as you change these things that are important. Conflict is likely to ensue. For instance, if your father is a doctor and is all caught up in his work, which is important to him, put his personality into a frustrated nurse. If your schoolteacher aunt is frail and feminine, think what her personality would be like in an attorney, what problems it might create for her. Write a scene.

Pathway 8.4. Listen to your character. Prolific novelist Joyce Carol Oates recommends a different method of getting to know your characters—that is, just start writing a scene with two characters *that you admittedly don't know anything about.* Put them in a situation and watch them react. Treat them as you would any new person you would meet. At first this seems impossible, but what Oates recommends is that you *listen* to them. In other words, allow various personality traits to emerge as you describe dialogue and action between them. This may take some time, but especially if you tend to write characters that become too predictable, this exercise can help you surprise even yourself.

Pathway 8.5. Looks can be deceiving. Pathway 7.7 asks you to write a description of a house or shop and then come to some conclusions about the people who live or work there based on these appearances. However, sometimes, especially with people themselves, looks can deceive us. Write a sketch of a character that lives or works in the house or business from Pathway 7.7. Focus on observing this character emerge from the building for the first time, and make his or her appearance surprising based on what you saw before. (Remember, you can use other senses besides or in addition to sight.) What can you convey about this character and how can a contrast between character and setting produce tension in what you write?

Pathway 8.6. Character conversations. Take the same character from Pathway 8.5, or a different one you're developing, and eavesdrop on daily life. How does this person interact with the grocery store clerk, a doctor, a babysitter, a police officer? What if a salesclerk makes an error? What kind of conversation does he or she make with family members over breakfast or coworkers on break? Such talks may not end up in a final story, but they will allow you to get to know your character well.

Pathway 8.7. Character reactions. This can be combined with Pathway 8.6, and shares similarities with 8.4, but here turn to putting your character into a scene with some consequence. Imagine your character in a particular situation. How would this person respond if he or she ran over an animal when driving a car or if a flight was canceled due to weather? What is this person's morning ritual and what if something interfered with it? How does he or she act on a date, whether with a new love interest, a long-time significant other, or a spouse—romantic, shy, teasing? Think about this character as you go about your daily activities: how would he or she do what you are doing or handle situations you are in? In the answers to these questions, as you can see, there will be seeds for many possible conflicts—external and internal. You may want to write several short beginnings of scenes, but try to choose one to develop into a story.

Pathway 8.8. Intimate knowledge. Take the character you've been working with over the past few exercises, and write a series of diary entries in that person's voice. Create in your mind a person that you know intimately, inside and out—family relationships; hopes and dreams; secrets; favorite colors, possessions, pets, movies, songs; insecurities and shameful memories; conflicts; even mundane details like how s/he takes a shower or what s/he eats for breakfast. See what new perspectives you gain on the looks, words, and behaviors of this character.

Pathway 8.9. Proving it. Make a list of general, judgmental, summary statements about people you know. Don't use their names, just the appropriate pronoun. Examples: "She's not a great student." "He's a real sweetheart." "She loves animals." "He's the best kind of geek." Once you have four or five of these, write a paragraph for each one where you demonstrate with specific descriptions, bits of dialogue, or actions that prove what you've claimed.

Pathway 8.10. Occupation and preoccupation. This idea is based on a classic writing exercise from John Gardner's *The Art of Fiction*. Describe a person walking along beside a lake, river, or ocean (the occupation). Work into this description the idea that the character has killed someone (the preoccupation). Murder, accident, mercy killing—that's up to you to decide. You also must decide how long ago this happened—fifteen years, fifteen minutes—and whether or not anyone else knows. BUT DO NOT MENTION THE DEATH. The objective is for you to try to get your style, syntax, and word choices to convey the tension in the character and situation. You might want to imagine that you will reveal this preoccupation a little later in the story, but right now you are defining the character and tone through the rhythms, sounds, and descriptions.

Pathway 8.11. Obituary. Write your main character's obituary. Long after the action of your story is over, what will become of him or her? What potential remains in his or her life? What further changes might occur and where will he or she end up?

Pathway 8.12. Secondary becomes primary. Write a sketch of one of your main characters' enemies or a secondary character. The point is not to end up with all of this information in your final story, but to view all the characters as potentially complex and sympathetic characters, even if they are not so in this particular story. You might even want to develop a separate, related story with this person as the main character.

FURTHER ANTHOLOGY READINGS

David Sedaris, "The Drama Bug" (creative nonfiction)

Judith Ortiz Cofer, "The Changeling" (poetry)

GUIDEPOST: EMPATHY

No ability in work and play is more important than understanding others.

The ability to get along with other people—even those who may be different from us personally—constitutes one of the most important and desirable skills in any situation. Perhaps nothing on earth causes so much day-to-day despair and frustration as working with those who don't have good "people skills." You can count on employers to seek to hire those skilled at understanding others (especially in an international or cross-cultural setting), negotiating, listening, and working effectively with others.

As an avid reader and creative writer, you have a distinct advantage in this regard. Through reading books that take you into other people's heads, capturing others' spirits in writing, and sharing others' perspectives in workshops, you learn an entire way of being that assumes that other people are worth thinking about and that other people have valid perspectives, even if those are different from yours. You learn to be an empathetic human being. I am not just making this up. Numerous social scientists have studied the impact of reading habits on people, and what they have found is that reading narrative renders people more sympathetic, patient, and kind in actual life situations. Reading news and technical information doesn't have the same effect.

Chapter 9

Plot

KEY ANTHOLOGY READINGS

Susan Minot, "Hiding" (fiction)

Tim O'Brien, "How to Tell a True War Story" (fiction)

Plot is an element of all the genres except poetry—and there are exceptions in some epic and narrative poetry—but we often misunderstand or forget the sly nature of plot. What can look like a simple set of events can become the most complex and vexing aspect of stories, plays, and even essays. Keep in mind the sneaky, covert, even underhanded way we think of the word's meaning when applied to political coups and bank robbery plans. People devise that kind of plot to lure someone into love or to assassinate a victim or overthrow a government. In writing, plot provides the framework for our characters, but, much more than that, it limits or frees our characters as we see fit and institutes entire worldviews. We can enjoy plots that delight us with the unexpected, but as writers we must make sure all the elements at least eventually come together. We learn to scheme and plan.

Plot requires that something happen; description, though often vital to a story, does not constitute the beginning of plot. However, plot is not the same as the mere events that happen in a story. **Plot** is the *arrangement* or *sequence* of events, a chain reaction where one event leads to another. The author makes decisions about what to include in a story, what information will be omitted, and in what order (not necessarily chronological) events will be introduced. Events recounted in a plot are almost always causally related (that is, one thing leads to another rather than events being random), even if only implicitly. In this chapter, we'll examine the ways in which various arrangements and decisions about what's included (and where) in a story influence the largest levels of our enjoyment and understanding.

CONFLICTS

John Gardner in *The Art of Fiction* notes, "In nearly all good fiction, the basic—all but inescapable—plot is this: A central character wants something, goes after it despite opposition (perhaps including his own doubts), and so arrives at a win, lose, or draw." I have never found a more succinct summary of what the task of plotting involves.

Perhaps the most clichéd plot line of them all is "Boy meets girl. Boy makes a play for girl. Boy fails to get girl, but tries again (and perhaps again). Boy finally gets girl." However, as we'll discuss more in the next section, it is most helpful when we also think of the events of a story as connected by reasons: "Boy and girl meet and get involved. But *because* the boy is rich the girl suspects he's just using her, and she gets angry and won't talk to him. *Because* he really cares, he sends her flowers every day to no avail and attempts to get her best friend on his side, but *because* she sees these gestures as trivial she won't budge. *Because* the boy sees that she's right, he gives up a substantial portion of his trust fund to establish a charitable foundation and names it after her, and she decides to give him another chance."

In most contemporary fiction, however, there might be an additional stage, wherein the girl and boy would find that they didn't really have much in common after all, and the boy would have to learn a hard lesson about impulsivity, and the girl might question her willingness to be won over. They might find that they do love each other, but that their relationship will continue to face challenges in his disapproving social sphere and her disinterest in sailing. Or the girl might be plagued by the idea that the guy still really just bought her affection. In other words, most interesting and profound problems are not entirely solvable. As we mature, we discover that even a happy ending may be qualified by mixed feelings or uncertain futures. Happily ever after is for children's stories.

Conflict and Complication

Stories generally begin with some kind of **conflict**, usually in the form of obstacles to something a character wants. You may have studied the classic conflicts—human vs. human, human vs. self, human vs. world (nature or society), or human vs. fate. However, most of these conflicts overlap and merge—for instance, in both the stories discussed in this chapter and Chapter 8, the main characters' conflicts with other characters and forces are only increased by the conflicts within themselves, their uncertainty about what they want or how to achieve it. The father in Susan Minot's "Hiding" (p. 420) clearly has mixed feelings about being a family man. The narrator of Tim O'Brien's "How to Tell a True War Story" (p. 447) struggles with his inability to "get the story right."

Yet if we have too many conflicts competing in one story, we might have a novel outline on our hands instead of a short story. A novel can sustain multiple conflicts woven together over the dozens or hundreds of pages of the book, but a short story's compression makes it necessary to focus on one or two. Be aware, however, that even conflicts that seem simple on the surface may have layers. The labels for types of conflict mentioned above may be too simplistic—if they help you think about the types of conflict that interest you, by all means, use them, but don't let them limit you. We may have grown used to the oversimplified, perhaps unrealistically clear conflicts involved in television cop shows and horror movies, but in many stories, novels, essays, and plays the conflict is harder to define. Though neither story's conflict is by any means simple, the domestic sources of conflict in Minot's "Hiding" overtake us more slowly than those life-and-death ones in O'Brien's "How to Tell a True War Story." Both provide compelling and thought-provoking situations.

Both of these stories also demonstrate how plot emerges from and is interwoven with character. Short story writer David Means notes that "the bare bones of a story—no matter how ornate or twisty a style might get—are always simple, rudimentary, and arriving from a deeply humane source." In order for a plot to feel organic rather than mechanical, it may be best not to set it up in outline form before you start, or at least not to do so rigidly. Give your characters some room to breathe and make choices, even if that really amounts to giving yourself some flexibility as you develop your story. Start with an idea, perhaps even an idea about how you want your story to end, but allow yourself in early drafts to follow your instincts, even if sometimes they lead you down paths that you'll later abandon. I like to say that a first draft is for finding out what your story is about. When you write, then, follow your idea, but try not to lead your characters too narrowly through specific events. You might have in mind the two or three major scenes or turning points in a story, but be open to the idea of arranging them and re-arranging. The various turning points and subconflicts in a story are what we refer to as **complications**, and they form variations on the central conflict. As in life, in fiction and drama, these arise from the flawed personalities of human beings. (See **Pathway 9.1**.)

There is nothing cornier than the convenient surprise ending based on pure chance, a device we call ***deus ex machina*** (Latin for "mechanistic god"). When we suddenly and miraculously clear an unresolvable problem, such as a character's financial need vanishing because of a surprise inheritance from a previously unknown relative, we may be insulting readers by failing to respect their sense of reality. We may also be tempted to sum up or state outright the "message" we hope readers will take from a story. However, if we force such tidy, unconvincing endings on a story—or even make various plot turns mid-story depend on them—we are not allowing the story to find its way to fulfillment. You might say that's like stalking a story rather than developing a relationship with one, and stories like that have the same creepy, overwrought feel about them. Instead, take your time, get to know your plot, let it come to you gradually. Trust your readers to get it.

Finding Conflict and Plot Ideas

Most plot ideas come from our observations of life around us. In creative non-fiction, this might seem easy, though it can be difficult to tell the mere situation from the compelling story, as Vivian Gornick puts it. No matter how super-ficially exciting or boring a series of events, it takes a particular lens to filter out their meaning or importance. In nonfiction, the challenge is to discern what about our experiences bears sharing with others. In fiction (or fictional plays), the challenge is to envision an entire series of events from scratch.

Consider three possible starting points for fictional plots: 1) an existing sto-ryline or set of events from life, 2) an initial situation from which you work forward, or 3) a stunning or concluding moment from which to work backward. The three work slightly differently, of course—with the first, you start out with some sense of the trajectory or narrative arc that we'll discuss in the next sec-tion of this chapter; you may have this kind of idea based on a classic story or on experiences you have been through. You may even want to start with a story you hear about from a third party, even a news outlet. You can pursue such stories through research and shape them into creative nonfiction, or you can mold the bare facts into rich fictionalized tales. (See **Pathways 9.2** and **9.3**.)

You may start with much less than that—with just a glimpse into an argu-ment someone has over coffee at the next table or with an imaginative leap out-ward from the barest idea. Once many years ago, as I drove (a bit too fast) to a late-night date, a car pulled slowly into my lane, and I honked my horn. As I veered past, I glanced over to see an elderly man gripping the steering wheel for all he was worth. Suddenly, I realized he had entered the highway from the hospital ramp, and that he probably was seldom out past midnight and had been at the hospital for some terrible reason—perhaps even the death of his wife or another family member. Notice that this one moment I observed could serve as either a beginning or ending, depending on the story's focus. Notice how my imagination immediately began filling in details.

Although this is a story that I have never written, it is this kind of thinking that will help you watch for story ideas in the world around you. **Pathways 9.4** and **9.5** will help you mine for ideas, but you shouldn't have trouble if you con-ceive of the world as full of stories. Your first job is to recognize them.

NARRATIVE ARCS

Freytag's Pyramid and Chronology

Much of what we still know to be true about plot goes back to Aristotle, but Gustav Freytag, a nineteenth-century German playwright and novelist, condensed Aristotle's ideas succinctly into the following plot elements: 1. **exposition/opening scene**, including the **inciting incident**, 2. **rising action**/complications/barriers, 3. **climax**/turning point, 4. **falling action**, and 5. **denouement**/resolution.

People over the centuries have found this structure, albeit with many variations, emotionally satisfying, perhaps in contrast to what happens in real life, where we often have no resolutions.

With these so-called formulas—only four basic types of conflict and now only five clear steps to laying out a plot—it might seem that writing a story is nothing more than creating a certain kind of jigsaw puzzle. Fit together precut pieces, and the story seemingly should work. However, in the writing you've no doubt already done, you realize it's never as simple as it sounds, especially not if your goal is to express the ineffable and mysterious in the world around us. For instance, it's one thing to write an accurate depiction of the life of a truck driver in a series of believable events, but another to make the story

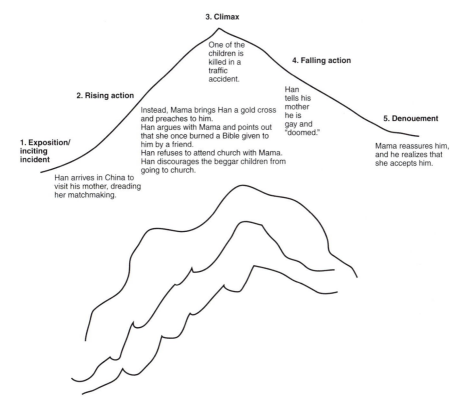

3. Climax

One of the children is killed in a traffic accident.

4. Falling action

2. Rising action

Instead, Mama brings Han a gold cross and preaches to him.
Han argues with Mama and points out that she once burned a Bible given to him by a friend.
Han refuses to attend church with Mama.
Han discourages the beggar children from going to church.

Han tells his mother he is gay and "doomed."

5. Denouement

1. Exposition/ inciting incident

Han arrives in China to visit his mother, dreading her matchmaking.

Mama reassures him, and he realizes that she accepts him.

Figure 9.1

Freytag's Pyramid Variations. Gustave Freytag originally drew a simple triangle to emphasize the rising tension, climax, and aftermath of classic story structure. Today, however, writers use many variations to help them get a visual sense of their stories' structures. Which of these shapes best describes Yiyun Li's "Son" (p. 405)?

a commentary about boredom and loneliness as a part of the human condition via the trucker's story.

Today, Freytag's pyramid is only a suggestion. It provides a structure that continues to work well for many stories. Erdrich's "Saint Marie" and Li's "Son" (discussed in Chapter 8) each basically follows this structure, where we are introduced to the situation, the conflicts are established and a few skirmishes happen (internally and between the two sets of main characters), and then a climactic turning point occurs a bit past halfway in each story. Afterward, we see the results of the characters' choices, and then the characters reflect change of some kind by the end.

Susan Minot's "Hiding" and Tim O'Brien's "How to Tell a True War Story," on the other hand, should provide good fodder for debate as you attempt to define major plot points in each of them. While Minot's story is told in chronological order with a flashback or two, O'Brien's story starts long after the main event occurs and moves around in time. The location or presence of a single inciting incident is highly debatable in each. Perhaps you could argue that the inciting incident in "Hiding" is in the first sentence when it's noted that Dad is not going to church with the rest of the family. Or perhaps it's when he yells at the kids to "Get down!" or when he "jerks his head" away when Mum brushes a pine needle from his collar. We could make an argument for any of these moments or others, but it begins to feel as though we are forcing the story into the formula when in reality the story accumulates details right up to the climactic scene where the kids and Mum hide in the linen closet. That definitely constitutes a climax, but an inciting incident is harder to pinpoint.

This is typical of stories today—writers play around much more with these structural elements than they once did, just the way poets take more liberties with forms like the sonnet or the sestina. We use the forms and structures to give us guidance, but feel free to steer around the edges when that better suits the story and when we're looking for ways to be fresh and innovative. Nonetheless, Freytag's pyramid still offers a good method for starting to think about plot. (See **Pathways 9.6** and **9.7**.)

A Freytag-type structure and chronological order often coincide, with perhaps the occasional flashback, but with a clear direction forward through time. However, this is not necessarily the case. "How to Tell a True War Story" jumps between numerous different moments in time that span more than twenty years. Surprisingly, even though Curt Lemon's death would in any traditional story scheme provide the climax to this story, O'Brien instead makes the water buffalo scene the actual turning point, signaled by Dave Jensen repeating that he has never seen anything like it before. (Sadly, they have probably seen other infantrymen killed, though not a helpless animal.) Look, however, at the construction of moments in the story, and you will see that even though they shift through time, they follow the Freytag structure. It's important to remember that, although they often coincide, the chronology and the emotional stages of a plot are not always the same.

The Benefits and Limitations of Chronology

"First this happened, and then this happened, and then finally this happened." We often get that kind of story from our family members or roommates. Even in this kind of story, memory often slips, and the teller will have to go back and fill in details forgotten the first time around. "Oh, wait, did I mention that I'd been waiting in line with Gianna when Ethan walked up?" That detail may change our entire view of the story, and when it's revealed matters.

Sticking to a straight chronology has many advantages, not the least of which is its simplicity in the construction of your stories. You will already be making complex choices about character development, setting, and scene, and most of the time it will be to your advantage to focus on those other elements before getting twisted up in a potential mess of time-shifting. Unless the manipulation of time will add a layer of depth your story needs or frame the story in a way that makes us see it more clearly, then chronology will likely serve you well.

Chronology also creates in a story a sense of inevitability, and it builds its own suspense. If we don't know what becomes of this character in the future, then we will be compelled to find out. Imagine a story in which a number of boys get stranded on an isolated island by a plane crash. If we knew from the beginning that they would ultimately be rescued (most of them), we might be less interested if they began to behave badly. On the other hand, if the author builds through a straightforward progression of worsening behavior through teasing, competition, laziness, scheming, lying, hallucination, accidental killing, and then intentional murder, we gradually accept the change in the boys and want to know where it will end. You may recognize this plot as coming from William Golding's *Lord of the Flies*, or one of its ancestors, even in film and television. In this and many other instances, the clear and direct chronology carries us into the story along with the characters and sweeps us up in what happens to them, almost as though it were happening to us as well.

A chronological story also remains usually easy to follow. Don't get me wrong. Time flows in any short story, play, or memoir. Unlike poetry and certain kinds of personal or lyric essays that are sometimes (though not always) more static, most kinds of narratives require the quality of **profluence**, or the sense of forward direction, of time passing, both in terms of the entire span covered by the story and in terms of the moment-to-moment sensations recorded. Profluence, however, may be easier to ascertain in a chronological piece of writing, for the very reason that the passage of time in the story parallels the passage of time in the reading, even if the pace is not the same.

This is perhaps more true in the novel than it is in the short story. In a short story, a temporary dislocation in time can be thrilling and the experience of undergoing the frisson of confusion can help us understand quickly a character's emotions; in a novel, this can become a tedious game. That's why so many novels that jump around in time find clear ways of indicating exactly where and when we are at each new chapter, even if they are out of chronological order. Sometimes this may be a year or date indicated at the beginning of a chapter; other times it might consist of setting details that give away a particular time period, such as music or other popular culture references or well-known events. One of the reasons this guidance becomes so important in novels is that they are far more likely than short stories to contain multiple **plot lines**, or different, perhaps even at first seemingly unrelated groups of characters or time periods. A short story's compression makes it common to focus on only one or two at most, but simplicity at this level allows for experimentation with other aspects of the prose, including time shifts.

However, remember that causality and motivation remain paramount to any story. Even stories with seemingly random moments cobbled together must contain some kind of thread, or they become meaningless. **Pathway 9.8** focuses on creating threads of meaning.

Each story has to find its own balance of experimentation and comprehensibility, and you will want to sometimes abandon chronology for a variety of possible reasons. In some ways, this is a "because it's there" issue. One of the great powers of writing things down is that we can fiddle with them—we write our memoirs in order to reflect on past events, and even alter how they affect us, not just to copy them. We write stories and plays in order to imagine possible futures and to reimagine pasts. And as we have become more and more familiar and comfortable with electronic media—which by their nature contain various access points and orders—we find more resonance with stories that don't follow what may seem like a lock-step chronology.

Chronology's main disadvantage may be that it sometimes fails to draw in readers because the situation set-up might not be the most inviting part of a story. It's one thing, for instance as in *Lord of the Flies*, if you have a plane crash to start with. Even there, however, the opening of the story must include context about who all the various characters are and what they bring to the island. In short stories, in particular, your readers may not have the leisurely mind-set of settling in for a good, long read and easing into the story with a panorama of the setting and all the background of the characters involved. We'll talk more about this need to start in the middle of the action in Chapter 11.

In addition, there may be something that your readers need to know right from the beginning even though it may take a while for your main character to realize or reveal it to other characters. Otherwise the character's actions may make no sense to readers or may lose their dramatic appeal. Sometimes we're tempted to include a huge "reveal" late in the story, for both characters and readers. However, these tend to feel as though the narrator has simply withheld information and can be annoying. Sometimes it's better instead to give readers information out of order so that they are not confused. Sometimes a writer wants or even needs to meddle with time for narrative purposes.

Alternatives to Chronology

Plots, as Kurt Vonnegut noted, are not "accurate representations of life," but "ways of keeping readers reading," and there are many structural methods that writers use to do so. Narrative arc and chronology are just two ways. Jerome Stern's *Making Shapely Fiction*, for just one example of many, outlines sixteen "shapes," including the Façade, the Iceberg, the Onion, the Visitation, and the Bear at the Door.

If you have difficulty fitting your stories into any of the types I describe here or that you find analyzed elsewhere, don't worry. These descriptions should raise your awareness of what you are doing so that you may improve your own stories, no matter what shape or narrative arc or tradition they are closest to. They are meant to be suggestive rather than proscriptive, as is most of the advice in this book. Here are a few common alternative structures in prose fiction and creative nonfiction, along with a few words of encouragement and caution.

Frame devices, flashbacks, and flash-forwards. These form three major ways that time is altered in prose. Flashbacks and flash-forwards shift time either back or forward in your writing. The term "*flash*back" in itself suggests that the shift in time should be momentary and not interrupt the overall flow of time too much. They pause profluence. When you find yourself inserting a flashback, ask yourself whether your story would stand without it or whether it goes on too long. However, if your story involves memory, self-questioning, conflict that involves different versions of events, and so on, flashbacks may be vital. They allow authors to provide background information or preview consequences as the action progresses. In many stories these form a natural-feeling occasional interruption of memory or brief scenes that fill us in on important information.

A frame device brackets a central story with an opening and closing from a different time (or times). "How to Tell a True War Story" opens with Rat Kiley's letter-writing and closes with the narrator's lecture, both after the main events. Both point out the lack of civilians' understanding of the experience of war, and this strong purpose justifies the use of the frame device. Notice that O'Brien comes back in the middle of the story to Kiley's letter. Often, a frame device needs to be incorporated a few times within a story or we lose its connection. The opening half of the frame often reconnects to the end of the story and constitutes a flash-forward. Sometimes, in fact, the ending frame simply circles around to the opening moment of the story. Though he doesn't return to the opening moment, O'Brien references the same obscene line after his narrator's presentation that Kiley voiced about Curt Lemon's sister, thus providing a strong thread throughout.

Braided narrative can refer to a variety of ways in which "strands" or seemingly different threads are woven together by alternating sections in a story or novel. Though most hair braids contain three strands, on the page you can weave together two, three, even four. Sometimes all of the story lines will eventually come together and sometimes they inform each other more allusively. Braiding can be a great way to shake up typical subject matter that you might otherwise approach in a predictable way. It's important to remember, too, that though the typical way braided narratives are set up on the page is with section breaks between them, the weaving can actually be closer and without distinct breaks. Annie Dillard's essay "Total Eclipse" (p. 325) offers a good example of a braided piece. (See **Pathway 9.9.**)

Vignettes are small scenes written without transition between them and sometimes without apparent connection (at least at first). Sometimes the term is used for single vignettes that are essentially short-short or flash stories (as discussed in Chapter 4). Writing in vignettes can work well when you wish to capture a more timeless feeling in a story, requiring less profluence than we generally strive for. Writing a story in brief, disconnected scenes works well in this situation, as some of the causal connections and explanations are eliminated. We are left as readers to ponder what the connections are and think about the "missing" parts of the narrative. Vignettes are often used for lyric essays, and stories written this way often take on a poetic sensibility. They also work well to examine a theme in a short space over a long period of time, letting the particular moments stand in for years, even decades of events. (See **Pathway 9.10.**)

Reverse and undone chronology. The most radical—and probably the most difficult—alternative structure is to tell a story backward, starting with the final events and moving steadily back in time. Theoretically, this should be easy, but creating sense this way is a challenge. The film *Memento* is well-known for using reverse chronology in order to capture the disorienting experience of a man with amnesia who is trying to figure out what happened to him. The film also uses a braided structure with one plot line that ran chronologically in addition to the one that ran in reverse. Only by the end of the film do the two plot lines merge.

Though perhaps most common in film, reverse chronology can be used in any genre, even poetry. Harold Pinter's play *Betrayal*, which was later made into a movie, follows an extramarital affair backward from two years after the affair is over to the night it begins; this structure suffuses even the excitement of the affair's outset with regret. One example in fiction is Julia Alvarez's *How the Garcia Girls Lost Their Accents*, which combines chronology in the story of a woman who returns from the United States to visit the Dominican Republic where she was born with the reversed story of how the family made its way in New York and, ultimately, why they left the Dominican Republic. The story is told as an uncovering of family history, a kind of archaeology, where going further back in time makes sense.

Novels and films that move around in time do so in various ways, but in whatever way they do so, the messing with time is not casual, but a crucial aspect of the story.

MOVING AROUND IN TIME

Writers manipulate time. Even in a story that is told chronologically, you will create the illusion of moving through time at a faster pace than time actually passes as you read the page. We write scenes to feel *as though* we are experiencing the story in real time, but we seldom are. We have the power as writers to create moments in slow motion or to ask for them in film or on stage. We also have the power to condense years or decades or even eons into a few short lines or paragraphs of text. We can telescope time, we can compress it, we can cut it into pieces, and this forms one of the most potent techniques at our disposal, no matter the genre in which we write.

One primary means of indicating our intentions about time is to write transitions or use line breaks to indicate shifts in both place and time; another is to use verb tenses to establish the various times that comprise our works. Never underestimate the importance of verb tenses.

In spoken language we choose tenses seemingly naturally, but it's good to keep in mind that other languages have sometimes fewer tenses (such as Chinese, which indicates time with adverbs or other added words) or more (such as French, which has an entire "historical" past tense used only in formal writing, usually about the distant past). In other words, there are many methods for indicating in writing that time is moving along or jumping back and forth. If you need to, be sure to review verb tenses so that you have a full understanding of their nuances.

"Hiding" and "How to Tell a True War Story" use two different primary tenses—Minot's in present, O'Brien's in past. Nonetheless, even O'Brien's story has a current moment from which the story is told—the present tense is used in the first sentence to inform us "This is true." The narrator also notes in the third section of the story that "It happened to *me*, nearly twenty years ago," and by the story's end the narrator reminds us that it is now "[t]wenty years later" and that nowadays he gives readings and lectures. For most of the story, this narrator is looking far into the past, and he signals us by various means when he moves from one time frame to another. Tense shifts becomes one signal, extra line spaces are another, and at other times O'Brien uses simple statements about time. O'Brien uses present tense when he is examining the way that we tell stories—in letters we write, in stories we tell, in his more philosophical contemplations of what a true war story is, when he notes that his narrator's present life involves telling these stories. Yet the main focus of this narrative, he emphasizes, remains long in the past, and only the combination of these two main verb tenses reflects the divided reality the narrator lives—haunted by the past and living in a different present.

Today in fiction we tend to see a lot of present tense—stories that not only *use* the present tense but that are written entirely in present tense, even events that clearly must have happened well before the narrator could have recorded them. This is said to make the story more "immediate," as though it is happening right before our eyes—or, perhaps more accurately, as if it is happening in a movie. There may be a scintilla of truth to that idea, though writers have been telling enthralling stories long before this fad of present-tense writing. It's a good thing to experiment with, and sometimes this suspension of time sets a story on just the right edge of uncertainty.

However, be aware of the limitations of an all–present tense narration, as it can render your story incoherent and muddy and can disallow the perspective we get with a retrospective narrator. The different tenses exist for a good reason—to help us distinguish one time from another and to distinguish what states of affairs are continuous and long-term versus those that last for a more fixed duration. The variety of tenses provides a tool that a writer doesn't want to do without.

Minot's story is written in a continuous present tense and provides a great example of how and when that works well. The story depicts one day in the life of a family, a Sunday in particular, when the mother and children go off to church, then the family goes ice skating, returns home, and then the mother and children play a prank on the father, which he ends up not noticing. Unlike in O'Brien's story, in Minot's we are seeing the world from a child's point of view and it is a short-term world. To the narrator of this story, there is not much analysis of the situation, just a depiction of it through which readers can come to their own conclusions about the issues in this family. The narrative voice is nonjudgmental even though we as readers can clearly see the marriage failing in front of us and the mother's pain. A continuous present tense only augments that sense of being there.

Note that plays unfold in real-time because they are performed in front of an audience. However, even in plays, authors can choose to represent a focused, single scene or events that happen over a period of years. Even poems can include spans of time. Each author makes choices that augment their themes, and verb tenses, as well as transitional words and phrases, play key roles. (See **Pathway 9.11** for a technique to help you clarify time and tense shifts.)

PLOT AND WORLDVIEW

As we come to the close of this chapter, I want to add one note that is often not discussed about plot, and that is how different kinds of plots reflect different worldviews. I won't dwell on this, but you might want to discuss it further in class or among your classmates because in order to shape the plot of any given story you write, you might need to become more aware of what worldviews you hold and which one or ones will be at play in that story.

One classic tradition entails a short story written to instruct and entertain and to come to a basically happy ending, even if not a perfect one. In O. Henry's "The Gift of the Magi," for instance, a young couple's failure to communicate and their vanity combine to result in the loss of the things they most prize, but in the end they still have each other and a lesson learned. They are the better in the long run for their experiences. Over the course of the twentieth century and now well into the twenty-first century, we've had many changes of belief and attitude, and our stories reflect that. No longer is a God-like narrative perspective standard, and no longer is the perfect denouement at the end of most stories even common. Nowadays, we are far more likely to cut off a story before the denouement or to find ourselves with a character who has not actually changed for the better by the end.

So remember when and how you start and end your stories—and how you structure them in between—plays as powerful a role in deciding their overall tone and attitude as any particular characters you devise or lines you write. If your story is not coming across the way you wanted it to, don't forget to look at your plotting. (See **Pathway 9.12**.)

PATHWAYS

Pathway 9.1. Desire's influence. Combine a character's desire with events. First, define the main thing that your character wants. For instance, Isabella really wants that great new job she's applied for. Then make a list of moments in which your character has to react to various things that happen. For example—

- Isabella rips her shirt at work and her boss watches like a creep.
- Isabella walks home and notices a person in danger.
- Isabella's friend Gustav calls and tells her he's depressed.

Continue on this way for a page or more, and then begin to connect these events to Isabella's motivation. You will pick and choose from the events, not using all of them, but once you have picked the three most compelling, write the story about Isabella's wish for that new, better job (or whatever) with your scenes already somewhat defined.

Pathway 9.2. Transform an existing plot. Start with a few basics of a situation in one of the stories or plays in this book or from other reading. It's a truism of creative writing that there are no original plots, only original developments of plots. The same set of events or characters can be good inspiration for distinct stories. Take off in a new direction from someone else's situation or basic idea. Do not copy but transform this situation into a new one.

Pathway 9.3. News plots. Bring in a news story that might form the basis for a story or play. Start writing based on the situation reported, but change the names and let your imagination fill in the whys, hows, and other gaps. Start or end with the situation reported in the news. Don't overlook your local news sources with their often small but personal stories.

Pathway 9.4. Inciting moments. For a few days, listen for interesting bits of dialogue, agitated individuals, and crises among both strangers and people you know. Watching random people's conflicts is often a great way to start your imagination off on a new story. Sometimes even a single line of overheard dialogue that reveals a wish, desire, or argument can open up an entire fictional plot. Choose one to use as the opening moment of a story.

Pathway 9.5. Group exercise: Randomized plot starters. On small, separate strips of paper, each person in your group or class should write down: a) a description of a main character, b) something that character wants, and c) the first obstacle keeping the character away from what he or she wants. Pass around a "hat" and collect a), then mix them up and have each person draw one out. Do the same with b), then c), so that each person has a random person, desire, and obstacle. Now go home and start a story with this material.

Pathway 9.6. Plot diagram. Use the basic structure of Freytag's pyramid (**Figure 9.1**) to outline a story you've already written or one you're working on. Note that not everyone constructs such formal outlines *before* working on a story, but even being able to locate a few turning points will help you keep in mind where your story is going. You may also want to change the shape of the pyramid—using a longer downside, a plateau at the top, various zig-zag ups and downs, or even another shape (like a spiral or a V) that you feel better reflects your story.

Pathway 9.7. Plot map. If Pathway 9.6 seems too limiting, or if your story doesn't yet have that particular a shape, draw a rough map of all the locations contained in your story. Note on your map how many and which scenes occur in each setting. This can help you determine if you have an appropriate number of locations and scenes, but also help you plan transitions between locations and scenes.

Pathway 9.8. Group exercise: Events into plot. E. M. Forster noted that "The king died, and then the queen died" constitutes only events, whereas "The king died, and the queen died of grief" becomes a plot. In groups of five or six, go around in a circle, each adding the next step in a series of events involving the same couple of characters. As you work in your group, don't speculate about why anything has happened, just agree upon a list of events or actions, with each person contributing one action in turn. Then for homework, each take the list home and create causal statements that connect the events into a conceivable plot. You don't need at this point to write the story itself, but bring back your ideas for the significance of these events to your group and see how they compare. Notice if at any point the original chronology might not best serve the ultimate story.

Pathway 9.9. Braided story. Take two ideas that you have thought of writing two completely separate stories about and braid or weave them together. Put the woman who is obsessed with skydiving with the single mother who holds down three waitressing jobs. Put the child's temper tantrum in the grocery store in Poughkeepsie alongside the fire burning in a building in Calcutta. See what happens, and figure out what two of your obsessions have to do with each other and how they might enrich each other. You might want to start several pieces like this and then pick the one where you find the most connection or suggestive juxtaposition after a couple of pages or a few scenes.

Pathway 9.10. Triptych. Write three short-short pieces of 500 words each on a related theme. The theme can be a single character, a place, or something more tenuous like household chores or what happens after hours. Let each one capture a single moment that casts light on, but is not necessarily continuous with, the other two.

Pathway 9.11. Time shifts. Take a highlighter to your story draft and mark each spot where time shifts, no matter how slightly. Make sure that your shifts are clearly indicated by tenses, transitional phrases, paragraphing, and line breaks.

Pathway 9.12. Plot points. Bring to class the first few pages of a short story in progress or a previously completed one. Exchange your manuscript with a classmate, and read your peer's story draft. This time, don't pay attention to style or other issues. Identify the major plot points, and comment only on a) whether causal connections emerge between the different plot points and the main character's motivations, and b) what worldview you think this plot implies. With b) you may start in a general way (optimistic? pessimistic?), but tease out the implications a bit more if you can.

FURTHER ANTHOLOGY READINGS

Annie Dillard, "Total Eclipse" (creative nonfiction)

Itamar Moses, "Men's Intuition" (drama)

GUIDEPOST: FORESIGHT

Events merely occur, but a writer can interpret and shape them.

The idea of planning or even outlining a story or play or screenplay probably seems ordinary enough. You've done enough writing to know that at various stages thinking through the architecture can help you build the building. This method—by which we take the chaotic input of our senses, our feelings, and unpredictable events, and shape them into art—is great training for learning how to anticipate possibilities and plan for them in myriad situations.

By this practiced exercise of your imagination, you learn to anticipate the results of actions and behaviors. When you take a character and set him on a certain path, you are already thinking about what will befall him. Of course, sometimes new possibilities will occur to you as you write, and these may change the course of your story, but you will already be thinking about where things are going from the moment change occurs. Part of your task is always anticipatory.

Think about the usefulness of this ability. No matter what work situation you are in, you will be focused on the consequences of steps you may take on your own behalf or that of your organization. We call this *vision*, and it requires an ability to imagine not only success but also potential failure and wide-ranging impacts. Vision means understanding technical or specialized information and being able to see it in terms of human consequences. Sometimes a lack of vision has dire effects, as when in 1986 the space shuttle *Challenger* exploded shortly after take-off, killing the entire crew. Technical reports later showed that the O-rings sealing the joints of the rocket fuel booster had never been tested at the low temperature readings expected at lift-off. A few engineers mentioned this, but none of them noted what would happen if those O-rings failed. They did fail, and consequently the ship exploded. In many ways, the failure to stop that rocket launch was a failure of narrative.

But there are more positive stories of those who have the insight to foresee needs or desires in our culture and step in to fulfill them. Often we don't identify these people as writers per se, but many of them have broad training in the humanities that have emphasized narrative continuity and storytelling—history, literature, and so on. In fact, recent studies show that a preponderance of people classified as "leaders"—in all walks of life, from business to politics—have humanities educations. Apple and Google are famous for hiring philosophers and English majors because, as former Google staffer and high-tech entrepreneur Santosh Jayaram noted in the *Wall Street*

Journal in 2012, in order to find undeveloped areas ripe for development, exactly what you do is "tell stories" and ask questions.

That is not to say, of course, that creative writers can magically see into the future. The downside to this powerful mind-set is that writers can sometimes imagine *too much* and have a hard time telling the difference between what is certain and what is likely. Yet, as long as you continue to make the distinction between what you know and what you foresee as possible, your ability to devise plots and strategize about what might happen next can only help you see potential and direction.

Chapter **10**

Point of View and Voice

KEY ANTHOLOGY READINGS
Junot Díaz, "Edison, New Jersey" (fiction)
Chris Offutt, "Out of the Woods" (fiction)

In general usage we think of "point of view" as an opinion, someone's attitude about any one of a number of things. At a family gathering, the quiet aunt who has held everybody together in tough times might be asked, "What's your point of view?" In creative writing, the meaning of **point of view** is not entirely divorced from its common meaning, but refers more specifically to the perspective from which the story is told and which is signaled by the preponderance of certain pronouns (I, you, he, she, and so on). The point of view in a piece of writing, in other words, is not necessarily that of the author. Point of view applies to the fictionalized perspective from which a given story is told; **voice**, on the other hand, applies to either a particular character's way of speaking or narrating, or the author's perspective that determines the feeling and sense of the story and attitudes toward the characters. Both characters and authors have voices, but a given piece of writing usually has only one point of view.

Choosing points of view that will best express your personal perspective can be less simple than it seems, and this chapter focuses on how both your own individuality and that of your characters can come through in your writing. Because the importance of point of view is often understated, I also include a wide range of references here outside of this textbook. I recommend that you seek some of these out if you're not already familiar with them, in order to fully examine the range of options available and the crucial role of this element.

FIRST, SECOND, AND THIRD PERSON

By now, you are probably familiar with the basic definitions of first-, second-, and third-person narrative. The most common types are as follows: the **first-person narrator**, who is a character in the story and refers to him- or herself as "I" and other characters as "he" or "she," and the **third-person narrator**, who refers to all the characters in a story as "he" or "she." **Second-person narrators**, who rely on the pronoun "you," are far less common. As you experiment with point of view, you'll find startling the enormity of its impact.

First Person

On the surface, first-person narration seems the simplest, easiest, least complicated point of view, even in fiction and poetry. In creative nonfiction, of course, the first-person narrator prevails, and we usually assume that this narrator *is* the author. This is not necessarily so, as noted in Chapter 2, and, of course, in fiction, it isn't so at all. Whatever the genre, however, the first-person point of view creates the illusion that readers almost know the narrator—or else are getting an up-close-and-personal view of the inside of a particular mind.

This perspective serves to intensify readers' feelings toward a given narrator—either we are on his or her side and hope that what the character wants comes true, or we feel alienated, disgusted, horrified, or annoyed with a narrator. Sometimes we feel that same combination of positive and negative feelings that we may have toward a family member or friend. For instance, the narrator in Junot Díaz's "Edison, New Jersey" (p. 315) admits that he's a petty criminal who sometimes turns "into a motherfucker who'll put a fist through anything." However, the narrator exhibits honorable traits as well, noticing the beauty of the baby ducks, lavishing gifts on his girlfriend, giving the young woman a ride into the city, bearing up under poor treatment. How we feel about him may depend on our own values, but we can't deny his complexity.

First-person narrators, then, offer an intimate feel to our storytelling, and are great when you have a main character that you really want to be the center of your fictional universe. The downside of first-person narration is that readers can't know much of anything that the narrator doesn't know. There are some exceptions—as "Edison, New Jersey" makes clear, readers can see things differently from a first-person narrator. However, what we don't see in this story is, for example, how others view either the narrator or Wayne, or what goes on in the mind of the young woman. Does the narrator's boss perhaps suspect he's stealing out of the cash register? Does the girl simply use the narrator in a spat with her wealthy boss? In other words, we don't usually get much of a panorama with first-person narrators, but what we do get is closeness and familiarity with a narrator that we'll understand all the better by being in his or her head. (See **Pathways 10.1** and **10.2**.)

However, you should also add to your repertoire different ways of managing that quality of first-person narration. For instance, it's also possible to create a **peripheral first-person narrator**, one who takes on a somewhat voyeuristic tone by not being the center of a story, but seeming to watch it from the sidelines. Nick Carraway in F. Scott Fitzgerald's *The Great Gatsby* and Chief Bromden in Ken Kesey's *One Flew Over the Cuckoo's Nest* are this kind of narrator—Carraway is an outsider to the East Coast wealthy set that Fitzgerald's novel focuses on, and Kesey's Bromden provides a lens through which we view the fatal power struggle between a cruel psych ward nurse and one of her patients. Both of these novels benefit from a first-person narrator who remains slightly removed from the main action.

There are also many novels and some short stories that combine **multiple first-person limited** points of view. Louise Erdrich's "Saint Marie," discussed in Chapter 6, for instance, forms part of a larger novel, *Love Medicine*, in which several other characters narrate some of the chapters; the novel speaks through seven different first-person narrators and a third-person narrator to give a panoramic view of the life of a Native American community over a sixty-year span. This technique is less common in short fiction, but it achieves a combination of first-person intimacy with a sweeping view of events and attitudes that can create an epic sensation and a sense of history and change.

Second Person

Second-person narrators, using the pronoun "you" in a primary way, can work in one of three ways. One is the **epistolary** style. "Epistolary" comes from the word "epistle," which means a letter, and often these types of stories have a strong first-person narrator in the form of a character who writes letters, or, as in the case of Julio Cortázar's "Letter to a Young Lady in Paris" (p. 308), just one letter. Sometimes, one or more characters can be given voice this way, as they write letters (or e-mails or text messages) back and forth to each other. The term, however, has evolved to include reference to any essay or story or even poem directed at a particular person or persons, generally another character in the piece. In Andre Dubus III's "Tracks and Ties" (p. 339), the form of letters isn't used, but the entire essay addresses the narrator's former friend. That the narrator speaks directly to his dead friend draws us with him into his mixed feelings about his friend's sad end.

Other forms of the second person can be a bit trickier to handle and involve either using "you" to generalize what is a first-person, personal experience, or to address readers more directly, usually to implicate the readers in the emotions of the story.

The first of these—what I refer to as the **"I" substitute** second person—often creates a compromise between a first-person narrator and the third-person use of "one." The pronoun "one" used to be more commonly used than it is today, and it smacks of a kind of formal essay writing done in a different era. "One need only walk outside to smell the fresh air" has the scent to us today of dusty tomes and stuffy, lace doily–covered rooms rather than invigorating breezes across pines or dunes, so instead we often use, especially in speech, the more common, casual "you." This point of view is unusual in writing, but is appropriate for a story where you want to assert, for instance, that your or your character's experience typifies a larger group. Lisa Gabriele's "The Guide to Being a Groupie" begins:

> 1. Be a girl. Be born sad. Be from a big family, or be an only child. Either way, make sure your parents are distracted and overwhelmed with life. . . . You are twelve. You learn to stay out of the way of what's going to happen. (Nerve.com)

The details of the story, though it is told in second person, are specific enough that they apply to just one person, a hidden character of sorts. Yet there is something about this experience of being a teenage girl that might seem trivial and unimportant if told simply in the first-person point of view. So, Gabriele has tried the bold second person to communicate that this experience has happened to girls over and over, and that, as much as it ultimately harms them, they still may want to know how to hang out with the band. Though specific, the story gestures toward the universal.

In the **Dear Reader** use of second person, in which readers are addressed directly, as though receiving a personal communication, we sometimes feel drawn in as a confidante, as the friendly recipient of an expository narrative, as in *Jane Eyre*. Other writers, however, turn this mode upside down and create narrators aggressive toward their readers. One example is Jamaica Kincaid's well-known "A Small Place" essay, later expanded into a book. Kincaid speaks to readers as tourists who might visit the island of Antigua. In challenging such readers, Kincaid notes, "An ugly thing, that is what you are when you become a tourist, an ugly, empty thing, a stupid thing." In this way, the second-person narration addressed to readers becomes a means to confront them and put them on the spot. This use of second person is more common in nonfiction as a form of social criticism, and it can be effective, though it also runs the risk of turning readers away. Writers using this strategy walk a fine line in terms of tone, but this point of view can work well when you have strong feelings about an issue you don't feel is being honestly or adequately faced. Note that this version of second person and the epistolary type mentioned above both also involve a first-person narrator's strong presence. These are points of view that emphasize a relationship between the narrator and the other character or readers.

Sometimes the use of the second-person pronoun challenges us to pin down its exact use. In Rachel Hadas's poem "Mnemonic" (p. 382), for instance, the pronoun only appears once and is followed by the pronoun "us":

> Poems accumulate; before you know it
> thicken to books, and books remember for us.

In a poem about the difficulty of memory, it seems perhaps the narrator speaks to herself, using "you" for "I," but also that she speaks to an audience as well, of those who need to appreciate that poetry forms cultural memory beyond the flaws of individual people's.

Second-person narrators are usually difficult to sustain over longer narratives. Creating a novel as an exchange of letters between two or more characters or otherwise rotating through different narrators can work well, but maintaining a substitute for "I" or an accusatory tone toward an audience over a long work, for instance, can grow tedious. In longer work, bursts of emotional intensity are by necessity balanced with quieter passages and moments of reflection or respite, and the continual high pitch created by second-person narration, especially of the confrontational or reader-involving kind, forms a risky gamble, sometimes one worth taking but never without forethought. (See **Pathways 10.3** and **10.4.**)

Objective, Omniscient, and Limited Third Person

We associate **third-person narrators**—which don't contain an "I" or "you," but only the other-oriented characters described by "he," "she," and "they" in pronoun form—with an all-knowing God or with a mechanical camera that records events. Neither of these extremes is precisely true, but they form good shorthand for thinking about two of the three types of third-person narration.

Objective third-person narrators seem to be exactly that—objective. Like journalists or documentary filmmakers, they describe what goes on in front of them with an unerring eye for detail but without obviously interpreting or inserting the feelings of either narrator or characters. The objective narrator often feels remote, but this can allow us to see more clearly and therefore to absorb more readily what is happening to the characters. As Anton Chekhov, who is credited with being the father of the contemporary short story, noted, "When you want to touch a reader's heart, try to be colder. It gives their grief, as it were, a background against which it stands out in greater relief." The objective point of view, in a sense, sacrifices our sympathy for the narrator in order to create more for the characters in the story. Ernest Hemingway's story "Hills Like White Elephants" (discussed in detail in Chapter 13) demonstrates how this point of view can create a quiet sense of the desperation of *two* characters, not just one. Often, the objective point of view allows for a focus on action where interpretation needs to be cast back upon the reader.

Also referred to as the **dramatic point of view**, the objective comes closest in prose to the way that plays and screenplays (other than voice-overs) are written, with their focus on the action and dialogue discussed in more detail in Chapter 11. In "Night Visits" by Simon Fill (p. 357), for example, there is no interpreting narrator to give us the background about why Tom is so distraught. We have to piece that together through the dialogue, first with Liz and then with the mysterious patient Emily. Unless there is a voice-over (or the occasional aside to the audience), this is always true in drama and films.

Objective point of view relies to an extreme extent on the "show, don't tell" adage, and often becomes difficult when a character would not clearly feel a particular emotion at a given time. Although an extreme example, even in "Hills Like White Elephants," for instance, we get at least one glimmer of narrative interpretation when we're told that the other people are waiting "reasonably" for the train, implying that "the man" believes "the girl" is not reasonable. It's easy to see that in a play or screenplay this feeling would have to be shifted into dialogue, actions, or facial expressions, and it's easy to see that the desperation of the girl expressed clearly in her dialogue would perhaps be easier to convey than the man's coldness toward her.

These few examples show that even the most objective story is not fully objective, but clearly partakes of the long tradition of the God-like **third-person omniscient point of view**, which can see into the minds and hearts of every character in a piece of writing or even beyond to things that no character knows. This type of narrator knows what different characters are doing in different rooms, countries, and even decades and can let readers know any bit of backstory needed in any given moment.

One classic third-person omniscient work is *A Tale of Two Cities* by Charles Dickens, who begins the novel with the magisterial statement, "It was the best of times, it was the worst of times." No ordinary mortal could know that, and so we know from the outset that a larger consciousness is at work.

Although there will be a main character or characters in third-person omniscient narratives, we may not feel as close to them as we might. After all, their minds are no more transparent to us than anyone else's. One Canadian writer, Marie-Claire Blais, has turned this aspect of omniscient narration into an experimental advantage—her elusive novel *Deaf to the City*, for instance, consists of a single paragraph that moves through the mind of one character after another sequentially. No single character takes on the status of protagonist; rather, the book ends up capturing the complex array of emotions and experiences of the human condition for a cast of different people.

When you're deciding whether or not you want to try writing a story from a third-person omniscient viewpoint, one question to ask yourself is the extent to which you feel able to understand the host of characters in the work. Also contemplate the effort required to smooth the transition between one person's thoughts, ideas, and attitudes and those of another character or several other characters. Sometimes it can be awkward and jarring to suddenly find yourself privy to a second or third character's internal thoughts, and for that reason when not well done omniscient point of view can feel gossipy and unfocused rather than God-like. That kind of "head-hopping" does not necessarily establish true omniscience, which requires the larger consciousness of a separate, all-knowing narrator who will have opinions and knowledge beyond that of any character. This can be difficult to maintain, and perhaps for this reason pure omniscience is not as popular as it once was; we now are more likely to view this as arrogant or foolhardy. Yet for a panoramic feel that opens up information across time, space, and various characters, third-person omniscient can't be beat.

The type of point of view that we call **third-person limited omniscient** or **third-person limited** partakes of omniscience in that the narrator can read another person's internal thoughts and feelings, but usually only one character's. In other words, this narrator is all-knowing but not about everyone. In actuality and practice, third person strongly limited to one character is probably closer to first-person narration than it is to the other two kinds of third person. The narrative voice stays close to the relevant character, almost as though we were in that persona's mind. Our narrator in Chris Offutt's "Out of the Woods" (p. 458) notes exactly what the main character, Gerald, thinks, how he decides to make the trip to pick up his brother-in-law, what he notices on the drive, and how he reacts to the news that Ory has died.

Although third-person limited point of view feels close to first person, however, the tiny distance between third-person limited and first person can be crucial. The narrator may, for example, back away a little bit and show us a somewhat wider perspective on things. In fact, a third-person limited narrator may even shift slightly to another character's perspective without too much interruption. Notice in "Out of the Woods" how when Gerald meets Sheriff Johnson, they "watched each other." Though we quickly move back to Gerald's thoughts (he "didn't like cops"), third-person point of view allows Offutt to step back and briefly note how the suspicions go both ways. Though neither of the characters yet knows it, Gerald is, after all, getting ready to stash Ory's body and drive off. Offutt prepares us for this eccentric behavior partly through the sheriff's moment of suspicion. Just as an objective narrator can momentarily become omniscient, a narrator limited to one character can shift momentarily to another, allowing an author to give us a crucial bit of perspective. (Experiment with third person in **Pathways 10.5** and **10.6**.)

Malleability of Point of View

Almost all of us *speak* in the first person, using the pronoun "I" to refer to ourselves and "mine" to refer to our actions, thoughts, and feelings. It's hard to imagine coming home from school or work to tell your family or roommates about your day completely in the third-person point of view. Imagine my coming home and saying to my husband, "Hey, Bruce, how was your day? Lisa's was terrific. She ran into an old friend and had a chat. But Lisa's a little annoyed at you since it seems you didn't feed the cats." Absurd. Only a few narcissistic celebrities can be caught speaking this way.

In fact, we also make great fun of anyone who uses what we call "the royal we," a holdover from times when kings, queens, emperors, and empresses governed on the supposed basis that they spoke for both their own individual selves and the entire body politic. Still, the occasional story or novel, or even piece of nonfiction, is written from the plural first-person "we" point of view, especially when trying to capture a community experience or sense of being part of the anonymous crowds. In Jeffrey Eugenides' *The Virgin Suicides*, for example, a group of brothers narrates for an entire bewildered community. (See **Pathway 10.7**.)

Karen Russell's story, discussed more at length in Chapter 15, provides a rare example of a single first-person narrative voice that switches from a primarily plural ("we") consciousness to one focused on "I." Although this isn't exactly shifting narrators completely, the move from a plural to a single mind-set reflects the content of the story—the narrator being returned to human society after years living in a wolf pack. The mere change in pronouns points out the emphasis on individuality in human society, for better and worse.

Every written narrative essentially has a first-person narrator lurking somewhere, even if that person is not an acknowledged part of the story or is plural. In today's published work—at least outside of genre fiction—first-person and third-person limited narration dominate. Some critics speculate that this change of perspective is societal—we live in an age when belief even in an omniscient God, much less an omniscient narrator, is not guaranteed, and our cultural attitude about knowledge recognizes much smaller spheres than the massive authority of one or two institutions or political leaders. Even in genre fiction, many writers have sworn off omniscience. As George R. R. Martin notes, "None of us have an omniscient viewpoint; we are alone in the universe. We hear what we can hear. . . . we are very limited." Most people today share this sense of the boundaries of an individual's (and maybe even humanity's) understanding.

There remain arguments, however, for the use of omniscient point of view. Robert Boswell notes in *The Half-Known World*, "The closer to true omniscience the writer pushes his narrator, the greater the opportunity for conveying the human state of half-knowledge." In other words, writers have the ability to show directly how two (or more) different characters are seeing things and that each of them misses certain pieces of the puzzle. We see this technique in Julio Ortega's "Las Papas" (p. 466) where the narrator shares mainly thoughts from an adult character, but occasionally notes what the child is thinking as well. In David James Poissant's fable-like "The History of Flight" (p. 476), we see not only what the main character experiences, but also how other townspeople feel, and even what the flying fish think.

What I hope these examples make clear is that point of view is highly malleable. All the common categories shown in **Table 10.1** can merge and overlap. When you set out to write a story, sometimes a particular point of view will come seemingly out of thin air and seem right. We often identify with our characters, even if they differ markedly from ourselves. Making this kind of move can help you maintain some consistency of narrative voice over the duration of writing in a voice that is perhaps (especially in fiction) not your own.

And this malleability makes point of view challenging. You can take a step back in a particular moment and sound almost like an objective third-person narrator, even when you are narrating in first person. When narrating in a limited third person focused on one particular character, you can step to the side just a bit and let us know what another character thinks—that's the power of third person. Should such shifts in point of view become too obvious or convenient, you risk your entire narrative fabric unraveling. However, done unobtrusively and purposefully, they can render a particular moment all the more vivid and surprising.

NARRATIVE DISTANCE

All of the various choices you have in terms of point of view contribute to how close or how far readers feel from the actions and emotions of a story at any given moment, what we refer to as **narrative distance**. "Objective," of course, implies that a teller is standing away from the action and can observe without involvement that might interfere with understanding. Omniscience sometimes has a similar feeling about it, in that the narrator seems to float above the world and share sympathy with or judge not-so-kindly the whole range of characters. These two points of view will foster a sense of space between reader and characters, and frequently are considered best for action-oriented stories.

Third-person limited and first person can also be referred to as categories of **subjective** point of view because of the way they filter actions and dialogue through a particular character's knowledge and perspective. These two points of view, then, create closeness between readers and characters. Sometimes, of course, this can be used to create an opposite kind of effect, where being inside a character's head is rather unappealing. You can see some of this effect in both Díaz's and Offutt's stories when their narrators focus on events like fouling someone else's bathroom or not believing a "foreigner" could really be a physician. But whether we like these characters or not, we see the world through

Table 10.1
Points of View. Works in bold are included in this book.

First-Person "I"		
Main character	Nowadays I take the bus home and the cash stays with me. I sit next to this three-hundred-pound rock-and-roll chick who washes dishes at Friendly's.	**"Edison, New Jersey" by Junot Díaz** *Other example:* **"Saint Marie" by Louise Erdrich**
Peripheral	She told me that her loneliness was sometimes awful. It wasn't the mountains—she had lived here all her life and wasn't interested in anywhere else—but the fact that no one was around to talk to. . . . Each time I visited, she went on and on.	**"Teeth" by Lee Gutkind** *Other example:* *The Great Gatsby* by F. Scott Fitzgerald
Third-Person "He" or "She"		
Objective	The American and the girl with him sat at a table in the shade, outside the building. It was very hot and the express from Barcelona would come in forty minutes.	**"Hills Like White Elephants" by Ernest Hemingway** *Other example:* "The Lottery" by Shirley Jackson
Omniscient	"What are you going to cook?" he [the child] asked. . . . "Chicken cacciatore," the man answered, but the child didn't believe him. He [the father] remembered what his mother had told him as a child: at harvest time, the largest potatoes would be roasted for everybody, and, in the fire, they would open up—just like flowers.	**"Las Papas" by Julio Ortega** *Other examples:* **"The History of Flight" by David James Poissant** "A Small, Good Thing" by Raymond Carver "The Story of an Hour" by Kate Chopin *Mansfield Park* and other novels by Jane Austen *One Hundred Years of Solitude* by Gabriel García Márquez

| Limited | He had asked his mother to stay at home; knowing she would not, he has feared, from the whole flight from San Francisco to Beijing, that she would be waiting at the terminal with an album of pictures, girls smiling at him out of the plastic holders, competing to please his eyes and win his heart. | **"Son" by Yiyun Li**

 Other example:

 "Out of the Woods" by Chris Offutt |

Second-Person *"You"*

Stand-in for "I" or "one"	Poems accumulate; before you know it / thicken to books, and books remember for us.	**"Mnemonic" by Rachel Hadas** *Other example:* "The Guide to Being a Groupie" by Lisa Gabriele
Epistolary	Years later, when I was twenty-six, she said in the *New York Times* you would tie her naked and spread-eagled on the bed, that you would take a bat to her. She said you'd hit her for any reason. But in Haverhill, Massachusetts, you were my best friend, my brother's too.	**"Tracks and Ties" by Andres Dubus III** *Other examples:* **"Letter to a Young Lady in Paris" by Julio Cortázar** **"Your Feet" by Pablo Neruda** *The Color Purple* by Alice Walker *The Perks of Being a Wallflower* by Stephen Chbosky
Dear Reader	I'm sure you have a few dog food questions of your own. To save us time, I've answered them in advance.	**"No Wonder They Call Me a Bitch" by Ann Hodgman** *Other examples:* "A Small Place" by Jamaica Kincaid *Jane Eyre* by Charlotte Brontë

their eyes. Even if we hope that we would not behave exactly like Gerald, we also feel the pressure that he is under from his wife's family and the way his trip changes him.

Even in creative nonfiction, where we might initially think that everything in the category must have a similar level of limited knowledge and personal intimacy provided by a first-person narrator, there are many ways to vary the level of narrative distance. We can have, for instance, an **effaced narrator**, similar to the peripheral narrator mentioned in **Table 10.1**. Truman Capote, for instance, in his "nonfiction novel" *In Cold Blood* never mentions himself per se, though his voice and interpretations permeate the book. The book is narrated from an omniscient point of view that's rare in nonfiction since we can't really ever know what another person is thinking. However, we can sometimes gather enough knowledge based on extensive interviewing or observation to justify this technique, especially when the subject matter has a wider scope or exists mainly outside our own personal experience. "The village of Holcomb stands on the high wheat plains of western Kansas," the book begins, "a lonesome area that other Kansans call 'out there.'" Capote characterizes the place as lonesome, but he edges close to Holcomb natives' perspective by noting how *other* Kansans refer to it. Even in creative nonfiction, we can vary our distance from a story. (See **Pathway 10.8**.)

As we choose a point of view, we consider a number of different issues, including 1) how our characters will come across from different viewpoints; 2) which perspective will allow us to get closer to our worldview; and, 3) whether particular characters' points of view can provide all the information we need to convey. But perhaps the most straightforward starting point is to contrast between character-driven stories that will benefit from our intimacy with certain characters over others, on the one hand, and, on the other, a story that is wider in scope with need for a focus on plot and duration. Looking at these different issues as you proceed with a story or essay will help you find the point-of-view sweet spot in all the possibilities.

UNRELIABLE NARRATORS

You've no doubt heard or read something where you didn't really trust what you were being told. Sometimes this happens when we engage in the political realm, as we are all familiar with the idea of "spin." We've all also got family members and friends who may be better known for the entertainment quality than the factual truth of what they say.

In written work as in life, we encounter **unreliable narrators**—some who lie outright and some who simply think about or experience things in an unusual or narrow way. Ann Hodgman in "No Wonder They Call Me a Bitch" (p. 387), an essay about taste-testing dog food, puts us on alert that she's up to something tricky; she imitates the form of a straightforward memoir about a new experience and her unusual research only to hint that there are sources of information, in the advertising world especially, that we shouldn't trust. Her slipperiness as a narrator reflects the point she's making.

Unreliable narrators are more common than you might think, and many narrators, of course, have their limits of knowledge, sympathy, intelligence, or perspective. Mark Twain's *The Adventures of Huckleberry Finn* and J. D. Salinger's *The Catcher in the Rye* both have somewhat unreliable narrators, as do more contemporary novels such as *Fight Club* by Chuck Palahniuk, *Life of Pi* by Yann Martel, and *Gone Girl* by Gillian Flynn, with varying degrees of deceit. Though most common in first person, any point of view can accommodate an unreliable narrator. For instance, in Cortázar's "Letter to a Young Lady in Paris," which combines first person with the epistolary second person, the unreliable narrator tells a bizarre tale of vomiting up bunnies as the rationale for destroying his friend's apartment. Though we may grow sympathetic to him, we hardly trust him.

In some ways, unreliable narrators are a character issue, and we've already discussed consistency and change of characters in Chapter 8. I mention unreliable narrators here, however, because it's important for you to be able to tell the difference between a calculatedly unreliable narrator and one that's just confusing and poorly defined. A narrator's unreliability must be set up as a consistent part of his or her personality, not as something that happens accidentally in the drafting of a story. (See **Pathway 10.9**.)

VOICE VS. CHARACTER

A character or a narrator-character may have a voice—he or she uses a complex or simple vocabulary, spews run-on sentences or speaks in brief epigrams, and so on—but **voice** considered overall is that of the author, and refers to the stylistic and thematic concerns of any given writer, whether in one particular work or over an entire body of work throughout a lifetime. Even if, for instance, no one told you that a particular poem was written by Emily Dickinson, you would be able to tell based on the epigrammatic brevity and hymn-like rhythms of all of her work. We can tell Ernest Hemingway from William Faulkner before we even start reading, just by the relative density of the words on the page. As Josip Novakovich puts it in *The Fiction Writer's Workshop*, "You must be in command of at least one voice: yours."

It's perhaps easiest if we talk about this issue from the realm of memoir, even though the points are just as relevant in fiction, poetry, and plays. When you sit down to write, you are not writing your actual self onto the screen or paper. As noted in Chapter 5, even when you are writing a memoir, ostensibly focused on you and events in your life, what exists on the page is a *character*, not a human being.

Both readers and writers seem to forget this distinction surprisingly often. The level of identification between writers of memoir and the persona on the page, or even writers of fiction and the characters they produce, can be intense. Once when I had submitted a short story in a writing workshop in graduate school, a classmate of mine opened the session by waxing prolific about how "insane" my narrator was, how she seemed to have "mental problems" and be "making up stories in her head almost like a schizophrenic." The words admittedly stung, even though I had fictionalized, intensified, and altered my own thoughts and concerns through my character. Might I actually be going crazy for imagining these kinds of things? Did I need to seek professional help? Was the character so far beyond the pale that no one would relate to her? After the story was published, however, I received numerous letters from readers who saw something of themselves in the desperate and hopeless character I portrayed. My life only superficially resembled that of my character, but I had used her to speak about my darkest moments, and that is something we should never hesitate to do through our writing, even if it risks others' judgment.

Strong connections exist between a writer and his or her work. But you will find it extremely helpful to create a buffer between yourself and what you write. This protects you from taking criticism too personally, but also from letting praise for your work swell your ego. Most of all, it allows you to see the narrators and characters you construct in your work more clearly. Even a nonfiction narrator can only ever represent a tiny fraction of who you are as an infinitely complex individual. (**Pathway 10.10** allows you to practice controlling mood and tone.)

Also realize that as an author, you probably don't yet have a singular voice, and probably you shouldn't yet be set on such a voice. Now is the time for you to experiment. An author's narrative voice may become recognizable over time and across various works, but it will also vary according to the characters and situations the author depicts. At this point in your writing life, try setting a particular type of narrative voice for one piece at a time. Explore different ones and free yourself from looking for "my voice." It will come out of you just as your spoken voice does, and it will develop over time.

PATHWAYS

Pathway 10.1. Five viewpoints. Write a story or memoir in five paragraphs with each one written from a different persona's first-person point of view. Don't simply tell the same moment from each person's perspective. Rather, tell a chronological story with each person covering the next moment in the series of events.

Pathway 10.2. Personification perspective. Choose an inanimate object (indoors or out) that sees a lot of action—a bicycle rack, an espresso machine, the door of a bar—and write a two-page story from its point of view.

Pathway 10.3. Second-person rant. Choose a subject about which you feel strongly, and choose one of the second-person points of view from which to write a one-page story or essay or a half-page poem about it. Think about how second-person can help you move beyond ranting when you consider the "you."

Pathway 10.4. Epistolary. Take a story or memoir that you've written at another time—even in high school—and rewrite it in second person, addressing it to one of the other people or characters. This can be especially powerful if you rewrite a memoir to someone in particular, but it can work well in fiction, too.

Pathway 10.5. Shifting third person. Sit down and look around your room. Write a paragraph about it that is "objective," describing merely what you see as if an outsider. Then write a paragraph from an omniscient perspective, including what you (in third person) think and feel about the space and objects in it, but also what a roommate, friend, or family member feels about it. Lastly, write a paragraph in the third-person limited point of view, almost as if writing from your own first-person perspective. What's the difference?

Pathway 10.6. Try another. Take a story you're working on already, then rewrite it from at least one other point of view.

Pathway 10.7. Plural point of view. Write a one-page story in the second person plural, speaking for a group large or small, specific or general, that you feel connected to—your family, you and your best friend, Latinas, New Yorkers, geeks, runners, etc.

Pathway 10.8. Effaced peripheral narrator. It's easy to see how a first-person narrator is a character, especially if that person is the main character or highly involved in the plot, but more difficult with effaced first-person narrators and third-person narrators. Write a short scene using a third-person peripheral narrator, thinking all the while consciously about who that narrator might be (besides you) and what attitudes he or she brings to this scene. Is your third-person narrator, for instance, forgiving of the story's characters, or judgmental? Is the voice well-educated or not? Pick one or two qualities with which to imbue your narrative voice.

Pathway 10.9. Unreliable narrator. Make a list of situations in which deceit plays a role. Then jot some ideas about which character would be most likely to narrate unreliably and why.

Pathway 10.10. Tone and voice. Take the subject you wrote about in Pathway 10.3 and try to find something funny or at least ironic in the same subject. Exaggerate that aspect as you write a second, humorous piece.

FURTHER ANTHOLOGY READINGS

Julio Cortázar, "Letter to a Young Lady in Paris" (fiction)
Andres Dubus III, "Tracks and Ties" (creative nonfiction)
Rachel Hadas, "Mnemonic" (poetry)
David James Poissant, "The History of Flight" (fiction)

GUIDEPOST: INDIVIDUALITY

A story and its teller can never be separated.

How we listen depends always on the person speaking. Are you skeptical? Enthralled? Disgustedly fascinated? Do you feel put on the spot or even downright attacked? It all depends on the tone and attitude of the speaker and your relationship with him or her. Besides, we take on different voices when we speak with different people. What you tell your mom about your escapades last Friday night may differ quite a lot from what you say to your friends who were with you. This ability to speak in different ways to different people, we hope, won't ever translate into being annoying or, worse, psychopathic. If we test our own boundaries of storytelling in life, we learn where our boundaries lie and what it is we are known for, in terms of sense of humor, intelligence, compassion, and so on.

As you create characters on the page—and especially as you think about the narrators who are conveying your stories and how you in turn must convey their personalities—you develop valuable skills at judging people. I don't mean judging them in a negative way, but *assessing* them and where their motivations, talents, weaknesses, and moral centers lie. This is a bit different from the empathy mentioned in Chapter 8—empathy involves seeing what we all have in common, how we all struggle and persist as humans in spite of our differences. Being able to estimate people's individual strengths and flaws doesn't mean harshly judging them in order to belittle them or toss them out. What it allows is for you to help them achieve their best—whether that is as a character in a story, as an employee, or as a fellow human being. Having this combination of empathy and judgment makes for a terrific managerial sense and an ability to work with people across the board, helping everyone find a role to play. Narrating, especially through a fictional character different from yourself, helps you see what that different perspective can add to your own.

Destination: **PLAYS**

Stories began in their oral telling, before writing had been invented. They were told in verse and song form, where the rhythms of music and rhyme helped their tellers recall and recite. These oral stories evolved into drama, where actors played out the roles of various characters and their actions could lend emphasis and vividness to emotions and events. Today, however, while many of you will have written stories, diaries, memoirs, and verses of some kind, few of you will have written a play. Many of you, though, will have performed in plays and skits, and will still have an instinctive feeling for the primacy of conflict, complication, action, and the spoken word that form the core of playwriting and screenwriting.

MAIN FEATURES OF PLAYS

Shared story elements. Plays—and their written form, which we call **scripts**, whether for a stage play or screenplay—may be either fictional or based in reality, and they share many of the elements of fiction and creative nonfiction—settings, characters, plots, and particular stances akin to point of view. Some of these elements must be used in somewhat different ways in scripts, however, because of some of the other features of plays mentioned below.

Collaboration. Scripts, whether for plays or screenplays, do much of the same work that fiction and creative nonfiction do; however, they do so in a way that focuses on the future collaboration of actors, directors, stage and costume and lighting designers, and an array of others involved in their production, sometimes even the audience.

Reliance on action and dialogue. Plays don't allow for much in the way of exposition, reflection, rumination, or description. For every thought or emotion a character has, playwrights must find an external way of showing it. Sometimes a character might explain something through dialogue, but it's far more effective for a character to stomp or throw an object across the stage than to say, "I'm mad." Playwrights work to *reveal*.

Although this book cannot fully examine all the aspects of playwriting, much less screenwriting, we examine drama's focus on words and actions in Chapter 11 and the collaborative and other unique aspects of both genres in Chapter 12.

Emphasis on performance. Although any given play may not ever be produced on stage or screen, they are all written with performance in mind. Performance takes place in a limited space and in real time. For that reason, both stage plays (from the ten-minute to the hour-long one-act, to the longer three-act) and screenplays (traditionally about an hour and a half long) have much more consistent length and form than poetry, creative nonfiction, and fiction. They also take into account effects that can be produced on stage or screen and the actual physical bodies of actors and audiences.

QUESTIONS ABOUT YOUR PLAYS

- **Is each character justified in your play?** It might help to look at the play and identify at least one important moment in which each character serves a particular function.
- **Is there a driving force or compelling desire that moves your play forward?** Often, in plays, a sense of time pressure or impending deadline helps propel the action and keep the audience enthralled.
- **Does your play bring deeper inner, psychological conflicts to the surface in speech and action?** Plays take place in visible spaces—on the surface, so to speak—but they move and engage us more when they illuminate the depths of the human psyche.
- **Have you kept your setting and character descriptions to the crucial aspects?** Remember that a play's producers would need flexibility and artistic freedom of their own to bring your play to life. You shouldn't hesitate to draw word pictures, but make sure they are necessary.
- **Does your play have a clear beginning, middle, and end?** Based on the parameters of performance, works on stage usually demand a more predictable pacing than that in prose and poetry. It's helpful to be able to clearly identify the three main phases of your ten-minute play: the rising conflict, climax, and resolution.
- **Have you begun your play** *in medias res,* **or in the middle of things?** In a short play, it's especially important to avoid long prologues and to draw potential viewers right into the story.
- **Have you included appropriate stage directions?** Actors have to be given some latitude, but remember that your stage directions outline the important element of action in your play and that these actions often speak as loudly as the dialogue. Be specific, be clear.
- **Could your play be performed?** Make sure that you can actually envision the setting and action of your play being manageable on a stage.
- **Does the dialogue both illuminate your characters and move the plot forward? Does it provide any necessary background without forcing the character to sound as though he or she is explaining to the audience?** Especially in the space of a compressed ten-minute play, every word of dialogue should work at multiple levels.
- **Have you used appropriate formatting for your play?** Scripts published in books use a different format than those in manuscript or production form. Make sure to follow the format given in Appendix A3.

Chapter 11

Action and Dialogue

KEY ANTHOLOGY READINGS

Itamar Moses, "Men's Intuition" (drama)
Michele Markarian, "Phoning It In" (drama)
Bara Swain, "Critical Care" (drama)

Action and dialogue form the basis of all narrative, just as imagery forms the basis of poetry. That is not to say that action and dialogue are never found in poetry, nor that imagery isn't a vital aspect of narrative. However, some poetry can work without a specific story, whereas the unfolding of events in seemingly real time is *crucial* in most creative nonfiction and fiction, and in drama this principle reaches its pinnacle. On the stage or screen, we do not go inside a character's mind or heart. Even when a character speaks to us about deep feelings, we have to see and hear the action to believe it. The dramatic forms of play and screenplay rely heavily on the actions we can see and the words we can hear spoken aloud to shape what we understand and believe.

Revered as the form of literature with the longest heritage, drama also reaches fully into the present not only on stage but in film, television, video, and now other forms of electronic entertainment. Significant differences exist between stage plays and movie-making (as well as between those and online games of all sorts and emerging hybrid genres). One thing to remember, however, is that, though we may think of Shakespeare in long verses on the page, when Shakespeare was writing, acting, and managing theaters that showcased his plays, much of the audience could not read. Up until that time, most audiences for drama contained a fairly high proportion of illiterate people, whose main engagement with narrative, ideas, and powerful, symbolic imagery was through drama and other performance media, such as oral storytelling and recitation of verses. Today, we seldom see scripts for movies, and similarly in Shakespeare's day people seldom saw the written plays that we now frequently encounter in books. Plays and screenplays are forms that deserve our attention both on page and stage (or screen), especially from writers hoping to master these forms. Watching a play or film, of course, helps sensitize us to how these forms work, but isn't the same as writing them.

In this chapter and the next, I will focus attention on issues central to writing action and dialogue in short plays, as well as performance in a variety of genres. One-act and ten-minute plays provide a beginning for experimenting with and understanding dramatic forms—we'll have time to look at a number of different examples and, similar to writing a story rather than a novel, you'll be able to master the shorter form with its fewer plot lines, settings, and characters. Dramatic work has in common with poetry a great need for condensation and distillation, and short plays give insight into this process. Remember that the principles of drama will help us write better dialogue and scene in our prose as well.

ACTION

We define **action** as the events of the plot that make up a narrative. Action, I should make clear, is not the same thing as mere activity. As Stuart Spencer notes in *The Playwright's Guidebook*:

> Dramatic action is not doing something. It is not physical activity. It is not characters moving around the stage, gesturing and performing business. It is not fight scenes, or dances, or behaving like large dogs, or preparing and then eating a meal. Characters onstage may do all these things with great exertion and extraordinary polish, but it will bring them no closer to dramatic action unless the fact of their wanting drives them to do so.

Chapters 8 and 9 deal with these same issues, but I bring them up again here to clarify how they work. In terms of character, actions arise, as Spencer points out, from characters' motivations. In terms of plot, each action must affect or move the plot forward. If some behavior or activity doesn't have these two features, it doesn't really constitute action and should probably be cut. (See **Pathways 11.1** and **11.2**.)

Forceful and Subtle Action

It's easy to discern the action in Itamar Moses's "Men's Intuition" (p. 438)—the two characters dash around the dorm room, tussle, grab a gun and a hockey stick, and engage in a physical confrontation that brings into clear focus their different personalities and traits. Those elements of their character have led to their misunderstandings and less than admirable behaviors offstage and prior to this moment.

However, the outward events of a story, play, or screenplay may even be negligible, understated, or calm, but if they have a strong desire behind them, the characters' movements, gestures, and words all become part of meaningful action. For example, the entire action of Michele Markarian's "Phoning It In" (p. 414) consists of the two onstage characters talking to each other and to others on their phones while they sit on a bench. In Bara Swain's "Critical Care" (p. 522), the onstage events of the play occur in a café where two women—a mother and daughter—sit at a table drinking coffee and looking at menus. While Markarian's play implies via the phones the involvement of others, the action of Swain's takes place primarily in and around the dialogue between the two women on stage with references to outside events. In this family, people criticize each other over seemingly trivial things, and the main character, Carol, seems particularly difficult to please—even the coffee is too strong. Her actions are all tied to an impossible-to-fulfill desire of hers to be as well-off and as comfortably married as her sister seems to be, even though her sister's husband is near death. Although Carol makes a few dramatic gestures, most of the physical action in this play remains subtle.

In Medias Res

In spite of the different levels of physicality in their action, Moses's, Markarian's, and Swain's plays all begin in the thick of things—when conflicts have been brewing and the characters already have histories with each other. The term *in medias res*, Latin for "in the middle of things," was first coined by Horace around 13 BC and signifies one of the key aspects of effective action. Too often, you may be tempted to ease into a story, set up the plot with all kinds of background information, and to gradually introduce your characters and their dilemmas. After all, you may have spent a lot of time thinking through these aspects of your characters and story. While this can work in novels and other longer works, and even when done succinctly in short prose, you want to make sure that your work draws readers in right away to a compelling situation or story. The background knowledge that you hold as the author may come to play a direct or indirect role in the story, but front-loading is usually not the most enthralling way to begin. And on stage or screen the opening moments determine whether or not someone will stay to hear the tale.

Notice where "Critical Care" begins: in the café after the two women have ordered and received their coffee. The background of this story weaves through in the women's dialogue—their references to "Evelyn's first husband," "Evelyn's second wedding," Jimmy visiting the orthodontist and being fifteen (though his father is "like eighty years old"), the red fox handbag and Burberry raincoat— all of these are part of the situation that it might be tempting to explain before the story starts. But Bain instead makes them part of the story and begins with Walter being in the hospital and Carol and Evelyn arguing over the discharge report.

In short plays, you have three main tasks in terms of action. One of these will be, of course, to understand each character's motivations and how to convey those through words and actions rather than any voice-over or exposition. Second, you will need a clear sense of conflict—plays and screenplays, more than any other genre, demand this immediacy in terms of struggle. In addition, you'll need to delineate a single scene (or a few extremely short ones) that can represent the larger situation that will necessarily surround the few minutes you are choosing to share. One of the major ways of doing this is to begin *in medias res* so that the scene you've chosen can unfold right away without a lot of waiting, but it is also important, especially in short plays, not to drag conclusions out either. As famed playwright and director David Mamet advised, "Get into the scene late, get out of the scene early." (See **Pathway 11.3**.)

HOW DIALOGUE WORKS

You might have heard someone compliment the dialogue in a novel or story by saying it sounds "real." Yet, what makes dialogue *sound* real is not actually realistic. Most of the time when people talk it wouldn't sound real when written down word for word: rather, it would sound boring. This is because a lot of talk consists of what we might call confetti—raining down in many small, almost meaningless bits. The confetti may add up to something—a party or a parade—but the individual bits of it aren't special. Most confetti, in fact, is made of scrap paper.

We can think of much of what people say in daily life in the same way. Much dialogue is repeated and ordinary and everyone says the exact same kinds of things—hi, how are you? keep the change, with all due respect, absolutely, awesome, where are you going? whatcha doing? what can I get for you? sorry to hear that, don't worry, never mind, I understand, I'm hungry, see you later, and so on. These phrases are necessary for our society to function and for us to get through the day.

However, effective dialogue, even in creative nonfiction, even in documentary film, must do more than get us through the day. Well-written dialogue is the result of a process of selection and distillation. Think about any interview with a famous person you've read or heard, and think of how much editing has gone into presenting a conversation—a lot is left out and only the most salient and fascinating parts are shown. It might help to think of your dialogue in fictional works the same way—there may be a much larger conversation that you *could* report with every word spoken, but your dialogue will be more effective if you compose it like poetry, with an eye to the strongest images and multiple layers of meaning or purpose. (See **Pathway 11.4**.)

In prose writing, unlike in dramatic forms, dialogue is not just one thing. **Table 11.1** shows some methods of working with dialogue in prose that will help you achieve just the right balance between scene and summary that is

Table 11.1

Modes of Dialogue. Note that all three of these forms of dialogue—direct, indirect, and summarized—can be blended and merged.

Direct Dialogue

"You have to pull your weight around here," we overheard Sister Josephine saying one night. We paused below the vestry window and peered inside.

"Does Mirabella try to earn Skill Points by shelling walnuts and polishing Saint-in-the-Box? No. Does Mirabella even know how to say the word *walnut*? Has she learned how to say anything besides a sinful 'HraaaHA!' as she commits frottage against the organ pipes? No."

There was a long silence.

"Something must be done," Sister Ignatius said firmly. The other nuns nodded, a sea of thin, colorless lips and kettle-black brows. "Something must be done," they intoned. That ominously passive construction; a something so awful that nobody wanted to assume responsibility for it.

—Karen Russell, "St. Lucy's Home for Girls Raised by Wolves" (p. 489)

- Comes closest to reproducing an actual conversation, word for word.
- Takes up a lot of space on the page, but usually reads fairly quickly.
- Emphasizes the nuances of precisely how a character expresses him- or herself.
- Used, of course, in dramatic forms, though sometimes characters may tell what another one said off-stage, thus reproducing a sense of indirect or summarized dialogue.
- Usually takes quotation marks and a new paragraph for each speaker, but some contemporary authors make exceptions (such as Junot Díaz).
- Plays and screenplays are formatted without quotation marks but designated by a centered character name above the spoken words.

Indirect Dialogue

She told me that her loneliness was sometimes awful. It wasn't the mountains—she had lived here all her life and wasn't interested in anywhere else—but the fact that no one was around to talk to.

—Lee Gutkind, "Teeth" (p. 373)

- Written like summary (not paragraphed with quotation marks).
- However, rises to a level of specificity that summary doesn't.
- Applies usually to a specific conversation and can be merged with direct dialogue to move efficiently through less key parts.
- Still often retains a lot of speakers' personalities.

(Continued)

Table 11.1   (Continued)

Summarized Dialogue	
The girlfriend calls sometimes but not often. She has found herself a new boyfriend, some zángano who works at a record store. —Junot Díaz, "Edison, New Jersey" (p. 315)	• Like all summary, doesn't go into great detail. • Used when it's important how a character learned something, but not the exact words that were said. • Moves quickly, so that we can focus on other, more central features of a story.

discussed in Chapter 7. Dialogue can be summarized, just like any other aspect of a story, and even within a scene you may want to use a balance of **direct** and **indirect dialogue.** Indirect dialogue, like summary, condenses a conversation, but it does so with almost the specificity that individual lines would have.

On stage and screen, however, all dialogue is direct unless a character sums up a conversation that happened offstage or off-screen. This is one reason why you may have noticed that when a novel is turned into a movie, so much of the novel is left out. Of course, a play or film usually is limited time-wise to a couple of hours, whereas we may take far many more to read a long novel. However, this also has to do with the fact that in dramatic forms, exposition and summary don't really exist. Exposition may still be spoken of, but what is meant by the term in drama is anything in the film that provides backstory; because this can't be done in a straightforward narrative paragraph, it is usually done via setting (a panorama of someone's belongings or of newspaper headlines and the like) or via conversation (a character refers to someone as "my husband" or tells another character an important bit of his or her past, as we noted about Swain's "Critical Care" above).

Direct dialogue, as a part of full-fledged scene, takes up a lot of time and space. For that reason, we expect a lot of it. We don't want it cluttered with a lot of confetti, but instead to be intensified by performing multiple purposes at once. The main purposes of dialogue are as follows: to reveal important qualities of the character who is speaking, to help advance the plot, and to provide needed background information.

Dialogue Reveals Character

Remember as you write dialogue that whatever is spoken will illuminate character. Sometimes it may be necessary for you to include a bit of confetti dialogue in your plays, stories, or essays, but you always want to take a hard look at your dialogue and ask what it conveys about its speaker. In other words, readers' understanding of your character should be developed and deepened through any dialogue that you put into his or her mouth. If the dialogue is too ordinary, the character may come across as boring even if seething or ecstatic inside. The words that come out of a character's mouth should sound uniquely his or hers. Otherwise, it may be better to summarize or excise them.

This may be trickier in plays, of course, as the dialogue forms a greater portion of the text. But even many aspects of character that we might take for granted or that might be given to us at least partly in exposition in prose can be expressed in dialogue. Think, for instance, about the educational level or intellect of a character. Many such issues of character are defined in dialogue, as well as in physical appearance—age, profession, ethnicity, regional origins (Southerners will sound different from Northerners and Westerners), wealth or poverty, even lifestyle. Even in the confetti moments, "Yo!" can distinguish a character from "Hey" or "How do you do?"

Personality, however, can be defined by other than these typical categories. In "Men's Intuition" we see from the first words they speak that although the two characters are both college students—roommates, in fact—they differ significantly. Both the strengths and weaknesses of their personalities emerge quickly—at first it seems we have a typical jock-versus-geek story. But the dialogue early on shows that Wendell is not only intelligent, but angry and tightly wound, that he's willing to manipulate Eric, perhaps unfairly. Eric, on the other hand, though definitely superficial, has a bit of practical wisdom when he asks a question like "Why are the light bulbs attached to a wall at eye level?" Eric and Wendell each has a realm of understanding missing in the other, and this is demonstrated not only in what they say but how they say it. (See **Pathways 11.5** and **11.6**.)

When working on dialogue, be aware of the extent to which your characters simply sound like you or whether you are able to give them different voices. As with actors, writers often have a range of characters they can "play" convincingly, and it's helpful to think about what your range is and how you might extend it. (See **Pathway 11.7**.)

Dialogue Moves the Plot Along

Another function of dialogue, is to move the plot or action forward. Sometimes, dialogue sets all the events of a narrative going. Look, for instance, at the opening of Junot Díaz's "Edison, New Jersey" (p. 315) when Wayne notes, "This guy better have a good excuse" for not answering the door. We see immediately the tension between the deliverymen and their wealthy customers that provides the motivation for the narrator to take a defiant risk later in the story. In other stories, key turning points in the plot can be highlighted by a line of dialogue, such as when the nuns in Karen Russell's "St. Lucy's Home for Girls Raised by Wolves" (p. 489) intone "Something must be done" about the sister who continues to misbehave.

In Moses's "Men's Intuition" the turning point occurs when Wendell changes from talking about actual brain teasers to confronting Eric about sleeping with a girl that Wendell went out with; the physical fight between them erupts from this one utterance.

Wherever you write dialogue, make sure that it serves the overall story by intensifying the conflict or connecting to the purpose and trajectory of the story. There is a role for **non sequiturs**, or things that don't contribute or even connect to the main issues of a story, but usually these are used to create the effect of absurdity, humor, or madness. Otherwise, rather than mimicking idle chitchat, your dialogue should reveal new obstacles or problems for the characters, create a tension between two characters, articulate a tension that has been brewing, or bring that conflict to a head. In each of these ways, dialogue establishes relevance to the plot. (See **Pathway 11.8.**)

Dialogue Provides Background

Especially in plays, much of the context of the dramatic situation must be given through dialogue. However, it's a great rule of thumb to remember that you should never have a character telling another character something that he or she already knows, just to inform the audience of the fact. Detective shows on television are particularly obnoxious about doing this—how many times does one CSI explain to another how Luminol works to reveal blood spatter? Even when the one getting a lecture is a trainee, we know that the explanation is for the audience, not the character on TV. Anyone working in the crime field would already have to know how Luminol works; otherwise, they'd never be hired.

That is not to say that there aren't many moments in prose and plays where dialogue is used to good effect in explaining backstory or giving information needed to understand what is going on. Swain's "Critical Care" provides great examples. Though the play is set in a café and follows a conversation between a mother and daughter, other members of the family are the topic of their conversation, and they discuss a range of events both recent and distant. Carol complains that at the hospital her sister has looked at her "like I stole her prom date or something." Her daughter rejoinders with "You did, Mom. . . . You stole Aunt Evelyn's prom date. Everyone knows that." Although this event doesn't take place on stage and in fact happened many years earlier, it is crucial to our understanding of the characters. Even the fact that Theresa needs to remind her mother of this speaks volumes about the competition between the supposedly mature sisters. A play about family drama appropriately contains many examples of backstory included in dialogue.

In almost every work of literature other than some poems, we receive at least some clarifying information about the past or other out-of-sight elements through the characters' spoken words. Of course, you may also choose to reveal such things via **prologue** or flashback, but the succinct nature of most dialogue corresponds well to information that needs to be present but doesn't need to be elaborate. For instance, as Hollywood script consultant Michael Hauge puts it:

> Telling backstory also means offering necessary bits of information in shorter, sometimes "tossed off" or oblique dialogue. My favorite of this is in Richard Tuggle's screenplay for *Escape from Alcatraz*. A fellow prisoner is remarking on the hero's cold, tough personality, and asks, "What kind of childhood did you have?"
>
> "Short" is his only answer, and it's all we are ever told—or need to know—about his backstory.

This kind of smooth incorporation of information—where it emerges out of the immediate context of the story and doesn't even interrupt the flow of the larger action—is worth striving for no matter the genre in which you write, but especially in your writing for stage or screen. (See **Pathway 11.9**.)

DIALOGUE AND ACTION IN CONCERT

Balancing action and dialogue seems as though it should be easy. After all, if you've been writing prose, you will already have decided to some extent the challenging balance of scene and narrative summary. Yet once you are into those scenes, or begin to write scripts, you will notice that action and dialogue require a balance all their own within each scene.

This is not to say that a particular ratio of lines of dialogue to lines describing action will serve you well in either play or screenplay (though you will find plenty of such recommendations should you look). Each story has to find its balance of event and spoken word—some plays, for instance, Lynne Alvarez's "On Sundays," contain quite a lot of specific direction about the precise motions and movements of the actors; others, such as Moses's "Men's Intuition," contain relatively little with much of the accompanying gestures, expressions, and movements left largely up to directors and actors. Both are appropriate for their stories. In Alvarez's play, for example, since one character never speaks, any director would need a clear understanding of what's expressed by her body language, whereas in Moses's play, the dialogue indicates what is going on. Moses uses a light hand with stage directions for much of the discussion between Eric and Wendell, only sketching in the main actions and thus leaving in the director's hands aspects that would depend on stage size, layout, and the live dynamic between actors.

However, Moses provides us with a vision for the play in the opening stage directions as well as outlining important aspects of the action later on. We see in the former that, although the two characters dress differently, their separate sides of the room have some things in common, such as their piles of dirty laundry. When writing plays, you must maintain this fine balance, knowing when description of desired actions is necessary and when it should remain open to interpretation.

It can also be helpful to consider what actions can easily be done while we talk and which ones will alter the way we speak or whether we are even able to speak at all. On stage, we find ways to link these two—actions and words—even more closely than they often are in daily life. In Swain's "Critical Care," for instance, we are amused by the moment when, there in the café, Carol raises her legs to show her daughter how Walter gave her "a ringside view of the family jewels" from his hospital bed. The conversational telling might easily have happened while the two women just sat at the table without much movement. However, Swain accomplishes at least two things by giving Carol this gesture—she creates action to complement the dialogue and she develops character by playing on the idea that while Walter was inappropriate in the hospital, Carol herself is inappropriate in the café.

If we were watching "Critical Care" being performed, we would react to the near-slapstick gestures of Carol, while at the same time her daughter's embarrassment augments this sense through her nervous laughter. As Carol continues her antics, Teresa says, "Cut it out, Mom! I can't breathe!" and tells her that she's "making a scene." Together, the action and dialogue reveal the hysterical, overwrought nature of Carol's personality and the difficulty that she ultimately expresses about aging and family relationships. In "On Sundays," on the other hand, Sylvia's silence and the obsessive nattering of Jules define not only their different characters, but the thematic gulf between them. Action and dialogue are complementary in each, though in different ways. (See **Pathway 11.10**.)

It's also worth noting when silence or inactivity is used to good effect. Note that almost every play uses at least one powerful moment of silence—Eric and Wendell staring at each other at the end of "Men's Intuition," Carol realizing that she can't find what she wants at the end of "Critical Care," the constant silence of Sylvia in "On Sundays." One use of the term **beat** refers to a brief pause in the dialogue for emphasis or added dramatic effect (you can see this in the script for Simon Fill's "Night Visits," discussed in Chapter 8). Either a lack of speech or a lack of movement can provide a compelling moment where an audience is waiting, expectant, almost leaning forward to see or hear what will happen next. These spaces allow readers and audiences time to process what's going on and to allow experiences to sink in. This is one reason why we may be more affected by a quieter movie that seems slowly to unfold than by an action-packed thriller where enough people die to fill a morgue. (See **Pathway 11.11** to experiment radically with silence on stage.) Nonstop action and dialogue at the volume of yelling don't allow our brains to connect deeply to a story. This same function is fulfilled by chapters, section breaks, stanza breaks, and even, to a miniaturized degree, line breaks in poems.

In fact, the term **beat** may also be used to refer to any given moment, emotion, gesture, expression, or other behavior into which we might divide a scene in a play. In other words, as a poem has stanzas and stanzas have lines, a play has acts, and acts have scenes, and scenes have beats. If you note the beats in your own scenes, you can see in what way they balance or fail to balance various kinds of action and dialogue, as well as the themes of your play overall. (See **Pathway 11.12.**)

What this means is that action and dialogue—and the breaks in them—are strongly connected to pacing in your work. We may want to cram the most we possibly can into a short work—the most action, the most talk, the most information, the whole family, all the boyfriends or girlfriends, the entire long duration of torture that was high school—but we must pay attention to the spaces as well as to the fullness of our stories and our plays. We must find ways for the balance of action and dialogue to include quietude. In that way, the words and actions we choose to include will stand out more clearly. You will learn to balance not only scene and exposition, not only action and dialogue, but activity and lull in your work. You will master pacing on the page and on the stage.

THE OBJECTIVE CORRELATIVE

Creative writing and other kinds of writing often share goals—many journalists and medical writers, for instance, hope for their work to have an impact on how people think and live their lives. Creative writing, however, differs from these other kinds of writing in perhaps one key way: its goal is to recreate experience and emotion in readers. It works often on a subconscious level where the story or image becomes as near to reality for us as any phantasm can. Poetry, creative nonfiction, fiction, and drama rely on and expect transformations of thought to be absorbed at the level of feeling, more than factual information.

T. S. Eliot's formulation of the **objective correlative** is one helpful way to think about how this can happen in your writing. He said:

> The only way of expressing emotion in the form of art is by finding an "objective correlative"; in other words, a set of objects, a situation, a chain of events which shall be the formula of that particular emotion; such that when the external facts, which must terminate in sensory experience, are given, the emotion is immediately evoked.

Even though Eliot put it that way in 1919, no one has said it better yet. Writers and critics, of course, continue to debate the exact parameters and definitions of the objective correlative. Can only an object itself constitute one—say, for instance, a gun that appears and produces an immediate sensation of threat or fear? It's easy to confuse the term "objective" for something that relates only to objects, and this misunderstanding often leads to the idea that an objective correlative is merely a clunky symbol crammed clumsily into a story or play. However, that's not the case, and the answer to the question about the gun would actually be no, for the entire situation of that gun and the people around it would have to contribute to that sense of threat. If the gun is a decorative old flintlock dueling pistol attached to the wall, then we might find it signals a certain stuffy rather than scary feel. For the gun to become part of an objective correlative, it must exist in a framework of character and action that renders its appearance suddenly and thoroughly terrifying, not just maybe. The opening scene of *Pulp Fiction* provides a good example. The film begins with a couple in a diner talking, seemingly idly, about robbing banks, then moving on to the idea of robbing restaurants. At the point when Pumpkin slams his pistol on the table in front of Honey Bunny, we feel a bit of alarm. Yet the objective correlative occurs really only when the average-looking couple begins kissing over the gun, reminiscent of Bonnie and Clyde. We know instantly in that moment that terrible violence will ensue. It ends up being the act of kissing over the gun that forms the objective correlative in this scene.

Similarly, in "Men's Intuition," the appearance of the gun creates a crisis for both the character Eric and the audience or reader of the play. As in *Pulp Fiction*, we at first don't realize the character's full intention, the depth of his frustration, or his willingness to act on it. Both guns bring a heightened sense of threat, but the gestures around those guns are perhaps even more important than the guns themselves and lead to different reactions. It is difficult with guns, of course, to escape the production of stereotypical reactions—*Pulp Fiction* and "Men's Intuition" do this by introducing them into unexpected settings and by humanizing the characters that hold them. There are, however, many more subtle objective correlatives, and such objects and gestures often form important pathways for larger feelings. In Markarian's "Phoning It In," for instance, the constantly ringing phone immediately lets us know that there will be problems in Brian and Stephanie's communication.

When circumstances and characters and objects coincide, they can create a kind of sudden recognition that brings the emotion to us. Sometimes it can be difficult to discern what's an objective correlative and what isn't—when an objective correlative can consist of actions, characters, and/or objects, then can't anything be considered one or part of one? I find it most useful to define the objective correlative in a narrow way—as just a specific item or action—but to consider also how the wider context affects it. Most of all, the objective correlative must evoke a specific emotion, sometimes even repeatedly, in a short, almost instant moment. You can think of these turning points from your own experiences, and the following one brought home for me how the elements of an objective correlative work.

A few years ago, I attended a party to which I'd only been invited because of my husband's position. Though I knew some of the people there, I wasn't comfortable. In addition, my husband and I had recently been working on a grant-funded project where a young employee had killed herself. We had considered her a friend, and I still felt like grieving, not partying.

People at the party began to loosen up with a little alcohol, and one powerful, unpleasant man began ranting about an absent colleague of mine who had run the project where we'd lost the young employee. This man began by saying that my colleague was responsible for the death of the young woman, about whom he clearly knew nothing. My mouth dropped open, and I made an attempt to protest. "No," I said, "she died due to a lack of health insurance. It had nothing to do with the job except that she had no benefits."

"She drove her to it," he shouted across the room at me. "She's a hateful devil, and that poor girl had a nervous breakdown because of her. She should be strung up."

My husband was in another room, and I could see that no one else around me cared enough or knew enough to correct this miscreant. This young woman had *not* had a nervous breakdown; she'd become schizoid, and all of us had spent hours and days getting her into the hospital and trying to arrange for her care when the hospital booted her out due to her lack of funds. I had recently attended the elaborate memorial service my colleague had held, and we had wept with her family, boyfriend, and friends. My face began to turn red, and I contemplated yelling at him, even though it wouldn't be wise. Suddenly, though, a friend of mine, sitting quietly next to me, reached over and picked up the pendant hanging from my neck. "That's a really cool necklace," she said. "Where'd you get it?"

This simple move, which was, first of all, positive and kind, shifted my attention from a battle I couldn't win and soothed me with its casual ordinariness. There was risk in it for my friend—she couldn't be sure how I would respond or whether others in the room would think her foolish for interrupting with something so trivial. Answering the question allowed my mind to escape into a different emotional space. This gesture of my friend reaching for the necklace will always stand in my mind as the perfect objective correlative for friendship, even though the word was never uttered.

Such highly charged moments help to create pivotal points in any genre, but they can be especially helpful in creating the kind of immediacy and tangible turning points required by drama. They give us fodder for showing rather than telling and remind us how actions and dialogues often carry feelings better than interpretation or labels. As any other literary concept, the objective correlative should not straitjacket or limit you; rather, it provides another tool for thinking about the action and emotions of your creative work. **Pathway 11.13** asks you to think about similar moments in your life when a situation and the people and objects in it brought or clarified an emotion or feeling to you in a brief moment.

PATHWAYS

Pathway 11.1. Character-activity-action. Sketch out two main characters (or use ones you've written about before). Define a dramatic struggle between the two of them (differing values, goals, or desires), and then decide which of them, if either, will get their way by scene's end. List at least five options for how this conflict might show itself in each character's behaviors. Note which options are more forceful and which more subtle. Explore which would both a) clearly demonstrate character and b) move the plot forward. Choose two or three behaviors for each to finally include in a two-page scene.

Pathway 11.2. Translations. Take your scene from Pathway 11.1 and translate your idea into the form of a psychological evaluation of the main character. Write it again as a three-line poem. Write it again as a fifteen-word single sentence. Write it as a news headline. Notice what the different forms and step-by-step distillation tell you about what's important in this scene.

Pathway 11.3. Mysterious box. Create two characters who live in the same house or apartment, and have them arrive home together to find an unlabeled, sealed box in the middle of the living room. One wants to open it, the other doesn't. OR . . . Put your characters on the street, where they encounter a similarly mysterious object. Use the package as the inciting incident that allows you to begin *in medias res*, and weave in what has led to this situation.

Pathway 11.4. A day of talk. Take a day to really pay attention to how you and people around you talk. Don't tell anyone when you are doing this—just let them go about their normal ways of speaking and acting, and try to go about yours. Write down as many interesting lines or snippets of interesting conversation as you can. At the end of the day, estimate the percentage of dialogue you heard that was ordinary versus distinctive.

Pathway 11.5. Notable lines. Take the list of conversational snippets that you wrote down for Pathway 11.4 and choose a few that you think might make good opening lines for a play or story. Start a new piece of paper for each snippet, copy the dialogue across the top, and then list as many fictional features of this character as you can based on that short bit of speaking—age, educational level, job, ethnicity, region, interests, personality traits. Even if the words were spoken by someone you know, remember to base your list of characteristics on the dialogue itself. Fictionalize. How might this line of dialogue lead to a story or play?

Pathway 11.6. No tags. Write a page where you identify two characters and then have them start talking. Do NOT use dialogue tags or attributions at all, though you might give the characters gestures or facial expressions. Mostly, though, define the characters through their speech styles.

Pathway 11.7. Group exercise: Inhabiting characters. Choose a fictional character from one of the stories in the book, preferably one the entire class has already read. Write a new moment that's not in the original story (though it might be referred to) for that character to inhabit, and try to become that character the way an actor would. Rehearse it. In class, read your passage aloud in the voice of your fictional persona, so that perhaps your classmates can guess which character you voiced. Afterward, discuss in your groups or as a whole class how speaking mannerisms and tones of voice influence our sense of character, aside from the content of the words spoken. As a reader, what signals did you try to give as to which persona you were? As a listener, what worked to signal you well and what didn't? How can any of this be translated to the page or script? How difficult was it for you to inhabit someone else's voice? What can you learn about writing dialogue for performance?

Pathway 11.8. Turning points. Create a list with at least ten lines of dialogue that, once spoken, would create inevitable reactions or trigger events. Try to avoid clichés, such as, "Honey, I want a divorce." Share these in class and choose one to start a play or story.

Pathway 11.9. Family backstory. Write a one-page scene in prose or a two-page scene in script form involving two members of a family facing a crisis. Include two or three pieces of backstory smoothly incorporated into the present scene, making sure there's a reason for them to come up other than a need for the reader or audience to be informed.

Pathway 11.10. Adaptation. Take any of your stories, memoirs, or even narrative poems that you have written before, and sketch out how you would write this content as a short play. Identify the characters, the setting to be recreated on stage, and the major scene or scenes. Then focus on how you would briefly describe actions vs. how much you could convey in the dialogue itself.

Pathway 11.11. Silent types. Create a two- to four-page scene in which two characters speak to each other only once or twice at most. This can be done in either prose or play form, but is actually more difficult in a play. How can you keep an imagined audience involved by actions rather than words? How can those reflect thoughts and feelings the characters have?

Pathway 11.12. Play outline and beats. Once you have an idea, do an outline for a one-scene, ten-minute play. Outlining what you will do page by page beforehand can help you manage the tight structure of this form. Structure a beginning, where you introduce your characters, including at least the main character's desire; a middle, where you bring the characters into conflict and begin a series of complications or raised stakes; and an end, where you resolve your story—happily or sadly or violently or anti-climactically or in any one of myriad other emotional possibilities. Also try to note what main beats your play-in-one-scene will contain.

Pathway 11.13. Objective correlatives. See how many instances of the objective correlative you can find from your own life. Think back on moments or scenes in which a feeling suddenly came clearly to you and you recognized an emotion unfolding. Make a list of as many as you can think of. Start a play, story, or memoir from one or more of them, perhaps changing the characters but keeping details and patterns of situation, character, and objects that allowed this emotion to crystallize for you.

FURTHER ANTHOLOGY READINGS

Lynne Alvarez, "On Sundays" (drama)

Junot Díaz, "Edison, New Jersey" (fiction)

Karen Russell, "St. Lucy's Home for Girls Raised by Wolves" (fiction)

GUIDEPOST: LISTENING SKILLS

Seeing—and hearing—is believing.

Consider, perhaps, that your writing as a whole is a kind of dialogue. That is, you do it so that you will be in conversation with other writers and with readers and audiences. When you talk with a friend, you do some listening as well as speaking, and that ebb and flow is what makes up a conversation. Whatever the circumstances, one of the ways you can ensure you are heard is to give people time to hear you and respond. Think of dialogue in this larger way, and you will not be afraid of the occasional silence and inaction in your writing.

But think of your working and living as a kind of stage play, and you may also become better at viewing your immediate situation with some dispassion and thus being able to listen to others around you. You will become attuned to what justifies a monologue versus when you (as a character in your own life) need to take a step back and let others speak.

The workshop model will teach you this in a tangible way. You may at times be unlucky enough to be in a workshop class where one or two people always seem to want to dominate the conversation. Your teacher may set up various means to prevent that—we're not so formal in Creative Writing classes as to use *Robert's Rules of Order*, but that is partly what those rules are about—giving each person a chance to participate in a discussion. If you are lucky, you will find that in a workshop you will come to value the range of feedback that different individuals offer. Keisha, for instance, will always hone right in on the missing motivation, while Raul will clobber the clichés, and Marilyn will be a master at structure.

You will, in other words, be learning to listen and to gauge immediate situations at several levels—that of eavesdropping to learn how people really do talk, to listening to your characters to see what they need to say and how they need to say it, to listening within your class and thinking about the variety of voices you hear. All these types of listening will help you in the future, as will your growing sensitivity to situations and how to respond to them. Any work involving customer service, education, politics, law, law enforcement, medicine, or business will require attentive listening and good sense about how to pace yourself and the employees that you may manage. And, if nothing else, learning to listen has the potential to make you a more considerate friend, partner, and parent.

Chapter 12

Performance

KEY ANTHOLOGY READINGS

Lynne Alvarez, "On Sundays" (drama)
William Borden, "The Blues Street Jazz Club Rehearses" (drama)

Writing **scripts**, for either stage plays or screenplays, is frequently compared to the practice of architecture. Architects *design* but they don't usually actually build the structures we live and work in. They create a plan by which others—from engineers to pipefitters, masons, electricians, carpenters, and other construction workers—take further steps to actually raise a building. The same thing will be true for any plays that you might write that you are lucky enough to have produced: as a playwright or screenwriter, you will make the first step—arguably the most important one—and then the producers, directors, designers (set, lighting, costume, and sound), technical staff, and actors and actresses will take over. In writing plays, even short ones, you have to keep in mind this mix of people. Theater and film are fundamentally collaborative arts and only through the collaboration of many people does a script come to life. "I believe movement can finish a phrase of language," notes novelist and playwright Ntozake Shange. "I have seen that happen on stage. I have felt it. The interaction is symbiotic, if it's really being done correctly."

In this chapter, we'll examine a few of the unique aspects of dramatic forms and touch on the implications for performances of poetry and prose. Unlike the practice of writing, which is usually best done in solitude, performances thrive on a multitude of people from collaborators to audiences.

THEATRICALITY

Storytelling began before writing, and at one point all writing was intended for performance, partly because what was written had first been told or performed aloud. That's no longer true. Although we will talk later in this chapter about ways of performing poetry and prose, we don't sit down to write a poem or novel or memoir thinking it necessary for someone to read it aloud. Great if they do, but we write those genres for the page. Plays, on the other hand, should be written to be performed whether they ever actually are or not, and the goal of performance makes drama unique.

Spectacle

Aristotle used the word **spectacle** to describe all the sensory effects created onstage—the costumes, settings, music, lighting, movements and voice qualities of the actors. Since Aristotle's time, of course, we have added all manner of special effects, even onstage, where automobiles may fly and horses stampede. There have always been spectacles of lights, smoke, and other effects on stage, and in recent years computer technology has allowed even more such stagecraft. *War Horse*, for example, was produced on stage (before ever becoming a film) with full-size horse puppets made from steel, leather, and aircraft cables. The other parts of a dramatic team usually produce the spectacle, but as a playwright, you will want to think about which gestures and movements, for example, you will want to specify to bring particular moments and points home to an audience. These may include an array of effects, including:

- soliloquies and asides that create complicity between the audience and the characters;
- architectural structures that emphasize power dynamics or other relationships;
- lighting, music, and other sounds that produce emotion based on their brightness, loudness, and other qualities; and
- gestures and pauses that emphasize words or moments in the play.

In Lynne Alvarez's "On Sundays" (p. 283), for example, Sylvia lives in a timeless, but confining translucent box while Jules comes and goes and grows older, and this onstage structure tells us a great deal about the relationship between them. Although William Borden's "The Blues Street Jazz Club Rehearses" (p. 296) calls for a "minimal" setting, the stage directions describe in detail the "heartbreaking melody" with which the play opens. Even before the first word is spoken by a character, we learn that the fine music emerges from a CD player rather than from the instruments the characters use. Immediately, Borden has established their amateurism, their fading dreams of musical greatness.

Spectacle, then, doesn't necessarily imply smoke bombs or screeching dinosaurs but concerns bringing ideas into a tangible space, rather than having readers imagine spaces and characters' physicality. Spectacle makes use of this palpability of the stage. (See **Pathway 12.1.**)

Physical Possibilities

The stage is more limited physically than places you may describe in prose but also has its own actual physical, material reality. Stages may vary—from the grand proscenium theaters of Broadway, which seat between 700 and 1,500 people, to smaller ones that take many forms including arena (in the round) and thrust (with the audience on three sides) stages. As a writer of plays, you have to remember that the stage has its limits and represents suggested places not real ones, possibilities rather than fixed and determined facts. On the other hand, the locales of your action will by necessity be more proscribed. Although in longer plays complicated scenery changes are commonplace, and even in shorter plays a stage may be set up with different areas representing different places, it's difficult to leap from place to place to place to place.

You also have to plan for the physicality of actors and audiences. Bodies will be encountering each other on stage, and the voyeuristic quality of theater never goes away. Humans love watching other humans, and this can often feel real and immediate to audiences. On the other hand, even when actors move to the front edge of the stage, they are only so close to the audience. Certainly the tradition of classical theater—where actors wore large masks with exaggerated expressions painted on them so people could see—emphasizes the broad gesture. This isn't always so today, but it remains true that at some point a whisper will become too quiet for an audience to hear. (See **Pathway 12.2**.)

Eternal Present

Unlike in poetry and prose, where we have a choice about the tenses we use, drama generally happens in the present tense, and as you work in this form, one major component is the issue of suspense—plays require that you keep something happening and that you keep the audience engaged. As Michael Wright notes in *Playwriting in Process*, "[w]hat's not said has its own subtext that makes the audience work a bit harder," and that mental participation keeps audiences involved. He notes that there's an immediacy when we watch plays that we must take advantage of when we write them.

Of course, plays may make use of time shifts—through set changes, through the aging of characters like Jules in "On Sundays," through references in the dialogue, as in "The Blues Street Jazz Club Rehearses," most pointedly through the use of voice-overs, which often indicate someone looking back on the action of the play (or film) from a later time. When we return to the action of the play, however, it remains in present tense, unfolding in front of the audience's eyes and ears in real time.

Sketch of Exposition

In a script, the exposition occurs in **setting descriptions** and **stage directions**. It is in these relatively short passages that you as a writer suggest the atmosphere, appearance of the characters, the movements and expressions of the actors, and anything else not conveyed in spoken dialogue. The first rule of thumb is to keep setting and stage directions to a minimum. Many of the details of this task will fall on a play or film's director.

"Stage direction" also refers to the simple terms used to instruct an actor where to go on the stage. If you've ever participated as an actor or even set-builder in high school or community theater, you are no doubt familiar with these terms, but they are reviewed in **Table 12.1**. Usually writers leave the exact **blocking**—or step-by-step choreography of a scene on stage—to the director, but occasionally it will be necessary to give a specific stage direction such as Lynne Alvarez does at the beginning of "On Sundays" when she notes "JULES enters stage right." In this way she emphasizes Jules's offstage world while Sylvia remains trapped on stage in her box; in this case, the writer needed to make sure that Jules *entered* and was not already on stage when the play began. In "The Blues Street Jazz Club Rehearses," however, note the flexibility of the characters' ages, each of them being in their "twenties or thirties," thus opening up the play for a variety of actors. (See **Pathway 12.3**.)

It's not that Borden doesn't have a vision for his characters—in fact, he delineates them clearly through what they say about their jobs and their affairs with each other, and he links both their financial struggles and their blasé attitude

Table 12.1
Stage Directions.

Stage right	toward the right while facing the audience
Stage left	toward the left while facing the audience
Upstage	away from the audience
Downstage	toward the audience
Center	the very middle side-to-side and front-to-back
Cross	moving across the stage to a particular point

Note that the stage is theoretically divided into three areas front-to-back and three or five right-to-left. The terms "right," "left," "center," "up," and "down" can be combined to indicate any of these specific positions on the stage, with up center being the middle back of the stage, down center being the middle front, and so on. Also note that "right" and "left" are based on the actor's perspective, not the audience's, since he or she is the one receiving the directions.

about love to the demands of their artistry. Obviously, they all sacrifice stability and perhaps even happiness to continue to be involved with the jazz scene. Yet Borden has also found a way not to require actual musicians to act in the play—he introduces the use of a CD player (which today could easily become a computer or other electronic music player) and makes their abilities and skills uncertain. This has the effect both of deepening the play's themes and making it more flexible to direct and perform. We'll come back to this issue, but the point here is for you to get in the habit of sketching rather than painting in full detail. Recognize which objects and other aspects of setting are vital and which gestures and movements you must specify in order for your meaning to be carried to the stage. The rest you should leave up to your collaborators. (See **Pathways 12.4, 12.5, and 12.6.**)

ONE SCRIPT, MANY PERFORMANCES

Theater Collaborators

Though the process of writing a play is usually separate from the production of plays on stage, you still need to keep in mind your collaborators when you write. Most simply, make sure that your play is actually possible to put on. For instance, when you write setting descriptions, think twice about specifying a set of particular elaborate mountain-climbing equipment with mounds of actual snow and a view of Glacier National Park in the background. Think about designers and set-builders who will have to turn your vision into reality. If you have sets that are too difficult or expensive to build, technical aspects that complicate matters inordinately (such as light and sound cues), or when you demand that you need a ghostly chorus of fifteen to stand behind the main action and chant a refrain, you are probably asking too much, especially if we are talking about a one-act (usually fifteen to twenty minutes long) or ten-minute play. These plays are usually put on as a set of three or more in one evening, and the theater personnel will already have three different playwrights' visions to deal with.

Also think of the directors and actors, even many of the other theater staff, such as costume and lighting designers, as fellow artists. They do not function as puppets that a playwright controls; rather they bring their own individual artistry to any play or screenplay. Sometimes a playwright will create a piece with a particular actor in mind—a role designed for someone's particular talents—but even if that person inhabits the role on stage first, many others will possibly go on to do so in their own ways. (See **Pathways 12.7 and 12.8.**)

Audience Collaborators

The collaboration of theater also extends to the audience. Anyone who has attended a play knows how the audience can affect our viewing—whether the theater space is large or small, sparsely attended or packed, whether the crowd hangs on every word and gesture or seems distracted, whether they're rowdy or circumspect—all of these things affect the meaning of a play. Playwrights, of course, have conflicting reactions to watching their work performed. The icono-clastic Nobel Prize–winner Harold Pinter noted in an interview that "audiences vary enormously. It's a mistake to care too much about them." Another Pulitzer Prize–winner, Stephen Sondheim, notes just the opposite when he says, "The last collaborator is your audience. . . . [W]hen the audience comes in, it changes the temperature of what you've written. . . . And so you start reshaping from an audience."

Sondheim points out that plays sometimes go through rewrites even once they are in production. Although this particular kind of revision is by no means universal, it's not uncommon and can add yet another layer to the collaboration that inheres in playwriting. It isn't that other kinds of writers never think of their readers, just that the repeated performances of plays are adaptable in a way that books cannot be. Perhaps this also has to do with the openness required of a playwright's personality—knowing already that directors, designers, and actors will add creative aspects to the play, it isn't so strange to think that as a writer you should stay open to the possibility of further changes in your own work. Plays continually evolve, long after they are "finished." Sondheim's own *West Side Story* provides a great example—the original 1957 play was itself an adaptation of Shakespeare's *Romeo and Juliet* and was adapted for a variety of productions, including an Academy Award–winning 1961 movie. In 2009 Arthur Laurents created a new version for Broadway, and the play lives on.

Practical aspects of creating works of literary art influence how and when changes are made. Film scripts, for instance, are revised constantly as the film is in production and even postproduction in the editing room, but once the film is made, it is distributed widely as a final product, and this step of getting film to audience demands enormous amounts of investment that would make revisions difficult. (This does increasingly happen, now that most "film" footage is digital, as with the release of "uncut" or "director's cut" versions—one of the first having been done for the sci-fi cult movie *Blade Runner*—but we continue to usually think of the commercially released film as definitive.) Similarly, over the past several hundred years, the production of books of poetry and prose required expensive printing and distribution methods. Although we note that things are "not written in stone"—an even older technology than the printing press—once a book is printed, it becomes difficult to change the material that's in it. At least those hundreds or thousands of copies will be circulating in the world for some time. This is changing somewhat, of course, with the advent of electronic versions of books and online venues for writing of all sorts, but the mentality surrounding plays remains uniquely open to multiple versions be-cause each production can be different.

Some of you will take to this openness, while others will struggle with it. It may be helpful at first to conceive of being a playwright as akin to being the person who hosts a party. You will do a lot of work that will result—if you're successful—in a grand event involving a lot of people. It will look simpler than it is. People may not notice the precision with which the food platters and drinks are refilled because they will be busy having a blast. Although you may not be at center stage, as the writer you will have orchestrated the entire event. Many writers take great pleasure in this influential yet offstage role.

DISTINCTIONS BETWEEN STAGE AND SCREEN

Although this book focuses its discussion of scripts on plays, many of you will also have an interest in movies. You may hope to work in Hollywood someday, writing mainstream movies or TV shows, or you may have more of an indie sensibility and hope to make films that will be shown at festivals or in art-houses across the country. There are dozens of terrific books and courses out there that will help you do so, but to get you started thinking about that possible future, here are a few ideas to help you move in that direction and learn from the other genres explored in this book.

First, remember that stories are stories. Many of the principles of character and plot and language use that we discuss in other chapters in this book will help you if and when you get to the point of working on screenplays or other filmmaking tasks.

Plays are different from screenplays, but plays can nonetheless be a great place to begin. Even smaller, independent film productions can get stuck in the fund-raising phase for long periods of time. As British screenwriter Frank Cottrell Boyce notes, "To get a movie into the world, someone needs to love it [the script] enough to spend millions of pounds [or dollars]—and years of their life. A play costs a few thousand and takes a couple of months." Boyce points out that if a play of yours is produced and well-liked, people in the film world may want to make the movie.

Plays require much collaboration, as noted above, but films require even more. With film, once the locations are found, the characters cast (**preproduction**), and the footage shot (**production**), there's another entire layer of technical work called **postproduction**, when the film is edited, the soundtrack produced, and sometimes computer-generated special effects are added. A film has wider parameters—the time that unfolds during filming over a period of days or weeks, possible changes in weather or other aspects of the physical settings, the greater complexity of filming over producing a stage play, and the increased opportunities to do multiple takes. Rewriting and changes to the original screenplay are even more common than changes to a play script. In addition, hours and hours of **raw footage**—what is shot on site—must be edited into an hour-and-a-half to two-hour time frame. This may constitute as little as thirty to forty hours of footage, but can reach two hundred or more—all to be edited down to a couple of hours of watching time. Shooting for the film *Titanic*, for instance, took one hundred sixty days and produced more than two million feet (or approximately three hundred hours) of raw footage that eventually was edited into the three-hour feature. Several scenes were cut or significantly altered through editing, due to test-audience reactions. Conceptual changes from the original screenplay often continue right through postproduction. Writers are offstage in the theater, but they can feel even more sidelined in the movie business.

Stage plays and screenplays usually have different scopes. That is not to say that stage plays never involve a wide range of settings, times, and different scales of events. The practical stage considerations mentioned in the previous section, however, don't theoretically apply to films. It's worth noting that including numerous or exotic locations in a screenplay will raise the production costs, but the medium of film is designed for swift jumps in location or time and the possibility of actions playing out against a variety of backgrounds, including large crowds and transient walk-ons. These elements may be suggested on stage, but they are expected elements in films and lead to often having a larger, rather sweeping scale of events and times. The same comparison does not hold true for screenplays and novels; novels tend to have the same kind of scope a screenplay can have, often even more fully developed. The comparative density and detail usually follow this order, most to least: novel, screenplay, play. Traditionally, the play is a pithy form rich in allusion and suggestion, the screenplay a panoramic form rich in visual detail, and the novel an introspective form that takes readers on a long trek. Of course, there are many exceptions to these characterizations.

Plays and films depend on different things to create a sense of closeness or intimacy. Although films tend to have larger visual scope than plays, they also allow for the **close-up** as well as the **long shot**. The spatial relationship between viewer and action is more consistent in a play—it may depend on where our seats are in the theater, and different stages have a variety of depths, but we usually remain at least ten or fifteen feet away from the actors and often far further, depending on the theater size and layout. In a film, on the other hand, we can zoom in to an intimate proximity to one character's nose hairs, and in another moment be looking down on the planet Earth from millions of miles above. Both of these options are important, but the close-up perhaps holds the most responsibility for the intimacy of film. We may not be inside characters' heads (though it is also easier in film to overlay a character's voice "in his head" than on stage), but we get close to their bodies. It's an illusion, of course, and stage productions have the benefit of actual bodies in front of us, but the appearance of closeness in film is a strong one. We seemingly stare directly into Ingrid Bergman's luminous eyes in the classic *Casablanca*, feel close enough to kiss the moody lips of Audrey Tautou in *Amélie*, and recoil from the gritty hands of Daniel Day Lewis in *There Will Be Blood*.

A play focuses more on the language, whereas a screenplay must take more into consideration the complex visual elements that will go into the final film. "A play," as Edward Albee said, "is a heard thing." Movies are definitely watched.

That doesn't mean that plays do not ever contain visual spectacle, as noted earlier in the chapter. While there is a visual aspect to stage plays, screenplays can be dominated by them.

Being aware of these differences and similarities can serve you in two ways. First, if you hope someday to write for the movies, you have a few pointers. But it's also true that these distinctions will help you be aware of the aspects of writing peculiar to plays and will help you create stronger dramatic work. (See **Pathways 12.9** and **12.10**.)

How do we use the terms "actor" and "actress"? In the time of Shakespeare, all actors were male, even the ones who played women—usually younger males played those roles—at least in England. By the sixteenth century, a few females acted on stage in Italy, France, and Spain, and illicitly in England during the years when Puritans outlawed theater completely (1642–1660). Warring factions had prevented Charles II from claiming the throne in England until 1660, but once he did one of his first actions was to establish a particular theater company that by law required females to play the roles of females. During his exile, Charles had been a huge fan of theater and had seen many women perform. So, for many years, the two separate terms **actors** and **actresses** were used to distinguish between the sexes on stage. However, today, we often use the simple one-word designation of actor to refer to anyone on stage of either gender. In this book, when I use the term "actor," I mean either a male or a female; however, if I speak of a particular female role, I will use the word "actress."

PERFORMING POETRY AND PROSE

The first chapter of this book focuses on the power of imagery and the connections between our bodily selves and the rhythms of poetry and prose. Those aspects of writing become paramount when you perform your own poetry and prose. Doing so can be a powerful experience that connects you to an audience in an almost theatrical way and that raises your awareness about the qualities of your work. Memorizing and/or reciting aloud a part or the whole of a piece of your own writing can reveal to you its nuances, strengths, and awkward spots.

Numerous overlapping groups of poets have concentrated on writing poetry (and sometimes prose) with its performance as a major consideration. You may have heard of—or even participated in—a **poetry slam**. Part poetry reading, part political and social activism, slams have evolved over the past twenty or so years into high-energy competitions in which audiences rate the poets' performances. These emerged almost simultaneously in New York and Chicago from different, but similarly inspired groups that saw themselves as anti-elitist and anti-establishment. In Chicago, white construction worker Marc Smith started a series of lively, blue-collar-oriented poetry readings held in bars and lounges; in New York, slam emerged out of the Nuyorican Poets Café, already a multicultural center for a variety of performing arts, including hip-hop. Both shared a sense that poetry had become too "snooty" and inaccessible to people. Slam has become a variegated movement with an orientation to youth, the working class, and people concerned with social discrimination based on race, gender, and sexual orientation. Well-known practitioners include Saul Williams, Taylor Mali, and Staceyann Chin. You might also hear other terms—**spoken word** or **performance poetry**. All of these categories overlap considerably, though the use of the term "spoken word" emerged a bit further back in the 1960s and featured both prose authors and poets, such as Spalding Gray and Gil Scott-Heron. Performance poetry is used more generally for any work particularly designed to be read or performed aloud or that includes nonverbal elements like music, dance, and visuals. Slams and other poetry and prose performance events have reawakened widespread interest in poetry, and their high-energy tone can be infectious. (See **Pathway 12.11**.)

Even beyond these particular performance-oriented movements, however, writers have been reading their work aloud for audiences virtually forever, certainly since the time of Homer in the seventh or eighth century BC. As noted in Chapter 2, rhyme helped oral storytellers remember their lines in verse narratives that people recited and listened to before literacy became widespread. Whether work is read aloud or memorized and recited, performance can bring another level of expression to works we usually absorb through our eyes from the page. **Pathway 12.12** will help you find some writers well known for performing their writing and may inspire you to do the same. In this way, you will find the power of the breath and heartbeat in your own work.

PATHWAYS

Pathway 12.1. Theatergoer. Go and see a play. This can be on your campus, in a community theater, or in a filmed version. Because you may not be as familiar with this genre as with poetry and prose forms, it's a great idea to see as many plays as possible when you begin writing them. Analyze the spectacle in any play you see. How has this production engaged you in a sensory fashion through setting, costumes, music, lighting, and actors' voices and notable gestures?

Pathway 12.2. Broad gestures. Take a look at one of the short stories or essays in this book. Reread it, looking for gestures and dialogue that you think would translate well—or not—in a stage adaptation. Make a list of each to discuss in class. How would you adapt this work for the stage?

Pathway 12.3. Stage blocking. Choose a stage form, and draw a rough sketch of the shape or find an example online. Block out a scene you have previously written by creating a square for each character, noting where they enter, act, and exit. Think about where each character will move and how they will interact.

Pathway 12.4. Setting analysis. Examine a few or all of the plays in this book and compare the setting descriptions and stage directions in each. Which one has the most? The least? Why do you think the playwrights have made the particular choices they have about how much to include?

Pathway 12.5. Group exercise: Stretching stagecraft. As a class, figure out a way to adapt Italo Calvino's "All at One Point" (p. 303) into a stage production. This might be difficult and challenging, and also fun to figure out. Assign roles (perhaps with your instructor as director), create movements and lines of dialogue, even discuss props and costumes and music if you like. Act it out.

Pathway 12.6. Group exercise: Song interpretation. Within your group, decide on a song (any kind, but one that everyone can have easy access to for listening purposes). At home, separately, define characters, setting, and other stage directions you would establish if you were creating a play for that song. Back in class, compare your different "productions."

Pathway 12.7. Casting. Once you have a draft of a ten-minute play, cast it in your head. Decide on actors for the parts. Do this twice: once with professional actors you're familiar with and then again with people in your own life, though you should avoid casting people on whom your characters are based. If your play is a family story, cast friends; if it's about your close friends, cast people you know only casually. Compare these two casts and think about what each set of collaborators might bring to your play. What do they tell you about how character is clarified in your play and which aspects of character you'll need to be most careful with?

Pathway 12.8. Group activity: Dramatic reading. Assign every person to a part in one of the plays in this book. In your separate groups, do dramatic readings of the plays. You need not move around and act them out, but inhabit your characters. See if there are any changes you'd like to make to the dialogue, perhaps based on more contemporary settings or what you bring to the part.

Pathway 12.9. Film treatment. Write a two- to five-page pitch or treatment for a movie. Remember to avoid stereotypes and clichéd Hollywood plots. This should be written in the present tense; introduce the main characters; also give the what, when, where, and why; outline three acts—Act I should set the scene and lay out the main conflicts, Act II should give two to six paragraphs of escalation of the conflict, culminating in a crisis, and Act III should dramatize the final crisis and any resolution.

Pathway 12.10. Close-up. On your phone, with yourself and/or a friend acting, film one extreme close-up that would be a part of the film you've outlined in Pathway 12.9. You've thought macro-level, now think micro. What close-up could reflect something important about the story you would tell? Think, too, about how you might convey this same moment on stage.

Pathway 12.11. Group activity: Poetry slam. Organize a poetry slam, spoken word event, or open mic in various genres either inside or outside your class. Research the competitive structure of slams and decide on the extent to which you want to make your event competitive. Find a space, organize performers, promote the event, and bring others together to read their work.

Pathway 12.12. Poetry videos. Access YouTube and search for "poetry reading," "slam poetry," or "spoken word." Perhaps even search YouTube for favorite writers of yours doing readings, or search for authors in this book, such as the slam and spoken word authors mentioned above. Among those in the book but outside the slam tradition, Lynn Emanuel and Al Young often read their poetry with musical accompaniment. Listen to several different types of readings and compare.

FURTHER ANTHOLOGY READINGS
Italo Calvino, "All at One Point" (fiction)
David Sedaris, "The Drama Bug" (creative nonfiction)
Lisel Mueller, "Spell for a Traveler" (poetry)
Mary Block, "Moving Song" (poetry)
Amber West, "Pirate's Admonition" (poetry)

GUIDEPOST: COLLABORATIVE SPIRIT

Our social nature must be remembered, even when we write alone.

Whatever we do as a profession in our lives, we must balance independence with an ability to understand our individual roles in a larger organization—and, I might add, in relation to the biological basis of all life on Earth. We are cooperative and competitive, singular and collective, and to be an effective person you must have a sense of both.

Most writers are individualists—one of our primary goals is to write something no one else has ever written, or to write something so well that no one can touch it in terms of quality. We find ourselves vying with other writers. Yet we all know that writers form a community surrounded by the larger community of avid readers. We support each other as writers, giving each other feedback on our work and fostering each other's growth with encouragement and faith in the importance of the endeavor of capturing human experience. We share words with each other.

As part of a society of writers—or whatever subsocieties you end up working or spending time in—we need to be aware of our interdependence with others. We write alone; if we are unread—or don't read others' work—then we remain alone. Only through sharing ourselves can we connect to the life around us.

Destination: HYBRID FORMS AND EMERGING MEDIA

Creative writing has reached a fascinating time in its practice and history. Because of the advent of the Internet, as well as increases in literacy across the world over the past hundred years, more people communicate their stories, verses, and opinions than ever before. As a result, we are witnessing a flowering not only of the amount of writing going on, but experiments with types and styles of storytelling and image production.

MAIN FEATURES OF THESE FORMS

Writers have always experimented with and merged forms, including novels written in the form of letters (the epistolary); dramatic monologues that combined qualities of fiction, drama, and poetry recitation; travelogues that became memoirs of self-discovery; novels that passed as nonfictional accounts; and memoirs that passed as fiction. Today, however, hybridity grows commonplace, or we simply notice it more, in a variety of contexts—racial, ethnic, national, cultural. In terms of expressive arts, new technologies have made it easier and easier for more people to take excellent photos, create and edit videos, record their own music, and combine sound elements from different sources, producing mash-ups and collages. It makes sense that in light of these changes, we would also feel more inclined to break the boundaries of traditional written genres as well.

In terms of hybrids within the written form, most common today are **prose poems** and **short shorts** (also known as **flash, sudden, micro**, or **postcard fiction and nonfiction**), all of which borrow from both prose and poetry forms discussed in Chapter 4. There are also many experiments ongoing that dance along the border between fiction and creative nonfiction, and writers who call for the letting go of firm distinctions. Perhaps the best known of these is David Shields, whose *Reality Hunger: A Manifesto* claims that our culture has become so fragmentary as not to be well represented in traditionally conceived narrative. There are also ongoing amalgamations of genres of fiction. Magical realism, for instance, melds fairy tale with emotional realism. Many novels have begun partaking of genre-fiction elements while maintaining high literary standards and originality—like Jonathan Lethem's *The Fortress of Solitude*, which draws a realistic story of urban boyhood affected by one magical element, or Michael Chabon's *The Yiddish Policemen's Union*, which contemplates issues of Jewish identity alongside a mystery whodunit. More about this is taken up in Chapter 15.

Perhaps because we live in the highly visual age of TV, movies, and billboards, many people today are interested in combining visual elements with written narrative in the form of **graphic novels**. Reflecting the same acknowledgement of high-quality science fiction and other genre fiction, comics that go beyond stereotypical superhero stories are now being recognized by the literary mainstream as an art form. "Graphic novel" typically refers to a book that, though written with the same combination of words and pictures as any comic book, focuses on one longer story (rather than serials) and concerns realistic or allegorical settings and characters, although the form emerged from science fiction works like Alan Moore's originally serialized 1987 *Watchmen*. Art Spiegelman's 1991 *Maus: A Survivor's Tale; My Father Bleeds History*, one of the most acclaimed of pioneers in this genre, demonstrates that even beyond the visual-verbal hybrid, this genre tends to mix fiction and creative nonfiction. *Maus* is based upon interviews that Spiegelman conducted with his father about his experiences during the Holocaust, yet depicts the Jews as mice, the Germans as cats, and the Poles as pigs.

More recently, the common nonfiction elements of some graphic novels have been more readily acknowledged as **graphic memoirs** with such works as *Blankets* by Craig Thompson, a story of young love and sexual discovery in conflict with the author's religious upbringing. A segment of his graphic travel memoir *Carnet de Voyage* (p. 528) demonstrates the evocative potential of this hybrid genre. This move toward graphic memoir has included authorship by many more women in the traditionally male-dominated comics world, with work such as *Persepolis: The Story of a Childhood*, Mariane Satrapi's account of her early years in Iran, and *Fun Home: A Family Tragicomic*, Alison Bechdel's exploration of her father's closeted homosexuality and its impact on her growing up.

The powerful combination of visuals and words can also be found in **digital storytelling**, in which authors can combine still visual images with video, voice-overs, and other sound elements using computer-based tools. Of course, like most of the visual arts, digital storytelling requires mastery of technical aspects, but most relevant software tools are becoming simpler to use and accessible to more people. Pioneered by the Center for Digital Storytelling, the genre now is offered as a particular course of study at many universities and in many short-term workshops.

Computer technology and the Internet have, of course, created multiple new forms of creative endeavor and expression, forms that are sometimes used to artistic ends and sometimes not. **Blogs**, as a primary example, are often used for political, social, business, and other reasons, but also offer a way for writers to reach readers with few limitations on length or purpose of work shared there. Generally, we think of blogs as informational, but occasionally as memoirs-in-the-making. Several blogs have, in fact, become so popular that their authors have obtained book contracts and revised and revamped their work for book form like Julie Powell's *Julie & Julia*, which originated with a blog chronicling her attempt to prepare recipes from master chef Julia Child. Today, however, much short form literature in poetry and fiction as well as creative nonfiction has moved permanently to **online literary magazines,** such as *Narrative* (mostly fiction), *Brevity* (short creative nonfiction), and *Mudlark* (poetry). There is a wealth of good (and, admittedly, also a wealth of bad) writing in all genres available on the Web, and opportunities for writers of all stripes to get their work out there when they are ready.

I also want to mention the future potential of **interactive games** of a variety of types, from early text-based **interactive fiction** or **hyperfiction** and **electronic poetry** to more current work in **cyberdrama** and the more commercial existence of **massively multiplayer online role-playing games** (MMORPGs). Debates rage about the potential for narrative art within computer games and other technology-driven forms, but generally the full potential remains untapped. As with much mass-market fiction, a lot of these games focus on fantasy and adventure settings and action rather than well-developed characters, realistic settings, or meaning. Because of the technical aspects of these fields, the writing of computer games does not usually fall within the realm of Creative Writing. If you have passion for this world, however, the training that you will get in Creative Writing may help you in taking these genres further into qualities of artistic merit on which literature is judged.

Although it is impossible to include comprehensive coverage of all the various new forms and media in which creative writing is happening today, I encourage you to follow your own interests in this regard and find work in these many genres that appeal to your sensibilities.

QUESTIONS ABOUT WRITING IN HYBRID FORMS AND EMERGING MEDIA

- **Have you mastered the nonwriting skills necessary?** Particularly the forms of narrative that use graphic and digital elements require an additional set of drawing, programming, and visual editing skills that differ somewhat from writing skills. Look for additional courses or mini-workshops that will augment any technical or artistic skills you need.
- **Does your idea suit a particular alternative genre or would it be better suited by a more traditional one?** Think early about how form and content relate to each other. Allow yourself to experiment with forms, but always remember the tried and true genres as well.
- **Are you familiar with other work in the new or hybrid genre that interests you?** The word "experimental" can be used in more than one way—either for work that is new to you in particular or for work that is unusual on the wider scene. Until you understand the latter, remember that what seems innovative to you may be similar to what others have done before you. Explore both your own personal experiments and those who have experimented before you.

- **Does your work keep a "beginner's mind"?** I encourage you to allow your hybrid and new media work to be playful, edgy, and exploratory. Particularly flash forms of fiction and nonfiction provide great forums for trying out a lot of different stories quickly and help keep us from getting stuck in a rut.
- **Do your flash fiction and creative nonfiction stories contain all the elements of a story rather than just an anecdote or scene?** Sometimes when we start writing in very short forms, we simply write fragments. Remember that these forms partake of the kind of condensation found in poetry—they should feel complete even though they are short.

PART II

Writing Life Matters

Chapter 13

Reading as a Writer

This chapter contains one simple gem of advice: if you wish to write well, you should develop a lifelong habit of impassioned reading. Certainly, this is the reason why students of Creative Writing are also almost always required to simultaneously study the field of Literature. Important though it is, however, taking courses in the history of great literature is not enough. As a writer, you enter into what is essentially a conversation with other living writers and readers, and you will develop your own reading preferences and passions that you should follow outside the classroom. You will need to read as a writer with the intention of understanding the choices that other writers have made and what you might learn about the range of possibilities for your own work.

Today, we have many opportunities for how we spend our time. We are not stuck by the fireside with an oil lamp and nothing for entertainment but a few books. We can instead watch TV, go out to the movies, listen to thousands of tunes available in an instant, immerse ourselves in online worlds, or spend all of our hours Tweeting and Facebooking with our friends. I don't mean to suggest that you not partake of those other media, only that you also reserve some time for reading (whether in book form or using an e-reader) and that you read widely and voraciously. It may seem that pouring out your soul on the page is the most important aspect of your writing, but if you are writing anything but a diary, you must think both about your need to express yourself and the need to make others understand what you are saying. Think of living literature as a world that you share with others, both those who read and others who also write.

In other words, put bluntly, if you don't read, who can you possibly expect to read what you write? Writing is a two-way street even beyond the Creative Writing workshop. Reading and writing both depend on the effort for us to understand our lives and our cultural moment in language that refreshes our perspective and insight. "You think your pain and your heartbreak are unprecedented in the history of the world, but then you read," notes James Baldwin. "It was books that taught me that the things that tormented me most were the very things that connected me with all the people who were alive, or who had ever been alive." As writers, part of our responsibility is to support this literate culture of a shared humanity.

READING: THE CRUCIAL FACTOR

In a practical sense, reading will help you understand the techniques that writers have learned over the years to be effective at communicating their ideas and feelings. These strategies change over time—for instance, the God-like third-person narrators of most nineteenth-century novels have given way to more common use today of more intimate first-person narrators who speak like our friends. This reflects our more casual social mores today, and, yet, if we understand the full range of options, we clearly have more choices in deciding what's best in a given piece of our own work.

This kind of knowledge takes time to develop. You may have heard of the "10,000-hour rule," popularized by Malcolm Gladwell in his book *Outliers: The Story of Success* and based on the research of Swedish psychologist K. Anders Ericsson in the early 1990s. Ericsson discovered that there is a direct correlation between musical ability and hours that a person has practiced playing the violin, such that "the elite performers had each totaled [at least] ten thousand hours of practice." The study found that, contrary to our belief that innate talent makes the difference in how high someone rises in a certain artistic pursuit, the amount of time spent working in that field matters far, far more.

This pattern has held through numerous other studies and across various fields. Even in situations where we have an image of young geniuses, such as Mozart, who composed great works by the time he was twenty-one, researchers have discovered that, in fact, such individuals most likely start earlier and work harder than other people. Mozart, for instance, composed less spectacular work throughout his childhood and didn't create his finest work until he had been at it for a long time. In addition, Mozart spent years writing arrangements of other composers' work before he began to write truly original music.

This latter point brings us back to why it is so important for writers to read: the creativity research shows that knowledge within the domain of any given field is the basis upon which creative work is built. Sometimes we have the idea that our own ideas might be tainted by too many "influences" from other work, and as you study Creative Writing you will likely see imitative and derivative pieces that pale in comparison to the writers they parrot. Yet, this phase of absorbing other writers' accomplishments is often necessary to fully understand what it is that you can contribute to the ongoing conversation of literature and what is unique about you as a writer.

In recent decades, some enlightening studies have been done of creative writers, their personalities, and their lives. I encourage you to look up the actual studies by the likes of James C. Kaufman, Jane Piirto, Teresa Amabile, Nancy Andreasen, and D. K. Simonton; although couched in the technical language of the field of psychology, they give insight into the various life factors that contribute to creative success. Some of these images of what writers are like we will take up further in Chapter 16, but virtually all successful writers are known to be avid readers. An almost universal finding of the research is that accomplished writers work assiduously at learning their craft and that reading (and/or listening to oral storytelling) provides one of the major avenues for doing so.

Sherman Alexie, in "Superman and Me" (p. 279), even says about his avid reading that "I was trying to save my life" as he struggled with poverty and low expectations for Native American children on the reservation. His experience may be personally different from yours, and many aspects of a given writer's methods and choices differ from one to another. Perhaps you "write what you know," or perhaps you launch out into unknown territory as a way to explore. Perhaps you are devoted almost exclusively to fiction, believing that is where your talent lies, or perhaps you are drawn to the practice of exploring different forms. You may have pursued the realistic stories of characters based on people that you know, or you may be drawn to poetry that focuses on nuances of language itself. Advice about being a writer is, therefore, appropriately variable and flexible. *Vive la différence!* However, one fact doesn't vary: Writers read—hungrily, attentively, constantly. (See **Pathways 13.1, 13.2,** and **13.3.**)

HOW TO READ AS A WRITER

Close Reading

Writers need to read differently from other readers. When a casual reader first opens a book, he or she is usually simply caught up in the story, turning the pages to find out what happens, or relating to the characters as though they are real people, even if they live in a fantasy world. Our parents may have given us stories to read when we were children that contain a moral that we absorb, like Shel Silverstein's *The Giving Tree* with its story of sacrifice and selflessness. Many people read this way—just for the amusement, content, or lesson—and this transparent approach to reading can give great pleasure.

As writers, we may still initially have this kind of response, and get caught up in a story or have our breath taken away by the beauty or horror of an image in a poem. However, as we go on to become writers, we set aside the emotional reaction and learn to analyze the way the text works. You do something similar when recommending books to friends or doing other kinds of writing, especially papers for Literature or other academic courses, but reading as a writer involves a somewhat different kind of analysis. We read to understand how a writer achieved the effects that first moved us. We ask basic questions about how a writer has structured a piece and the choices a writer has made about style. We react to characters and personae less as though they are people we are just encountering on the street and more as though we need to understand what they are made of, what produces their personalities on the page. We notice the order in which the story is told, whether chronological or otherwise. We examine how the sentences or lines set up a rhythm that augments or undermines the pace of events described.

Literary scholars may also use these tools of what we call **close reading**, but their purposes differ significantly from a creative writer's purpose. Today's literary scholars are usually concerned with the larger social and cultural implications of a piece of literature and less so in how it functions internally. Although much of what we understand about narrative emerged from scholars of previous decades—and they created a variety of theories regarding language use and structure—the purpose of close reading techniques for current scholars is to support their wider cultural observations and theories with specific analysis (an evidence-conclusion structure). Writers, on the other hand, need to analyze and then resynthesize the techniques and strategies of what they read in order to be able to use or adapt these methods in their own efforts at writing well. In *Reading Like a Writer*, Francine Prose says, "I can remember the novels and stories that seemed to me revelations: wells of beauty and pleasure that were also textbooks, private lessons in the art of fiction."

In reading as writers, then, we seek to understand the choices that masterful writers have made. Like any dancer who must be shown the moves of the masters, sometimes with teachers' hands directly manipulating their limbs into position, we can learn from careful observation of strategies and techniques successfully used by other writers. We learn to attend to the particular use of individual words and their connotations and associations, and to the juxtapositions and placement of words and passages. Because everything we write is removed from reality by the language we use, there are numerous options for expressing any one event, emotion, or thought. As writers we must know the effects of these particular choices if we are to have any control over our results at all, and these are skills that we get better and better at the more we read and the more we think consciously about them.

Pleasure and Displeasure

Our first impulse when we read something that we don't understand is to label it "stupid" and accuse the writer of writing badly. This is understandable, and sometimes it's even true. But most often an "I don't get it" reaction indicates merely a gap between your own understanding of the language and the author's. Because schoolbooks are written at particular "grade levels," their content has been matched to the general ability of students at any given age. So, as you set out to grow as a writer, and to move beyond the general population's understanding of language, you should even seek out reading material that seems unfamiliar in its style, subject matter, or difficulty, especially work that has been highly praised but that you are uncertain how to approach. This is how you will grow and learn the subtleties of language. Otherwise, you will be like a mathematician who can do no more than balance a checkbook or an ice skater who doesn't know how to leap into the air. (See **Pathway 13.4.**)

It's important to keep in mind that there is no shame in being uncertain of your interpretations of something you read or to find that others are reading your writing in a way that you didn't intend. There are many aspects of creative writing that are subtle and open to various interpretations. This is part of the nature and joy of stories and poems as opposed to thesis-driven writing that may present a compelling argument, but the goal of which is to *tell* us what to think and gain our agreement. Many of these creative writing qualities are slippery and challenging—how, for instance, do we know that a writer is being ironic as opposed to sincere? Sometimes writing—such as Michael Palmer's "The Cord" (p. 472) and Lia Purpura's "On Looking Away" (p. 480)—will contain a layer of meaning about the elusive quality of language and play with language in an intentionally mysterious way.

However, we shouldn't ever forget that the reason why most of us have aspired to write is that at some point we have been inspired by the pleasures of reading. As we talk about our own work and that of published writers, we should feel free to praise as well as critique and to revel as well as analyze. (See **Pathway 13.5.**)

TWO CASE STUDIES: HEMINGWAY AND WOJAHN

This section takes close looks at two pieces of writing in order to demonstrate how you might approach reading as a writer. Though usually we approach a text the first time without all the clutter of comments and arrows, allow these two examples to demonstrate some of the kinds of things you might try to notice as you read other work. Ernest Hemingway's "Hills Like White Elephants" may be familiar to you—whether or not it is, you'll be able to see how you can add to your insights about a writer's techniques beyond a first reading. David Wojahn's poem "Cold Glow: Icehouses" should provide some guidance for approaching a text that seems at first difficult and mysterious, in other words, how to unpack a densely layered piece of writing that is new to you. Both of these works can be read in myriad other ways—this depth and multiple aspects are what make these works literary. I will highlight particular qualities, but each of these works can benefit by numerous readings. I simply want to invite you to practice this kind of assessment and perceiving on your own.

Ernest Hemingway is considered one of the "greats" of the mid-twentieth century, and he's often taught in Literature courses for his mastery of the minimalist style. That minimal style is one of the places that we can start with a close reading of "Hills Like White Elephants." If you've read this story before, you probably noticed immediately that most of the story is written in brief exchanges of dialogue, that the paragraphs and sentences are short, and that there isn't much description. In addition, many times the first reaction to a quick read of this story is to wonder what it is exactly that the couple is arguing about since the subject of their argument is never quite named. Since most advice about writing is to be specific and to include rich detail and active vocabulary, we see right away that Hemingway's work is designed to unsettle us.

However, even going beyond a discussion of the euphemistic treatment of abortion that was a scandalous topic in Hemingway's time, we might learn even more about the specific unconventional methods he uses to create the story's overwhelming unease.

HILLS LIKE WHITE ELEPHANTS

The hills across the valley of the Ebro were long and white. On this side there was no shade and no trees and the station was between two lines of rails in the sun. Close against the side of the station there was the warm shadow of the building and a curtain, made of strings of bamboo beads, hung across the open door into the bar, to keep out flies. The American and the girl with him sat at a table in the shade, outside the building. It was very hot and the express from Barcelona would come in forty minutes. It stopped at this junction for two minutes and went on to Madrid.

> Description is kept to a minimum throughout, and there are few adjectives. Note how the adjectives in this first paragraph all have potentially sexual connotations. "Long" and "white," for instance, might evoke how the girl appeared stretched out nude. Later references to the "skin" of the hills adds to this sense. See below for shifts in the adjectives' tone.

> Brief characterizations tell us a lot. The female is referred to as a "girl," the male as a "man," so we see he is older than she is. In addition, because he is referred to as "the American," we wonder if she is not.

"What should we drink?" the girl asked. She had taken off her hat and put it on the table.

"It's pretty hot," the man said.

"Let's drink beer."

"Dos cervezas," the man said into the curtain.

"Big ones?" a woman asked from the doorway.

"Yes. Two big ones."

The woman brought two glasses of beer and two felt pads. She put the felt pads and the beer glasses on the table and looked at the man and the girl. The girl was looking off at the line of hills. They were white in the sun and the country was brown and dry.

"They look like white elephants," she said.

"I've never seen one," the man drank his beer.

"No, you wouldn't have."

"I might have," the man said. "Just because you say I wouldn't have doesn't prove anything."

The girl looked at the bead curtain. "They've painted something on it," she said. "What does it say?"

"Anis del Toro. It's a drink."

"Could we try it?"

The man called "Listen" through the curtain. The woman came out from the bar.

"Four reales."

"We want two Anis del Toro."

"With water?"

"Do you want it with water?"

"I don't know," the girl said. "Is it good with water?"

"It's all right."

"You want them with water?" asked the woman.

"Yes, with water."

"It tastes like licorice," the girl said and put the glass down.

Brief characterizations tell us a lot. The female is referred to as a "girl," the male as a "man," so we see he is older than she is. In addition, because he is referred to as "the American," we wonder if she is not.

Notice the use of "it" throughout. There are only two places where what it refers to is named: here with the hat and below with the "operation."

Here, the antecedent, though not named, is clear enough. H. eases us into his unusual use of "it."

Here, the adjective "felt" takes on double meaning and stands in for both "feelings" and people "feeling" each other physically. But by the end of the paragraph, the adjectives refer to something drying up, perhaps more than just the landscape.

The couple begins to bicker, though it seems trivial.

Because she can't read the sign and because she hasn't tried this alcoholic beverage, whereas he has, we get a picture of his greater worldliness and experience. The girl perhaps doesn't even speak Spanish, the language of the country where they are.

Notice the time leap here. H. has eliminated the blow-by-blow of the waitress bringing the new drinks.

"That's the way with everything."

"Yes," said the girl. "Everything tastes of licorice. Especially all the things you've waited so long for, like absinthe."

"Oh, cut it out."

"You started it," the girl said. "I was being amused. I was having a fine time."

"Well, let's try and have a fine time."

"All right. I was trying. I said the mountains looked like white elephants. Wasn't that bright?"

"That was bright."

"I wanted to try this new drink. That's all we do, isn't it—look at things and try new drinks?"

> An indication of her impatience with their tourism and partying.

"I guess so."

The girl looked across at the hills.

"They're lovely hills," she said. "They don't really look like white elephants. I just meant the coloring of their skin through the trees."

> A surprising word choice since we don't think of hills as having skin. Shows she's thinking of something else.

"Should we have another drink?"

"All right."

The warm wind blew the bead curtain against the table.

> Their disagreement ebbs for a moment.

"The beer's nice and cool," the man said.

"It's lovely," the girl said.

"It's really an awfully simple operation, Jig," the man said. "It's not really an operation at all."

> Here the meaning of "it" changes suddenly without an antecedent. "It" is followed by "operation," but we only gradually come to see what kind of operation he means. The conflict is escalating.

The girl looked at the ground the table legs rested on.

"I know you wouldn't mind it, Jig. It's really not anything. It's just to let the air in."

The girl did not say anything.

"I'll go with you and I'll stay with you all the time. They just let the air in and then it's all perfectly natural."

> Another shift of meaning without clear antecedent.

"Then what will we do afterward?"

"We'll be fine afterward. Just like we were before."

"What makes you think so?"

"That's the only thing that bothers us. (It)'s the only thing that's made us unhappy."

> And another.

The girl looked at the bead curtain, put her hand out and took hold of two of the strings of beads.

"And you think then we'll be all right and be happy."

"I know we will. You don't have to be afraid. I've known lots of people that have done (it)."

> Here he shifts back to the operation and stays on it somewhat relentlessly for a while.

"So have I," said the girl. "And afterward they were all so happy."

"Well," the man said, "if you don't want to you don't have to. I wouldn't have you do (it) if you didn't want to. But I know (it)'s perfectly simple."

"And you really want to?"

"I think (it)'s the best thing to do. But I don't want you to do (it) if you don't really want to."

"And if I do (it) you'll be happy and things will be like they were and you'll love me?"

"I love you now. You know I love you."

"I know. But if I do (it) then it will be nice again if I say things are like white elephants, and you'll like (it)?"

> The meaning of "it" begins to shift again.

"I'll love (it) I love (it) now but I just can't think about (it) You know how I get when I worry."

"If I do (it) you won't ever worry?"

"I won't worry about that because (it)'s perfectly simple."

"Then I'll do (it). Because I don't care about me."

"What do you mean?"

"I don't care about me."

"Well, I care about you."

"Oh, yes. But I don't care about me. And I'll do (it) and then everything will be fine."

"I don't want you to do (it) if you feel that way."

> The girl stood up and walked to the end of the station. Across, on the other side, were fields of grain and trees along the banks of the Ebro. Far away, beyond the river, were mountains. The shadow of a cloud moved across the field of grain and she saw the river through the trees.

By this point, the description contains no adjectives at all. She sees a river rather than hills through the trees. Because the hills have been described as having "skin," they might be reminiscent of a pregnant belly. She no longer focuses on the hills, only on the moving river.

"And we could have all this," she said. "And we could have everything and every day we make (it) more impossible."

"What did you say?"

"I said we could have everything."

"We can have everything."

"No, we can't."

"We can have the whole world."

"No, we can't."

"We can go everywhere."

"No, we can't. (It) isn't ours any more."

"(It)'s ours."

"No, (it) isn't. And once they take (it) away, you never get (it) back."

"But they haven't taken (it) away."

"We'll wait and see."

"Come on back in the shade," he said. "You mustn't feel that way."

"I don't feel any way," the girl said. "I just know things."

"I don't want you to do anything that you don't want to do—"

"Nor that isn't good for me," she said. "I know. Could we have another beer?"

"All right. But you've got to realize—"

"I realize," the girl said. "Can't we maybe stop talking?"

This "it" might refer to a number of things—happiness, innocence, a future together, the unborn child.

He doesn't understand or refuses what she means.

These two "its" seem to make direct reference to the child.

He interprets "it" as perhaps his own happiness or their relationship.

They sat down at the table and the girl looked across at the hills on the dry side of the valley and the man looked at her and at the table.

> A repetition of an adjective that portends more than a dry landscape.

"You've got to realize," he said, "that I don't want you to do it if you don't want to. I'm perfectly willing to go through with it if it means anything to you."

> the abortion

> the pregnancy

"Doesn't it mean anything to you? We could get along."

> the child

"Of course it does. But I don't want anybody but you. I don't want any one else. And I know it's perfectly simple."

> He shifts topic back to the operation.

"Yes, you know it's perfectly simple."

"It's all right for you to say that, but I do know it."

"Would you do something for me now?"

"I'd do anything for you."

"Would you please please please please please please please stop talking?"

He did not say anything but looked at the bags against the wall of the station. There were labels on them from all the hotels where they had spent nights.

> Another indicator about the nature of their relationship. It seems to be based on touring and is perhaps of a temporary nature.

"But I don't want you to," he said, "I don't care anything about it."

"I'll scream," the girl said.

The woman came out through the curtains with two glasses of beer and put them down on the damp felt pads. "The train comes in five minutes," she said.

> Another sign of change in the adjectives. The feeling is sodden.

"What did she say?" asked the girl.

> Another hint that perhaps the girl doesn't speak the language and is therefore dependent on the man.

"That the train is coming in five minutes."

The girl smiled brightly at the woman, to thank her.

"I'd better take the bags over to the other side of the station," the man said. She smiled at him.

"All right. Then come back and we'll finish the beer."

He picked up the two heavy bags and carried them around the station to the other tracks. He looked up the tracks but could not see the train. Coming back, he walked through the barroom, where people waiting for the train were drinking. He drank an Anis at the bar and looked at the people. They were all waiting reasonably for the train. He went out through the bead curtain. She was sitting at the table and smiled at him.

> This last main descriptive paragraph contains one adjective (aside from "bead," which is a necessary identifier for the type of curtain). Not only do the bags feel heavy, but likely this adjective refers to the unpleasant feelings of the man.

"Do you feel better?" he asked.

"I feel fine," she said. "There's nothing wrong with me. I feel fine."

Hemingway's reputation is one of hyper-masculinity. Yet, as we read this story again and again, we see that Hemingway's nearly objective narrator portrays both the male and female characters as sympathetic, with perhaps the vulnerability of the "girl" being most prominent. Not only does close reading allow us to make clear sense of the obliquely stated conflict at the center of the story, but it allows us to see the precise techniques that make this story work the way it does. In addition to reading carefully, we can also sometimes learn a great deal by mimicking in some way a particular writer's style. (See **Pathway 13.6**.)

So, how do you approach, on the other hand, something that you've never read before that is challenging in different ways than the euphemism-shrouded abortion of "Hills"? David Wojahn's allusive poem "Cold Glow: Icehouses" offers a good model for unpacking a text that, rather than sparse, seems dense with a strange combination of specifics. This poem confronts you with a particular morning when the speaker remembers watching a lake freeze over, but then shifts to a figure from history before startling us with a personal confession of grief. Wojahn has spoken elsewhere about his belief that our individual experiences are "in a pact with memory beyond ourselves," and this poem works to bring that connection to light. First, read the unmarked poem and see what you notice about it. Then, I will demonstrate a few ways to open up its meaning. We may not have noticed exactly the same things, as poems can be read in many ways.

COLD GLOW: ICEHOUSES

Because the light this morning is recondite
like figures behind curtains from a long way off,
because the morning is cold and this room is heatless,
I've gone without sleep, I brood.
The protocol of memory: the faucet dripping
into a sponge, then thinking of the way
I saw White Bear Lake freeze over
twenty years ago in Minnesota, the carp oblivious below.

I thought last night of Solomon Petrov,
a Ukranian rabbi in my college science books
afflicted with total recall, a pathological memory
that made perspective impossible.
Once for doctors he *remembered* running for a train
in Petersburg in winter. They recorded
his quickened pulse, body temperature plunging.
The death by fever of his first wife Tania
was not remembered, but continually relived.

And memory is not accomplishment.
Last night again you described for me
our child pulled dead from your womb. In sleep you talked
to yourself and the child, who passed unnamed
wholly into memory. Now you wanted peace,
some distance. And every memory, said Solomon Petrov,
must proceed unchanged in the mind, going on
like smoke to designate itself again
like a second-floor window where I stood as a boy
to watch the fishermen park their cars
on the lake, icehouse lights in the evening below.

Or our child whose name is ash,
is only a thought too hurtful to free.
Mornings like these, he floats at the window, waiting
and mouthing his name, there through a tangent of ice,
his face and hands ashimmer.

COLD GLOW: ICEHOUSES

Because the light this morning is recondite

like figures behind curtains from a long way

   off,

because the morning is cold and this room is

   heatless,

I've gone without sleep, I brood.

The protocol of memory: the faucet

   dripping

into a sponge, then thinking of the way

I saw White Bear Lake freeze over

twenty years ago in Minnesota, the carp

   oblivious below.

I thought last night of Solomon Petrov,

a Ukranian rabbi in my college science books

afflicted with total recall, a pathological

   memory

that made perspective impossible.

Once for doctors he *remembered* running for

   a train

in Petersburg in winter. They recorded

his quickened pulse, body temperature

   plunging.

The death by fever of his first wife Tania

was not remembered, but continually

   relived.

Glow usually implies warmth, so expectations are undermined early.

Notice the harsh "k" **sounds** in first half of the poem—because, recondite, like, curtains, cold, etc.

W. uses unusual **diction**, so we have to work a bit. "Recondite" means "hard to understand," and we need to pause to get all its meanings, whereas we might think a simpler word like "dim" simply applied to the light. The image in the next line helps us get it, even if the word is unfamiliar.

W. uses several recurring **images**, but the iced-in carp become one of the most powerful by the end of the poem.

Notice the different times referred to throughout (underlined). The speaker jumps around in memory, but indicates the time of each.

The poem does not have regular meter or form, but the **rhythm** still works to aid the mood. Notice how over the first two stanzas, a predominance of long vowels gives way to short ones, perhaps like the feeling of waking up slowly, then beginning to tick off thoughts quickly.

Petrov's story takes us even further back in time, and W. recounts a tragedy in Petrov's life before in the third stanza focusing on his own.

And memory is not accomplishment.

Last night again you described for me

our child pulled dead from your womb.

   In sleep you talked

to yourself and the child, who passed

   unnamed

wholly into memory. Now you wanted peace,

some distance. And every memory, said Sol-

   omon Petrov,

must proceed unchanged in the mind, going

   on

like smoke to designate itself again

like a second-floor window where I stood as

   a boy

to watch the fishermen park their cars

on the lake, icehouse lights in the evening

   below.

Or our child whose name is ash,

   is only a thought too hurtful to free.

Mornings like these, he floats at the window,

   waiting

and mouthing his name, there through a

   tangent of ice,

his face and hands ashimmer.

We return to "last night" and the speaker's own tragedy and reason for insomnia.

Though "ch," "sh," soft "c" and "s" sounds have been used before, here they become more frequent, creating a whispering feel to the end of the poem.

This powerful image connects to the "cold glow" in that it upends our expectations for childbirth.

The speaker evokes Petrov again. At first he might seem a strange, irrelevant person, but the way his pathological memory forced him to relive his experiences reminds the speaker of the situation in which his partner constantly relives the stillbirth of their child. All of the disparate elements of the poem begin to coalesce.

The speaker also returns to his childhood memory and the morning where the poem started.

In the final stanza, W uses one of his rare **strong enjambments** with the line ending "waiting." Note how appropriate that is to the sense of being haunted and enduring through difficult times.

In the last image of the lost child, W. evokes the carp again, floating in the near-frozen lake. Both fish and infant seem distant and unaware of the death that awaits them (whether via ice fishing or stillbirth), yet are strongly remembered.

I've pointed out a few things about imagery, sound and rhythm, line breaks, and how Wojahn shifts us back and forth through time, the way one's mind might grasp at a variety of memories on a painfully sleepless night. What I encourage you to do individually, in groups, or as a class is to continue to explore this poem even more. With more readings, the poem continues to open its treasures to you.

Having just read Hemingway's story, we might also compare how differently felt is each couple's loss of a potential child. What else do you notice about the story and the poem when you begin to compare them? What other elements of inspiration and craft might help you clarify this comparison? You can apply these same reading skills to your favorite authors. (See **Pathway 3.7.**)

Notice also that you're developing a vocabulary for commenting on manuscripts for workshop, as discussed in Chapter 14. While more of the comments you make in that setting may be suggesting changes as well as noting elements of craft well-mastered, these readings demonstrate a good method of commenting on manuscripts.

PATHWAYS

Pathway 13.1. Literary social networking. Join an online literary social networking site. Goodreads.com, Shelfari.com, and Librarything.com all offer great, easy-to-use ways of talking with others about the books you love and the books that you are reading. They allow you to list, rate, organize, and comment on books. It's a great way to let others know what you think of a particular book and to get ideas for future reading from like-minded readers. Your teacher may want to assign particular groups or your entire class to create connections and share lists of books you have read or are currently reading. But you can also tailor your membership to your own reading needs and keep it going long after the class has ended.

Pathway 13.2. Read reviews. The social networking sites mentioned in **Pathway 13.1** (as well as most online booksellers) house millions of informal book reviews by average readers, but you might also want to find more professional book reviews to peruse every week or so. My own habit is to read the *New York Times Book Review* every week; when I see a book that interests me, I go and add it to my "want to read" list on Goodreads.

Pathway 13.3. Your reading. Write a short piece like Alexie's "Superman and Me" about what role reading played in your childhood.

Pathway 13.4. Branch out. Explore the work of new writers. For instance, you might look up writers you're introduced to in classes and read more of their work. Some of these writers you may not have read before, and yet they are highly accomplished storytellers, playwrights, and poets that may teach you a lot. Choose at least one writer in this book's anthology whose work you are drawn to, and read an entire book or another play by that person.

Pathway 13.5. Literary magazines. Sometimes we feel intimidated by "great authors." Reading more recent writing in literary magazines can be a way to try out writers who may or may not be famous, and there is a lot of great writing available for free in online literary magazines. Newpages (www.newpages.com) provides links to hundreds of publications. Peruse the available magazines in Newpages' "Big List of Literary Magazines" (www.newpages.com/literary-magazines/complete.htm) and pick one to order or subscribe to. What genres and styles can you identify? What do you learn from reading the author biographies or the submission guidelines? If you've been writing for a while, do you think your writing would fit alongside this work? Why or why not? If you're just starting out, what kind of inspiration do you find here?

Pathway 13.6. Imitation. Write a pastiche of Hemingway's "Hills Like White Elephants." This story is deceptively simple, clearly the result of much winnowing. We may not want to be as spare as he is all of the time, but he can teach us much about the carefully placed word or phrase in a story, about how behavior *reveals* emotion, and about economy of expression. In order to help you to think further about style and necessary elements, write a short-short story (one of two or so pages) similar in certain ways to "Hills Like White Elephants."

- It should contain only two main characters in a conflict of some sort.
- The conflict should never be stated outright, even though both are aware of what the underlying conflict is.
- Allow other, smaller, even trivial conflicts to arise as substitutes and symbols of the fundamental or more important conflict.
- Avoid using much description, but make the description you do use count. Pay special attention to the few well-placed richer words you use. Remember how the richer words in his first paragraph could be associated with the sexual. Try to use the connotations of words to create a similar (not necessarily sexual) underlying association in your story.
- Reflect on what worldview this minimalist style implies, and how that worldview and that style suit you. Is it an undue struggle for you to write this way, or does it come easily? What does that imply about your philosophies and attitudes?

Pathway 13.7. Mimic favorite passage. Now that you've tried out the pastiche method, choose one of your favorite, most beloved published paragraphs or a short passage—one you think particularly beautiful or effective—and alter the content but follow the sentence structure and style to learn how it works.

Chapter 14

After Brainstorming

KEY ANTHOLOGY READINGS

Tony Hoagland, "America" (poetry)

Al Zolynas, "Love in the Classroom" (poetry)

Michael Blumenthal, "On Not Bringing Your Mother
   to Creative Writing Class" (on writing)

Throughout this book, the Pathways provide brainstorming and development activities that constitute the beginnings and sometimes middles of the writing process. In this chapter, we focus on one unusual aspect of Creative Writing: the workshop and how it can enhance your revisions.

In most courses we take in school, we write something and then it's done. Even for a semester-long term paper, we seldom devote more than two or three months. This provides a good model for some of the writing done in the "real world." Journalism, grant writing, project reports, and other deadline-driven text production require that we complete work in a specific time frame. As my editor at a large magazine was fond of saying, "I don't need it to be perfect: I need it now." For those of us, however, who want to achieve artistic levels and/or pursue longer projects, this model falters. It may even give students of Creative Writing a wrong impression about the actual level of energy and time it takes for writers to produce a full-length novel or perfect their short work. "I have rewritten—often several times—every word I have ever written," noted Vladimir Nabokov in his memoir *Speak, Memory*. "My pencils outlast my erasers."

WHY WE WORKSHOP

The Creative Writing workshop is an unusual mode of teaching and learning, and it's therefore worth addressing how to make the most of your workshop experience, either in this course or in later courses you may take. Your course may include some lecture, small-group assignments, and peer-evaluation work;

it may include an online or other multimedia component as well. However, the classic Creative Writing workshop consists of all the students and their instructor gathered together in a circle to discuss student manuscripts one at a time. In most other fields, even if you work collaboratively and discuss your reading in small groups, you will be focused on received wisdom—great works of literature, scientific theories and data, mathematical formulas long ago worked out. That is not to say that those fields do not continue to evolve—they certainly do and you might be involved in exciting cutting-edge research even as an undergraduate. But to sit around in a room full of people with all their attention focused on *your* work occurs primarily in the arts.

Mind you, plenty of writers hone their craft and publish widely without ever having taken a workshop course. The workshop process has its pros and cons, and if you were to toss out a handful of rice in a crowd, you'd likely hit at least one workshop detractor, even among writers. Here we pause to take a look at the reasons why the Creative Writing workshop nonetheless prevails and what it can offer you.

Writing as Process

In your previous writing experiences, you might have heard terms like prewriting, free writing, brainstorming, outlining, planning, drafting, and revising. These are generally acknowledged, in that order, as the stages that we all go through as we produce any written work. First, we get ideas, then we use various means to develop them, then we concentrate on getting the ideas down, then we refine them. You may even have used peer evaluations or have had a teacher who reviewed your work and gave you feedback building up to your "final" draft or portfolio.

In Creative Writing, the same basic principles apply, but the process for individual writers often varies considerably and creative work follows few formulas. In fact, originality and difference, rather than predictability and businesslike efficiency, are valued. Perhaps because there remains more mystery in the success (or failure) of a piece of creative writing than most kinds of text, in this field we rely on the unusual process of mulling things over together in a group. We introduce workshop discussion and feedback between the stages of drafting and revising, placing more emphasis on exploring the myriad possible directions in which a piece of writing may be developed after its initial draft than in most other writing contexts.

We all almost always start with ugly first drafts. As you begin to put words on the page—whether it's for the first story or poem you've ever written or for the four hundredth—it will come out new and raw. It will need training. There are many analogies we can use. You might prefer to think of your early drafts as puppies, for instance. When you bring a puppy home from the dog shelter, it will no doubt be cute and pull at your heartstrings. Yet it will mess on your floor, chew up your shoes, and demand all kinds of attention before it will become a well-trained dog that will come when called and quit yanking on the leash. Not every dog will win obedience trials or best-in-show prizes—and we don't want to train the spirit out of them—but every dog given care will grow into its potential.

Think of your drafts as living things, things that will change and adapt, that have more potential for excellence than may be obvious the first time you see them typed as words on the page. Understand that even the first several drafts may not fulfill the original idea in your head, but that because words are infinitely malleable, they can continue to improve as long as you are invested in them. Let yourself write. Don't hold back. But know that you will come to the time of reckoning and that our early attempts can almost always be improved upon. Get in the habit of trying out different methods. (See **Pathway 14.1**.)

Discussion of your manuscript in a workshop implies the extent to which it might be improved. In fact, without this prospect, there would be little purpose to the workshop, and that's good to keep in mind when you are facing public commentary about your work, which can seem to be a grueling experience, especially the first time you experience it. You may be used to receiving written criticism from instructors, but seldom is such criticism discussed openly in a room with other participants. Many nonwriters who have witnessed Creative Writing workshops say, "I could never do that. It puts you on the spot so much. It must be really hard to bear." True—it can be hard—but if you are part of a supportive group, it can also be wonderfully productive. And it provides excellent training for a world in which tenacity and a willingness to take risks are highly valued and in which a person must not collapse at the merest of challenges.

Community

One of the main ways workshops are useful to writers is that discussion, interaction, and community form a counterbalance to the solitary act of writing itself. Although there are some writing projects that involve coauthoring or collaborative work—or in the case of plays and screenplays the future contributions of directors, actors, and designers—most writing is done alone at a computer keyboard. While this alone-time forms a significant, inevitable portion of the writer's life, and which we generally embrace, it can be lonely and make us distractible.

Having a community of your peers in a workshop gives you a set of like-minded individuals with whom to compare notes about the methods and strategies that work and don't work in your writing, as well as in your writing process. This doesn't always go smoothly, admittedly, but the workshop can reveal truths even when it's going awkwardly. Although there can be missteps there, the workshop remains "a very human situation," as long-term teacher Philip Gross puts it. Take a look at Tony Hoagland's "America" (p. 385) and Al Zolynas's "Love in the Classroom" (p. 535). Zolynas announces in his title that he feels powerful affection for his students and notes their efforts to please him. Hoagland, on the other hand, initially finds one of his students "full of shit." Yet both of these poems ultimately reveal the way in which the intense sharing of the writing class creates this vital encounter with our human qualities. This kind of encounter provides the heartbeat of great writing—both in the lives we draw from in our writing and in the workshop. (See **Pathway 14.2.**)

Although occasionally personality conflicts arise between writers in a group, you will also likely find "writer friends" who will help keep you focused and alleviate the sense of isolation. If you're interested in continuing as a writer after the course, I encourage you to exchange information with the writers whose work shares sensibilities with your own and continue these friendships outside of class. Most writers rely over their careers for the support, encouragement, and sometimes goad of their writer-friends, which is discussed more in Chapter 15.

Testing Ground

In Creative Writing circles, you'll notice that the word "workshop" is used not just as a noun but also as a verb. We "workshop" in order to test our writing and the effects we hope it will have on readers. Workshop readers differ from our family and close friends outside of writing—those people may encourage us too much out of loyalty and affection or discourage us too much because of a lack of understanding of our writing's possibilities. Let those people read your work, too, if you wish—they provide an "everyman" or "everywoman" perspective with its own value—but remember that more knowledgeable and dispassionate perspectives will likely help you improve your writing more. Your teacher will be more experienced, but as you and your classmates gain understanding, you will bring additional eyes and ideas to the discussion of each other's work.

One of the other fundamental assumptions of the workshop, then, is that you will be writing for others to read. This may seem obvious, but it's not uncommon to hear someone say when faced with feedback in a workshop, "Well, I just wrote it to please myself." If you truly want to write only for yourself, then there is no need to go beyond the diary form and no need to show it to anyone else, *ever.* Many diaries (of well-known people) do end up being published, and certainly many a popular blog began with a much smaller audience of friends and family in mind. But everyone in a workshop is testing his or her work for a potentially wider audience.

You may be surprised by how far your original vision for your work is from what you have actually put on paper. The character you thought showed admirable grit and spirit may be seen by your peers as pig-headed and unappealing. Someone may note that a description of your favorite place is marred by clichés. Or you may realize—before anyone even says anything—that your language could be more precise—"lavender" would be far better a word than "purple" in capturing a sense of shimmering early-morning light. Workshops should provide a safe place for you to have these realizations before you someday seek publication and send your work out on its own. (See **Pathway 14.3.**)

Knowing Thyself

As you participate in workshops, you should also develop an awareness of what particular strategies work best for you. For many types of writing, you may have been instructed about formulas for developing your ideas—starting with a thesis statement, for instance, or outlining specific steps in your paper. There are formulas in creative writing, too—for instance, you might think of Freytag's pyramid as one—but creative writing tends to be much more idiosyncratic and unpredictable. Just as writers strive for unique and recognizable styles in their writing, they often indulge eccentricities in their habits and methods. Workshops are a great place to share ideas about how, where, when, and under what circumstances we write, though we can't be prescriptive. Each writer has to do what works for him or her.

For instance, writing well takes something of a split consciousness. While you will probably lean more to one side or the other, all writers must both be able to get on a roll, accessing their deepest emotions, and also be able to step back, organize their thoughts, and criticize their own work. Some writers start with a kind of outpouring where thoughts and words flow quickly and they pay little attention to grammar and so forth. Other writers tend to start with an outline or a list of scenes and proceed much more methodically. There are, of course, many variations on work habits and patterns, but it helps to know what your tendency is. Then if you have a poem, story, essay, or play that isn't working out, you can think about trying something different. Knowing your own habits as a writer will often help you think of new ways to stay on track. (See **Pathway 14.4.**)

You may not even notice that you have a set of writing habits until you encounter that dreaded phenomenon of writer's block—a common, usually short-term period when a person just can't seem to write. Should you encounter writer's block—and most writers do at some point or another—remember that many problems in the writing itself can be traced back to a disruption or dysfunction in the process that you are using. If you have a sense of what your own personal process is, then you are far more likely to be able to identify how to help yourself and your writing. Sometimes changing one small habit is enough to get your words flowing again.

HOW WE WORKSHOP

Different instructors conduct workshops with different rules of the road. Some instructors disallow the author who's up for discussion from speaking during the process; others merely ask that the writer refrain from overexplaining or defending his or her own work, but allow the writer to answer and ask questions. Some ask that the work—or a selected part—be read aloud by the author or another workshop member. Most of the time, workshops consist of an entire class discussing the work; other times students workshop in smaller groups. Some are done completely online, others face to face without written commentary, though even most face-to-face workshops demand careful commentary in writing as well as in conversation.

There are reasons behind all these various choices. They may be based on practicality—how many students there are in a course, how often you meet and how much class time you have, whether an online class is synchronous or asynchronous. Or they may be based on deeply philosophical choices about empowerment and participation. It is fair for you to expect the particular practices of your course to be explained clearly to you, but you should understand that they may not be the same from one course to another. Because of this, these guidelines are somewhat general, and you will likely refine them for the particular process and success of your course.

However, one commonality among all workshops is that their goal is to help the writer improve the work at hand. You have analyzed your reading in many other contexts before, but this may be quite different in its method. When we read our peers' manuscripts in workshops, we want to keep in mind that the purposes are different from those of a review, which is written to help *readers*, or a paper in a literature course, which is to help other *scholars* and *critics* think in new ways about work they have studied but not written themselves. Instead, our critiques will be designed to help the *writers* themselves. **Table 14.1** charts similarities and differences between reading for reviewing, scholarship, and workshops, and **Pathway 14.5** allows you to practice this distinction.

Giving Comments

- Workshop should not be an endeavor where we tell other people how to write their work. It may seem like that at times, and suggestions abound, but as you critique, remember that the purpose is to assist the *writer* in better fulfilling his or her vision, not to change the vision to your own. You may call into question the writer's vision, but always respect the author's ownership of that work.
- Read manuscripts well in advance of class time. Read the manuscript at least twice—once for an overall impression and again to look at the details of how it is working as a piece of writing. You will want your own work to be read carefully and with respect, so please do that for others in return.
- Be productive, neither overly harsh nor overly generous. In other words, be honest, but diplomatic, never vicious. Remember to offer praise as well as criticism, as sometimes your fellow authors may not be sure of what's strongest in their work.

Table 14.1
Types of Commentary. Comparison of reading and writing for reviews, scholarly literary criticism, and workshop critiques.

Similarities			
	All three contain some evaluation, beyond just description.		
	Almost always, there should be a balance between praise and criticism or a sense of proportion. Outright trashing a work or over-the-top adoration indicates a bias or laziness rather than a helpful engagement with the text.		
	All use the vocabulary of the craft elements and discuss some aspects of the subjects of Chapters 1 through 12, as well as the genre designations described in the **Destination** chapters.		
Differences			
	Reviews	**Literary Criticism**	**Workshop Critiques**
	The most based on evaluation or judgment	May include implicit judgment, but focuses much more on interpretation	May evaluate whether elements are working but focuses on helping the author to see rather than judging
	Written to help readers choose books	Written for readers within a community of scholars to discuss ideas about literature, culture, and history	Written for the author of the work to help make it better
	Found online in Goodreads and in professional book review sites; also in newspapers and magazines	Found in literature courses and scholarly journals and books	Found in creative writing courses and workshops; sometimes an editor will also do this kind of reading

(Continued)

Table 14.1   (Continued)

	Reviews	Literary Criticism	Workshop Critiques
	Must include overview (such as plot summary) since readers won't have yet read the work	Usually includes an overview to give context	Doesn't need an overview since the author and any other workshop participants will have read the same thing
	Because of the brevity of the form, uses only brief quotes to give flavor	Quotes generously from text to prove points	Can include occasional quote as an example of what you mean, but usually done right on manuscript pages
	Readers will not have the work in front of them	Readers won't have the work in front of them, but may have it nearby for reference	Everyone should have the same manuscript in front of them for constant reference
	Short and in brief paragraph form	Long and often containing sections and long block quotes and footnotes	Combines marginal comments and underlining or highlighting right on manuscript as well as an "end comment" to summarize impressions
	Uses only a few select details to give a flavor; concentrates on overview	Attends to details to draw out an overall argument about the meaning or importance of the work	Attends to both how details are contributing to the whole work and how the manuscript is working overall

- It can even be helpful to divorce from the idea of "positive" and "negative" feedback and focus on strategies like "pointing," where you make observations, such as "New character introduced on p. 4" or "Style shift here." Your comments should facilitate the writer's exploring further development and making choices about where the work will go next, not merely fixing up errors.

- Remember that it's fine to have initial emotional reactions to what you read, but you must go beyond that to help the writer understand how it is working and not working. It is never enough just to say, "I didn't like this story" or "I loved this poem." You need to offer practical observations and suggestions, so that your group learns specifically *how* to succeed.

- Make both **marginal comments**—written in the margins as you read and encounter powerful images or moments of confusion—and an **end comment** of at least several lines summarizing what you think of the piece's strengths and weaknesses overall.

- Remember to address several layers: content, organization, style, as well as punctuation and grammar. You may also write more succinct reactions—"good," "awesome," "weird," "I don't understand," "confusing," "funny," and so forth. Remember that marginal comments help explain and support the overall impression your end comment suggests.

- If you are stumped about how to comment or what to say, go back to the various elements you have discussed in class or recently read about in the book and try to think of how each one is handled in the poem, essay, story, or play under consideration. Use the **Destination** lists to help focus your comments.

- I also suggest that you make sure to sign your name to your comments. On a practical level, that way it is easy for classmates to check with you about anything they can't read or don't fully understand. In addition, we should all be willing to stand behind our comments, and including your name will help you keep a helpful and productive tone.

Tips for Making Your Workshop Productive

- Creative writing workshops are often very open and casual, but keep in mind the professional purposes and maintain a focus on these. Most Creative Writing courses, for instance, allow for the use of any language that seems appropriate in a given piece of writing. A character may even insult another character with profanity. However, that does not mean that such language is appropriate between students within a discussion session. Maintain professional respect.

- Know when to let go. Sometimes you may feel very strongly that a certain change should be made in someone else's manuscript. Debating such points is central to the workshop process, but you must also know when to move on in the limited time you have.

- Listen to what other people are saying. You might note verbally that you agree with another comment, but try to bring up new points instead of repeating already-made ones. One practice that I enjoy is asking the class to rap on their desks or the table when they agree with a comment; that gives an excellent sense of how many share a perception without anyone having to repeat the point. (And it's fun.)

- Remember that you and all of your peers are commenters-in-training, just as you are writers-in-training, and cut each other some slack in this regard. Not every comment will be helpful. If someone makes a comment awkwardly, try not to take offense. You will all be experimenting with that line between going too easy and being too harsh. Don't take it personally if someone errs a bit on either side.

Receiving Comments

- First, remember that it is your *manuscript* and not *you* that is being evaluated.
- Sometimes it can be overwhelming to receive a whole pile of marked-up manuscripts. What do you do with all those comments? What if some of them conflict with each other? What if you think some of them are off the wall? First, remember that the piece of writing is still *yours*, and you are the one to make decisions about what to do. As the writer, you always have to sift through workshop comments and decide which ones are most useful and sympathetic with your sensibilities. The goal of workshop is never to produce "committee-written" writing.
- Often it helps to develop a strategy for going through the manuscripts you receive back from a class. Read through all the comments and see if there are any commonalities—things that come up over and over again. You may want to transfer major comments to a separate, clean manuscript, selecting the most helpful comments as you go through and ending up with a master copy to work with as you revise. Or you may simply want to make a list of main points that you can then organize before you set to work.
- You'll often find that even when some of your classmates make what seem like opposite comments, they are still pointing to the same problem. For instance, one person might say, "I really like this character, and I'd like you to do more with her," whereas another will say, "This character isn't central to the story—just get rid of her." Obviously, there's an issue with this character. *You* will have to decide how important she is to your vision of the story and whether to delete her or further develop her. Learn to look at comments not always for the solution they offer you, but for simply the issues they point out.
- If you remain overwhelmed by the amount or nature of comments you've received, ask your instructor to help you sort them out. And remember that your instructor's comments will be based on the most experience and may be the most valuable of them all.

REVISION

"Good writing," as Truman Capote put it, "is rewriting." Many writers continue working on one idea or even one piece of writing for years, even decades. Poet Dean Young is particularly articulate about the tensions inherent in the sometimes arduous process of revision. "We must risk a loss of passionate connection," he notes in *The Art of Recklessness*, "to distance ourselves from our work, to grow a little cold to it in order to revise, in order to look at a poem as a series of decisions. . . . At this point, we insist on writing being a series of devices." This can, Young says, be a "trauma," but it is necessary.

However universal the process of revising is, there is no one right way to do it. I offer here some suggestions that students have found useful over the years and that you and your instructor can adapt to your particular situations and purposes.

- Think about how much time away from a manuscript you'll need to develop the detached eye necessary for clear-headed revision. Try to find the sweet spot between still being connected to intense feelings that inspired your writing and feeling so much distance that you no longer care about it. The latter isn't likely to happen in one short semester, but it's worth noting for your future writing what these time frames are for you.
- Don't be afraid to try things. Many times we are hesitant to really change our original precious words. We get defensive about our first vision, and sometimes we hesitate to really dig in and significantly alter a manuscript. We tend to make merely cosmetic changes—like a new manicure or a new haircut—instead of performing the radical surgery that could remove the malignant tumor from our story or poem. If you find yourself refusing to try something even though you thought it was a good idea, ask yourself what you have to lose. You might lose an hour or two or three, but if you save the earlier version of your manuscript you can always go back to it should your radical surgery fail. A piece of writing differs from a human life: you get as many chances as you want and your writing is almost infinitely malleable. **Pathways 14.6** and **14.7** offer a couple of methods for opening up your work beyond fixing minor errors.
- On the other hand, resist the urge to start over and write something completely different instead of revising. Trust that you did write something of value and that your first interest in your subject or idea contains at least a seed of genuine merit. Save a new idea for a new piece.
- Always, always, always start your revision in a new version of your computer document. This should allow you to produce even radical changes freely and without fear because you will still have a copy of your original manuscript should your revision go awry. This seldom happens, but it can, and your revisions will be much less constrained if you have the security blanket of saved multiple versions. Create a system for keeping track—most people add a

number to the title of their original document, like so: My Story2. You may end up with My Story8 before you know it, and that usually benefits the work.

- You may also want to keep a "scrap" file for passages that you delete from your original manuscript. Even though these should still be available in the original document if you're working with a second version, it sometimes helps to have these passages separated out. You can go back and see if there are any additional story, essay, poem, or play ideas embedded there. Perhaps you decided that your current manuscript was too full of other images or ideas and that these didn't fit, but that doesn't mean that you can't pursue them separately at a later time. In this way, your scrap document can become part of your journal or other idea file and provide inspiration should you feel in need of new ideas to pursue.

- Think of revision as a multi-step process in itself. You may comb through your manuscript several times looking at a different issue each time. Often it is easier to do this rather than try to hold in your mind all the different aspects that need work at once. You may go back and forth between this kind of focused work and a more holistic approach where you step back and just read like any reader.

- In particular, start revising the "larger" issues first, then move through a process of refinement. For instance, if you are going to be deleting or adding large chunks of text, then there's no use correcting spelling errors at that stage. Large-scale issues might include overall organization and structure, major character development, trying out a different point of view, adding clearer setting or backstory, developing exposition into scene (or the reverse), and so on. After you've worked on these issues, move to middle-scale issues, such as transitions, paragraph coherence and flow, varieties of sentence structure, tweaking figurative language and diction, and so on. Then and only then move to the details of correct grammar, punctuation, and spelling. The issues, of course, will differ when you are revising poems, but when you work on an entire set of poems for a portfolio, it can still be helpful to conceive of them as a larger entity; for instance, perhaps before you begin working on individual poems, you want to think about what order you'll put them in and how they resonate with each other.

- When you start revising, it's often helpful to write down two or three main goals for this particular revision. If you understand that revision may be an ongoing process for some time, you'll understand that this revision won't necessarily be the last. So, what do you want to concentrate on *this time*? Keep focused on those aspects.

- Revision takes an overlapping but distinct set of skills from writing first drafts, and you might want to try creating a separate space in your life for it. For instance, if you write late at night, you might want to try revising during the day.

Ideally, revision involves just as much creativity and inspiration as writing the first draft. Too often, however, we try to cram it into a short period of time at the end of a semester when we are exhausted by deadlines and other projects, and it therefore becomes an object of dread. If you begin thinking about your revisions earlier and grant them the same openness, excitement, and solid time that you give to your first drafts, you will find revising a pleasure as you watch your work achieve new insight, depth, and beauty. If you know from the beginning of your writing process that you're on a journey—sometimes unpredictable, sometimes filled with false turns, but usually one that will end with a stronger poem, story, essay, or play—you will have the courage and energy to stick with it. And stick with it you must, in order to continue to develop as a writer.

PATHWAYS

Pathway 14.1. Sentence tweaking. Choose an opening of one of the poems, essays, stories, or plays you've written. Then rewrite it at least ten times with the same basic meaning, but altering sentence structure, vocabulary, tone, and complexity. You could even change the perspective from which events or objects are viewed. Try your variations out and see what impact they have on your piece. Read different versions to people and see which one pulls them in the most.

Pathway 14.2. Workshop poem. Write your own poem (like Zolynas and Hoagland) about the workshop experience—the camaraderie, the hostility, the ego, the vulnerability, the different personalities, the shared concerns, the sense of safe haven or lion's den or other way you feel about the experience. For once, don't share it with the class, but tuck it away to look at in a year or two and see how it brings the experience back to you.

Pathway 14.3. Missives. One day when you're out beyond your usual campus haunts, try giving out copies of a piece of your work—on the bus, at the airport, at the grocery store. This could be a single poem or a small folded flyer or chapbook of prose. Making copies can get expensive, so only make ten or so to give out. Make sure to include a "pass it on" message (else it be immediately thrown away). Think about how it feels to have your work out there on its own.

Pathway 14.4. Habits. Make a list that describes your writing habits—times of day, days of the week, frequency, locations, props (cigarettes, candy, music, journals), and so on. Think of as many as possible. Then, over the next week or so, try changing one of these habits—write more often, write in a different place, turn off (or on) the music—and see what happens.

Pathway 14.5. Practice critiques. After you've looked carefully at **Table 14.1**, choose a short amateur video from the Internet. Watch it three times, the first time jotting notes about how you might review it for other potential viewers, then how you might approach it through a scholarly lens (what it says about our culture, how its technical effects work, what physics principles are in operation, or whatever other field you want to draw on), then how you would express your reaction to the video's maker in the interest of kindly helping that person make an even better video next time. Share these in class and discuss what the differences are.

Pathway 14.6. Cut-up exercise. Print out one of your complete manuscripts printed on one side of the page only. Number on the right side of the page each and every separate paragraph (or if working on poetry or drama, label each line, stanza, or bit of dialogue). Then cut them all apart and begin rearranging your piece. Allow this to be a fluid process, but think about what different organizational principle you might use. Instead of chronology, for instance, you might try a reverse chronology or a set of image associations that make the piece less linear. (This can be especially effective in poetry.) Work this into as good a new shape as you can, and then tape all the pieces together in page-size lots. Then go back to your computer and retype a new document or open a new copy of your earlier document and create a new draft, adjusting and creating needed transitions along the way. What do you learn about your original draft?

Pathway 14.7. Minimizing. Create a new copy of one of your manuscripts and delete as much as possible out of it. That will likely mean every adverb, adjective, and even some articles. But it might also mean taking out nonessential characters and background material. Whittle at least in half. This will not likely be the final version of your work that you'll want to keep, but it will be a great way to see what the skeleton of your piece consists of. Then you can go back in and restore enriching parts or alter the background and details you had to make them more relevant. You will learn which aspects of setting, description, and plot are most crucial.

Chapter **15**

The Literary
vs. Genre Debate

KEY ANTHOLOGY READINGS

Italo Calvino, "All at One Point" (fiction)

Stuart Dischell, "She Put on Her Lipstick in the Dark" (poetry)

Leon Stokesbury, "Unsent Message to My Brother in His Pain" (poetry)

Pablo Neruda, "Your Feet" (poetry)

Toni Morrison, "Peril" (on writing)

This chapter will make some people mad, maybe even you. Maybe even your instructor. Talking about literary quality is a dicey proposition because, no matter how much we share standards, it remains somewhat subjective. That's not the same as *completely* subjective or *only* a matter of opinion, but it means that no one correct answer will satisfy everyone the way it might for a calculus problem or a question about the location of the pineal gland deep between the two hemispheres of the brain. Of course, if you rise to the level of math theory or look at variations of human and animal anatomy, you will uncover that norms are debatable in those areas as well. But when someone writes a bad story, no bridge falls down, no oil rig explodes into flames, and no one dies on the operating table. This makes our work in some ways less fraught—we are not likely to kill anyone—but in other ways more fraught—it can be difficult to tell great writing from so-so or even poor writing. We often even enjoy or find useful writing that does not meet the standards of literature.

I offer no gospel here, but merely open the door for discussions among you and your classmates and instructor. For some years, the writing world has separated out "literary" writing from what is most often called "genre" writing in the fiction world, "hack" writing in the nonfiction world, "doggerel" in the poetry world, and "skits" in the world of drama, or by other similar language. Often these terms have been used to dismiss or insult writing in those categories, and this has given rise to a fair amount of understandable resentment on the part of their practitioners and devotees. However, it has not been without reason that we have categorized the Harlequin romance novel as inferior to the novels of Jane Austen and Charlotte Brontë, or questionable self-help books like *Chicken Soup for the Soul* and *The Happiness Project* as less profound than James Baldwin's *Notes of a Native Son* or Henry Adams's *The Education of Henry Adams*.

Parallel debates exist for all genres, but the ones about literary vs. genre fiction, in particular, sometimes grow to a level of melodramatic invective all their own. However, today, some terms of these debates shift and slide. The popularity of genres such as science fiction and fantasy—partly fueled by the predominance of ever more sophisticated and believable special effects at the movies—and the general decline in reading for pleasure have forced the major publishing houses to place more emphasis on genre fiction. Small publishers are stepping in to provide a forum for those who write literary and experimental fiction (and some are still published by major houses), but some authors wish to appeal to a wider readership, and many writers also have a genuine dedication to genre work that influenced them. For both of these reasons, some writers with the finest literary chops have begun to work—if not in genre fiction per se—with genre elements. Some writing partakes of both genre elements and literary excellence.

It can be difficult in this environment to tell a sell-out from someone forging new ground, and you may sometimes wonder about the motivations of an author who includes elements of romance, sci-fi, fantasy, action-adventure, crime, spy, mystery, and other genres. Writers, however, have always struggled between the necessities of economics and those of art. What we have to be willing to do is examine the work itself and see what we find there.

GENRE FICTION AND ACADEMIC VALUES

When I use the term "genre fiction," I don't mean each and every work that contains magic, ghosts, murders, spaceships, or even vampires. Mary Shelley's *Frankenstein* is not genre fiction. Neither is Margaret Atwood's *Oryx and Crake* (futuristic post-apocalypse), Gabriel García Márquez's *One Hundred Years of Solitude* (magic), Muriel Spark's *The Driver's Seat* (murder), or Henry James's *The Turn of the Screw* (ghosts).

On the other hand, few people will argue for much in the way of lasting value for certain series-oriented work, such as the Twilight or Echelon books, perhaps even the entire book list for Harlequin romances. L. Ron Hubbard, James Patterson, Robert Ludlum, Terry Goodkind—these writers may have earned a lot of money and may have provided many an hour of entertainment, but few would claim they have created work of enduring importance except as a phenomenon, perhaps of interest to sociologists but not to those who study the nuances of language and writing. Nonetheless, many writers work within genre categories and simultaneously sometimes aspire to more than the most basic level of entertainment. Though they may not step far outside the confines of their genres, we admire their work and its cultural significance—Stephen King, Harlan Ellison, Ray Bradbury, J. R. R. Tolkien, and J. K. Rowling, for instance.

So, it might be useful to think of three basic categories, understanding all the while that there are no hard and fast lines—1) "trash" writers (which we may still enjoy), 2) genre writers whose work transcends its genre in some ways, and 3) literary writers who completely break down the boundaries and make the literary indistinguishable from genre. Several stories in the Anthology of this book provide examples of the literary use of otherworldly and futuristic elements. Italo Calvino's "All at One Point" (p. 303) is part of a collection of stories, *Cosmicomics*, that focuses on scientific theories and brings them to life through whimsical reinterpretations. Author Salman Rushdie calls it "possibly the most enjoyable story collection ever written," and notes that it "combines scientific erudition, wild fantasy and a humane wit." The story, like much science fiction, takes place in outer space in a futuristic-seeming past before the Big Bang theoretically occurred, but "All at One Point" engages language and meaning at a literary level. It is entirely possible to employ some of the conventions of genres you like without abandoning the challenges and rewards of ambitious writing. Note also the ways in which Julio Cortázar, David James Poissant, and Karen Russell create fable-like qualities and play with our usual sense of reality.

Much of the debate about literary vs. genre fiction assumes that literary fiction is "realist" or "naturalist" writing, and, although this has been perhaps mostly true it has never been narrowly true. In most Creative Writing courses, you will be asked to write in this vein, though different instructors feel more comfortable with some genre elements than others. Some Creative Writing instructors forbid sci-fi or other recognizably genre elements. There are reasons for this, the main one being that much work that we would categorize as purely genre has been written to a set formula for a mass paperback market and has little ambition other than to sell books to readers who like repeated similar experiences. These books are not known for their artistic, revelatory qualities.

I like to compare them to McDonald's hamburgers. They are made the same way, over and over and over and over and over again. We've all eaten them—and at times they even tasted great because we were hungry, had high caloric need, or wanted something familiar. In fact, some hamburgers are indeed better than others—some restaurants use a better quality of beef than others or give you fresher fixings. Some restaurants now offer sirloin burgers with blue cheese, caramelized onions, or other fancy ingredients. No matter how high the quality, however, they are still hamburgers. You don't need to attend chef school to become a fry cook.

On the other hand, what if you want to make something more complicated? Beef bourguignon or mole sauce or baklava? While each of these dishes has a basic definition, even fundamental similarities in their various recipes, they require skill, delicacy, and gustatory sensitivity to make well. They may acknowledge a debt of precedence—the wide variety of mole recipes, for instance, have been passed down through generations of families—but it is common with these dishes for chefs to put their own personal touches on them and to innovate outside traditional bounds. These aren't always snooty or fancy recipes—the slow simmering beef bourguignon, for example, started off as a way that country people could do other tasks while a meal cooked and allowed them to tenderize tough cuts of meat. However, it takes skill to prepare and over the years has become a much refined classic of French cuisine. And what if you want to take your girlfriend or boyfriend or spouse out for a special dinner? You sit down to a table set for a six-course meal, and you will find silverware you may not be sure what to do with or how to use. Once someone shows you or you figure out how to eat it, you will usually find the meal not just good, but excellent. You may taste things you've never tasted before.

This analogy might give some tangible sense of why most Creative Writing programs do not teach straight genre-fiction writing. There are people who do those things well—and there are even a few academic programs that do specialize in them or offer courses (as they do in children's book writing). Briefly put, the reasons these genres are not usually central are threefold:

- A lot of genre fiction requires little instruction to read, to understand, or to emulate—you can generally appreciate that on your own;
- Workshops are labor intensive, demanding small classes and a lot of individualized instruction; it is only more nuanced writing tasks that deserve and require this intensive attention; and
- Colleges and universities are places of intellectual and higher learning, and they place value on the arts beyond their commercial appeal; the expectation for both instructors and students in Creative Writing is that we will participate in these loftier purposes of higher education.

These reasons contain within them deep issues of debate and cognitive dissonance. National discussions about the "dumbing down" of higher education run parallel with attacks on the "elitism" or "out of touch" nature of academia. This is a similar debate to the one about "literary" vs. "genre" fiction and other forms of less-than-highbrow writing. Whichever way you lean in these debates, the situation now is that Creative Writing programs will expect you to respect literary values and qualities in your work. Don't, however, assume that means no magic or murder in your pages. (See **Pathways 15.1, 15.2,** and **15.3.**)

THE MANY ROLES OF WRITERS IN SOCIETY

Early in this book, I ask you to think about your motivations for wanting to write. A closely related issue has to do with what purpose your writing itself might have in the world, beyond the individual goals it fulfills for you. Obviously, these two things will influence each other—if your main desire in wanting to write is to seek fame and wealth in Hollywood or to become the next Stephenie Meyer cranking out Twilight novels, then that will delimit your potential purposes. On the other hand, if you want to write challenging and perhaps difficult work in the tradition of the language poets, your work may have lasting impact but within a smaller sphere. If you are motivated mainly for reasons of psychological healing, then you may not even seek a public venue for your writing. Just as there are many paths to becoming a writer, there are a variety of personal and social functions writing fulfills. How you feel about genre fiction—or nonliterary nonfiction, poetry, or plays—may have to do with your attitudes about the larger purposes of creative works.

By way of contrast, if you decide to be a veterinarian, you have one main professional purpose—to keep animals alive and well. There may be secondary purposes (supporting your family, helping pet owners when they lose a beloved animal, keeping the public safe from rabies, and so on), and you may choose particular settings and specialties (whether to work with domestic pets, horses and farm animals, exotics, or in a zoo setting), but the overarching mission of your work remains clear and straightforward.

Writers as a group have no such singular direction. Even if we whittle off categories of writing such as journalism, business and technical writing, grant writing, report writing, and so on, and focus only on so-called creative writing, there are myriad ways we might conceive of ourselves and our contributions to society. Through the Guideposts in this book, we have focused on "transferable skills" that the study of Creative Writing might bring to other realms, but here I want to pause and talk about the "usefulness" of the practice of writing creatively. We should never forget that creative writing matters in and of itself.

Entertainment "versus" Enlightenment

In taking on the literary vs. genre debate, we're engaging the issue of what we should value most about the many roles our writing can play. Most of the time, the choices writers have in this regard are discussed along the binary terms of entertainment *versus* enlightenment, as though the two do not overlap. However, even much entertainment writing becomes a source of social commentary and criticism. Early science fiction writers such as H. G. Wells, Aldous Huxley, Ray Bradbury, Ursula Le Guin, and Harlan Ellison are known today as classics of social criticism. Humorists such as David Sedaris and P. J. O'Rourke, albeit in very different ways, both comment on social mores and politics in the contemporary world. By definition, of course, going to see a play or movie entertains us, while the best of them also inspire in us broader understanding—as examples, consider the movie *Dr. Strangelove*, with its satirical look at war-mongering, or the more recent gay-focused *Brokeback Mountain* or the anti-totalitarian *V for Vendetta*. As Michael Chabon, who has himself written novels that combine genre elements with literary aspirations, notes, "Entertainment is a sacred pursuit when done well. When done well, it raises the quality of human life."

So, while entertainment and enlightenment are not the same thing, they are by no means mutually exclusive. In many ways, the entertainment potential opens us up to the deeper meanings that many works of writing contain. Writing that aspires to artistic merit usually emphasizes these deeper meanings, but whatever motivates your own writing, try not to think in divisive terms. Allow your motivations to grow, accumulate, and shift over time.

Sympathy and Social Change

Probably the most widely offered rationale for the importance of literature is that it reflects reality back to us for a closer look and helps us to understand the reality in which we live, in terms both of our general human qualities and also the particulars of our time. We can see our world more clearly once it has been distilled into poems, essays, stories, and plays. The conversion of experience into writing gives not only the writer, but readers as well, enough distance that our vision clears. This helps us to understand our cultural moment, the social forces that influence human behavior, and the prevalent attitudes that may seem normal as we live them, but which are actually highly contingent on a variety of factors.

In this way, writing offers the opportunity to affect the way that readers see the world around them. As C. S. Lewis put it, "Literature adds to reality, it does not simply describe it." If we see when we glance in the mirror on our way out the door to school or work that something green is stuck in our teeth, we can remove it. This might mean we get the job or the person we have a crush on responds positively. In a larger way, literature allows us to raise awareness of inhumane situations, to foster sympathy for people different from ourselves, to show the world the horror of something everyone else seems to be ignoring.

To be able to see large-scale social change as the direct result of a piece of writing is, however, rare. There are rousing speeches, such as Martin Luther King, Jr.'s "I Have a Dream," and books, plays, and movies that gradually help to shift social consciousness, such as Rachel Carson's nonfiction environmental meditation *Silent Spring* and Tony Kushner's poignant take on the AIDS crisis in his play *Angels in America*. However, few creative writers want their work to be merely a form of political activism. If we did, we would more likely simply turn directly to political activism. In the realm of creative writing—though the line often blurs— we are committed to writing from something other than a desire to impose a political agenda. Otherwise we would be writing propaganda, and although that is always a choice writers have, like advertising and instruction manuals, it is not what we usually aspire to as creative writers. Instead, we often seek to create a world and individuals more aware of themselves, more open to others, and more open to cultural change. The manifesto assignment in Pathway 6.7 can be revisited over time to make you aware of issues you can speak to.

Respecting and Affecting the Individual

Most often, as novelist Russell Banks notes, "Change occurs only at the edges, one human being at a time." It isn't so much that authors write with a fixed social or political agenda in mind, but that they reflect the importance of individual consciousness and the value of each person's existence. In your own workshop, you will see a variety of imagistic impressions and points of view—some may be basically optimistic, others darker than dark. Some will reflect values and beliefs that you do not share, or will ask you to think of something in a new way. One of the main things we do in our classes is foster an appreciation of this diversity of purpose and message.

Yet, even though we experience the possibility of our own self-expression as an individual thing, its importance goes beyond each of us. Collectively, the activity of creating new writing works against repression and asserts that each person's life has meaning and potential for greatness. This may seem most obvious when we talk about forms of nonfiction like the memoir, which has seen a rise in popularity and which often nowadays reflects some particular aspect of an otherwise ordinary person's life story, as opposed to that of a celebrity or historical figure. But this is also true for the fictionalized lives we see in novels, plays, and movies as well and in the distilled visions of poems.

In the practice of writing, we have the opportunity to explore the very particular aspects of our personalities, beliefs, and circumstances. Sometimes this very insistence puts us at odds with a world in which we may be seen as functionaries or employees, here to fulfill a certain role, rather than as quirky individuals with a right to exist for our own sake. (See **Pathway 15.4.**)

Writing as Rebellion

Often this willingness to plumb the depths of our own experience renders writers a little bit "different." Notoriously, we say what might not otherwise be expressed in polite company. In fact, the stereotype of artists of all kinds—whether writers, painters, or musicians—often includes an element of downright craziness. Lord Byron was most famously described as "mad, bad, and dangerous to know," and many writers embrace this role of social rebel.

One important distinction in this regard has to do with the difference between behavioral rebellion for its own sake and more serious intellectual rebellion that sets some writers at odds with their governments or societies (or other governments and societies). In many countries with repressive forms of government, writers really do risk their own lives and liberty to write what they believe, or to write expressively at all. The Russian-Jewish novelist Isaac Babel, for instance, underwent arrest, imprisonment, and execution at the hands of the Stalinist government between 1939 and 1940, simply for resisting the channeling of his work into propaganda. More recently, after the release of his novel *The Satanic Verses* in 1988, Indian-British author Salman Rushdie received a death sentence from an imam in Iran who disapproved of the book; he spent years in hiding and in fear for his life, with a nearly three-million-dollar bounty on his head. In many parts of the world, writers are still frequently arrested, even murdered; PEN International sponsors an annual Day of the Imprisoned Writer every November 15. Journalists take the brunt of such arrests, but sometimes poets, novelists, and playwrights are attacked simply because the backdrop of their work reflects their misgivings about the systems in which they live. Imagine, if you can, being threatened with punishment or imprisonment for writing a story in which a police officer misbehaved or a character grew bored waiting in line at an over-bureaucratized driver's license bureau.

Sometimes, however, even work that later seems to contain no major political content threatens the societal status quo. The Marquis de Sade, for instance, had no intention of overthrowing any government, but his ribald writing about violent sexual practices and criticism of the Catholic Church made him so objectionable to late-eighteenth-century mores that he ended up in an insane asylum for the better part of his adult life. Even short of imprisonment, numerous writers' work has been suppressed by being banned or denied publication. James Joyce's *Ulysses*, D. H. Lawrence's *Lady Chatterley's Lover*, Henry Miller's *Tropic of Cancer*, Vladimir Nabokov's *Lolita*, Kurt Vonnegut's *Slaughterhouse-Five*, even J. D. Salinger's *The Catcher in the Rye*—these are just a few of the books that have faced such challenges. Attempts to ban them from schools remain ongoing today.

To many of us, these concerns seem far away—what do these issues have to do with you as you develop as a writer? For one, as Toni Morrison notes in "Peril" (p. 436), the "suppression of [any] writers is the earliest harbinger of the steady peeling away" of all our rights. For another, an awareness of this worldwide current and historical situation should make us feel grateful for the freedom of expression we currently enjoy once we reach adulthood.

It also might help you if you are a person who does not take part in the more superficially obvious elements of the rebellious-writer stereotype. Many students I have met over the years have feared that they just didn't have the necessary eccentricity to be a writer. Others have wasted a lot of time pursuing that image (through partying, for instance) more than working on their own writing. Intelligent readers, however, know that true rebellion lies in the words, not in the antics of a writer. Often the greater shifts in our paradigms come to us from writers who live calm, even modest lives—Henry David Thoreau, for instance, who laid the groundwork for environmental awareness with his quiet reflections on nature in *Walden*, or Emily Dickinson, who published few poems in her rather isolated life, but whose originality had an enormous influence on the use of unconventional forms in modern poetry.

In other words, become aware of your own personality and its relationship to the solitude and the occasional social fortitude required by a range of writing styles and purposes. Mostly, your writing will take you where it needs to go, but be prepared for the variety of destinations that might entail, from the quiet spaces you will always need to produce your work to the sudden way in which you might find yourself a lightning rod for social issues. (See **Pathway 15.5.**)

LITERARY QUALITIES

What does it mean for a piece of writing to have literary value? This is the question that raises the issue of subjectivity in the study of Creative Writing. The first thing to remember is that there can be other kinds of value, as we have discussed above—Harriet Beecher Stowe's *Uncle Tom's Cabin* provides a classic example. Now almost uniformly acknowledged to be dreadfully written, the novel nonetheless scandalized the nation about the cruelties of slavery after its publication in 1852 and helped galvanize abolitionist feelings and ready the country for the painful Civil War. We read it today more as a powerful historical document than a great novel, even though it had an important social impact.

However, even light entertainment can have a significant value in our lives, and there should be nothing shameful in that. For example, I like to read crime fiction, sometimes even true-crime. I don't do it often, but when I need a real break—and we all sometimes do—a shift to a plainly moralistic world where things are clear-cut right and wrong refreshes me in its difference from my "real life." (On the other hand, often I find myself simply irritated at the clichéd characters, dull descriptions, ludicrous plot gaps, assertions, and assumptions in such work.) This occasional reading doesn't poison my literary appreciations, nor does it help me become a better writer except by counter-example. However, it serves a function for me, and it's important that we not abandon completely these other values when we talk about literary value per se. These different values often overlap, but they are not always the same.

The list I provide here of some of the main components acknowledged to define literary value should be merely a starting point. Discuss these among your classmates or friends, ask your instructor about his or her standards, and continue to develop your own sense of what makes writing into something deserving the title of art.

The following qualities are most commonly held to define works of literary distinction:

- often associated with "realism," but that doesn't define it
- distinguishable style
- depth of meaning and unusual insight
- often contains elements of social criticism
- usually character-driven with complex human nature on display
- ambitions beyond mere entertainment
- lasting value
- complexity calling for rereading
- pleasure in the language, not just the plot
- non-formulaic/original

This last item on the list raises some hackles, as much realist literary fiction shares conventions in ways that some think are just as formulaic as those of specific genres. In fact, criticism is sometimes aimed at Creative Writing classes for producing writing that all sounds the same. Without a doubt, this sometimes happens, but it is not the *goal* of Creative Writing instruction, and the goal matters. Similarity of plot, themes, style, and characters *is* the goal of many mass-appeal genre novels. Creative Writing books like this one, and assignments that your instructor may give, often seem to be offering a set of rules for writers to follow. But what we hope to do is teach techniques that you will master, adapt, and alter to your storytelling needs. If we reach a time when Creative Writing instructors are giving students narrow formulas for their work, then we will have reached a time when literary writing will have become just another genre. Instead, Creative Writing attempts to allow you to find and hone your own specific voice and to find forms that may take from guidelines rather than formulas. (See **Pathway 15.6**.)

MELODRAMA, SENTIMENTALITY, AND STEREOTYPE

One of the primary challenges in our writing is the fine line between powerful emotion and overwrought emotion. Sentimentality and melodrama are hard qualities to define, and, as with many other borders, we don't always agree exactly where they fall. As novelist Graham Greene notes, "Sentimentality— that's what we call the sentiment we don't share." We can easily recognize this in people—the friend who always seems hysterical or spitting mad over every little thing or the relative who coos at cute puppies but won't adopt one. The first of these I would define as **melodramatic** and the second as **sentimental**. Melodrama may be more outward, louder, outsize in its expression, but both of these qualities feel false. If we can't believe in the degree of feeling, then it's true that we can't share it, and this lack of sharing feeling is not only a difference of opinion. It can mean a failure to communicate honestly and with precision. What both melodrama and sentimentality have in common is "too muchness."

Writing that gets labeled nonliterary tends to oversimplify emotions, thus leading to cliché in both plot and character. In genres other than fiction, we can think of memoirs that ooze self-pity rather than give us insight into illness or the loss of a loved one. In poetry, we can think of the kind of verses that stereotypical grandmothers might write, all with sing-song rhymes and superficial praise of children or flowers. In plays, we can think of what would happen if Itamar Moses (p. 438) hadn't made the gun a water-gun or if Simon Fill (p. 357) hadn't changed up the dynamics of the doctor-patient relationship. Oversimplification leads to melodrama or sentimentality leads to stereotype and cliché. And so on.

This doesn't mean that all writing that's rich and descriptive is melodramatic or sentimental; rather, melodrama means describing something with an amount of emotion it doesn't merit or hasn't earned on the page. Even someone writing in a spare, stripped-down style can be guilty of cliché and melodrama. For instance, if we say either, "The long-separated lovers raced toward each other like freight trains on a collision course," or, "The lovers ran toward each other like trains colliding," we get the wrong impression in both long and short versions. We not only get the wrong impression of the emotions (impending disaster instead of joy), but we also see that the implication of such speed is not quite deserved. The figure of speech doesn't fit the situation.

Pathway 15.7 asks you to look at numerous poems in comparison to greeting cards. Note that the poems may exhibit bald emotion—Leon Stokesbury's "Unsent Message to My Brother in His Pain" (p. 519) begs and worries, Pablo Neruda's "Your Feet" (p. 446) lusts and celebrates, and Stuart Dischell's "She Put on Her Lipstick in the Dark" (p. 336) expresses longing and regret for a love unfulfilled. However, they allow the emotions to arise through description and specificity rather than overstatement.

Melodrama, then, also applies more widely to situations and characters who try to force unearned or undeserved emotion out of readers, especially when an author labels feelings rather than simply showing a moment and letting readers feel their own feelings. This quality often relates to the quality of abstraction—if a writer seems to be in love with the idea of love, then his writing will tend to sentimentalize the feeling rather than showing it in all its specificity. In fact, common foci of sentimentality include things like babies, childhood, motherhood, the fidelity of dogs, and other abstract ideas such as nationality, religion, and friendship. When emotions are common—as is love of mother or love of country—we may respond, but feel unmoved by a shallow presentation. Our strong feelings can be conveyed best if we respect others' ability to also feel and let them respond to the specific moments we describe. Think of yourself as shining a flashlight on what you have discovered, not running through the streets shrieking and screaming about it.

As you continue writing, you will experiment with many such boundaries. When is emotion earned or not earned? Which word is the right word? When is a character strong and when does he become arrogant? When another character begins taking over as your first-person narrator, how do you tell when she's gotten so far from your own experience that she'll feel like a lie? When does this plot hold together too well and when does it fall too far apart? The boundary between literary writing and genre fiction (or hack nonfiction or doggerel poetry or skits) is as blurred as any of these. It is worth, however, thinking about qualities that will stand the test of time.

PATHWAYS

Pathway 15.1. Near future. Write a two-page story set in the future, but within your expected lifespan. Avoid the clichés of science fiction writing: spaceships, apocalypse, funny-looking aliens.

Pathway 15.2. Magical realism. Write a two-page story containing an element of magic or fantasy, but allow yourself only *one* such element in an otherwise realistic story.

Pathway 15.3. The uncriminal gun. Write a poem or scene with a gun in it. But make sure that the gun, though meaningful, does not fulfill its stereotypes. You are not allowed to have it go off at all or for it to be used to threaten anyone directly in a crime.

Pathway 15.4. Individuality conflict. When has a role you play (at a job, in school, or in your family) conflicted with your individuality? Write about how you resolved the conflict.

Pathway 15.5. Dream big. Write about what you want your writing to do in the world. Why might it be important for you to write in whatever form you prefer? If you don't feel it is important yet, how might it become important? Write it beautifully, with all your expressive heart and any techniques you've already studied. Be specific, personal, and quirky.

Pathway 15.6. Most important element. Choose one of the list of literary qualities above and write a one-page paper about which one you think is most important to literary writing. Obviously, all these aspects work together, but which one matters most to you right now? Why? Give at least a couple of examples of how it works in specific writing.

Pathway 15.7. Greeting card poems. Bring in a greeting card that contains a poem or verse rather than a joke. This might be a birthday card, Valentine's Day card, anniversary card, sympathy card, get well card, or one for any of a number of other holidays and occasions. Compare your greeting card poems with some of the following poems in this book:

- Valentine's Day: Dischell's "She Put on Her Lipstick in the Dark" (p. 336) or Neruda's "Your Feet" (p. 446)
- Get Well: Stokesbury's "Unsent Message to My Brother in His Pain" (p. 519)
- Father's Day: Gallagher's "3 A.M. Kitchen: My Father Talking" (p. 340)
- Mother's Day: Cofer, "The Changeling" (p. 307)
- Grief/Sympathy: Becker's "The Children's Concert" (p. 291) or Emanuel's "The Out-of-Body Experience" (p. 344)

What differences do you notice? Why might the poems in this book be valued as "literature" when the ones in cards are not?

Now, try writing the worst possible love poem you can. Fill it with abstractions, clichés, and rhythms and sounds that either don't reflect the emotions you'd otherwise be trying to express, or try using a fixed meter (such as iambic pentameter) that you stick to without subtlety or nuance. Make it as bad (abstract, generic) as you can.

Then write a new one about the same person, but make the poem the opposite of that poem. Be specific. Don't idealize, generalize, or use any clichés. Try a more natural or subtle rhythm. Perhaps use only slant or off-rhyme and stay away from a rigid iambic pentameter. Make your line lengths vary. Don't use the word "love." Instead, prove it by paying the closest attention you've ever paid to anything and reaching beyond stereotyped ideas about love.

Chapter **16**

The Writing Life

KEY ANTHOLOGY READINGS

Gary Soto, "What the Federal Bailout Means to Me" (poetry)

Connie May Fowler, "Connie May Is Going to Win the Lottery
This Week" (on writing)

Creative Writing is not one of those courses that students dread for its academic difficulty or the weed-out mentality of professors. In this chapter, however, we will discuss the sometimes daunting realities that writers face as they leave college and begin to make a living—either the difficulties of continuing to write when your career doesn't focus on writing or the challenges of linking your writing to a career path.

It may seem too soon to think about such things, and I want to emphasize that as far as your study of Creative Writing goes, the focus on the craft of writing itself is of the greatest importance in your development right now. Obsessing about practicalities too early will likely not be helpful. However, because the exact role writing will play in your life (or even whether it will play any major role) will depend partly on your ongoing choices, a heads-up is in order. Thinking in advance about where you hope your writing life will go can help you make it go there. Keep in mind, though, that this information is best left simmering like a pot of chili in a slow-cooker. You can't determine your future at microwave speed, and art does not respond well to being zapped.

PROFESSION OR AVOCATION?

As we've discussed throughout this book, studying Creative Writing can help you fulfill many different possibilities. You may be dedicated to pursuing life as a full-time writer—writing plays for Broadway, publishing collections of poems, forging social awareness through true stories, or penning the next great American novel. Or you may focus your career aspirations elsewhere and use what you learn in Creative Writing classes to help you communicate better, work both independently and cooperatively, and be more observant. Many people find fulfillment in more casual writing—blogging, writing stories for their children, keeping a diary. Any of these is a positive outcome of your study of Creative Writing. Yet, you will likely find that, no matter which path as a writer you choose to take, it will not be ordinary. There is something special about the writing life. Robert Graves noted, "To be a poet is a condition, not [merely] a profession."

Intrinsic Rewards

Amateur writers are often looked askance at in the publishing world and by literary experts. It is indeed true that sometimes they lack sophistication about the elements of writing and haven't made the commitment to excellence or paid the dues required to become a professional writer, though it's also true that sometimes they write beautifully, even if they only ever share their work with a small group of relatives and friends.

However, you should be aware that even of those who study Creative Writing, go on for advanced degrees, and continue to perfect their work and publish throughout their lifetimes, very few will become the likes of Toni Morrison or David Sedaris—household names widely read and widely respected. Only a small minority will even go on to gain the notoriety of David Foster Wallace or Aimee Bender with their cult-like followings. In other words, few of you will become famous writers, published internationally and able to make better than a modest income from your writing alone. To be honest, many of you will not make a living from your creative writing at all. For some that's because you are already devoted to other professions, but even those who wish they could live on writing alone will find themselves seeking other ways of making a living out of necessity. No matter your level of devotion, in a certain sense, every writer faces a culture that, as Gary Soto puts it in "What the Federal Bailout Means to Me" (p. 517), prefers to "deal in numbers, not words."

This is not said to discourage you, though it can be daunting.

In fact, the persistence of people's desire to write in spite of harsh economic realities and the many other demands of their personal and professional lives should indicate to us what a vital, enjoyable, and rewarding process it is. The origins of the word "amateur," after all, are the same as those for "amatory," from the Latin *amare*, to love. No matter how professional we become, we write first and foremost out of our love of language and story. In fact, numerous studies by psychologists such as Alfie Kohn and Mihaly Csikszentmihalyi and behavioral economists such as Bruno Frey show that people who engage in creative activities for intrinsic rather than extrinsic reasons are actually more creative. We should, in fact, keep the "beginner's mind" of the amateur at all phases of a writing life, no matter how professionalized our writing becomes.

Keeping Writing in Your Life

If you have a single-minded devotion to writing, these issues raise the question of how you are going to live and, if you already have other career plans, the question of how writing might fit into your life. Prior to the advent of a system of free public education, reading and writing were practices reserved for an elite class of people. Now, those of us who emerge with a passion for writing out of a working- or middle-class background have to think about how to support ourselves and our writing lives. Even those of us from more well-off backgrounds may face family skepticism about the importance of writing and may feel a need to prove our practical usefulness and to contribute to the family coffers. Whichever category you fall into, you should be thinking about how to survive as a writer long term. If you take this for granted, you may not survive as a writer at all.

One long-term literary editor, Ted Solataroff, noticed that about half of the brilliant new writers he published for the first time would soon disappear entirely from the writing scene. In outlining the challenges inherent in maintaining a writing life, he notes the "uncertainty, rejection and disappointment." He goes on to say that "how well a writer copes with rejection determines whether he has a genuine literary vocation or just a literary flair," partly because it "is precisely this struggle with rejection that helps the young writer develop his main defense against the narcissism that prompts him to speak out in the first place." He warns writers that the desire to write should be separated from the desire to publish and notes that most writers "fix the turning point in their writing lives when the intrinsic interest of what they were doing began to take over and generate a sense of necessity." Remember that once you leave school and the assignments given by your instructors, there are very few people who will care at all whether you continue to write. Don't obsess about it, but take some steps now to ready yourself for that time and remember that whatever you do, however you spend your time, it can be fodder for your writing. (See **Pathway 16.1.**)

HOW WRITERS MAKE A LIVING

We all know that no employer advertises an open position for "The Next Great Novelist." If you ever see such an ad, a scammer probably wants to sell you a cheap anthology containing your work and will end up asking you to pay him, not the other way around. In this section, we will look at a few of the various ways that writers have made a living in the past hundred years and look forward to how you can begin to envision opportunities for yourself. Although I direct this section more toward those who wish for writing to be central in their lives, notice that many well-known writers have had completely separate careers in addition to their writing.

Different Trajectories

Most of even the writers who succeed commercially or critically often go through many years before they become well-known. Even some writers who achieved great fame—such as Emily Dickinson, Franz Kafka, James Agee, Sylvia Plath, and Henry Darger—did so only after their deaths. Others achieve some level of renown but have difficulty publishing consistently or supporting themselves just from their writing even at the height of their careers. These include such well-known fiction writers as Edward P. Jones, Annie Proulx, Barbara Pym, and William Faulkner, and all but a handful of poets. Some writers don't publish significant work until they are in their thirties, forties, or even older than fifty—Henry Adams, Charles Bukowski, Raymond Chandler, and Tillie Olsen fall into this category. Even writers who seem to burst onto the literary scene at a younger age often have years of apprenticeship before they do so. Many have worked "odd jobs" or in other fields to support themselves—Ralph Ellison, Tennessee Williams, Jonathan Safran Foer, for example. While J. R. R. Tolkien led a comfortable life supported by his academic profession as a linguist, J. K. Rowling struggled as a single mother on welfare while she finished a draft of the first Harry Potter novel. Some writers continue, even after they become well-known, to alternate between working strictly to make money and then focusing on writing for periods of time with the help of grants, residencies, and other honorary stipends. Connie May Fowler, a best-selling novelist, notes in "Connie May Is Going to Win the Lottery This Week" (p. 364) that her retirement plan is tenuous at best.

As noted in Chapter 1, there are many different motivations for becoming a writer, and there are also many different pathways to developing and remaining one over a lifetime. Though most successful writers are well-educated, it's different from many professions in that there is no certification process. No one particular set of skills and knowledge is required. Certified public accountants (CPAs), doctors, nurses, psychologists, lawyers, veterinarians, and various types of engineers all pass licensing exams of one kind or another and have to have a seal of approval from the government and professional organizations in order to practice their trade. Even public elementary and high school teachers must have state certification, and many other jobs, such as those in construction contracting and physical therapy, require licensing. Writing, on the other hand, is one of the least regulated professions in the world. Anyone can try a hand at it, and the only external proofs of competence or success are publication, awards, and readership, which may not come for many years after a writer begins to write—or ever. This variability and openness of the writing world may be a challenge, but it also offers many opportunities.

Luck and hard work grant some writers at least some income from their writing, though few would claim that as their main motivation. And many writers never make a living from their writing at all. We'll discuss below some variations on how they survive. The two main methods writers use are 1) to pursue work related to words, which most likely involves teaching and/or editing, and 2) to separate writing from work, whether by following a different career and writing in one's "spare time" or by putting paid work on the sideline and doing only enough to get by.

Working with Words

There is a hint in the biographies and in more contemporary interviews and articles of well-known authors about how you may conceive of making a living as a writer even if you don't hit the bestseller list. Many writers do achieve a decent living working with words. Often, however, these paying jobs are not simply sitting at the computer working on one's own novel, memoir, poems, or plays. They often involve other kinds of writing—journalistic, business, technical, medical, or other more commercial forms of writing. Some writers—such as F. Scott Fitzgerald, Salman Rushdie, Dorothy Sayers, Don DeLillo, and Joseph Heller—have even spent time working as advertising copywriters before their creative work could support them. Others make a living editing, which involves working with others' words to improve them.

Often working with words involves teaching, at either the high school or college and university level. Education is in itself a demanding career with requirements that can take away from time and energy devoted to writing, but it also offers helpful opportunities to think about language and its subtleties on a nearly constant basis. In addition, many teaching positions allow summers that writers can devote to writing. Many well-known writers today have earned their livings in the classroom—Tobias Wolff, Junot Díaz, Zadie Smith, Jonathan Safran Foer, and Billy Collins are all college or university professors, and James Joyce, Aldous Huxley, Frank McCourt, and Nick Hornby taught high school before their publications supported them. Even commercially oriented Stephen King worked as a high school history teacher, writing in the wee hours of the morning before work, until he had a hit with *Carrie*.

Separating Work and Writing

Another approach to the writing life is hinted at by Mark Twain's early stint as a riverboat pilot and by the diverse paths of many other writers. There are some writers who strive to keep their art separate from their jobs or who seek wide-ranging experiences to fuel their writing. Revered physician-writers like William Carlos Williams and Anton Chekhov, and contemporary ones such as Abraham Verghese, Pauline Chen, and Chris Adrian, have day jobs that certainly keep them in close touch with the dramas of human life and provide them with much material for their work. Many popular writers of legal and crime novels, such as Dashiell Hammett and John Grisham, emerged from backgrounds as attorneys, police officers, private detectives, and journalists covering crime beats. Authors like Carl Sagan and Neil deGrasse Tyson (scientists), Philip Larkin (a librarian), and Thomas Lynch (an undertaker) consider their "other" work as primary as their writing.

Even more likely, writers work in other professions throughout their lifetimes in order to support themselves and their families while they write. These include the likes of poets T. S. Eliot, who highly valued his "peaceful, but interesting" work as a bank clerk, and Wallace Stevens, who spent most of his adult life as an insurance executive and even declined a teaching position at Harvard because it would have required him to give up his vice-presidency at the insurance company. Harper Lee worked for many years as an airline reservationist, and Zora Neale Hurston as an anthropological researcher. (See **Pathway 16.2**.)

Various methods of making a living while maintaining a writing life entail living conditions particular to these choices. New York City, for one thing, remains the center of the publishing world in spite of the presence of the Internet, and many writers consider an apprenticeship in the literary scene there crucial for contacts and inspiration. On the other hand, some writers don't greet the idea of urban living happily and seek to find a smaller, though perhaps thriving, local writing community. In addition, subsisting on a series of transient jobs may be fine if you are young and healthy, but if and when you decide to have a family or you encounter health challenges, a more stable income may be something you desire. We also each have our own desires and psychological needs when it comes to material comfort, and self-knowledge will help you chart your own path forward.

CHARTING YOUR OWN FUTURE

Over the course of your life as a writer, you may use one or a variety of the strategies that other writers have used. It's helpful to get to know yourself well in order to predict how you will fare in each of these scenarios. How much support can you count on, especially in your early years, from your parents or grandparents? Do you hope to have a family of your own that you can support and children that you'll hope to send to college? Do you already have a family with children or even grandchildren who count on you? How important is it to you to have the usual benefits of full-time professional careers, such as vacations, holidays, various kinds of insurance, and a retirement plan? Do you find that you thrive in or that you become bored and stifled by a routine? How much instability are you comfortable with? What are the worlds that fascinate you and motivate your writing, and will you have access to them in any given walk of life? **Pathway 16.3** asks you to take a look at yourself and steps you might take—not to lock your plans in place, but to help you envision what you will need in your life to make it possible to keep writing. From time to time, it's a good idea to revisit these questions and make up ones of your own that can lend insight into not only what you want to do, but how you want to live.

Steps to Take Now

What can you do now to increase the chances that you will have a long writer's life? Some people would say, "Nothing." Indeed, there is an element of chance in any hopeful writer's life that cannot and should not be denied. No one path guarantees success. However, there are some things you can do that will help you.

One is simply preparing yourself for the challenges of a writing life. If you expect instant success, you will have a hard time; if, on the other hand, you understand ahead of time that challenges and difficulties are not unusual for new writers, then you'll be prepared to face them. You'll feel less alone and encouraged that others have also faced the inevitable rejections with patience and endurance.

It is important that you establish a network of people who will support you in your work as a writer. Writing is generally a solitary activity, and it can be lonely, so balancing with a social life will help you immensely. But it's also important that this social aspect of your life be one that fosters rather than distracts from your writing life. It may be tricky to tell at times whether your friendships are fostering or hampering your work as a writer, and even if you establish helpful friendships now, their nature may change over time. Writing is a complex psychological universe, and many factors intervene, including professional jealousy and simple disagreements that can eventually undermine a friendship. Many famous literary friendships—like that of Emily Dickinson and Thomas Wentworth Higginson, of George Sand and Gustave Flaubert, of Wordsworth and Coleridge—last lifetimes, whereas others—of C. S. Lewis and J. R. R. Tolkien, of Camus and Sartre, of Hemingway and Fitzgerald—eventually grow dysfunctional and end. There have been many famous supportive (and competitive) literary friendships. Recently, Robert Silvers and Barbara Epstein have edited two volumes of *The Company They Kept: Writers on Unforgettable Friendships*, which give insight into the power of these relationships. At some points in our lives, it may be enough to have friends that get us "out of the house," whereas at other times those very friends may demand too much time away from our actual work.

It's especially great to have knowledgeable people you trust who will read and give opinions on your work even once you're out of school. Your workshop classes may fulfill some of this need now, but your workshop classes will eventually end. As suggested in Chapter 14, you shouldn't waste classes and other opportunities to create lasting friendships with people who share your sensibilities and whose work you respect. You may eventually move on from the writer friends you make in college, but learning to establish such relationships now will help you create new ones later on. And they may provide long-term emotional sustenance and practical assistance in the years to come. (See **Pathway 16.4.**)

Looking Ahead in Academia

Many writers support themselves and their families via teaching, a largely enjoyable and rewarding career helping students achieve success and take part in a continual conversation about writing. However, teaching at the college and university level takes an advanced degree, and teaching at the elementary and high school levels usually takes certification based on particular training courses and testing. These are also extremely competitive and demanding careers, especially at the college and university level. Therefore, if you hope to pursue this avenue, you should begin early to lay the groundwork. This means primarily, of course, doing the most excellent writing you can do and applying yourself seriously to the task of learning as much as you can while you are in school.

You also will want to begin establishing closer-than-average relationships with a few of your teachers so that they might know you well enough in the future to write good letters of recommendation for you. Again, while this seems to be something you won't need to think about for another year or two, you might want to begin early to talk to your professors and find out what it has taken for them to be in their positions. This kind of "informational interviewing" may give you a better idea of whether or not academia is a realistic or desirable possibility for you.

You can also begin familiarizing yourself early on with application processes for graduate schools, as these are quite different from undergraduate procedures, and to look around at different MFA and PhD programs in Creative Writing, Education, and related fields that might interest you. Your professors and your college or university's career center will be good sources for ways to begin. If there is a graduate program at your university, you might also want to try to meet some enrolled students and ask them for advice. And, of course, there are myriad websites that you can find to help you with particulars.

If you have an interest in pursuing graduate school in Creative Writing and/ or an academic career, the point is to not wait. Get involved with available student literary magazines, start a peer writing group, go to readings, and see what other ways you can get involved. Teaching careers will always demand this kind of involvement from you, and so it's great to get a taste of it now.

Developing Your Knowledge of the Literary World

Start now in getting familiar with the literary landscape. This involves the avid reading we discussed in Chapter 13, but it may also involve learning about the publishing industry, attending conferences, and reading book reviews and other sources that will both heighten your sense of what good writing is and give you a grasp of the "other" side of a writing life. In other words, good writing is the key factor in your future, but understanding the basics of the various publishing processes and how agents work and what they can do for you will be an asset as well.

One of the prime ways that you may be able to explore the world of publishing is through internships and other extracurricular opportunities offered by your college or university. The practical experience of working on a student literary magazine or helping with a national-level journal will give you a thorough understanding of what it means to take a story or poem from manuscript to published form, how to choose artwork to enhance the literary experience, and all the technical terms for steps along the way. An internship with a more commercial publication might also give you experience with interviewing, article-writing, fact-checking, advertising and layout, and other related skills, all of them possibly relevant to your own life as a writer. In addition, your college or university may offer opportunities such as serving on a committee that brings in guest authors to campus, helping out at a book or literary festival, or interviewing authors for publications—all of these will give you invaluable exposure to practicing writers and insight into how they work and live. There may also be service learning experiences that may help you test out teaching as an option. If your home department doesn't offer such opportunities, look for a campus-wide office for internships and service opportunities, and, failing that, look for them yourself in your community. The practical experience of putting together a newsletter for a church, synagogue, mosque, or a pet-rescue group or cycling club will serve you well. (See **Pathway 16.5**.)

The Changing Publishing World

The rise of the digital in contemporary society has changed our practices of reading and writing. You know this intuitively even if you don't remember what life was like before the Internet. We are in the midst of technological changes that compare with the very first invention of movable type printing by Johannes Gutenberg in the mid-1400s. The effect of these technological changes will not be clear for some time to come, though plenty of pundits argue on both sides of the divide between "culturally destructive" and "wonderfully liberating." As writers, no matter how we feel about them, we must live with and learn to make the most of these changes, as we certainly cannot stop them. We can try to offset losses of interest in the written word by finding new ways to use the word in film, gaming, and other electronic environments, and we can also find exciting new opportunities for our writing and communication of ideas via means not previously available.

These new technologies are not the main subject of this book—for one thing, they change all the time in terms of software and other tools, as well as in terms of general innovations in form. The Twitter story, for instance, may be in today and out tomorrow. However, many of the writing Pathways in this book may be easily adapted to an online environment, and I encourage you to explore online resources for learning about writers, writing, and your professional goals.

You should also learn as much as you can about technology related to computer skills and the Internet. Because so much of publishing is moving online these days, it is foolish not to learn as much as you can about creating, maintaining, writing for, and editing web pages, blogs, and social networking sites. In addition, if you are in one of the more collaborative endeavors of writing plays or screenplays, you will need to understand the technologies involved. In five years, no doubt, it will all be different than it is now, and the quality of your fundamental writing skills will last much, much longer, but if you want to work with words, there's no reason not to add these technology skills to your repertoire. Most of them are relatively easy and inexpensive to acquire, and most high schools, colleges, universities, libraries, and community centers offer workshops and short classes to help you get started.

Writers from Toni Morrison to Mary Roach have spent time in various editorial capacities in the publishing world, and today many writers have opportunities as social media managers, commercial website authors, and the like as well as in more traditional editorial roles. Remember that other types of writing can be honorable ways of making a living, and that journalism, magazine writing, tech writing, and business writing don't have to be sensationalist or dishonest. You may find in time that they drain some of your creative energy, and you may decide that the living you can earn that way isn't worth the sacrifice of time and focus, but, on the other hand, you may find that you enjoy exercising your writing skills in a number of different ways and that writing, any kind of writing, helps you develop your language skills better than other kinds of employment tasks. There is no one right answer, but respect for other kinds of writing is a good place to start when you're exploring your options.

Most creative writers still feel a great deal of devotion to our books—we like the feel of paper and the smell of ink, we enjoy curling up with something that is not plugged in and the ability to concentrate on a story or poem without the interrupting chime of an instant message arriving. But consider that you live in a very exciting time and that you will help to define the next great paradigms and patterns of story and language through new media.

Other Realms

Whether you are planning to become a Creative Writing or English major or are taking an introductory course in the subject to fulfill a casual interest or a general education requirement, you can also think about all the other courses you are taking in the context of your future writing life. In other words, even if you plan to pursue some other career first and foremost, writing can be important to you and it can help foster that other career. More and more, for instance, medical schools and law schools judge their applicants partly by how "well rounded" those contenders are and how well and humanely they are able to communicate with others. In technological or social science fields, you may be regularly called upon to translate ideas for wider audiences. Being sensitive to language use and having an ear for crucial elements of a story will serve you well in those professions as well as in the writing life.

Even if you don't plan on making another career your main focus, however, you will find that courses outside English and Creative Writing may often benefit you as you pursue your writing. If you have taken courses in science or technology, there may be opportunities for you to work with research scientists or civil engineers or the like, interpreting their work in forms more popular than the technical material they write themselves. So, even when you take a psychology or business course, keep an eye out for areas in which you might enjoy a bit of expertise later on. Keep an eye on the images, characters, and stories in those fields.

Some of you may have additional passions that are academic—maybe you love botany, for instance, or you're fascinated with the cultures of Asia. If so, by all means, pursue a minor or a second major in addition to your Creative Writing or English major, or pursue Creative Writing as a minor. On the other hand, if your other passion is surfing or cooking, or if you have learned a lot raising your five children, continue to pursue understanding and learning about those things outside of school. You don't have to always "write what you know," but depth of understanding will enrich your work and give it a compelling confidence.

The good news is that you can retain a vital writing life even if you don't become an instant bestseller. Many writers develop followings of readers who sustain a public interest in their work even when it is not at the top of the charts. Writers also support each other as readers, and you may have very meaningful communities of writers and readers within the context of small press publishing, literary magazines, and blogging. Many publishers recognize that less sensationalist and less popular work may have value, and they continue to support such work.

There are many directions you might go with what you've learned about Creative Writing. My hope is that you will continue to write, that you will continue to read, and that you will share with others the power of words.

PATHWAYS

Pathway 16.1. Writing hopes. Write a reflection on what role you hope writing to have in your life. What types of writing ("creative" or not) do you see yourself doing the most? Will you do that as part of your job or on your own or both? Will you seek publication? If so, in what kind of venue—book publishers, self-publishing, blogging, online or print literary magazines, professional publications, etc.?

Pathway 16.2. Writers' jobs. Research the life of one or more writers you admire. Did this writer pursue work with words (teaching or editing) or separate his or her work life from writing? What jobs did he or she hold over the years? If a watershed moment occurred, after which the author could make a living purely from writing, how old was he or she when that happened?

Pathway 16.3. Writing life plan. Create a long-term plan for writing in your life. Even if you don't intend to become a creative writer, per se, think about all the writing you will have to do or want to do and how you might make it a more enjoyable part of your work or personal life. If you are intent upon continuing as a creative writer, think about a two-year plan (courses you will take, events you will attend, projects you have in mind), then perhaps a five-year or ten-year span of time (graduate school, travel or other activities that will inspire you, writers you want to meet, larger book projects you have in mind, thoughts about future reading, and so on). You may want to discuss details and parameters of this with your instructor and/or look online about planning strategies.

Pathway 16.4. Writer-friends. Make a list of readers who will help you improve your work outside of classes—particularly astute friends, an online community, and writer-friends you hope to hang onto after your class ends. Make a list of people whose work you'd be willing to keep critiquing outside of class.

Pathway 16.5. Literary event. Attend one or more literary events on your campus—a poetry slam, visiting author reading, open mic night, or other such event. Make a list of observations and discuss with your class or friends what such events have to do with the writing life.

PART III

Anthology

Fiction   **James Agee**

KNOXVILLE: SUMMER, 1915

We are talking now of summer evenings in Knoxville, Tennessee, in the time that I lived there so successfully disguised to myself as a child. It was a little bit mixed sort of block, fairly solidly lower middle class, with one or two juts apiece on either side of that. The houses corresponded: middle-sized gracefully fretted wood houses built in the late nineties and early nineteen hundreds, with small front and side and more spacious back yards, and trees in the yards, and porches. These were softwooded trees, poplars, tulip trees, cottonwoods. There were fences around one or two of the houses, but mainly the yards ran into each other with only now and then a low hedge that wasn't doing very well. There were few good friends among the grown people, and they were not poor enough for the other sort of intimate acquaintance, but everyone nodded and spoke, and even might talk short times, trivially, and at the two extremes of the general or the particular, and ordinarily nextdoor neighbors talked quite a bit when they happened to run into each other, and never paid calls. The men were mostly small businessmen, one or two very modestly executives, one or two worked with their hands, most of them clerical, and most of them between thirty and forty-five.

But it is of these evenings, I speak.

Supper was at six and was over by half past. There was still daylight, shining softly and with a tarnish, like the lining of a shell; and the carbon lamps lifted at the corners were on in the light, and the locusts were started, and the fire flies were out, and a few frogs were flopping in the dewy grass, by the time the fathers and the children came out. The children ran out first hell bent and yelling those names by which they were known; then the fathers sank out leisurely in crossed suspenders, their collars removed and their necks looking tall and shy. The mothers stayed back in the kitchen washing and drying, putting things away, recrossing their traceless footsteps like the lifetime journeys of bees, measuring out the dry cocoa for breakfast. When they came out they had taken off their aprons and their skirts were dampened and they sat in rockers on their porches quietly.

It is not of the games children play in the evening that I want to speak now, it is of a contemporaneous atmosphere that has little to do with them: that of the fathers of families, each in his space of lawn, his shirt fishlike pale in the unnatural light and his face nearly anonymous, hosing their lawns. The hoses were attached at spiggots that stood out of the brick foundations of the houses. The nozzles were variously set but usually so there was a long sweet stream of spray, the nozzle wet in the hand, the water trickling the right forearm and the peeled-back cuff, and the water whishing out a long loose and low-curved cone, and so gentle a sound. First an insane noise of violence in the nozzle, then the still irregular sound of adjustment, then the smoothing into steadiness and a pitch as accurately tuned to the size and style of stream as any violin. So many qualities of sound out of one hose: so many choral differences out of those several hoses that were in earshot. Out of any one hose, the almost dead silence of the release, and the short still arch of the separate big drops, silent as a held breath, and the only noise the flattering noise on leaves and the slapped grass at the fall of each big drop. That, and the intense hiss with the intense stream; that, and that same intensity not growing less but growing more quiet and delicate with the turn of the nozzle, up to that extreme tender whisper when the water was just a wide bell of film. Chiefly, though, the hoses were set much alike, in a compromise between distance and tenderness of spray (and quite surely a sense of art behind this compromise, and a quiet deep joy, too real to recognize itself), and the sounds therefore were pitched much alike; pointed by the snorting start of a new hose; decorated by some man playful with the nozzle; left empty, like God by the sparrow's fall, when any single one of them desists: and all, though near alike, of various pitch; and in this unison. These sweet pale streamings in the light lift out their pallors and their voices all together, mothers hushing their children, the hushing unnaturally prolonged, the men gentle and silent and each snail-like withdrawn into the quietude of what he singly is doing, the urination of huge children stood loosely mili-tary against an invisible wall, and gentle happy and peaceful, tasting the mean goodness of their living like the last of their suppers in their mouths; while the locusts carry on this noise of hoses on their much higher and sharper key. The noise of the locust is dry, and it seems not to be rasped or vibrated but urged from him as if through a small orifice by a breath that can never give out. Also there is never one locust but an illusion of at least a thousand. The noise of each locust is pitched in some classic locust range out of which none of them varies more than two full tones: and yet you seem to hear each locust discrete from all the rest, and there is a long, slow, pulse in their noise, like the scarcely defined arch of a long and high set bridge. They are all around in every tree, so that the noise seems to come from nowhere and everywhere at once, from the whole shell heaven, shivering in your flesh and teasing your eardrums, the boldest of all the sounds of night. And yet it is habitual to summer nights, and is of the great order of noises, like the noises of the sea and of the blood her preco-cious grandchild, which you realize you are hearing only when you catch yourself listening. Meantime from low in the dark, just outside the swaying horizons of the hoses, conveying always grass in the damp of dew and its strong green-black smear of smell, the regular yet spaced noises of the crickets, each a sweet cold silver noise three-noted, like the slipping each time of three matched links of a small chain.

But the men by now, one by one, have silenced their hoses and drained   5 and coiled them. Now only two, and now only one, is left, and you see only ghostlike shirt with the sleeve garters, and sober mystery of his mild face like the lifted face of large cattle enquiring of your presence in a pitchdark pool of meadow; and now he too is gone; and it has become that time of evening when people sit on their porches, rocking gently and talking gently and watching the street and the standing up into their sphere of possession of the trees, of birds hung havens, hangars. People go by; things go by. A horse, drawing a buggy, breaking his hollow iron music on the asphalt; a loud auto; a quiet auto; people in pairs, not in a hurry, scuffling, switching their weight of aestival body, talking casually, the taste hovering over them of vanilla, strawberry, pasteboard and starched milk, the image upon them of lovers and horsemen, squared with clowns in hueless amber. A street car raising its iron moan; stopping, belling and starting; stertorous; rousing and raising again its iron increasing moan and swimming its gold windows and straw seats on past and past and past, the bleak spark crackling and cursing above it like a small malignant spirit set to dog its tracks; the iron whine rises on rising speed; still risen, faints; halts; the faint stinging bell; rises again, still fainter, fainting, lifting, lifts, faints forgone: forgotten. Now is the night one blue dew.

Now is the night one blue dew, my father has drained, he has coiled
    the hose.
Low on the length of lawns, a frailing of fire who breathes.
Content, silver, like peeps of light, each cricket makes his comment
    over and over in the drowned grass.
A cold toad thumpily flounders.
Within the edges of damp shadows of side yards are hovering children
    nearly sick with joy of fear, who watch the unguarding of a telephone
    pole.
Around white carbon corner lamps bugs of all sizes are lifted elliptic,
    solar systems. Big hardshells bruise themselves, assailant: he is fallen
    on his back, legs squiggling.
Parents on porches: rock and rock: From damp strings morning glories:
    hang their ancient faces.
The dry and exalted noise of the locusts from all the air at once enchants
    my eardrums.

On the rough wet grass of the back yard my father and mother have spread quilts. We all lie there, my mother, my father, my uncle, my aunt, and I too am lying there. First we were sitting up, then one of us lay down, and then we all lay down, on our stomachs, or on our sides, or on our backs, and they have kept on talking. They are not talking much, and the talk is quiet, of nothing in particular, of nothing at all in particular, of nothing at all. The stars are wide and alive, they seem each like a smile of great sweetness, and they seem very near. All my people are larger bodies than mine, quiet, with voices gentle and meaningless like the voices of sleeping birds. One is an artist, he is living at home. One is a musician, she is living at home. One is my mother who is good to me. One is my father who is good to me. By some chance, here they are, all on this earth; and who shall ever tell the sorrow of being on this earth, lying, on quilts, on the grass, in a summer evening, among the sounds of night. May God bless my people, my uncle, my aunt, my mother, my good father, oh, remember them kindly in their time of trouble; and in the hour of their taking away.

After a little I am taken in and put to bed. Sleep, soft smiling, draws me unto her: and those receive me, who quietly treat me, as one familiar and well-beloved in that home: but will not, oh, will not, not now, not ever; but will not ever tell me who I am.

On Writing   **Sherman Alexie**

SUPERMAN AND ME

I learned to read with a Superman comic book. Simple enough, I suppose. I cannot recall which particular Superman comic book I read, nor can I remember which villain he fought in that issue. I cannot remember the plot, nor the means by which I obtained the comic book. What I can remember is this: I was 3 years old, a Spokane Indian boy living with his family on the Spokane Indian Reservation in eastern Washington state. We were poor by most standards, but one of my parents usually managed to find some minimum-wage job or another, which made us middle-class by reservation standards. I had a brother and three sisters. We lived on a combination of irregular paychecks, hope, fear and government surplus food.

My father, who is one of the few Indians who went to Catholic school on purpose, was an avid reader of westerns, spy thrillers, murder mysteries, gangster epics, basketball player biographies and anything else he could find. He bought his books by the pound at Dutch's Pawn Shop, Goodwill, Salvation Army and Value Village. When he had extra money, he bought new novels at supermarkets, convenience stores and hospital gift shops. Our house was filled with books. They were stacked in crazy piles in the bathroom, bedrooms and living room. In a fit of unemployment-inspired creative energy, my father built a set of bookshelves and soon filled them with a random assortment of books about the Kennedy assassination, Watergate, the Vietnam War and the entire 23-book series of the Apache westerns. My father loved books, and since I loved my father with an aching devotion, I decided to love books as well.

I can remember picking up my father's books before I could read. The words themselves were mostly foreign, but I still remember the exact moment when I first understood, with a sudden clarity, the purpose of a paragraph. I didn't have the vocabulary to say "paragraph," but I realized that a paragraph was a fence that held words. The words inside a paragraph worked together for a common purpose. They had some specific reason for being inside the same fence. This knowledge delighted me. I began to think of everything in terms of paragraphs. Our reservation was a small paragraph within the United States. My family's house was a paragraph, distinct from the other paragraphs of the LeBrets to the north, the Fords to our south and the Tribal School to the west. Inside our house, each family member existed as a separate paragraph but still had genetics and common experiences to link us. Now, using this logic, I can see my changed family as an essay of seven paragraphs: mother, father, older brother, the deceased sister, my younger twin sisters and our adopted little brother.

At the same time I was seeing the world in paragraphs, I also picked up that Superman comic book. Each panel, complete with picture, dialogue and narrative was a three-dimensional paragraph. In one panel, Superman breaks through a door. His suit is red, blue and yellow. The brown door shatters into many pieces. I look at the narrative above the picture. I cannot read the words, but I assume it tells me that "Superman is breaking down the door." Aloud, I pretend to read the words and say, "Superman is breaking down the door." Words, dialogue, also float out of Superman's mouth. Because he is breaking down the door, I assume he says, "I am breaking down the door." Once again, I pretend to read the words and say aloud, "I am breaking down the door." In this way, I learned to read.

5   This might be an interesting story all by itself. A little Indian boy teaches himself to read at an early age and advances quickly. He reads *Grapes of Wrath* in kindergarten when other children are struggling through *Dick and Jane*. If he'd been anything but an Indian boy living on the reservation, he might have been called a prodigy. But he is an Indian boy living on the reservation and is simply an oddity. He grows into a man who often speaks of his childhood in the third-person, as if it will somehow dull the pain and make him sound more modest about his talents.

A smart Indian is a dangerous person, widely feared and ridiculed by Indians and non-Indians alike. I fought with my classmates on a daily basis. They wanted me to stay quiet when the non-Indian teacher asked for answers, for volunteers, for help. We were Indian children who were expected to be stupid. Most lived up to those expectations inside the classroom but subverted them on the outside. They struggled with basic reading in school but could remember how to sing a few dozen powwow songs. They were monosyllabic in front of their non-Indian teachers but could tell complicated stories and jokes at the dinner table. They submissively ducked their heads when confronted by a non-Indian adult but would slug it out with the Indian bully who was 10 years older. As Indian children, we were expected to fail in the non-Indian world. Those who failed were ceremonially accepted by other Indians and appropriately pitied by non-Indians.

I refused to fail. I was smart. I was arrogant. I was lucky. I read books late into the night, until I could barely keep my eyes open. I read books at recess, then during lunch and in the few minutes left after I had finished my classroom assignments. I read books in the car when my family traveled to powwows or basketball games. In shopping malls, I ran to the bookstores and read bits and pieces of as many books as I could. I read the books my father brought home from the pawnshops and secondhand. I read the books I borrowed from the library. I read the backs of cereal boxes. I read the newspaper. I read the bulletins posted on the walls of the school, the clinic, the tribal offices, the post office. I read junk mail. I read auto-repair manuals. I read magazines. I read anything that had words and paragraphs. I read with equal parts joy and desperation. I loved those books, but I also knew that love had only one purpose. I was trying to save my life.

Despite all the books I read, I am still surprised I became a writer. I was going to be a pediatrician. These days, I write novels, short stories, and poems. I visit schools and teach creative writing to Indian kids. In all my years in the reservation school system, I was never taught how to write poetry, short stories or novels. I was certainly never taught that Indians wrote poetry, short stories and novels. Writing was something beyond Indians. I cannot recall a single time that a guest teacher visited the reservation. There must have been visiting teachers. Who were they? Where are they now? Do they exist? I visit the schools as often as possible. The Indian kids crowd the classroom. Many are writing their own poems, short stories and novels. They have read my books. They have read many other books. They look at me with bright eyes and arrogant wonder. They are trying to save their lives. Then there are the sullen and already defeated Indian kids who sit in the back rows and ignore me with theatrical precision. The pages of their notebooks are empty. They carry neither pencil nor pen. They stare out the window. They refuse and resist. "Books," I say to them. "Books," I say. I throw my weight against their locked doors. The door holds. I am smart. I am arrogant. I am lucky. I am trying to save our lives.

Poetry **Agha Shahid Ali**

STARS

When through night's veil they continue to seep, stars
in infant galaxies begin to weep stars.

After the eclipse, there were no cheap stars
How can you be so cheap, stars?

5   How grateful I am you stay awake with me
till by dawn, like you, I'm ready to sleep, stars!

If God sows sunset embers in you, Shahid,
all night, because of you, the world will reap stars.

Drama   **Lynne Alvarez**

ON SUNDAYS

Characters

SYLVIA: *A young dancer whom we see during one day of her life.*

JULES: *A dapper man whom we see throughout his life beginning in
    his late twenties and ending when he is seventy-eight.*

A BEAST

Scene 1

*It is noon on a Sunday in a large, modern city. Traffic is heard, and
people's voices as they pass.*

   *Downstage right is a large box with transparent sides. It is open at the
top. SYLVIA is in her bedroom; perhaps there is a pastel-colored makeup
table and a mirror, a chair, some fluttery, transparent curtains. She is
going through her morning ablutions.*

   *At her foot is the flipping tail of a beast. It lies still and then twitches as
if to brush a fly away. She doesn't notice it.*

   *JULES enters stage right. He is in his late twenties at this time. He has
neatly combed, short, dark hair under his derby hat. He has a thin, neat
mustache. He is wearing a summer suit and swings a cane. A newspaper is
folded under his arm. He is dapper and charming, with a tinge of sadness.
He whistles softly to himself and seems quite happy.*

   *He walks past the box as if it were a window. He catches sight of himself
in one of the smooth sides and stops to adjust his hat, his tie, his mustache.
He smiles, twirls his cane and continues.*

   *As he passes the side of the box, he catches a glimpse of SYLVIA and
stops abruptly.*

JULES: Ooh la la!

*(He is delighted. His actions are exaggerated, mimelike. He looks around
cautiously to see if anyone is watching. He backs up and tries to
see the entire figure. To do this, he cranes his neck in all kinds of positions;
he stoops, he stands on tiptoe. Finally, he gets down on the floor.)*

   Impossible!

*(He gets up, dusts himself off, and using the smooth side, adjusts his mus-
tache. He smiles at himself and tips his hat to himself.)*

   Ahh. C'est la vie! *(He tips his hat to SYLVIA as he passes the door.)* And
   a good day to you . . . *(He looks around and adds softly:)* My lovely.

(He exits and immediately reappears. It is later in the afternoon and he looks wilted. His jacket is unbuttoned, his hat slanted over his forehead. He walks slower. There is something defeated in his posture. His newspaper has obviously been opened and refolded, but not carefully.

He walks very slowly across the stage, looking at his feet. As he approaches the door side of the box, he lifts his head. He makes an effort to appear self-composed. He buttons his coat, straightens his posture. He adjusts his hat and walks very purposefully to the box, tips his hat, and starts to move past. He catches himself. He stops and pensively and hopefully addresses SYLVIA.)

> Roberta? . . . *(Pause.)* . . . Emily? . . . Blanche? . . . *(His tone becomes more pleading.)* Cynthia? . . . Diane? . . . Joyce? . . . Lillian? Rebecca? . . . Christine? . . . Aurora? . . . Daphne? *(He waits for a response, sighs deeply, and starts to proceed. He stops suddenly, snaps his fingers.)* Ah-ha! *(He returns to the door.)* Sylvia? . . . Sylvia, is that you?

(He almost collapses and rests his head on his arm, pressing against the box.)

Scene 2

It is noon the following Sunday. SYLVIA is now preparing breakfast, the beast's tail is longer. SYLVIA is careful to step over it whenever she crosses to set or clear the table. She is preoccupied.

JULES enters, dressed as he always is, but he is carrying a bouquet of flowers. He approaches the box.

JULES: I'm sorry. I couldn't come before. I want to apologize.

(He looks around self-consciously. He moves closer so he won't be overheard. He faces the audience and speaks over his shoulder, trying to appear nonchalant to passersby.)

> I brought you flowers. See?

(He tries to find a place to offer them to SYLVIA. He holds them to the door, but they are not taken. He puts them on the ground and waits to see if she will reach out. Finally, he throws them over the top into the box. SYLVIA finds them and puts them on her morning table.)

> I realize I took advantage of you last Sunday. You probably aren't Sylvia . . . You look like Sylvia . . . but then perhaps you're not. *(Clears his throat.)* In any event I want to tell you that I am sorry I took advantage of your . . . unusual position . . . and poured my troubles out like that. I had no right. I'm sorry. *(He waits.)* Of course, I expect that you will hold what I told you in the highest regard and not disclose it to anyone. I hope I can trust you in this respect. *(He waits.)* You seem discreet. You appear to have that quality. *(He waits for a moment.)* In fact, Sylvia . . .

May I call you Sylvia? You seem to possess more than discretion, much more. *(He becomes more and more passionate in his speech.)* You have an aura of calm. Self-possession, I'd say. Yes. But beyond that . . . *(He looks around insidiously.)* May I take the liberty . . . Yes, I will take the liberty of saying you project mystery and . . . and . . .

(He turns and kneels fervently before the door, his hands clasped together near his heart. The beast's tail coils around SYLVIA'S ankle. She kicks it impatiently.)

Romance! Yes. Romance.

(He tries to embrace the box. Then he jumps to his feet and adjusts his clothing and his mustache.)

I feel foolish. Thank you for your patience. *(He is about to leave.)* I hope you will let me see you again.

(He takes out a date book from his pocket and flips through the pages, nodding and muttering. After some consideration, he adds:)

Let me see. Let me see . . . Ahhhh. Yes. I could come see you on Sundays.

(He tips his hat and exits.)

Scene 3
JULES comes out with a paper bag with a handle, a Sunday newspaper with the magazine and comic sections, a portable radio, a folding chair, and a tiny, round table.

He is wearing a flower in his lapel and comes out humming.

He puts the table down near the box and opens the chair. He pulls a handkerchief from his breast pocket and flamboyantly opens it and uses it as a tablecloth. Next he takes a paper cup from the bag and a plate. He puts the paper cup in the center of the table and puts the flower from his lapel in it.

JULES: Good morning, my love. I've brought brunch and the *News*. The flower is perfectly formed. *Magnifique!*

(As he speaks and gets comfortable, eats and reads the paper, SYLVIA will be getting dressed to go out. The beast, which lies at her feet, switching his tail, raises a paw and tears whatever she puts on. Her clothes are made of colorful crepe paper. She leaves the shreds on and continues dressing. JULES now takes out a thermos of coffee, another cup, a sweet roll, pats of butter, a plastic knife, sugar, a container of milk and strawberries.)

(He begins to butter the sweet roll and eat strawberries while he chats.)

How fresh the strawberries are this time of year. The smallest ones are best, bittersweet. How fragrant this coffee is. It's Hawaiian and Indonesian. A blend. How crisp and sweet is this roll, and how creamy the butter is. It's a tender yellowish white. It makes me think of youth.

(JULES picks up the paper, glances through the comic section quickly. Once in a while he lets out a quick, sharp laugh. When he finishes, he folds it into a paper airplane and shoots it into the box. He sits down and reads another section, the Metropolitan section.)

My, my. Listen to this. "A wounded and lost whale wandered the shores of New York within forty feet of Coney Island beach before a police launch herded the forlorn mammal back to the open sea. The launch got between the whale and the shore and tried to steer him to the open sea as the disoriented whale repeatedly tried to enter several bays. 'He was injured,' the police chief said. 'You could see the cut marks on his back. He nudged the launch like it was his girl. We got worried he was going to try to have some fun with it, if you know what I mean,' the police chief continued." Ahem . . . *(He looks around nervously.)* . . . My . . . my . . . *(Continues.)* "The police launch lost track of the whale but it was reported that the whale will most likely stay in the area for a while. The police chief added, 'They usually hang around. Sometimes they lose a mate and hang around waiting for it to return.'"

(JULES reaches out and touches the box tenderly. It begins to rain, light at first and then harder.)

(He fishes in his bag and takes out a collapsible umbrella, which he opens. He sits sipping coffee, holding the umbrella over his head.)

Scene 4

SYLVIA, *dressed now, tries to leave. The beast blocks her way. There are several attempts. JULES comes rushing in. He carries his coat over his arm.*

JULES: I hope you'll forgive that I'm late!

(He spreads his jacket on the ground near the door. He sits down there. He is animated, sparkling.)

But I went to the beach! It was delightful! Delicious. Three sea gulls circled the ocean and dove in. Seven women were having a picnic on a pink blanket. Nine couples were laughing on the boardwalk . . . *(Pause.)* I counted them. I like to know what is going on. The world interests me. No! It fascinates me! If only you were there.

(SYLVIA taps on the glass and tries in vain to get JULES'S attention. He stands up and takes out a piece of paper from his breast pocket. He unfolds it and takes an oratorical stance, half-facing the box and yet visible to the audience.)

I wrote a poem for you. *(He reads very grandly.)*

"The sea roars and swells
above me
my lone heart leaps
that dolphin part of me."

(He folds the paper and returns it to his pocket. He looks longingly at the box. SYLVIA looks longingly out. He doesn't see her.)

That dolphin part of me.

Scene 5

During this scene SYLVIA wrestles with the beast, who claws her. She bleeds.

It is an overcast Sunday. Years have passed for JULES. This is noted by two things. First, the mirrored sides of the box are streaked with dirt; and second, some flowers, branches, pieces of paper, newspaper, and cloth have accumulated around the bottom of the box as if driven there by wind.

JULES enters. He walks slowly, almost decrepitly, his hat in one hand, leaning on a cane. His hair is unkempt, with visible gray in it. He has a few days' growth of beard; his clothes are rumpled. He walks as if he is physically weak rather than old.

JULES: Well, I'm here. *(He pauses.)* It's been some time now. I don't know precisely how much. But it's been quite some time. You don't look well, I may add. You've changed. *(He pauses.)* Don't worry, though. I've only come . . . This will only be a short visit. For many reasons. *(His voice is tightly controlled.)* You may have noticed that I . . . don't feel too well. It's no wonder with all that's happened. In any event, you've failed to say anything about it. Is that your usual discretion? Well, let me tell you . . . your silence . . .

(He starts to lose control of his voice. As he talks, he absently starts to pick up the trash around the box or will wipe at a streak with part of his sleeve.)

is . . . more . . . than . . . I can . . . tolerate! I will not be treated . . . *(He loses his place. He clears his throat.)* I was ill, you see. A touch of flu. Can you see how pale I've become? How thin? My sources of revenue, my *usual* sources dried up, disappeared and I . . . I was . . . you might say, I was reluctant to leave my home. After all, it is my home, with all my special objects about me, little things I collect, a lifetime, if you wish. And I became afraid to step out. No telling who might come, and I hadn't a cent. Of course, in better health I would have set about . . . set about establishing new sources. Much more stable ones. I had several ideas in fact . . . and . . . *(He clears his throat.)* then these two men burst through the door. Unasked, uncalled for. It was humiliating. I was in my bed-clothes . . . indeed, I had retired to my bedclothes some time before, days, perhaps a week . . . Needless to say, I was frightened but maintained a calm presence. "Please leave as you came in," I told them. But they ignored me, in my own house. I would have thrown them out, mind you, although I'm usually quite polite. They were uninvited. I don't know how they knew my name. They read it from a piece of paper and asked me if that was my name. "Why, yes, it is," I answered. "And now will you kindly leave. I'm very tired." But they wouldn't, you know. They looked official. Officious. (He laughs.) Like officious ice cream men, really. All in white. It made me laugh. Then one of them said, "Will ya look at this pitiful mess." Now, yes, I was very weak and may have had my eyes closed, but I heard that. I heard that. (He is quite upset.) "This pitiful mess" they called it, my home. Who are they to say that? What do they know about beauty, I ask you? But that wasn't the worst. They took me away. It took two of them. But I had worse to contend with. Yes. Your silence haunted me then. Your silence became a burden. All those days upon days. I worried about it. I fretted. Once or twice they told me I screamed out in my sleep. It was agony. (He steps away from the box.) And all that time. Not a word, not a note, not a sigh on my account. I paced, I cursed, I spit on you. Yes, I did, and several times. I vowed to come back and end this once and for all just as soon . . . just as soon as I . . . was able.

(He clears his throat and straightens his clothes. He empties his hat and pockets of trash and puts his derby on his head.)

I will no longer be humiliated. I will no longer be ignored.

(He raises his cane and beats the box until he breaks through one side.)

Do you hear? Some response is necessary! Some response is necessary! Some response is necessary! I will no longer tolerate . . . tolerate . . . emptiness!

(He stands back, satisfied with what he has done and stalks off without looking back. SYLVIA is wrestling with the beast. She takes its tail and wraps it around its throat and kills it. She lies there breathing heavily.)

Scene 6

There is a curtain of pastel strips of paper inside the box. We can't see SYLVIA at all. JULES comes in carrying a paper shopping bag over one arm. He is dressed again as before, neatly, although not as precisely as at first. He leans more on his cane and is obviously older. His hair is white. He also carries a broom.

He approaches smiling. The box looks in sad shape. It is even dirtier, and the glass is cracked. More debris is cluttering around its base. The dead beast lies there, too, discarded.

JULES: *(Looking at the box, walking entirely around it.)* Tsch . . . tsch . . . tsch . . . a little the worse for wear . . . tsch . . . tsch . . . But you know. It is time, time we made our peace. I have had you in my heart all these years . . . as if a sliver from one of these mirrors had entered it and settled there . . . My . . . my . . . *(He puts his bag down and begins to sweep away the debris.)* Yes, a sliver. So I have come back to you . . . my lovely. Do you remember how I called you that? There are many things I must tell you. There are things I must explain to you. . . . Just a minute. *(He sweeps some of the debris offstage and returns.)* It looks better already. No one has taken care of you. Not the way I would have. *(He sweeps, walking all the way around the box. As he reappears, he looks older, perhaps more bent, slower.)* I have made mistakes. Incredible errors for a person who is basically careful, civilized sometimes to a fault. One of which I hope to expiate with you. There are so many things I never told you that would have perhaps . . . perhaps softened things between us. . . . Just a moment . . . *(He sweeps the remaining debris offstage.)* There. Quite an improvement. But that is not all. Voilà!

(He extracts a large bottle of Windex and a rag from his bag. He begins to clean the glass.)

So many things I never ventured to tell you. Never dared to mention because I might disturb some imperceptibly delicate balance. . . . But no matter. Now I can say . . . Now I will say what I please.

(He clears his throat and straightens his derby in the newly cleaned mirror. He makes a face at himself and smiles, tips his hat, almost forgetting his place for a moment.)

Now where was I? Oh, yes . . . Ahem. You see. You may wonder why I never approached you physically. It's not that I don't think that way. Quite the opposite is true. However, physical relationships are . . . I suppose you might say they are difficult for me, but that doesn't mean I haven't admired . . . ardently . . . the smoothness of an arm I have glimpsed . . . *(He tries to peer into the box, slants his hat roguishly.)* or the slenderness of a leg, a length of calf, the velvet flow of hair . . . why even now its perfume wafts, floats to me and makes me drowsy. . . .

(In his cleaning, JULES has turned a corner around the box. He continues talking. When he reappears, he has a slight wispy white goatee.)
(SYLVIA steps out from behind the curtain. She is in tights and a leotard and wears a wreath on her head, streamers.)

And you have inspired me. I have often aspired to be as quiet and accepting as you, not to complain or exclaim, not to pile my emotions and desires against you here as if they were leaves and debris blown in by the wind. I have tried to emulate your steadfastness, your virtuous simplicity.

(He again turns the corner and reappears with a longer beard. Steps back and reviews his work.)

Aha. My lovely. You are once again nearly as I remember you.

(He steps close to wipe a speck away and catches sight of himself. He cannot see SYLVIA, who steps up to the glass. She tries to find an opening in order to leave, but cannot. She is dejected because she can find no way out.)

Oo la la. I have grown old. Who would have thought . . .

(He shakes his head and puts away the Windex. Now he is removing small specks of dirt that only he can see.)

But I must hurry to tell you more. Soon it will be too late.

(A strong wind comes up. We hear it. Then it blows JULES's hat away.)

(Talking over the wind.) I believe . . . in fact I am sure that I have learned from your higher qualities. It has been painful, in fact at times it has been excruciatingly painful to never receive a word of love or feel your affection . . . but now I see that although one may never actually receive tokens of love . . .

(The wind almost blows him over. He holds on to the box. SYLVIA hears the wind; she studies the opening at the top of the box and jumps. Large leaves, as big as he, blow onstage and settle against him or the box.)

(Struggling physically and vocally against the wind.) That doesn't matter. What is left, you see . . . oh, my dear, here is the beauty of it all . . . although you never receive the smallest hint, the vaguest gesture or the slightest trace of love . . . *(His voice rises.)* . . . you can always . . . without fail . . . *give it.* Voilà! That is a life! *(He laughs happily.)* C'est vrai, ma cherie . . . my lovely . . .

(He recovers himself enough to continue polishing the box. For a moment, poised to turn the corner, he tilts his head jauntily, twirls his mustache.)

Now. Let me tell you a joke I overheard. It was quite humorous and I remember it perfectly . . .

(He steps around the corner and his voice is cut off by the wind. He does not reappear this time. The stage begins to fill with huge, gold, orange, and brown leaves. SYLVIA climbs out of the box, looks around, and scampers behind it.)

END OF PLAY

Poetry   **Robin Becker**

THE CHILDREN'S CONCERT

Once a month when I was twelve
    and my sister was ten
our mother would drop us at
    The Philadelphia Academy of Music

for the Saturday children's concerts.   5
    We'd sit in the enormous dark
hall with the other children and I'd
    whisper to my sister

that our mother was never coming back,
    that she'd abandoned us there,   10
that she was driving to meet our father
    and take a plane to Europe.

My sister called me a liar
    and her eyes filled
with tears. The musicians had started   15
    on Mozart, but I was whispering

about how we would feel when all the other
    children had gone and we
were left standing in our navy winter coats
    on the grim Philadelphia street.   20

I did not know then that I would grow
    to love the eighteenth century,
that my sister would take her own life
    one winter day in Philadelphia,

that childhood could be so final a thing.   25

Poetry   **Mary Block**

MOVING SONG

The things fit into boxes fairly well.
I picked through hats and tiny plastic bags
with buttons for forgotten coats, the shells
I couldn't leave to wither with the rags
5   and dusty shoes, the fraying underwear,
the shampoo growing black around its neck
and blue beads interspersed with tufts of hair,
the things I never threw away. The flecks
of river write the borough's sturdy name
10   on all the windows in the empty space
we fill with things we always say and frame
with garbage cans. We've got a little place
for this. We'll leave the dead man's dust unswept
and tuck ourselves between the things we kept.

On Writing **Michael Blumenthal**

ON NOT BRINGING YOUR MOTHER TO CREATIVE WRITING CLASS

"'I write for myself and strangers,' is what Gertrude Stein said, and that, I think, is whom all real writers write for," I tell my Friday morning non-fiction writing seminar.

"In most of our early life," I continue, "if we write at all, we are writing for those we are already intimate with—parents, teachers, friends, lovers, aunts and uncles . . . people we don't need to convince to take an interest in us. But once we begin writing for strangers—for people who have better and more urgent things to do than be interested in our private happenings and small tragedies—the going gets tough."

Sarah has brought a piece to class about her family's Hanukkah celebration, entitled "Other People's Plans," for today's discussion. She came to class, on this occasion, with a genteel-looking, salt-and-pepper haired woman in her late 50s or early 60s.

"Would you mind," Sarah asks, "if my mother sat in on our seminar today?"   5

Reluctantly, but feeling that, with Sarah's mother already in the room, I have no other choice, I agree. Her mother smiles at me sweetly.

"I think this essay," Sarah's mother, obviously not averse to class participation, raises her hand as soon as Sarah has finished reading her essay aloud, "is extremely well-written and beautifully told."

Sarah's "essay" is about lighting the candles with her family on the first night of Hanukkah, only to discover that she had misread the calendar— that it wasn't the first night of Hanukkah at all. *"It has always been my responsibility to arrange the family celebration of 'The first candle of Hanukkah,'"* the essay begins.

"Probably the first thing any writer needs to do, from the very beginning," I say to the class, "is to *engage* the reader's curiosity and interest… to convince them that this essay is, in some meaningful sense, about *them*, and not only about you."

"I think," interrupts Sarah's mother, "it is a very wonderful beginning to this essay. . . I am immediately interested in how this writer will carry out her family responsibilities."

"I used to look at the calendar, find the day where it said 'The first day of Hanukkah,' *and prepare everything for the great event on the evening* before,"   10 Sarah's essay continues in a prose style hardly distinctive from anyone else's in the class.

"One sure thing that helps a writer interest strangers," I say, "is the presence of a unique and thoroughly engaging voice . . . a voice like nobody else's. Take, for example, the work of Joan Didion or Truman Capote . . . or of Hemingway or Gertrude Stein. Or, more locally, of Shalom Alechem or Agnon."

"I think it is a very engaging voice in this piece," says Sarah's mother. "It is totally believable."

"This year's celebration was going to be no different," Sarah's piece goes on. *"I took a quick glance at the calendar,* not *suspecting anything different, and found out that we were supposed to celebrate on Wednesday night."*

"Then," I continue, "there's the question of a writer's loyalty. Writers, if they are any good at their work, must develop a loyalty, above all, to the piece of writing in question—*not* to some abstract ideal of the truth, or, even, to the facts themselves, but to the ideal of being both interesting and, in some deeper sense, *psychologically* true . . ."

15   "Which is why," I add, "those who are already privy to the facts may not be the best or the most reliable audience."

"I like it," says Sarah's mother. "This is exactly how it happened."

"When my husband returned with the required amount of donuts, starting with a little surprise on his face that there had been no rush at all at the bakery," writes Sarah, *"I became suspicious. But, to my shame, this did not happen."*

"One of the major risks for the personal essayist," I say, "is that the too frequent use of personal and possessive pronouns—*my shame, my husband, our family, etc.*—will make the piece seem too clearly intended for an already intimate audience, and the reader feel all the more excluded from the concerns of the piece—will make it all the more difficult for the personal essayist to arrive at something that speaks more *im*personally to the reader."

"I don't feel excluded from this piece *at all*," says Sarah's mother. "I was there, and this is *exactly* how it happened."

20   Most of the other students yawn and cough into their fists. For some reason, no one can rival Sarah's mother's enthusiasm for discussing Sarah's essay.

"I've always felt," I say to the class, "that one of the best things a beginning writer can do is to write with a sign above their desk that says, in large letters, 'NO ONE GIVES A DAMN ABOUT ME UNLESS I CAN MAKE THEM.' The problem for most young writers is that they are too accustomed to showing their work to those who are already, somehow, invested in their lives. While in life we have to *work* at alienating our intimates, we have the opposite problem in literature: we have to work hard to interest *strangers*."

Sarah's essay goes on: *"The great moment came. Everybody gathered around our big dining table, which was covered with a white tablecloth. My old father was the guest of honor, causing much happiness with the money he gave my daughters. The first candle was lit, everybody sang 'Maoz Zur,' and then we ate the donuts."*

"The effective essay," I say, glancing discretely at my watch, "is, in part, effective because it allows the *readers*—by providing them with enough specific detail and creating an actual sensual and physical atmosphere—to somehow *reenact* the writer's experience. It makes of the *writer's* personal sadness or loss or shame—through the impersonal and sensual mechanisms of art—the *reader's* sadness, loss or shame."

"I was fascinated by this piece," Sarah's mother offers proudly. "It was so filled with intimate details. I could *see* the white tablecloth again, and taste the donuts."

"But very gradually, the truth began to dawn on me," begins the last   25 paragraph of Sarah's essay. *"And when I looked at my calendar again, more carefully this time, I was really ashamed. So the first thing I did was call my old father, tell him of my mistake, and apologize to him."*

"Wonderful," Sarah's mother mutters under her breath with the palpable relief of someone who has been unable to sleep on her own excitement.

I should, I realize by now, feel grateful to Sarah and her mother for having, so unwittingly and poignantly, illustrated the points I've tried so hard to make to my class about the impersonality of art. But this, I remind myself, is Israel, and art, like most everything else in this country, has a slight "all in the family" quality to it. The problem here, to paraphrase a remark of Wallace Stevens' about humanity in general, is not that people aren't intimate, but that they're intimate with everyone.

"Well," I say, feeling guiltily grateful that the hour is coming to an end, "it's time to quit for today. Next week, we'll discuss Onat's essay, 'Portrait of a Moment.'"

Onat, now seeming to have caught the fever of Sarah's mother's passion, waves her hand into the air. "Would you mind," she says, "if I brought my husband?"

Drama   **William Borden**

THE BLUES STREET JAZZ CLUB REHEARSES
Characters

DON: Twenties or thirties, saxophonist.
BEVERLY: Twenties or thirties, drummer.
FRANK: Twenties or thirties, trumpet player.
SALLY: Twenties or thirties, keyboard player.
ALICE: Twenties or thirties, bass player.

Setting

Minimal.

Time
The present.

A bluesy, winsome saxophone winds a heartbreaking melody through the dark theater. Soft blue light up on DON, a sax to his lips, his fingers caressing the keys. The music tears our hearts out, it's so sad and so beautiful. DON takes the sax away from his lips, but the music continues. Light up, whiter. DON lays down the sax, lights a cigarette, listens to the music. He wears an old sweatshirt, trousers. BEVERLY enters. A drum solo begins on the music. She mimes the drumming. As the drum solo reaches a crescendo of complex virtuosity, DON turns off the CD player. BEVERLY continues the drum solo, then stops.

BEVERLY: You quit smoking.

(He nods, takes a drag.)

BEVERLY: Where are the others?

(He looks at his watch.)

BEVERLY: They're always late. *(She watches him a moment.)* Are you seeing Alice again?

(He tries to ignore her.)

BEVERLY: That explains it.
DON: I'm smoking because I want to smoke!
BEVERLY: Your lungs are the color of prunes!
DON: Alice loves me.
BEVERLY: Your breath sounds like a chain saw.
DON: She came over last night.
BEVERLY: Don't tell me.

DON: She was as seductive as ever.

BEVERLY: I don't know what love is. What is it? Heartbreak?

DON: That's country western.

BEVERLY: A good orgasm?

DON: You went to the Beethoven concert, didn't you?

BEVERLY: Dying for each other?

DON: Opera. Gounod.

BEVERLY: Habit? A habit you can't break?

(He gives her a look, stubs out his cigarette.)

BEVERLY: Quitting again?

(He nods. She smiles knowingly.)

DON: Alice wants you to—

(FRANK enters, interrupting them. He carries a trumpet case.)

FRANK: I'm here, I'm here, I'm here because I'm here—how you doin', you guys, huh?

(FRANK takes a battered trumpet out of the case, puts on a CD. A trumpet wails as he puts the trumpet to his lips and pretends to play. DON turns off the CD player.)

FRANK: What the hell? Is this a rehearsal or not? Don? Beverly?

(DON lights a cigarette.)

BEVERLY: He started again.

FRANK: *(To DON.)* You can't play the sax and smoke.

DON: Dexter Gordon smoked.

FRANK: You ruin it for the group. You're not the only one, you know. The sound depends on all of us.

(DON stubs out the cigarette. FRANK turns on the CD player. A trumpet wails. FRANK puts his trumpet to his lips. BEVERLY "drums." A sax comes in. FRANK and BEVERLY look at DON. A few beats. He puts the sax to his lips. A keyboard comes in. The three of them hesitate, look around. SALLY enters, drops her coat, "plays" a keyboard. A few beats. FRANK turns off the player.)

BEVERLY: You're late.

FRANK: You missed a few notes.

SALLY: My fingers are stiff. Damn computer all day. I'm getting that carpal tunnel thing. Mail order adult videos — you know how many people want *My Back Door's Open and I'm Lonely for You*?

DON: Sounds like a country western song.

SALLY: It's number one this week.

BEVERLY: You watch?

SALLY: Descriptions on the box covers.

DON: How can you work there?

SALLY: When I was a telemarketer I was always pissing people off. Now I make people happy.

DON: Perverts.

SALLY: We don't use that term. Except as a compliment.

DON: It's filth.

SALLY: You're a mechanic. Your hands are black.

BEVERLY: His lungs are black.

SALLY: Did you start again?

FRANK: Alice.

SALLY: Oh God.

DON: She loves me.

SALLY: You're pitiful. Is she coming?

BEVERLY: Why wouldn't she come? She loves him.

SALLY: You loved him. Once.

BEVERLY: I loved you, too.

SALLY: You weren't going to tell that.

BEVERLY: I enjoyed it. Didn't you?

SALLY: Yes.

(Beat.)

FRANK: She should be here. She playing trombone tonight? Guitar? Clarinet? I wish she'd make up her mind.

DON: *(To BEVERLY.)* Alice—last night—said she wanted you to—

SALLY: I don't want to hear about Alice.

(FRANK puts on a CD. Discordant jazz. To BEVERLY.)

SALLY: Why didn't you ever call?

BEVERLY: I was afraid.

SALLY: Of me?

(FRANK begins to "play.")

BEVERLY: What you'd think of me?

SALLY: I thought you loved me.

(DON begins to "play.")

BEVERLY: Why does it have to be me who calls?

(On the CD the piano takes a solo. FRANK and DON look at BEVERLY. Finally she "plays." A few beats. ALICE enters. She wears a stained

*waitress's uniform. She watches them a moment, listens, exits, returns
dragging an acoustic bass. She "plays" as the bass on the CD takes a solo.
The others watch. When the solo ends, they quietly applaud. BEVERLY
turns off the player.)*

ALICE: Sorry I'm late.
FRANK: Nice finger work.
ALICE: I love Don.
BEVERLY: He started smoking.
SALLY: Again.
ALICE: Don't blame me.
FRANK: Sally and BEVERLY—

(DON lights a cigarette.)

ALICE: I don't care. I made a hundred and three in tips. Two dollars in
    pennies.
FRANK: I leave pennies. Just to get rid of them.
ALICE: Take them to the bank. My legs ache.
SALLY: What was the special?
ALICE: Maybe I'm getting that fibromyalgia. Meat loaf.
FRANK: Again?
DON: *(To ALICE.)* I love you.
BEVERLY: I don't need this.
DON: I would've loved you if you'd've let me.
BEVERLY: We tried it.
DON: We could try it again.
FRANK: Beverly . . .
BEVERLY: *(To SALLY.)* Do we still have that Brubeck we used to play?
FRANK: *(To BEVERLY.)* I've always loved you. Since we were kids.
BEVERLY: *(To SALLY.)* What's it called?
ALICE: *(To DON.)* You still love her.
DON: *(To ALICE.)* I love you.
SALLY: *(To BEVERLY.)* I love you.
FRANK: *(To BEVERLY.)* I dream about you.

*(BEVERLY looks at FRANK, at SALLY. DON coughs. ALICE takes away
his cigarette.)*

BEVERLY: *(To ALICE.)* He's used to me, that's all. I'm like a bad habit.
ALICE: Is that what love is? A habit?
SALLY: I've watched hundreds of those videos, looking for love.
FRANK: It's a hurt, here. *(In the heart.)*
DON: Here it is. *(He pulls out a CD.)*
FRANK: You know love when you see it.

SALLY: *(To BEVERLY.)* Do you?

ALICE: Don't you?

FRANK: *(To BEVERLY.)* Since we were seven. You were swinging in that old green porch swing. You were barefoot. The chain squeaked.

(He actually plays the trumpet, a series of squeaks.)

FRANK: Back and forth. Kicking your bare legs.

(He plays a few more squeaks.)

BEVERLY: Why didn't you tell me?

FRANK: I was just the trumpet player.

DON: I know love when I see it.

SALLY: You can't see love.

(ALICE puts on the CD. One by one they begin to "play." Light eases to a smoky blue, as in a nightclub, then fades as the music fades.)

END OF PLAY

Poetry   **James Byrne**

SESTINA FOR R

(with repetitions of two lines by Edna St. Vincent Millay)

Dawn and again your voice cracks
like a vessel too thin for certain
vibrations. Demisting the window,
you rock gently from side-to-side,
your hand waving with a rhythm   5
that holds you to it as if by a drug.

Your doctor prescribes the same drug
on every visit, widening the cracks
in your downcast face. Deadly rhythm.
If treatment and health go side-by-side,   10
untreatable is your face at the window.
You're the same sunk vessel, for certain.

Like a vessel too thin for certain
vibrations, you re-alight in '91: a drug
binge at The Brain. Memory's window   15
props open, reconfiguring wisecracks
from the promo video. On the outside
you were a zeitgeister, the rhythm

of the club — the core of its rhythm.
What plans you had. Fame, for certain.   20
But the pilled-up crew at your side
guided a thin vessel. Love was the drug
fooled by its addiction. The cracks
widen in your profile at the window.

Who are you waiting for at the window?   25
The streetlamps click off to the rhythm
of a lit horizon. Chimney cracks
proffer terraced light to a certain
vibration, until the light, like a drug,
fires the body, flush full on the side   30

of your face (as if warmed from inside).
This is your life at the window.
Fear-hogged, shocked quiet by drug

after drug. Frail now, less of rhythm,
35   like a vessel too thin for certain
vibrations. Furrowed are the cracks.

Outside, traffic cargoes to a rhythm.
You hear a ghost sonata tap the window.
I listen in closely until your voice cracks.

Fiction   **Italo Calvino**

ALL AT ONE POINT

Through the calculations begun by Edwin P. Hubble on the galaxies' velocity of recession, we can establish the moment when all the universe's matter was concentrated in a single point, before it began to expand in space.

Naturally, we were all there—*old Qfwfq said*—where else could we have been? Nobody knew then that there could be space. Or time either: what use did we have for time, packed in there like sardines?

I say "packed like sardines," using a literary image: in reality there wasn't even space to pack us into. Every point of each of us coincided with every point of each of the others in a single point, which was where we all were. In fact, we didn't even bother one another, except for personality differences, because when space doesn't exist, having somebody unpleasant like Mr. Pber^t Pber^d underfoot all the time is the most irritating thing.

How many of us were there? Oh, I was never able to figure that out, not even approximately. To make a count, we would have had to move apart, at least a little, and instead we all occupied that same point. Contrary to what you might think, it wasn't the sort of situation that encourages sociability; I know, for example, that in other periods neighbors called on one another; but there, because of the fact that we were all neighbors, nobody even said good morning or good evening to anybody else.

In the end each of us associated only with a limited number of acquaintances. The ones I remember most are Mrs. Ph(i)Nk$_o$, her friend De XuaeauX, a family of immigrants by the name of Z'zu, and Mr. Pber^t Pber^d, whom I just mentioned. There was also a cleaning woman—"maintenance staff" she was called—only one, for the whole universe, since there was so little room. To tell the truth, she had nothing to do all day long, not even dusting—inside one point not even a grain of dust can enter—so she spent all her time gossiping and complaining.

Just with the people I've already named we would have been overcrowded; but you have to add all the stuff we had to keep piled up in there: all the material that was to serve afterwards to form the universe, now dismantled and concentrated in such a way that you weren't able to tell what was later to become part of astronomy (like the nebula of Andromeda) from what was assigned to geography (the Vosges, for example) or to chemistry (like certain beryllium isotopes). And on top of that, we were always bumping against the Z'zu family's household goods: camp beds, mattresses, baskets; these Z'zus, if you weren't careful, with the excuse that they were a large family, would begin to act as if they were the only

5

ones in the world: they even wanted to hang lines across our point to dry their washing.

But the others also had wronged the Z'zus, to begin with, by calling them "immigrants," on the pretext that, since the others had been there first, the Z'zus had come later. This was mere unfounded prejudice—that seems obvious to me—because neither before nor after existed, nor any place to immigrate from, but there were those who insisted that the concept of "immigrant" could be understood in the abstract, outside of space and time.

It was what you might call a narrow-minded attitude, our outlook at that time, very petty. The fault of the environment in which we had been reared. An attitude that, basically, has remained in all of us, mind you: it keeps cropping up even today, if two of us happen to meet—at the bus stop, in a movie house, at an international dentists' convention—and start reminiscing about the old days. We say hello—at times somebody recognizes me, at other times I recognize somebody—and we promptly start asking about this one and that one (even if each remembers only a few of those remembered by the others), and so we start in again on the old disputes, the slanders, the denigrations. Until somebody mentions Mrs. $Ph(i)Nk_0$—every conversation finally gets around to her—and then, all of a sudden, the pettiness is put aside, and we feel uplifted, filled with a blissful, generous emotion. Mrs. $Ph(i)Nk_0$, the only one that none of us has forgotten and that we all regret. Where has she ended up? I have long since stopped looking for her: Mrs. $Ph(i)Nk_0$, her bosom, her thighs, her orange dressing gown—we'll never meet her again, in this system of galaxies or in any other.

Let me make one thing clear: this theory that the universe, after having reached an extremity of rarefaction, will be condensed again has never convinced me. And yet many of us are counting only on that, continually making plans for the time when we'll all be back there again. Last month, I went into the bar here on the corner and whom did I see? Mr. Pber^t Pber^d. "What's new with you? How do you happen to be in this neighborhood?" I learned that he's the agent for a plastics firm, in Pavia. He's the same as ever, with his silver tooth, his loud suspenders. "When we go back there," he said to me, in a whisper, "the thing we have to make sure of is, this time, certain people remain out . . . You know who I mean: those Z'zus . . ."

I would have liked to answer him by saying that I've heard a number of people make the same remark, concluding: "You know who I mean . . . Mr. Pber^t Pber^d . . ."

To avoid the subject, I hasten to say: "What about Mrs. $Ph(i)Nk_0$? Do you think we'll find her back there again?"

10   "Ah, yes . . . She, by all means . . ." he said, turning purple.

For all of us the hope of returning to that point means, above all, the hope of being once more with Mrs. Ph(i)Nk$_0$. (This applies even to me, though I don't believe in it.) And in that bar, as always happens, we fell to talking about her, and were moved; even Mr. Pber^t Pber^d's unpleasantness faded, in the face of that memory.

Mrs. Ph(i)Nk$_0$'s great secret is that she never aroused any jealousy among us. Or any gossip, either. The fact that she went to bed with her friend, Mr. De XuaeauX, was well known. But in a point, if there's a bed, it takes up the whole point, so it isn't a question of *going* to bed, but of *being* there, because anybody in the point is also in the bed. Consequently, it was inevitable that she should be in bed also with each of us. If she had been another person, there's no telling all the things that would have been said about her. It was the cleaning woman who always started the slander, and the others didn't have to be coaxed to imitate her. On the subject of the Z'zu family—for a change!—the horrible things we had to hear: father, daughters, brothers, sisters, mother, aunts: nobody showed any hesitation even before the most sinister insinuation. But with her it was different: the happiness I derived from her was the joy of being concealed, punctiform, in her, and of protecting her, punctiform, in me; it was at the same time vicious contemplation (thanks to the promiscuity of the punctiform convergence of us all in her) and also chastity (given her punctiform impenetrability). In short: what more could I ask?

And all of this, which was true of me, was true also for each of the others. And for her: she contained and was contained with equal happiness, and she welcomed us and loved and inhabited all equally.

We got along so well all together, so well that something extraordinary was bound to happen. It was enough for her to say, at a certain moment: "Oh, if I only had some room, how I'd like to make some noodles for you boys!" And in that moment we all thought of the space that her round arms would occupy, moving backward and forward with the rolling pin over the dough, her bosom leaning over the great mound of flour and eggs which cluttered the wide board while her arms kneaded and kneaded, white and shiny with oil up to the elbows; we thought of the space that the flour would occupy, and the wheat for the flour, and the fields to raise the wheat, and the mountains from which the water would flow to irrigate the fields, and the grazing lands for the herds of calves that would give their meat for the sauce; of the space it would take for the Sun to arrive with its rays, to ripen the wheat; of the space for the Sun to condense from the clouds of stellar gases and burn; of the quantities of stars and galaxies and galactic masses in flight through space which would be needed to hold suspended every galaxy, every nebula, every sun, every planet, and at the same time we thought of it, this space was inevitably being formed, at the same time that Mrs. Ph(i)Nk$_0$ was uttering those words: ". . . ah, what noodles, boys!"

the point that contained her and all of us was expanding in a halo of distance in light-years and light-centuries and billions of light-millennia, and we were being hurled to the four corners of the universe (Mr. Pber^t Pber^d all the way to Pavia), and she, dissolved into I don't know what kind of energy-light-heat, she, Mrs. Ph(i)Nk$_o$, she who in the midst of our closed, petty world had been capable of a generous impulse, "Boys, the noodles I would make for you!," a true outburst of general love, initiating at the same moment the concept of space and, properly speaking, space itself, and time, and universal gravitation, and the gravitating universe, making possible billions and billions of suns, and of planets, and fields of wheat, and Mrs. Ph(i)Nk$_o$s, scattered through the continents of the planets, kneading with floury, oil-shiny, generous arms, and she lost at that very moment, and we, mourning her loss.

Poetry   **Judith Ortiz Cofer**

THE CHANGELING

As a young girl
vying for my father's attention,
I invented a game that made him look up
from his reading and shake his head
as if both baffled and amused.   5

In my brother's closet, I'd change
into his dungarees—the rough material
molding me into boy shape; hide
my long hair under an army helmet
he'd been given by Father, and emerge   10
transformed into the legendary Che
of grown-up talk.

Strutting around the room,
I'd tell of life in the mountains,
of carnage and rivers of blood,   15
and of manly feasts with rum and music
to celebrate victories *para la libertad.*
He would listen with a smile
to my tales of battles and brotherhood
until Mother called us to dinner.   20

She was not amused
by my transformations, sternly forbidding me
from sitting down with them as a man.
She'd order me back to the dark cubicle
that smelled of adventure, to shed   25
my costume, to braid my hair furiously
with blind hands, and to return invisible,
as myself,
to the real world of her kitchen.

Fiction   Julio Cortázar

LETTER TO A YOUNG LADY IN PARIS

Andrea, I didn't want to come live in your apartment in the calle Suipacha. Not so much because of the bunnies, but rather that it offends me to intrude on a compact order, built even to the finest nets of air, networks that in your environment conserve the music in the lavender, the heavy fluff of the powder puff in the talcum, the play between the violin and the viola in Ravel's quartet. It hurts me to come into an ambience where someone who lives beautifully has arranged everything like a visible affirmation of her soul, here the books (Spanish on one side, French and English on the other), the large green cushions there, the crystal ashtray that looks like a soap-bubble that's been cut open on this exact spot on the little table, and always a perfume, a sound, a sprouting of plants, a photograph of the dead friend, the ritual of tea trays and sugar tongs . . . Ah, dear Andrea, how difficult it is to stand counter to, yet to accept with perfect submission of one's whole being, the elaborate order that a woman establishes in her own gracious flat. How much at fault one feels taking a small metal tray and putting it at the far end of the table, setting it there simply because one has brought one's English dictionaries and it's at this end, within easy reach of the hand, that they ought to be. To move that tray is the equivalent of an unexpected horrible crimson in the middle of one of Ozenfant's painterly cadences, as if suddenly the strings of all the double basses snapped at the same time with the same dreadful whiplash at the most hushed instant in a Mozart symphony. Moving that tray alters the play of relationships in the whole house, of each object with another, of each moment of their soul with the soul of the house and its absent inhabitant. And I cannot bring my fingers close to a book, hardly change a lamp's cone of light, open the piano bench, without a feeling of rivalry and offense swinging before my eyes like a flock of sparrows.

You know why I came to your house, to your peaceful living room scooped out of the noonday light. Everything looks so natural, as always when one does not know the truth. You've gone off to Paris, I am left with the apartment in the calle Suipacha, we draw up a simple and satisfactory plan convenient to us both until September brings you back again to Buenos Aires and I amble off to some other house where perhaps . . . But I'm not writing you for that reason, I was sending this letter to you because of the rabbits, it seems only fair to let you know; and because I like to write letters, and maybe too because it's raining.

I moved last Thursday in a haze overlaid by weariness, at five in the afternoon. I've closed so many suitcases in my life, I've passed so many hours preparing luggage that never manages to get moved anyplace, that

Thursday was a day full of shadows and straps, because when I look at valise straps it's as though I were seeing shadows, as though they were parts of a whip that flogs me in some indirect way, very subtly and horribly. But I packed the bags, let your maid know I was coming to move in. I was going up in the elevator and just between the first and second floors I felt that I was going to vomit up a little rabbit. I have never described this to you before, not so much, I don't think, from lack of truthfulness as that, just naturally, one is not going to explain to people at large that from time to time one vomits up a small rabbit. Always I have managed to be alone when it happens, guarding the fact much as we guard so many of our privy acts, evidences of our physical selves which happen to us in total privacy. Don't reproach me for it, Andrea, don't blame me. Once in a while it happens that I vomit up a bunny. It's no reason not to live in whatever house, it's no reason for one to blush and isolate oneself and to walk around keeping one's mouth shut.

When I feel that I'm going to bring up a rabbit, I put two fingers in my mouth like an open pincer, and I wait to feel the lukewarm fluff rise in my throat like the effervescence in a sal hepatica. It's all swift and clean, passes in the briefest instant. I remove the fingers from my mouth and in them, held fast by the ears, a small white rabbit. The bunny appears to be content, a perfectly normal bunny only very tiny, small as a chocolate rabbit, only it's white and very thoroughly a rabbit. I set it in the palm of my hand, I smooth the fluff, caressing it with two fingers; the bunny seems satisfied with having been born and waggles and pushes its muzzle against my skin, moving it with that quiet and tickling nibble of a rabbit's mouth against the skin of the hand. He's looking for something to eat, and then (I'm talking about when this happened at my house on the outskirts) I take him with me out to the balcony and set him down in the big flower-pot among the clover that I've grown there with this in mind. The bunny raises his ears as high as they can go, surrounds a tender clover leaf with a quick little wheeling motion of his snout, and I know that I can leave him there now and go on my way for a time, lead a life not very different from people who buy their rabbits at farmhouses.

Between the first and the second floors, then, Andrea, like an omen of what my life in your house was going to be, I realized that I was going to vomit a rabbit. At that point I was afraid (or was it surprise? No, perhaps fear of the same surprise) because, before leaving my house, only two days before, I'd vomited a bunny and so was safe for a month, five weeks, maybe six with a little luck. Now, look, I'd resolved the problem perfectly. I grew clover on the balcony of my other house, vomited a bunny, put it in with the clover and at the end of a month, when I suspected that any moment . . . then I made a present of the rabbit, already grown enough, to señora

5

de Molina, who believed I had a hobby and was quiet about it. In another flowerpot tender and propitious clover was already growing, I awaited without concern the morning when the tickling sensation of fluff rising obstructed my throat, and the new little rabbit reiterated from that hour the life and habits of its predecessor. Habits, Andrea, are concrete forms of rhythm, are that portion of rhythm which helps to keep us alive. Vomiting bunnies wasn't so terrible once one had gotten into the unvarying cycle, into the method. You will want to know why all this work, why all that clover and señora de Molina. It would have been easier to kill the little thing right away and . . . Ah, you should vomit one up all by yourself, take it in two fingers and set it in your opened hand, still attached to yourself by the act itself, by the indefinable aura of its proximity, barely now broken away. A month puts a lot of things at a distance; a month is size, long fur, long leaps, ferocious eyes, an absolute difference. Andrea, a month is a rabbit, it really makes a real rabbit; but in the maiden moment, the warm bustling fleece covering an inalienable presence . . . like a poem in its first minutes, "fruit of an Idumean night" as much one as oneself . . . and afterwards not so much one, so distant and isolated in its flat white world the size of a letter.

With all that, I decided to kill the rabbit almost as soon as it was born. I was going to live at your place for four months: four, perhaps with luck three—tablespoonsful of alcohol down its throat. (Do you know pity permits you to kill a small rabbit instantly by giving it a tablespoon of alcohol to drink? Its flesh tastes better afterward, they say, however, I . . . Three or four tablespoonsful of alcohol, then the bathroom or a package to put in the rubbish.)

Rising up past the third floor, the rabbit was moving in the palm of my hand. Sara was waiting upstairs to help me get the valises in . . . Could I explain that it was a whim? Something about passing a pet store? I wrapped the tiny creature in my handkerchief, put him into my overcoat pocket, leaving the overcoat unbuttoned so as not to squeeze him. He barely budged. His minuscule consciousness would be revealing important facts: that life is a movement upward with a final click, and is also a low ceiling, white and smelling of lavender, enveloping you in the bottom of a warm pit.

Sara saw nothing, she was too fascinated with the arduous problem of adjusting her sense of order to my valise-and-footlocker, my papers and my peevishness at her elaborate explanations in which the words "for example" occurred with distressing frequency. I could hardly get the bathroom door closed; to kill it now. A delicate area of heat surrounded the handkerchief, the little rabbit was extremely white and, I think, prettier than the others. He wasn't looking at me, he just hopped about and was being content, which was even worse than looking at me. I shut him in the

empty medicine chest and went on unpacking, disoriented but not unhappy, not feeling guilty, not soaping up my hands to get off the feel of a
final convulsion.

I realized that I could not kill him. But that same night I vomited a little
black bunny. And two days later another white one. And on the fourth
night a tiny grey one.

You must love the handsome wardrobe in your bedroom, with its great   10
door that opens so generously, its empty shelves awaiting my clothes. Now
I have them in there. Inside there. True, it seems impossible; not even Sara
would believe it. That Sara did not suspect anything, was the result of my
continuous preoccupation with a task that takes over my days and nights
with the singleminded crash of the portcullis falling, and I go about hard-
ened inside, calcined like that starfish you've put above the bathtub, and at
every bath I take it seems all at once to swell with salt and whiplashes of
sun and great rumbles of profundity.

They sleep during the day. There are ten of them. During the day they
sleep. With the door closed, the wardrobe is a diurnal night for them
alone, there they sleep out their night in a sedate obedience. When I leave
for work I take the bedroom keys with me. Sara must think that I mistrust
her honesty and looks at me doubtfully, every morning she looks as
though she's about to say something to me, but in the end she remains
silent and I am that much happier. (When she straightens up the bedroom
between nine and ten, I make noise in the living room, put on a Benny
Carter record which fills the whole apartment, and as Sara is a *saetas* and
pasodobles fan, the wardrobe seems to be silent, and for the most part it is,
because for the rabbits it's night still and repose is the order of the day.)

Their day begins an hour after supper when Sara brings in the tray with
the delicate tinkling of the sugar tongs, wishes me good night—yes, she
wishes me, Andrea, the most ironic thing is that she wishes me good
night—shuts herself in her room, and promptly I'm by myself, alone with
the closed-up wardrobe, alone with my obligation and my melancholy.

I let them out, they hop agilely to the party in the living room, sniffing
briskly at the clover hidden in my pockets which makes ephemeral lacy
patterns on the carpet which they alter, remove, finish up in a minute.
They eat well, quietly and correctly; until that moment I have nothing to
say, I just watch them from the sofa, a useless book in my hand—I who
wanted to read all of Giraudoux, Andrea, and López's Argentine history
that you keep on the lower shelf—and they eat up the clover.

There are ten. Almost all of them white. They lift their warm heads
toward the lamps in the living room, the three motionless suns of their
day; they love the light because their night has neither moon nor sun nor
stars nor streetlamps. They gaze at their triple sun and are content. That's

when they hop about on the carpet, into the chairs, ten tiny blotches shift like a moving constellation from one part to another, while I'd like to see them quiet, see them at my feet and being quiet—somewhat the dream of any god, Andrea, a dream the gods never see fulfilled—something quite different from wriggling in behind the portrait of Miguel de Unamuno, then off to the pale green urn, over into the dark hollow of the writing desk, always fewer than ten, always six or eight and I asking myself where the two are that are missing, and what if Sara should get up for some reason, and the presidency of Rivadavia which is what I want to read in López's history.

15   Andrea, I don't know how I stand up under it. You remember that I came to your place for some rest. It's not my fault if I vomit a bunny from time to time, if this moving changed me inside as well—not nominalism, it's not magic either, it's just that things cannot alter like that all at once, sometimes things reverse themselves brutally and when you expect the slap on the right cheek—. Like that, Andrea, or some other way, but always like that.

It's night while I'm writing you. It's three in the afternoon, but I'm writing you during their night. They sleep during the day. What a relief this office is! Filled with shouts, commands, Royal typewriters, vice presidents and mimeograph machines! What relief, what peace, what horror, Andrea! They're calling me to the telephone now. It was some friends upset about my monasterial nights, Luis inviting me out for a stroll or Jorge insisting—he's bought a ticket for me for this concert. I hardly dare to say no to them, I invent long and ineffectual stories about my poor health, I'm behind in the translations, any evasion possible. And when I get back home and am in the elevator—that stretch between the first and second floors—night after night, hopelessly, I formulate the vain hope that really it isn't true.

I'm doing the best I can to see that they don't break your things. They've nibbled away a little at the books on the lowest shelf, you'll find the backs repasted, which I did so that Sara wouldn't notice it. That lamp with the porcelain belly full of butterflies and old cowboys, do you like that very much? The crack where the piece was broken out barely shows, I spent a whole night doing it with a special cement that they sold me in an English shop—you know the English stores have the best cements—and now I sit beside it so that one of them can't reach it again with its paws (it's almost lovely to see how they like to stand on their hind legs, nostalgia for that so-distant humanity, perhaps an imitation of their god walking about and looking at them darkly; besides which, you will have observed—when you were a baby, perhaps—that you can put a bunny in the corner against the wall like a punishment, and he'll stand there, paws against the wall and very quiet, for hours and hours).

At 5 A.M. (I slept a little stretched out on the green sofa, waking up at every velvety-soft dash, every slightest clink) I put them in the wardrobe and do the cleaning up. That way Sara always finds everything in order, although at times I've noticed a restrained astonishment, a stopping to look at some object, a slight discoloration in the carpet, and again the desire to ask me something, but then I'm whistling Franck's *Symphonic Variations* in a way that always prevents her. How can I tell you about it, Andrea, the minute mishaps of this soundless and vegetal dawn, half-asleep on what staggered path picking up butt-ends of clover, individual leaves, white hunks of fur, falling against the furniture, crazy from lack of sleep, and I'm behind in my Gide, Troyat I haven't gotten to translating, and my reply to a distant young lady who will be asking herself already if . . . why go on with all this, why go on with this letter I keep trying to write between telephone calls and interviews.

Andrea, dear Andrea, my consolation is that there are ten of them and no more. It's been fifteen days since I held the last bunny in the palm of my hand, since then nothing, only the ten of them with me, their diurnal night and growing, ugly already and getting long hair, adolescents now and full of urgent needs and crazy whims, leaping on top of the bust of Antinoös (it is Antinoös, isn't it, that boy who looks blindly?) or losing themselves in the living room where their movements make resounding thumps, so much so that I ought to chase them out of there for fear that Sara will hear them and appear before me in a fright and probably in her nightgown—it would have to be like that with Sara, she'd be in her nightgown—and then . . . Only ten, think of that little happiness I have in the middle of it all, the growing calm with which, on my return home, I cut past the rigid ceilings of the first and second floors.

I was interrupted because I had to attend a committee meeting. I'm continuing the letter here at your house, Andrea, under the soundless grey light of another dawn. Is it really the next day, Andrea? A bit of white on the page will be all you'll have to represent the bridge, hardly a period on a page between yesterday's letter and today's. How tell you that in that interval everything has gone smash? Where you see that simple period I hear the circling belt of water break the dam in its fury, this side of the paper for me, this side of my letter to you I can't write with the same calm which I was sitting in when I had to put it aside to go to the committee meeting. Wrapped in their cube of night, sleeping without a worry in the world, eleven bunnies; perhaps even now, but no, not now— In the elevator then, or coming into the building; it's not important now where, if the when is now, if it can happen in any now of those that are left to me.

Enough now, I've written this because it's important to me to let you know that I was not all that responsible for the unavoidable and helpless destruction of your home. I'll leave this letter here for you, it would be indecent if the mailman should deliver it some fine clear morning in Paris. Last night I turned the books on the second shelf in the other direction; they were already reaching that high, standing up on their hind legs or jumping, they gnawed off the backs to sharpen their teeth—not that they were hungry, they had all the clover I had bought for them, I store it in the drawers of the writing desk. They tore the curtains, the coverings on the easy chairs, the edge of Augusto Torres' self-portrait, they got fluff all over the rug and besides they yipped, there's no word for it, they stood in a circle under the light of the lamp, in a circle as though they were adoring me, and suddenly they were yipping, they were crying like I never believed rabbits could cry.

I tried in vain to pick up all the hair that was ruining the rug, to smooth out the edges of the fabric they'd chewed on, to shut them up again in the wardrobe. Day is coming, maybe Sara's getting up early. It's almost queer, I'm not disturbed so much about Sara. It's almost queer, I'm not disturbed to see them gamboling about looking for something to play with. I'm not so much to blame, you'll see when you get here that I've repaired a lot of the things that were broken with the cement I bought in the English shop, I did what I could to keep from being a nuisance . . . As far as I'm concerned, going from ten to eleven is like an unbridgeable chasm. You understand: ten was fine, with a wardrobe, clover and hope, so many things could happen for the better. But not with eleven, because to say eleven is already to say twelve for sure, and Andrea, twelve would be thirteen. So now it's dawn and a cold solitude in which happiness ends, reminiscences, you and perhaps a good deal more. This balcony over the street is filled with dawn, the first sounds of the city waking. I don't think it will be difficult to pick up eleven small rabbits splattered over the pavement, perhaps they won't even be noticed, people will be too occupied with the other body, it would be more proper to remove it quickly before the early students pass through on their way to school.

Fiction   **Junot Díaz**

EDISON, NEW JERSEY

The first time we try to deliver the Gold Crown the lights are on in the house but no one lets us in. I bang on the front door and Wayne hits the back and I can hear our double drum shaking the windows. Right then I have this feeling that someone is inside, laughing at us.

This guy better have a good excuse, Wayne says, lumbering around the newly planted rosebushes. This is bullshit.

You're telling me, I say but Wayne's the one who takes this job too seriously. He pounds some more on the door, his face jiggling. A couple of times he raps on the windows, tries squinting through the curtains. I take a more philosophical approach; I walk over to the ditch that has been cut next to the road, a drainage pipe half filled with water, and sit down. I smoke and watch a mama duck and her three ducklings scavenge the grassy bank and then float downstream like they're on the same string. Beautiful, I say but Wayne doesn't hear. He's banging on the door with the staple gun.

At nine Wayne picks me up at the showroom and by then I have our route planned out. The order forms tell me everything I need to know about the customers we'll be dealing with that day. If someone is just getting a fifty-two-inch card table delivered then you know they aren't going to give you too much of a hassle but they also aren't going to tip. Those are your Spotswood, Sayreville and Perth Amboy deliveries. The pool tables go north to the rich suburbs—Livingston, Ridgewood, Bedminster.

You should see our customers. Doctors, diplomats, surgeons, presidents of universities, ladies in slacks and silk tops who sport thin watches you could trade in for a car, who wear comfortable leather shoes. Most of them prepare for us by laying down a path of yesterday's *Washington Post* from the front door to the game room. I make them pick it all up. I say: Carajo, what if we slip? Do you know what two hundred pounds of slate could do to a floor? The threat of property damage puts the chop-chop in their step. The best customers leave us alone until the bill has to be signed. Every now and then we'll be given water in paper cups. Few have offered us more, though a dentist from Ghana once gave us a six-pack of Heineken while we worked.

Sometimes the customer has to jet to the store for cat food or a newspaper while we're in the middle of a job. I'm sure you'll be all right, they say. They never sound too sure. Of course, I say. Just show us where the silver's at. The customers ha-ha and we ha-ha and then they agonize over leaving, linger by the front door, trying to memorize everything they own, as if they don't know where to find us, who we work for.

Once they're gone, I don't have to worry about anyone bothering me. I put down the ratchet, crack my knuckles and explore, usually while Wayne is smoothing out the felt and doesn't need help. I take cookies from the kitchen, razors from the bathroom cabinets. Some of these houses have twenty, thirty rooms. On the ride back I figure out how much loot it would take to fill up all that space. I've been caught roaming around plenty of times but you'd be surprised how quickly someone believes you're looking for the bathroom if you don't jump when you're discovered, if you just say, Hi.

After the paperwork's been signed, I have a decision to make. If the customer has been good and tipped well, we call it even and leave. If the customer has been an ass—maybe they yelled, maybe they let their kids throw golf balls at us—I ask for the bathroom. Wayne will pretend that he hasn't seen this before; he'll count the drill bits while the customer (or their maid) guides the vacuum over the floor. Excuse me, I say. I let them show me the way to the bathroom (usually I already know) and once the door is shut I cram bubble bath drops into my pockets and throw fist-sized wads of toilet paper into the toilet. I take a dump if I can and leave that for them.

Most of the time Wayne and I work well together. He's the driver and the money man and I do the lifting and handle the assholes. Tonight we're on our way to Lawrenceville and he wants to talk to me about Charlene, one of the showroom girls, the one with the blowjob lips. I haven't wanted to talk about women in months, not since the girlfriend.

I really want to pile her, he tells me. Maybe on one of the Madisons.

10   Man, I say, cutting my eyes towards him. Don't you have a wife or something?

He gets quiet. I'd still like to pile her, he says defensively.

And what will that do?

Why does it have to *do* anything?

Twice this year Wayne's cheated on his wife and I've heard it all, the before and the after. The last time his wife nearly tossed his ass out to the dogs. Neither of the women seemed worth it to me. One of them was even younger than Charlene. Wayne can be a moody guy and this is one of those nights; he slouches in the driver's seat and swerves through traffic, riding other people's bumpers like I've told him not to do. I don't need a collision or a four-hour silent treatment so I try to forget that I think his wife is good people and ask him if Charlene's given him any signals.

He slows the truck down. Signals like you wouldn't believe, he says.

15   On the days we have no deliveries the boss has us working at the show-room, selling cards and poker chips and mankala boards. Wayne spends

his time skeezing the salesgirls and dusting shelves. He's a big goofy guy—I don't understand why the girls dig his shit. One of those mysteries of the universe. The boss keeps me in the front of the store, away from the pool tables. He knows I'll talk to the customers, tell them not to buy the cheap models. I'll say shit like, Stay away from those Bristols. Wait until you can get something real. Only when he needs my Spanish will he let me help on a sale. Since I'm no good at cleaning or selling slot machines I slouch behind the front register and steal. I don't ring anything up, and pocket what comes in. I don't tell Wayne. He's too busy running his fingers through his beard, keeping the waves on his nappy head in order. A hundred-buck haul's not unusual for me and back in the day, when the girlfriend used to pick me up, I'd buy her anything she wanted, dresses, silver rings, lingerie. Sometimes I blew it all on her. She didn't like the stealing but hell, we weren't made out of loot and I liked going into a place and saying, Jeva, pick out anything, it's yours. This is the closest I've come to feeling rich.

Nowadays I take the bus home and the cash stays with me. I sit next to this three-hundred-pound rock-and-roll chick who washes dishes at the Friendly's. She tells me about the roaches she kills with her water nozzle. Boils the wings right off them. On Thursday I buy myself lottery tickets—ten Quick Picks and a couple of Pick 4s. I don't bother with the little stuff.

The second time we bring the Gold Crown the heavy curtain next to the door swings up like a Spanish fan. A woman stares at me and Wayne's too busy knocking to see. Muñeca, I say. She's black and unsmiling and then the curtain drops between us, a whisper on the glass. She had on a t-shirt that said *No Problem* and didn't look like she owned the place. She looked more like the help and couldn't have been older than twenty and from the thinness of her face I pictured the rest of her skinny. We stared at each other for a second at the most, not enough for me to notice the shape of her ears or if her lips were chapped. I've fallen in love on less.

Later in the truck, on the way back to the showroom Wayne mutters, This guy is dead. I mean it.

The girlfriend calls sometimes but not often. She has found herself a new boyfriend, some zángano who works at a record store. *Dan* is his name and the way she says it, so painfully gringo, makes the corners of my eyes narrow. The clothes I'm sure this guy tears from her when they both get home from work—the chokers, the rayon skirts from the Warehouse, the lingerie—I bought with stolen money and I'm glad that none of it was earned straining my back against hundreds of pounds of raw rock. I'm glad for that.

20   The last time I saw her in person was in Hoboken. She was with *Dan*
and hadn't yet told me about him and hurried across the street in her high
clogs to avoid me and my boys, who even then could sense me turning,
turning into the motherfucker who'll put a fist through anything. She
flung one hand in the air but didn't stop. A month before the zángano, I
went to her house, a friend visiting a friend, and her parents asked me how
business was, as if I balanced the books or something. Business is outstanding, I said.
     That's really wonderful to hear, the father said.
     You betcha.
     He asked me to help him mow his lawn and while we were dribbling
gas into the tank he offered me a job. A real one that you can build on.
Utilities, he said, is nothing to be ashamed of.
     Later the parents went into the den to watch the Giants lose and she
took me into her bathroom. She put on her makeup because we were going
to a movie. If I had your eyelashes, I'd be famous, she told me. The Giants
started losing real bad. I still love you, she said and I was embarrassed for
the two of us, the way I'm embarrassed at those afternoon talk shows where
broken couples and unhappy families let their hearts hang out.

25   We're friends, I said and Yes, she said, yes we are.
     There wasn't much space so I had to put my heels on the edge of the bath-
tub. The cross I'd given her dangled down on its silver chain so I put it in my
mouth to keep it from poking me in the eye. By the time we finished my legs
were bloodless, broomsticks inside my rolled-down baggies and as her
breathing got smaller and smaller against my neck, she said, I do, I still do.

Each payday I take out the old calculator and figure how long it'd take me
to buy a pool table honestly. A top-of-the-line, three-piece slate affair
doesn't come cheap. You have to buy sticks and balls and chalk and a score
keeper and triangles and French tips if you're a fancy shooter. Two and a
half years if I give up buying underwear and eat only pasta but even this
figure's bogus. Money's never stuck to me, ever.
     Most people don't realize how sophisticated pool tables are. Yes, tables
have bolts and staples on the rails but these suckers hold together mostly
by gravity and by the precision of their construction. If you treat a good
table right it will outlast you. Believe me. Cathedrals are built like that.
There are Incan roads in the Andes that even today you couldn't work a
knife between two of the cobblestones. The sewers that the Romans built
in Bath were so good that they weren't replaced until the 1950s. That's the
sort of thing I can believe in.
     These days I can build a table with my eyes closed. Depending on how
rushed we are I might build the table alone, let Wayne watch until I need
help putting on the slate. It's better when the customers stay out of our

faces, how they react when we're done, how they run fingers on the lacquered rails and suck in their breath, the felt so tight you couldn't pluck it if you tried. Beautiful, is what they say and we always nod, talc on our fingers, nod again, beautiful.

The boss nearly kicked our asses over the Gold Crown. The customer, an asshole named Pruitt, called up crazy, said we were *delinquent*. That's how the boss put it. Delinquent. We knew that's what the customer called us because the boss doesn't use words like that. Look boss, I said, we knocked like crazy. I mean, we knocked like federal marshals. Like Paul Bunyan. The boss wasn't having it. You fuckos, he said. You butthogs. He tore us for a good two minutes and then *dismissed* us. For most of that night I didn't think I had a job so I hit the bars, fantasizing that I would bump into this cabrón out with that black woman while me and my boys were cranked but the next morning Wayne came by with that Gold Crown again. Both of us had hangovers. One more time, he said. An extra delivery, no overtime. We hammered on the door for ten minutes but no one answered. I jimmied with the windows and the back door and I could have sworn I heard her behind the patio door. I knocked hard and heard footsteps.

We called the boss and told him what was what and the boss called the house but no one answered. OK, the boss said. Get those card tables done. That night, as we lined up the next day's paperwork, we got a call from Pruitt and he didn't use the word delinquent. He wanted us to come late at night but we were booked. Two-month waiting list, the boss reminded him. I looked over at Wayne and wondered how much money this guy was pouring into the boss's ear. Pruitt said he was *contrite* and *determined* and asked us to come again. His maid was sure to let us in.

What the hell kind of name is Pruitt anyway? Wayne asks me when we swing onto the parkway.

Pato name, I say. Anglo or some other bog people.

Probably a fucking banker. What's the first name?

Just an initial, C. Clarence Pruitt sounds about right.

Yeah, Clarence, Wayne yuks.

Pruitt. Most of our customers have names like this, court case names: Wooley, Maynard, Gass, Binder, but the people from my town, our names, you see on convicts or coupled together on boxing cards.

We take our time. Go to the Rio Diner, blow an hour and all the dough we have in our pockets. Wayne is talking about Charlene and I'm leaning my head against a thick pane of glass.

Pruitt's neighborhood has recently gone up and only his court is complete. Gravel roams off this way and that, shaky. You can see inside the other houses, their newly formed guts, nailheads bright and sharp on the fresh timber. Wrinkled blue tarps protect wiring and fresh plaster. The driveways are mud and on each lawn stand huge stacks of sod. We park in front of Pruitt's house and bang on the door. I give Wayne a hard look when I see no car in the garage.

40   Yes? I hear a voice inside say.

We're the delivery guys, I yell.

A bolt slides, a lock turns, the door opens. She stands in our way, wearing black shorts and a gloss of red on her lips and I'm sweating.

Come in, yes? She stands back from the door, holding it open.

Sounds like Spanish, Wayne says.

45   No shit, I say, switching over. Do you remember me?

No, she says.

I look over at Wayne. Can you believe this?

I can believe anything, kid.

You heard us didn't you? The other day, that was you.

50   She shrugs and opens the door wider.

You better tell her to prop that with a chair. Wayne heads back to unlock the truck.

You hold that door, I say.

We've had our share of delivery trouble. Trucks break down. Customers move and leave us with an empty house. Handguns get pointed. Slate gets dropped, a rail goes missing. The felt is the wrong color, the Dufferins get left in the warehouse. Back in the day, the girlfriend and I made a game of this. A prediction game. In the mornings I rolled onto my pillow and said, What's today going to be like?

Let me check. She put her fingers up to her widow's peak and that motion would shift her breasts, her hair. We never slept under any covers, not in spring, fall or summer and our bodies were dark and thin the whole year.

55   I see an asshole customer, she murmured. Unbearable traffic. Wayne's going to work slow. And then you'll come home to me.

Will I get rich?

You'll come home to me. That's the best I can do. And then we'd kiss hungrily because this was how we loved each other.

The game was part of our mornings, the way our showers and our sex and our breakfasts were. We stopped playing only when it started to go wrong for us, when I'd wake up and listen to the traffic outside without waking her, when everything was a fight.

She stays in the kitchen while we work. I can hear her humming. Wayne's shaking his right hand like he's scalded his fingertips. Yes, she's fine. She has her back to me, her hands stirring around in a full sink, when I walk in.

I try to sound conciliatory. You're from the city?   60
A nod.
Where about?
Washington Heights.
Dominicana, I say. Quisqueyana. She nods. What street?
I don't know the address, she says. I have it written down. My mother   65
and my brothers live there.
I'm Dominican, I say.
You don't look it.
I get a glass of water. We're both staring out at the muddy lawn.
She says, I didn't answer the door because I wanted to piss him off.
Piss who off?   70
I want to get out of here, she says.
Out of here?
I'll pay you for a ride.
I don't think so, I say.
Aren't you from Nueva York?   75
No.
Then why did you ask the address?
Why? I have family near there.
Would it be that big of a problem?
I say in English that she should have her boss bring her but she stares at   80
me blankly. I switch over.

He's a pendejo, she says, suddenly angry. I put down the glass, move next to her to wash it. She's exactly my height and smells of liquid detergent and has tiny beautiful moles on her neck, an archipelago leading down into her clothes.

Here, she says, putting out her hand but I finish it and go back to the den.

Do you know what she wants us to do? I say to Wayne.

Her room is upstairs, a bed, a closet, a dresser, yellow wallpaper. Spanish *Cosmo* and *El Diario* thrown on the floor. Four hangers' worth of clothes in the closet and only the top dresser drawer is full. I put my hand on the bed and the cotton sheets are cool.

Pruitt has pictures of himself in his room. He's tan and probably has been to more countries than I know capitals for. Photos of him on vacations, on beaches, standing beside a wide-mouth Pacific salmon he's hooked. The size of his dome would have made Broca proud. The bed is made and his wardrobe spills out onto chairs and a line of dress shoes follows the far wall. A bachelor. I find an open box of Trojans in his dresser beneath a stack of boxer shorts. I put one of the condoms in my pocket and stick the rest under his bed.

85   I find her in her room. He likes clothes, she says.

A habit of money, I say but I can't translate it right; I end up agreeing with her. Are you going to pack?

She holds up her purse. I have everything I need. He can keep the rest of it.

You should take some of your things.

I don't care about that vaina. I just want to go.

90   Don't be stupid, I say. I open her dresser and pull out the shorts on top and a handful of soft bright panties fall out and roll down the front of my jeans. There are more in the drawer. I try to catch them but as soon as I touch their fabric I let everything go.

Leave it. Go on, she says and begins to put them back in the dresser, her square back to me, the movement of her hands smooth and easy.

Look, I say.

Don't worry. She doesn't look up.

I go downstairs. Wayne is sinking the bolts into the slate with the Makita. You can't do it, he says.

95   Why not?

Kid. We have to finish this.

I'll be back before you know it. A quick trip, in out.

Kid. He stands up slowly; he's nearly twice as old as me.

I go to the window and look out. New gingkoes stand in rows beside the driveway. A thousand years ago when I was still in college I learned something about them. Living fossils. Unchanged since their inception millions of years ago. You tagged Charlene, didn't you?

100   Sure did, he answers easily.

I take the truck keys out of the toolbox. I'll be right back, I promise.

My mother still has pictures of the girlfriend in her apartment. The girlfriend's the sort of person who never looks bad. There's a picture of us at the bar where I taught her to play pool. She's leaning on the Schmelke I stole for her, nearly a grand worth of cue, frowning at the shot I left her, a shot she'd go on to miss.

The picture of us in Florida is the biggest—shiny, framed, nearly a foot tall. We're in our bathing suits and the legs of some stranger frame the right. She has her butt in the sand, knees folded up in front of her because she knew I was sending the picture home to my moms; she didn't want my mother to see her bikini, didn't want my mother to think her a whore. I'm crouching next to her, smiling, one hand on her thin shoulder, one of her moles showing between my fingers.

My mother won't look at the pictures or talk about her when I'm around but my sister says she still cries over the breakup. Around me my mother's

polite, sits quietly on the couch while I tell her about what I'm reading and
how work has been. Do you have anyone? she asks me sometimes.

Yes, I say.   105

She talks to my sister on the side, says, In my dreams they're still
together.

We reach the Washington Bridge without saying a word. She's emptied his
cupboards and refrigerator; the bags are at her feet. She's eating corn chips
but I'm too nervous to join in.

Is this the best way? she asks. The bridge doesn't seem to impress her.

It's the shortest way.

She folds the bag shut. That's what he said when I arrived last year. I   110
wanted to see the countryside. There was too much rain to see anything
anyway.

I want to ask her if she loves her boss, but I ask instead, How do you like
the States?

She swings her head across at the billboards. I'm not surprised by any
of it, she says.

Traffic on the bridge is bad and she has to give me an oily fiver for the
toll. Are you from the Capital? I ask.

No.

I was born there. In Villa Juana. Moved here when I was a little boy.   115

She nods, staring out at the traffic. As we cross over the bridge I drop
my hand into her lap. I leave it there, palm up, fingers slightly curled.
Sometimes you just have to try, even if you know it won't work. She turns
her head away slowly, facing out beyond the bridge cables, out to Manhattan
and the Hudson.

Everything in Washington Heights is Dominican. You can't go a block
without passing a Quisqueya Bakery or a Quisqueya Supermercado or a
Hotel Quisqueya. If I were to park the truck and get out nobody would
take me for a deliveryman; I could be the guy who's on the street corner
selling Dominican flags. I could be on my way home to my girl. Everybody's
on the streets and the merengue's falling out of windows like TVs. When
we reach her block I ask a kid with the sag for the building and he points
out the stoop with his pinkie. She gets out of the truck and straightens the
front of her sweatshirt before following the line that the kid's finger has
cut across the street. Cuídate, I say.

Wayne works on the boss and a week later I'm back, on probation, painting
the warehouse. Wayne brings me meatball sandwiches from out on the road,
skinny things with a seam of cheese gumming the bread.

Was it worth it? he asks me.

He's watching me close. I tell him it wasn't.   120

Did you at least get some?

Hell yeah, I say.

Are you sure?

Why would I lie about something like that? Home-girl was an animal. I still have the teeth marks.

125 Damn, he says.

I punch him in the arm. And how's it going with you and Charlene?

I don't know, man. He shakes his head and in that motion I see him out on his lawn with all his things. I just don't know about this one.

We're back on the road a week later. Buckinghams, Imperials, Gold Crowns and dozens of card tables. I keep a copy of Pruitt's paperwork and when the curiosity finally gets to me I call. The first time I get the machine. We're delivering at a house in Long Island with a view of the Sound that would break you. Wayne and I smoke a joint on the beach and I pick up a dead horseshoe crab by the tail and heave it in the customer's garage. The next two times I'm in the Bedminster area Pruitt picks up and says, Yes? But on the fourth time she answers and the sink is running on her side of the phone and she shuts it off when I don't say anything.

Was she there? Wayne asks in the truck.

130 Of course she was.

He runs a thumb over the front of his teeth. Pretty predictable. She's probably in love with the guy. You know how it is.

I sure do.

Don't get angry.

I'm tired, that's all.

135 Tired's the best way to be, he says. It really is.

He hands me the map and my fingers trace our deliveries, stitching city to city. Looks like we've gotten everything, I say.

Finally. He yawns. What's first tomorrow?

We won't really know until the morning, when I've gotten the paperwork in order but I take guesses anyway. One of our games. It passes the time, gives us something to look forward to. I close my eyes and put my hand on the map. So many towns, so many cities to choose from. Some places are sure bets but more than once I've gone with the long shot and been right.

You can't imagine how many times I've been right.

140 Usually the name will come to me fast, the way the numbered balls pop out during the lottery drawings, but this time nothing comes: no magic, no nothing. It could be anywhere. I open my eyes and see that Wayne is still waiting. Edison, I say, pressing my thumb down. Edison, New Jersey.

Creative Nonfiction   **Annie Dillard**

TOTAL ECLIPSE

I

It had been like dying, that sliding down the mountain pass. It had been like the death of someone, irrational, that sliding down the mountain pass and into the region of dread. It was like slipping into fever, or falling down that hole in sleep from which you wake yourself whimpering. We had crossed the mountains that day, and now we were in a strange place—a hotel in central Washington, in a town near Yakima. The eclipse we had traveled here to see would occur early the next morning.

I lay in bed. My husband, Gary, was reading beside me. I lay in bed and looked at the painting on the hotel room wall. It was a print of a detailed and lifelike painting of a smiling clown's head, made out of vegetables. It was a painting of the sort which you do not intend to look at, and which, alas, you never forget. Some tasteless fate presses it upon you; it becomes part of the complex interior junk you carry with you wherever you go. Two years have passed since the total eclipse of which I write. During those years I have forgotten, I assume, a great many things I wanted to remember—but I have not forgotten that clown painting or its lunatic setting in the old hotel.

The clown was bald. Actually, he wore a clown's tight rubber wig, painted white; this stretched over the top of his skull, which was a cabbage. His hair was bunches of baby carrots. Inset in his white clown makeup, and in his cabbage skull, were his small and laughing human eyes. The clown's glance was like the glance of Rembrandt in some of the self-portraits: lively, knowing, deep, and loving. The crinkled shadows around his eyes were string beans. His eyebrows were parsley. Each of his ears was a broad bean. His thin, joyful lips were red chili peppers; between his lips were wet rows of human teeth and a suggestion of a real tongue. The clown print was framed in gilt and glassed.

To put ourselves in the path of the total eclipse, that day we had driven five hours inland from the Washington coast, where we lived. When we tried to cross the Cascades range, an avalanche had blocked the pass.

A slope's worth of snow blocked the road; traffic backed up. Had the avalanche buried any cars that morning? We could not learn. This highway was the only winter road over the mountains. We waited as highway crews bulldozed a passage through the avalanche. With two-by-fours and walls of plyboard, they erected a one-way, roofed tunnel through the avalanche. We 5 drove through the avalanche tunnel, crossed the pass, and descended several thousand feet into central Washington and the broad Yakima valley, about which we knew only that it was orchard country. As we lost altitude, the snows disappeared; our ears popped; the trees changed, and in the trees were strange birds. I watched the landscape innocently, like a fool, like a diver in the rapture of the deep who plays on the bottom while his air runs out.

The hotel lobby was a dark, derelict room, narrow as a corridor, and seemingly without air. We waited on a couch while the manager vanished upstairs to do something unknown to our room. Beside us on an overstuffed chair, absolutely motionless, was a platinum-blond woman in her forties wearing a black silk dress and a strand of pearls. Her long legs were crossed; she supported her head on her fist. At the dim far end of the room, their backs toward us, sat six bald old men in their shirt-sleeves, around a loud television. Two of them seemed asleep. They were drunks. "Number six!" cried the man on television, "Number six!"

On the broad lobby desk, lighted and bubbling, was a ten-gallon aquarium containing one large fish; the fish tilted up and down in its water. Against the long opposite wall sang a live canary in its cage. Beneath the cage, among spilled millet seeds on the carpet, were a decorated child's sand bucket and matching sand shovel.

Now the alarm was set for six. I lay awake remembering an article I had read downstairs in the lobby, in an engineering magazine. The article was about gold mining.

In South Africa, in India, and in South Dakota, the gold mines extend so deeply into the earth's crust that they are hot. The rock walls burn the miners' hands. The companies have to air-condition the mines; if the air conditioners break, the miners die. The elevators in the mine shafts run very slowly, down, and up, so the miners' ears will not pop in their skulls. When the miners return to the surface, their faces are deathly pale.

10   Early the next morning we checked out. It was February 26, 1979, a Monday morning. We would drive out of town, find a hilltop, watch the eclipse, and then drive back over the mountains and home to the coast. How familiar things are here; how adept we are; how smoothly and professionally we check out! I had forgotten the clown's smiling head and the hotel lobby as if they had never existed. Gary put the car in gear and off we went, as off we have gone to a hundred other adventures.

It was before dawn when we found a highway out of town and drove into the unfamiliar countryside. By the growing light we could see a band of cirrostratus clouds in the sky. Later the rising sun would clear these clouds before the eclipse began. We drove at random until we came to a range of unfenced hills. We pulled off the highway, bundled up, and climbed one of these hills.

II

The hill was five hundred feet high. Long winter-killed grass covered it, as high as our knees. We climbed and rested, sweating in the cold; we passed clumps of bundled people on the hillside who were setting up telescopes and fiddling with cameras. The top of the hill stuck up in the middle of the sky. We tightened our scarves and looked around.

East of us rose another hill like ours. Between the hills, far below, was the highway which threaded south into the valley. This was the Yakima valley; I had never seen it before. It is justly famous for its beauty, like every planted valley. It extended south into the horizon, a distant dream of a valley, a Shangri-la. All its hundreds of low, golden slopes bore orchards. Among the orchards were towns, and roads, and plowed and fallow fields. Through the valley wandered a thin, shining river; from the river extended fine, frozen irrigation ditches. Distance blurred and blued the sight, so that the whole valley looked like a thickness or sediment at the bottom of the sky. Directly behind us was more sky, and empty lowlands blued by distance, and Mount Adams. Mount Adams was an enormous, snow-covered volcanic cone rising flat, like so much scenery.

Now the sun was up. We could not see it; but the sky behind the band of clouds was yellow, and, far down the valley, some hillside orchards had lighted up. More people were parking near the highway and climbing the hills. It was the West. All of us rugged individualists were wearing knit caps and blue nylon parkas. People were climbing the nearby hills and setting up shop in clumps among the dead grasses. It looked as though we had all gathered on hilltops to pray for the world on its last day. It looked as though we had all crawled out of spaceships and were preparing to assault the valley below. It looked as though we were scattered on hilltops at dawn to sacrifice virgins, make rain, set stone stelae in a ring. There was no place out of the wind. The straw grasses banged our legs.

Up in the sky where we stood the air was lusterless yellow. To the west   15
the sky was blue. Now the sun cleared the clouds. We cast rough shadows on the blowing grass; freezing, we waved our arms. Near the sun, the sky was bright and colorless. There was nothing to see.

It began with no ado. It was odd that such a well-advertised public event should have no starting gun, no overture, no introductory speaker. I should have known right then that I was out of my depth. Without pause or preamble, silent as orbits, a piece of the sun went away. We looked at it through welders' goggles. A piece of the sun was missing; in its place we saw empty sky.

I had seen a partial eclipse in 1970. A partial eclipse is very interesting. It bears almost no relation to a total eclipse. Seeing a partial eclipse bears the same relation to seeing a total eclipse as kissing a man does to marrying him, or as flying in an airplane does to falling out of an airplane. Although the one experience precedes the other, it in no way prepares you for it. During a partial eclipse the sky does not darken—not even when 94 percent of the sun is hidden. Nor does the sun, seen colorless through protective devices, seem terribly strange. We have all seen a sliver of light in the sky; we have all seen the crescent moon by day. However, during a partial eclipse the air does indeed get cold, precisely as if someone were standing between you and the fire. And blackbirds do fly back to their roosts. I had seen a partial eclipse before, and here was another.

What you see in an eclipse is entirely different from what you know. It is especially different for those of us whose grasp of astronomy is so frail that, given a flashlight, a grapefruit, two oranges, and fifteen years, we still could not figure out which way to set the clocks for Daylight Saving Time. Usually it is a bit of a trick to keep your knowledge from blinding you. But during an eclipse it is easy. What you see is much more convincing than any wild-eyed theory you may know.

You may read that the moon has something to do with eclipses. I have never seen the moon yet. You do not see the moon. So near the sun, it is as completely invisible as the stars are by day. What you see before your eyes is the sun going through phases. It gets narrower and narrower, as the waning moon does, and, like the ordinary moon, it travels alone in the simple sky. The sky is of course background. It does not appear to eat the sun; it is far behind the sun. The sun simply shaves away; gradually, you see less sun and more sky.

20   The sky's blue was deepening, but there was no darkness. The sun was a wide crescent, like a segment of tangerine. The wind freshened and blew steadily over the hill. The eastern hill across the highway grew dusky and sharp. The towns and orchards in the valley to the south were dissolving into the blue light. Only the thin river held a trickle of sun.

Now the sky to the west deepened to indigo, a color never seen. A dark sky usually loses color. This was a saturated, deep indigo, up in the air. Stuck up into that unworldly sky was the cone of Mount Adams, and the alpenglow was upon it. The alpenglow is that red light of sunset which holds out on snowy mountaintops long after the valleys and tablelands are dimmed. "Look at Mount Adams," I said, and that was the last sane moment I remember.

* * *

I turned back to the sun. It was going. The sun was going, and the world was wrong. The grasses were wrong; they were platinum. Their every detail of stem, head, and blade shone lightless and artificially distinct as an art photographer's platinum print. This color has never been seen on earth. The hues were metallic; their finish was matte. The hillside was a nineteenth-century tinted photograph from which the tints had faded. All the people you see in the photograph, distinct and detailed as their faces look, are now dead. The sky was navy blue. My hands were silver. All the distant hills' grasses were finespun metal which the wind laid down. I was watching a faded color print of a movie filmed in the Middle Ages; I was standing in it, by some mistake. I was standing in a movie of hillside grasses filmed in the Middle Ages. I missed my own century, the people I knew, and the real light of day.

I looked at Gary. He was in the film. Everything was lost. He was a platinum print, a dead artist's version of life. I saw on his skull the darkness of night mixed with the colors of day. My mind was going out; my eyes were receding the way galaxies recede to the rim of space. Gary was light-years away, gesturing inside a circle of darkness, down the wrong end of a telescope. He smiled as if he saw me; the stringy crinkles around his eyes moved. The sight of him, familiar and wrong, was something I was remembering from centuries hence, from the other side of death: yes, *that* is the way he used to look, when we were living. When it was our generation's turn to be alive. I could not hear him; the wind was too loud. Behind him the sun was going. We had all started down a chute of time. At first it was pleasant; now there was no stopping it. Gary was chuting away across space, moving and talking and catching my eye, chuting down the long corridor of separation. The skin on his face moved like thin bronze plating that would peel.

The grass at our feet was wild barley. It was the wild einkorn wheat which grew on the hilly flanks of the Zagros Mountains, above the Euphrates valley, above the valley of the river we called *River*. We harvested the grass with stone sickles, I remember. We found the grasses on the hillsides; we built our shelter beside them and cut them down. That is how he used to look then, that one, moving and living and catching my eye, with the sky so dark behind him, and the wind blowing. God save our life.

From all the hills came screams. A piece of sky beside the crescent sun was   25
detaching. It was a loosened circle of evening sky, suddenly lighted from the back. It was an abrupt black body out of nowhere; it was a flat disk; it was almost over the sun. That is when there were screams. At once this disk of sky slid over the sun like a lid. The sky snapped over the sun like a lens cover. The hatch in the brain slammed. Abruptly it was dark night, on

the land and in the sky. In the night sky was a tiny ring of light. The hole where the sun belongs is very small. A thin ring of light marked its place. There was no sound. The eyes dried, the arteries drained, the lungs hushed. There was no world. We were the world's dead people rotating and orbiting around and around, embedded in the planet's crust, while the earth rolled down. Our minds were light-years distant, forgetful of almost everything. Only an extraordinary act of will could recall to us our former, living selves and our contexts in matter and time. We had, it seems, loved the planet and loved our lives, but could no longer remember the way of them. We got the light wrong. In the sky was something that should not be there. In the black sky was a ring of light. It was a thin ring, an old, thin silver wedding band, an old, worn ring. It was an old wedding band in the sky, or a morsel of bone. There were stars. It was all over.

III

It is now that the temptation is strongest to leave these regions. We have seen enough; let's go. Why burn our hands any more than we have to? But two years have passed; the price of gold has risen. I return to the same buried alluvial beds and pick through the strata again.

I saw, early in the morning, the sun diminish against a backdrop of sky. I saw a circular piece of that sky appear, suddenly detached, blackened, and backlighted; from nowhere it came and overlapped the sun. It did not look like the moon. It was enormous and black. If I had not read that it was the moon, I could have seen the sight a hundred times and never thought of the moon once. (If, however, I had not read that it was the moon—if, like most of the world's people throughout time, I had simply glanced up and seen this thing—then I doubtless would not have speculated much, but would have, like Emperor Louis of Bavaria in 840, simply died of fright on the spot.) It did not look like a dragon, although it looked more like a dragon than the moon. It looked like a lens cover, or the lid of a pot. It materialized out of thin air—black, and flat, and sliding, outlined in flame.

Seeing this black body was like seeing a mushroom cloud. The heart screeched. The meaning of the sight overwhelmed its fascination. It obliterated meaning itself. If you were to glance out one day and see a row of mushroom clouds rising on the horizon, you would know at once that what you were seeing, remarkable as it was, was intrinsically not worth remarking. No use running to tell anyone. Significant as it was, it did not matter a whit. For what is significance? It is significance for people. No people, no significance. This is all I have to tell you.

In the deeps are the violence and terror of which psychology has warned us. But if you ride these monsters deeper down, if you drop with them farther over the world's rim, you find what our sciences cannot locate or name, the substrate, the ocean or matrix or ether which buoys the rest, which gives goodness its power for good, and evil its power for evil, the unified field: our complex and inexplicable caring for each other, and for our life together here. This is given. It is not learned.

The world which lay under darkness and stillness following the closing of the lid was not the world we know. The event was over. Its devastation lay round about us. The clamoring mind and heart stilled, almost indifferent, certainly disembodied, frail, and exhausted. The hills were hushed, obliterated. Up in the sky, like a crater from some distant cataclysm, was a hollow ring.

You have seen photographs of the sun taken during a total eclipse. The corona fills the print. All of those photographs were taken through telescopes. The lenses of telescopes and cameras can no more cover the breadth and scale of the visual array than language can cover the breadth and simultaneity of internal experience. Lenses enlarge the sight, omit its context, and make of it a pretty and sensible picture, like something on a Christmas card. I assure you, if you send any shepherds a Christmas card on which is printed a three-by-three photograph of the angel of the Lord, the glory of the Lord, and a multitude of the heavenly host, they will not be sore afraid. More fearsome things can come in envelopes. More moving photographs than those of the sun's corona can appear in magazines. But I pray you will never see anything more awful in the sky.

You see the wide world swaddled in darkness; you see a vast breadth of hilly land, and an enormous, distant, blackened valley; you see towns' lights, a river's path, and blurred portions of your hat and scarf; you see your husband's face looking like an early black-and-white film; and you see a sprawl of black sky and blue sky together, with unfamiliar stars in it, some barely visible bands of cloud, and over there, a small white ring. The ring is as small as one goose in a flock of migrating geese—if you happen to notice a flock of migrating geese. It is one 360th part of the visible sky. The sun we see is less than half the diameter of a dime held at arm's length.

The Crab Nebula, in the constellation Taurus, looks, through binoculars, like a smoke ring. It is a star in the process of exploding. Light from its explosion first reached the earth in 1054; it was a supernova then, and so bright it shone in the daytime. Now it is not so bright, but it is still exploding. It expands at the rate of seventy million miles a day. It is interesting

30

to look through binoculars at something expanding seventy million miles a day. It does not budge. Its apparent size does not increase. Photographs of the Crab Nebula taken fifteen years ago seem identical to photographs of it taken yesterday. Some lichens are similar. Botanists have measured some ordinary lichens twice, at fifty-year intervals, without detecting any growth at all. And yet their cells divide; they live.

The small ring of light was like these things—like a ridiculous lichen up in the sky, like a perfectly still explosion 4,200 light-years away: it was interesting, and lovely, and in witless motion, and it had nothing to do with anything.

It had nothing to do with anything. The sun was too small, and too cold, and too far away, to keep the world alive. The white ring was not enough. It was feeble and worthless. It was as useless as a memory; it was as off kilter and hollow and wretched as a memory.

35   When you try your hardest to recall someone's face, or the look of a place, you see in your mind's eye some vague and terrible sight such as this. It is dark; it is insubstantial; it is all wrong.

The white ring and the saturated darkness made the earth and the sky look as they must look in the memories of the careless dead. What I saw, what I seemed to be standing in, was all the wrecked light that the memories of the dead could shed upon the living world. We had all died in our boots on the hilltops of Yakima, and were alone in eternity. Empty space stoppered our eyes and mouths; we cared for nothing. We remembered our living days wrong. With great effort we had remembered some sort of circular light in the sky—but only the outline. Oh, and then the orchard trees withered, the ground froze, the glaciers slid down the valleys and overlapped the towns. If there had ever been people on earth, nobody knew it. The dead had forgotten those they had loved. The dead were parted one from the other and could no longer remember the faces and lands they had loved in the light. They seemed to stand on darkened hilltops, looking down.

IV

We teach our children one thing only, as we were taught: to wake up. We teach our children to look alive there, to join by words and activities the life of human culture on the planet's crust. As adults we are almost all adept at waking up. We have so mastered the transition we have forgotten we ever learned it. Yet it is a transition we make a hundred times a day, as, like so many will-less dolphins, we plunge and surface, lapse and emerge. We live half our waking lives and all of our sleeping lives in some private, useless, and insensible waters we never mention or recall. Useless, I say. Valueless, I might add—until someone hauls their wealth up to the surface and into the wide-awake city, in a form that people can use.

I do not know how we got to the restaurant. Like Roethke, "I take my waking slow." Gradually I seemed more or less alive, and already forgetful. It was now almost nine in the morning. It was the day of a solar eclipse in central Washington, and a fine adventure for everyone. The sky was clear; there was a fresh breeze out of the north.

The restaurant was a roadside place with tables and booths. The other eclipse-watchers were there. From our booth we could see their cars' California license plates, their University of Washington parking stickers. Inside the restaurant we were all eating eggs or waffles; people were fairly shouting and exchanging enthusiasms, like fans after a World Series game. Did you see . . .? Did you see . . .? Then somebody said something which knocked me for a loop.

A college student, a boy in a blue parka who carried a Hasselblad, said to us, "Did you see that little white ring? It looked like a Life Saver. It looked like a Life Saver up in the sky."

And so it did. The boy spoke well. He was a walking alarm clock. I   40
myself had at that time no access to such a word. He could write a sentence, and I could not. I grabbed that Life Saver and rode it to the surface. And I had to laugh. I had been dumbstruck on the Euphrates River, I had been dead and gone and grieving, all over the sight of something which, if you could claw your way up to that level, you would grant looked very much like a Life Saver. It was good to be back among people so clever; it was good to have all the world's words at the mind's disposal, so the mind could begin its task. All those things for which we have no words are lost. The mind—the culture—has two little tools, grammar and lexicon: a decorated sand bucket and a matching shovel. With these we bluster about the continents and do all the world's work. With these we try to save our very lives.

There are a few more things to tell from this level, the level of the restaurant. One is the old joke about breakfast. "It can never be satisfied, the mind, never." Wallace Stevens wrote that, and in the long run he was right. The mind wants to live forever, or to learn a very good reason why not. The mind wants the world to return its love, or its awareness; the mind wants to know all the world, and all eternity, and God. The mind's sidekick, however, will settle for two eggs over easy.

The dear, stupid body is as easily satisfied as a spaniel. And, incredibly, the simple spaniel can lure the brawling mind to its dish. It is everlastingly funny that the proud, metaphysically ambitious, clamoring mind will hush if you give it an egg.

Further: while the mind reels in deep space, while the mind grieves or fears or exults, the workaday senses, in ignorance or idiocy, like so many computer terminals printing out market prices while the world blows up, still transcribe their little data and transmit them to the warehouse in the skull. Later, under the tranquilizing influence of fried eggs, the mind can sort through this data. The restaurant was a halfway house, a decompression chamber. There I remembered a few things more.

The deepest, and most terrifying, was this: I have said that I heard screams. (I have since read that screaming, with hysteria, is a common reaction even to expected total eclipses.) People on all the hillsides, including, I think, myself, screamed when the black body of the moon detached from the sky and rolled over the sun. But something else was happening at that same instant, and it was this, I believe, which made us scream.

The second before the sun went out we saw a wall of dark shadow come speeding at us. We no sooner saw it than it was upon us, like thunder. It roared up the valley. It slammed our hill and knocked us out. It was the monstrous swift shadow cone of the moon. I have since read that this wave of shadow moves 1,800 miles an hour. Language can give no sense of this sort of speed—1,800 miles an hour. It was 195 miles wide. No end was in sight—you saw only the edge. It rolled at you across the land at 1,800 miles an hour, hauling darkness like plague behind it. Seeing it, and knowing it was coming straight for you, was like feeling a slug of anesthetic shoot up your arm. If you think very fast, you may have time to think, "Soon it will hit my brain." You can feel the deadness race up your arm; you can feel the appalling, inhuman speed of your own blood. We saw the wall of shadow coming, and screamed before it hit.

45 This was the universe about which we have read so much and never before felt: the universe as a clockwork of loose spheres flung at stupefying, unauthorized speeds. How could anything moving so fast not crash, not veer from its orbit amok like a car out of control on a turn?

Less than two minutes later, when the sun emerged, the trailing edge of the shadow cone sped away. It coursed down our hill and raced eastward over the plain, faster than the eye could believe; it swept over the plain and dropped over the planet's rim in a twinkling. It had clobbered us, and now it roared away. We blinked in the light. It was as though an enormous, loping god in the sky had reached down and slapped the earth's face.

Something else, something more ordinary, came back to me along about the third cup of coffee. During the moments of totality, it was so dark that drivers on the highway below turned on their cars' headlights. We could see the highway's route as a strand of lights. It was bumper-to-bumper down there. It was eight-fifteen in the morning, Monday morning, and people were driving into Yakima to work. That it was as dark as night, and eerie as hell, an hour after dawn, apparently meant that in order to *see* to drive to work, people had to use their headlights. Four or five cars pulled off the road. The rest, in a line at least five miles long, drove to town. The highway ran between hills; the people could not have seen any of the eclipsed sun at all. Yakima will have another total eclipse in 2086. Perhaps, in 2086, businesses will give their employees an hour off.

From the restaurant we drove back to the coast. The highway crossing the Cascades range was open. We drove over the mountain like old pros. We joined our places on the planet's thin crust; it held. For the time being, we were home free.

Early that morning at six, when we had checked out, the six bald men were sitting on folding chairs in the dim hotel lobby. The television was on. Most of them were awake. You might drown in your own spittle, God knows, at any time; you might wake up dead in a small hotel, a cabbage head watching TV while snows pile up in the passes, watching TV while the chili peppers smile and the moon passes over the sun and nothing changes and nothing is learned because you have lost your bucket and shovel and no longer care. What if you regain the surface and open your sack and find, instead of treasure, a beast which jumps at you? Or you may not come back at all. The winches may jam, the scaffolding buckle, the air conditioning collapse. You may glance up one day and see by your head-lamp the canary keeled over in its cage. You may reach into a cranny for pearls and touch a moray eel. You yank on your rope; it is too late.

Page 326

Apparently people share a sense of these hazards, for when the total eclipse ended, an odd thing happened.   50

When the sun appeared as a blinding bead on the ring's side, the eclipse was over. The black lens cover appeared again, backlighted, and slid away. At once the yellow light made the sky blue again; the black lid dissolved and vanished. The real world began there. I remember now: we all hurried away. We were born and bored at a stroke. We rushed down the hill. We found our car; we saw the other people streaming down the hillsides; we joined the highway traffic and drove away.

We never looked back. It was a general vamoose, and an odd one, for when we left the hill, the sun was still partially eclipsed—a sight rare enough, and one which, in itself, we would probably have driven five hours to see. But enough is enough. One turns at last even from glory itself with a sigh of relief. From the depths of mystery, and even from the heights of splendor, we bounce back and hurry for the latitudes of home.

Poetry **Stuart Dischell**

SHE PUT ON HER LIPSTICK IN THE DARK

I really did meet a blind girl in Paris once.
It was in the garden of a museum
Where I saw her touching the statues.
She had brown hair and an aquamarine scarf.

5   It was in the garden of the museum
I told her I was a thief disguised as a guard.
She had brown hair and an aquamarine scarf.
She told me she was a student from Grenoble.

I told her I was not a thief disguised as a guard.
10   We had coffee at the little commissary.
She said she had time till her train to Grenoble.
We talked about our supreme belief in art.

We had coffee at the little commissary
Then sat on a bench near the foundry.
15   We talked about our supreme belief in art.
She leaned her head upon my chest.

We kissed on a bench near the foundry.
I closed my eyes when no one was watching.
She leaned her head upon my chest.
20   The museum was closing. It was time to part.

I really did meet a blind girl in Paris once.
I never saw her again and she never saw me.
In a garden she touched the statues.
She put on her lipstick in the dark.

25   I close my eyes when no one is watching.
She had brown hair and an aquamarine scarf.
The museum was closing. It was time to part.
I never saw her again and she never saw me.

Fiction   **E. L. Doctorow**

EXCERPT FROM *WORLD'S FAIR*

Startled awake by the ammoniated mists, I am roused in one instant from glutinous sleep to grieving awareness; I have done it again. My soaked thighs sting. I cry, I call Mama, knowing I must endure her harsh reaction, get through *that*, to be rescued. My crib is on the east wall of their room. Their bed is on the south wall. "Mama!" From her bed she hushes me. "Mama!" She groans, rises, advances on me in her white nightgown. Her strong hands go to work. She strips me, strips the sheets, dumps my pajamas and the sheets, and the rubber sheet under them, in a pile on the floor. Her pendulous breasts shift about in the nightgown. I hear her whispered admonitions. In seconds I am washed, powdered, clean-clothed, and brought to secret smiles in the dark. I ride, the young prince, in her arms to their bed, and am welcomed between them, in the blessed dry warmth between them. My father gives me a companionable pat and falls back to sleep with his hand on my shoulder. Soon they are both asleep. I smell their godlike odors, male, female. A moment later, as the faintest intimation of daylight appears as an outline of the window shade, I am wide awake, blissful, guarding my sleeping parents, the terrible night past me, the dear day about to dawn.

These are my earliest memories. I liked when morning came to climb down from their bed and watch my parents. My father slept on his right arm, his legs straight, his hand coming over the pillow and bending at the wrist against the headboard. My mother lay curled with the curve of her broad back touching his. Together under the covers they made a pleasing shape. The headboard knocked against the wall as they stirred. It was baroque in style, olive green, with a frieze of small pink flowers and dark green leaves along its fluted edges. On the opposite wall were the dresser and mirror of the same olive green and fluted edges. Sprays of the pink flowers were set above the oval brass drawer pulls. In my play I liked to lift each handle and let it fall back to hear the clink. I understood the illusion of the flowers, looking at them, believing them and then feeling the raised paint strokes with my fingertips. I had less fondness for the bedroom curtains of sheer white over the window shades and for the heavy draperies framing the curtains. I feared suffocation. I shied away from closets, the dark terrified me mostly because I wasn't sure it was breathable.

I was an asthmatic child, allergic to everything, I was attacked continually in the lungs, coughing, wheezing, needing to be steamed over inhalators. I was the mournful prodigy of medicine, I knew the mustard plaster, the nose drop, the Argyrol throat swab. I was plugged regularly with thermometers and soap water enemas. My mother believed pain was curative.

If it didn't hurt it was ineffective. I shouted and screamed and went down fighting. I argued for the cherry-red mercurochrome for my scraped knees and I got the detested iodine. How I howled. "Oh stop the nonsense," my mother said, applicating me with strokes of searing pain. "Stop it this instant. You make a fuss over nothing."

Creative Nonfiction   **Andre Dubus III**

TRACKS AND TIES

Years later, when I was twenty-six, she said in the *New York Times* you would tie her naked and spread-eagled on the bed, that you would take a bat to her. She said you'd hit her for any reason. But in Haverhill, Massachusetts, you were my best friend, my brother's too. I was fifteen and you two were fourteen and in 1974 we walked the avenues on cold gray days picking through dumpsters for something to beat off to. We'd beat off to anything, though I was shy about it and couldn't do it just anywhere.

One February morning we skipped school and went downtown. It was ten or eleven degrees and the dirty snow piled along both sides of River Street had become ice; the air made my lungs hurt and our noses, ears, and fingers felt burned, but you wore your faded blue jean jacket with the green magic marker peace signs drawn all over it. You wore sneakers and thin fake denim pants that looked more purple than blue. It was so cold I pulled the rubber band from my ponytail and let my hair down around my neck and leather-jacketed shoulders. Your hair was long too, brown and stringy. My brother, barely fourteen, needed a shave.

We had a dollar between us so we sat in a booth at Vahally's Diner and drank coffee with so much milk and sugar in it you couldn't call it coffee anymore. The Greek man behind the counter hated us; he folded his black hairy forearms across his chest and watched us take our free refills until we were giddy with caffeine. You went for your seventh cup and he yelled something at you in Greek. On the way out you stole two dollars someone had left on their check under a sugar shaker.

You paid our way on the city bus that was heated and made a loop all the way through town, along the river, up to the Westgate shopping center, then back again. We stayed on it for two hours, taking the loop six times. In the far rear, away from the driver, you took out your black-handled Buck knife and carved a peace sign into the aluminum-backed seat in front of you. For a while I looked out the window at all the red brick factory buildings, the store-fronts with their dusty windows, bright neon price deals taped to the bottom and top. Barrooms on every block. I probably thought of the high school algebra I was flunking, the gym class I hated, the brown mescaline and crystal meth and THC my sister was selling. The bus was warm, too warm, and more crowded than before. A woman our mothers' age sat in her overcoat and scarf in the seat in front of you both. Her back was to you and I'm sure she heard you laughing but she didn't see my brother hunched forward in his seat, jerking back and forth on his penis and coming in no time, catching it all in his hand. I think I looked away and I don't remember what he did with it.

5   After the bus, we made our way through the narrow factory streets, most of the buildings' windows covered with gray plywood, though your mother still worked at Schwartz's Shoe, on the fifth floor, when she wasn't drinking. We walked along the railroad tracks, its silver rails flush with the packed snow, the wooden ties gone under. And we laughed about the summer before when we three built a barricade for the train, a wall of broken creosote ties, an upside-down shopping cart, cinder blocks, and a rusted oil drum. We covered it with brush, then you siphoned gas from a Duster behind Schwartz's and poured it on. My brother and I lit it, air sucked by us in a whoosh, and we ran down the bank across the parking lot into the abandoned brewery to the second floor to watch our fire, to wait for the Boston & Maine, to hear the screaming brakes as it rounded the blind curve just off the trestle over the river. But a fat man in a good shirt and tie showed up at the tracks, then a cop, and we ran laughing to the first floor where we turned on the keg conveyor belt, lay on it belly-first, and rode it up through its trap door over and over.

As we made our way through town it began to snow. My brother and I were hungry, but you were never hungry; you were hawny, you said. One morning, as we sat in the basement of your house and passed a homemade pipe between us, your mother upstairs drunk on Kappy's vodka and Pepsi, singing to herself, you said: "I'm always hawny in the mawnin'."

My brother and I laughed and you didn't know why, then you inhaled resin on your next hit and said, "Shit man, the screem's broken."

"The *what?*"

"The screem. You know, the *screem*. Like a screem door?"

By the time we reached the avenues the snow had blanketed the streets. There were two sisters on Seventh who lived in the projects that always had motorcycles in front of them, and trash, and bright-colored babies' toys. Trish and Terry were older, sixteen and seventeen and so skinny their breasts looked like prunes beneath their shirts, but they had dark skin and long hair and sometimes, if they were high, they'd suck you. But there was a day party on the first floor of their building, and it had only been two weeks since Harry Wright and Kevin McConigle, rent collectors for Fat Billy, both twenty-three or -four, beat us up, you and me, just walked us out of a pot party we were both quiet at, walked us off the front porch into the mud then kicked and punched us until they were through. So we kept walking, heading for a street close to the highway where we knew three girls who would fuck if you had wine and rubbers, though after the wine they didn't mention the rubbers.

10   On Cedar Street, cars spun out snow as they drove from the curb or the corner store. You let out a yelp and a holler and went running after a Chevy that had just pulled away, skidding slightly as it went. You ran low, bent over so the driver wouldn't see you, and when you reached the

back bumper you grabbed it and squatted on your sneakers, your butt an inch or two from the road. And you skied away, just like that, the snow shooting out from under the wheels of the car, out from under your Zayre Department Store sneakers, blue exhaust coughing out its pipe beside you.

In the spring and summer we hopped trucks. A mile from the highway was a crosswalk on Main with a push-button traffic signal pole that we three leaned against until a truck came along and one of us pressed the button to turn red. I was the decoy that day, for a white refrigerator truck from Shoe City Beef. It stopped at the line, and I crossed the street jerking my head like a chicken to keep his attention from the mirrors while you two ran around to the back and climbed up on the foot-wide iron ledge at the bottom of its rear doors. As soon as I got to the sidewalk I heard the driver shift from neutral to first, heard him give it the gas. I waited for a car to drive by from the opposite direction, then I ran out into the street behind the truck, which was only shifting up to second. You and my brother stood on the ledge waiting, smiling, nodding your heads for me to hurry. I reached the ledge just as the truck moved into higher gear and I grabbed the bolt lock on its back doors and pulled myself up, the truck going faster now, shifting again, dipping and rattling through a low spot in the road. You both held an iron handle on opposite sides of the door so I stayed down, gripping the bolt lock with both hands, sitting on the ledge.

A car horn behind us honked and the driver, some man who combed his hair to the side like a teacher, shook his head and honked his horn again. You gave him the finger and we laughed but it was a scared laugh because the truck wasn't slowing down as it got to the gas stations and Kappy's Liquor near the highway, it was speeding up. Before, we'd jumped off into the grass of the highway ramp, but now we couldn't; he took the turn without leaving third gear and you yelled: "He *knows*! He friggin' *knows*!" My brother wasn't smiling anymore, and he stuck his head around the corner and let the growing wind hit him in the face, run through the hair on his cheeks as he squeezed the handle with both hands and I wanted to stand, to get my feet on something solid, but there was no room and now the driver was in fourth gear, heading north on 495, going fifty, then sixty, then sixty-five. He moved to the middle lane and I tried not to look down at the zip of the asphalt a foot beneath my dangling boots, but it was worse looking out at the cars, at the drivers looking at us like we might be a circus act they should catch sometime. Some honked as they passed so I looked up at you, at the side of your face as you looked around the corner, the June wind snapping your hair back past your forehead and ears, your mouth open in a scream I could barely hear. You smiled and shook your head at my brother then down at me, your brown eyes wet from the wind, your cheeks flushed in a satisfaction so deep I had to look back at the cars behind us, at the six or seven I was convinced would run me over one after the other, after my fingers failed. Miles later, at the tollbooths of the New Hampshire line, the truck slowed to a stop and we jumped off exhausted, our fingers stiff, and thumbed home.

That fall you went to the trade school, my brother joined me at the high school, and I saw you six years later in an all-night store in Monument Square. I was buying cigarettes for my college girlfriend. She waited in the car. It was winter. The floor was dirty with people's slush and mud tracks, the overhead light was fluorescent and too bright, and I was waiting my turn at the register when I saw you, watching me, smiling as you walked up. You carried a carton of ice cream and a quart of Coke. I had on a sweater and a jacket but you wore only a T-shirt, green Dickie work pants, and sneakers. You were taller than me, lean, and your young black mustache and goatee made you look sinister until you started talking in that high voice that hadn't changed since you'd told us you were hawny in the mawnin'. You said you were living down on the avenues, that you were getting married soon. I said congratulations, then I was at the counter asking for a pack of Parliaments and you touched me on the shoulder, said to say hi to my brother. I said I would. At the door I glanced back at you and watched you dig into your front pocket for crumpled bills. You nodded and smiled at me, winked even, and as I left the store, the cold tightening the skin on my face, I remembered the time your mother went to visit her sister in Nebraska for a whole month. I could never understand why she went alone, why she'd leave her family like that to go off for a visit. Then my mother told me it was detox she went to, some twenty-eight-day program in Boston. When I told you I knew, you laughed and said, "Nah," but you swallowed twice and walked away to do nothing in particular.

Six months after I saw you in the store my brother and I got invitations to your wedding. We didn't go.

15   Four more years and you were dead.

I heard about it after you were buried. They said your wife stabbed you in the back. That was it; she stabbed you. But a year later I was behind the bar at McMino's Lounge and Fat Billy's son, Bill Jr., told me what really happened, that you were cooked, always thinking your wife was cheating on you, always beating her up. That night you ran outside off the porch to go kill the guy you thought she was fucking. This was down on one of the avenues, behind the projects, and you took the trail in back of your house. But your wife opened your black-handled Buck knife and chased after you, screaming. She was short and small, barely five feet, and just as you reached the weeds she got to you and drove it in low, sinking the blade into your liver, snipping something called the portal artery. You went down without a sound. You curled up in a heap. But your wife spent four hours at a neighbor's house crying before they called anyone, and then it was the cops, and you were gone.

I served Bill Jr. another White Russian and for a second I felt sure it was him she went to that night, and I thought about hitting him for not making a faster call, but I felt no heat in my hands, no pull inside me. And I've always hated woman beaters. Part of me thought you got what you deserved. I left Bill Jr. to finish his too-sweet drink.

The following winter I was living in New York City, in a one-room studio with my girlfriend. It was late on a Sunday morning and we both sat with our feet up on the couch reading the *New York Times*. Outside our barred window snow fell on parked cars, on the sidewalk and street. I got tired of the movie section and picked up a story about three women in prison, all there for the same reason, for killing the husbands who beat them. And your wife was one of them; they gave her full name, *your* name. They wrote how she chased you outside and stabbed you. They described the town you both lived in as economically depressed, once a thriving textile town but no more. I lowered the paper and started to tell my girlfriend all about you, but she and I weren't doing so well, both past wanting to hear anything extra about each other, so I pulled on my boots and jacket and went walking. I crossed Third Avenue and Second and First. A car alarm went off in front of some Chinese laundry. I stuck my hands in my pockets and wished I'd worn a hat. I passed an empty basketball court, then I waited for the traffic on FDR Drive and walked the last block to the East River. To my right and left were bridges over to Queens. Though from where I stood I could see only the backs of warehouses, dry weeds five feet tall, then the gray river, swirling by fast.

The snow had stopped and I started walking along the cobblestone walk. One morning I skipped school and cut through back yards to your house. I didn't know your mother was home from Nebraska and I almost stepped back when she answered the door. She'd dyed her brown hair black, she wore sweatpants and a sweater, she had a cold sore on her bottom lip, and she'd gained weight, but she smiled and kissed me on the cheek and invited me in. The small kitchen was clean and warm. It smelled like coffee and cinnamon rolls. She put one on a napkin and handed it to me. I thanked her, and while I chewed the sweet buttery bread, she lit up a cigarette and asked about my mother. Then you came downstairs in just your jeans, no shirt, your chest pale and thin, your nipples pink, and your mother rushed over and kissed and hugged you like you'd been gone and just gotten home. And you didn't pull away, you hugged her back, and when your eyes caught mine, you lowered your face into the hair at her shoulder, and kept hugging.

Poetry   **Lynn Emanuel**

THE OUT-OF-BODY EXPERIENCE,

the extraterrestrial view,
  as though to die
    were to fly around
  in the airplane
5   of the mind
  looking down on
    (from a great distance,
  dwarfed and vivid)
    the Amazonian
10 wandering of the guts
      exposed,
  looking at that me that is
    unkempt and wild, a trickle
  from the tidal pool,
15   wandering, wavering, and free.

Not to close things, but to open them,
  is the line drawn
    ruthlessly
  the way mother drew
20   her open sewing scissor
  over the swollen belly
    of the melon.

So this is the way out,
  the sweet dishevelment, the delight
25   of disorder,
  to let go, and suddenly,
    we are in the cemetery,
  dressed in the strict black dress
    the paperweight
30 of the Bible on my chest.

All the willows weeping,
  are not symbols for me
    but symbols for me
  they stand, staunchly
35   rooted in the black

rainy margin of this
    aerial photograph:
I am the river
    going over the spillway
like oiled bath water,   40
    a colder cold, a dark
dark.

The comma at the end of the title of this poem is correct, but we have left it off—with the
author's consent—in textual references to avoid confusion.

Fiction   **Louise Erdrich**

SAINT MARIE

So when I went there, I knew the dark fish must rise. Plumes of radiance had soldered on me. No reservation girl had ever prayed so hard. There was no use in trying to ignore me any longer. I was going up there on the hill with the black robe women. They were not any lighter than me. I was going up there to pray as good as they could. Because I don't have that much Indian blood. And they never thought they'd have a girl from this reservation as a saint they'd have to kneel to. But they'd have me. And I'd be carved in pure gold. With ruby lips. And my toenails would be little pink ocean shells, which they would have to stoop down off their high horse to kiss.

I was ignorant. I was near age fourteen. The length of sky is just about the size of my ignorance. Pure and wide. And it was just that—the pure and wideness of my ignorance—that got me up the hill to Sacred Heart Convent and brought me back down alive. For maybe Jesus did not take my bait, but them Sisters tried to cram me right down whole.

You ever see a walleye strike so bad the lure is practically out its back end before you reel it in? That is what they done with me. I don't like to make that low comparison, but I have seen a walleye do that once. And it's the same attempt as Sister Leopolda made to get me in her clutch.

I had the mail-order Catholic soul you get in a girl raised out in the bush, whose only thought is getting into town. For Sunday Mass is the only time my father brought his children in except for school, when we were harnessed. Our soul went cheap. We were so anxious to get there we would have walked in on our hands and knees. We just craved going to the store, slinging bottle caps in the dust, making fool eyes at each other. And of course we went to church.

5   Where they have the convent is on top of the highest hill, so that from its windows the Sisters can be looking into the marrow of the town. Recently a windbreak was planted before the bar "for the purposes of tornado insurance." Don't tell me that. That poplar stand was put up to hide the drinkers as they get the transformation. As they are served into the beast of their burden. While they're drinking, that body comes upon them, and then they stagger or crawl out the bar door, pulling a weight they can't move past the poplars. They don't want no holy witness to their fall.

Anyway, I climbed. That was a long-ago day. There was a road then for wagons that wound in ruts to the top of the hill where they had their buildings of painted brick. Gleaming white. So white the sun glanced off in dazzling display to set forms whirling behind your eyelids. The face of God you could hardly look at. But that day it drizzled, so I could look all

I wanted. I saw the homelier side. The cracked whitewash and swallows nesting in the busted ends of eaves. I saw the boards sawed the size of broken windowpanes and the fruit trees, stripped. Only the tough wild rhubarb flourished. Goldenrod rubbed up their walls. It was a poor convent. I didn't see that then but I know that now. Compared to others it was humble, ragtag, out in the middle of no place. It was the end of the world to some. Where the maps stopped. Where God had only half a hand in the creation. Where the Dark One had put in thick bush, liquor, wild dogs, and Indians.

I heard later that the Sacred Heart Convent was a catchall place for nuns that don't get along elsewhere. Nuns that complain too much or lose their mind. I'll always wonder now, after hearing that, where they picked up Sister Leopolda. Perhaps she had scarred someone else, the way she left a mark on me. Perhaps she was just sent around to test her Sisters' faith, here and there, like the spot-checker in a factory. For she was the definite most-hard trial to anyone's endurance, even when they started out with veils of wretched love upon their eyes.

I was that girl who thought the black hem of her garment would help me rise. Veils of love which was only hate petrified by longing—that was me. I was like those bush Indians who stole the holy black hat of a Jesuit and swallowed little scraps of it to cure their fevers. But the hat itself carried smallpox and was killing them with belief. Veils of faith! I had this confidence in Leopolda. She was different. The other Sisters had long ago gone blank and given up on Satan. He slept for them. They never noticed his comings and goings. But Leopolda kept track of him and knew his habits, minds he burrowed in, deep spaces where he hid. She knew as much about him as my grandma, who called him by other names and was not afraid.

In her class, Sister Leopolda carried a long oak pole for opening high windows. It had a hook made of iron on one end that could jerk a patch of your hair out or throttle you by the collar—all from a distance. She used this deadly hook-pole for catching Satan by surprise. He could have entered without your knowing it—through your lips or your nose or any one of your seven openings—and gained your mind. But she would see him. That pole would brain you from behind. And he would gasp, dazzled, and take the first thing she offered, which was pain.

She had a stringer of children who could only breathe if she said the word. I was the worst of them. She always said the Dark One wanted me most of all, and I believed this. I stood out. Evil was a common thing I trusted. Before sleep sometimes he came and whispered conversation in the old language of the bush. I listened. He told me things he never told anyone but Indians. I was privy to both worlds of his knowledge. I listened

10

to him, but I had confidence in Leopolda. She was the only one of the bunch he even noticed.

There came a day, though, when Leopolda turned the tide with her hook-pole.

It was a quiet day with everyone working at their desks, when I heard him. He had sneaked into the closets in the back of the room. He was scratching around, tasting crumbs in our pockets, stealing buttons, squirting his dark juice in the linings and the boots. I was the only one who heard him, and I got bold. I smiled. I glanced back and smiled and looked up at her sly to see if she had noticed. My heart jumped. For she was looking straight at me. And she sniffed. She had a big stark bony nose stuck to the front of her face for smelling out brimstone and evil thoughts. She had smelled him on me. She stood up. Tall, pale, a blackness leading into the deeper blackness of the slate wall behind her. Her oak pole had flown into her grip. She had seen me glance at the closet. Oh, she knew. She knew just where he was. I watched her watch him in her mind's eye. The whole class was watching now. She was staring, sizing, following his scuffle. And all of a sudden she tensed down, posed on her bent kneesprings, cocked her arm back. She threw the oak pole singing over my head, through my braincloud. It cracked through the thin wood door of the back closet, and the heavy pointed hook drove through his heart. I turned. She'd speared her own black rubber overboot where he'd taken refuge in the tip of her darkest toe.

Something howled in my mind. Loss and darkness. I understood. I was to suffer for my smile.

He rose up hard in my heart. I didn't blink when the pole cracked. My skull was tough. I didn't flinch when she shrieked in my ear. I only shrugged at the flowers of hell. He wanted me. More than anything he craved me. But then she did the worst. She did what broke my mind to her. She grabbed me by the collar and dragged me, feet flying, through the room and threw me in the closet with her dead black overboot. And I was there. The only light was a crack beneath the door. I asked the Dark One to enter into me and boost my mind. I asked him to restrain my tears, for they was pushing behind my eyes. But he was afraid to come back there. He was afraid of her sharp pole. And I was afraid of Leopolda's pole for the first time, too. I felt the cold hook in my heart. How it could crack through the door at any minute and drag me out, like a dead fish on a gaff, drop me on the floor like a gutshot squirrel.

15   I was nothing. I edged back to the wall as far as I could. I breathed the chalk dust. The hem of her full black cloak cut against my cheek. He had left me. Her spear could find me any time. Her keen ears would aim the hook into the beat of my heart.

What was that sound?

It filled the closet, filled it up until it spilled over, but I did not recognize the crying wailing voice as mine until the door cracked open, brightness, and she hoisted me to her camphor-smelling lips.

"He *wants* you," she said. "That's the difference. I give you love."

Love. The black hook. The spear singing through the mind. I saw that she had tracked the Dark One to my heart and flushed him out into the open. So now my heart was an empty nest where she could lurk.

Well, I was weak. I was weak when I let her in, but she got a foothold   20
there. Hard to dislodge as the year passed. Sometimes I felt him—the brush of dim wings—but only rarely did his voice compel. It was between Marie and Leopolda now, and the struggle changed. I began to realize I had been on the wrong track with the fruits of hell. The real way to overcome Leopolda was this: I'd get to heaven first. And then, when I saw her coming, I'd shut the gate. She'd be out! That is why, besides the bowing and the scraping I'd be dealt, I wanted to sit on the altar as a saint.

To this end, I went up on the hill. Sister Leopolda was the consecrated nun who had sponsored me to come there.

"You're not vain," she said. "You're too honest, looking into the mirror, for that. You're not smart. You don't have the ambition to get clear. You have two choices. One, you can marry a no-good Indian, bear his brats, die like a dog. Or two, you can give yourself to God."

"I'll come up there," I said, "but not because of what you think."

I could have had any damn man on the reservation at the time. And I could have made him treat me like his own life. I looked good. And I looked white. But I wanted Sister Leopolda's heart. And here was the thing: sometimes I wanted her heart in love and admiration. Sometimes. And sometimes I wanted her heart to roast on a black stick.

She answered the back door where they had instructed me to call. I stood   25
there with my bundle. She looked me up and down.

"All right," she said finally. "Come in."

She took my hand. Her fingers were like a bundle of broom straws, so thin and dry, but the strength of them was unnatural. I couldn't have tugged loose if she was leading me into rooms of white-hot coal. Her strength was a kind of perverse miracle, for she got it from fasting herself thin. Because of this hunger practice her lips were a wounded brown and her skin deadly pale. Her eye sockets were two deep lashless hollows in a taut skull. I told you about the nose already. It stuck out far and made the place her eyes moved even deeper, as if she stared out the wrong end of a gun barrel. She took the bundle from my hands and threw it in the corner.

"You'll be sleeping behind the stove, child."

It was immense, like a great furnace. There was a small cot close behind it.

"Looks like it could get warm there," I said.   30

"Hot. It does."

"Do I get a habit?"

I wanted something like the thing she wore. Flowing black cotton. Her face was strapped in white bandages, and a sharp crest of starched white cardboard hung over her forehead like a glaring beak. If possible, I wanted a bigger, longer, whiter beak than hers.

"No," she said, grinning her great skull grin. "You don't get one yet. Who knows, you might not like us. Or we might not like you."

35   But she had loved me, or offered me love. And she had tried to hunt the Dark One down. So I had this confidence.

"I'll inherit your keys from you," I said.

She looked at me sharply, and her grin turned strange. She hissed, taking in her breath. Then she turned to the door and took a key from her belt. It was a giant key, and it unlocked the larder where the food was stored.

Inside there was all kinds of good stuff. Things I'd tasted only once or twice in my life. I saw sticks of dried fruit, jars of orange peel, spice like cinnamon. I saw tins of crackers with ships painted on the side. I saw pickles. Jars of herring and the rind of pigs. There was cheese, a big brown block of it from the thick milk of goats. And besides that there was the everyday stuff, in great quantities, the flour and the coffee.

It was the cheese that got to me. When I saw it my stomach hollowed. My tongue dripped. I loved that goat-milk cheese better than anything I'd ever ate. I stared at it. The rich curve in the buttery cloth.

40   "When you inherit my keys," she said sourly, slamming the door in my face, "you can eat all you want of the priest's cheese."

Then she seemed to consider what she'd done. She looked at me. She took the key from her belt and went back, sliced a hunk off, and put it in my hand.

"If you're good you'll taste this cheese again. When I'm dead and gone," she said.

Then she dragged out the big sack of flour. When I finished that heaven stuff she told me to roll my sleeves up and begin doing God's labor. For a while we worked in silence, mixing up the dough and pounding it out on stone slabs.

"God's work," I said after a while. "If this is God's work, then I've done it all my life."

45   "Well, you've done it with the Devil in your heart then," she said. "Not God."

"How do you know?" I asked. But I knew she did. And I wished I had not brought up the subject.

"I see right into you like a clear glass," she said. "I always did."

"You don't know it," she continued after a while, "but he's come around here sulking. He's come around here brooding. You brought him in. He knows the smell of me, and he's going to make a last ditch try to get you back. Don't let him." She glared over at me. Her eyes were cold and lighted. "Don't let him touch you. We'll be a long time getting rid of him."

So I was careful. I was careful not to give him an inch. I said a rosary, two rosaries, three, underneath my breath. I said the Creed. I said every scrap of Latin I knew while we punched the dough with our fists. And still, I dropped the cup. It rolled under that monstrous iron stove, which was getting fired up for baking.

And she was on me. She saw he'd entered my distraction.   50

"Our good cup," she said. "Get it out of there, Marie."

I reached for the poker to snag it out from beneath the stove. But I had a sinking feel in my stomach as I did this. Sure enough, her long arm darted past me like a whip. The poker lighted in her hand.

"Reach," she said. "Reach with your arm for that cup. And when your flesh is hot, remember that the flames you feel are only one fraction of the heat you will feel in his hellish embrace."

She always did things this way, to teach you lessons. So I wasn't surprised. It was playacting, anyway, because a stove isn't very hot underneath right along the floor. They aren't made that way. Otherwise a wood floor would burn. So I said yes and got down on my stomach and reached under. I meant to grab it quick and jump up again, before she could think up another lesson, but here it happened. Although I groped for the cup, my hand closed on nothing. That cup was nowhere to be found. I heard her step toward me, a slow step. I heard the creak of thick shoe leather, the little *plat* as the folds of her heavy skirts met, a trickle of fine sand sifting, somewhere, perhaps in the bowels of her, and I was afraid. I tried to scramble up, but her foot came down lightly behind my ear, and I was lowered. The foot came down more firmly at the base of my neck, and I was held.

"You're like I was," she said. "He wants you very much."   55

"He doesn't want me no more," I said. "He had his fill. I got the cup!"

I heard the valve opening, the hissed intake of breath, and knew that I should not have spoke.

"You lie," she said. "You're cold. There is a wicked ice forming in your blood. You don't have a shred of devotion for God. Only wild cold dark lust. I know it. I know how you feel. I see the beast . . . the beast watches me out of your eyes sometimes. Cold."

The urgent scrape of metal. It took a moment to know from where. Top of the stove. Kettle. Lessons. She was steadying herself with the iron poker. I could feel it like pure certainty, driving into the wood floor. I would not remind her of pokers. I heard the water as it came, tipped from the spout, cooling as it fell but still scalding as it struck. I must have twitched beneath her foot, because she steadied me, and then the poker nudged up beside my arm as if to guide. "To warm your cold ash heart," she said. I felt how patient she would be. The water came. My mind went dead blank. Again. I could only think the kettle would be cooling slowly in her hand. I could not stand it. I bit my lip so as not to satisfy her with a sound. She gave me more reason to keep still.

"I will boil him from your mind if you make a peep," she said, "by filling up your ear."

60   Any sensible fool would have run back down the hill the minute Leopolda let them up from under her heel. But I was snared in her black intelligence by then. I could not think straight. I had prayed so hard I think I broke a cog in my mind. I prayed while her foot squeezed my throat. While my skin burst. I prayed even when I heard the wind come through, shrieking in the busted bird nests. I didn't stop when pure light fell, turning slowly behind my eyelids. God's face. Even that did not disrupt my continued praise. Words came. Words came from nowhere and flooded my mind.

Now I could pray much better than any one of them. Than all of them full force. This was proved. I turned to her in a daze when she let me up. My thoughts were gone, and yet I remember how surprised I was. Tears glittered in her eyes, deep down, like the sinking reflection in a well.

"It was so hard, Marie," she gasped. Her hands were shaking. The kettle clattered against the stove. "But I have used all the water up now. I think he is gone."

"I prayed," I said foolishly. "I prayed very hard."

"Yes," she said. "My dear one, I know."

65   We sat together quietly because we had no more words. We let the dough rise and punched it down once. She gave me a bowl of mush, unlocked the sausage from a special cupboard, and took that in to the Sisters. They sat down the hall, chewing their sausage, and I could hear them. I could hear their teeth bite through their bread and meat. I couldn't move. My shirt was dry but the cloth stuck to my back, and I couldn't think straight. I was losing the sense to understand how her mind worked. She'd gotten past me with her poker and I would never be a saint. I despaired. I felt I had no inside voice, nothing to direct me, no darkness, no Marie. I was about to throw that cornmeal mush out to the birds and make a run for it, when the vision rose up blazing in my mind.

I was rippling gold. My breasts were bare and my nipples flashed and winked. Diamonds tipped them. I could walk through panes of glass. I could walk through windows. She was at my feet, swallowing the glass after each step I took. I broke through another and another. The glass she swallowed ground and cut until her starved insides were only a subtle dust. She coughed. She coughed a cloud of dust. And then she was only a black rag that flapped off, snagged in bob wire, hung there for an age, and finally rotted into the breeze.

I saw this, mouth hanging open, gazing off into the flagged boughs of trees.

"Get up!" she cried. "Stop dreaming. It is time to bake."

Two other Sisters had come in with her, wide women with hands like paddles. They were evening and smoothing out the firebox beneath the great jaws of the oven.

"Who is this one?" they asked Leopolda. "Is she yours?"   70

"She is mine," said Leopolda. "A very good girl."

"What is your name?" one asked me.

"Marie."

"Marie. Star of the Sea."

"She will shine," said Leopolda, "when we have burned off the dark   75
corrosion."

The others laughed, but uncertainly. They were mild and sturdy French, who did not understand Leopolda's twisted jokes, although they muttered respectfully at things she said. I knew they wouldn't believe what she had done with the kettle. There was no question. So I kept quiet.

"*Elle est docile,*" they said approvingly as they left to starch the linens.

"Does it pain?" Leopolda asked me as soon as they were out the door.

I did not answer. I felt sick with the hurt.

"Come along," she said.   80

The building was wholly quiet now. I followed her up the narrow stair-case into a hall of little rooms, many doors. Her cell was the quietest, at the very end. Inside, the air smelled stale, as if the door had not been opened for years. There was a crude straw mattress, a tiny bookcase with a picture of Saint Francis hanging over it, a ragged palm, a stool for sitting on, a crucifix. She told me to remove my blouse and sit on the stool. I did so. She took a pot of salve from the bookcase and began to smooth it upon my burns. Her hands made slow, wide circles, stopping the pain. I closed my eyes. I expected to see blackness. Peace. But instead the vision reared up again. My chest was still tipped with diamonds. I was walking through windows. She was chewing up the broken litter I left behind.

"I am going," I said. "Let me go."

But she held me down.

"Don't go," she said quickly. "Don't. We have just begun."

I was weakening. My thoughts were whirling pitifully. The pain had   85
kept me strong, and as it left me I began to forget it; I couldn't hold on. I began to wonder if she'd really scalded me with the kettle. I could not re-member. To remember this seemed the most important thing in the world. But I was losing the memory. The scalding. The pouring. It began to vanish. I felt like my mind was coming off its hinge, flapping in the breeze, hanging by the hair of my own pain. I wrenched out of her grip.

"He was always in you," I said. "Even more than in me. He wanted you even more. And now he's got you. Get thee behind me!"

I shouted that, grabbed my shirt, and ran through the door throwing it on my body. I got down the stairs and into the kitchen, even, but no matter what I told myself, I couldn't get out the door. It wasn't finished. And she knew I would not leave. Her quiet step was immediately behind me.

"We must take the bread from the oven now," she said.

She was pretending nothing happened. But for the first time I had gotten through some chink she'd left in her darkness. Touched some doubt. Her voice was so low and brittle it cracked off at the end of her sentence.

"Help me, Marie," she said slowly.

90   But I was not going to help her, even though she had calmly buttoned the back of my shirt up and put the big cloth mittens in my hands for taking out the loaves. I could have bolted for it then. But I didn't. I knew that something was nearing completion. Something was about to happen. My back was a wall of singing flame. I was turning. I watched her take the long fork in one hand, to tap the loaves. In the other hand she gripped the black poker to hook the pans.

"Help me," she said again, and I thought, Yes, this is part of it. I put the mittens on my hands and swung the door open on its hinges. The oven gaped. She stood back a moment, letting the first blast of heat rush by. I moved behind her. I could feel the heat at my front and at my back. Before, behind. My skin was turning to beaten gold. It was coming quicker than I thought. The oven was like the gate of a personal hell. Just big enough and hot enough for one person, and that was her. One kick and Leopolda would fly in headfirst. And that would be one-millionth of the heat she would feel when she finally collapsed in his hellish embrace.

Saints know these numbers.

She bent forward with her fork held out. I kicked her with all my might. She flew in. But the outstretched poker hit the back wall first, so she rebounded. The oven was not so deep as I had thought.

There was a moment when I felt a sort of thin, hot disappointment, as when a fish slips off the line. Only I was the one going to be lost. She was fearfully silent. She whirled. Her veil had cutting edges. She had the poker in one hand. In the other she held that long sharp fork she used to tap the delicate crusts of loaves. Her face turned upside down on her shoulders. Her face turned blue. But saints are used to miracles. I felt no trace of fear.

95   If I was going to be lost, let the diamonds cut! Let her eat ground glass!

"Bitch of Jesus Christ!" I shouted. "Kneel and beg! Lick the floor!"

That was when she stabbed me through the hand with the fork, then took the poker up alongside my head, and knocked me out.

It must have been a half an hour later when I came around. Things were so strange. So strange I can hardly tell it for delight at the remembrance.

For when I came around this was actually taking place. I was being worshiped. I had somehow gained the altar of a saint.

I was laying back on the stiff couch in the Mother Superior's office. I looked around me. It was as though my deepest dream had come to life. The Sisters of the convent were kneeling to me. Sister Bonaventure. Sister Dympna. Sister Cecilia Saint-Claire. The two French with hands like paddles. They were down on their knees. Black capes were slung over some of their heads. My name was buzzing up and down the room, like a fat autumn fly lighting on the tips of their tongues between Latin, humming up the heavy blood-dark curtains, circling their little cosseted heads. Marie! Marie! A girl thrown in a closet. Who was afraid of a rubber overboot. Who was half overcome. A girl who came in the back door where they threw their garbage. Marie! Who never found the cup. Who had to eat their cold mush. Marie! Leopolda had her face buried in her knuckles. Saint Marie of the Holy Slops! Saint Marie of the Bread Fork! Saint Marie of the Burnt Back and Scalded Butt!

I broke out and laughed.

They looked up. All holy hell burst loose when they saw I'd woke. I still did not understand what was happening. They were watching, talking, but not to me.

"The marks . . ."

"She has her hand closed."

"Je ne peux pas voir."

I was not stupid enough to ask what they were talking about. I couldn't tell why I was laying in white sheets. I couldn't tell why they were praying to me. But I'll tell you this: it seemed entirely natural. It was me. I lifted up my hand as in my dream. It was completely limp with sacredness.

"Peace be with you."

My arm was dried blood from the wrist down to the elbow. And it hurt. Their faces turned like flat flowers of adoration to follow that hand's movements. I let it swing through the air, imparting a saint's blessing. I had practiced. I knew exactly how to act.

They murmured. I heaved a sigh, and a golden beam of light suddenly broke through the clouded window and flooded down directly on my face. A stroke of perfect luck! They had to be convinced.

Leopolda still knelt in the back of the room. Her knuckles were crammed halfway down her throat. Let me tell you, a saint has senses honed keen as a wolf. I knew that she was over my barrel now. How it happened did not matter. The last thing I remembered was how she flew from the oven and stabbed me. That one thing was most certainly true.

"Come forward, Sister Leopolda." I gestured with my heavenly wound. Oh, it hurt. It bled when I reopened the slight heal. "Kneel beside me," I said.

She kneeled, but her voice box evidently did not work, for her mouth opened, shut, opened, but no sound came out. My throat clenched in noble delight I had read of as befitting a saint. She could not speak. But she was beaten. It was in her eyes. She stared at me now with all the deep hate of the wheel of devilish dust that rolled wild within her emptiness.

110   "What is it you want to tell me?" I asked. And at last she spoke.

"I have told my Sisters of your passion," she managed to choke out. "How the stigmata . . . the marks of the nails . . . appeared in your palm and you swooned at the holy vision. . . ."

"Yes," I said curiously.

And then, after a moment, I understood.

Leopolda had saved herself with her quick brain. She had witnessed a miracle. She had hid the fork and told this to the others. And of course they believed her, because they never knew how Satan came and went or where he took refuge.

115   "I saw it from the first," said the large one who put the bread in the oven. "Humility of the spirit. So rare in these girls."

"I saw it too," said the other one with great satisfaction. She sighed quietly. "If only it was me."

Leopolda was kneeling bolt upright, face blazing and twitching, a barely held fountain of blasting poison.

"Christ has marked me," I agreed.

I smiled the saint's smirk into her face. And then I looked at her. That was my mistake.

120   For I saw her kneeling there. Leopolda with her soul like a rubber over-boot. With her face of a starved rat. With the desperate eyes drowning in the deep wells of her wrongness. There would be no one else after me. And I would leave. I saw Leopolda kneeling within the shambles of her love.

My heart had been about to surge from my chest with the blackness of my joyous heat. Now it dropped. I pitied her. I pitied her. Pity twisted in my stomach like that hook-pole was driven through me. I was caught. It was a feeling more terrible than any amount of boiling water and worse than being forked. Still, still, I could not help what I did. I had already smiled in a saint's mealy forgiveness. I heard myself speaking gently.

"Receive the dispensation of my sacred blood," I whispered.

But there was no heart in it. No joy when she bent to touch the floor. No dark leaping. I fell back into the white pillows. Blank dust was whirling through the light shafts. My skin was dust. Dust my lips. Dust the dirty spoons on the ends of my feet.

Rise up! I thought. Rise up and walk! There is no limit to this dust!

Drama   **Simon Fill**

NIGHT VISITS
Characters

TOM: A second-year resident in medicine, twenty-eight.
LIZ: A nurse, twenty-seven.
EMILY: Gentle, looks about twenty-three.

Time

The present.

Location

An examination room in a hospital.

(A hospital examination room. White. Patient gowns hang all over. We hear wind outside. TOM lies on the examining table, asleep. Twenty-eight. In a doctor's outfit. LIZ enters. Twenty-seven. Nurse's uniform. Quiet moment to herself, then notices the gowns and TOM.)

TOM: *(Eyes closed.)* I'm not seeing patients anymore, Liz. *(Quickly, lightly, sounding upbeat and energetic.)* It's over. It's over. It's over. It's over. It's over. It's over. It's over. It's over. It's over. It's over. It's over. It's over. It's over. It's over. It's over. Do you have a problem with it being over? You better not. Is it not really over? I don't think so.
LIZ: Tom. One more. That's all.
TOM: Seeing one patient in your thirty-fifth hour of being awake is the equivalent of seeing fifteen hundred in your first.
LIZ: You can't refuse to see patients. You're a resident.
TOM: Shit.

(He gets up.)

TOM: You look . . . nice.
LIZ: Got a date.
TOM: Doctor?
LIZ: No.
TOM: Yes. Yes. YES! Good for *you.*
LIZ: You are such a freak. *(Looks out window.)* Windy outside.
TOM: It's a bad night.
LIZ: I know. We all do.
TOM: . . . What? Oh. I'm. . .fine.
LIZ: We all loved Katie, Tom.
TOM: Yeah. Thanks. No, I mean it.

LIZ: She was a great nurse. I wish I'd known her more.
TOM: You're okay, Liz. I hate to admit it.

(He hits her lightly on the arm.)

LIZ: You are such a freak. *(Beat.)* This patient—Doug gave her a shot of methicillin, he's busy now. Watch her ten minutes, see if she's allergic. She was . . . in a car . . .
TOM: Look. Katie's accident was a year ago.
LIZ: To the day.
TOM: I'm not really doing anything to this patient anyhow.
LIZ: You mean that?
TOM: *(Very dramatic.)* Have I *ever* lied to you before?
LIZ: Yeah.
TOM: No, 'bout something serious.
LIZ: Yeah.
TOM: You're—you're—you're—

(Jokingly, he grabs a tiny knee hammer.)

LIZ: You gonna test my reflexes? You are such a . . .!
TOM: What!
LIZ: *(Beat. Softly, with great fondness.)* Little boy. This patient. The accident involved only her. After it, she disappeared. They found her in a church. Sitting on the floor. Surrounded herself with lit wish candles. Hundreds. She'd been there hours. When they asked her why, she said, "I'm cold."

(She gives him a chart. He stares at her.)

LIZ: Emily. I know, I know. She's odd, this one. Another sweet nobody. Passed a psych consult, but otherwise, she won't talk. Here twenty-one hours. Won't leave till she feels she's "okay." She's a little banged up, but fine. She could go now. She won't. Bring her upstairs when you're done. *(Beat. Studies TOM with suspicion.)* No.
TOM: I'm good at this. She'll feel better. She'll leave.
LIZ: Won't work. We tried everything. Social services was called. They'll be here soon. *(Looks at robes.)* I wish we had another free room.
TOM: You didn't carry those up from a broken dryer at three in the morning.
LIZ: Dr. Pitnick, that was nice. Someday you'll make a good nurse.
TOM: I'll get her to go.
LIZ: Won't happen. *(Looks him up and down.)* You need a compliment. Badly. *(Beat.)* Serious now. You okay?
TOM: Funny. When Katie died, I prayed every night for a month.
LIZ: What about?

TOM: If I told anyone, Liz, I'd tell you. *(Lightly.)* It was very self-involved. *(Beat.)* I'm fine. Thanks. Have a good date. You're not as cute as you think you are.

LIZ: *(Smiles.)* I'll send her down. See you tomorrow.

(She exits. Pause. The sound of wind. He looks out the window. He is overcome and starting to break down. A knock. He recovers himself.)

TOM: *(Cheerful.)* Dr. Pitnick's house of optimism and laundry!

(EMILY enters. She looks about twenty-three. Gentle. Bruised face and arms.)

TOM: *(Grins. A quick patter. His "routine.")* Just kidding. There's no optimism here. Don't mean to be unprofessional. I expect you to stay silent. *(Looks at chart, then her arm, checking where the shot was given.)* Hope that didn't hurt too much. I hate shots. We're gonna get you to feel okay. I usually do this by showing patients how impressive they are in comparison to me. Some patients protest. For good reason. I expect you to stay silent. They call me the funny doctor. *(To self.)* This is like one of my dates in high school. *(Looks at her.)* Did I detect a glint of humanity?

(She smiles a little.)

TOM: I bet no one upstairs tried to crack you up. Their mistake. Do you feel sorry for yourself?

(She shakes her head.)

TOM: You ought to. You gotta listen to me. But if you talk to me, you get to listen to me less. 'Round here, I'm considered aversion therapy for introverts. *(Whispers.)* Of course, being the funniest doctor 'round here is a weak claim. *(Beat. Back to normal.)* Look. I know what you went through was serious. I know. I do. But sometimes when you think you're alone, when you most think that, you . . . aren't. *(Beat.)* Sorry. I'm expecting a lot here. I mean, it's not like you're God or anything. No offense.

(Silence. He raises his hands in surrender, looks out the window. Pause.)

EMILY: Why would I be offended you don't think I'm God? That's pretty queer.

TOM: I'm not the one who surrounded myself with wish candles in a church.

EMILY: Does that unnerve you? Dr. Tom?

TOM: *(Beat.)* How'd you know my name was Tom?

EMILY: *(Mock mystical.)* Woo woo.

(Beat. She points at his name tag.)

TOM: Oh. Wow. I need some sleep. Sorry. I shouldn't say that.

EMILY: *(Lightly teasing.)* C'mon. This is all about you. *(Beat. Sincere.)* You look tired. You okay?

TOM: Great. My patient's asking me if I'm okay. Are you?

EMILY: You want me to leave, don't you?

TOM: I . . . *(Looks at her face and arms. Gentle.)* These bruises'll disappear on their own in a few days. They hurt?

EMILY: No, they feel great. Sorry. Not that bad. Thanks. You're nice.

TOM: I'm only nice when I'm tired.

EMILY: How often you tired?

TOM: Always. You're gonna be fine.

EMILY: I'm not important. What?

TOM: Nothing.

EMILY: What?

TOM: *(Warmly ironic.)* I WISH someone'd said that in your chart!

(She smiles.)

EMILY: You're weird.

TOM: I know.

EMILY: When the accident happened, I hit a divider, everything stopped. I didn't know where I was. For some reason, I thoughta my dad. He died four years ago. Nothing to do with cars. I . . . loved him. After he was gone, I never felt his loss. I . . . Something happened.

(Pause.)

TOM: You tell anyone this?

EMILY: Do you count? *(Beat.)* I got out of the car, looked around to make sure no one was hurt. Then I ran.

(Silence.)

You all right?

TOM: Yeah. Sure. I'm gonna get you outta here. In good shape.

EMILY: *(Lightly.)* I'm a nobody. And I dress poorly.

TOM: What's the one thing you could do to give your life meaning?

EMILY: Accessorize?

(Beat. He smiles. She looks off.)

EMILY: You can't see wind.

TOM: What?

EMILY: You can't see it, but it's there.

TOM: *(Beat.)* Is it? When the accident happened, who were you with?

EMILY: That's an odd question.

TOM: Who were you with?

EMILY: Why?

TOM: Answer it!

EMILY: No one! *(Beat.)* I was hurt, and for the first time I felt, *knew,* I'm with no one. My father, he's really . . . gone . . .

(Pause.)

You understand what I'm saying?

TOM: *(Thinks with care, then nods slowly.)* I'm sorry. *(Beat.)* You okay?

EMILY: *(Upset. Snippy.)* With doctors like you, who needs accidents!

TOM: Sorry.

EMILY: I . . . No, don't feel bad for me. I don't. My father . . . I loved him.

TOM: Did he love you?

EMILY: Yes, but that's not as important.

TOM: You okay?

EMILY: Keep asking that, and you won't be.

TOM: *(Softly.)* Sorry.

EMILY: Stop apologizing, you didn't kill him. *(Beat.)* When I left the accident, a few blocks away I passed a homeless woman. I asked her for the nearest good church. One that was honest, that wasn't about exclusion. She said nothing. I asked again, and she goes, "Here."

(She points to her heart.)

TOM: *(Softly.)* Oh.

EMILY: You enjoy helping this nobody?

TOM: Who? You?

EMILY: You know a lot about this. *(Beat.)* Who was it?

TOM: You're my patient.

EMILY: So? There's doctor-patient privilege. I won't tell anyone.

TOM: I'm trying to make *you* all right.

EMILY: You're almost there. This'll help. Or don't you open up to nobodies?

TOM: Is this a trick?

EMILY: Yes. You got me to like you.

TOM: *(Beat.)* My wife, Katherine. She was a nurse here in pediatrics. We grew up together in Brooklyn, but in high school I was too shy to ask her out. We ran into each other when she'd graduated from college, at a reading of James Joyce by an Irish actor. Joyce was her favorite writer. She and I dated. At that point, I was well on my way to becoming the "funny doctor." She was quiet and funnier, in that good way the most serious people are. After two months, I proposed. Now that was funny. She didn't answer. We kept dating. Every day for two months after that I proposed. Silence. I thought, "This woman either likes me or is totally insensate." At the end of that time she gave me a copy of *Finnegan's Wake*, her favorite book. At college I'd read it and almost finished. The first page, that is. But I loved her so much I slogged through the book. Boy, did I love her. On page fifty, at the bottom, in pencil, someone'd written something. I looked closely. It said, "Yes. I'll marry you."

(Pause.) I called her up and told her Joyce had accepted my proposal of marriage. *(Pause.)* She was driving to Riverdale, a favor, to pick up a friend's kid at school. I know she was starting to think about children herself. She said she wanted them to have "my looks and her sense of humor." Another car, an old lady who shouldn't have been driving, who had a history of epilepsy . . . and . . . you know the rest. The other woman lived. *(Beat.)* I asked Katie once why she wrote "yes" to me on page fifty. She said, "I knew you loved me, but I wasn't sure how much." *(Pause.)* Don't look so serious.

EMILY: *(Gently.)* The line you draw between yourself and other people, it doesn't exist. Not how you think. You know that, you'll let her inside of you, even if she's gone.

TOM: *(Softly.)* Hey. Thanks.

EMILY: *(With affection.)* You gonna believe that? Or are you just another punk doctor?

(Long pause.)

TOM: Yeah, I do. *(Beat.)* Yeah. *(Beat.)* What do you charge? I don't know if my insurance covers this.

EMILY: This was good.

TOM: I can't treat you for premature nostalgia. It isn't my specialty. You gonna stay or go?

EMILY: Quiet in here.

TOM: *(Light. Gentle.)* That tough being a nobody?

(She smiles.)

TOM: Funny. When Katie died, I prayed every night for a month. It was very self-involved.

EMILY: No, it was just about her. You asked that she be okay. You never worried about yourself. That's incredibly rare, even for people who love each other. *And* you're a nonbeliever.

TOM: *(Beat.)* How'd you know that?

EMILY: Who listens to prayers?

TOM: I don't get it.

EMILY: Who listens to prayers?

TOM: Nobody! *(Beat. A slow realization.)* Nobody. You could leave the
hospital now.
EMILY: Thanks for the permission.

(She gathers her things.)

EMILY: Oh, and Tom?
TOM: Yeah?
EMILY: Your insurance doesn't cover it.

*(She leaves. Pause. The sound of wind. He looks out the window. He opens
it. When the wind enters the room, the robes fill with air, as if inhabited by
ghosts. They sway beautifully. Tableau. Blackout.)*

END OF PLAY

On Writing   **Connie May Fowler**

CONNIE MAY IS GOING TO WIN THE LOTTERY THIS WEEK

As far as I can tell, no one in my family—not even a distant cousin or spinster aunt—ever had any money. Paternal? Maternal? Black? White? Native American? Doesn't matter. Generations upon generations of my people have remained poor as dirt since our DNA first crawled out of the swamp on the back of a tadpole.

The reasons why poverty clings with the ferocity of acid to my family make no sense. We are hard workers, all: sharecroppers, itinerant preachers, circus performers, street singers, writers . . .

Oh, wait. I spy a pattern. Even when we're able to get off the farm, we follow our bliss, but our bliss rarely intersects with any activity that has greater than a fifty-fifty chance of generating cash in amounts that would cease our endless hand-wringing. And that is why my retirement plan— the Bliss Plan—is totally dependent on me winning the lottery.

The job that I have held the longest is that of writer. In fact, I don't remember a time when I didn't write. I also don't remember a time when it provided a living wage.

5   Seriously. For illustrative purposes only, let's say I receive $100,000 for a book that takes me three years to complete (I'm being optimistic). My agent takes 15% of the $100,000, which leaves me with about $85,000. Various state and federal taxes extract another 30%. Now divide that number by three. I'm not a math whiz, but I'm pretty sure this means that my take-home pay for a job in which I reveal to the world my most painful truths, and get awards and fan mail for doing so, is $19,800. I know, I know; it's more than some people make but let's be honest: it stinks.

And because The Third Law of The Universe states, "There shall be only ten living writers at any given moment who actually get rich following their bliss and you're not one of them (and by the way, you're not going to win the lottery, either)," I have always worked other jobs.

Let me list some of them now in no particular order: bartender, waitress, maid, TV host, antique dealer, college professor, construction worker, actor, clothing store clerk, proofreader, door-to-door hawker of crap. Of the eleven stated professions, two provided no remuneration but I thought they might lead to something.

Currently, I'm an antique dealer and giver of how-to-write seminars. Thanks to the robust nature of the American economy, no one I know is buying nineteenth-century brooches, and folks these days will teach themselves how to write, thank you very much.

If there is a silver lining, I suppose it would be that I'm brilliantly maintaining the family tradition of, as my mother was so fond of saying, not having a pot to pee in or a window to throw it out of.

Writing is not for the faint of heart or the greedy. It is a mad act born of necessity. I must write. If I go too long without spinning a tale, I get all kinds of crazy. Thirty years ago, long before I penned my first novel, I was a poet. Faithful to the calling, I wrote every day, revised compulsively, and sent out pieces of my heart—SASE included—to strangers at literary magazines, occasionally getting published but mainly not.

As part of the dedication to my art, and in the wake of my mother's   10
death, I decided to quit college, be a full-time poet, and see the world. As with the Bliss Plan, what could go wrong? I used my inheritance to fuel my dream: the $150 my mother left behind in her checking account.

I caught a ride with four guys—two of them I knew from a couple of classes we'd taken together and two were strangers. All four were from Saudi Arabia and on their way to Spokane, Washington, to sojourn with fellow countrymen. They were perfect gentlemen, only occasionally allowing me to pay for gas.

You're already suspecting, I'm sure, that this story has all the signs of being a sordid, tragic affair. And you're right. It was terrible. They dumped me in Spokane in a cold, wheezy apartment, picked up their buddies, and headed to Cuba via Mexico, where they thought Fidel would train them to be fighters so that they could return home and overthrow the Saudi royal family. What a plan!

Because this essay isn't about that little adventure, all I can tell you of their fate is that Cuba wouldn't allow the bozos into the country and I was stuck penniless 2,000 miles from home with winter fast approaching.

I'm from Florida. How could I have known that in Spokane pretty much everything—and I mean everything save bars and pizza joints—closes down for the winter and that if you don't have a job by, say, the end of August, you probably aren't going to get one?

My poetry wasn't going well. It was overwrought with abandonment   15
issues and perpetual whining about the weather. But I had two things in my favor: The writing was preventing me from going totally berserk and the landlady felt sorry for me. That, and she wanted me to keep paying the rent on the tenement apartment, which was, by the way, chock full of disgruntled ghosts who routinely scared the bejeezus out of me.

My landlady hooked me up with a local construction crew. I swear. To this day I have no idea why the foreman hired me but I'm forever grateful that he did. I'll tell you right now, I'm not a hammer-n-nail gal. So you can imagine my relief when he put a trowel in my hand and taught me how to smear stucco mud on lath.

I was the only female on the crew and none of the males, except for the foreman, spoke to me. In fact, they didn't even look at me. When we broke for lunch, they sat on one side of the room and I sat on the other. This was a huge relief because even I could not imagine a conversation that included references to the Denver Broncos, that sweet piece of meat down at Lefty's, competitive puking, and Sylvia Plath.

The gig was minimum wage but it was enough to keep me in paper and typewriter ribbon. That's really all I wanted: just enough money to support my habit.

By my second day on the job, I knew something was terribly wrong. My eyes were scarlet. Each time I blinked, it felt as if the undersides of my lids were lined with sandpaper. I feared I had pink eye and, in retrospect, this possibility may have fueled my co-workers' refusal to speak to me, and their insistence on maintaining a healthy distance.

20   On day three, my eyes began oozing toxic glue. In the cold air, the glue quickly dried, encasing my peepers in an amber crust. The foreman sent me to his doctor, who assured me I did not have pink eye, which was curable. I was, said the doctor, allergic to the stucco mud and he recommended that I immediately quit my job.

Easy for him to say. I didn't relish the idea—however romantic—of being a *homeless* poet. And the sending and resending of rejected poems required cash. My tenure as a construction worker had been so brief that I hadn't yet saved bus fare for the long trip back home across the broad continent. So, against doctor's orders, I did the only logical thing a girl in my situation could: I continued to smear stucco eight hours a day, five days a week, even as my condition grew rapidly worse.

My red-rimmed eyes swelled shut. I gazed at the world through a lens fading to black. The inflammation, oozing, and crusting blossomed anew, globular and hideous, with each arced stroke of the trowel. I worked—whether it was in construction or poetry—with a wet washrag in one hand, which I used to unglue my lids.

Fearing I was going to be a blind poet, I prepared. I watched—between hot washrag compressions—*The Miracle Worker.* I went to the library one cold evening—a fresh dusting of snow lighting my way—and checked out a manual on sign language, because I had become confused as to what actually happened when you lost your sight. I practiced walking around my apartment with my eyes closed, counting how many steps between the bed and the bathroom (twenty-three).

I kept my job through the winter and came home in the spring, a notebook bursting with not bad poetry. My eyes would not clear up for another four weeks, and when they did, I snagged a job as a waitress at Bennigan's. It was there that I ran into the University of Tampa provost; by luck or providence, the hostess seated him in my section. He told me to come to his office the following week and he'd reinstate my scholarship. I did and he did and the rest is history. My dream came true. I became the only thing I had ever really wanted to be in this life: a writer who, if things got dicey, had enough cash to get out of town.

As for my eyes, I can see just fine if I'm wearing my glasses but that is   25
the result of age, not demon stucco mud.

My experience being doggedly committed to a nowhere job so that my
higher calling of Artist/Writer could be fulfilled has served me well. I'm
proud that for six months of my life I worked among people who wouldn't
so much as say hello but who, when I quit, lined up and shook my hand,
man by man. I earned their respect, not their friendship. And that was
okay because I had sought neither.

Writing is a tough vocation made all the more difficult by changing
delivery systems, archaic business models, and imploding economies. You
write your heart out and some clown you don't even know takes a sucker
punch at you in the media, and manners and tradition dictate that you
remain silent.

But it's the best of jobs. In the early morning I sip my hot tea and browse
the masters: Virginia Woolf, Gabriel García Márquez, Flannery O'Conner,
Zora Neale Hurston, William Faulkner. I might throw in some poets:
Neruda, Eliot, Lorca, Ellison, Oliver, Donne. Their words ferry me into my
writer's skin. And then I begin. One word at a time—sentence by paragraph
by chapter—I chase my bliss.

I know my retirement plan sucks, and that my next part-time job might
entail picking up bottles along the highway. But that's okay. I don't need
riches. All I need is time to write and a roof over my head. I have so many
more stories to tell.

On Writing; Poetry   **Tess Gallagher**

ODE TO MY FATHER

On Saturdays my father would drive my mother and my three brothers and me into town to shop and then to wait for him while he drank in what he called "the beer joints." We would sit for hours in the car watching the townspeople pass, commenting on their dress and faces, trying to figure out what they did with the rest of their lives. Although it was just a game we played to pass the time, I think it taught me to see deeply at a very young age. Every hour or so my mother would send me on a round of the taverns to try for a sighting of my father. I would peck on the windows and the barmaid would shake her head "no" or motion down the dim aisle of faces to where my father would be sitting on his stool, forgetting, forgetting us all for a while. Back at the car, my brothers were quarreling, then crying. My mother had gone stiff. These times were the farthest I would ever get from home.

My father's drinking and the quarrels he had with my mother because of it terrorized my childhood. There is no other way to put it. And if terror and fear are necessary to the psychic stamina of a poet, I had them in steady doses—just as inevitably as I had the rain. I learned that the world was not just, that any balance was temporary, that the unreasonableness could descend at any minute, thrashing aside everything and everyone in its path. Love, through all this, was constant, though it had a hoary head. Its blow, brutal as any evil, was perhaps more so for how it raked the quick of my being. The body remembers too, though not with malice, but as one might gaze uncomprehendingly at photographs of family friends, now deceased—but somehow important.

I remember the day I became aware that other families lived differently. I was showering in the junior high school's gym with my best friend, Molly, when she noticed the welts on my back. I could not see them and so could not share her awe and worry for me. What had happened to me? What had I done? Who had done this?

I was sixteen when I had my last lesson from the belt and my father's arm. I had learned that no words, no pleading would save me. I stood still in the yard, in full view of the neighbors, and took "what was coming to me." I looked steadily ahead, without tears or cries, as a tree must look while the saw bites in, then deepens to the core. I felt my spirit reach its full defiance. I stood somehow in the power of my womanhood that day and knew I had passed beyond humiliation. If a poet must know that physical pain and unreasonable treatment can be turned aside by an ultimate act of the will, I learned this then. I did not feel sorry for myself. I did not stop the loving. It was our hurt not to have another way to settle these things. For we had no language between us in those numb years of my changing, of my large hope toward the world. All through my attempts in the poems, this need has been building, the need to forge a language that would give these dead and living lives a way to speak. There was often the feeling that the language might come too late, might even do damage, might not be equal to the love. All these fears. Finally no choice.

The images of these two primal figures, mother and father, condense 5 now into a view of my father's work-thickened hands and my mother's back, turned in hopeless anger at the stove where she fixed eggs for my father in silence. My father gets up from the table, shows me the open palms of his hands: "Threasie," he says, "get an education. Don't get hands like these."

Years later, after returning from a trip to Ireland, it was the work of these hands that I wanted to celebrate and to acknowledge for my father. He had recently retired from the docks and liked to play cards with the men down at Chinook Tavern. I would drive down and pick him up when the game ended at 2:00 A.M. Sometimes I would go early enough to have a beer with his friends in the back room and to listen to them kid him. "Hey Okie, how'd an ole geezer like you get a good lookin' daughter like that?" My father would laugh and wink, giving his head a quick little dip and rise. He didn't need to say anything. They called him Okie because he'd come from Oklahoma and he liked to be called that.

When he got home, we put the coffee pot on and sat at the kitchen table and talked. I don't remember when we began this sort of talking but I think now it happened because my father had caught sight of his death. He had suffered a heart attack while I had been in Ireland and this had given him more to say. When I'd been a child fishing with him in the salmon derbies he had talked more than he usually did—talked "to make the fish bite"—for just when you got to the most interesting place in the story, the fish were sure to bite. And they did. But this night there was another kind of talking. My father knew I was going the next day to a job in another part of the country. He might not see me again. He began to tell me his life. And though he told it all plainly and without pity for himself— only some verbal turning of the palms upward—the rhythms of his speech, his vulnerability before me had a power and beauty I did not want to see lost to the world.

The next day I got on a bus and waved good-bye to him and my mother. The bus was crammed with people headed for Seattle. They were talking and adjusting their packages. The woman sitting next to me had some knitting to work on. I took out my notebook with its pale green-white pages, frog-belly green they were. I was thinking this is no place to write this; this is too important a poem to be writing here. I put the book on my knees and tried to hear my father's voice, to get it to speak through me. This was the only place, the only time.

3 A.M. Kitchen: My Father Talking

For years it was land working me, oil fields,
cotton fields, then I got some land. I
worked it. Them days you could just about
make a living. I was logging.

5   Then I sent to Missouri. Momma
come out. We got married.
We got some kids. Five kids.
That kept us going.

We bought some land near the water.
10   It was cheap then. The water
was right there. You just looked out
the window. It never left the window.

I bought a boat. Fourteen footer.
There was fish out there then.
15   You remember, we used to catch
six, eight fish, clean them right
out in the yard. I could of fished to China.

I quit the woods. One day just
walked out, took off my corks, said that's
20   it. I went to the docks.
I was working winch. You had to watch
to see nothing fell out of the sling. If
you killed somebody you'd
never forget it. All
25   those years I was just working
I was on edge, every day. Just working.

You kids. I could tell you
a lot. But I won't.

It's winter. I play a lot of cards
30   down at the tavern. Your mother.
I have to think of excuses

to get out of the house. You're
wasting your time, she says. You're wasting
your money.

You don't have no idea, Threasie.   35
I run out of things
to work for. Hell, why shouldn't I
play cards? Threasie,
some days now I just don't know.

Poetry   **Sherine Gilmour**

LITTLE BOYS

Beside me there is a little boy, who sleeps
and kicks his tiny legs. Outside in the snowy night,
a man is shouting "I'm gonna' kill you" on the street.

The sound seeps in, slurred red ghosts slip through mortar, bricks.
5   I turn away—relieved to see my husband's bum in pale moonlight
bare, exposed by wayward sheets. He's such a child when he sleeps.

I reach for him, but he dreams so deep.
My fingers trace his leg, the boyhood scar from racing bikes
in traffic. Again, the street. Another shout, something tumbles, hits the
    street.

10   I think: Knife scar on his hand. Burn mark on his arm, ashy, pink.
I remember the first date, a trick where he ignited
his sock with a lighter. I hold our little boy close as he nurses into sleep,

and what happens to little boys? He's told me of the beatings,
faced the wall, bruises dark as well water. I'm terrified
15   about the nights years ago his father shouted "kill you" from the street,

and his mother hid in the kitchen. Earlier, the baby peed
on him. I thought he grunted "cocksucker" and ran over. All in my mind,
husband fine, baby a symphony of warbling coo's in clean PJs, ready for
    sleep.

I touch this man, he was everything I ever wanted. Now I need
20   this baby more. In bed I think, "If you ever hurt our boy, I'll
choke you against the wall, then leave." Ah, hush now, my little sweetheart
    sleeps
beside me and sighs. Men outside keep shouting "I'm going to kill you" on
    the street.

Creative Nonfiction   **Lee Gutkind**

TEETH

After breakfast, her husband looked up from across the table and announced that he was taking her into town to have all her teeth pulled out. It took a while for the meaning of his words to penetrate. Even when he said he was getting her a new set of teeth, she stared at him blankly. The memory of that morning nearly six months ago pained her even now.

"My teeth ain't perfect, but they never give me or my husband no trouble," she said, rolling her eyes and shaking her head back and forth slowly. "And suddenly, there he wanted to go and pull them all out. I've never been so surprised in all my life."

She was sitting on a stoop in front of the tarpaper-covered cabin in which she and her husband lived, petting the old coon dog, curled in a grimy heap at her feet, and watching the tractor-trailer trucks whoosh by. Each time a truck went up the road, she would wave and smile. The truckers would invariably wave back, as they roared by, bellowing smoke.

She told me that her loneliness was sometimes awful. It wasn't the mountains—she had lived here all her life and wasn't interested in anywhere else—but the fact that no one was around to talk to. The gloomy shadow that fell across her face blatantly telegraphed her desperation. Each time I visited, she went on and on, could hardly stop herself from talking and questioning me about my travels. She was enthralled by my motorcycle and the stories I told about Santa Fe, New Mexico; Amarillo, Texas; Pine Bluff, Arkansas—places far away from where she lived now. She wanted to see the world, which to her was anywhere beyond her own confining backyard.

The woman was a river of fat. Her body bulged and rippled in every direction, and her eyes, tucked into her pasty skin, looked like raisins pressed into cookie dough. Her hair was dirty gray, tangled and woolly, but you could tell her face had once been pretty. When she showed me her picture as an infant, I remarked that she looked like the Ivory Snow baby. Blushing, she covered her mouth and turned away. That was how we had first got on the subject of her teeth.

One day in town her husband was approached by the new dentist, a handsome young man in a white shirt and a blue-and-red-striped tie, who said his house needed a new roof. Would he be interested in installing it in return for money or services?

Her husband was a short, wiry old man of seventy-two, who resembled a chicken hawk, with a hooked nose and arms that bowed out like furled wings. He hunched forward when he walked, as if he were about to take off flying. He told the dentist he would think on it for a while.

That evening, after supper, he stooped down and peered into her mouth, testing each of her teeth with his thumb and forefinger to see how well they were rooted. "Smile," he told her. "Laugh." She followed his instructions to the letter, as was her habit. Over the next few days, he watched her every chance he got. It was early autumn when he finally went back into town to make the deal. She never knew anything about it.

The woman explained that she and her husband had very little use for cash, bartering for almost everything they needed. They traded vegetables, cultivated on their tiny patch of land, for fruit—corn for peaches, tomatoes for apples, pickles for pears, beets for pretty "blue-fire" plums. He chopped wood in return for mason jars. Periodically, he repaired a car for a guy who owned a dry goods store in town in exchange for clothes for both of them. By bartering instead of buying and selling, they hardly paid Uncle Sam a penny's worth of taxes.

10   Last summer, he raised a barn for some city folks, recently retired near here, in return for an old engine from a '64 Buick and a side of beef. The engine went into a pickup truck they had gotten for 150 dozen eggs. Paid out over a period of three months, the eggs came from their chicken coops out back. The pickup was then swapped to the owner of a local filling station for credit for two hundred gallons of gas, plus an assortment of parts and tools. Meanwhile, she boiled up the beef on the old black cast-iron stove that had belonged to his grandfather and canned and stored most of it in the cold-cellar cave under the house. She cut the remainder of the beef in strips and hung them like wet socks above the stove, smoking and shriveling them down to jerky. From the spring to the fall, her husband went fishing each evening after dinner. When he collected a big batch of trout, she stewed them in the pressure cooker until the whole fish, bones and all, was white and meaty like tuna. This was what they would eat next winter and the winters thereafter. Their cave was stocked with years of stuff.

Her husband never talked about his work and what was owed to him in the way of goods and services, and she never asked. Despite her significant contribution, the actual swapping wasn't her business. Years ago, her daddy had told her in no uncertain terms exactly what she needed to know to get herself through life. He was a man much like her husband, didn't owe anyone and never wasted anything. No words were wasted in conversation, unless some specific point was to be made. Otherwise, silence was golden.

One night, however, her father came outside and squeezed down on the stoop beside her. They lived in an old house along the side of the road, about the same size as the one in which she and her husband lived now. But her father only rented it for fifty dollars a month. Neither her father nor his father before him had ever owned a piece of property straight out.

At the time, she didn't know that the old man was dying from cancer. Her mother had also died from cancer, and she had had to quit school in the sixth grade to take care of the rest of the kids and keep house. Recently, her two older brothers had joined the army, while the younger kids were sent to foster homes. Now, she and her father were home alone. She was fifteen at the time.

They sat side by side as the night grew colder. The moon shimmered in the glittering dish of sky, but the air felt like rain. Suddenly he cleared his throat. The sound of his voice made her feel uncomfortable, similar to how she felt trying on a new pair of boots.

"What else is there in life?" He said this as if in summation after a long conversation, which she had somehow missed. Then he paused. She would never forget his face as they sat there. His hard, sharp features seemed to disintegrate in the darkness. The glitter reflecting from the moonlight faded from the blue of his eyes. "You work to eat, you eat to live, you live to work." He sighed. "That's all there are to it." 15

That philosophy repelled me and was the reason I was not ever going to be happy shoe-dogging with my father or staying around Pittsburgh making a life with the likes of Steve Mayerstein and Melvin Herwald—any of that old crowd from school. I didn't know, exactly, what was ahead of me when I first got on a motorcycle—I certainly had little confidence I could make it as a writer—but anything was better than limiting my life plan to mere survival and maintaining the status quo, which was so uninspiring.

But this woman's notions of escape were too vague to be transformed into a reality. She lacked direction—and a concrete dream. Robert Meyers had anchored my possibilities. Gave me permission to try to turn my dreams of a different and better life into reality by verbalizing what I had been hereto afraid to even imagine. I wouldn't be here, on my big, black R-60 BMW road warrior, living this life from one end of the country to the other, without that vital exchange between teacher and student.

The next morning, the man who was soon to become her husband made himself known. Miraculously, all of the details had been worked out between the man and her father in advance, without her having the slightest idea of what was happening. The following afternoon, the man came and took her away. Two weeks later, her father died.

She cleared her throat and motioned toward the house with her fat, flesh-soaked arm. "We came right here to these two acres and moved into an old shed out back. It ain't there no more. Tore it down to salvage the wood for this place. First we made sure we had good water, then we started building. From start to finish it took two years to get all set up. The winters were awful, but the summers weren't too bad."

20   All this happened some thirty years ago. Her husband had been married once before. His first wife died or left him, she wasn't sure, and his children, whom she never met, were all grown up and living somewhere in another part of the state. Once in a great while, there was a letter, which he would read carefully, his lips moving, then stuff into his pocket, shaking his head and muttering. He would go on, muttering and cursing, shaking his head, for days at a time, without so much as an explanation.

Her own brothers and sisters all lived near here, but hardly ever stopped by or invited her to visit. Like most everyone else, they were more than a little afraid of her somber, silent husband.

Once again, she paused to wave at a trucker, barreling up the narrow two-lane highway. Their shack had been built unusually close to the asphalt. Even from up in the sleeping loft inside, you could hear the cinders and feel the wind when the trucks rumbled by. She said she was so shocked and angry when she found out about the deal her husband had made with the new dentist that she started screaming and yelling. "I had never acted that way before, but I just couldn't help myself. All of a sudden, I went crazy. My husband didn't know what to do."

He had turned away, glaring in silence out the window. It was still early. The sun was just beginning its ascent up the hill toward them. His eyes narrowed. Time passed as he stared down the road. His brows, thick and hairy, cast a shadow, like umbrellas over his eyelids. When the sunlight reached up as far as their house, he got up and finished dressing. He bit off a plug of tobacco, stuffed it under his cheek, put on his old grimy baseball cap, climbed into his pickup, and turned her over. When he saw his wife come out onto the porch, he threw the truck into reverse, backed up, and leaned out the window. He wanted to have his say one more time. "We shook hands on a new set of teeth. It's owed to me."

She turned and walked back into the house without a word. He peeled out onto the asphalt, his tires spitting gravel.

25   In no time, her best clothes were out of the drawer and piled on the bed. She found an old suitcase, cleaned it inside and out carefully before laying in her clothes. The last time she had been on any sort of trip was when her husband had come to take her from her daddy. They didn't have a suitcase then. All her possessions, including her mother's big black roasting pan, fit easily into a medium-sized cardboard box. Her father carried the box down to the road and they waited together until the man who was to become her husband arrived. The whole thing—packing, waiting, and driving away—all took about ten minutes. It went by in a blur, one moment stacked up on top of another.

Thinking back, she realized that her life had ended right about then. She had been isolated with this man who hardly talked to her and whom she hardly knew, a man who had refused to discuss his past for over thirty

years. At least with her father there was evidence of some roots and another life somewhere behind the one he had been living. But this man's
world was bleak, both behind and beyond. He offered little more than a
nod or a grunt for sustenance each day. Her father's words, uttered with
such sadness and resignation on that damp, dark night so many centuries
ago, came back to her now. You work to eat, you eat to live, you live to
work. That's all there are to it.

All right. She had lived her life in accordance with her father's wishes,
had never asked for anything from anyone, never shirked her responsibilities or wasted a breath. She had always done whatever her husband had
told her to do—and more. But giving up a part of her own body simply for
the sake of a business deal was too much. It was going too far. A person
has a God-given right to own certain things, especially when they were
born with them.

The last thing she did before leaving was to go out to the pump house
and peer into the mirror. The image she saw glaring back at her was awful.
She was too old, too fat, and too dirty. But, if anything, her face had held
up best of all. There was still a spark, a hint of the beauty that might have
been.

Her daddy, who never had more than a dollar in his pocket at any one
time, had always bragged that the Good Lord had made him rich by blessing him with a daughter with a million-dollar smile. Even now, she could
hear the distant echo of his praise. She wasn't going to let that damn bastard she married squash the memory by pulling out her teeth.

She looked up at me. The shroud that had fallen over her face as she told
her story momentarily lifted. "Used to be my husband would leave me
alone from early morning until supper. But now, things is different. He's
liable to ride by anytime, just to check and see if I'm still here. Sometimes
I hide out behind the chicken coops and wait for him. When the house
looks empty, he'll stop to see where I am. He always pretends he's come back
for tools or materials, but I know I got him worried. It serves him right."

She dug her fingers into her scalp, shook her head vehemently, scratching simultaneously before continuing. "I left the house that morning,
hitchhiked into town, and bought a ticket for Davenport, Iowa. Davenport
was the only city in the state I could think of. My daddy traveled all over
the country when he was younger. He told me you could drive for half a
day in any one direction in Iowa and not see anything else but a green
carpet of corn, just bending and stretching in the distance."

She pushed her big blubbery legs out into the grass, right near where
the old coon dog was lying. Once in a while, the dog would thrash around
and thump its tail against the ground. A couple of times, it pushed itself
up and crawled over on top of us. The woman had on brown double-knit
slacks worn through at the knees. Her blouse was white with alternating

pink and blue pastel stripes, although the colors were graying from repeated washings. This was the outfit she wore as she climbed aboard the
bus and headed toward Davenport. Her clothes looked a lot better back
then, she said.

It took nearly three hours to get to Pittsburgh, where they stopped and
idled in the depot for about forty-five minutes. She did not get off the bus.
They stopped twice on the highway in Ohio and once more in Indiana, but
she remained in her seat, guarding her suitcase.

"I tell you, I've never done so much thinking in my entire life as I did
on that bus, looking through the window, reading the neon signs and
watching the headlights from the cars. Most of the people around me were
sleeping, and none of them were too friendly. Not that I tried to do much
talking. To tell the truth, I was scared half to death."

She wasn't actually thinking, she explained, as much as she was dreaming—with her eyes open. Her window was like an imaginary TV screen, and
she could see the images of her past reflected before her. She saw her father
carrying the cardboard box down to the side of the road. As the cancer took
its toll, he had shriveled up like an old root. Then she saw the man who was
to be her husband pull up. He put the cardboard box into the bed of the
truck, opened up the passenger door, and helped her inside.

35   "I remember looking right into his face as he done this, the first time I
had ever looked him full in the face. And then, as I sat in the darkness on
that bus, I pictured how he looked earlier that morning when he leaned
across the table and told me he was going to take away my teeth. And you
know what? He was the same. Those thirty years we had spent together
had bloated me like a balloon and wrecked up my face but, except for a
little more gray in his whiskers, that bastard ain't changed one bit."

She paused, shook her head, chuckled, then shook her head again and
again. It wasn't easy to suddenly accept the reality of what had happened.
The shiny sadness of her life reflected in her eyes.

I looked away, down behind the tarpaper shack toward the outhouse
across the field. It had a three-hole bench. There were four or five old cars
dumped into a gully behind the outhouse and an abandoned windowless
school bus, teetering on the edge.

"I never made it to Davenport," she said, after a while. "But I got all the
way to Chicago. You ever been to the bus station in Chicago? More people
there than I ever seen, all in one place. Half of them don't speak English, and
none of them was white. The moment I got off that bus, seeing all them colored and hearing all that foreign commotion, I was completely confused. I
was hungry, but didn't want to spend any money. I also wanted to clean up a
little, but with all them people, I was afraid to make a decision."

After a while, she found herself a bench back in the corner, out of the
way, and sat down to try to think things out. She still had her ticket to

Davenport, Iowa, but didn't particularly want to go there any more. She didn't want to go anywhere, as a matter of fact. She wasn't willing to move one inch from where she was. She must have dozed off, for the next thing she remembered was feeling a hand on her shoulder, shaking her gently. Someone was saying her name. No one would know her name in Chicago, so maybe she really was back home, about to emerge from a terrible dream.

But when she finally opened her eyes, an elderly man with horn-rimmed   40
glasses and a tiny, pinched nose introduced himself as a representative of the Traveler's Aid Society, whatever that was. The man's voice was soft and reassuring. As he talked, he picked up her bag, wrapped his arm around her ample shoulders, helped her up, and led her across the bus station.

When her husband had discovered her missing, the man explained, he had contacted their minister, who somehow traced her to Pittsburgh and subsequently to Chicago. There was also a Traveler's Aid representative waiting at the Davenport bus station, just in case she had made it that far.

They were moving at a brisk pace, passing the ticket counters and neatly wending their way through the milling crowd. She felt like a piece of livestock. "Where are you taking me?"

"There's a bus to Pittsburgh leaving in about ten minutes. Your husband already wired the money." He smiled and continued to talk to her in his quiet and reassuring manner, as they pushed through a big set of swinging doors and headed on down a broad cement runway toward a long line of idling buses. Drivers in neatly pressed gray uniforms stood by the doors of their respective vehicles, puffing cigarettes and punching tickets, as she and the man hurried by.

"But I already have a ticket to Davenport, Iowa."

"You can cash it in when you get back home . . ." He paused, all the   45
while continuing to lead her down along the row of buses. "Of course, I can't force you to do anything you don't want to do." He shrugged and smiled apologetically. "I can't even help you make up your mind."

By this time, they were approaching the bus to Pittsburgh. She felt his hand on her back, urging her gently toward the bus. He handed a ticket and her suitcase to the driver.

Meanwhile, she hesitated, momentarily resisting the pressure on her back. She tried desperately to think things out, but her mind was blank, as was her future.

With nothing better to do, she walked up the steps, dropped into a seat by the window, and closed her eyes. She did not allow herself to open her eyes until hours later, when the bus pulled into Pittsburgh. She was so confused and embarrassed, she had completely forgotten to say goodbye to the man with the horn-rimmed glasses who had helped her.

Now she looked up at me, smiling and winking. "My husband came to meet me." The thought evidently amused her, for she shook her head back and forth, chuckling. "On the way home, we talked things over, got every-thing out in the open for the very first time. I told him how lonely I was, how it wasn't fair the way he constantly mistreated me. I said that I should be consulted in his decisions about how we spend our money. I told him that I didn't have enough clothes, that I wanted to go into town more often, and that, because he was such a damn hermit, I didn't have no friends or family." She nodded emphatically. "I let him have it with both barrels. He had never allowed no one to talk to him that way before in his entire life."

50   I stood up. More than two hours had passed since we had first started talking. The sky was clouding over. In this part of western Pennsylvania, rain erupts suddenly, swallowing the hillsides and ravaging the roads. Besides, I was getting cold, sitting so long on that stoop. And my pants were filthy, where the old coon dog had tracked mud all over me. I walked briskly back to my motorcycle.

"He tries to be nice," she said, as she followed along behind me. "But you really can't change him. You couldn't ever change my daddy either," she added. "When you come right down to it, they was both dark and silent men."

I nodded, pulled on my helmet and kicked down on the starter. The machine cranked to life as I straddled the seat. From past experience, I knew that I couldn't wait for the right moment to leave. Otherwise, I'd be waiting forever. I had to depart even while she was still in the act of talking.

She planted her foot in my path and grabbed my arm. "You know, he drove by two or three times while we was sitting here talking. He'll want to know who you are and everything that was said. Hell," she said, smiling and winking, finally stepping out of the way, so that I could pull out, "I ain't telling him nothing. It serves him right."

The woman prepared herself extra special for her husband's homecoming that evening.

55   She went into the pump house and sponged herself down from head to toe, ran a brush through her hair a hundred times, scrubbed the grime from her fingers until the half-moons of her nails were white. Back in the house, in the loft where they slept, she got out the nice green cotton jumper-dress with the pretty yellow and white floral design and laid it out on the quilt. He had bought her the dress the day she came home. She had only taken it out of the box once, the following Sunday when they went to church.

After preparing dinner and setting the table nice and neat, she went back upstairs and put on the dress. Then she dusted herself with some fancy-smelling powder she had ordered through a magazine and gotten in the mail. She was just about ready, when his truck crackled outside on the gravel. He walked into the house. She could hear him move about downstairs, looking into the big pot on the cast-iron stove, sniffing what was for dinner. But not until he walked across the room and started up the ladder toward the loft, did she reach into the water glass on the nightstand beside their bed. Only then did she put in her new teeth.

Poetry   **Rachel Hadas**

MNEMONIC

Impossible to remember where or how
the talk went. Parties; quarrels with old friends;
dwindling band of survivors.
Wings of aspirations
5   clipped. Stirred widdershins,
batter slops over the side
of the mixing bowl. Compote
of tropes. Abstract the daily
quota; spread out; re-
10   distribute into parcels of energy.
Poems accumulate; before you know it
thicken to books, and books remember for us.

Growing
old

Rachel Hadas. "Mnemonic" from *Literary Imagination*, vol. 10, no. 3 (2008): 302. © 2008
Association for Literary Scholars, Critics and Writers. By permission Oxford University Press.

Poetry   **Terrance Hayes**

THE GOLDEN SHOVEL

after Gwendolyn Brooks

I. 1981

When I am so small Da's sock covers my arm, we
cruise at twilight until we find the place the real

men lean, bloodshot and translucent with cool.
His smile is a gold-plated incantation as we

drift by women on bar stools, with nothing left   5
in them but approachlessness. This is a school

I do not know yet. But the cue sticks mean we
are rubbed by light, smooth as wood, the lurk

of smoke thinned to song. We won't be out late.
Standing in the middle of the street last night we   10

watched the moonlit lawns and a neighbor strike
his son in the face. A shadow knocked straight.

Da promised to leave me everything: the shovel we
used to bury the dog, the words he loved to sing,

his rusted pistol, his squeaky Bible, his sin.   15
The boy's sneakers were light on the road. We

watched him run to us looking wounded and thin.
He'd been caught lying or drinking his father's gin.

He'd been defending his ma, trying to be a man. We
stood in the road, and my father talked about jazz,   20

how sometimes a tune is born of outrage. By June
the boy would be locked upstate. That night we

got down on our knees in my room. *If I should die*
before I wake, Da said to me, *it will be too soon.*

II. 1991

25   Into the tented city we go, we-
akened by the fire's ethereal

afterglow. Born lost and cool-
er than heartache. What we

know is what we know. The left
30   hand severed and school-

ed by cleverness. A plate of weekdays cooking. The hour lurk-

ing in the afterglow. A late-
night chant. Into the city we

35   go. Close your eyes and strike
a blow. Light can be straight-

ened by its shadow. What we
break is what we hold. A sing-

ular blue note. An outcry sin-
40   ged exiting the throat. We

push until we thin, thin-
king we won't creep back again.

While God licks his kin, we
sing until our blood is jazz,

45   we swing from June to June.
We sweat to keep from we-

eping. Groomed on a die-
t of hunger, we end too soon.

Poetry   **Tony Hoagland**

AMERICA

Then one of the students with blue hair and a tongue stud
Says that America is for him a maximum-security prison

Whose walls are made of RadioShacks and Burger Kings, and MTV episodes
Where you can't tell the show from the commercials,

And as I consider how to express how full of shit I think he is,   5
He says that even when he's driving to the mall in his Isuzu

Trooper with a gang of his friends, letting rap music pour over them
Like a boiling Jacuzzi full of ballpeen hammers, even then he feels

Buried alive, captured and suffocated in the folds
Of the thick satin quilt of America   10

And I wonder if this is a legitimate category of pain,
or whether he is just spin doctoring a better grade,

And then I remember that when I stabbed my father in the dream last night,
It was not blood but money

That gushed out of him, bright green hundred-dollar bills   15
Spilling from his wounds, and—this is the weird part—,

He gasped, "Thank god—those Ben Franklins were
Clogging up my heart—

And so I perish happily,
Freed from that which kept me from my liberty"—   20

Which is when I knew it was a dream, since my dad
Would never speak in rhymed couplets,

And I look at the student with his acne and cell phone and phony ghetto
     clothes
And I think, "I am asleep in America too,

And I don't know how to wake myself either,"   25
And I remember what Marx said near the end of his life:

"I was listening to the cries of the past,
When I should have been listening to the cries of the future."

But how could he have imagined 100 channels of 24-hour cable
30   Or what kind of nightmare it might be

When each day you watch rivers of bright merchandise run past you
And you are floating in your pleasure boat upon this river

Even while others are drowning underneath you
And you see their faces twisting in the surface of the waters

35   And yet it seems to be your own hand
Which turns the volume higher?

Creative Nonfiction   **Ann Hodgman**

NO WONDER THEY CALL ME A BITCH

I've always wondered about dog food. Is a Gaines-burger really like a hamburger? Can you fry it? Does dog food "cheese" taste like real cheese? Does Gravy Train actually make gravy in the dog's bowl, or is that brown liquid just dissolved crumbs? And exactly what *are* by-products?

Having spent the better part of a week eating dog food, I'm sorry to say that I now know the answers to these questions. While my dachshund, Shortie, watched in agonies of yearning, I gagged my way through can after can of stinky, white-flecked mush and bag after bag of stinky, fat-drenched nuggets. And now I understand exactly why Shortie's breath is so bad.

Of course, Gaines-burgers are neither mush nor nuggets. They are, rather, a miracle of beauty and packaging—or at least that's what I thought when I was little. I used to beg my mother to get them for our dogs, but she always said they were too expensive. When I finally bought a box of cheese-flavored Gaines-burgers—after twenty years of longing—I felt deliciously wicked.

"Dogs love real beef," the back of the box proclaimed proudly. "That's why Gaines-burgers is the only beef burger for dogs with real beef and no meat by-products!" The copy was accurate: meat by-products did not appear in the list of ingredients. Poultry by-products did, though—right there next to preserved animal fat.

One Purina spokesman told me that poultry by-products consist of   5
necks, intestines, undeveloped eggs and other "carcass remnants," but not feathers, heads, or feet. When I told him I'd been eating dog food, he said, "Oh, you're kidding! Oh, *no!*" (I came to share his alarm when, weeks later, a second Purina spokesman said that Gaines-burgers *do* contain poultry heads and feet—but *not* undeveloped eggs.)

Up close my Gaines-burger didn't much resemble chopped beef. Rather, it looked—and felt—like a single long, extruded piece of redness that had been chopped into segments and formed into a patty. You could make one at home if you had a Play-Doh Fun Factory.

I turned on the skillet. While I waited for it to heat up I pulled out a shred of cheese-colored material and palpated it. Again, like Play-Doh, it was quite malleable. I made a little cheese bird out of it; then I counted to three and ate the bird.

There was a horrifying rush of cheddar taste, followed immediately by the dull tang of soybean flour—the main ingredient in Gaines-burgers. Next I tried a piece of red extrusion. The main difference between the meat-flavored and cheese-flavored extrusions is one of texture. The "cheese" chews like fresh Play-Doh, whereas the "meat" chews like Play-Doh that's been sitting out on a rug for a couple of hours.

Frying only turned the Gaines-burger black. There was no melting, no sizzling, no warm meat smells. A cherished childhood illusion was gone. I flipped the patty into the sink, where it immediately began leaking rivulets of red dye.

10   As alarming as the Gaines-burgers were, their soy meal began to seem like an old friend when the time came to try some *canned* dog foods. I decided to try the Cycle foods first. When I opened them, I thought about how rarely I use can openers these days, and I was suddenly visited by a long-forgotten sensation of can-opener distaste. *This* is the kind of unsavory place can openers spend their time when you're not watching! Every time you open a can of, say, Italian plum tomatoes, you infect them with invisible particles of by-product.

I had been expecting to see the usual homogeneous scrapple inside, but each can of Cycle was packed with smooth, round, oily nuggets. As if someone at Gaines had been tipped off that a human would be tasting the stuff, the four Cycles really were different from one another. Cycle-1, for puppies, is wet and soyish. Cycle-2, for adults, glistens nastily with fat, but it's passably edible—a lot like some canned Swedish meatballs I once got in a Care package at college. Cycle-3, the "lite" one, for fatties, had no specific flavor; it just tasted like dog food. But at least it didn't make me fat.

Cycle-4, for senior dogs, had the smallest nuggets. Maybe old dogs can't open their mouths as wide. This kind was far sweeter than the other three Cycles—almost like baked beans. It was also the only one to contain "dried beef digest," a mysterious substance that the Purina spokesman defined as "enzymes" and my dictionary defined as "the products of digestion."

Next on the menu was a can of Kal Kan Pedigree with Chunky Chicken. Chunky *chicken?* There were chunks in the can, certainly—big, purplish-brown chunks. I forked one chunk out (by now I was becoming more callous) and found that while it had no discernible chicken flavor, it wasn't bad except for its texture—like meat loaf with ground-up chicken bones.

In the world of canned dog food, a smooth consistency is a sign of low quality—lots of cereal. A lumpy, frightening, bloody, stringy horror is a sign of high quality—lots of meat. Nowhere in the world of wet dog foods was this demonstrated better than in the fanciest I tried—Kal Kan's Pedigree Select Dinners. These came not in a can but in a tiny foil packet with a picture of an imperious Yorkie. When I pulled open the container, juice spurted all over my hand, and the first chunk I speared was trailing a long gray vein. I shrieked and went instead for a plain chunk, which I was able to swallow only after taking a break to read some suddenly fascinating office equipment catalogues. Once again, though, it tasted no more alarming than, say, canned hash.

Still, how pleasant it was to turn to *dry* dog food! Gravy Train was the first I tried, and I'm happy to report that it really does make a "thick, rich, real beef gravy" when you mix it with water. Thick and rich, anyway. Except for a lingering rancid-fat flavor, the gravy wasn't beefy, but since it tasted primarily like tap water, it wasn't nauseating either.

My poor dachshund just gets plain old Purina Dog Chow, but Purina also makes a dry food called Butcher's Blend that comes in Beef, Bacon & Chicken flavor. Here we see dog food's arcane semiotics at its best: a red triangle with a *T* stamped into it is supposed to suggest beef; a tan curl, chicken; and a brown *S,* a piece of bacon. Only dogs understand these messages. But Butcher's Blend does have an endearing slogan: "Great Meaty Tastes—without bothering the Butcher!" *You know, I wanted to buy some meat, but I just couldn't bring myself to bother the butcher . . .*

Purina O.N.E. ("Optimum Nutritional Effectiveness") is targeted at people who are unlikely ever to worry about bothering a tradesperson. "We chose chicken as a primary ingredient in Purina O.N.E. for several reasonings," the long, long essay on the back of the bag announces. Chief among these reasonings, I'd guess, is the fact that chicken appeals to people who are—you know—*like us.* Although our dogs do nothing but spend eighteen-hour days alone in the apartment, we still want them to be *premium* dogs. We want them to cut down on red meat, too. We also want dog food that comes in a bag with an attractive design, a subtle typeface, and no kitschy pictures of slobbering golden retrievers.

Besides that, we want a list of the Nutritional Benefits of our dog food— and we get it on O.N.E. One thing I especially like about this list is its constant references to a dog's "hair coat," as in "Beef tallow is good for the dog's skin and hair coat." (On the other hand, beef tallow merely provides palatability, while the dried beef digest in Cycle provides palatability *enhancement.*)

I hate to say it, but O.N.E was pretty palatable. Maybe that's because it has about 100 percent more fat than, say, Butcher's Blend. Or maybe I'd been duped by the packaging; that's been known to happen before.

As with people food, dog snacks taste much better than dog meals. They're better looking too. Take Milk-Bone Flavor Snacks. The loving-hands-at-home prose describing each flavor is colorful; the writers practically choke on their own exuberance. Of bacon they say, "It's so good, your dog will think it's hot off the frying pan." Of liver: "The only taste your dog wants more than liver—is even more liver!" Of poultry: "All

15

20

those farm fresh flavors deliciously mixed in one biscuit. Your dog will bark with delight!" And of vegetable: "Gardens of taste! Specially blended to give your dog that vegetable flavor he wants—but can rarely get!"

Well, I may be a sucker, but advertising *this* emphatic just doesn't convince me. I lined up all seven flavors of Milk-Bone Flavor Snacks on the floor. Unless my dog's palate is a lot more sensitive than mine—and considering that she steals dirty diapers out of the trash and eats them, I'm loath to think it is—she doesn't detect any more difference in the seven flavors than I did when I tried them.

I much preferred Bonz, the hard-baked, bone-shaped snack stuffed with simulated marrow. I liked the bone part, that is; it tasted almost exactly like the cornmeal it was made of. The mock marrow inside was a bit more problematic: in addition to looking like the sludge that collects in the treads of my running shoes, it was bursting with tiny hairs.

I'm sure you have a few dog food questions of your own. To save us time, I've answered them in advance.

> Q. *Are those little cans of Mighty Dog actually branded with the sizzling word* BEEF, *the way they show in the commercials?*

25

> A. You should know by now that that kind of thing never happens.

> Q. *Does chicken-flavored dog food taste like chicken-flavored cat food?*
> A. To my surprise, chicken cat food was actually a little better—more chickeny. It tasted like inferior canned pâté.

> Q. *Was there any dog food that you just couldn't bring yourself to try?*
> A. Alas, it was a can of Mighty Dog called Prime Entree with Bone Marrow. The meat was dark, dark brown, and it was surrounded by gelatin that was almost black. I knew I would die if I tasted it, so I put it outside for the raccoons.

Poetry   **Fady Joudah**

SLEEPING TREES

Between what should and what should not be
Everything is liable to explode. Many times
I was told *who has no land has no sea*. My father
Learned to fly in a dream. This is the story
Of a sycamore tree he used to climb   5
When he was young to watch the rain.

Sometimes it rained so hard it hurt. Like being
Beaten with sticks. Then the mud would run red.

My brother believed bad dreams could kill
A man in his sleep, he insisted   10
We wake my father from his muffled screams
On the night of the day he took us to see his village.
No longer his village he found his tree amputated.
Between one falling and the next

There's a weightless state. There was a woman   15
Who loved me. Asked me how to say *tree*
In Arabic. I didn't tell her. She was sad. I didn't understand.
When she left, I saw a man in my sleep three times. A man I knew
Could turn anyone into one-half reptile.
I was immune. I thought I was. I was terrified of being   20

The only one left. When we woke my father
He was running away from soldiers. Now
He doesn't remember that night. He laughs
About another sleep, he raised his arms to strike a king
And tried not to stop. He flew   25
But mother woke him and held him for an hour,

Or half an hour, or as long as it takes a migration inward.
Maybe if I had just said it,
Shejerah, she would've remembered me longer. Maybe
I don't know much about dreams   30
But my mother taught me the law of omen. The dead
Know about the dying and sometimes

Catch them in sleep like the sycamore tree
My father used to climb

35   When he was young to watch the rain stream,
And he would gently swing.

Creative Nonfiction   **Stephen Kuusisto**

LETTER FROM VENICE

I came to Venice precisely because I was blind. The palazzos boasted of sunlight and stood beside the Grand Canal like wedding cakes. Water slapped the boat and somewhere a window opened and I heard a songbird. I guessed it was a Jamaican bluebird. I'd heard him before. A year ago I was standing at the Dunn's River Falls when a Jamaican minister took me by the hand. His palm was rough as a starfish. "Bluebirds sing all around here," he said. "You listen you can hear them above the falls." They were there, talking in the high, sunlit branches.

—*Digression*

Now I heard them on the Grand Canal. Then a small girl laughed and a man sang in a baritone voice. I imagined they were on a balcony and waving at the tourists floating beneath them.

Venice has endless distractions for the listener. I'd come here, in part, to prove it. Marsilio Ficino, the Florentine translator of Plato, wrote: *The world is just shapes and sounds.* Ficino said that sound equals form. This poses a challenge—could I, for instance, listen to the accidental music of a place like Venice while my wife explored the architecture? Could I find corresponding pleasure in merely listening?

As luck would have it, my literary agent called while I was pondering this in the New York Public Library. "I have a boondoggle for you," she said. "You can think of it as a romp." What followed was so improbable I could only guess it must be true. A design firm in Milan wanted me to appear in a magazine ad for interior lighting. My memoir *Planet of the Blind* had been translated into Italian under the title *Tutti i colori dei buio* (All the Colors of Darkness). Now the Italians wanted me to pose beneath stylish lights and say: *You can't imagine how I see light.* Of course my wife Connie and I and my guide dog Corky would be flown to Milan. All our expenses would be taken care of. Yes this was a boondoggle . . . Yes they could get us tickets to La Scala . . .

That night sitting in our kitchen Connie and I folded and spindled the journey. I worried about the tactlessness of appearing in an ad for interior lighting. Blindness is not a trifling subject. In my memoir I depict the effects of light and shade as being both shocking and oddly beautiful. My version of blindness still allows me to see colors and shapes, though they are often in-exact and more than a little troubling. But forget the aesthetics of the thing: over seventy percent of the blind remain unemployed in the United States. As a blind person I knew it was essential to portray the dignity of physical difference. But I also remembered the American poet Theodore Roethke, who wrote: *The eye, of course, is not enough. But the outer eye serves the inner, that's the point.* I decided that I liked the irony of the advertisement—*You*

5

can't imagine how I see light. This was about the inner eye. Roethke also said: *Literalness is the devil's weapon*. We decided we would go.

My own hearing had become careful and algebraic. If seeing is really an epicurean experience—if a stained glass window can take us higher like the Kama Sutra—then hearing has only its acquired nobility, sequenced and slow. I knew that I needed to go to Venice for "the Ficino Cure." I had to wander in a delirium of sound in a vast city with no cars. I had to get lost there. Connie could go her own way. We'd meet in the evening at Harry's Bar and she could tell me about San Zaccaria and I would tell her about getting lost while following the music of what happens.

First we would go to Milan. The lighting firm had retained the noted photographer Elliott Erwitt to photograph three blind artists. A Russian chess master and a concert pianist from Milan joined me in a villa on the outskirts of the city. Here we were: a crew of blind men who saw light with the inner eye. We were each in his way worried about the dignity of this enterprise. Each wondered if he'd made a mistake. We were upright and quiet. Eventually we were photographed in separate sessions and our paths never crossed again. We were free.

I was surprised by the odor of the stones. The Venetian mortar had a heady scent—the smell of galvanic particles, a chalky smell that was distinct from the ocean.

From the deck of the vaporetto I saw a sack of feathers: tropical feathers, green pastels—then, in the fast-changing light, this became a lemon dessert, a tower of ice—my blindness identified palazzos and clouds through cataracts and damaged retinas and announced that pillows were falling from a great ship. In reality the ship was a church blocking the sun. The pillows were boats piled with produce. "My Venice," it turned out, was a transparency, a slide that had been overexposed, or more properly, two slides that had been fitted neatly across my face. You can't imagine how I see light! Like the poet Wallace Stevens, I was "catching tigers in red weather." Some of the world's most renowned architecture stood before me and I was staring at the protoplasm of microbiology.

10   I turned to Connie, who is a resolute admirer of sunsets; a café observer—thinking to ask "What's that darkly groomed form over yonder?" but thought better of it for she was in a rapture of the quattrocento. And I, in turn, knew that I must find my own Venice because Marsilio Ficino had challenged me. The light about my head was incandescent, striking. It did not resolve into anything knowable. There was a kind of magnificence about this. I was passing through a prismatic cloud. Venice wore her mask of sea glass and I wore mine. I would dance with her. For music we'd take the ordinary buzz and din of the narrow passageways and canals.

After finding our hotel I made a solo foray into the Venetian alleys. I wasn't exclusively alone since I was accompanied by Corky. Corky was companionable, and unfazed by strange cities. She was also large and handsome with a noble head. Before I'd gone two steps a passing woman remarked: "Cane guida! Bellissima!" I nodded on Corky's behalf and then we sailed up a causeway—man and dog pushed by wind, each of us taking in the aromatic salts and musk of this place we'd never seen before. We turned left and Corky guided me through a medieval warren of slippery paving stones and jutting shops. She hugged the walls, evading a pack of schoolchildren shouting in French. I heard bells from a door, tourists speaking Japanese, and something heavy rolling on casters. The air was wet and cold. I heard caged birds from somewhere above and put out a hand. What was this, a morning glory trellis? I'd backed into a cul-de-sac, a fairy grot, a cave of waterweeds and acacia.

I was in equal parts a figure of struggle and peace; a walking lodestone _Retrospection_ of sorts. I touched my fingers to a cold window. A fine dust coated the glass. A light rain had begun falling, and since there was no one around I encouraged Corky to relieve herself there in the fairy grot. I stood listening. There were extraordinary songbirds calling from a second-story window. Laughter from above, a woman and a child . . . I couldn't make out the words. Two poets . . . The lyrical push of ordinary Italian . . .

I had to slow down. If I was going to listen to Venice properly I needed to hear the cadences of the place. I needed to stand still. Again I thought of Theodore Roethke: *A poet must be a good reporter; but he must be something a good deal more.* Whitman called this *loafing.* I thought of Whitman observing the parade of humanity with lewd concentration. Walt had a good ear. He loved opera and knew how to sit perfectly still.

At home in New York, Corky and I raced up and down the streets at _Digression_ breakneck speeds. Guide dogs move fast through traffic. We sailed past the expensive couples on their Rollerblades and took the joggers in Central Park by surprise. It was obvious that here in Venice we didn't need to rush anywhere. We could prevail over chaos by means of deliberation.

We trailed the sound of footsteps through a transverse intersection of alleys. Shop bells rang . . . someone opened a door . . . Corky followed a stranger into a shop and we found ourselves in a room full of hand-blown glass. We stood completely still. There was a deep silence. All eyes were watching us. I was certain that the shop's owner was horrified—a blind man with only a dog for company had appeared amid the exquisite glass! We were literally "a bull in a china shop"!

Then there was a noise of little shoes—paper slippers—a tiny person 15 was approaching . . . "Listen," a woman said. I heard the hum of breath moving over glass—she was playing a glass flute! Wind and sunlight pressed through dark leaves. I was sweetly transfixed. This was a shy, unasked-for gift . . . She played the delicate pipe and I imagined leaps of light on water. *A mind of grace is real and it comes by surprise,* I thought. The shop-keeper showed me glass butterflies, a glass cricket, fish, a glass bird with wings outstretched . . .

For the next hour I walked by ear. I broke the rules for the proper use of a dog guide by issuing vague directions, letting Corky wander aimlessly. Together we got good and lost. I tracked the sounds of bells and a scattering of wings and guessed that I'd arrived at St. Mark's Square. It was good not knowing where I was. The sun had come out and a balloon seller walked about in slow circles—maybe he had seeds for the birds instead of balloons. He had a litany of amiable phrases drawn from a dozen languages but none of the words revealed what he was selling. He had a sack of coins that I imagined was hanging from his belt. The coins and the rhythm of his walk were strophe and antistrophe. He sang to the far corners of the square. "Hello! Hello! Beautiful! Beautiful! *Willkommen! Tervetuloa!*" Coins slapped against his belt.

Intrusion —

"Are you all right?" The voice was British. Yes, I'd managed to find my way to St. Mark's Square. And Corky was standing stoically amidst thousands of pigeons. The tourists were photographing her.

Apparently a significant number of nuns were snapping our picture. Once the Englishman mentioned it I heard their cameras clicking. I told the Englishman that I was walking and listening with no true destination. He called to his wife. "These two have no idea where they're going," he said. "I mean he's just walking about and listening!" She asked if she could have my photograph. I let them take my picture and then I told them that I must run—it was time to feed the dog.

The sun was setting. I stopped on a bridge and stood for a time. A gondola slipped beneath us, the plash of its rudder sounded like the tail of a pheasant in the grass. I imagined the gondolier was going home to his wife and children. It was twilight and cold. If he looked back he'd see me leaning on the bridge and talking to myself. He wouldn't see the dog, just a

Retrospection
— 20

man wearing a leather jacket and sunglasses.

Twenty years ago at the Iowa Writers' Workshop I read philosophy like a halfhearted gardener. I sat under willows and read parts of Kant and Hegel. Now the gondola's hull was slapping the surface of the canal; the noise echoed under the bridge. Two women hurried past in the growing darkness; I could hear them admiring the dog in German. *Guesswork and understanding create a knowing man,* I thought. *The subjectivity of Kant . . . Why go anywhere when you can't see? Is it because the spirit of man and the world of form are identical? Because even with eyes shut my spirit and the narrow alleys of Venice were one and the same?*

I listened.

Walked.

Jazz piano drifted from somewhere. There was a nightclub nearby.

I walked some more.

The Venetians had more caged birds than any other people.   25

Then I was in a working-class district. The windows of the apartments were open to spring rain. Radios and televisions played from building after building. There was a clatter of dishes . . . I heard a tinny stereo playing the Rolling Stones—"Jumping Jack Flash" . . . From still another window I heard the voices of two men arguing. Wild laughter from a woman, a mezzo-soprano . . . The odd grace of being was in that laugh because the men stopped—then laughed along with her . . . They were laughing because twelve moons circled Jupiter . . . Because one of them had forgotten his left from his right . . .

Hearing poetry starts the psychological mechanism of prayer.

The phrase was Roethke's.

I sat alone in a tiny neighborhood park.

I was amazed at how quiet Venice suddenly was.

It was a city of wind . . .   30

Someone lowered a flag. There was the unmistakable sound of pulleys. It was time to walk.

Something strange was happening to me. I was surprisingly happy. Why not? I'd been drifting through the unfamiliar atmosphere with only the wind for a map. Was this what happened to sighted people as they wandered in churches and museums?

Corky stopped while I located a flight of steps with my foot. In the distance I heard a crowd. They were still far off. They made a strange buzz. I thought of Samson working his mill.

It appeared that I'd emerged from the vatic silence into a scene of great confusion. I wondered briefly if I'd walked onto a movie set because hundreds of people were shouting in a chorus. I had found my way into the middle of a street protest and I was completely ignorant about what was going on—I was Candide walking among the Bulgarians. Women were shouting. Gunshots rang out. No, they were firecrackers. Corky continued working and guided me through a knot of humanity as if we were in New York at rush hour. She pushed past a group of men who were banging trash can lids. I supposed that the look on my face suggested my incomprehension because someone tapped me on the arm and said: "It's a protest. The hotel workers are going on strike!" There were more firecrackers and then there were police whistles. There was a palpable feeling of anger mixed with hilarity. This was street theater and not a riot. We turned a corner and moved quickly away. I wanted to turn and wave but Corky was going at a good clip.

I wondered if Connie was viewing the paintings of Titian and   35
Tintoretto. Maybe she was drifting in a gondola around Santa Maria della Salute. Me? I was lost. A great baroque weather vane turned before me.

Venice—"queen of the seas"—her jewelry and clouds attracting me at random . . .

The next morning I listened on the Bridge of Sighs to the conversations of tourists.

Gondolas floated beneath the bridge.

Leaning at the rail, I overheard a woman talking about her dentist.

"Honest to God!" she said. "You'd think a dentist with his reputation would have noticed by now!"

40   I wanted to hear the rest, but the Bridge of Sighs swallowed her story.

"It's true!" said a man in another boat. "Just look at the way she dresses!"

"Vitamins," said a different man.

"It's just schoolbook Latin," a woman said.

"The great excitement of Manzoni when Napoleon died," said another woman.

45   No one noticed the bridge.

"Catherine of Siena," said a man.

"I fully intend to catch up with it!" said a woman.

There were gondolas with nothing but laughing people.

Was it the influence of Disney?

50   This was the Bridge of Sighs!

The doges of Venice marched their subjects across this span to the waiting prison where they most certainly died from starvation and torture. Later the Austrians marched the Venetians over this same bridge when the Austro-Hungarian Empire owned Venice during the nineteenth century. One can only imagine the Austrians and their efficient cruelties . . .

The gondolas slipped by and the tourists talked in floating zones of contentment.

The gondoliers had completely given up on their traditional role as tour guides. They worked their tillers in silence.

"She was a glowing bridesmaid," said a woman.

55   There were limits to how much listening I could do without the consoling balance of visual description. Connie took me to the Church of St. Mark's to see the mosaics and I listened as she described the strands of gold finer than hair that were woven through the marble floor.

The tesserae of the mosaic were smaller than chipped diamonds or the microscopic slices of platinum inside Rolex watches.

Connie's voice had a respectful softness. She was a guest. As a result she conveyed her appreciation for the things she saw.

We stood in the great church amidst a billion inlaid fragments of glass, marble, and tile.

Later we drifted through the city. Connie described the Rialto Bridge. With its baroque foppishness it looked temporary—as if it was erected for a wedding.

We saw Mozart's louvered window. The building was in the dark even at midday.   60

We saw a canal that had been dammed at both ends and then drained. Men were working at the foundations of a sinking palazzo with what appeared to be rubber mallets.

We noticed a horse on a thin bridge, improbable as an onion atop the queen's crown.

Three men wearing black tuxedos waved from a motorboat.

We drifted around the Church of Santa Maria della Salute. Gulls rose and fell against a backdrop of dark Adriatic clouds.

Lights appeared at the tall windows of the monastery.   65

We sat above the Grand Canal and sipped wine. The Venetian dusk called the bleached whiteness out of the stones. I talked about listening as a variation of sight-seeing. Connie was a professional trainer of guide dogs. Accordingly she knew a good deal about the art of hearing. More than once while training her dogs she assumed the role of a blind person by walking blindfolded through the streets of New York. As Huck Finn would say, "she has sand."

My Olympiad was to find aesthetic pleasure among the riches of the baroque with little or no visual help. The trouble with this plan was glaringly obvious—the sounds of a place were products of random nature— they were happenings of luck and factors of wind. Boats turned at their moorings. There was music from their chains. A window slid open because a little boy saw a calico cat on a ledge—the cat who got away last night—and now the boy was calling softly. This was the mysterious aleatoric work of the hourglass. But no listener could ever hear in the wind the exquisite formal arrangements of architecture. For this I would always require help. And something more—a nobility of descriptive engagement from my wife and from my friends . . .

The next morning Connie spotted a motor launch piled high with boxes of Jaffa oranges. The boat was in the hands of a single man who believed that with mind over matter he could squeeze his cargo beneath a miniature bridge. Connie described him as he drove his tower of crates into a mousehole. There was a groan, then a splintering of wood. The people atop the bridge broke into rowdy laughter. Salty, colorful words boomed back and forth. One man shouted: "The bridge is too slight for such a thing. Back up!" All the while the reckless captain worked feverishly to break the logjam. He kicked at crates of oranges and three of them tumbled into the canal where they bobbed like deck chairs thrown from a stricken ship. Now the crowd on the bridge shouted more instructions. "You need additional weight! We'll come down!" Four stout men climbed over the railing of the bridge and dropped into the flimsy motor launch. They lay down on top of the crates. They were willing the boat to sink lower. The captain prodded the ceiling of the bridge with his skinny arms. "If the canal rises they'll be stuck in there," said Connie. "I wonder if the Venetian water patrol carries the Jaws of Life?"

We watched as five men laughed their way under a bridge. Heft and hilarity were their only tools of navigation.

Had I been walking alone I would have missed this splendid moment. The predominance of the eye—that old magician! How he snaps us to attention whenever he discovers chaos. A friend calls on the phone and says: "I just saw the damnedest thing! A white cloth seemed to be dancing by itself under the trees. For a minute I thought it was a ghost. When I looked again I saw it was a squirrel with a man's handkerchief in its mouth."

The "willing suspension of disbelief" is the very faith of poetry, as Coleridge said. But it's also a prime ingredient in the gleam of the eye. I don't think it really matters whose eyes are gleaming. As long as my companion is a talkative enthusiast of the odd apparition, everything will be okay. I can know the world by proxy.

Walking in Venice in long, slow circles, I realized that sound is to shape as thirst is to hunger. Ficino understood the nature of the meal.

Dear Marsilio Ficino,

I travel with my wife. And yes, she sees better than 20/20. Ted Williams, the baseball player, also had 20/10 sight. In his heyday with the Boston Red Sox he saw the stitches on a fastball. Connie sees blackbirds flick their wings in the corn of southern Ohio. She drives at seventy miles per hour and notices red squirrels, pheasants, bob-headed quail, Arabian horses . . . Handmade signs for Ohio Swiss cheese, sausage, fresh dill pickles . . . In Venice she spots the unhistorical shops selling faux zebra hides—"in case you need to cover your piano," she says . . . And the shop displaying handmade women's shoes, but only for the left foot, a specialty trade . . .

And yes, dear Ficino, Connie reads me the menus in comic Italian, and the waiters look on with contempt—but their scorn turns to dismay when I tell them we're only ordering for the dog. And in turn we walk the palazzos with Corky heeling beside us and I see the interiors that Connie sees, hear her voice among the dazzling arches and feel that I have stepped through a thin wall of sleep into someone else's dream. And this is all right. Why not? We train all our days in the geometry of self so as not to get lost. Why not get lost in someone else's wonder?

* * *

On our last morning in Venice I went out alone. The air was bluish in my retinas . . . Trees clicked in a small park. A frenzied Pekinese followed me. He barked like a motorized winch in need of oil. He was a stray. There were strays all over Venice. *Once,* I thought, *they lived in the palaces.*

I walked. It was early and shopkeepers swept and launches delivered goods. Once more I was in no remarkable spot, I was merely standing beside a weathered door. I pressed my palms against the wood. It was rough as pumice, or the barnacled hull of a New England dory. Sometimes I believe that beneath the rutted surfaces of wood I can feel the grain, the pith of the tree. This was a black oak from Macedonia. In my mind's eye I could see where it stood on a great estate—saw the picnickers beneath it, some five hundred years ago. _ *Imagination*

Poetry   **Larry Levis**

AT THE GRAVE OF MY GUARDIAN ANGEL:
ST. LOUIS CEMETERY, NEW ORLEANS

for Gerald Stern

At sixteen I was so vulnerable to every influence
That the overcast light, making the trash of addicts & sunbathers suddenly
    clearer
On the paths of the city park, seemed death itself spreading its shade
Over the leaves, the swan boats, the gum wrappers, and the quarreling
    ducks.
It took nothing more than a few clouds straying over the sun,
And I would begin falling through myself like an anvil or a girl's comb or
    a feather
Dropped, tossed, or spiraling by pure chance down the silent air shaft of a
    warehouse,
The spiderweb in one fourth-floor window catching, in that moment, the
    sunset.
For in such a moment, to fall was to be simplified & pure,
With a neck snapped like a stem instead
Of whoever I turned out to be,
Wiping the window glass clear with one cuff
To gaze out at a two-hundred-year-old live oak tethering
The courtyard to its quiet,
The tree so old it has outlived even its life as a cliché,
And has survived, with no apparent effort, every boy who marched, like a
    wilderness
Himself, past it on his way to enlist in Lee's army,
And now it swells gently in the mist & the early sunlight.
So who saved me? And for what purpose?
Beneath the small angel cut from cheap stone, there was nothing
But my name & the years 1947–1949,
And the tense, muggy little quiet of a place where singing ends,
And where there is only the leftover colored chalk & the delusions of
    voodoo,
The small bones & X's on stones signifying the practitioner's absence,
Entirely voluntary, from the gnat swirl & humming of time;
To which the chalked X on stone is the final theory; it is even illiterate.
It is not even a lock of hair on a grave. It is not even
The small crowd of roughnecks at Poe's funeral, nor the blind drunkard
Laughing there, the white of his eyes the unfurling of a cold surf below
    a cliff—

Which is the blank wave sprawl of fact receding under the cries of   30
   gulls—
Which is not enough.

*

I should rush out to my office & eat a small, freckled apple leftover
From 1970 & entirely wizened & rotted by sunlight now,
Then lay my head on my desk & dream again of horses grazing, riderless &
   still saddled,
Under the smog of the freeway cloverleaf & within earshot of the music   35
   waltzing with itself out
Of the topless bars & laundromats of East L.A.

I should go back again & try to talk my friend out of his diet
Of methamphetamine & vodka yogurts & the look of resignation spread-
   ing over his face
Like the gray shade of a tree spreading over a sleeper in the park—

For it is all or nothing in this life, for there is no other.   40
And without beauty, Bakunin will go on making his forlorn & unreliable
   little bombs in the cold, & Oswald will adjust
The lenses on the scope of his rifle, the one
Friend he has carried with him all the way out of his childhood,
The silent wood of its stock as musical to him in its grain as any violin.
This must have been what they meant,   45
Lincoln & Whitman, joining hands one overcast spring afternoon
To stroll together through the mud of Washington at the end
Of the war, the tears welling up in both their eyes,
Neither one of them saying a word, their hands clasped tightly together
As they walk for block after block past   50
The bay, sorrel, chestnut, and dapple-gray tail swish of horses,
And waiting carriages, & neither one of them noticing, as they stroll &
   weave,
The harness gall on the withers of a mare,
Nor the gnats swarming over it, alighting now on the first trickle of blood
   uncaking from the sore;
And the underfed rib cage showing through its coat each time it inhales   55
Like the tines of a rake combing the battleground to overturn
Something that might identify the dead at Antietam.
The rake keeps flashing in the late autumn light.
And Bakunin, with a face impassive as a barn owl's & never straying from
   the one true text of flames?
And Lincoln, absentmindedly trying to brush away the wart on his cheek   60

As he dresses for the last time,
As he fumbles for a pair of cuff links in a silk-lined box,
As he anticipates some pure & frivolous pleasure,
As he dreams for a moment, & is a woman for a moment,
65   And in his floating joy has no idea what is going to happen to him in the
      next hour?
And Oswald dozing over a pamphlet by Trotsky in the student union?
Oh live oak, thoughtless beauty in a century of pulpy memoirs,
Spreading into the early morning sunlight
As if it could never be otherwise, as if it were all a pure proclamation of
      leaves & a final quiet—

                    *

70   But it's all or nothing in this life; it's smallpox, quicklime, & fire.
It's the extinct whistling of an infantry; it is all the faded rosettes of blood
Turning into this amnesia of billboards & the ceaseless *hunh?* of traffic.
It goes on & I go with it; it spreads into the sun & air & throws out a fast
      shade
That will never sleep, and I go with it; it breaks Lincoln & Poe into small
      drops of oil spreading
75   Into endless swirls on the water, & I recognize the pattern:

                    *

There there now, Nothing.
Stop your sniveling. Stop sifting dirt through your fingers into your glass
      of milk,
A milk still white as stone; whiter even. Why don't you finish it?
We'd better be getting on our way soon, sweet Nothing.
80   I'll buy you something pretty from the store.
I'll let you wear the flower in your hair even though you can only vanish
      entirely underneath its brown, implacable petals.
Stop your sniveling. I can almost see the all night diner looming
Up ahead, with its lights & its flashing sign a testimony to failure.
85   I can almost see our little apartment under the freeway overpass, the cups
      on the mantle rattling continually—
The Mojave one way; the Pacific the other.
At least we'll have each other's company.
And it's not as if you held your one wing, tattered as it was, in contempt
For being only one. It's not as if you were frivolous.
90   It's not like that. It's not like that at all.
Riding beside me, your seat belt around your invisible waist. Sweet Nothing.
Sweet, sweet Nothing.

Fiction   **Yiyun Li**

SON

Han, thirty-three years old, single, software engineer and recently natu-ralized American citizen, arrives at Beijing International Airport with a brand-new American passport and an old Chinese worry. He has asked his mother to stay at home; knowing she would not, he has feared, for the whole flight from San Francisco to Beijing, that she would be waiting at the terminal with an album of pictures, girls smiling at him out of the plastic holders, competing to please his eyes and win his heart. Han is a *zuanshi-wanglaowu*, a diamond bachelor, earning American dollars and holding American citizenship. But even when he was at lower levels—silver or gold or whatever he was—his mother never tired of matchmak-ing for him. At first Han said he would not consider marriage before he got his degree. Then it was a job, and then the green card. But now that Han has got his American citizenship, he is running out of excuses. He imagines the girls his mother has collected, all busy weaving sturdy nets to catch a big fish like him. Han is gay. He has no plan to marry any one of them, nor does he intend to explain this decision to his mother. Han loves his mother, but more so he loves himself. He does not want to bring un-necessary pains to his mother's life; he does not want to make any sacrifice out of filial duty, either.

But to his surprise, what his mother presents to him is not a picture album but a gold cross on a gold chain. A miniature of Jesus is pinned to the cross. "I special-ordered it for you," she says. "Feel it."

Han feels the cross, his finger avoiding the crucified figure. The cross is solid and heavy in his hand. "Twenty-four-karat gold," his mother says. "As pure as our faith."

"That sounds like the oath we took when we joined the Communist Youth League. *Our faith in communism is as pure and solid as gold*," Han says.

"Han, don't make such inappropriate jokes."   5

"I'm not joking. What I'm saying is that many things are circulated and recycled. Language is one of them. Faith is another one. They are like the bills in our wallets. You can buy anything with them, but they themselves hold no meaning," Han says. His mother tries to smile, but he sees the dis-appointment she cannot hide. "Sorry, Mama. Of course we can't go on without the paper bills in our wallet."

"You talk a lot now, Han," his mother says.

"I'll shut up then."

"No, it's good you talk more than before. You've always been a quiet child. Baba would be happy to know that you've opened up."

10   "It's not easy to shut up in America. They value you not by what's inside you, but by what's pouring out of your mouth," Han says.

"Yes, of course," Han's mother says, quickly agreeing. "But Baba would say you have to learn to listen before you open your mouth. Baba would say the more you talk, the less you gain."

"Mama, Baba is dead," Han says. He watches his mother blink and try to find words to fill the vacuum arising between them, and he lets her struggle. For as long as Han remembers, his mother has always been a parrot of his father. The last time Han was on vacation, a few months after his father's death, he was horrified to overhear his mother's conversation with several neighbors. "Han says there's nothing wrong for old people to wear bright colors," his mother said of the red and orange T-shirts he had bought in bulk for his mother and her friends and neighbors. "Han says we should live for our own comforts, not others' opinions." It saddened him back then that his mother had to spend her life repeating her husband's, and then her son's, lines. But his sympathy must have been worn out by the seventeen hours in a crammed jet plane. "Mama, let's get out of here. It's getting late," Han says. He picks up his bags and starts to move toward the revolving glass door.

Han's mother catches up with him and makes a fuss taking over the biggest bag from Han. "Mama, I can handle it myself," Han says.

"But I can't walk empty-handedly with you. I'm your mother."

15   Han lets go of the bag. They walk silently. Men in suits and women in dresses come up to them, talking to Han about the best hotel deals they have, and Han waves them away. Half a step behind him, his mother apologizes to the hawkers, explaining that they are going home. No, not too far and no need for an overnight place, she says when the hawkers do not give up their hope, and apologizes more.

It upsets Han that his mother is humble for no good reason. When they reach the end of the line at the taxi station, he says, "Mama, you don't have to apologize to those people."

"But they're trying to help us."

"They only care about the money in your pocket."

"Han." His mother opens her mouth, and then sighs.

20   "I know—I shouldn't be thinking about people this way, and money is not everything—except it is everything," Han says. He takes out the gold cross he has slipped into his pocket earlier. "Look, even your church encourages you to buy the twenty-four-karat-gold cross. Why? The more you spend on it, the purer your faith is."

Han's mother shakes her head. "Han, come to the church tomorrow with me and listen to our pastor. Ask him about his experience in the Cultural Revolution, and you would know what a great man he is."

"What can he tell me that I don't know?" Han says.

"Don't be so arrogant," his mother says, almost begging.

Han shrugs with exaggeration. They move slowly with the line. After a silent moment, Han asks, "Mama, are you still a member of the Communist Party?"

"No. I sent my membership card back before I was baptized."

"They let you do that! You are not afraid that they'll come back and 25 prosecute you for giving up your communist faith? Remember, Marx, your old god, says religion is the spiritual opium."

Han's mother does not reply. The wind blows her gray hair into her eyes, and she looks despondent. A yellow cab drives in, and Han helps his mother into the backseat. A good son she's got for herself, the cabbie compliments his mother, and she agrees, saying that indeed, he is a very good son.

Later that night, unable to sleep from the jet lag, Han slips out of the house and goes to an Internet café nearby. He tries to connect to the several chat rooms where he usually spends his evenings in America, flirting with other men and putting on different personalities for different IDs he owns, but after several failed trials, he realizes that the Internet police have blocked such sites in China. It's daytime in America, and people are busy working anyway. Han sits there for a moment, opening randomly any sites that are available. He feels sorry to have upset his mother earlier, even though she acted as if nothing unpleasant ever happened, and cooked a whole table of dishes for his homecoming. She did not mention the service for tomorrow, and he did not mention the gold cross, which he slipped into his suitcase, ready to forget.

Han is not surprised that his mother has become this devout person. In her letters to him after his father's death, she writes mostly about her newly discovered faith. What bothers Han is that his mother would have never thought of going to the church if his father were still alive. His father wouldn't have allowed anyone, be it a man or a god, to take a slice of her attention away; she wouldn't have had the time for someone else, either, his father always requiring more than she could give. His father's death should be a relief for his mother. She should have started to enjoy her life instead of putting on another set of shackles for herself. Besides, what kind of church does she go to, and what god does she worship, if the whole thing exists in broad daylight in this country? Han remembers reading, in *The New York Times* once, a report about the underground churches in China. He decides to find the article and translate it for his mother. If she wants to be a Christian, she had better believe in the right god. She needs to know these people, who risk their freedom and lives going to shacks and caves for their faith. Han remembers the pictures from the report, those believers' eyes squinting at the reporter's camera, dispassionate and fearless. Han respects anybody leading an underground life; he himself, being gay, is one of them.

But of course the website of *The New York Times* is blocked, Han realizes a minute later. He searches for the seminaries and organizations referred to in the article, and almost laughs out loud when he finds a report about the Chinese Christian Patriots Association, the official leader of all the state-licensed churches. The association is coordinating several seminars for a national conference, focusing on the role of Christian teachings in the latest theories of communist development in the new millennium. God on the mission to help revive Marxism, Han thinks.

30   After two hours of sleep, Han wakes up, and is happy to find the printed article in his pocket, black words on white paper. He walks into his father's study. His mother, sitting at the desk, looks up from behind her bifocals. "Did you have a good sleep?" she asks.

"Yes."

"I've got breakfast ready," his mother says, and puts down a brochure she is reading. Han takes it up, reads a few pages, and tosses it back to his mother's side of the desk. It's a collection of poems written by different generations of believers in mainland China over the past century.

"In your spare time—I know you're busy in America—but if you have some time to spare, I have some good books for you to read," his mother says.

Han says nothing and goes into the kitchen. He has accepted, in the past ten years, handouts and brochures and several pocket-sized Bibles from people standing in the streets. He lets the young men from the Mormon Church into his kitchen and listens to them for an hour or two. He stands in the parking lots of shopping centers and allows the Korean ladies to preach to him in broken English. He goes to the picnics of the local Chinese church when he is invited, and he does not hang up when people from the church spend a long time trying to convert him. He is never bothered by the inconvenience caused by these people. Once he was stopped outside a fast food restaurant in Cincinnati by a middle-aged woman who insisted on holding both his hands in hers and praying for his soul. He listened and watched a traffic cop write a ticket for his expired meter; even then he did not protest. Han finds it hard to turn away from these people, their concerns for his soul so genuine and urgent that it moves him. Other times, when he sees people standing in the street with handwritten signs that condemn, among many other sinners, homosexuals, he cannot help laughing in their faces. These people, who love or hate him for reasons only good to themselves, amuse Han, but it's because they are irrelevant people, and their passion won't harm him in any way. He imagines his mother being one of them; the mere thought of it irritates him.

She follows him to the kitchen. "You can always start with reading the Bible," she says and puts a steaming bowl of porridge in front of Han. "Purple rice porridge, your favorite."

"Thanks, Mama."   35

"It's good for you," Han's mother says. Han does not know if she is talking about food, or religion. She sits down on the other side of the table and watches him eat. "I've talked to many people," she says. "Some of them didn't believe me at first, but after they came to the church with me, and read the Bible, their lives were changed."

"My life's good enough. I don't need a change," Han mumbles.

"It's never too late to know the truth. Confucius said: If one gets to know the truth in the morning, he can die in the evening without regret."

"Confucius said: When one reaches fifty, he is no longer deceived by the world. Mama, you are sixty already, and you still let yourself be deceived. Wasn't your communist faith enough of an example?" Han says. "Look here, Mama, I have printed out this lovely message for you. Read it yourself. The church you go to, the god you talk about—it's all made up so people like you can be tricked. Don't you know that all the state-licensed churches recognize the Communist Party as their only leader? Maybe someday you will even come up with the old conclusion that God and Marx are the same."

Han's mother takes the sheet of paper. She seems not surprised, or disappointed. When she finishes reading, she puts the printout carefully in the trash can by the desk, and says, "No cloud will conceal the sunshine forever."   40

"Mama, I did not come home to listen to you preach. I've been in America for ten years, and enough people have tried to convert me, but I'm sitting here the same person as ten years ago. What does that tell you?"

"But you're my son. I have to help you even if they've failed."

"You could have helped me before. Remember, you burned my Bible," Han says, and watches her body freeze. He knows that she has forgotten the incident, but he has chosen not to. The Bible was a gift from his best friend when they were thirteen. They were in love without realizing it; innocent boys they were then, their hands never touching. Han did not know what made the boy seek out the Bible, a tightly controlled publication that one could never see in a bookstore or anywhere he knew, as a birthday gift for him. He did not know what trouble the boy had gone through to get the Bible, but he knew, at the time, that it was the most precious gift he had ever got. It would have remained so, well kept and carried along to each city he moved to, a souvenir of the first love, except that his mother made a fire with the Bible and dumped the ashes into the toilet bowl. She did not know the hours he had spent with his best friend after school, sitting together and reading the Bible, finding a haven in the book while their classmates were competing to join the Communist Youth

League. They had loved the stories, the bigness of the book that made their worries tiny and transient. When their classmates criticized them for being indifferent to political activities, they laughed it off secretly, both knowing that the Bible allowed them to live in a different, bigger world.

The Bible was discovered by Han's father and then burned by his mother. Afterward, Han was no longer able to face his friend. He made up excuses to stay away from his friend; he found fault with his friend and argued with him for any trivial reason. Their friendship—their love—did not last long afterward. It would have been doomed anyway, a first love that was going nowhere, but the way it ended, someone other than himself was to be blamed. "Remember, it's you who burned the Bible," Han says.

45 "Yes," his mother says, trying hard to find words. "But Baba said it was not appropriate to keep it. It was a different time then."

"Yes, a different time then because it was Baba who gave out orders, and it was the communist god you both worshipped. And now Baba is gone, and you've got yourself a new god to please," Han says. "Mama, why can't you use your own brain to think?"

"I'm learning, Han. This is the first decision that I've made on my own." A wrong decision it is, but Han only smiles out of pity and tolerance.

Later, when his mother cautiously suggests a visit to the church, Han says he will accompany her for the bus ride. It won't hurt to go in and listen, his mother says, but Han only nods noncommittally.

West Hall, the church that Han used to ride his bicycle past on his way to high school years ago, remains the same gray nondescript building inside the rusty iron fence, but the alleys around were demolished, and the church, once a prominent landmark of the area, is now dwarfed by the surrounding shopping centers. Han watches people of all ages enter the church, nodding at one another politely. He wonders how much these people understand of their placing their faiths in the wrong hands, and how much they care about it.

50 A few steps away from the entrance, Han's mother stops. "Are you coming in with me?" she asks.

"No, I'll sit in the Starbucks and wait for you."

"Starbucks?"

"The coffee shop over there."

Han's mother stretches and looks at it, no doubt the first time she has noticed its existence. She nods without moving. "Mama, go in now," Han says.

55 "Ah, yes, just a moment," she says and looks around with expectation. Soon two little beggars, a boy and a girl, run across the street to her. Brother and sister they seem to be, both dressed up in rags, their hands and faces smeared with dirt and soot. The boy, seven or eight years old,

holds out a hand when he sees Han. "Uncle, spare a penny. Our baba died with a large debt. Our mama is sick. Spare a penny, please. We need money to send our mama to the hospital."

The girl, a few years younger, follows suit and chants the same lines. Han looks at the boy. There is a sly expression in the boy's eyes that makes Han uncomfortable. He knows they are children employed for the begging job, if not by their parents, then by relatives or neighbors. The adults, older and less capable of moving people with their tragedies, must be monitoring the kids from not far away. Han shakes his head. He does not have one penny for such kids; on his previous vacations, he even fought with the kids, who grabbed his legs tightly and threatened not to loose their grip until they were paid. Han is not a stingy person. In America he gives away dollar bills to the musicians playing in the street, quarters and smaller change for homeless people who sit at the same spot all day long. They are honest workers according to Han's standard, and he gives them what they deserve. But child laborers are not acceptable, and people using the children deserve nothing. Han pushes the boy's hand away, and says, "Leave me alone."

"Don't bother Uncle," Han's mother says to the children, and they both stop chanting right away. Han's mother takes out two large bills from her purse, and gives one to each child. "Now come with Granny," she says. The children carefully put the money away and follow Han's mother to the church entrance.

"Wait a minute, Mama," Han says. "You pay them every week to go to church with you?"

"It can only benefit them," Han's mother says.

"But this is not right."   60

"It doesn't hurt anyone. They would have to beg in the street otherwise."

"It hurts my principles," Han says. He takes out several bills from his wallet and says to the boy, "Now listen. I will pay you double the amount if both of you return the money to her and do not go to the church today."

"Han!"

"Hold it, Mama. Don't say a word," Han says. He squats down and flips the bills in front of the children's eyes. The girl looks up at the boy, and the boy looks up at Han's mother for a moment and then looks down at the money. The cunning and the calculation in the boy's eyes infuriate Han; he imagines his mother deceived even by such small children. "Come on," he says to the boy, still smiling. A few seconds later, the boy accepts Han's money and gathers the bill from his sister's hand and returns the two bills to Han's mother. "Good," Han says. "You can go now."

The children walk away, stopping people in the sidewalk and repeating   65
their begging lines. Han turns to his mother with a smile. "What did this tell you, Mama? The only thing that matters to them is money."

"Why did you do that?" his mother says.

"I need to protect you."

"I don't need your protection," Han's mother says.

"You can say that, Mama," Han says. "But the truth is, I'm protecting you, and it's my duty to do this."

70   "What right do you have to talk about the truth?" his mother says, and turns away for the church.

Han tries to convince himself that he is not upset by his mother's words. Still, he feels hurt. He is his mother's son. The boy who accepted the money from him is a son, too, but someday he will become a husband, a father, maybe sending his sons and daughters into the street to beg, maybe giving them a better life. Han will never become a father—he imagines himself known to the world only as someone's son. Not many men would remain only as sons all their lives, but Jesus is one. It's not easy being a son with duties, Han thinks, and smiles bitterly to himself. What right does he have? His right is that he lives with his principles. He works. He got laid off, struggled for a few months, but found work again. He pays his rent. He greets his neighbors. He goes to the gym. He watches news channels but not reality shows. He sponsors a young girl's education in a rural province in China, sending checks regularly for her tuition and her living expenses. He masturbates, but not too often. He does not believe in long-term relationships, but once in a while, he meets men in local bars, enjoys physical pleasure with them, and uses condoms. He flirts with other men, faceless as he himself is, on the Internet, but he makes sure they talk about arts too. He loves his mother. He sends two thousand dollars to her every year, even though she has said many times that she does not need the money. He sends the money still, because he is her son, and it's his duty to protect her and nurture her, as she protected and nurtured him in his younger years. He saves up his vacation and goes home to spend time with her, but what happens when they are together? A day into the vacation and they are already hurting each other.

Han walks across the street to the Starbucks. He feels tired and sad, but then it is his mother's mistake, not his, that makes them unhappy, and he decides to forgive her. A few steps away from the coffee shop, there is a loud squealing noise of tires on the cement road. Han turns and looks. Men and women are running toward a car, where a crowd has already gathered. A traffic accident, people are yelling, a kid run over. More people swarm toward the accident, some dialing the emergency number on their cellphones, others calling their friends and family, reporting a traffic accident they are witnessing, gesturing as they speak, full of excitement. A man dressed in old clothes runs toward the crowd. "My child," he screams.

Han freezes, and then starts walking again, away from the accident. He does not want to see the man, who must have been smoking in a shaded corner a block or two away, cry now like a bereaved parent. He does not want to know if it's the young girl with the singsong voice, or her brother with the sly smile in his eyes, that was run over. Traffic accidents happen every day in this city. People pay others to take their driving tests for them or buy their driver's licenses directly from the black market; cars do not yield to pedestrians, pedestrians do not fear the moving vehicles. If he does not look, it could be any child, a son, a daughter, someone irrelevant and forgettable.

But somehow, Han knows it's the boy. It has to be the boy, ready to deceive anyone who is willing to be deceived. The boy will remain a son and never become a father. He will be forgotten by the crowd once his blood is rinsed clean from the ground; his sister will think of him but soon she will forget him, too. He will live on only in Han's memory, a child punished not for his own insincerity but someone else's disbelief.

Han sits in Starbucks by the window and waits for his mother. When she finally walks out of the church, the street is cleared and cleaned, not a trace of the accident left. Han walks out to meet his mother, his hands shaking. Across the street she smiles at him, hope and love in her eyes, and Han knows she has already forgotten the unpleasant incident from two hours earlier. She will always forgive him because he is her son. She will not give up her effort to save his soul because he is her son. But he does not want to be forgiven, or saved. He waits until his mother safely arrives at his side of the street, and says without looking at her, "Mama, there is something I want you to know. I'll never get married. I only like men."

Han's mother does not speak. He smiles and says, "A shock, right? What would Baba say if he knew this? Disgusting, isn't it?"

After a long moment, Han's mother says, "I've guessed. That's why I didn't try matchmaking for you this time."

"So you see, I'm doomed," Han says. "I'm one of those—what did we say of those counterrevolutionaries back then?—stinky and hard and untransformable as a rock in an outhouse pit."

"I wouldn't say so," Han's mother says.

"Admit it, Mama. I'm doomed. Whoever your god is, he wouldn't be fond of people like me."

"You're wrong," Han's mother says. She stands on tiptoe and touches his head, the way she used to touch his head when he was younger, to reassure him that he was still a good boy even after he did something wrong. "God loves you for who you are, not what others expect you to be," she says. "God sees everything, and understands everything."

Of course, Han wants to make a joke. Her god is just like a Chinese parent, never running out of excuses to love a son. But he stays quiet when he looks up at his mother, her eyes so eager and hopeful that he has to avert his own.

Drama   Michele Markarian

PHONING IT IN

Characters

Brian
Stephanie

Setting

A city park.

Time

The present.

AT THE CURTAIN: *BRIAN and STEPHANIE are seated on a bench. They are holding hands.*

BRIAN: You know, I really love you.
STEPHANIE: Oh, that's nice. I really love you, too.
BRIAN: Really?
STEPHANIE: Yeah. Really. *(BRIAN tries to speak. Cell phone rings.)* Excuse me. *(Answers cell phone.)* Hello? Oh, hi! Hi! How are you? I'm—oh. Oh. Really? Really? You like him that much? Of course it's a lot! Carrie! Come on! You're telling me you want to marry the guy, well, that's liking someone an awful lot. Wouldn't you say? Oh. Yeah. *(Nods head.)* Okay. Carrie, I'm kind of—oh, is that your buzzer? It could be him? All right, I'll let you go. Bye. *(She hangs up.)* Sorry.
BRIAN: What was that about?
STEPHANIE: Oh, Carrie's just—*(Cell phone rings.)* Excuse me. *(She picks up phone.)* Hello? *(She hangs up.)* Wrong number.
BRIAN: So anyway, I really—
STEPHANIE: I was telling you about Carrie. She wants to marry this guy.
BRIAN: What guy?
STEPHANIE: The guy she's been seeing!
BRIAN: What's wrong with that?
STEPHANIE: Brian, come on! I mean really!
BRIAN: What, really?
STEPHANIE: I mean, she's only been seeing him two months!
BRIAN: So?
STEPHANIE: You can't just marry someone you've been seeing for two months! It's not right!
BRIAN: Why not?

STEPHANIE: Well, jeez, we've been seeing each other for eight months.

BRIAN: Yeah? *(He leans closer.)*

STEPHANIE: Exactly!

BRIAN: What do you mean, exactly?

STEPHANIE: Exactly!

BRIAN: Are you saying that—you think we shouldn't—*(A cell phone rings.)* Excuse me. *(He answers phone.)* Hello? Scott. Yeah. Yeah, well, I'm kind of—no. No, not yet—*(He looks at STEPHANIE.)* What? What do you mean, don't do it? You said last week that—what? She *what*? Scott, are you sure? Uh-huh. Yeah. Yeah. Yeah, that's pretty serious. That's really serious. Just be sure you got your information right, buddy. You wouldn't want to—oh. That's your call-waiting. Okay. Good luck. *(He hangs up.)*

STEPHANIE: Who was that?

BRIAN. Scott. *(He looks glum.)*

STEPHANIE: Oh. *(BRIAN starts to speak, then stops.)* Why the face?

BRIAN: What face?

STEPHANIE: You know. *(She exaggerates glum face.)*

BRIAN: I don't wanna talk about it.

STEPHANIE: Is it about Scott? *(BRIAN nods.)* What about Scott?

BRIAN: I don't wanna talk about it.

STEPHANIE: Brian!

BRIAN: What?

STEPHANIE: I thought we agreed to tell each other everything!

BRIAN: This is—so wrong.

STEPHANIE: Maybe it's not so bad. Tell me.

BRIAN: Oh God. Where do I start? *(A cell phone rings.)*

STEPHANIE: Oh, Brian, I'm sorry. This could be Carrie. I'll just be a minute. *(She answers phone.)* Hello? Carrie? Hi! What? He *what*? Oh my God! *(She screams.)* That's incredible! Oh, Carrie! *(She jumps up.)* When? July? Oh, perfect! Seriously? Seriously? Oh, I'd be honored. Oh my God, yes! Oh, can I tell Brian? I love you too, sweetie. Tell Conrad congratulations! *(She hangs up. BRIAN sighs.)* Well?

BRIAN: Well what?

STEPHANIE: Aren't you going to ask what that was about?

BRIAN: Why?

STEPHANIE: Why? What is wrong with you? *(BRIAN sighs.)* Carrie is getting married.

BRIAN: That's nice.

STEPHANIE: To Conrad.

BRIAN: Conrad. Conrad. Wait a minute. Is that the guy she's been seeing for two months?

STEPHANIE: Yeah.

BRIAN: This is good news?

STEPHANIE: Yeah. She's my best friend.

BRIAN: But I thought you said it wasn't right.

STEPHANIE: What?

BRIAN: You said it wasn't right for a couple who's only been dating for two months to get married?

STEPHANIE: That was before.

BRIAN: Before what?

STEPHANIE: Before—I just had to get used to it, that's all.

BRIAN: You're unbelievable. How can you change your mind, just like that?

STEPHANIE: Brian, I didn't change my mind. I just—adjusted it, that's all.

BRIAN: Are all women this fickle?

STEPHANIE: What kind of stupid remark is that?

BRIAN: It's not stupid. It's—uh, I'm sorry. I think I'm still upset about Scott. He just told me—

STEPHANIE: And I can't believe that Conrad proposed to Carrie after only two months! *(She glares at BRIAN.)*

BRIAN: Yeah. *(Pause.)* Are you—not happy about this anymore?

STEPHANIE: We've been going out for eight months!

BRIAN: Yeah.

STEPHANIE: And—

BRIAN: What?

STEPHANIE: I'd just like to know where this relationship is going, that's all. *(BRIAN shrugs.)* Maybe it's time to just end things.

BRIAN: I don't know. *(Cell phone rings.)* I'm sorry. *(He answers phone.)* Hello? Oh, hey, Scott. How's it going? Really? Greg made it up? Why? You gotta be kidding me. I told you not to sleep with her. Yeah. Yeah, I know. No kidding. No kidding. Wow. That's great, Scottie. No, I mean it. That's really cool. Yeah, I'll be seeing you, man. What? Who, me? No, I haven't. Yeah, yeah, she is. *(He smiles at STEPHANIE.)* Yeah, yeah, I will, though. See ya. *(He hangs up.)*

STEPHANIE: I don't know what I was thinking.

BRIAN: About what?

STEPHANIE: Nothing. Never mind.

BRIAN: Stephanie, there's something I want to ask you.

STEPHANIE: Go ahead. *(Cell phone rings. She answers it.)* Hello? Carrie?

BRIAN: It's pretty important.

STEPHANIE: Wait a minute, Carrie, I can't hear you. *(She motions for BRIAN to stop talking. He sits back and sighs.)* What? I still can't hear you. Okay. *(She hangs up.)*

BRIAN: I think you know how I feel about you.

STEPHANIE: Oh?

BRIAN: You're a special girl—uh, I mean, woman. I feel like the luckiest—

(Cell phone rings. STEPHANIE answers it.)

STEPHANIE: Hello? Yeah, that's much better. Yeah. What? He *what?*
No! No way! Stop it! *No!* Carrie, that's not even funny, that's just plain
sick. No way. You tell him that there's no way in hell you're going to
marry him. Seriously. Lose him. You hear me? No, I won't tell Brian.
No, don't worry. I promise. I won't say a word. I'm sorry, sweetie. I'll
call you later. Bye. *(She hangs up.)*

BRIAN: As I was saying—

STEPHANIE: I can't believe it.

BRIAN: Don't tell me—I don't want to know.

STEPHANIE: I can't tell you. I promised Carrie I wouldn't.

BRIAN: Oh.

STEPHANIE: So what were you saying?

BRIAN: Stephanie, I—*(Cell phone rings.)* Wait a minute. Hello? Scott.
No, no I haven't. No! Just—leave it to me, will you? Yeah, yeah. Later.
(He hangs up.)

STEPHANIE: You didn't tell me what happened with Scott.

BRIAN: I don't want to talk about Scott.

STEPHANIE: What do you want to talk about?

BRIAN: Stephanie, I love you more than any woman I've ever been with.
I can't imagine living withou—

(Cell phone rings. STEPHANIE answers it.)

STEPHANIE: Hello? Who? Oh. Oh, you're very smooth. Very smooth. I
can't believe you told my oldest friend that I had a great ass. What do
you mean, it's true? You ask a girl to marry you and then you tell her
that her best friend has a great ass? What kind of sick pervert are you?
Oh. That kind. I'm not interested. And if you ever bother Carrie or me
ever again, I swear to God I'll have you arrested, you hear me? Same
to you! *(She hangs up.)*

BRIAN: What the hell was that about?

STEPHANIE: Don't even ask.

BRIAN: Yeah, I'm gonna ask! Some guy tells my girlfriend she has a
great ass, I wanna know about it!

STEPHANIE: It's no big deal. He's just a jerk.

BRIAN: How can you say that?

STEPHANIE: What?

BRIAN: It *is* a big deal! It—wait a minute. This isn't what I want to talk to you about. Stephanie, I love—

(Cell phone rings. STEPHANIE answers it.)

STEPHANIE: Hello? Carrie? Carrie, I can't understand you. Stop crying, sweetie. You what? You miss him? You think you overreacted? You want to take him back? Uh-uh, huh. Yeah. I just don't think it's a good idea, that's all. I—if you really want me to be your maid-of-honor I will, but don't you think—no. No. Yeah. Call him. *(She hangs up phone and stares straight ahead, dejected.)*

BRIAN: Stephanie? *(No answer.)* Stephanie? Stephanie, I—*(He realizes she's not listening, picks up his cell phone and dials a number. Cell phone rings.)*

STEPHANIE: Hello?

BRIAN: Stephanie, I love you. Will you marry me?

STEPHANIE: Who is this?

(She turns and looks at BRIAN, sees him on phone, and is surprised.)

END OF PLAY

Poetry   **Sandra McPherson**

TO A PENNY POSTCARD, © 1911

A woman's interested head, long sprigs of green,
and a loose, supple ribbon the blush
pink of the rose shaded by my apple tree
sashes it all.

What   5
do we live for,
if it is not
to make Life
less difficult
for one another.   10

Not one of the pharmacy cure-alls from its day:
They usually use the word "easy."

And who doesn't know many
who would answer the rhetorical query,
No, for me. Or no one else will.   15

Very pretty, the sprigs and the satin of the loopy bowknot
and the font where we find difficulty.
And rather intrepid, the look in the woman's eyes.
She probes the words at an angle;
her hair, full and clean, as if it could polish them.   20

She lived
but it's a long time since a penny.
I don't wonder how she lived.
We know, don't we?

Isn't life easier for us,   25
being sent this postcard
from a bygone mailbox
and a vanished heart—
yes, even extinct it makes life
less troublesome for me,   30
not quite lost each day. And pretty.

Fiction   **Susan Minot**

HIDING

Our father doesn't go to church with us but we're all downstairs in the hall at the same time, bumbling, getting ready to go. Mum knuckles the buttons of Chicky's snowsuit till he's knot-tight, crouching, her heels lifted out of the backs of her shoes, her nylons creased at the ankles. She wears a black lace veil that stays on her hair like magic. Sherman ripples by, coat flapping, and Mum grabs him by the hood, reeling him in, and zips him up with a pinch at his chin. Gus stands there with his bottom lip out, waiting, looking like someone's smacked him except not that hard. Even though he's seven, he still wants Mum to do him up. Delilah comes half-hurrying down the stairs, late, looking like a ragamuffin with her skirt slid down to her hips and her hair all slept on wrong. Caitlin says, "It's about time." Delilah sweeps along the curve of the banister, looks at Caitlin, who's all ready to go herself with her pea jacket on and her loafers and bare legs, and tells her, "You're going to freeze." Everyone's in a bad mood because we just woke up.

Dad's outside already on the other side of the French doors, waiting for us to go. You can tell it's cold out there by his white breath blowing by his cheek in spurts. He just stands on the porch, hands shoved in his black parka, feet pressed together, looking at the crusty snow on the lawn. He doesn't wear a hat but that's because he barely feels the cold. Mum's the one who's warm-blooded. At skiing, she'll take you in when your toes get numb. You sit there with hot chocolate and a carton of french fries and the other mothers and she rubs your foot to get the circulation back. Down on the driveway the car is warming up and the exhaust goes straight up, disappearing in thin white curls.

"Okay, monkeys," says Mum filing us out the door. Chicky starts down the steps one red boot at a time till Mum whisks him up under a wing. The driveway is wrinkled over with ice so we take little shuffle steps across it, blinking at how bright it is, still only half-awake. Only the station wagon can fit everybody. Gus and Sherman scamper in across the huge backseat. Caitlin's head is the only one that shows over the front. (Caitlin is the oldest and she's eleven. I'm next, then Delilah, then the boys.) Mum rubs her thumbs on the steering wheel so that her gloves are shiny and round at the knuckles. Dad is doing things like checking the gutters, waiting till we leave. When we finally barrel down the hill, he turns and goes back into the house, which is big and empty now and quiet.

We keep our coats on in church. Except for the O'Shaunesseys, we have the most children in one pew. Dad only comes on Christmas and Easter, because he's not Catholic. A lot of times you only see the mothers there.

When Dad stays at home, he does things like cuts prickles in the woods or tears up thorns, or rakes leaves for burning, or just stands around on the other side of the house by the lilacs, surveying his garden, wondering what to do next. We usually sit up near the front and there's a lot of kneeling near the end. One time Gus got his finger stuck in the diamond-shaped holes of the heating vent and Mum had to yank it out. When the man comes around for the collection, we each put in a nickel or a dime and the handle goes by like a rake. If Mum drops in a five-dollar bill, she'll pluck out a couple of bills for her change.

The church is huge. Out loud in the dead quiet, a baby blares out "Dah-Dee." We giggle and Mum goes "Ssshhh" but smiles too. A baby always yells at the quietest part. Only the girls are old enough to go to Communion; you're not allowed to chew it. The priest's neck is peeling and I try not to look. "He leaves me cold," Mum says when we leave, touching her forehead with a fingertip after dipping it into the holy water.

On the way home, we pick up the paper at Cage's and a bag of eight lollipops—one for each of us, plus Mum and Dad, even though Dad never eats his. I choose root beer. Sherman crinkles his wrapper, shifting his eyes around to see if anyone's looking. Gus says, "Sherman, you have to wait till after breakfast." Sherman gives a fierce look and shoves it in his mouth. Up in front, Mum, flicking on the blinker, says, "Take that out," with eyes in the back of her head.

Depending on what time of year it is, we do different things on the weekends. In the fall we might go to Castle Hill and stop by the orchard in Ipswich for cider and apples and red licorice. Castle Hill is closed after the summer so there's nobody else there and it's all covered with leaves. Mum goes up to the windows on the terrace and tries to peer in, cupping her hands around her eyes and seeing curtains. We do things like roll down the hills, making our arms stiff like mummies, or climb around on the marble statues, which are really cold, or balance along the edge of the fountains without falling. Mum says "Be careful" even though there's no water in them, just red leaves plastered against the sides. When Dad notices us he yells, "Get down."

One garden has a ghost, according to Mum. A lady used to sneak out and meet her lover in the garden behind the grape trellis. Or she'd hide in the garden somewhere and he'd look for her and find her. But one night she crept out and he didn't come and didn't come and finally when she couldn't stand it any longer, she went crazy and ran off the cliff and killed herself and now her ghost comes back and keeps waiting. We creep into the boxed-in place, smelling the yellow berries and the wet bark, and Delilah jumps—"What was that?"—trying to scare us. Dad shakes the wood to see if it's rotten. We run ahead and hide in a pile of leaves. Little twigs get in your mouth and your nostrils; we hold still underneath listening to the brittle

5

ticking leaves. When we hear Mum and Dad get close, we burst up to surprise them, all the leaves fluttering down, sputtering from the dust and tiny grits that get all over your face like gray ash, like Ash Wednesday. Mum and Dad just keep walking. She brushes a pine needle from his collar and he jerks his head, thinking of something else, probably that it's a fly. We follow them back to the car in a line, all scruffy with leaf scraps.

After church, we have breakfast because you're not allowed to eat before. Dad comes in for the paper or a sliver of bacon. One thing about Dad, he has the weirdest taste. Spam is his favorite thing or this cheese that no one can stand the smell of. He barely sits down at all, glancing at the paper with his feet flat down on either side of him, ready to get up any minute to go back outside and sprinkle white fertilizer on the lawn. After, it looks like frost.

10   This Sunday we get to go skating at Ice House Pond. Dad drives. "Pipe down," he says into the backseat. Mum faces him with white fur around her hood. She calls him Uncs, short for Uncle, a kind of joke, I guess, calling him Uncs while he calls her Mum, same as we do. We are making a racket.

"Will you quit it?" Caitlin elbows Gus.

"What? I'm not doing anything."

"Just taking up all the room."

Sherman's in the way back. "How come Chicky always gets the front?"

15   "'Cause he's the baby." Delilah is always explaining everything.

"I en not a baby," says Chicky without turning around.

Caitlin frowns at me. "Who said you could wear my scarf?"

I ask into the front seat, "Can we go to the Fairy Garden?" even though I know we won't.

"Why couldn't Rummy come?"

20   Delilah says, "Because Dad didn't want him to."

Sherman wants to know how old Dad was when he learned how to skate.

Dad says, "About your age." He has a deep voice.

"Really?" I think about that for a minute, about Dad being Sherman's age.

"What about Mum?" says Caitlin.

25   This isn't his department so he just keeps driving. Mum shifts her shoulders more toward us but still looks at Dad.

"When I was a little girl on the Boston Common." Her teeth are white and she wears fuchsia lipstick. "We used to have skating parties."

Caitlin leans close to Mum's fur hood, crossing her arms into a pillow. "What? With dates?"

Mum bats her eyelashes. "Oh sure. Lots of beaux." She smiles, acting like a flirt. I look at Dad but he's concentrating on the road.

We saw one at a football game once. He had a huge mustard overcoat and a bow tie and a pink face like a ham. He bent down to shake our tiny hands, half-looking at Mum the whole time. Dad was someplace else getting the tickets. His name was Hank. After he went, Mum put her sunglasses on her head and told us she used to watch him play football at BC. Dad never wears a tie except to work. One time Gus got lost. We waited until the last people had trickled out and the stadium was practically empty. It had started to get dark and the headlights were crisscrossing out of the parking field. Finally Dad came back carrying him, walking fast, Gus's head bobbing around and his face all blotchy. Dad rolled his eyes and made a kidding groan to Mum and we laughed because Gus was always getting lost. When Mum took him, he rammed his head onto her shoulder and hid his face while we walked back to the car, and under Mum's hand you could see his back twitching, trying to hide his crying.

We have Ice House Pond all to ourselves. In certain places the ice is bumpy and if you glide on it going *Aauuuuhhhh* in a low tone, your voice wobbles and vibrates. Every once in a while, a crack shoots across the pond, echoing just beneath the surface, and you feel something drop in the hollow of your back. It sounds like someone's jumped off a steel wire and left it twanging in the air.

I try to teach Delilah how to skate backwards but she's flopping all over the ice, making me laugh, with her hat lopsided and her mittens dangling on strings out of her sleeves. When Gus falls, he just stays there, polishing the ice with his mitten. Dad sees him and says, "I don't care if my son is a violin player," kidding.

Dad played hockey in college and was so good his name is on a plaque that's right as you walk into the Harvard rink. He can go really fast. He takes off—*whoosh*—whizzing, circling at the edge of the pond, taking long strides, then gliding, chopping his skates, crossing over in little jumps. He goes zipping by and we watch him: his hands behind him in a tight clasp, his face as calm as if he were just walking along, only slightly forward. When he sweeps a corner, he tips in, then rolls into a hunch, and starts the long side-pushing again. After he stops, his face is red and the tears leak from the sides of his eyes and there's a white smudge around his mouth like frostbite. Sherman, copying, goes chopping forward on collapsed ankles and it sounds like someone sharpening knives.

Mum practices her 3s from when she used to figure skate. She pushes forward on one skate, turning in the middle like a petal flipped suddenly in the wind. We always make her do a spin. First she does backward crossovers, holding her wrists like a tulip in her fluorescent pink parka, then stops straight up on her toes, sucking in her breath and dips, twisted, following her own tight circle, faster and faster, drawing her feet together. Whirring around, she lowers into a crouch, ventures out one balanced leg,

30

a twirling whirlpool, hot pink, rises again, spinning, into a blurred pillar or a tornado, her arms going above her head and her hands like the eye of a needle. Then suddenly: stop. Hiss of ice shavings, stopped. We clap our mittens. Her hood has slipped off and her hair is spread across her shoulders like when she's reading in bed, and she takes white breaths with her teeth showing and her pink mouth smiling. She squints over our heads. Dad is way off at the car, unlacing his skates on the tailgate but he doesn't turn. Mum's face means that it's time to go.

Chicky stands in the front seat leaning against Dad. Our parkas crinkle in the cold car. Sherman has been chewing on his thumb and it's a pointed black witch's hat. A rumble goes through the car like a monster growl and before we back up Dad lifts Chicky and sets him leaning against Mum instead.

35   The speed bumps are marked with yellow stripes and it's like sea serpents have crawled under the tar. When we bounce, Mum says, "Thank-you-ma'am" with a lilt in her voice. If it was only Mum, the radio would be on and she'd turn it up on the good ones. Dad snaps it off because there's enough racket already. He used to listen to opera when he got home from work but not anymore. Now we give him hard hugs and he changes upstairs then goes into the TV room to the same place on the couch, propping his book on his crossed knees and reaching for his drink without looking up. At supper, he comes in for a handful of onion-flavored bacon crisps or a dish of miniature corn-on-the-cobs pickled. Mum keeps us in the kitchen longer so he can have a little peace and quiet. Ask him what he wants for Christmas and he'll say, "No more arguing." When Mum clears our plates, she takes a bite of someone's hot dog or a quick spoonful of peas before dumping the rest down the pig.

In the car, we ask Dad if we can stop at Shucker's for candy. When he doesn't answer, it means *No*. Mum's eyes mean *Not today*. She says, "It's treat night anyway." Treats are ginger ale and vanilla ice cream.

On Sunday nights we have treats and BLTs and get to watch Ted Mack and Ed Sullivan. There are circus people on almost every time, doing cartwheels or flips or balancing. We stand up in our socks and try some of it. Delilah does an imitation of Elvis by making jump-rope handles into a microphone. Girls come on with silver shoes and their stomachs showing and do clappity tap dances. "That's a cinch," says Mum behind us.

"Let's see you then," we say and she goes over to the brick in front of the fireplace to show us. She bangs the floor with her sneakers, pumping and kicking, thudding her heels in smacks, not like clicking at all, swinging her arms out in front of her like she's wading through the jungle. She speeds up, staring straight at Dad who's reading his book, making us laugh even harder. He's always like that. Sometimes for no reason, he'll snap out of it, going, "What? What? What's all this? What's going on?" as if he's emerged from a dark tunnel, looking like he does when we wake him up and he hasn't put on his glasses yet, sort of angry. He sits there before dinner, popping black olives into his mouth one at a time, eyes never leaving his book. His huge glass mug is from college and in the lamplight you can see the liquid separate. One layer is beer, the rest is gin. Even smelling it makes you gag.

Dad would never take us to Shucker's for candy. With him, we do things outside. If there's a storm we go down to the rocks to see the waves—you have to yell—and get sopped. Or if Mum needs a nap, we go to the beach. In the spring it's wild and windy as anything, which I love. The wind presses against you and you kind of choke but in a good way. Sherman and I run, run, run! Couples at the end are so far away you can hardly tell they're moving. Rummy races around with other dogs, flipping his rear like a goldfish, snapping at the air, or careening in big looping circles across the beach. Caitlin jabs a stick into the wet part and draws flowers. Chicky smells the seaweed by smushing it all over his face. Delilah's dark bangs jitter across her forehead like magnets and she yells back to Gus lagging behind. Dad looks at things far away. He points out birds—a great blue heron near the breakers as thin as a safety pin or an osprey in the sky, tilting like a paper cutout. We collect little things. Delilah holds out a razor shell on one sandy palm for Dad to take and he says "Uh-huh" and calls Rummy. When Sherman, grinning, carries a dead seagull to him, Dad says, "Cut that out." Once in Maine, I found a triangle of blue and white china and showed it to Dad. "Ah yes, a bit of crockery," he said.

"Do you think it's from the Indians?" I whispered. They had made the arrowheads we found on the beach.

"I think it's probably debris," he said and handed it back to me. According to Mum, debris is the same thing as litter, as in Don't Be a Litterbug.

When we get home from skating, it's already started to get dark. Sherman runs up first and beats us to the door but can't open it himself. We are all used to how warm it was in the car so everybody's going "Brrrr," or "Hurry up," banging our feet on the porch so it thunders. The sky is dark blue glass and the railing seems whiter and the fur on Mum's hood glows. From the driveway Dad yells, "I'm going downtown. Be right back," slamming the door and starting the car again.

Delilah yells, "Can I come?" and Gus goes, "Me too!" as we watch the car back up.

"Right back," says his deep voice through the crack in the window and he rounds the side of the house.

"How come he didn't stop on the way home?" asks Caitlin, sticking out her chin.

"Yah," says Delilah. "How come?" We look at Mum.

She kicks the door with her boot. "In we go, totsies," she says instead of answering and drops someone's skate on the porch because she's carrying so much stuff.

Gus gets in a bad mood, standing by the door with his coat on, not moving a muscle. His hat has flaps over the ears. Delilah flops onto the hall sofa, her neck bent, ramming her chin into her chest. "Why don't you take off your coat and stay awhile?" she says, drumming her fingers on her stomach as slow as a spider.

"I don't have to."

50 "Yah," Sherman butts in. "Who says you're the boss?" He's lying on the marble tile with Rummy, scissor-kicking his legs like windshield wipers.

"No one," says Delilah, her fingers rippling along.

On the piano bench, Caitlin is picking at her split ends. We can hear Mum in the kitchen putting the dishes away.

Banging on the piano fast because she knows it by heart, Caitlin plays "Walking in a Winter Wonderland." Delilah sits up and imitates her behind her back, shifting her hips from side to side, making us all laugh. Caitlin whips around. "What?"

"Nothing." But we can't help laughing.

"Nothing what?" says Mum coming around the corner, picking up mittens and socks from the floor, snapping on the lights.

55 Delilah stiffens her legs. "We weren't doing anything," she says.

We make room for Mum on the couch and huddle. Gus perches at the edge, sideways.

"When's Dad coming back?" he says.

"You know your father," says Mum vaguely, smoothing Delilah's hair on her lap, daydreaming at the floor but thinking about something. When Dad goes to the store, he only gets one thing, like a can of black bean soup or watermelon rind.

"What shall we play?" says Sherman, strangling Rummy in a hug.

60 "Yah. Yah. Let's do something," we say and turn to Mum.

She narrows her eyes into spying slits. "All rightee. I might have a little idea."

"What?" we all shout, excited. "What?" Mum hardly ever plays with us because she has to do everything else.

She rises, slowly, lifting her eyebrows, hinting. "You'll see."

"What?" says Gus and his bottom lip loosens nervously.

65 Delilah's dark eyes flash like jumping beans. "Yah, Mum. What?"

"Just come with me," says Mum in a singsong and we scamper after her. At the bottom of the stairs, she crouches in the middle of us. Upstairs behind her, it's dark.

"Where are we going?" asks Caitlin, and everybody watches Mum's face, thinking of the darkness up there.

"Hee hee hee," she says in her witch voice. "We're going to surprise your father, play a little trick."

"What?" asks Caitlin again, getting ready to worry, but Mum's already creeping up the stairs so we follow, going one mile per hour like her, not making a peep even though there's no one in the house to hear us.

Suddenly she wheels around. "We're going to hide," she cackles.

"Where?" we all want to know, sneaking along like burglars.

Her voice is hushed. "Just come with me."

At the top of the stairs it is dark and we whisper.

"How about your room?" says Delilah. "Maybe under the bed."

"No," says Sherman breathlessly. "In the fireplace." We all laugh because we could never fit in there.

Standing in the hall, Mum opens the door to the linen closet and pulls the light-string. "How about right here?" The light falls across our faces. On the shelves are stacks of bedcovers and rolled puffs, red and white striped sheets and pink towels, everything clean and folded and smelling of soap.

All of a sudden Caitlin gasps, "Wait—I hear the car!"

Quickly we all jumble and scramble around, bumbling and knocking and trying to cram ourselves inside. Sherman makes whimpering noises like an excited dog. "Ssshhh," we say or "Hurry, Hurry," or "Wait." I knee up to a top shelf and Sherman gets a boost after me and then Delilah comes grunting up. We play in here sometimes. Gus and Chicky crawl into the shelf underneath, wedging themselves in sideways. Caitlin half-sits on molding with her legs dangling and one hand braced against the doorframe. When the rushing settles, Mum pulls out the light and hikes herself up on the other ledge. Everyone is off the ground then, and quiet.

Delilah giggles. Caitlin says "Ssshhh" and I say "Come on" in a whisper. Only when Mum says "Hush" do we all stop and listen. Everyone is breathing; a shelf creaks. Chicky knocks a towel off and it hits the ground like a pillow. Gus says, "I don't hear anything." "Ssshhh," we say. Mum touches the door and light widens and we listen. Nothing.

"False alarm," says Sherman.

Our eyes start to get used to the dark. Next to me Delilah gurgles her spit.

"What do you think he'll do?" whispers Caitlin. We all smile, curled up in the darkness with Mum, thinking how fooled he'll be, coming back and not a soul anywhere, standing in the hall with all the lights glaring not hearing a sound.

"Where will he think we've gone?" We picture him looking around for a long time, till finally we all pour out of the closet.

"He'll find out," Mum whispers. Someone laughs at the back of his throat, like a cricket quietly ticking.

Delilah hisses, "Wait—"

85 "Forget it," says Caitlin, who knows it's a false alarm.

"What will he do?" we ask Mum.

She's in the darkest part of the closet, on the other side of the light slant. We hear her voice. "We'll see."

"My foot's completely fallen asleep," says Caitlin.

"Kick it," says Mum's voice.

90 "Ssshhh," lisps Chicky, and we laugh at him copying everybody.

Gus's muffled voice comes from under the shelf. "My head's getting squished."

"Move it," says Delilah.

"Quiet!"

And then we really do hear the car.

95 "Silence, monkeys," says Mum, and we all hush, holding our breaths. The car hums up the hill.

The motor dies and the car shuts off. We hear the door crack, then clip shut. Footsteps bang up the echoing porch, loud, toe-hard and scuffing. The glass panes rattle when the door opens, resounding in the empty hall, and then the door slams in the dead quiet, reverberating through the whole side of the house. Someone in the closet squeaks like a hamster. Downstairs there isn't a sound.

"Anybody home?" he bellows, and we try not to giggle.

Now what will he do? He strides across the deep hall, going by the foot of the stairs, obviously wondering where everybody's gone, stopping at the hooks to hang up his parka.

"What's he doing?" whispers Caitlin to herself.

100 "He's by the mitten basket," says Sherman. We all have smiles, our teeth like watermelon wedges, grinning in the dark.

He yells toward the kitchen, "Hello?" and we hunch our shoulders to keep from laughing, holding on to something tight like our toes or the shelf, or biting the side of our mouths.

He starts back into the hall.

"He's getting warmer," whispers Mum's voice, far away. We all wait for his footsteps on the stairs.

But he stops by the TV room doorway. We hear him rustling something, a paper bag, taking out what he's bought, the bag crinkling, setting something down on the hall table, then crumpling up the bag and pitching it in the wastebasket. Gus says, "Why doesn't he—?" "Ssshhh," says Mum like spitting and we all freeze. He moves again—his footsteps turn and bang on the hollow threshold into the TV room where the rug pads the sound.

105 Next we hear the TV click on, the sound swelling and the dial switching *tick-ah tikka tikka tick* till it lands on a crowd roar, a football game.

We can hear the announcer's voice and the hiss-breath behind it of cheering.

Then it's the only sound in the house.

"What do we do now?" says Delilah only half-whispering. Mum slips down from her shelf and her legs appear in the light, touching down.

Still hushed, Sherman goes, "Let's keep hiding."

The loud thud is from Caitlin jumping down. She uses her regular voice. "Forget it. I'm sick of this anyway." Everyone starts to rustle. Chicky panics, "I can't get down," as if we're about to desert him.

"Stop being such a baby," says Delilah, disgusted.

110

Mum doesn't say anything, just opens the door all the way. Past the banister in the hall it is yellow and bright. We climb out of the closet, feet-feeling our way down backward, bumping out one at a time, knocking down blankets and washcloths by mistake. Mum guides our backs and checks our landings. We don't leave the narrow hallway. The light from downstairs shines up through the railing and casts shadows on the wall—bars of light and dark like a fence. Standing in it we have stripes all over us. "Hey look," we say whispering, with the football drone in the background, even though this isn't anything new—we always see this, holding out your arms and seeing the stripes. Lingering near the linen closet, we wait. Mum picks up the tumbled things, restacking the stuff we knocked down, folding things, clinching a towel with her chin, smoothing it over her stomach and then matching the corners left and right, like crossing herself, patting everything into neat piles. The light gets like this every night after we've gone to bed and we creep into the hall to listen to Mum and Dad downstairs. The bands of shadows go across our nightgowns and pajamas and we press our foreheads against the railing trying to hear the mumbling of what Mum and Dad are saying down there. Then we hear the deep boom of Dad clearing his throat and look up at Mum. Though she is turned away, we still can see the wince on her face like when you are waiting to be hit or right after you have been. So we keep standing there, our hearts pounding, waving our hands through the flickered stripes, suddenly interested the way you get when it's time to take a bath and you are mesmerized by something. We're stalling, waiting for Mum to finish folding, waiting to see what she's going to do next because we don't want to go downstairs yet, where Dad is, without her.

Creative Nonfiction   **Dinty W. Moore**

SON OF MR. GREEN JEANS
A Meditation on Missing Fathers

Allen, Tim

Best known as the father on ABC's *Home Improvement* (1991–99), the popular comedian was born Timothy Allen Dick on June 13, 1953. When Allen was eleven years old, his father, Gerald Dick, was killed by a drunk driver while driving home from a University of Colorado football game.

Bees

"A man, after impregnating the woman, could drop dead," critic Camille Paglia suggested to Tim Allen in a 1995 *Esquire* interview. "That is how peripheral he is to the whole thing."

"I'm a drone," Allen responded. "Like those bees?"

"You are a drone," Paglia agreed. "That's exactly right."

Carp

5   After the female Japanese carp gives birth to hundreds of tiny babies, the father carp remains nearby. When he senses approaching danger he will suck the helpless babies into his mouth, and hold them safely there until the coast is clear.

Divorce

University of Arizona psychologist Sanford Braver tells a disturbing story of a woman who felt threatened by her husband's close bond with their young son. The husband had a flexible work schedule, but the wife did not, so the boy spent the bulk of his time with the father.

The mother became so jealous of the tight father-son relationship that she eventually filed for divorce, and successfully fought for sole custody. The result was that instead of being in the care of his father while the mother worked, the boy was now left in daycare.

Emperor Penguins

Once a male emperor penguin has completed the act of mating, he remains by the female's side for the next month to determine if he is indeed about to become a father. When he sees a single greenish white egg emerge from his mate's egg pouch, he begins to sing.

Scientists have characterized his song as "ecstatic."

Father Knows Best

In 1949 Robert Young began *Father Knows Best* as a radio show. Young   10
played Jim Anderson, an average father in an average family. The show
later moved to television, where it was a substantial hit.

Young's successful life, however, concluded in a tragedy of alcohol
and depression. In January 1991, at age eighty-three, he attempted sui-
cide by running a hose from his car's exhaust pipe to the interior of the
vehicle. The attempt failed because the battery was dead and the car
wouldn't start.

Green Genes

In Dublin, Ireland, a team of geneticists has been conducting a study to
determine the origins of the Irish people. By analyzing segments of DNA
from residents across different parts of the Irish countryside, then comparing this DNA with corresponding DNA segments from people elsewhere
in Europe, the investigators hope to determine the derivation of Ireland's
true forefathers.

Hugh Beaumont

The actor who portrayed the benevolent father on the popular TV show
Leave It to Beaver was a Methodist minister. Tony Dow, who played older
brother Wally, reports that Beaumont didn't care much for television and
actually hated kids.

"Hugh wanted out of the show after the second season," Dow told the
Toronto Sun. "He thought he should be doing films and things."

Inheritance

My own Irish forefather was a newspaperman, owned a popular night-   15
club, ran for mayor, and smuggled rum in a speedboat during Prohibition.
He smoked, drank, ate nothing but red meat, and died of a heart attack
in 1938.

His one son—my father—was only a teenager when his father died. I
never learned more than the barest details about my grandfather from my
father, despite my persistent questions. Other relatives tell me that the relationship had been strained.

My father was a skinny, eager-to-please little boy, battered by allergies,
and not the tough guy his father had apparently wanted. My dad lost his
mother at age three and later developed a severe stuttering problem, perhaps as a result of his father's sharp disapproval. My father's adult vocabulary was outstanding, due to his need for alternate words when faltering
over hard consonants like *b* or *d*.

The stuttering grew worse over the years, with one noteworthy exception: after downing a few shots of Canadian whiskey my father could muster a stunning, honey-rich Irish baritone. His impromptu vocal performances became legend in local taverns, and by the time I entered the scene my father was spending every evening visiting the working class bars. Most nights he would stumble back drunk around midnight; some nights he was so drunk he would stumble through a neighbor's back door, thinking he was home.

Our phone would ring. "You'd better come get him."

20   As a boy I coped with this embarrassment by staying glued to the television—shows like *Father Knows Best* and *Leave It to Beaver* were my favorites. I desperately wanted someone like Hugh Beaumont to be my father, or maybe Robert Young.

Hugh Brannum, though, would have been my absolute first choice. Brannum played Mr. Green Jeans on *Captain Kangaroo,* and I remember him as kind, funny, and extremely reliable.

Jaws

My other hobby, besides watching other families on television, was an aquarium. I loved watching as my tropical fish drifted aimlessly through life, and I loved watching guppy mothers give birth. Unfortunately guppy fathers, if not moved to a separate tank, will often come along and eat their young.

Kitten

Kitten, the youngest daughter on *Father Knows Best,* was played by Lauren Chapin.

Lauren Chapin

Chapin's father, we later learned, molested her, and her mother was a severe alcoholic. After *Father Knows Best* ended in 1960, Chapin's life came apart. At sixteen she married an auto mechanic. At eighteen she became addicted to heroin and began working as a prostitute.

Masculinity

25   Wolf fathers spend the daylight hours away from the pack—hunting—but return every evening. The wolf cubs, five or six to a litter, will rush out of the den when they hear their father approaching and fling themselves at him, leaping up to his face. The father will back up a few feet and disgorge food for the cubs, in small, separate piles.

Natural Selection

When my wife, Renita, confessed to me her desire to have children, the very first words out of my mouth were, "You must be crazy." Convinced that she had just proposed the worst idea imaginable, I stood from my chair, looked straight ahead, and literally marched out of the room. This was not my best moment.

Ozzie

Oswald Nelson, at thirteen, was the youngest person ever to become an Eagle Scout. Oswald went on to become Ozzie Nelson, the father in *Ozzie and Harriet*. Though the show aired years before the advent of reality television, Harriet was indeed Ozzie's real wife, Ricky and David were his real sons, and eventually Ricky and David's wives were played by their actual spouses. The current requirements for Eagle Scout make it impossible for anyone to ever beat Ozzie's record.

Penguins, Again

The female emperor penguin "catches the egg with her wings before it touches the ice," Jeffrey Moussaieff Masson writes in his book *The Emperor's Embrace*. She then places the newly laid egg on her feet, to keep it from contact with the frozen ground.

At this point both penguins will sing in unison, staring down at the egg. Eventually the male penguin will use his beak to lift the egg onto the surface of his own feet, where it will remain until hatching.

Not only does the penguin father endure the inconvenience of walking around with an egg balanced on his feet for months on end, he will also forgo food for the duration.

Quiz

1. What is Camille Paglia's view on the need for fathers?   30
2. Did Hugh Beaumont hate kids, and what was it he would rather have been doing than counseling the Beav?
3. Who played Mr. Green Jeans on *Captain Kangaroo*?
4. Who would you rather have as your father: Hugh Beaumont, Hugh Brannum, a wolf, or an emperor penguin?

Religion

In 1979 Lauren Chapin, the troubled actress who played Kitten, had a religious conversion. She credits her belief in Jesus with saving her life. After *his* television career ended, Methodist Minister Hugh Beaumont became a Christmas tree farmer.

Sputnik

On October 4, 1957, *Leave It to Beaver* first aired. On that same day the Soviet Union launched Sputnik I, the world's first artificial satellite. Sputnik I was about the size of a basketball, took roughly ninety-eight minutes to orbit the earth, and is often credited with escalating the Cold War and launching the U.S.-Soviet space race.

Years later, long after *Leave It to Beaver* ended its network run, a rumor persisted that Jerry Mathers, the actor who played Beaver, had died at the hands of the Soviet-backed communists in Vietnam. Actress Shelley Winters went so far as to announce it on the *Tonight Show*. But the rumor was false.

Toilets

Leave It to Beaver was the first television program to show a toilet.

Using Drugs

35　The presence of a supportive father is essential to helping children avoid drug problems, according to the National Center of Addiction and Substance Abuse at Columbia University. Lauren Chapin may be a prime example here. Tim Allen would be one, too. Fourteen years after his father died at the hands of a drunk driver, Allen was arrested for dealing drugs and spent two years in prison.

I also fit the gloomy pattern. Though I have so far managed to avoid my father's relentless problems with alcohol, I wasted about a decade of my life hiding behind marijuana, speed, and various hallucinogens.

Vasectomies

I had a vasectomy in 1994.

Ward's Father

In an episode titled "Beaver's Freckles," we learn that Ward Cleaver had "a hittin' father," but little else is ever revealed about Ward's fictional family. Despite Wally's constant warning—"Boy, Beav, when Dad finds out he's gonna clobber ya!"—Ward does not follow his own father's example and never hits his sons on the show. This is an example of xenogenesis.

Xenogenesis

(zen'u̲-jen'u̲-sis), n. <u>Biol</u>. 1. heterogenesis 2. the supposed generation of offspring completely and permanently different from the parent.

40　Believing in xenogenesis—though at the time I couldn't define it, spell it, *or* pronounce it—I changed my mind about having children about four years after I walked out on my wife's first suggestion of the idea.

Luckily this was five years before my vasectomy.

Y Chromosomes

The Y chromosome of the father determines a child's gender, and it is unique in that its genetic code remains relatively unchanged as it passes from father to son. The DNA in other chromosomes is more likely to get mixed between generations, in a process called recombination. What this means, apparently, is that boys have a higher likelihood of directly inheriting their ancestral traits.

Once my wife convinced me to risk being a father—this took many years and considerable prodding—my Y chromosomes chose the easy way out: our only child is a daughter.

Maria, so far, has inherited many of what people say are the Moore family's better traits—humor, a facility with words, a stubborn determination.

It is yet to be seen what she will do with the negative ones.

Zappa

Similar to the persistent "Beaver died in Vietnam" rumor of the late 1960s, Internet discussion lists of the late 1990s were filled with assertions that the actor who played Mr. Green Jeans, Hugh "Lumpy" Brannum, was in fact the father of musician Frank Zappa.

Brannum, though, had only one son, and that son was neither Frank Zappa nor this author.

Too bad.   45

On Writing   Toni Morrison

PERIL

Authoritarian regimes, dictators, despots are often, but not always, fools. But none is foolish enough to give perceptive, dissident writers free range to publish their judgments or follow their creative instincts. They know they do so at their own peril. They are not stupid enough to abandon control (overt or insidious) over media. Their methods include surveillance, censorship, arrest, even slaughter of those writers informing and disturbing the public. Writers who are unsettling, calling into question, taking another, deeper look. Writers—journalists, essayists, bloggers, poets, playwrights—can disturb the social oppression that functions like a coma on the population, a coma despots call peace; and they stanch the blood flow of war that hawks and profiteers thrill to.

That is their peril.

Ours is of another sort.

How bleak, unlivable, insufferable existence becomes when we are deprived of artwork. That the life and work of writers facing peril must be protected is urgent, but along with that urgency we should remind ourselves that their absence, the choking off of a writer's work, its cruel amputation, is of equal peril to us. The rescue we extend to them is a generosity to ourselves.

5   We all know nations that can be identified by the flight of writers from their shores. These are regimes whose fear of unmonitored writing is justified because truth is trouble. It is trouble for the warmonger, the torturer, the corporate thief, the political hack, the corrupt justice system, and for a comatose public. Unpersecuted, unjailed, unharassed writers are trouble for the ignorant bully, the sly racist, and the predators feeding off the world's resources. The alarm, the disquiet, writers raise is instructive because it is open and vulnerable, because if unpoliced it is threatening. Therefore the historical suppression of writers is the earliest harbinger of the steady peeling away of additional rights and liberties that will follow. The history of persecuted writers is as long as the history of literature itself. And the efforts to censor, starve, regulate, and annihilate us are clear signs that something important has taken place. Cultural and political forces can sweep clean all but the "safe," all but state-approved art.

I have been told that there are two human responses to the perception of chaos: naming and violence. When the chaos is simply the unknown, the naming can be accomplished effortlessly—a new species, star, formula, equation, prognosis. There is also mapping, charting, or devising proper nouns for unnamed or stripped-of-names geography, landscape, or population. When chaos resists, either by reforming itself or by rebelling against imposed order, violence is understood to be the most frequent response and the most rational when confronting the unknown, the catastrophic, the wild, wanton, or incorrigible. Rational responses may be censure, incarceration in holding camps, prisons, or death, singly or in war. There is however a third response to chaos, which I have not heard about, which is stillness. Such stillness can be passivity and dumb-foundedness; it can be paralytic fear. But it can also be art. Those writers plying their craft near to or far from the throne of raw power, of military power, of empire building and countinghouses, writers who construct meaning in the face of chaos must be nurtured, protected. And it is right that such protection be initiated by other writers. And it is imperative not only to save the besieged writers but to save ourselves. The thought that leads me to contemplate with dread the erasure of other voices, of unwritten novels, poems whispered or swallowed for fear of being overheard by the wrong people, outlawed languages flourishing underground, essayists' questions challenging authority never being posed, unstaged plays, canceled films—that thought is a nightmare. As though a whole universe is being described in invisible ink.

Certain kinds of trauma visited on peoples are so deep, so cruel, that unlike money, unlike vengeance, even unlike justice, or rights, or the goodwill of others, only writers can translate such trauma and turn sorrow into meaning, sharpening the moral imagination.

A writer's life and work are not a gift to mankind; they are its necessity.

Drama   **Itamar Moses**

MEN'S INTUITION

Characters

WENDELL: A male college student, skinny, rumpled clothing.
ERIC: His roommate, hockey jersey, backwards cap.

Setting

Eric and Wendell's dorm room, on a large college campus.

Time

Evening.

(Lights up on a dorm room: two desks, two chairs, two computers, two twin-sized beds, two piles of dirty laundry, two doors, one of which leads to the hallway, and one of which leads to a closet. ERIC, nineteen, hockey jersey, backwards cap, is seated at one of the desks, with papers, pens, a calculator, and an open economics textbook in front of him. WENDELL, also nineteen, in jeans and a button-down, is pacing. ERIC's desk is by the front door. WENDELL's desk is by the closet door. A hockey stick leans against the wall by the closet.)

WENDELL: So? Did you figure it out?

ERIC: No. Dude, you gotta give me a clue. It's, like, impossible.

WENDELL: Just keep in mind that every word counts. It's important to employ exacting attention to detail with respect to the given circumstances.

ERIC: Oh. (*Pause.*) What?

WENDELL: Do you remember what the question was?

ERIC: Oh, um. There's two guards. One always lies, one always tells the truth. And there's, um, two doors. One leads to certain death, and one leads to freedom. And you gotta . . . I have to figure out . . . you can ask only one question, and you have to figure out . . . I don't know.

WENDELL: That's all right, Eric, we can try a different one.
I know it's a little bit difficult to conceive of, after all:
Someone who always lies.

ERIC: Dude, I don't see why I have to do *any* of these. This isn't even what the test is even about.

WENDELL: Hey, *you* asked *me* for help, uh, man, so if you don't really—

ERIC: No, I know, I know, so, like, thanks, or whatever, but could we at least do it faster, though? I gotta get out of here. I'm going out tonight.

WENDELL: A little bit of patience is required for this. Let's do another one.

ERIC: Aww, maaaan . . .

WENDELL: Three lightbulbs are attached to a wall at eye level.

ERIC: Could you just explain to me how it works? Like, what's in the book?

WENDELL: There is an adjacent room containing three switches, each
of which operates one of the lightbulbs. Each room is visually inaccessible from the other.

ERIC: Visually what?

WENDELL: Inaccessible. You can't see one from the other.

ERIC: Wendell, I gotta say—

WENDELL: Do you want to pass this test or not? Listen: Eric—

ERIC: Call me E.

WENDELL: I'm not calling you E.

ERIC: Everyone else does.

WENDELL: I'm not starting to call you E just because your goddamn
coach—

ERIC: I don't have a lot of time, okay?

WENDELL: Which is why it's important that we hurry up and—

ERIC: Dude! It's an econ midterm! What the fuck do these brain
tweezers have to do with economics?

WENDELL: "Teasers."

ERIC: What?

WENDELL: "Brain *teasers*." And the reason I am doing this, as I
thought I explained, is that much of the material is intuitive.

ERIC: Oh. (*Pause.*) It's what?

WENDELL: You just, sort of . . . You either get it or you don't, Eric. These
puzzles will place you in the appropriate state of mind to . . . get it.

ERIC: I don't—

WENDELL: Okay, so: There's three lightbulbs attached to a wall at eye
level.

ERIC: Why are lightbulbs attached to a wall at eye level?

WENDELL: I don't know.

ERIC: Is it, like, a strip club?

WENDELL: No.

ERIC: Cause that'd be sweet. (*He chuckles to himself.*)

WENDELL: It is not a strip club. They're attached to the wall because they
just *are*, okay? There's an adjacent room with three switches. You, uh, you
can't see the lightbulbs from the switch room, okay? Operating the
switches however you like, and then going to check the status of the bulbs
only once, how can you determine which switch operates which bulb?
Got it? Go.

ERIC: Wendell—

WENDELL: Go.

(ERIC tries to get to work, scribbles some notes, drums his fingers, plays with his hat, and gives up more or less immediately. WENDELL simply stares at him.)

It doesn't look like you're making much progress.

ERIC: Wendell, dude, no, all right? Enough. Just explain to me how economics works. I'm supposed to meet this girl later. Just *explain* it to me.

WENDELL: A girl? Well. That *is* important. I'll do what I can to speed this up.

(He stands, slowly.) Shall we try just one more?

ERIC: I don't know. *(Standing.)* If this is all you're planning to make me study, I should really just—

WENDELL: You can't *go*. Didn't your coach say, if you don't pass this class, you can't, you won't be allowed to—

ERIC: Yeah, but, this isn't helping. I gotta—

(ERIC heads for the door. WENDELL moves quickly and blocks his path.)

WENDELL: One more.

ERIC: No.

WENDELL: One more, one more, all right: Here it is. Listen carefully: There's a gun in a desk drawer.

ERIC: Dude—

WENDELL: And you fucked my girlfriend.

(Pause.)

ERIC: What? *(Pause.)* Hey. Hey, let's go back to the one with the two guards—

WENDELL: You heard me.

ERIC: What are you talking about?

WENDELL: You know what I'm talking about.

ERIC: Who told you that?

WENDELL: So it happened.

ERIC: Dude, no, I asked who *told* you that. *(Pause.)* She's not your girlfriend.

WENDELL: Oh, is that right? Why don't *you* teach *me* something, what do *you* call a girl that somebody is going out with? What's *your* term for that? Is it, like, "Ho," or something, Eric?

ERIC: Call me E.

WENDELL: No.

ERIC: You went out with her *one time*. You didn't even kiss her.

WENDELL: Just tell me what happened. I want to hear it from you.

ERIC: Dude, no. *(Pause.)* I ran into her at a party.

WENDELL: No. Tell me exactly what happened, Eric.

ERIC: E.

WENDELL: *I'm not fucking calling you E!*

ERIC: Hey, keep it on the ice!

WENDELL: *What!?*

ERIC: Keep it on the ice, dude.

WENDELL: *What ice!?*

ERIC: It means "calm down."

WENDELL: If you want me to calm down, then tell me what happened.

ERIC: We talked at the party. I thought she was cute. She asked me back to her room. That was pretty much that.

WENDELL: *No. No. Tell me everything that happened!*

ERIC: What the fuck is wrong with you? It didn't even *matter*. It was just this *thing*.

WENDELL: What did you *say* to her? What *hand gestures* did you make? What were you *wearing*? When did she laugh, how did you make her laugh? Tell me every word you said, *every single word—*

ERIC: (overlapping) Why? Why do you want to know all that stuff?

WENDELL: *Because I don't understand!*

You went to a party? That's your fucking explanation? You probably weren't even planning on it, some *buddy* of yours drags you, "Hey, E, let's go to this party," you so then you, you *run into* this girl. And you talk. And, and, and what happens *then*? What fucking *alchemy* takes place at that point, to turn, to turn *that* into . . . into *this*?

Can you just *explain* it to me? Because I don't get it.

ERIC: I don't know what to tell you, man. It just happened.

WENDELL: Is she the girl you're meeting later?

ERIC: What? Oh. No. That's a different girl. (*Pause.*) Are you going to get out of my way? Wendell?

WENDELL: No.

ERIC: Dude, don't make me have to, like, move you.

WENDELL: I wouldn't try that if I were you.

ERIC: What are you talking about?

WENDELL: You weren't listening, Eric. To the last puzzle.

ERIC: What, the thing about the drawer? The gun in the—

(*A quick beat. Then, WENDELL jerks, as though he's going to run to his desk, but ERIC sprints there first and opens the drawer. He laughs, high-pitched, a bit relieved.*)

You had me goin' there, man. You really had me goin' there. (*He chuckles, tension draining.*) I'm sorry, okay? I really am. I'll make it up to you.

I'll take you out, we'll meet some girls. I'll hook you up. Tonight's kind of no good, this is really just a thing for the hockey team, but, seriously, next weekend maybe, okay?

(As he talks, ERIC turns his back on WENDELL to open the closet. He takes out his letterman jacket and puts it on.)

And, you know, thanks for the help with the studying. Even if we didn't get to the actual, you know, econ. Coach'll work somethin' out, I guess.

WENDELL: You didn't pay close enough attention, Eric. You have to listen to every single word.
ERIC: What?
WENDELL: I didn't say the gun was in *my* drawer.

(Another quick beat, but this time ERIC is much too far away. WENDELL pulls open ERIC'S desk drawer and pulls out a gun. He points it at ERIC's head.)

ERIC: Dude, what the fuck?
WENDELL: You're not leaving, Eric.
ERIC: That is not real.
WENDELL: Listen to me—
ERIC: That is not real, man. Is that real? That is not real. Is that *loaded?*
WENDELL: Who knows? That wasn't in the given circumstances of the brain teaser. You can only work with what you have. So. What now?
ERIC: Quit fucking around, man. I'm sorry, all right? Just tell me what to do. I'll do anything you say, just tell me what to do.
WENDELL: You were about to leave, Eric, you've obviously got it all figured out. You don't need me to teach you anything. What's the solution? How do you get through the door? Huh? What do you think you can—

(Suddenly, ERIC grabs his hockey stick from where it leans against the wall by the closet. He swings it with incredible precision and knocks the gun from WENDELL'S hand. A brief moment of stunned motionless silence from both of them as the new circumstances are absorbed. Then ERIC charges, stick held out in front of him body-check style, and slams WEN-DELL up against the front door. He punches WENDELL in the stomach. WENDELL drops to the ground, where ERIC kicks him several times.)

(A silence. Both of them are breathing hard. WENDELL curls up into a ball. ERIC throws his stick away, and looks around for the gun. He picks it up from the floor where it fell, and hefts it, curiously. He finds a plug in the "cartridge" and pulls it out. Water spills onto the floor. WENDELL sees. ERIC puts the water gun down.)

WENDELL: (*weakly, with a rueful chuckle*) Blam. (*Pause.*) Nice slapshot.

ERIC: I'm an All-American wing. (*Pause.*) Wendell. Wendell, I . . . uh . . .
You shouldn't have done that, man. You didn't need to, uh . . . to do that.

(*ERIC sits, not sure what to do. A long pause. Breathing. At last . . .*)

Wendell?

WENDELL: Mhm.

ERIC: So . . . uh . . . what's the answer? To the thing with the lightbulbs?

WENDELL: Are you kidding me?

ERIC: No. Tell me. What's the answer? Just explain it to me.

WENDELL: You turn on two of the switches for a few minutes. Then
you turn one of them off, and go into the other room. One of the
bulbs will be on, easy. But this way you can also figure out which of
the other two was on before you came in.
Because you feel it. And it's warm.

(*They stare at each other, ERIC down at the floor, and WENDELL up from
it. Fade to black.*)

END OF PLAY

Poetry   **Lisel Mueller**

SPELL FOR A TRAVELER

From the harbor of sleep bring me the milk of childhood,
from the ocean of silence bring me a grain of salt,
from the city of chances bring me my lucky number,
from the lookout of morning bring me a speckled egg,
5   from the palace of mirrors send me my old, lost self,
from the hill of bones send me a drop of your blood.

From the province of spring everlasting
bring back a rose that remains half-open,
from the drydock of mute old men
10   bring back the miracle of a tear,
from the delta of good intentions
bring back the seed that will change a life.

From the fields of the dispossessed bring me a donkey
with Byzantine eyes, from the wells of the mad
15   bring me the bell and lantern of heaven.

From the bay of forgetfulness come back with my name,
from the cave of despair come to me empty-handed,
from the strait of narrow escapes come back, come back.

Poetry   **Harryette Mullen**

TREE

Yes
I'm grounded
like all the little bushes
attached to the earth at the ankles

What saves me is   5
my madness
the racket of birds
singing loud in my tangled hair

Poetry **Pablo Neruda**

YOUR FEET

When I can not look at your face
I look at your feet.

Your feet of arched bone,
your hard little feet.

5 I know that they support you,
and that your gentle weight
rises upon them.

Your waist and your breasts,
the doubled purple
10 of your nipples,
the sockets of your eyes
that have just flown away,
your wide fruit mouth,
your red tresses,
15 my little tower.

But I love your feet
only because they walked
upon the earth and upon
the wind and upon the waters,
20 until they found me.

Fiction   **Tim O'Brien**

HOW TO TELL A TRUE WAR STORY

This is true.

I had a buddy in Vietnam. His name was Bob Kiley, but everybody called him Rat.

A friend of his gets killed, so about a week later Rat sits down and writes a letter to the guy's sister. Rat tells her what a great brother she had, how together the guy was, a number one pal and comrade. A real soldier's soldier, Rat says. Then he tells a few stories to make the point, how her brother would always volunteer for stuff nobody else would volunteer for in a million years, dangerous stuff, like doing recon or going out on these really badass night patrols. Stainless steel balls, Rat tells her. The guy was a little crazy, for sure, but crazy in a good way, a real daredevil, because he liked the challenge of it, he liked testing himself, just man against gook. A great, great guy, Rat says.

Anyway, it's a terrific letter, very personal and touching. Rat almost bawls writing it. He gets all teary telling about the good times they had together, how her brother made the war seem almost fun, always raising hell and lighting up villes and bringing smoke to bear every which way. A great sense of humor, too. Like the time at this river when he went fishing with a whole damn crate of hand grenades. Probably the funniest thing in world history, Rat says, all that gore, about twenty zillion dead gook fish. Her brother, he had the right attitude. He knew how to have a good time. On Halloween, this real hot spooky night, the dude paints up his body all different colors and puts on this weird mask and hikes over to a ville and goes trick-or-treating almost stark naked, just boots and balls and an M-16. A tremendous human being, Rat says. Pretty nutso sometimes, but you could trust him with your life.

And then the letter gets very sad and serious. Rat pours his heart out. He says he loved the guy. He says the guy was his best friend in the world. They were like soul mates, he says, like twins or something, they had a whole lot in common. He tells the guy's sister he'll look her up when the war's over.

So what happens?   5

Rat mails the letter. He waits two months. The dumb cooze never writes back.

A true war story is never moral. It does not instruct, nor encourage virtue, nor suggest models of proper human behavior, nor restrain men from doing the things men have always done. If a story seems moral, do not believe it. If at the end of a war story you feel uplifted, or if you feel that some small bit of rectitude has been salvaged from the larger waste, then you have been made the victim of a very old and terrible lie. There is no rectitude whatsoever. There is no virtue. As a first rule of thumb, therefore, you can tell a true war story by its absolute and uncompromising allegiance to obscenity and evil. Listen to Rat Kiley. Cooze, he says. He does not say bitch. He certainly does not say woman, or girl. He says cooze. Then he spits and stares. He's nineteen years old—it's too much for him—so he looks at you with those big sad gentle killer eyes and says *cooze*, because his friend is dead, and because it's so incredibly sad and true: she never wrote back.

You can tell a true war story if it embarrasses you. If you don't care for obscenity, you don't care for the truth; if you don't care for the truth, watch how you vote. Send guys to war, they come home talking dirty.

Listen to Rat: "Jesus Christ, man, I write this beautiful fuckin' letter, I slave over it, and what happens? The dumb cooze never writes back."

10　The dead guy's name was Curt Lemon. What happened was, we crossed a muddy river and marched west into the mountains, and on the third day we took a break along a trail junction in deep jungle. Right away, Lemon and Rat Kiley started goofing. They didn't understand about the spookiness. They were kids; they just didn't know. A nature hike, they thought, not even a war, so they went off into the shade of some giant trees—quadruple canopy, no sunlight at all—and they were giggling and calling each other yellow mother and playing a silly game they'd invented. The game involved smoke grenades, which were harmless unless you did stupid things, and what they did was pull out the pin and stand a few feet apart and play catch under the shade of those huge trees. Whoever chickened out was a yellow mother. And if nobody chickened out, the grenade would make a light popping sound and they'd be covered with smoke and they'd laugh and dance around and then do it again.

It's all exactly true.

It happened, to *me*, nearly twenty years ago, and I still remember that trail junction and those giant trees and a soft dripping sound somewhere beyond the trees. I remember the smell of moss. Up in the canopy there were tiny white blossoms, but no sunlight at all, and I remember the shadows spreading out under the trees where Curt Lemon and Rat Kiley were playing catch with smoke grenades. Mitchell Sanders sat flipping his yo-yo. Norman Bowker and Kiowa and Dave Jensen were dozing, or half dozing, and all around us were those ragged green mountains.

Except for the laughter things were quiet.

At one point, I remember, Mitchell Sanders turned and looked at me, not quite nodding, as if to warn me about something, as if he already *knew*, then after a while he rolled up his yo-yo and moved away.

It's hard to tell you what happened next. 15

They were just goofing. There was a noise, I suppose, which must've been the detonator, so I glanced behind me and watched Lemon step from the shade into bright sunlight. His face was suddenly brown and shining. A handsome kid, really. Sharp gray eyes, lean and narrow-waisted, and when he died it was almost beautiful, the way the sunlight came around him and lifted him up and sucked him high into a tree full of moss and vines and white blossoms.

In any war story, but especially a true one, it's difficult to separate what happened from what seemed to happen. What seems to happen becomes its own happening and has to be told that way. The angles of vision are skewed. When a booby trap explodes, you close your eyes and duck and float outside yourself. When a guy dies, like Curt Lemon, you look away and then look back for a moment and then look away again. The pictures get jumbled; you tend to miss a lot. And then afterward, when you go to tell about it, there is always that surreal seemingness, which makes the story seem untrue, but which in fact represents the hard and exact truth as it *seemed*.

In many cases a true war story cannot be believed. If you believe it, be skeptical. It's a question of credibility. Often the crazy stuff is true and the normal stuff isn't, because the normal stuff is necessary to make you believe the truly incredible craziness.

In other cases you can't even tell a true war story. Sometimes it's just beyond telling.

I heard this one, for example, from Mitchell Sanders. It was near dusk 20 and we were sitting at my foxhole along a wide muddy river north of Quang Ngai. I remember how peaceful the twilight was. A deep pinkish red spilled out on the river, which moved without sound, and in the morning we would cross the river and march west into the mountains. The occasion was right for a good story.

"God's truth," Mitchell Sanders said. "A six-man patrol goes up into the mountains on a basic listening-post operation. The idea's to spend a week up there, just lie low and listen for enemy movement. They've got a radio along, so if they hear anything suspicious—anything—they're supposed to call in artillery or gunships, whatever it takes. Otherwise they keep strict field discipline. Absolute silence. They just listen."

Sanders glanced at me to make sure I had the scenario. He was playing with his yo-yo, dancing it with short, tight little strokes of the wrist.

His face was blank in the dusk.

"We're talking regulation, by-the-book LP. These six guys, they don't say boo for a solid week. They don't got tongues. *All* ears."

25   "Right," I said.
      "Understand me?"
      "Invisible."
      Sanders nodded.
      "Affirm," he said. "Invisible. So what happens is, these guys get them-
selves deep in the bush, all camouflaged up, and they lie down and wait
and that's all they do, nothing else, they lie there for seven straight days
and just listen. And man, I'll tell you—it's spooky. This is mountains. You
don't *know* spooky till you been there. Jungle, sort of, except it's way up in
the clouds and there's always this fog—like rain, except it's not raining—
everything's all wet and swirly and tangled up and you can't see jack, you
can't find your own pecker to piss with. Like you don't even have a body.
Serious spooky. You just go with the vapors—the fog sort of takes you
in . . . And the sounds, man. The sounds carry forever. You hear stuff
nobody should *ever* hear."

30   Sanders was quiet for a second, just working the yo-yo, then he smiled
at me.
      "So after a couple days the guys start hearing this real soft, kind of
wacked-out music. Weird echoes and stuff. Like a radio or something, but
it's not a radio, it's this strange gook music that comes right out of the
rocks. Faraway, sort of, but right up close, too. They try to ignore it. But it's
a listening post, right? So they listen. And every night they keep hearing
that crazyass gook concert. All kinds of chimes and xylophones. I mean,
this is wilderness—no way, it can't be real—but there it *is,* like the mountains are tuned in to Radio fucking Hanoi. Naturally they get nervous.
One guy sticks Juicy Fruit in his ears. Another guy almost flips. Thing is,
though, they can't report music. They can't get on the horn and call back
to base and say, 'Hey, listen, we need some firepower, we got to blow away
this weirdo gook rock band.' They can't do that. It wouldn't go down. So
they lie there in the fog and keep their mouths shut. And what makes it
extra bad, see, is the poor dudes can't horse around like normal. Can't joke
it away. Can't even talk to each other except maybe in whispers, all hush-
hush, and that just revs up the willies. All they do is listen."
      Again there was some silence as Mitchell Sanders looked out on the
river. The dark was coming on hard now, and off to the west I could see the
mountains rising in silhouette, all the mysteries and unknowns.
      "This next part," Sanders said quietly, "you won't believe."
      "Probably not," I said.

35   "You won't. And you know why?" He gave me a long, tired smile. "Because it happened. Because every word is absolutely dead-on true."
      Sanders made a sound in his throat, like a sigh, as if to say he didn't care
if I believed him or not. But he did care. He wanted me to feel the truth, to
believe by the raw force of feeling. He seemed sad, in a way.

"These six guys," he said, "they're pretty fried out by now, and one night they start hearing voices. Like at a cocktail party. That's what it sounds like, this big swank gook cocktail party somewhere out there in the fog. Music and chitchat and stuff. It's crazy, I know, but they hear the champagne corks. They hear the actual martini glasses. Real hoity-toity, all very civilized, except this isn't civilization. This is Nam.

"Anyway, the guys try to be cool. They just lie there and groove, but after a while they start hearing—you won't believe this—they hear chamber music. They hear violins and cellos. They hear this terrific mama-san soprano. Then after a while they hear gook opera and a glee club and the Haiphong Boys Choir and a barbershop quartet and all kinds of weird chanting and Buddha-Buddha stuff. And the whole time, in the background, there's still that cocktail party going on. All these different voices. Not human voices, though. Because it's the mountains. Follow me? The rock—it's *talking*. And the fog, too, and the grass and the goddamn mongooses. Everything talks. The trees talk politics, the monkeys talk religion. The whole country. Vietnam. The place talks. It talks. Understand? Nam—it truly *talks*.

"The guys can't cope. They lose it. They get on the radio and report enemy movement—a whole army, they say—and they order up the firepower. They get arty and gunships. They call in air strikes. And I'll tell you, they fuckin' crash that cocktail party. All night long, they just smoke those mountains. They make jungle juice. They blow away trees and glee clubs and whatever else there is to blow away. Scorch time. They walk napalm up and down the ridges. They bring in the Cobras and F-4s, they use Willie Peter and HE and incendiaries. It's all fire. They make those mountains burn.

"Around dawn things finally get quiet. Like you never even *heard* quiet before. One of those real thick, real misty days—just clouds and fog, they're off in this special zone—and the mountains are absolutely deadflat silent. Like Brigadoon—pure vapor, you know? Everything's all sucked up inside the fog. Not a single sound, except they still *hear* it.

"So they pack up and start humping. They head down the mountain, back to base camp, and when they get there they don't say diddly. They don't talk. Not a word, like they're deaf and dumb. Later on this fat bird colonel comes up and asks what the hell happened out there. What'd they hear? Why all the ordnance? The man's ragged out, he gets down tight on their case. I mean, they spent six trillion dollars on firepower, and this fatass colonel wants answers, he wants to know what the fuckin' story is.

"But the guys don't say zip. They just look at him for a while, sort of funny like, sort of amazed, and the whole war is right there in that stare. It says everything you can't ever say. It says, man, you got *wax* in your ears. It says, poor bastard, you'll never know—wrong frequency—you

40

don't *even* want to hear this. Then they salute the fucker and walk away, because certain stories you don't ever tell."

You can tell a true war story by the way it never seems to end. Not then, not ever. Not when Mitchell Sanders stood up and moved off into the dark.

It all happened.

45   Even now, at this instant, I remember that yo-yo. In a way, I suppose, you had to be there, you had to hear it, but I could tell how desperately Sanders wanted me to believe him, his frustration at not quite getting the details right, not quite pinning down the final and definitive truth.

And I remember sitting at my foxhole that night, watching the shadows of Quang Ngai, thinking about the coming day and how we would cross the river and march west into the mountains, all the ways I might die, all the things I did not understand.

Late in the night Mitchell Sanders touched my shoulder.

"Just came to me," he whispered. "The moral, I mean. Nobody listens. Nobody hears nothin'. Like that fatass colonel. The politicians, all the civilian types. Your girlfriend. My girlfriend. Everybody's sweet little virgin girlfriend. What they need is to go out on LP. The vapors, man. Trees and rocks—you got to *listen* to your enemy."

And then again, in the morning, Sanders came up to me. The platoon was preparing to move out, checking weapons, going through all the little rituals that preceded a day's march. Already the lead squad had crossed the river and was filing off toward the west.

50   "I got a confession to make," Sanders said. "Last night, man, I had to make up a few things."

"I know that."

"The glee club. There wasn't any glee club."

"Right."

"No opera."

55   "Forget it, I understand."

"Yeah, but listen, it's still true. Those six guys, they heard wicked sound out there. They heard sound you just plain won't believe."

Sanders pulled on his rucksack, closed his eyes for a moment, then almost smiled at me. I knew what was coming.

"All right," I said, "what's the moral?"

"Forget it."

60   "No, go ahead."

For a long while he was quiet, looking away, and the silence kept stretching out until it was almost embarrassing. Then he shrugged and gave me a stare that lasted all day.

"Hear that quiet, man?" he said. "That quiet—just listen. There's your moral."

In a true war story, if there's a moral at all, it's like the thread that makes the cloth. You can't tease it out. You can't extract the meaning without unraveling the deeper meaning. And in the end, really, there's nothing much to say about a true war story, except maybe "Oh."

True war stories do not generalize. They do not indulge in abstraction or analysis.

For example: War is hell. As a moral declaration the old truism seems   65
perfectly true, and yet because it abstracts, because it generalizes, I can't believe it with my stomach. Nothing turns inside.

It comes down to gut instinct. A true war story, if truly told, makes the stomach believe.

This one does it for me. I've told it before—many times, many versions—but here's what actually happened.

We crossed that river and marched west into the mountains. On the third day, Curt Lemon stepped on a booby-trapped 105 round. He was playing catch with Rat Kiley, laughing, and then he was dead. The trees were thick; it took nearly an hour to cut an LZ for the dustoff.

Later, higher in the mountains, we came across a baby VC water buffalo. What it was doing there I don't know—no farms or paddies—but we chased it down and got a rope around it and led it along to a deserted village where we set up for the night. After supper Rat Kiley went over and stroked its nose.

He opened up a can of C rations, pork and beans, but the baby buffalo   70
wasn't interested.

Rat shrugged.

He stepped back and shot it through the right front knee. The animal did not make a sound. It went down hard, then got up again, and Rat took careful aim and shot off an ear. He shot it in the hindquarters and in the little hump at its back. He shot it twice in the flanks. It wasn't to kill; it was to hurt. He put the rifle muzzle up against the mouth and shot the mouth away. Nobody said much. The whole platoon stood there watching, feeling all kinds of things, but there wasn't a great deal of pity for the baby water buffalo. Curt Lemon was dead. Rat Kiley had lost his best friend in the world. Later in the week he would write a long personal letter to the guy's sister, who would not write back, but for now it was a question of pain. He shot off the tail. He shot away chunks of meat below the ribs. All around us there was the smell of smoke and filth and deep greenery, and the evening was humid and very hot. Rat went to automatic. He shot randomly, almost casually, quick little spurts in the belly and butt. Then he reloaded, squatted down, and shot it in the left front knee. Again the animal fell hard and tried to get up, but this time it couldn't quite make it. It wobbled and went down sideways. Rat shot it in the nose. He bent forward and whispered something, as if talking to a pet, then he shot it in the throat. All the while the baby buffalo was silent, or almost silent, just a light bubbling sound where the nose had been. It lay very still. Nothing moved except the eyes, which were enormous, the pupils shiny black and dumb.

Rat Kiley was crying. He tried to say something, but then cradled his rifle and went off by himself.

The rest of us stood in a ragged circle around the baby buffalo. For a time no one spoke. We had witnessed something essential, something brand-new and profound, a piece of the world so startling there was not yet a name for it.

75   Somebody kicked the baby buffalo.

It was still alive, though just barely, just in the eyes.

"Amazing," Dave Jensen said. "My whole life, I never seen anything like it."

"Never?"

"Not hardly. Not once."

Kiowa and Mitchell Sanders picked up the baby buffalo. They hauled it across the open square, hoisted it up, and dumped it in the village well.

80   Afterward, we sat waiting for Rat to get himself together.

"Amazing," Dave Jensen kept saying. "A new wrinkle. I never seen it before."

Mitchell Sanders took out his yo-yo. "Well, that's Nam," he said. "Garden of Evil. Over here, man, every sin's real fresh and original."

How do you generalize?

War is hell, but that's not the half of it, because war is also mystery and terror and adventure and courage and discovery and holiness and pity and despair and longing and love. War is nasty; war is fun. War is thrilling; war is drudgery. War makes you a man; war makes you dead.

85   The truths are contradictory. It can be argued, for instance, that war is grotesque. But in truth war is also beauty. For all its horror, you can't help but gape at the awful majesty of combat. You stare out at tracer rounds unwinding through the dark like brilliant red ribbons. You crouch in ambush as a cool, impassive moon rises over the nighttime paddies. You admire the fluid symmetries of troops on the move, the harmonies of sound and shape and proportion, the great sheets of metal-fire streaming down from a gunship, the illumination rounds, the white phosphorus, the purply orange glow of napalm, the rocket's red glare. It's not pretty, exactly. It's astonishing. It fills the eye. It commands you. You hate it, yes, but your eyes do not. Like a killer forest fire, like cancer under a microscope,

any battle or bombing raid or artillery barrage has the aesthetic purity of absolute moral indifference—a powerful, implacable beauty—and a true war story will tell the truth about this, though the truth is ugly.

To generalize about war is like generalizing about peace. Almost everything is true. Almost nothing is true. At its core, perhaps, war is just another name for death, and yet any soldier will tell you, if he tells the truth, that proximity to death brings with it a corresponding proximity to life. After a firefight, there is always the immense pleasure of aliveness. The trees are alive. The grass, the soil—everything. All around you things are purely living, and you among them, and the aliveness makes you tremble. You feel an intense, out-of-the-skin awareness of your living self—your truest self, the human being you want to be and then become by the force of wanting it. In the midst of evil you want to be a good man. You want decency. You want justice and courtesy and human concord, things you never knew you wanted. There is a kind of largeness to it, a kind of godliness. Though it's odd, you're never more alive than when you're almost dead. You recognize what's valuable. Freshly, as if for the first time, you love what's best in yourself and in the world, all that might be lost. At the hour of dusk you sit at your foxhole and look out on a wide river turning pinkish red, and at the mountains beyond, and although in the morning you must cross the river and go into the mountains and do terrible things and maybe die, even so, you find yourself studying the fine colors on the river, you feel wonder and awe at the setting of the sun, and you are filled with a hard, aching love for how the world could be and always should be, but now is not.

Mitchell Sanders was right. For the common soldier, at least, war has the feel—the spiritual texture—of a great ghostly fog, thick and permanent. There is no clarity. Everything swirls. The old rules are no longer binding, the old truths no longer true. Right spills over into wrong. Order blends into chaos, love into hate, ugliness into beauty, law into anarchy, civility into savagery. The vapors suck you in. You can't tell where you are, or why you're there, and the only certainty is overwhelming ambiguity.

In war you lose your sense of the definite, hence your sense of truth itself, and therefore it's safe to say that in a true war story nothing is ever absolutely true.

Often in a true war story there is not even a point, or else the point doesn't hit you until twenty years later, in your sleep, and you wake up and shake your wife and start telling the story to her, except when you get to the end you've forgotten the point again. And then for a long time you lie there watching the story happen in your head. You listen to your wife's breathing. The war's over. You close your eyes. You smile and think, Christ, what's the *point?*

This one wakes me up.

90　　In the mountains that day, I watched Lemon turn sideways. He laughed and said something to Rat Kiley. Then he took a peculiar half step, moving from shade into bright sunlight, and the booby-trapped 105 round blew him into a tree. The parts were just hanging there, so Dave Jensen and I were ordered to shinny up and peel him off. I remember the white bone of an arm. I remember pieces of skin and something wet and yellow that must've been the intestines. The gore was horrible, and stays with me. But what wakes me up twenty years later is Dave Jensen singing "Lemon Tree" as we threw down the parts.

You can tell a true war story by the questions you ask. Somebody tells a story, let's say, and afterward you ask, "Is it true?" and if the answer matters, you've got your answer.

For example, we've all heard this one. Four guys go down a trail. A grenade sails out. One guy jumps on it and takes the blast and saves his three buddies.

Is it true?

The answer matters.

95　　You'd feel cheated if it never happened. Without the grounding reality, it's just a trite bit of puffery, pure Hollywood, untrue in the way all such stories are untrue. Yet even if it did happen—and maybe it did, anything's possible—even then you know it can't be true, because a true war story does not depend upon that kind of truth. Absolute occurrence is irrelevant. A thing may happen and be a total lie; another thing may not happen and be truer than the truth. For example: Four guys go down a trail. A grenade sails out. One guy jumps on it and takes the blast, but it's a killer grenade and everybody dies anyway. Before they die, though, one of the dead guys says, "The fuck you do *that* for?" and the jumper says, "Story of my life, man," and the other guy starts to smile but he's dead.

That's a true story that never happened.

Twenty years later, I can still see the sunlight on Lemon's face. I can see him turning, looking back at Rat Kiley, then he laughed and took that curious half step from shade into sunlight, his face suddenly brown and shining, and when his foot touched down, in that instant, he must've thought it was the sunlight that was killing him. It was not the sunlight. It was a rigged 105 round. But if I could ever get the story right, how the sun seemed to gather around him and pick him up and lift him high into a tree, if I could somehow recreate the fatal whiteness of that light, the quick glare, the obvious cause and effect, then you would believe the last thing Curt Lemon believed, which for him must've been the final truth.

Now and then, when I tell this story, someone will come up to me afterward and say she liked it. It's always a woman. Usually it's an older woman of kindly temperament and humane politics. She'll explain that as a rule she hates war stories; she can't understand why people want to wallow in all the blood and gore. But this one she liked. The poor baby buffalo, it made her sad. Sometimes, even, there are little tears. What I should do, she'll say, is put it all behind me. Find new stories to tell.

I won't say it but I'll think it.

I'll picture Rat Kiley's face, his grief, and I'll think, *You dumb cooze.*   100

Because she wasn't listening.

It *wasn't* a war story. It was a *love* story.

But you can't say that. All you can do is tell it one more time, patiently, adding and subtracting, making up a few things to get at the real truth. No Mitchell Sanders, you tell her. No Lemon, no Rat Kiley. No trail junction. No baby buffalo. No vines or moss or white blossoms. Beginning to end, you tell her, it's all made up. Every goddamn detail—the mountains and the river and especially that poor dumb baby buffalo. None of it happened. *None* of it. And even if it did happen, it didn't happen in the mountains, it happened in this little village on the Batangan Peninsula, and it was raining like crazy, and one night a guy named Stink Harris woke up screaming with a leech on his tongue. You can tell a true war story if you just keep on telling it.

And in the end, of course, a true war story is never about war. It's about sunlight. It's about the special way that dawn spreads out on a river when you know you must cross the river and march into the mountains and do things you are afraid to do. It's about love and memory. It's about sorrow. It's about sisters who never write back and people who never listen.

Fiction   **Chris Offutt**

OUT OF THE WOODS

Gerald opened his front door at dawn, wearing only a quickly drawn-on pair of jeans. His wife's four brothers stood in the ground fog that filtered along the ridge. The oldest brother had become family spokesman after the father's death, and Gerald waited for him to speak. The mother was still boss but everything had to filter through a man.

"It's Ory," the oldest one said. "He got shot and is in the hospital. Somebody's got to fetch him."

The brothers looked at Gerald from below their eyebrows. Going after Ory wasn't a chore anyone wanted, and Gerald was new to the family, married to Kay, the only sister. He still needed to prove his worth. If he brought Ory home, maybe they'd cut the barrier that kept him on the edge of things, like he was nothing but a third or fourth cousin.

"Where's he at?" Gerald said.

5   "Wahoo, Nebraska. Ory said it would take two days but was easy to find."

"My rig won't make it."

"You can take the old Ford. She'll run till doomsday."

"Who shot him?"

The oldest brother flashed him a mean look. The rest were back to looking down, as if they were carpenters gauging the amount of linoleum needed for a job.

10   "Some woman," the oldest brother said.

Kay began to cry. The brothers left and Gerald sat on the couch beside Kay. She hugged her knees and bit a thumbnail, gasping in a throaty way that reminded him of the sounds she made in bed. He reached for her. She shrugged from his hand, then allowed his touch.

"Him leaving never made sense," Kay said. "He hadn't done nothing and nobody was after him. He didn't tell a soul why. Just up and went. Be ten years come fall."

"I'll go get him," Gerald whispered.

"You don't care to?"

15   "No."

"For my brothers?"

"For you."

She snuggled against him, her damp face pressed to his neck. She was tiny inside the robe. He opened the front and she pushed against his leg.

The next day he left in the black pickup. Gerald was thirty years old and had never been out of the county. He wore a suit that was snug in the shoulders, and short in the legs. It had belonged to his father, but he didn't figure anyone would notice. He wished he owned a tie. The dogwoods and redbuds had already lost their spring color. The air was hot. Four hours later he was in Indiana, where the land was flat as a playing card. There was nowhere to hide, no safety at all. Even the sun was too bright. He didn't understand how Ory could stand such open ground.

Illinois was equally flat but with less green to it. Gerald realized that he was driving through a season, watching spring in reverse. The Illinois dirt was black as manure and he pulled over to examine it. The earth was moist and rich. It smelled of life. He let it trickle between his fingers, thinking of the hard clay dirt at home. He decided to stop and get some of this good dirt on the way back.

He drove all day and crossed the Mississippi River at night. At a rest area, he unrolled a blanket and lay down. He was cold. Above him the stars were strewn across the sky. They seemed to be moving down, threatening to press him against the ground. Something bright cut across the night, and he thought someone had shot at him until he realized it was a shooting star. The hills at home blocked so much sky that he'd never seen one. He watched the vast prairie night until fading into sleep.

The eerie light of a flatland dawn woke him early. The sun wasn't visible and the world seemed to glow from within. There were no birds to hear. He could see his breath. He drove west and left the interstate at Wahoo and found the hospital easily. A nurse took him to a small room. Everything was white and the walls seemed to emit a low hum. He couldn't place the smell. A man came into the room wearing a white coat. He spoke with an accent.

"I am Dr. Gupte. You are with the family of Mr. Gowan?"

"You're the doctor?"

"Yes." He sighed and opened a manila folder. "I'm afraid Mr. Gowan has left us."

"Done out, huh. Where to?"

"I'm afraid that is not the circumstance."

"It's not."

"No, he had a pulmonary thromboembolism."

"Is that American?"

"I'm afraid you will excuse me."

Dr. Gupte left the room and Gerald wondered who the funny little man really was. He pulled open a drawer. Inside was a small mallet with a triangular head made of rubber, perfect for nothing. A cop came in the room, and Gerald slowly closed the drawer.

"I'm Sheriff Johnson. You the next of kin?"

"Gerald Bolin."

They watched each other in the tiny room under the artificial light. Gerald didn't like cops. They got to carry a gun, drive fast, and fight. Anybody else got thrown in the pokey for doing the same thing.

"Dr. Gupte asked me to come in," the sheriff said.

"He really is a doctor?"

"He's from Pakistan."

40   "Run out of your own, huh."

"Look, Mr. Bolin. Your brother-in-law got a blood clot that went to his lung. He died from it."

Gerald cleared his throat, scanned the floor for somewhere to spit, then swallowed it. He rubbed his eyes.

"Say he's dead."

The sheriff nodded.

45   "That damn doctor ain't worth his hide, is he."

"There's some things to clear up."

The sheriff drove Gerald to his office, a small space with a desk and two chairs. A calendar hung from the wall. The room reminded Gerald of the hospital without the smell.

"Ory was on a tear," the sheriff said. "He was drinking and wrecked his car at his girlfriend's house. She wouldn't let him in and he broke the door open. They started arguing and she shot him."

"Then he got a blood clot."

50   The sheriff nodded.

"Did he not have a job?" Gerald said.

"No. And there's some money problems. He went through a fence and hit a light post. He owed back rent at a rooming house. Plus the hospital."

"Car bad hurt?"

"It runs."

55   "Did he own anything?"

"Clothes, a knife, suitcase, a little twenty-two pistol, a pair of boots, and a radio."

"What all does he owe?"

"Twelve hundred dollars."

Gerald walked to the window. He thought of his wife and all her family waiting for him. They'd given him a little money, but he'd need it for gas on the ride back.

60   "Can I see her?" he said.

"Who?"

"The woman that shot him."

The sheriff drove him a few blocks to a tan building made of stone. Near the eaves were narrow slits to let light in. They went through heavy doors into a common room with a TV set and a pay phone. Four cells formed one wall. A woman sat on a bunk in one of the cells, reading a magazine. She wore an orange jumpsuit that was too big for her.

"Melanie," the sheriff said. "You have a visitor. Ory's brother-in-law."

The sheriff left and Gerald stared through the bars. Her hair was dark purple. One side was long, the other shaved. Each ear had several small gold hoops in a row that reminded Gerald of a guide for a harness. A gold ring pierced her left nostril. She had a black eye. He wanted to watch her for a long time, but looked at his boots instead.

"Hidy," he said.

She rolled the magazine into a tube and held it to her good eye, looking at Gerald.

"I come for Ory," Gerald said, "but he's died on me. Just thought I'd talk to you a minute."

"I didn't kill him."

"I know it."

"I only shot him."

"A blood clot killed him."

"Do you want to screw me?"

Gerald shook his head, his face turning red. She seemed too young to talk that way, too young for jail, too young for Ory.

"Let me have a cigarette," she said.

He passed one through the bars and she took it without touching his hand. A chain was tattooed around her wrist. She inhaled twin lines of smoke from her mouth into her nose. The ash was long and red. She sucked at the filter, lifting her lips to prevent them from getting burned. She blew a smoke ring. Gerald had never seen anyone get so much out of a single cigarette.

"Wish it was menthol," she said. "Ory smoked menthol."

"Well."

"What do you want," she said.

"I don't know. Nothing I don't guess."

"Me neither, except out of here."

"Don't reckon I can help you there."

"You talk just like Ory did."

"How come you to shoot him?"

"We had a fight, and he like, came over drunk. He wanted something he gave me and I wouldn't give it back. It was mine. He busted the lock and started tearing everything up, you know, looking for it. I had a little pistol in my vanity and I like, got it out."

Melanie finished the cigarette and he gave her another one, careful not to look at the ring in her nose. Behind her was a stainless steel toilet with a sink on top where the tank should be. When you washed your hands, it flushed the toilet. He thought of the jail at home with its putrid hole in the floor and no sink at all.

"What was it he was wanting so bad?"

"A wig," she said. "It was blond and he liked me to wear it. Sometimes I wore it in bed."

"You shot him over a wig."

90   "I was scared. He kept screaming, 'Give me back my wig.' So I, you know, shot him. Just once. If I knew he'd get that blood clot, I wouldn't have done it."

Gerald wondered how old she was but didn't want to insult her by asking. He felt sorry for her.

"He give you that eye?"

"The cops did. They think me and Ory sell dope but we don't, not really. Nothing heavy. Just to, like, friends."

"Why do you do that?" he said.

"Deal?"

95   "No. Cut your hair and stick that thing in your nose."

"Shut up," she said. She began yelling. "I don't need you. Get away from me. Get out of here!"

The sheriff came into the common room and took Gerald outside. The sky was dark with the smell of rain. He wanted to stand there until the storm swept over him, rinsing him of the jail. He underwent a sudden sense of vertigo, and for a moment he didn't know where he was, only that he was two days from anything familiar. He didn't even know where his truck was.

"She's a hard one," the sheriff said.

"I don't want no charges pressed against her."

100   "That's not up to you."

"She didn't kill him."

"I don't know about Kentucky," the sheriff said, "but in Nebraska, shooting people's a crime. Look, there's been a big wreck on Ninety-two and five people are coming to the hospital. They need the space. We got to get your brother-in-law to a funeral home."

"Can't afford it."

"The hospital's worse. It charges by the day."

105   "What in case I take his stuff and leave."

"The county'll bury him."

"That'll run you how much?"

"About a thousand."

"That's a lot of money."

110   The sheriff nodded.

"Tell you what," Gerald said. "I'll sell you his car for one dollar. You can use it to pay off what all he owes. There's that radio and stuff. Plus I'll throw in a hundred cash."

"You can't buy a body."

"It ain't yours to sell or mine to buy. I just want to get him home. Family wants him."

"I don't know if it's legal."

"He ain't the first person to die somewhere else. My cousin's aunt came   115
in on a train after getting killed in a wreck. They set her off at the Rocksalt station. She was in a box."

The sheriff puffed his cheeks and blew air. He went to his office and dialed the courthouse and asked for a notary public. Half an hour later the car belonged to the city of Wahoo. It was a Chevelle and for a moment Gerald wondered if he'd made a mistake. They were pretty good cars.

The sheriff drove them to the hospital. Gerald pulled the money out and started counting.

"Keep it," the sheriff said.

"Give it to Melanie. She wants menthol cigarettes."

"You and Ory aren't a whole lot alike, are you."   120

"I never knew him that good."

"The only man I saw give money away was my daddy."

"Was he rich?"

"No," said the sheriff, "Daddy was a farmer."

"You all worked this flat land?"   125

"It worked him right back into it."

Gerald followed the sheriff into the hospital and signed several forms. An orderly wheeled in a gurney with the body on it, covered with a white cloth. He pushed it to an exit beside the emergency room. Three ambulances drove into the lot and paramedics began moving the injured people into the hospital. The orderlies left the gurney and went to help. A state police car stopped behind the ambulances.

"I have to talk to them," the sheriff said. "Then I'll get an ambulance to drop the body down at the train station."

The sheriff left the car and walked to the state trooper. Nobody was looking at Gerald. He pushed the gurney into the lot and along the side of the building. A breeze rippled the cloth that covered Ory. Gerald held it down with one hand but the gurney went crooked. He let go of the cloth and righted the gurney and the wind blew the cloth away. Ory was stretched out naked with a hole in his side. He didn't look dead, but Gerald didn't think he looked too good either. He looked like a man with a bad hangover that he might shake by dinner.

Gerald dropped the tailgate of his pickup and dragged Ory into the   130
truck. He threw his blanket over him and weighted the corners with tire tools, the spare, and a coal shovel. He drove the rest of the day. In Illinois, he stopped and lay down beside the truck. Without the blanket he was cold, but he didn't feel right about taking it back from Ory. Gerald thought

about Ory asking Melanie to wear the blond wig. He wondered if it made a difference when they were in bed.

He woke with frost on him. A buzzard circled high above the truck. He drove into the rising sun, thinking that he'd done everything backward. No matter when he drove, he was always aimed at the sun. Mist lifted above the land as the frost gave way. At the next exit, Gerald left the interstate for a farm road and parked beside a plowed field.

He carried the shovel over a wire fence. The dirt was loose and easy to take. It would make a fine garden at home. His body took over, grateful for the labor after three days of driving. A pair of redwing blackbirds sat on a power line, courting each other, and Gerald wondered how birds knew to go with their own kind. Maybe Ory knew he was in the wrong tree and that's why he wanted Melanie to wear a wig. Gerald tried to imagine her with blond hair. He suddenly understood that he wanted her, had wanted her at the jailhouse. He couldn't figure why. It bothered him that he had so much desire for a woman he didn't consider attractive.

He climbed in the back and mounded the dirt to balance the load. As he traveled south, he reentered spring. The buds of softwood trees turned pale green. Flocks of starlings moved over him in a dark cloud, heading north. By nightfall, he crossed the Ohio River into Kentucky. In four hours he'd be home. He was getting sleepy, but coffee had stopped doing him any good. He slid into a zone of the road, letting the rhythm of motion enter his body. A loud noise made him jerk upright. He thought he'd had a flat until he saw that he'd drifted across the breakdown lane and onto the edge of the median. He parked and lay down in the bench seat. He was lucky not to have been killed. The law would have a hard time with that— two dead men, one naked and already stiff, and a load of dirt.

When he woke, it was light and he felt tired already. At a gas station he stared at the rest room mirror, thinking that he looked like the third day of a three-day drunk. The suit was ruined. He combed his hair with water and stepped into the sun. A dog was in the back of his pickup, digging. Gerald yelled, looking for something to grab. The dog saw him and jumped off the truck and loped away. Gerald shoved dirt over Ory's exposed hand. A man came behind him.

135   "Shoo-eee," the man said. "You waited long enough didn't you."

Gerald grunted. He was smoothing the dirt, replacing the weights along the blanket's edge. The man spoke again.

"Had to take one to the renderers myself last week. Got some kind of bug that killed it in three days. Vet said it was a new one on him."

"A new one."

"I put mine in a garbage bag. Keeps the smell in better than dirt."

140   "It does."

"Did yours up and not eat, then lay down and start breathing hard?"

"More or less."

"It's the same thing. A malady, the vet called it."

"A malady."

Gerald got in the truck and decided not to stop until he was home. The 145 stench was bad and getting worse. He wondered if breathing a bad smell made your lungs stink. The land started to roll, the crests rising higher as he traveled east. The sun was very hot. It seemed to him as if summer had arrived while he was gone. He'd been to winter and back.

Deep in the hills, he left the interstate for a blacktop road that turned to dirt, following the twists of a creek. He stopped at the foot of his wife's home hill. Kay would be up there, at her mom's house with all her family. They would feed him, give him whiskey, wait for him to tell what happened. He brushed off his suit and thought about the events, collecting them in sequence. He told the story in his head. He thought some more, then practiced again. Ory had quit drinking and taken a good job as manager of a department store. He'd gotten engaged to a woman he'd met at church, but had held off telling the family until he could bring her home. She was nice as pie, blond headed. He was teaching her to shoot a pistol and it went off by accident. She was tore all to pieces about it. He'd never seen anyone in such bad shape. All she did was cry. It was a malady.

Gerald drove slowly up the hill. Later, he could tell the truth to the oldest brother, who'd tell the rest. They'd appreciate his public lie and he'd be in with the family. He parked in the yard beside his mother-in-law's house. Dogs ran toward the truck, then kids. Adults stepped onto the porch and Gerald could see them looking for Ory in the cab. Kay came out of the house. She smiled at him, the same small smile that she always used, and he wondered how she'd look in a wig.

He got out of the truck and waited. Everything was the same—the house, the trees, the people. He recognized the leaves and the outline of the branches against the sky. He knew how the light would fall, where the shadows would go. The smell of the woods was familiar. It would be this way forever. Abruptly, as if doused by water, he knew why Ory had left.

Fiction   Julio Ortega

LAS PAPAS

He turned on the faucet of the kitchen sink and washed off the knife. As he felt the splashing water, he looked up through the front window and saw the September wind shaking the tender shoots of the trees on his street, the first hint of fall.

He quickly washed the potatoes one by one. Although their coloring was light and serene, they were large and heavy. When he started to peel them, slowly, using the knife precisely and carefully, the child came into the kitchen.

"What are you going to cook?" he asked. He stood there waiting for an answer.

"Chicken cacciatore," the man answered, but the child didn't believe him. He was only six, but he seemed capable of objectively discerning between one chicken recipe and another.

5   "Wait and see," he promised.

"Is it going to have onions in it?" asked the child.

"Very few," he said.

The child left the kitchen unconvinced.

He finished peeling the potatoes and started to slice them. Through the window he saw the growing brightness of midday. That strong light seemed to paralyze the brilliant foliage on the trees. The inside of the potatoes had the same clean whiteness, and the knife penetrated it, as if slicing through soft clay.

10   Then he rinsed the onions and cut into them, chopping them up. He glanced at the recipe again and looked for seasonings in the pantry. The child came back in.

"Chicken is really boring," the child said, almost in protest.

"Not this recipe," he said. "It'll be great. You'll see."

"Put a lot of stuff in it," the child recommended.

"It's going to have oregano, pepper, and even some sugar," he said.

15   The child smiled, approvingly.

He dried the potato slices. The pulp was crisp, almost too white, more like an apple, perhaps. Where did these potatoes come from? Wyoming or Idaho, probably. The potatoes from his country, on the other hand, were grittier, with a heavy flavor of the land. There were dark ones, almost royal purple like fruit, and delicate yellow ones, like the yolk of an egg. They say there used to be more than a thousand varieties of potato. Many of them have disappeared forever.

The ones that were lost, had they been less firmly rooted in the soil? Were they more delicate varieties? Maybe they disappeared when control of the cultivated lands was deteriorating. Some people say, and it's probably true, that the loss of even one domesticated plant makes the world a little poorer, as does the destruction of a work of art in a city plundered by invaders. If a history of the lost varieties were written it might prove that no one would ever have gone hungry.

Boiled, baked, fried, or stewed: the ways of cooking potatoes were a long story in themselves. He remembered what his mother had told him as a child: at harvest time, the largest potatoes would be roasted for everybody, and, in the fire, they would open up—just like flowers. That potato was probably one of the lost varieties, the kind that turned into flowers in the flames.

Are potatoes harvested at night in the moonlight? He was surprised how little he knew about something that came from his own country. As he thought about it, he believed *harvest* wasn't even the correct term. *Gathering? Digging?* What do you call this harvest from under the earth?

For a long time he had avoided eating them. Even their name seemed unpleasant to him, *papas*. A sign of the provinces, one more shred of evidence of the meager resources, of underdevelopment—a potato lacked protein and was loaded with carbohydrates. French-fried potatoes seemed more tolerable to him: they were, somehow, in a more neutralized condition.

At first, when he began to care for the child all by himself, he tried to simplify the ordeal of meals by going out to the corner restaurant. But he soon found that if he tried to cook something it passed the time, and he also amused himself with the child's curiosity.

He picked up the cut slices. There wasn't much more to discover in them. It wasn't necessary to expect anything more of them than the density they already possessed, a crude cleanliness that was the earth's flavor. But that same sense transformed them right there in his hands, a secret flowering, uncovered by him in the kitchen. It was as if he discovered one of the lost varieties of the Andean potato: the one that belonged to him, wondering, at noon.

When the chicken began to fry in the skillet, the boy returned, attracted by its aroma. The man was in the midst of making the salad.

"Where's this food come from?" the child asked, realizing it was a different recipe.

"Peru," he replied.

"Not Italy?" said the child, surprised.

"I'm cooking another recipe now," he explained. "Potatoes come from Peru. You know that, right?"

"Yeah, but I forgot it."

"They're really good, and there are all kinds and flavors. Remember mangoes? You really used to like them when we went to see your grandparents."

30   "I don't remember them either. I only remember the lion in the zoo."

"You don't remember the tree in Olivar Park?"

"Uh-huh. I remember that."

"We're going back there next summer, to visit the whole family."

"What if there's an earthquake?"

35   The boy went for his Spanish reader and sat down at the kitchen table. He read the resonant names out loud, names that were also like an unfinished history, and the man had to go over to him every once in a while to help explain one thing or another.

He tasted the sauce for the amount of salt, then added a bit of tarragon, whose intense perfume was delightful, and a bit of marjoram, a sweeter aroma.

He noticed how, outside, the light trapped by a tree slipped out from the blackened greenness of the leaves, now spilling onto the grass on the hill where their apartment house stood. The grass, all lit up, became an oblique field, a slope of tame fire seen from the window.

He looked at the child, stuck on a page in his book; he looked at the calm, repeated blue of the sky; and he looked at the leaves of lettuce in his hands, leaves that crackled as they broke off and opened up like tender shoots, beside the faucet of running water.

As if it suddenly came back to him, he understood that he must have been six or seven when his father, probably forty years old, as he was now, used to cook at home on Sundays. His father was always in a good mood as he cooked, boasting beforehand about how good the Chinese recipes were that he had learned in a remote hacienda in Peru. Maybe his father had made these meals for him, in this always incomplete past, to celebrate the meeting of father and son.

40   Unfamiliar anxiety, like a question without a subject, grew in him as he understood that he had never properly acknowledged his father's gesture; he hadn't even understood it. Actually, he had rejected his father's cooking one time, saying that it was too spicy. He must have been about fifteen then, a recent convert devoutly practicing the religion of natural foods, when he left the table with the plate of fish in his hands. He went out to the kitchen to turn on the faucet and quickly washed away the flesh boiled in soy sauce and ginger. His mother came to the kitchen and scolded him for what he had just done, a seemingly harmless act, but from then on an irreparable one. He returned to the table in silence, sullen, but his father didn't appear to be offended. Or did he suspect that one day his son's meal would be refused by his own son when he served it?

The emotion could still wound him, but it could also make him laugh. There was a kind of irony in this repeating to a large extent his father's gestures as he concocted an unusual flavor in the kitchen. However, like a sigh that only acquires some meaning by turning upon itself, he discovered a symmetry in the repetitions, a symmetry that revealed the agony of emotions not easily understood.

Just like animals that feed their young, we feed ourselves with a promise that food will taste good, he said to himself. We prepare a recipe with painstaking detail so that our children will recognize us in a complete history of flavor.

He must have muttered this out loud because the child looked up.

"What?" he said, "Italian?"

"Peruvian," he corrected. "With a taste of the mountains, a mixture of   45
Indian, Chinese, and Spanish."

The child laughed, as if he'd heard a private joke in the sound of the words.

"When we go to Lima, I'll take you around to the restaurants," he promised.

The child broke into laughter again.

"It tastes good," said the child.

"It tastes better than yesterday's," the man said.   50

He poured some orange juice. The boy kneeled in the chair and ate a bit of everything. He ate more out of curiosity than appetite.

He felt once again that brief defenselessness that accompanies the act of eating one's own cooking. Behind that flavor, he knew, lurked the raw materials, the separate foods cooked to render them neutral, a secret known only to the cook, who combined ingredients and proportions until something different was presented to eyes and mouth. This culinary act could be an adventure, a hunting foray. And the pleasure of creating a transformation must be shared, a kind of brief festival as the eaters decipher the flavors, knowing that an illusion has taken place.

Later, he looked for a potato in the pantry and he held it up against the unfiltered light in the window. It was large, and it fit perfectly in his barely closed hand. He was not surprised that the misshapen form of this swollen tuber adapted to the contour of his hand; he knew the potato adapted to different lands, true to its own internal form, as if it occupied stolen space. The entire history of his people was here, he said to himself, surviving in a territory overrun and pillaged several times, growing in marginal spaces, under siege and waiting.

He left the apartment, went down the stairs and over to the tree on the hillock. It was a perfect day, as if the entire history of daytime were before him. The grass was ablaze, standing for all the grass he had ever seen. With both hands, he dug, and the earth opened up to him, cold. He placed the potato there, and he covered it up quickly. Feeling slightly embarrassed, he looked around. He went back up the stairs, wiping his hands, almost running.

55   The boy was standing at the balcony, waiting for him; he had seen it all.

"A tree's going to grow there!" said the boy, alarmed.

"No," he said soothingly, "potatoes aren't trees. If it grows, it will grow under the ground."

The child didn't seem to understand everything, but then suddenly he laughed.

"Nobody will even know it's there," he said, excited by such complicity with his father.

Poetry   **Alicia Suskin Ostriker**

THE ORANGE CAT

for Vikram Seth

The orange cat on the porch
Regards the tiny bird
Out on the pine tree limb
And yawns without a word.

The morning air is mild,   5
The tawny hillsides seem
Halfway from sleep to waking;
The cat appears to dream,

Which is of course illusion;
A harsh jay on the hill   10
Is answered by three quail
Clucks, and a warbler's trill.

The cat who is not hungry
Can listen in repose
To bird calls, with that pleasant   15
Touch of desire's throes

We feel before a painting
Of nude or odalisque,
The lust without the pain,
Arousal without risk   20

Of failure, mild *frisson*—
Like drink, and no hangover,
Sex without friction, love
Minus the awkward lover.

Poetry   **Michael Palmer**

THE CORD

To whistle or whisper
To breathe along the bone

To twist the torso so
(That we drink the grey water)

5   To loose the limbs
(That we bathe in their dust)

To laugh, just as monsters must—
mouths open, tongues taut

To itch and to scratch
10 just as monsters must

To trace the sleeve of praise
against the liquid dark

To elevate our offerings
of burnt flesh and mint

15 (Line the windcaves
with panther skins)

To see voices yes
under light's duress

To conduct the streaming pit
20 (That we live in it yes?)

for C.E. at 70

Creative Nonfiction   **Anne Panning**

REMEMBERING, I WAS NOT THERE

It is 1963. My mother, Barbara Louise Griep, works at the family cream-
ery, sells buckets of ice cream and bricks of butter, saves wages for the
wedding. She has already purchased yards and yards of creamy white
satin and made, by herself, one hundred cloth-covered buttons to go down
the back. She sits home nights with pins held between her teeth: stitch and
hem. Her older sisters wash dishes and laugh; her mother, my grandmother Lucille, is not happy with the engagement, and says so. My mother's soon-to-be-husband, Lowell William Arthur Panning, is out driving
country roads, crushing and tossing empty beer cans out the window of
his light blue '57 Chevy Custom.

Do not marry him, I wish to warn her. He's wild already, though oddly
charming with his square black glasses, his white T-shirt, his loose rolled-
up jeans. His hair rolls back at the forehead like an Elvis or better, a Buddy
Holly with narrow boy's hips, the beginning of pockmarks.

I would stop them surely, but this: *impossible.* They cannot hear me. I
am born two whole years later, the first baby daughter with black hair like
an Indian's, cloudy gray eyes that would magically turn gold years later.
There is already the first son, James, with black piercing eyes from the
start. We will thrill them, James and I, blinking, innocent, adorable bun-
dles. My mother will give up The School of Nursing. She will give up delicate white hose and the starched white caps with pointed wings she has so
dreamed of wearing.

I wish to sit them both down, say *don't.* You will destroy yourselves,
everything dear. You will make your lives harder than they have to be.

My father, Lowell W. A. Panning, is finishing up his studies at Lee's Barber   5
College on 7th Street in St. Paul. He learns about scalp diseases, shaving
with a straightedge, crew cuts, dandruff, and proper placement of comb
and scissors in the hands. A barber? Just months ago he was almost a professional baseball player with the Milwaukee Braves, the Chicago Cubs,
the Minnesota Twins. The scouts were there with clipboards, Lowell W. A.
Panning was on the mound, bases were loaded, and he struck the batter
out—other fantastic feats. The scouts buzzed with offers, shook the nimble
hands of my father that would become so adept at haircuts mere months
later.

So close.

The next weekend my father was caught with vodka and beer, kicked
off the team: the end, but *almost.* This is the story of his life—*almost*—and
he will tell me this tale of near-fame and glory repeatedly as I get older, as

I learn of his many defeats. He will tell the story belching over a six-pack at age forty-one.

The day before the wedding, my father's grandfather dies. This is the William Arthur of my father's namesake. He has a long sober face from generations of no touch, no hugs in the Panning family. He dies from lack of affection and love—a dry, curled-up gray heart. My mother and father call each other up on the phone: what do we do, what do we do about the wedding? It is too late to cancel or postpone. Both know it.

That night, my mother goes to sleep in the north bedroom for the last time, feet curled up in her nightgown. The room is painted soft yellow, and shadows of maple leaves move across the wall like waving hands: goodbye. She places her palms together and presses them under the pillow; she's eighteen. She has been a good girl her whole life. She wonders if her Lowell W. A. Panning is sad about the death. She, herself, feels no sadness. She worries; she convinces herself this is what people do: marry. She knows she will change him; he will be better. And herself? She puts herself on hold, stops, to become a wife.

10   My father is out on the farm, on the porch, listening to the creak of the old windmill. Beer flows. His sparkling bachelorhood wavers in front of him. He contemplates kissing all the fun that is his life good-bye for a wife. His father, my grandfather Wilbert, cuffs him on the head, untucks his soiled undershirt, and sighs. "This is about booze," my grandfather says, fat and angry. "Dammit. You have to take care of that girl." He goes inside.

My father loves her. He thinks she is a prize. Plus, he has been waiting for her to finish high school so they can finally do it, marry. His only gripe is the wedding day falls on pheasant hunting opener. In a secret way he cannot explain, he would rather be out with his shotgun.

He hopes he can be a good barber, provider. How can I tell him he will do so well at one but not the other?

When my mother walks down the papered aisle, it crunches. I am in the shadows, tiny and invisible, marveling at her golden hair, her long slender back, her dark brown eyes that are fixed steadily on the cross in front of her. I am the little girl she will someday tell, "I have never got anything I have wanted, Anne. Do you know how that feels? Nothing. Be careful with marriage." Even though she is not.

I will cause her my own share of grief later, but on their wedding day, when Minnesota winds blow cool and the church bell rings, I watch her in wonder and alarm, my hands up over my open mouth. *Help. Don't.* I watch her in fear, scared for myself.

* * *

The honeymoon is a no-big-deal. They drive up to a motel in Ham Lake   15
with no television and no swimming pool. It is not even two hours away
from the town they both grew up in. The sun on my mother's head makes
her warm and sleepy. My father rubs her cheek with a knuckle as a semi-
truck passes. My mother holds her shiny diamond up in the air and wig-
gles her fingers. The glitter alerts me to the new anti-life that is forming—one
minus one equals zero. I see figures of them both melting into a black hole
I might fall into. I see my mother fascinated by her new wifeness, and
shudder. My father stops at the store for a twelve-pack. Just in case we get
thirsty, he says, but fools neither of them.

Still 1963, and already a Panning's Barber Shop. John Kennedy is shot, and
my father swoons into Reggie's Bar next door. The ceramic barber's chair
is left pumped up high, spinning. It is dark in the bar and my father is
crying. He doesn't know why, but I could tell him. I could tell him it is not
being loved and touched as a child, a cold mother and cold father and little
food for so many years—lost youth. These are his problems, I could tell
him, but don't.

My mother is at home, sewing brass buttons onto her hand-knit cardi-
gan. The television is on, but she is not surprised. She has enough sense to
know anyone that good, that groomed, is bound to die in office. She
doesn't cry, but lets out a long, dry wail and is fine. She needs a friend.
Everyone is gone. She has given up her life. She irons, reads, cleans, gets
ready to have a baby. What is a national tragedy to her when she has already lost it all?

When I do finally spring to life, after James, there are only three of us at
home: boy, girl, mom. I learn to think of father as absent, invisible. I learn
to take care of my mother, who is really just a girl. I learn to be quiet so she
doesn't yell. At age four, I tell my mother that I can get a job so there is
more money. At age six, I learn to walk in my shoes carefully so they don't
wear out. I learn to misunderstand men at age ten when I see James getting a BB gun when there is supposedly no money for me to join Junior
Great Books Club.

My father sails in and out. He dances drunk and lets James and me
hang on his flexed biceps when he's in the mood. Take a picture of me and
the kids like this! he shouts at my mother, then throws up. And my mother
. . . my mother. I see it happening, I know it will happen, I try to warn her.
She does not leave him when everything screams *leave*. She's in it for the
kids, she tries to believe and stand by. I am unfortunately old enough to
grasp it all.

Before I was born, I knew this would happen.   20

Fiction   **David James Poissant**

THE HISTORY OF FLIGHT

All day the fish flew, and the girl watched them.

Bass bellied into the sky. Koi muscled up from their manicured ponds. Marlins, with their serrated backs, sawed the clouds.

From her favorite branch on her favorite climbing tree in her front yard, the girl watched and wondered at the beauty of the fish: perch swarming rooftops, sharks torpedoing, blender-faced and gray, guppies that made patchwork skirts of the sky.

It wasn't just her street, her town, her state. All over the country, aquariums were emptying out, pet stores boarding up, restaurants shutting down.

5   The local Red Lobster, unable to support itself on shellfish and Cheddar Bay Biscuits, stood empty, door padlocked, its OPEN sign unlit.

The birds appeared confused.

The girl had woken to an empty goldfish bowl. She'd slept with her window open, and, now, Mr. Fins was gone, out the window and into the night.

So, the girl climbed her tree and sat and watched, and the fish flew. They fattened the skies, fins paddling, gills like bellows opening and puffing shut. They were free now, the fish. Their mouths *O*ed the air. The girl waved, and the fish with whiskers waggled them.

The girl missed her goldfish, but, otherwise, she was enjoying this turn of events. She liked the sky so full of scales it hurt, sometimes, to look.

10   Others were not so pleased: the ship captains with their empty nets; grandfathers on docks, their cane poles unbent and the grandchildren bored; Roman Catholics who didn't mind so much the proliferation of the Ichthus symbol but who were at a loss for what to do on Fridays.

The girl saw those around her unhappy, and so she called out to those fish nearest her. "Come back," she called, and the fish, had they been able to laugh, would have guffawed. They cartwheeled and spun. They touched the treetops with the tips of their fins.

The fish were wary of the girl, and why shouldn't they have been? How many centuries had humans caught them? How long, stuffed or tanked, had fish gussied up these people's walls? The fish preferred this new arrangement. They liked their sky without hooks in it. They liked their skyways harpoon-free. People stood, openmouthed, while fish shadows darkened their faces, and the fish liked that too.

Skimming the earth, the fish dive-bombed and somersaulted and sashayed. And if, once in a while, a minnow suffocated in a keyhole or a mackerel fried on a power line, if, every now and then, a smokestack gassed a flock of smelt, was this worse than the ocean's oil and toxic sludge, its hypodermic needles and plastic six-pack rings?

Could they, the fish would have whooped, and those who could croak—the catfish, the chub—croaked with all they had in them.

The fish learned semaphore. Their bodies, shimmering, made brilliant   15 flags. But the men and women below knew no semaphore, and so the fish learned to make pictures, shapes in the sky: Smiley faces. Skulls and crossbones. A fist with middle finger raised.

Each morning, the girl climbed her tree, and each morning she called to the fish. "Come back," she called each morning, and each morning, inasmuch as they could, the fish jeered.

The girl got angry. She saw the fish saddled, imagined them bridled and reined. She imagined spurs for her Converse and the kicks she'd give a grouper's side to get it going.

But it wasn't a ride the girl wanted.

"Come down!" she said to the fish.

But the fish, having worked very hard at getting free, weren't having it.   20 Eons, they'd stuck to lakes and streams, to oceans and to seas. Ages, they'd tread water, forgoing limb and thumb. They'd even resisted blowholes, most of them. The fish were of the water and only of the water, before, suddenly, they weren't. And, now that they weren't, they weren't going back in, ever.

The girl called, "Come down right now!"

"We can't *hear* you!" the fish would have said had they been able to make words leave their mouths. Instead, they zigzagged and careened. They slapped the trees with their tails.

Conditions worsened. The fish bumped satellite dishes and knocked over antennas. All over the country, TV signals were going out. Angry customers clogged phone lines while cable companies lost millions on repairs.

But the fish weren't just a nuisance. One whale shark took out a Boeing 747. The same day, a smaller craft went down in a fog of salmon, fish confettied before the propellers locked. Air traffic controllers pulled headsets from their heads and threw up their hands. By that afternoon, flights were grounded, all of them.

Everywhere, it seemed, people were out of work, the sea captains with   25 nothing to fish for and the pet stores with no fish to sell, the Red Lobster employees with no tables to wait and the pilots with no planes to fly. The grandfathers, without hooks to bait or fish to pull from lines, told the same stories over and over—always, grandfathers told the same stories over and over, but, now, even more so—while, in deckchairs or splayed on docks, grandchildren writhed.

The unemployed sought other incomes, and it wasn't long before many turned to methamphetamines, to heroin and cocaine, before many stood under streetlamps and lifted skirts or lowered pants at passing cars—the flight attendants and Red Lobster line cooks, the seafarers and PetSmart employees. Even the grandfathers and grandchildren—bored, disconsolate—raised their hemlines, dropped their drawers.

The girl watched all of this in despair.

"Come down," the girl called to the fish. "It's for your own good!" Though, even as she said this, the girl knew it was not true. What she meant was: *Come down that we might find a use for you. Come down before it's too late.*

"Please," she said.

30   But, now, it was as if the fish really *couldn't* hear. They'd foregone all attempts at communication. No more semaphore. Not even the occasional lewd pictogram. The fish traversed the skies as though no one roamed below.

"Please!" she cried. "Our grandchildren are addicted to meth and dropping their pants at the traffic!"

The fish coursed, indifferent, overhead.

The girl came down from her tree and searched her garage and found an old, weather-beaten kite. She cut the string from the kite and returned to the yard with the spool in her hands. She climbed the tree, and she knew what she must do.

She didn't want to see the fish hurt, didn't want them back in the water or pushed onto plates. She only wanted to stop what she worried was coming, and perhaps this way—

35   She pictured the fish moored like zeppelins, saw them paraded like Thanksgiving Day Macy's balloons. She saw them over football stadiums, cameras strapped to their heads. She wondered whether, caught, the fish might be bolted to car dealership sidewalks. Closing her eyes, the girl could almost see them already, fish bobbing in tandem with the bright, inflatable men that somehow made Americans want to buy cars.

Or, perhaps the fish needed only to be caught the way balloons are caught, or kites. Perhaps this would become the fashion, a fish for every wrist.

And there was this, if nothing else: A balloon could still be loosed. A kite could still catch a gust and be gone. And, if the fish must be caught, there lingered the knowledge—delicate, profane—that something caught can always get away.

The girl moved to the end of her favorite branch, and, when the very next fish sidled by, a tuna—fat and blue-backed—she lassoed its tail. The tuna reared back, bucked. It thrashed and heaved. It all but pulled the girl from her branch before, exhausted, it hung, a comic book speech bubble empty overhead.

The girl climbed down from her tree. She secured the fish to the kite string and the kite string to her wrist. Then she ran through town, tuna in tow. She ran down Main Street and through the town square. She ran round the fountain and along the library steps.

"Look," she said. "I've caught one!"   40

But already the people were unpacking their ammo and oiling their guns.

"Wait," the girl said. "You don't have to do that. We can catch them, see?" She gave the string a tug, and the tuna bobbed, obedient.

The people nodded. They attached their scopes and their silencers. They donned their bandoliers. One man was trying to load the cannon on the courthouse lawn.

"Wait!" the girl cried, and the townspeople—the grandfathers and grandchildren, the sea captains and their crews, the restaurant workers in their aprons and the pilots in their aviator glasses, even the PetSmart employees, some of whom loved fish very much—all turned their gun muzzles to the sky.

Above, the fish watched, amused. They circled and funneled and schooled   45
between clouds. They were lithe. They were fast. They were not worried. This, why this would be the exact opposite of shooting fish in a barrel.

But the fish were wrong.

The first was a sturgeon, hollow-point to the eye.

Next, shotguns peppered a congregation of sardines.

The girl looked away. She reeled in her line. She held the tuna to her chest.

"I'm sorry," the girl said. "I'm sorry. I'm sorry."   50

But the tuna wouldn't look at her. She was no different, no better than the rest of them. Maybe she'd wanted to help. Maybe, had she tried earlier, she'd have kept them alive. Except that, maybe, in the end, a bullet was a knife was a noose was the string of a kite.

The girl looked up.

And then—as in the days to come—the fish began to fall.

Creative Nonfiction   **Lia Purpura**

ON LOOKING AWAY: A PANORAMIC

Once I saw:

at an exhibition, balanced on its points, a blowfish, inflated, shellacked. Its empty stomach was mottled pink, brown, and cream. Its mouth was open, the lips a thin, stretched O of surprise. So easy someone had made it to forget the working insides, to forget, so we might tilt toward the light a hollow balloon of pleasure. Dip safely a finger into the spaces between flared needles.

And once . . .

But it wasn't just once. There are so many things to consider looking away from.

Once an emerald dragonfly landed in front of me on a cashier's thin arm. Its jittery sheen articulated as she moved and made her smaller by that trick, partial, and barely seen.

5   Tattoos are sad things. So one-time-only. The need to be marked so openly displayed and then, well, that little picture is all you get. And how much the poor image is meant to hold: such a record of need, all painstaking decision or quick impetuousness recorded on the skin. The snapshot of the big event and not the big event itself (the one that lives behind the skin, always, always unseen) makes anyone forever the guy with his old war stories. About Johnnie. Remember him? True love you had for that guy. Like a brother . . . wife gave me his medal. . . . Heraldry, desire, homage crushed down to shamrock, Tasmanian devil, or, demurely—let's not go too far, let's not go crazy—a sweet-pea vine at the ankle. Muted registers, in case of disappointment. Muted regions of the body, in case of having-to-learn-to-live-with.

Once I saw them.

But how that came to be involves a complicated set of strategies, the history of our own Office of War Information, a break with the Geneva Conventions. I saw the bloated faces of the evil tyrant's sons. Browned. Potatoed. Like things hauled from saltwater. It must be that proof is dilatory, elastic, as expansive as the very early morning hours devoted to a single task. After all, "It is not a practice the United States engages in on a normal basis" said Secretary of State Donald Rumsfeld. And "I honestly believe that these two are particularly bad characters, and that it's important for the Iraqi people to see them, to know they're gone, to know they're dead and to know they're not coming back." For *this* purpose the faces are shown, for the purpose of identifying monsters. For surely monsters look like monsters—see? Enduringly. And as surely, there is a child in bed, insistent, *but, but-ing* in the buttery light of happy endings: *what about the troll/witch/dragon—are they really dead?* Surely there is a mother imposing *sleep now, shhhh.* (And surely, the child—didn't you?—gathers the loose threads of the story into her hand, since threads show in even the best stories, and asks: *what happened to the beanstalk after?* And: *did they eat the witch they kicked into the oven?* And: *aren't there more witches out there? I know this story goes on,* thinks the child. . . .)

Once I saw her.   10
   But then, just like that, the next summer she was gone. When I called the director of the state fair, his secretary told me that people complained and said she was inappropriate and was being exploited. In her air-conditioned trailer with her newspaper and knitting, sitting, tiny legs crossed, tiny bonnet of blue calico and little calico apron kindling questions (how old *is* she? is she from this century? were, maybe, people smaller then?). The seat a little too high, just an inch, so her feet would dangle, making her even more specimenlike. Polite yet brief about the questions. Oh, she was a lovely person, and she liked her work and chose to do it, the state fair director's secretary told me. Velvet rope between her and the quiet people filing by. Nothing about her left you exactly breathless. Gravitational issues though: the onlookers' sudden, unexpected shame, embarrassment—no clue that this would happen—like entering a river, and suddenly the river is alive, minnows uncomfortably nibbling at toes, the current tugging. Soon an iciness not at all refreshing.
   Most everyone hurried through.

One might resist:
   touching a chicken to clean it, and retreat from its smallness and loose, bumpy skin where once feathers were and were scalded off. One might refuse the articulated movement of its legs while washing it under the water in the sink and still eat the chicken. Cooked by another: *Mediterranean. Fantastique.* Wined and buttered breast and thigh and leg transformed. Under pineapple, so you don't have to see. And can finally eat.

One might resist: 15
   the article about a mother, hot water, steel wool, her child. One might resist the phrase "her child." One might start to read, and knowing at once what's coming, seeing where it's going *(bathtub, peroxide, wound,* and *squirt)* turn away. Feel the sheer drop-off, the height scaled fast and the sharp rocks shift underfoot. One might keep the article, file it, because all around the air is thinning. Because such helplessness splinters anyone. If

you're not a mother, or a father, you don't know what it's like to want—and maybe only once, and maybe only glancingly—to do anything, anything to make the crying stop, to stop your own helplessness in the face of it. How, even if only for a moment, you feel broken apart. And that's when the shards start flying.

Remember the last time you had a speck in the eye? How you could think of nothing else?

But you closed your eyes to stop the irritation.

But you took a deep breath and the moment passed.

20   Right?

Here is a boy whose eye could be fixed. In the West. In America. But in the photo it's slipping inward. And here is his mother whose black, body-long burqa, when she squats, makes her look like a mountain. A mountain of slag from a freshly dug ditch. Whose entire face is covered with meshing. Here is a mother whose eyes are graphed, whose cheek is graphed when he flies to her and presses hard for a kiss. What is a kiss through mesh—a graphed breath? Here is a mother who cannot find the eyes of her son. Here is a boy with a mountain for a mother. A newspaper lays these things before you, at your feet—good dog—in black and white, and black and white allows the incremental 1-2-3 of understanding. A reader says I see, I see. Then leaves. For orange juice. Water. Small pleasures/consolations of tea.

If I am going to stay with these children (the girl's name is Sylena), I have to consider what they turn towards. Heliotropically. Tiny, back-bent sup-plicants searching under beds, around corners: *Mom, where are you?* Child-as-heliostat fixed to reflect the sun's rays, continuously, even as the sun turns away. And heliotropes: any kind of small, reddish-purple flower from Heliopolis, city of ruins, ruined, with a modern city superimposed, oh site of hurry and bustle, with ghost words and echoes, our ears too dulled to gauge a cry—of protest? exhaustion? hunger rising? And here, still standing in the city, my city, the story of the terrible bathtub, the story a reader might choose—*I* chose, because I am on trial here—to pass over one recent morning, to concentrate instead on the interesting demolition, 10th Avenue, the whole west side of the building torn off, the rooms like holes, empty, except for one.

With a white bathtub.

That stops me.

25   Ladder built back to the scene I keep turning away from.

The tub is clean. Very clean of the bodies (her body) (Sylena's) (and the soaps and towels heaped on the floor would have been wet, and worse). (And here comes the wet bed that the child didn't, didn't mean to, that I couldn't, I cannot . . . fix, clean. Fold away.)

And look! There are Murphy beds, still, in this part of town. See them in the torn up apartments! Remember the velvet ropes across the rooms in the Tenement Museum and the Murphy beds there. I remember that . . . safely now. I'm safe for now.

I paid my admission.

Then this comes:

How would all the tenement children live in just two rooms?

Crammed, I suppose. Crammed into, like these specimens I'm here to see, I'm not turning away from. Here in the museum of things gone terribly wrong, the Mütter Museum of Medical Oddities, in Philadelphia. All the specimens: a loud carbuncle in plaster, on the back of a neck, like a scream. A smallpox pustule like an open mouth, its lips pulled down in sorrow in the photograph. The (forgive me) macaroni & cheese-with-ketchup face of a syphilitic. The gorgeous phrase "cavity of the sacrum" followed by photos of Frederik Ruysch's tiny, mounted fetal skeletons, some playing miniature bone-and-ligament violins, some jarred and injected with wax, talc, cinnabar, oil of lavender, alcohol, black pepper, colored pigments to better illustrate the transience of life and other allegorical lessons. And some he draped with embroidered lace. And to some he gave a mesentery handkerchief to accompany postures of grief.

The word *caries.* The words *phial* and *lancet* and *paregoric.* And *mercury pastille.*   30

One fetus—like Da Vinci's Hyperion Man, limbs out to measure the breadth of the known universe with its body—is really one star of conjoined twins, a head at either end and arms and legs as shining points. A star in the process of exploding, but caught. A star that didn't explode at all. Among such pinkness and tension and sadness, among the weightless beings strung up and clamped to best show their features, heads bent below a meniscus of poison, heads cresting the terrible solutions—I sat down. I stepped into their sleep.

And when I peered around to see their open backs, where the seam of them split, and the heat clanked on in the ancient radiators, and a toilet somewhere loudly flushed and the lobby voices were pistons churning the room . . . what was the difference, *sitting with?*

I read the medieval explanation about these bodies: God's anger. The Devil's hand at work. Some fear, danger, tragedy striking a mother straight through to her child. I looked and looked past reason to the useless necks again. To *sit with* you have to look into the gap in your understanding, not drive the conversation, not know where it's going. Not know beforehand at all where it's heading. I read once, *there is a quality of legend about freaks . . . like a person in a fairy tale who stops and demands that you answer a riddle.* That's the space. That open field, where you're sitting

with, and don't have the answer, but an atmosphere of response is
forming.

I'm reading about a death-row inmate called "Little Lew." And though
here he is, framed in his neat newspaper photo, he is hard to see for all his
running—away from home at seven, then a little blur escaping from ju-
venile detention. Little Lew, who, by twelve, was already a father. (He's
flying now.) Who loved guns from early on ("I can't even explain why. Just
had to have one."). At 5′3″ and 117 pounds, he's feather-blown. Of his
weight, say *Welter:* "to roll," "to roll about, as in mud," and used figura-
tively as in: "they weltered in sin." "To be soaked, stained or bathed," as in:
"the corpses weltered in their own blood." As in: "Leoma Chmielewski,"
after Lew shot her in the face during a robbery.

35   It took nine corrections officers to hold him down while the IV tubes
were inserted in his arms.

The prisons' chief said he would have preferred not to have cameras
involved in the execution process.

Of the drugs used to anesthetize, paralyze, and kill (sodium pentothal,
pancuronium bromide, and potassium chloride), the first, the article
states, can mask symptoms of an agonizing death by suffocation. It's
banned by the American Veterinary Medical Association.

There were no signs that Williams suffered "once his struggles ceased"
the article continues. "But that does not mean he did not feel pain" the
article also reads.

Little kids playing hide-and-seek close their eyes and suppose no one
can see them.

Safe, safe, safe.

40   Here's Little Lew's little picture, stamp-sized on page 1 of the paper.
Below it *See Killer p. A2, Columbus Dispatch*, no picture, just words. But I
see him there. I see him and see him. He is an argument hanging in air. He
is a memory no one wants. He's stubborn. Little Lew who ran away keeps
turning up unannounced. Shoots the face off my peace right now.

Right now I was sketching his face, the mustache and beard that encircled his open mouth. Two easy concentricities, my favorite design to
draw. One circle inside another. It's on the necklace I wear, a lozenge of
silver with a bronze washer soldered on. I believe in the circle. Small circle
on a larger one, my child always with me that way.

I also collect washers I find in the street. You'd be surprised at how
many there are to be found. I have three already from Columbus, Ohio,
where I'm living for a few weeks. At home I have small pea-sized ones, and
large ones I can barely palm. Pocked, rusty, and scratched; smooth and
bright. Lots from Baltimore and from New York. Sometimes I think I
should catalog them with little tags and note the circumstances under

which they were found. One has a raised pattern like a prayer ring, a chaplet, whose bumps you thumb along while reciting your Our Fathers and Hail Marys. One is black; one is toothed like a kid's sketch of the sun. Easy to slide into my little mania. Even a friend of mine looks for them now. He finds them everywhere, though it took him a while to see them. I told him he had to train his eye for the object he desired, to practice being alert for the shape and sudden shine. And then they would come to him.

Two weeks after Lew was executed, another man lay strapped to the same gurney. The *Columbus Dispatch* reported that it took a team of prison health workers twenty minutes to find the veins on murderer John Glen Roe and to insert the shunts that would hold the needles carrying the lethal drugs. Family members of his victim, Donette Crawford, held hands and watched the execution on closed-circuit TV.

And where did they go after that? After the warden announced he was dead and Donette's sister, Michelle, raised up the hands of her father and sister's fiancé and said "Yes." After they saw the last breath, and were certain he was gone—where did they go? At 10:24 in the morning—out to breakfast? For a walk? To the cemetery? Where do you go and what do you do after watching an execution?

Here's another scene about staying to see: 45

Once I wanted to squat down and be with the yellows and greens and trace the U of a crushed frog's jawline. Its missing belly was a washed-out place. The middle was a smear, a wetness in the ease of light rain. And then its legs picked up again. Bent close to it, I wanted to sing aloud the song in my head, "Everyday is Like Sunday," and it could've been Sunday when this happened, it was still fresh. I was looking for its hand, the longer index finger and little thumb (I'll call them "hand," "finger" and "thumb") pressed white to the bone on the blue asphalt. Why stand over it? Why want to stay if the day is so joyously unfolding? The frog was all mouth. The crush opened and spread it and made it as wide as the day was wide. But I was dragged away. I had plans, a talk to give. Spring air, rain, all the bodies filing into the auditorium—I wanted to stay, but there was so much going on. Only now can I return to it. The yellows and greens and reds gone pink in the rain and spreading. Some brown from tires, and the treads evident. The sky was uncolored and *silent and gray*, the song was saying. But the frog wasn't silent and gray. Not at all.

And another:

At the El Greco show at the Met, the paintings soar because they are huge and because the figures themselves are so radically elongated. I'm finally face to face with the one I've been searching for, the one I've known since I was a child, looking through my parents' art books, "St. Martin and the Beggar." And because the painting is so large, I'm eye to eye with the beggar's hands, his terribly, painfully long, knobbed knuckles. And the others, too, gathered around it comment on his hands. And isn't this the way children go about looking, those for whom such attention is sanctioned, for whom finding is daily, who state simply, aloud, or pose as a question: *why are his knuckles so long?* Travel up the ripple of the beggar's arm to St. Martin's silver armor and over his white-rumped horse into the gray sky behind them. Travel up the leg of the beggar, bent unnaturally in at the knee, the effect lengthening the foot. You come to it, bring all your desire to the painting because you seek in it a mood, a sensation. So that you can say, by way of sight, "the beggar, pained and cold, is receiving a portion of St. Martin's cloak," and be in the presence of something unspeakable, by way of the unnatural bend of the body, the graying and bluing of the body, which is part agony, part beauty.

And this one, occuring on a day like any other day:

50   Days after the photo of an Iraqi prisoner is released, the famous one where he is made to stand on a box with wires attached to his hands, black hood on his head and black cloak over his body (he was told not to move or he'd be electrocuted), I walk past a church in Bolton Hill, in Baltimore, on the north side of which is a Tiffany stained-glass Christ in flowing robes. The leaded panes emanate from Christ's hands, his body inclines toward the street, bending, as if to whisper to me. And the superimposition rises. The images converge. It's the spring of 2004, and I will be able to say this in America and know, reader, you, too, will have seen the hooded prisoner. First the words: *is he not Christ?* about the prisoner come. Then—though I am not Christian—all those who inhabit Christ's body populate the glass, and it lights, and the wash of light is suddenly made of motes, of little sharpened points, of heads and bodies like small fists, upthrust. Christ has found the prisoner's posture, Christ took it on. Or always knew. And since I have seen, since Christ looked into me—what a prisoner I must be. Or speck. Or mote. Or single light.

What to say in a situation like this, when seeing, you are unexpectedly seen?

Once I saw something that could've been a horror but wasn't—my friend's arm around his daughter, first at rest on the small of her back, then wrapping further to make a full circle. It was beautiful. Loving. There was no swarm of bees in the girl's stomach. I didn't have to see, in her place, that other girl, too big on a man's lap, on the bus in Warsaw, being "dandled"— awful word that came to me and was everafter poisoned—and try, in a language I hardly spoke, to say "stop." I didn't have to see, for once, as a mother and leap up. Or remember anything with my body.

* * *

I look away. And if she's still there, and she is, the girl in the bathtub, the girl in the article held by the words, and her name is Sylena—if I look away and she is still there, then I am not free.

How to stay with her? As if with the dying, by way of a vigil, which is to form, with others, a house of shelter, to make a green respite, a *hospice*, a place a traveler might rest while passing though? I watched the sun at the window over the—how strange the precision while my friend was dying—*cafe curtains*. The cool June afternoon resounded with, only once but loudly, a car alarm, and neighbors' voices. I watched from the foot of the bed past the boxes of meds and the useless hundreds of vitamin bottles, and didn't turn away from the moment of passing, though it was more like a ceasing. Because nothing stepped forth in the form of announcement, no herald. The light was just part of the branches scratching, and the scratching bore no message. It was June 24th. I did not turn away. The knob of the bed was an anchor, burnished. Like—may I veer, just briefly here?—the bare breasts on the statue of the muse on 33rd and Charles Street, her bronze breasts shining from touch, from men late at night, boys after school just touching for luck, and why not, walking with buddies and laughing, everyone does, it's just a moment to be alive. So alive.

The bedposts were mahogany and they shone too, from years and years   55 of touching.

In Tod Browning's film *Freaks*, the side-show performers "live by a code unto themselves," says the narrator at the begining. The pinheads, the dwarfs, the bearded woman, the worm-man in a sack, the Siamese twins live in a camp in their carved and painted folksy caravans. The interesting tension in the film is between the arc of the story line and the viewer's desire to see the freaks, to be allowed to see and not have to turn away, a kind of sanctioned privacy. The camera lingers over them and gives each the space to perform his or her own calling-card trick or accomplishment. The woman who used her feet as deftly as hands. The limbless man who moved like a worm and who rolled his own cigarettes with his teeth and struck a match and smoked. Beyond this, we are aware of waiting for *something* to happen. And it does. All the freaks, seeking revenge on the duplicitous "normal" performer, assemble under a rickety caravan to launch their attack; it's raining, the freaks are crawling on their bellies in the mud toward the beautiful/evil one to do her in. But then, they all fall together in a crumple and each of them is lost to the pile, and their singularity, yes, their *nobility*, dissolves.

Once there was a green elephant and a purple elephant and they lived in a house together. The house and the elephants were part of a old German children's game I played with at my grandmother's house. They lived together in other ways, as shapes and textures, quite aside from being elephants, and now they come back to me as the pleasure of colors paired up in the garden world of alyssum and lavender, purple aster and moss. The elephants sat squatly with their fat legs out in front and stomachs curved over. And the little wrinkles in their trunks were nice elephant touches. They were made of soapstone and were nicked with fingernail scratches. But they lived as colors best.

Today, purple calls sun down to light the soft green of thyme, undried and fuzzily growing. Green and purple pair themselves so the eye might gather on clover, lamb's ear, morning glory.

What did the colors do to my eye?

60   Not once have I forgotten that the elephants were contorted, stubby, disproportionate.

Reader, I finished the article. About Sylena.

When I finished I had an inkling about a word. The word *strafe* came forth, unbidden. I looked it up for confirmation: *to punish. To reprimand viciously. From the German.*

What did I see, after I read? After I read, I stared out at the backyard and made a calming list: apple tree, loblolly, morning glory, ash. Rose-of-Sharon, tiger lily. 1-2-3 of black telephone wires against the blue sky, the Every Good Boy (Does Fine) for the invisible notes to climb. Checked the porthole of leaves that lets me see through to the next street. Sunk a bit into the deep brown of the shed. Opened the window a little for breeze.

What did I see while reading?

65   That once I used steel wool as a ball of tinsel in a pinch.

That when I said *fuck you* to my great aunt, and she washed my mouth out with soap (as soap occurred in the article, too), I studied the scratches in the very dull, very clean silver spiggots and, so close, saw the green spot where a drip wore the porcelain away.

Such focus made me dizzy, even then. "Custody of the eyes," my friend, a former nun tells me, is the practice of training your sight to focus only on the meditation, task, prayer in front of you, and you let nothing else in. But what if the object in front of you swims, dares swim away?

I will tell you a silver spiggot can swim. And the sky be white. And a faucet bear a hurricane.

I focused on the green porcelain spot as if it were the sun. I found I could make it be many pictures—a mossy rock, a turtle's back. But I tried to keep it the sun. I was maybe eight at the time.

70   Even then I focused hard.

I felt I might be tested on the things I saw.

Fiction   **Karen Russell**

ST. LUCY'S HOME FOR GIRLS RAISED BY WOLVES

> Stage 1: The initial period is one in which everything is new, exciting, and interesting for your students. It is fun for your students to explore their new environment.
>
> —from *The Jesuit Handbook on Lycanthropic Culture Shock*

At first, our pack was all hair and snarl and floor-thumping joy. We forgot the barked cautions of our mothers and fathers, all the promises we'd made to be civilized and ladylike, couth and kempt. We tore through the austere rooms, overturning dresser drawers, pawing through the neat piles of the Stage 3 girls' starched underwear, smashing lightbulbs with our bare fists. Things felt less foreign in the dark. The dim bedroom was windowless and odorless. We remedied this by spraying exuberant yellow streams all over the bunks. We jumped from bunk to bunk, spraying. We nosed each other midair, our bodies buckling in kinetic laughter. The nuns watched us from the corner of the bedroom, their tiny faces pinched with displeasure.

"*Ay caramba,*" Sister Maria de la Guardia sighed. "*Que barbaridad!*" She made the Sign of the Cross. Sister Maria came to St. Lucy's from a halfway home in Copacabana. In Copacabana, the girls are fat and languid and eat pink slivers of guava right out of your hand. Even at Stage 1, their pelts are silky, sun-bleached to near invisibility. Our pack was hirsute and sinewy and mostly brunette. We had terrible posture. We went knuckling along the wooden floor on the calloused pads of our fists, baring row after row of tiny, wood-rotted teeth. Sister Josephine sucked in her breath. She removed a yellow wheel of floss from under her robes, looping it like a miniature lasso.

"The girls at our facility are *backwoods,*" Sister Josephine whispered to Sister Maria de la Guardia with a beatific smile. "You must be patient with them." I clamped down on her ankle, straining to close my jaws around the woolly XXL sock. Sister Josephine tasted like sweat and freckles. She smelled easy to kill.

We'd arrived at St. Lucy's that morning, part of a pack fifteen-strong.   5
We were accompanied by a mousy, nervous-smelling social worker; the baby-faced deacon; Bartholomew, the blue wolfhound; and four burly woodsmen. The deacon handed out some stale cupcakes and said a quick prayer. Then he led us through the woods. We ran past the wild apiary, past the felled oaks, until we could see the white steeple of St. Lucy's rising out of the forest. We stopped short at the edge of a muddy lake. Then the

deacon took our brothers. Bartholomew helped him to herd the boys up the ramp of a small ferry. We girls ran along the shore, tearing at our new jumpers in a plaid agitation. Our brothers stood on the deck, looking small and confused.

Our mothers and fathers were werewolves. They lived an outsider's existence in caves at the edge of the forest, threatened by frost and pitchforks. They had been ostracized by the local farmers for eating their silled fruit pies and terrorizing the heifers. They had ostracized the local wolves by having sometimes-thumbs, and regrets, and human children. (Their condition skips a generation.) Our pack grew up in a green purgatory. We couldn't keep up with the purebred wolves, but we never stopped crawling. We spoke a slab-tongued pidgin in the cave, inflected with frequent howls. Our parents wanted something better for us; they wanted us to get braces, use towels, be fully bilingual. When the nuns showed up, our parents couldn't refuse their offer. The nuns, they said, would make us naturalized citizens of human society. We would go to St. Lucy's to study a better culture. We didn't know at the time that our parents were sending us away for good. Neither did they.

That first afternoon, the nuns gave us free rein of the grounds. Everything was new, exciting, and interesting. A low granite wall surrounded St. Lucy's, the blue woods humming for miles behind it. There was a stone fountain full of delectable birds. There was a statue of St. Lucy. Her marble skin was colder than our mother's nose, her pupil-less eyes rolled heavenward. Doomed squirrels gamboled around her stony toes. Our diminished pack threw back our heads in a celebratory howl—an exultant and terrible noise, even without a chorus of wolf brothers in the background. There were holes everywhere!

We supplemented these holes by digging some of our own. We interred sticks, and our itchy new jumpers, and the bones of the friendly, unfortunate squirrels. Our noses ached beneath an invisible assault. Everything was smudged with a human odor: baking bread, petrol, the nuns' faint woman-smell sweating out beneath a dark perfume of tallow and incense. We smelled one another, too, with the same astounded fascination. Our own scent had become foreign in this strange place.

We had just sprawled out in the sun for an afternoon nap, yawning into the warm dirt, when the nuns reappeared. They conferred in the shadow of the juniper tree, whispering and pointing. Then they started towards us. The oldest sister had spent the past hour twitching in her sleep, dreaming of fatty and infirm elk. (The pack used to dream the same dreams back then, as naturally as we drank the same water and slept on the same red scree.) When our oldest sister saw the nuns approaching, she instinctively bristled. It was an improvised bristle, given her new, human limitations. She took clumps of her scraggly, nut-brown hair and held it straight out from her head.

Sister Maria gave her a brave smile.

"And what is your name?" she asked.

The oldest sister howled something awful and inarticulable, a distillate of hurt and panic, half-forgotten hunts and eclipsed moons. Sister Maria nodded and scribbled on a yellow legal pad. She slapped on a name tag: HELLO, MY NAME IS _____! "Jeanette it is."

The rest of the pack ran in a loose, uncertain circle, torn between our instinct to help her and our new fear. We sensed some subtler danger afoot, written in a language we didn't understand.

Our littlest sister had the quickest reflexes. She used her hands to flatten her ears to the side of her head. She backed towards the far corner of the garden, snarling in the most menacing register that an eight-year-old wolf-girl can muster. Then she ran. It took them two hours to pin her down and tag her: HELLO, MY NAME IS MIRABELLA!

"Stage 1," Sister Maria sighed, taking careful aim with her tranquilizer dart. "It can be a little overstimulating."

> Stage 2: After a time, your students realize that they must work to adjust to the new culture. This work may be stressful and students may experience a strong sense of dislocation. They may miss certain foods. They may spend a lot of time daydreaming during this period. Many students feel isolated, irritated, bewildered, depressed, or generally uncomfortable.

Those were the days when we dreamed of rivers and meat. The full-moon nights were the worst! Worse than cold toilet seats and boiled tomatoes, worse than trying to will our tongues to curl around our false new names. We would snarl at one another for no reason. I remember how disorienting it was to look down and see two square-toed shoes instead of my own four feet. Keep your mouth shut, I repeated during our walking drills, staring straight ahead. Keep your shoes on your feet. Mouth shut, shoes on feet. Do not chew on your new penny loafers. Do not. I stumbled around in a daze, my mouth black with shoe polish. The whole pack was irritated, bewildered, depressed. We were all uncomfortable, and between languages. We had never wanted to run away so badly in our lives; but who did we have to run back to? Only the curled black grimace of the mother. Only the father, holding his tawny head between his paws. Could we betray our parents by going back to them? After they'd given us the choicest part of the woodchuck, loved us at our hairless worst, nosed us across the ice floes and abandoned us at St. Lucy's for our own betterment?

Physically, we were all easily capable of clearing the low stone walls. Sister Josephine left the wooden gates wide open. They unslatted the windows at night so that long fingers of moonlight beckoned us from the woods. But we

knew we couldn't return to the woods; not till we were civilized, not if we
didn't want to break the mother's heart. It all felt like a sly, human taunt.

It was impossible to make the blank, chilly bedroom feel like home. In
the beginning, we drank gallons of bathwater as part of a collaborative
effort to mark our territory. We puddled up the yellow carpet of old news-
papers. But later, when we returned to the bedroom, we were dismayed to
find all trace of the pack musk had vanished. Someone was coming in and
erasing us. We sprayed and sprayed every morning; and every night, we
returned to the same ammonia eradication. We couldn't make our scent
stick here; it made us feel invisible. Eventually we gave up. Still, the pack
seemed to be adjusting on the same timetable. The advanced girls could
already alternate between two speeds: "slouch" and "amble." Almost
everybody was fully bipedal.

Almost.

20   The pack was worried about Mirabella.

Mirabella would rip foamy chunks out of the church pews and replace
them with ham bones and girl dander. She loved to roam the grounds
wagging her invisible tail. (We all had a hard time giving that up. When
we got excited, we would fall to the ground and start pumping our back-
sides. Back in those days we could pump at rabbity velocities. *Que horror!*
Sister Maria frowned, looking more than a little jealous.) We'd give her
scolding pinches. "Mirabella," we hissed, imitating the nuns. "No." Mirabella cocked her ears at us, hurt and confused.

Still, some things remained the same. The main commandment of wolf
life is Know Your Place, and that translated perfectly. Being around other
humans had awakened a slavish-dog affection in us. An abasing, belly-to-
the-ground desire to please. As soon as we realized that someone higher
up in the food chain was watching us, we wanted only to be pleasing in
their sight. Mouth shut, I repeated, shoes on feet. But if Mirabella had this
latent instinct, the nuns couldn't figure out how to activate it. She'd go
bounding around, gleefully spraying on their gilded statue of St. Lucy,
mad-scratching at the virulent fleas that survived all of their powders and
baths. At Sister Maria's tearful insistence, she'd stand upright for roll call,
her knobby, oddly muscled legs quivering from the effort. Then she'd collapse right back to the ground with an ecstatic *oomph!* She was still loping
around on all fours (which the nuns had taught us to see looked unnatural
and ridiculous—we could barely believe it now, the shame of it, that we
used to locomote like that!), her fists blue-white from the strain. As if she
were holding a secret tight to the ground. Sister Maria de la Guardia would
sigh every time she saw her. *"Caramba!"* She'd sit down with Mirabella
and pry her fingers apart. "You see?" she'd say softly, again and again.
"What are you holding on to? Nothing, little one. Nothing."

Then she would sing out the standard chorus, "Why can't you be more like your sister Jeanette?"

The pack hated Jeanette. She was the most successful of us, the one furthest removed from her origins. Her real name was GWARR!, but she wouldn't respond to this anymore. Jeanette spiffed her penny loafers until her very shoes seemed to gloat. (Linguists have since traced the colloquial origins of "goody two-shoes" back to our facilities.) She could even growl out a demonic-sounding precursor to "Pleased to meet you." She'd delicately extend her former paws to visitors, wearing white kid gloves.

"Our little wolf, disguised in sheep's clothing!" Sister Ignatius liked to joke with the visiting deacons, and Jeanette would surprise everyone by laughing along with them, a harsh, inhuman, barking sound. Her hearing was still twig-snap sharp. Jeanette was the first among us to apologize; to drink apple juice out of a sippy cup; to quit eyeballing the cleric's jugular in a disconcerting fashion. She curled her lips back into a cousin of a smile as the traveling barber cut her pelt into bangs. Then she swept her coarse black curls under the rug. When we entered a room, our nostrils flared beneath the new odors: onion and bleach, candle wax, the turnipy smell of unwashed bodies. Not Jeanette. Jeanette smiled and pretended like she couldn't smell a thing.

I was one of the good girls. Not great and not terrible, solidly middle of the pack. But I had an ear for languages, and I could read before I could adequately wash myself. I probably could have vied with Jeanette for the number one spot, but I'd seen what happened if you gave in to your natural aptitudes. This wasn't like the woods, where you had to be your fastest and your strongest and your bravest self. Different sorts of calculations were required to survive at the home.

The pack hated Jeanette, but we hated Mirabella more. We began to avoid her, but sometimes she'd surprise us, curled up beneath the beds or gnawing on a scapula in the garden. It was scary to be ambushed by your sister. I'd bristle and growl, the way that I'd begun to snarl at my own reflection as if it were a stranger.

"Whatever will become of Mirabella?" we asked, gulping back our own fear. We'd heard rumors about former wolf-girls who never adapted to their new culture. It was assumed that they were returned to our native country, the vanishing woods. We liked to speculate about this before bedtime, scaring ourselves with stories of catastrophic bliss. It was the disgrace, the failure that we all guiltily hoped for in our hard beds. Twitching with the shadow question: *Whatever will become of me?*

We spent a lot of time daydreaming during this period. Even Jeanette. Sometimes I'd see her looking out at the woods in a vacant way. If you interrupted her in the midst of one of these reveries, she would lunge at

25

you with an elder-sister ferocity, momentarily forgetting her human cat-
echism. We liked her better then, startled back into being foamy old
Jeanette.

30   In school, they showed us the St. Francis of Assisi slide show, again and
again. Then the nuns would give us bags of bread. They never announced
these things as a test; it was only much later that I realized that we were under
constant examination. "Go feed the ducks," they urged us. "Go practice compassion for all God's creatures." *Don't pair me with Mirabella,* I prayed, *anybody but Mirabella.* "Claudette"—Sister Josephine beamed—"why don't you
and Mirabella take some pumpernickel down to the ducks?"

"Ohhkaaythankyou," I said. (It took me a long time to say anything;
first I had to translate it in my head from the Wolf.) It wasn't fair. They
knew Mirabella couldn't make bread balls yet. She couldn't even undo the
twist tie of the bag. She was sure to eat the birds; Mirabella didn't even try
to curb her desire to kill things—and then who would get blamed for the
dark spots of duck blood on our Peter Pan collars? Who would get penal-
ized with negative Skill Points? Exactly.

As soon as we were beyond the wooden gates, I snatched the bread
away from Mirabella and ran off to the duck pond on my own. Mirabella
gave chase, nipping at my heels. She thought it was a game. "Stop it," I
growled. I ran faster, but it was Stage 2 and I was still unsteady on my two
feet. I fell sideways into a leaf pile, and then all I could see was my sister's
blurry form, bounding towards me. In a moment, she was on top of me,
barking the old word for tug-of-war. When she tried to steal the bread out
of my hands, I whirled around and snarled at her, pushing my ears back
from my head. I bit her shoulder, once, twice, the only language she would
respond to. I used my new motor skills. I threw dirt, I threw stones. "Get
away!" I screamed, long after she had made a cringing retreat into the
shadows of the purple saplings. "Get away, get away!"

Much later, they found Mirabella wading in the shallows of a distant
river, trying to strangle a mallard with her rosary beads. I was at the lake;
I'd been sitting there for hours. Hunched in the long cattails, my yellow
eyes flashing, shoving ragged hunks of bread into my mouth.

I don't know what they did to Mirabella. Me they separated from my
sisters. They made me watch another slide show. This one showed images
of former wolf-girls, the ones who had failed to be rehabilitated. Long-
haired, sad-eyed women, limping after their former wolf packs in white
tennis shoes and pleated culottes. A wolf-girl bank teller, her makeup
smeared in oily rainbows, eating a raw steak on the deposit slips while her
colleagues looked on in disgust. Our parents. The final slide was a bolded
sentence in St. Lucy's prim script:

35   DO YOU WANT TO END UP SHUNNED BY BOTH SPECIES?

After that, I spent less time with Mirabella. One night she came to me, holding her hand out. She was covered with splinters, keening a high, whining noise through her nostrils. Of course I understood what she wanted; I wasn't that far removed from our language (even though I was reading at a fifth-grade level, halfway into Jack London's *The Son of the Wolf*).

"Lick your own wounds," I said, not unkindly. It was what the nuns had instructed us to say; wound licking was not something you did in polite company. Etiquette was so confounding in this country. Still, looking at Mirabella—her fists balled together like small, white porcupines, her brows knitted in animal confusion—I felt a throb of compassion. *How can people live like they do?* I wondered. Then I congratulated myself. This was a Stage 3 thought.

> Stage 3: It is common that students who start living in a new and differ-
> ent culture come to a point where they reject the host culture and with-
> draw into themselves. During this period, they make generalizations
> about the host culture and wonder how the people can live like they do.
> Your students may feel that their own culture's lifestyle and customs
> are far superior to those of the host country.

The nuns were worried about Mirabella, too. To correct a failing, you must first be aware of it as a failing. And there was Mirabella, shucking her plaid jumper in full view of the visiting cardinal. Mirabella, battling a raccoon under the dinner table while the rest of us took dainty bites of peas and borscht. Mirabella, doing belly flops into compost.

"You have to pull your weight around here," we overheard Sister Jose-   40
phine saying one night. We paused below the vestry window and peered inside.

"Does Mirabella try to earn Skill Points by shelling walnuts and polish-ing Saint-in-the-Box? No. Does Mirabella even know how to say the word *walnut*? Has she learned how to say anything besides a sinful 'HraaaHA!' as she commits frottage against the organ pipes? No."

There was a long silence.

"Something must be done," Sister Ignatius said firmly. The other nuns nodded, a sea of thin, colorless lips and kettle-black brows. "Something must be done," they intoned. That ominously passive construction; a some-thing so awful that nobody wanted to assume responsibility for it.

I could have warned her. If we were back home, and Mirabella had come under attack by territorial beavers or snow-blind bears, I would have warned her. But the truth is that by Stage 3 I wanted her gone. Mirabella's inability to adapt was taking a visible toll. Her teeth were ground down to nubbins; her hair was falling out. She hated the spongy, long-dead foods we were served, and it showed—her ribs were poking through her uniform.

Her bright eyes had dulled to a sour whiskey color. But you couldn't show Mirabella the slightest kindness anymore—she'd never leave you alone! You'd have to sit across from her at meals, shoving her away as she begged for your scraps. I slept fitfully during that period, unable to forget that Mirabella was living under my bed, gnawing on my loafers.

45   It was during Stage 3 that we met our first purebred girls. These were girls raised in captivity, volunteers from St. Lucy's School for Girls. The apple-cheeked fourth-grade class came to tutor us in playing. They had long golden braids or short, severe bobs. They had frilly-duvet names like Felicity and Beulah; and pert, bunny noses; and terrified smiles. We grinned back at them with genuine ferocity. It made us nervous to meet new humans. There were so many things that we could do wrong! And the rules here were different depending on which humans we were with: dancing or no dancing, checkers playing or no checkers playing, pumping or no pumping.

The purebred girls played checkers with us.

"These girl-girls sure is dumb," my sister Lavash panted to me between games. "I win it again! Five to none."

She was right. The purebred girls were making mistakes on purpose, in order to give us an advantage. "King me," I growled, out of turn. "*I say king me!*" and Felicity meekly complied. Beulah pretended not to mind when we got frustrated with the oblique, fussy movement from square to square and shredded the board to ribbons. I felt sorry for them. I wondered what it would be like to be bred in captivity, and always homesick for a dimly sensed forest, the trees you've never seen.

Jeanette was learning how to dance. On Holy Thursday, she mastered a rudimentary form of the Charleston. "*Brava!*" The nuns clapped. "*Brava!*"

50   Every Friday, the girls who had learned how to ride a bicycle celebrated by going on chaperoned trips into town. The purebred girls sold seven hundred rolls of gift-wrap paper and used the proceeds to buy us a yellow fleet of bicycles built for two. We'd ride the bicycles uphill, a sanctioned pumping, a grim-faced nun pedaling behind each one of us. "Congratulations!" the nuns would huff. "Being human is like riding this bicycle. Once you've learned how, you'll never forget." Mirabella would run after the bicycles, growling out our old names. HWRAA! GWARR! TRRRRRRR! We pedaled faster.

At this point, we'd had six weeks of lessons, and still nobody could do the Sausalito but Jeanette. The nuns decided we needed an inducement to dance. They announced that we would celebrate our successful rehabilitations with a Debutante Ball. There would be brothers, ferried over from the Home for Man-Boys Raised by Wolves. There would be a photographer from the *Gazette Sophisticate*. There would be a three-piece jazz band from West Toowoomba, and root beer in tiny plastic cups. The brothers! We'd almost forgotten about them. Our invisible tails went limp. I should have been excited; instead, I felt a low mad anger at the nuns. They knew we weren't ready to dance with the brothers; we weren't even ready to talk to them. Things had been so much simpler in the woods. That night I waited until my sisters were asleep. Then I slunk into the closet and practiced the Sausalito two-step in secret, a private mass of twitch and foam. Mouth shut—shoes on feet! Mouth shut—shoes on feet! Mouthshutmouthshut . . .

One night I came back early from the closet and stumbled on Jeanette. She was sitting in a patch of moonlight on the windowsill, reading from one of her library books. (She was the first of us to sign for her library card, too.) Her cheeks looked dewy.

"Why you cry?" I asked her, instinctively reaching over to lick Jeanette's cheek and catching myself in the nick of time.

Jeanette blew her nose into a nearby curtain. (Even her mistakes annoyed us—they were always so well intentioned.) She sniffled and pointed to a line in her book: "The lake-water was reinventing the forest and the white moon above it, and wolves lapped up the cold reflection of the sky." But none of the pack besides me could read yet, and I wasn't ready to claim a common language with Jeanette.

The following day, Jeanette golfed. The nuns set up a miniature putt-putt course in the garden. Sister Maria dug four sandtraps and got old Walter, the groundskeeper, to make a windmill out of a lawn mower engine. The eighteenth hole was what they called a "doozy," a minuscule crack in St. Lucy's marble dress. Jeanette got a hole in one.

On Sundays, the pretending felt almost as natural as nature. The chapel was our favorite place. Long before we could understand what the priest was saying, the music instructed us in how to feel. The choir director—aggressively perfumed Mrs. Valuchi, gold necklaces like pineapple rings around her neck—taught us more than the nuns ever did. She showed us how to pattern the old hunger into arias. Clouds moved behind the frosted oculus of the nave, glass shadows that reminded me of my mother. The mother, I'd think, struggling to conjure up a picture. A black shadow, running behind the watery screen of pines.

We sang at the chapel annexed to the home every morning. We understood that this was the humans' moon, the place for howling beyond purpose. Not for mating, not for hunting, not for fighting, not for anything but the sound itself. And we'd howl along with the choir, hurling every pitted thing within us at the stained glass. "Sotto voce." The nuns would frown. But you could tell that they were pleased.

> Stage 4: As a more thorough understanding of the host culture is acquired, your students will begin to feel more comfortable in their new environment. Your students feel more at home, and their self-confidence grows. Everything begins to make sense.

"Hey, Claudette," Jeanette growled to me on the day before the ball. "Have you noticed that everything's beginning to make sense?"

60   Before I could answer, Mirabella sprang out of the hall closet and snapped through Jeanette's homework binder. Pages and pages of words swirled around the stone corridor, like dead leaves off trees.

"What about you, Mirabella?" Jeanette asked politely, stooping to pick up her erasers. She was the only one of us who would still talk to Mirabella; she was high enough in the rankings that she could afford to talk to the scruggliest wolf-girl. "Has everything begun to make more sense, Mirabella?"

Mirabella let out a whimper. She scratched at us and scratched at us, raking her nails along our shins so hard that she drew blood. Then she rolled belly-up on the cold stone floor, squirming on a bed of spelling-bee worksheets. Above us, small pearls of light dotted the high, tinted window.

Jeanette frowned. "You are a late bloomer, Mirabella! Usually, everything's begun to make more sense by Month Twelve at the latest." I noticed that she stumbled on the word *bloomer*. HraaaHA! Jeanette could never fully shake our accent. She'd talk like that her whole life, I thought with a gloomy satisfaction, each word winced out like an apology for itself.

"Claudette, help me," she yelped. Mirabella had closed her jaws around Jeanette's bald ankle and was dragging her towards the closet. "Please. Help me to mop up Mirabella's mess."

65   I ignored her and continued down the hall. I had only four more hours to perfect the Sausalito. I was worried only about myself. By that stage, I was no longer certain of how the pack felt about anything.

At seven o'clock on the dot, Sister Ignatius blew her whistle and frog-marched us into the ball. The nuns had transformed the rectory into a very scary place. Purple and silver balloons started popping all around us. Black streamers swooped down from the eaves and got stuck in our hair like bats. A full yellow moon smirked outside the window. We were greeted by blasts of a saxophone, and fizzy pink drinks, and the brothers.

The brothers didn't smell like our brothers anymore. They smelled like pomade and cold, sterile sweat. They looked like little boys. Someone had washed behind their ears and made them wear suspendered dungarees. Kyle used to be a blustery alpha male, BTWWWR!, chewing through rattlesnakes, spooking badgers, snatching a live trout out of a grizzly's mouth. He stood by the punch bowl, looking pained and out of place.

"My stars!" I growled. "What lovely weather we've been having!"

"Yeees," Kyle growled back. "It is beginning to look a lot like Christmas." All around the room, boys and girls raised by wolves were having the same conversation. Actually, it had been an unseasonably warm and brown winter, and just that morning a freak hailstorm had sent Sister Josephina to an early grave. But we had only gotten up to Unit 7: Party Dialogue;

we hadn't yet learned the vocabulary for Unit 12: How to Tactfully Acknowledge Disaster. Instead, we wore pink party hats and sucked olives on little sticks, inured to our own strangeness.

The nuns swept our hair back into high, bouffant hairstyles. This made   70
us look more girlish and less inclined to eat people, the way that squirrels are saved from looking like rodents by their poofy tails. I was wearing a white organdy dress with orange polka dots. Jeanette was wearing a mauve organdy dress with blue polka dots. Linette was wearing a red organdy dress with white polka dots. Mirabella was in a dark corner, wearing a muzzle. Her party culottes were duct-taped to her knees. The nuns had tied little bows on the muzzle to make it more festive. Even so, the jazz band from West Toowoomba kept glancing nervously her way.

"You smell astoooounding!" Kyle was saying, accidentally stretching the diphthong into a howl and then blushing. "I mean—"

"Yes, I know what it is that you mean," I snapped. (That's probably a little narrative embellishment on my part; it must have been months before I could really "snap" out words.) I didn't smell astounding. I had rubbed a pumpkin muffin all over my body earlier that morning to mask my natural, feral scent. Now I smelled like a purebred girl, easy to kill. I narrowed my eyes at Kyle and flattened my ears, something I hadn't done for months. Kyle looked panicked, trying to remember the words that would make me act like a girl again. I felt hot, oily tears squeezing out of the red corners of my eyes. *Shoesonfeet!* I barked at myself. I tried again. "My! What lovely weather—"

The jazz band struck up a tune.

"The time has come to do the Sausalito," Sister Maria announced, beaming into the microphone. "Every sister grab a brother!" She switched on Walter's industrial flashlight, struggling beneath its weight, and aimed the beam in the center of the room.

Uh-oh. I tried to skulk off into Mirabella's corner, but Kyle pushed me   75
into the spotlight. "No," I moaned through my teeth, "noooooo." All of a sudden the only thing my body could remember how to do was pump and pump. In a flash of white-hot light, my months at St. Lucy's had vanished, and I was just a terrified animal again. As if of their own accord, my feet started to wiggle out of my shoes. *Mouth shut,* I gasped, staring down at my naked toes, *mouthshutmouthshut.*

"Ahem. The time has come," Sister Maria coughed, "to do the Sausalito." She paused. "The Sausalito," she added helpfully, "does not in any way resemble the thing that you are doing."

Beads of sweat stood out on my forehead. I could feel my jaws gaping open, my tongue lolling out of the left side of my mouth. What were the steps? I looked frantically for Jeanette; she would help me, she would tell me what to do.

Jeanette was sitting in the corner, sipping punch through a long straw and watching me pant. I locked eyes with her, pleading with the mute intensity that I had used to beg her for weasel bones in the forest. "What are the steps?" I mouthed.

"The steps!"

80   "The steps?" Then Jeanette gave me a wide, true wolf smile. For an instant, she looked just like our mother. "Not for you," she mouthed back.

I threw my head back, a howl clawing its way up my throat. I was about to lose all my Skill Points, I was about to fail my Adaptive Dancing test. But before the air could burst from my lungs, the wind got knocked out of me. *Oomph!* I fell to the ground, my skirt falling softly over my head. Mirabella had intercepted my eye-cry for help. She'd chewed through her restraints and tackled me from behind, barking at unseen cougars, trying to shield me with her tiny body. *"Caramba!"* Sister Maria squealed, dropping the flashlight. The music ground to a halt. And I have never loved someone so much, before or since, as I loved my littlest sister at that moment. I wanted to roll over and lick her ears, I wanted to kill a dozen spotted fawns and let her eat first.

But everybody was watching; everybody was waiting to see what I would do. "I wasn't talking to you," I grunted from underneath her. "I didn't want your help. Now you have ruined the Sausalito! You have ruined the ball!" I said more loudly, hoping the nuns would hear how much my enunciation had improved.

"You have ruined it!" my sisters panted, circling around us, eager to close ranks. "Mirabella has ruined it!" Every girl was wild-eyed and itching under her polka dots, punch froth dribbling down her chin. The pack had been waiting for this moment for some time. "Mirabella cannot adapt! Back to the woods, back to the woods!"

The band from West Toowoomba had quietly packed their instruments into black suitcases and were sneaking out the back. The boys had fled back towards the lake, bow ties spinning, snapping suspenders in their haste. Mirabella was still snarling in the center of it all, trying to figure out where the danger was so that she could defend me against it. The nuns exchanged glances.

In the morning, Mirabella was gone. We checked under all the beds. I pretended to be surprised. I'd known she would have to be expelled the minute I felt her weight on my back. Walter came and told me this in secret after the ball, "So you can say yer good-byes." I didn't want to face Mirabella. Instead, I packed a tin lunch pail for her: two jelly sandwiches on saltine crackers, a chloroformed squirrel, a gilt-edged placard of St. Bolio. I left it for her with Sister Ignatius, with a little note: "Best wishes!" I told myself I'd done everything I could.

85   "Hooray!" the pack crowed. "Something has been done!"

We raced outside into the bright sunlight, knowing full well that our sister had been turned loose, that we'd never find her. A low roar rippled through us and surged up and up, disappearing into the trees. I listened for an answering howl from Mirabella, heart thumping—what if she heard us and came back? But there was nothing.

We graduated from St. Lucy's shortly thereafter. As far as I can recollect, that was our last communal howl.

> Stage 5: At this point your students are able to interact effectively in the new cultural environment. They find it easy to move between the two cultures.

One Sunday, near the end of my time at St. Lucy's, the sisters gave me a special pass to go visit the parents. The woodsman had to accompany me; I couldn't remember how to find the way back on my own. I wore my best dress and brought along some prosciutto and dill pickles in a picnic basket. We crunched through the fall leaves in silence, and every step made me sadder. "I'll wait out here," the woodsman said, leaning on a blue elm and lighting a cigarette.

The cave looked so much smaller than I remembered it. I had to duck my head to enter. Everybody was eating when I walked in. They all looked up from the bull moose at the same time, my aunts and uncles, my sloe-eyed, lolling cousins, the parents. My uncle dropped a thighbone from his mouth. My littlest brother, a cross-eyed wolf-boy who has since been successfully rehabilitated and is now a dour, balding children's book author, started whining in terror. My mother recoiled from me, as if I was a stranger. TRRR? She sniffed me for a long moment. Then she sank her teeth into my ankle, looking proud and sad. After all the tail wagging and perfunctory barking had died down, the parents sat back on their hind legs. They stared up at me expectantly, panting in the cool gray envelope of the cave, waiting for a display of what I had learned.

"So," I said, telling my first human lie. "I'm home."

Creative Nonfiction   **David Sedaris**

THE DRAMA BUG

The man was sent to our class to inspire us, and personally speaking, I thought he did an excellent job. After introducing himself in a relaxed and genial manner, he started toward the back of the room, only to be stopped midway by what we came to know as "the invisible wall," that transparent barrier realized only by psychotics, drug fiends, and other members of the show business community.

I sat enthralled as he righted himself and investigated the imaginary wall with his open palms, running his hands over the seemingly hard surface in hopes of finding a way out. Moments later he was tugging at an invisible rope, then struggling in the face of a violent, fantastic wind.

You know you're living in a small town when you can reach the ninth grade without ever having seen a mime. As far as I was concerned, this man was a prophet, a genius, a pioneer in the field of entertainment—and here he was in Raleigh, North Carolina! It was a riot, the way he imitated the teacher, turning down the corners of his mouth and riffling through his imaginary purse in search of gum and aspirin. Was this guy funny or what!

I went home and demonstrated the invisible wall for my two-year-old brother, who pounded on the very real wall beside his playpen, shrieking and wailing in disgust. When my mother asked what I'd done to provoke him, I threw up my hands in mock innocence before lowering them to retrieve the imaginary baby that lay fussing at my feet. I patted the back of my little ghost to induce gas and was investigating its soiled diaper when I noticed my mother's face assume an expression she reserved for unspeakable horror. I had seen this look only twice before: once when she was caught in the path of a charging, rabid pig and then again when I told her I wanted a peach-colored velveteen blazer with matching slacks.

5   "I don't know who put you up to this," she said, "but I'll kill you myself before I watch you grow up to be a clown. If you want to paint your face and prance around on street corners, then you'll have to find some other place to live because I sure as hell won't have it in my house." She turned to leave. *"Or in my yard,"* she added.

Fearful of her retribution, I did as I was told, ending my career in mime with a whimper rather than the silent bang I had hoped for.

The visiting actor returned to our classroom a few months later, removing his topcoat to reveal a black body stocking worn with a putty-colored neck brace, the result of a recent automobile accident. This afternoon's task was to introduce us to the works of William Shakespeare, and once again I was completely captivated by his charm and skill. When the words became confusing, you needed only to pay attention to the actor's face and hands to understand that this particular character was not just angry, but vengeful. I loved the undercurrent of hostility that lay beneath the surface of this deceptively beautiful language. It seemed a shame that people no longer spoke this way, and I undertook a campaign to reintroduce Elizabethan English to the citizens of North Carolina.

"Perchance, fair lady, thou dost think me unduly vexed by the sorrowful state of thine quarters," I said to my mother as I ran the vacuum cleaner over the living-room carpet she was inherently too lazy to bother with. "These foul specks, the evidence of life itself, have sullied not only thine shag-tempered mat but also thine character. Be ye mad, woman? Were it a punishable crime to neglect thine dwellings, you, my feeble-spirited mistress, would hang from the tallest tree in penitence for your shameful ways. Be there not garments to launder and iron free of turbulence? See ye not the porcelain plates and hearty mugs waiting to be washed clean of evidence? Get thee to thine work, damnable lady, and quickly, before the products of thine very loins raise their collected fists in a spirit born both of rage and indignation, forcibly coaxing the last breath from the foul chamber of thine vain and upright throat. Go now, wastrel, and get to it!"

My mother reacted as if I had whipped her with a short length of yarn. The intent was there, but the weapon was strange and inadequate. I could tell by the state of my room that she spent the next day searching my dresser for drugs. The clothes I took pride in neatly folding were crammed tight into their drawers with no regard for color or category. I smelled the evidence of cigarettes and noticed the coffee rings on my desk. My mother had been granted forgiveness on several previous occasions, but mess with mine drawers and ye have just made thyself an enemy for life. Tying a feather to the shaft of my ballpoint pen, I quilled her a letter. "The thing that ye search for so desperately," I wrote, "resideth not in mine well-ordered chamber, but in the questionable content of thine own character." I slipped the note into her purse, folded twice and sealed with wax from the candles I now used to light my room. I took to brooding, refusing to let up until I received a copy of Shakespeare's collected plays. Once they were acquired, I discovered them dense and difficult to follow. Reading the words made me feel dull and stupid, but speaking them made me feel powerful. I found it best to simply carry the book from room to room, occasionally skimming for fun words I might toss into my ever fragrant vocabulary. The dinner hour became either unbearable or excruciating, depending on my mood.

"Methinks, kind sir, most gentle lady, fellow siblings all, that this barn- 10 yard fowl be most tasty and succulent, having simmered in its own sweet juices for such a time as it might take the sun to pass, rosy and full-fingered, across the plum-colored sky for the course of a twilight hour. 'Tis crisp yet juicy, this plump bird, satisfied in the company of such finely roasted neighbors. Hear me out, fine relations, and heed my words, for methinks it adventurous, and fanciful, too, to saddle mine fork with both fowl *and* carrot at the exact same time, the twin juices blending together in a delicate harmony which doth cajole and enliven mine tongue in a spirit of unbridled merriment! What say ye, fine father, sisters, and infant brother, too, that we raise our flagons high in celebration of this hearty feast, prepared lovingly and with utmost grace by this dutiful woman we have the good fortune to address as wife, wench, or mother!"

My enthusiasm knew no limits. Soon my mother was literally begging me to wait in the car while she stepped into the bank or grocery store.

I was at the orthodontist's office, placing a pox upon the practice of dentistry, when the visiting actor returned to our classroom.

"You missed it," my friend Lois said. "The man was so indescribably powerful that I was practically crying, that's how brilliant he was." She positioned her hands as if she were supporting a tray. "I don't know what more I can say. The words, they just don't exist. I could try to explain his realness, but you'd never be able to understand it. Never," she repeated. "Never, never, never."

Lois and I had been friends for six months when our relationship suddenly assumed a competitive edge. I'd never cared who made better grades or had more spending money. We each had our strengths; the important thing was to honor each other for the thing that person did best. Lois held her Chablis better than I, and I respected her for that. Her frightening excess of self-confidence allowed her to march into school wearing a rust-colored Afro wig, and I stood behind her one hundred percent. She owned more records than I did, and because she was nine months older, also knew how to drive a car and did so as if she were rushing to put out a fire. *Fine*, I thought, *good for her*. My superior wisdom and innate generosity allowed me to be truly happy for Lois up until the day she questioned my ability to understand the visiting actor. The first few times he visited, she'd been just like the rest of them, laughing at his neck brace and rolling her eyes at the tangerine-sized lump in his tights. *I* was the one who first identified his brilliance, and now she was saying I couldn't understand him? Methinks not.

15 "Honestly, woman," I said to my mother on our way to the dry cleaner, "to think that this low-lying worm might speak to me of greatness as though it were a thing invisible to mine eyes is more than I can bear. Her words doth strike mine heart with the force of a punishing blow, leaving me both stunned and highly vexed, too. Hear me, though, for I shall bide my time, quietly, and with cunning, striking back at the very hour she doth least expect it. Such an affront shall not go unchallenged, of that you may rest assured, gentle lady. My vengeance will hold the sweet taste of the ripest berry, and I shall savor it slowly."

"You'll get over it," my mother said. "Give it a week or two and I'm sure everything will be back to normal. I'm going in now to get your father's shirts and I want you to wait here, *in the car*. Trust me, this whole thing will be forgotten about in no time."

This had become her answer to everything. She'd done some asking around and concluded I'd been bitten by what her sister referred to as "the drama bug." My mother was convinced that this was a phase, just like all the others. A few weeks of fanfare and I'd drop show business, just like I had the guitar and my private detective agency. I hated having my life's ambition reduced to the level of a common cold. This wasn't a bug, but a full-fledged virus. It might lay low for a year or two, but this little germ would never go away. It had nothing to do with talent or initiative. Rejection couldn't weaken it, and no amount of success would ever satisfy it. Once diagnosed, the prognosis was terminal.

The drama bug seemed to strike hardest with Jews, homosexuals, and portly girls, whose faces were caked with acne medication. These were individuals who, for one reason or another, desperately craved attention. I would later discover it was a bad idea to gather more than two of these people in an enclosed area for any length of time. The stage was not only a physical place but also a state of mind, and the word *audience* was defined as anyone forced to suffer your company. We young actors were a string of lightbulbs left burning twenty-four hours a day, exhausting ourselves and others with our self-proclaimed brilliance.

I had the drama bug and Lois had a car. Weighing the depth of her momentary transgression against the rich rewards of her private chariot, I found it within my bosom to forgive my wayward friend. I called her the moment I learned the visiting actor had scheduled a production of *Hamlet* set to take place in the amphitheater of the Raleigh Rose Garden. He himself would direct and play the title role, but the other parts were up for grabs. We auditioned, and because we were the youngest and least experienced, Lois and I were assigned the roles of the traveling players Hamlet uses to bait his uncle Claudius. It wasn't the part I was hoping for, but I accepted my role with quiet dignity. I had a few decent speeches and planned to work them to the best of my ability.

Our fellow cast members were in their twenties and thirties and had   20 wet their feet in such long-running outdoor dramas as *The Lost Colony* and *Tender Is the Lamb*. These were professionals, and I hoped to benefit from their experience, sitting literally at their feet as the director paced the lip of the stage addressing his clenched fist as "poor Yorick."

I worshiped these people. Lois slept with them. By the second week of rehearsal, she had abandoned Fortinbras in favor of Laertes, who, she claimed, had a "real way with the sword." Unlike me, she was embraced by the older crowd, attending late-night keg parties with Polonius and Ophelia and driving to the lake with the director while Gertrude and Rosencrantz made out in the backseat. The killer was that Lois was nowhere near as committed as I was. Her drama bug was the equivalent of a twenty-four-hour flu, yet there she was, playing bumper pool with Hamlet himself while I practiced lines alone in my room, dreaming up little ways to steal the show.

It was decided that as traveling players, Lois and I would make our entrance tumbling onto the outdoor stage. When she complained that the grass was irritating her skin, the director examined the wee pimples on her back and decided that, from this point on, the players would enter skipping. I had rehearsed my tumble until my brain lost its mooring and could be heard rattling inside my skull, and now, on the basis of one complaint, we were skipping? He'd already cut all my speeches, leaving me with the one line "Aye, my lord." That was it, three lousy syllables. A person could wrench more emotion out of a sneeze than all my dialogue put together. While the other actors strolled the Rose Garden memorizing their vengeful soliloquies, I skipped back and forth across the parking lot repeating, "Aye, my lord," in a voice that increasingly sounded like that of a trained parrot. Lois felt silly skipping and spoke to the director, who praised her instincts and announced that, henceforth, the players would enter walking.

The less I had to do, the more my fellow actors used me as a personal slave. I would have been happy to help them run lines, but instead, they wanted me to polish their crowns or trot over to a car, searching the backseat for a misplaced dagger.

"Looking for something to do? You can help Doogan glow-tape the props," the director said. "You can chase the spiders out of the dressing room, or better yet, why don't you run down to the store and get us some drinks."

25   For the most part, Lois sat in the shade doing nothing. Not only did she refuse to help out, but she was always the first one to hand me a large bill when placing an order for a thirty-cent diet soda. She'd search through her purse, bypassing the singles in favor of a ten or a twenty. "I need to break this anyway," she'd say. "If they charge you extra for a cup of ice, tell them to fuck themselves." During the rehearsal breaks she huddled in the stands, gossiping with the other actors while I was off anchoring ladders for the technicians.

When it came time for our big scene, Lois recited her lines as if she were reading the words from the surface of some distant billboard. She squinted and paused between syllables, punctuating each word with a question mark. "Who this? Has seen with tongue? In venom steeped?"

If the director had a problem with her performance, he kept it to himself. I, on the other hand, was instructed to remove the sweater from around my neck, walk slower, and drop the accent. It might have been easier to accept the criticism had he spread it around a little, but that seemed unlikely. She could enter the scene wearing sunglasses and eating pizza and that was "fine, Lois. Great work, babe."

By this time I was finding my own way home from rehearsal. Lois couldn't give me a ride, as she was always running off to some party or restaurant with what she referred to as "the gang from Elsinore."

"I can't go," I'd say, pretending I had been invited. "I really need to get home and concentrate on my line. You go ahead, though. I'll just call my mother. She'll pick me up."

"Are we vexed?" my mother would ask, pulling her station wagon into the parking lot.   30

"We are indeed," I answered. "And highly so."

"Let it go," she said. "Ten years from now I guarantee you won't re-member any of these people. Time passes, you'll see." She frowned, study-ing her face in the rearview mirror. "Enough liquor, and people can forget anything. Don't let it get to you. If nothing else, this has taught you to skim money while buying their drinks."

I didn't appreciate her flippant attitude, but the business with the change was insightful.

"Round everything off to the nearest dollar," she said. "Hand them their change along with their drinks so they'll be less likely to count it— and never fold the bills, keep the money in a wad."

My mother had the vengeful part down. It was the craft of acting I   35
thought she knew nothing about.

We were in dress rehearsal when the director approached Lois regard-ing a new production he hoped to stage that coming fall. It was to be a musical based on the lives of roving Gypsies. "And you," he said, "shall be my lusty bandit queen."

Lois couldn't sing; everyone knew that. Neither could she act or play the tambourine. "Yours is the heart of a Gypsy," he said, kneeling in the grass. "The vibrant soul of a nomad."

When I expressed an interest, he suggested I might enjoy working behind the scenes. He meant for me to hang lights or lug scenery, to become one of those guys with the low-riding pants, their tool belts bur-dened with heavy wrenches and thick rolls of gaffer tape. Anyone think-ing I might be trusted with electrical wiring had to be a complete idiot, and that's what this man was. I looked at him clearly then, noticing the way his tights made a mockery of his slack calves and dumpy little basket. Vibrant soul of a nomad, indeed. If he were such a big stinking deal, what was he doing in Raleigh? His blow-dried hair, the cheap Cuban-he·' shoes, and rainbow-striped suspenders—it was all a sham. Why tights with suspenders when their only redeeming feature was tha stayed up on their own—that's how they got their name, tights. And acting? The man performed as if the audience were deaf. He shouted his lines, grinning like a jack-o'-lantern and flailing his arms as if his sleeves were on fire. His was a form of acting that never fails to embarrass me. Watching him was like opening the door to a singing telegram: you know it's supposed to be entertaining, but you can't get beyond the sad fact that this person actually thinks he's bringing some joy into your life. Somewhere he had a mother who sifted through a shoe box of mimeographed playbills, pouring herself another drink and wondering when her son would come to his senses and swallow some drain cleaner.

I finally saw Hamlet for who he really was and recognized myself as the witless Yorick who had blindly followed along behind him.

40   My mother attended the opening-night performance. Following my leaden "Aye, my lord," I lay upon the grassy stage as Lois poured a false vial of poison into my ear. As I lay dying, I opened my eyes just a crack, catching sight of my mother stretched out on her hard, stone pew, fighting off the moths that, along with a few dozen seniors, had been attracted by the light.

There was a cast party afterward, but I didn't go. I changed my clothes in the dressing room, where the actors stood congratulating one another, repeating the words "brilliant" and "intense" as if they were describing the footlights. Horatio asked me to run to the store for cigarettes, and I pocketed his money, promising to return "with lightning speed, my lord."

"You were the best in the whole show," my mother said, stopping for frozen pizza on our way home. "I mean it, you walked onto that stage and all eyes went right to you."

It occurred to me then that my mother was a better actor than I could ever hope to be. Acting is different than posing or pretending. When done with precision, it bears a striking resemblance to lying. Stripped of the costumes and grand gestures, it presents itself as an unquestionable truth. I didn't envy my mother's skill, neither did I contradict her. That's how convincing she was. It seemed best, sitting beside her with a frozen pizza thawing on my lap, to simply sit back and learn.

Poetry   **Christopher Shannon**

APOLLO (AT) ELEVEN

The television went white with snow.
The black sky hard-boiled the moon.
He felt a humming around him,
a full-body halo of chalkboard dust; breathing
on a spoon, he watched himself disappear.   5
Being young was like falling through a glass of water.
His father drifted by, moving for an aspirin,
while Apollo worked out trajectories
on his slingshot, strummed chords
on his lyre. It was his turn to shovel the walk,   10
and he did, because his father was so grave.
He loped forward, past the flag pole,
his boots imprinting the snow with little maps.

                    ~

His boots imprinted the dust with little maps.
He loped forward with a flag on a pole,   15
but diffidently, as if to his father's grave.
That liar. It was his first moonwalk;
he was as tense as a cord thumbed on a slingshot.
Those on board Apollo worked out trajectories.
The astronaut drifted, moving as an aspirin   20
falling through a glass of water.
He feared he might disappear, like breath from a spoon,
or an angel's halo, if it were made of chalk dust.
He felt a humming around him.
His wide eyes were hard-boiled moons,   25
televisions white with snow.

On Writing   Frederick Smock

A POET'S EDUCATION

> *If I had to limit myself to one criticism of academics it would be this—*
> *they distrust their responses. They feel that if a response can't be*
> *defended intellectually, it lacks vitality.*

> —Richard Hugo

I

In my years of teaching creative writing, I have had the good fortune of learning from many fine students. One of them was a ten-year-old girl. She wrote a poem from the point of view of a coconut, I recall. I had brought to the class a sackful of the oddest fruits and vegetables I could find at the market: ugli fruit, star fruit, okra, kumquats, and the like. And a coconut. Each child selected one, played with it a bit, sniffed it, tasted it. Then, to generate poems, I asked a series of questions, such as, "Who is this one's best friend?" "What is this one's favorite game?" "Where does this one like to go for vacation?" To which this 4th-grade girl wrote, "I never have to go on vacation / because I carry the waves inside me."

The other students gasped. They felt the beauty in those lines and could not help it—they gasped.

Children are natural poets. They have wild and crazy imaginations. They delight in metaphor, rhyme, and word-play. And yet, somehow, many of them have that poetic gift taught right out of them. On a recent visit to my campus, Billy Collins remarked, "High school is where poetry goes to die." I know what he means. When I was in high school, I had an English teacher who was always asking us to "find the hidden meaning" in the poem. She was not a poet herself, obviously. I confess, I did not like poetry when I was in high school. But I also kept reading it, in private, convinced there must be another way.

Nowadays, I belong to a wide circle of poets, and not one of us (that I know) tries to *hide* the meaning of his or her poems. Instead, we work to make our meanings plain. This is not to deny the pleasures of complexity or ambiguity. But asking students to find "the hidden meaning" tells them, straight off, that whatever *they* felt upon reading the poem must have been wrong—because it was not hidden! A quicker way to squelch the poetic sensibility hardly exists.

5   To put it rather bluntly, poems are not written in order to be discussed in classrooms. Rather, poems, are written to be read in a lonely communion somewhere—beside a lake, under a blanket with a flashlight, in a hammock—one-to-one, poet to reader. And yet, discuss them in classrooms we do. So we must be sensitive to the beating heart of the poem. We

do not want to euthanize it, and dissect it, and leave its carcass on the seminar table.

II

What happens to children as they grow up? They seem to lose that simple, weird, loving relationship with words. A good poet—or a good reader—is one who has not lost his or her glee with language.

When my son was little, I read him many books. Some of those books I read him many, many times. There was one sentence in particular, I recall, that always delivered him into paroxysms of delight. It appears in the original *Paddington Bear* story, by Michael Bond. Mr. Brown has just discovered the little bear cub huddling in a corner of Paddington station, and he escorts him into the cafeteria for a bite to eat. Mr. Brown sits him at a table, and soon returns "carrying two steaming cups of tea and a large plate piled high with sticky cakes." The delicious sounds of that line absolutely thrilled my son. (Read that phrase aloud to yourself—I dare you not to grin.) My son always insisted that I read that sentence again, and again, several times over, before he would allow me to go forward with the story.

As the poet Karl Shapiro once noted, "The proper response to a work of art is joy—even hilarity."

III

Another English teacher at my high school started her class by asking us, "What is the author trying to say?" As if Emily Dickinson and Walt Whitman and William Carlos Williams have tried but ultimately failed to say what they wanted—and yet *we*, pimply adolescents sitting bored and distracted in Mrs. Wilson's third period English class, *we* would at last figure out what those great poets had left unfinished. We would "fix" Dickinson and Whitman and Williams, once and for all.

Poets know that meaning can be a difficult and slippery thing. Sometimes meaning does not make itself known even to the poet until late in the writing process—if then. Sometimes it happens later, when readers suggest possible meanings that the poet had not thought of, and yet which seem entirely plausible. Indeed, meaning can be accidental. Randall Jarrell said that a poet is someone sitting at a desk hoping to be struck by lightning! Charles Simic said that a poem owes everything to chance, for the simple fact that no one can will a memorable phrase into being. John Ciardi said that the question is not *what* a poem means, but *how* it means. These things can be confusing to the student-poet.

On the first day of class, I go ahead and tell my students the secret to good writing: *the right word in the right place every time.*

They laugh. Then they get serious: "You mean that, don't you?"

I tell them that I am only paraphrasing what has been said of Flaubert: *le mot juste*. Flaubert, who lived every day "in fear of the false, which kept him confined to his couch for weeks or months on end in the dread that he would never be able to write another word without compromising himself in the most grievous of ways," as the novelist W. G. Sebald put it.

We certainly do not want to turn our literature or creative writing students into neurasthenics. And yet, writing *is* serious business. There is an inner call to truth and justice that makes every writer a moralist, at least about his or her own work. If the modern industrialized, digitalized world seems to diminish the value of the individual, then art may well be the last refuge of the humanized soul. "When we are told in dozens of insidious ways that our lives don't matter, we may be forced to insist, often far too loudly, that they do," the poet Richard Hugo wrote, in *The Triggering Town*. "A creative writing class may be one of the last places you can go where your life still matters."

15   "Poetry's work," wrote the poet and Zen adept Jane Hirshfield, in *Nine Gates: Entering the Mind of Poetry*, "is the clarification and magnification of being. Here, as elsewhere in life, attentiveness only deepens what it regards." When that regard is turned to the self, salvation can happen.

Should not all students, therefore, practice creative writing? Certainly all writing is in some ways creative. For several hundred years, in the western world, the penning of verses was a required part of every student's education.

What happened?

IV

Look into almost any high school classroom in America these days, and you will see that learning is being conducted in the service of testing, and what very little poetry that gets taught is usually for quantitative reasons. (Mostly that old curmudgeon Robert Frost.) Students can be seen cramming for their standardized exams. There is no glee to be observed in those classrooms. Any laughter you might hear is almost certainly nervous laughter.

It is the *experience* of poetry that seems to have been lost. And poetry is nothing if not an experience. There is really nothing standardized about it, and perhaps this is why not much poetry gets taught anymore.

A poem is not a word puzzle to be figured out, though some teachers approach it that way. A poem is not a linguistic Rubik's cube. It is not even primarily an intellectual event, I believe. In my experience, a poem enters the body not so much through the brain as through the skin, the gut, the hands, the heart. . . . Emily Dickinson said that she knew a good poem when she felt like the top of her head was going to blow off, or when she got goosebumps up her spine. Robert Frost said that poetry is a way of taking life by the throat.

Poetry, then, is physical. Words embody our experience of the world. Words body forth the meaning of our lives. A poem even resembles the human form: "The broken torso of the poem," Lawrence Durrell wrote in one of his poems. A poem has a skin (sound), and a skeleton (nouns), and muscles (verbs). Poetry is visceral. A poem is often more real to us than the news that we see on evening television, especially if it stays with us and matches itself to our breath, to our heartbeat. Thus does poetry *live*.

20

There is no sure way to test for that deep identification with the written word. It can scarcely even be explained. A reader's love of words—and the deep effect of a poem's embrace—do not submit themselves to quantitative measurement.

V

My thinking about poetry does not amount to a theory, or a system, much less a philosophy. In fact, my classroom probably runs more like a shop class than a literature class. I tell my students that writing a poem is like building a birdhouse—you can talk all day about the aesthetics of the thing, but if no birds come to live in it, then it is not much good, is it?

Or: the ability to write poetry is a gift, like a mule—you have to work it to get anything done. Because the only way to begin to approach the secret of writing—*the right word in the right place every time*—is this: *you must practice the craft.* There is no way around it; you must go *through* it.

Wendell Berry, the aged Kentucky poet, still refers to himself as an amateur poet. Some practitioners in other fields, I have noticed, take to calling themselves master-artists. A poet would never do this. For one, it's bad luck. For another, the poet is never the master; the craft is the master, and the poet serves a lifelong apprenticeship. This idea is not original with me—it is at least as old as the oldest Japanese haiku. When I talk about this in class, some student invariably objects: "You mean, we will never be any good?"

No, that is not what I mean. What I mean is this: you might get good— you might even get very good—but you will never get perfect. And so, relax. The pressure is off. You can take the rest of your life to learn how to write a poem, if you wish, and then, well, what a marvelous life you will have led!

25

Let me take an example from the visual arts: A fortunate stroke of paint appears on the painter's canvas out of nowhere. Well. Not out of *no-where*. It has been long prepared for. Or, the artist has long prepared to recognize its worthiness. Talent makes for good luck. Some ability at craft is required for the fortunate accident to happen. An artist-friend of mine was asked at a recent show, "How long did it take you to paint this painting?" She replied, "All my life."

Or, to take an example from golf: Arnold Palmer, playing a casual round with friends, once holed out on a chip shot from the sand trap. "Lucky shot," one of his friends said. To which Palmer is said to have replied, "Right. But I notice, the more I practice, the luckier I get."

VI

Not all of my students go on to become professional writers. I expect, however, that my students turn out to be cultured individuals. And I believe that any cultured person ought to be able—equally—to speak a foreign language, play a musical instrument, cook a decent pasta marinara, and write a poem. I also want my students to have beautiful lives. Their chance at this is enhanced if they can also create beauty. To craft the beautiful is nothing less than to attend imaginatively to the beneficent spirit of the universe.

VII

Sometimes, the sophistication of my students can amaze me. For just one example, a young woman named Sunny Allen, whom I had not seen since she was a student in my (Kentucky) Governor's School for the Arts class in the late 1990s, recently turned up working on a phonetic transcription method of writing poems. How impressive is that? (She had come into my class already smart, and I just hoped that she graduated not any less smart.)

30   Her recent study of Italian has led her to consider what she calls "consonant clusters" as a way of slowing down the poetic line. What does this mean? To cluster consonants at the endings and beginnings of consecutive words is to create a musical thickness, to radically slow down the reading of a line. It is to write for both sound *and* meaning. The untitled poem that she showed me reads, in its entirety:

> *That winged thing made this, yes,*
> *from the bright strike of its hard hoof*
> *alighting to earth. Let our paths still,*
> *here, on this day, where the blue of the*
> *sky and the blue of the waves are the*
> *one blue stretched out world sized.*

One cannot read this poem quickly. It does what all poetry tries to do: slow the reader down long enough for the world to be perceived, appreciated, pleasured in. The thickness of this poem also begs for it to be read again and again, layering it ever deeper in the sensitive reader's mind and heart.

In poetry, sound cannot be sacrificed to meaning. Indeed, sound often *is* meaning. No one asks you to explain a favorite piece of music. That would be both reductive and pedantic. Yet this is precisely what too many of us do with poetry.

VIII

The question naturally arises: Can creative writing be taught? I believe so. Can it take a student with little or no talent and turn him or her into a writer? Well, probably not. However, "talent," like "meaning," is a slippery term.

One student of mine, who struggled mightily in my poetry class, en-   35
tered a highly productive phase only after reading some Gary Snyder poems and making a literary pilgrimage to the American northwest, to visit the grave of poet and writer Raymond Carver. This student has gone on to publish poems in the venerable *Evergreen Review,* where I cannot get published. As a teacher, I cannot be jealous that Gary Snyder and Raymond Carver taught him whereas I could not. A good teacher does not want disciples. A good teacher wants freethinkers. For their part, students crave inspiration, and where they find that inspiration can often be quite unpredictable.

Students are so ready to take on the world. Sometimes, the best a teacher can do is show them a few things, then get out of the way. I am thinking of a scene in Francois Truffaut's film *Small Change.* A second-form teacher is exhorting her class to read a dramatic passage with some real feeling, but her students just drone on; not until the teacher steps outside for a smoke does she hear, through the open windows above, one of her students get up and declaim the passage with flair, and urgency, and passion. All it takes, sometimes, is for the teacher to just leave the room.

What is more, teaching does not always move in a straight line toward its stated aims. My college requires that faculty identify three learning outcomes for each course taught; I would hope that I satisfy those three outcomes, and also that I teach my students a great deal more than just those three.

The model for the teacher in the film *Dead Poets Society,* Samuel Pickering, once said:

> . . . To educate for the future, one must educate for the moment. Classes should sprawl beyond particular subjects. In digressions lie lessons. Expose students to possibilities. Let them know about your fondness for china, birds, tag sales, and gardening. Talk to them about economics and sociology, to be sure, but also about places you have been and things you have

seen and thought. Instill the awareness that for the interested person days and nights glitter.

40   Of my own professors in college, I confess to you that I do not recall all that much of what they might have said in their lectures, at least not at this great remove in time, anyway. However, I do still recall—and with some precision—the humor and the gentleness and the kindness that they modeled for us. Is there any lesson more important than this?

To quote my friend Wendell Berry once again, in conversation with a few colleagues: "Do you want to know how good a teacher I was? Go and talk to my students twenty years from now, and see what kind of people they have turned out to be." In these assessment-crazed times, I think this is fairly cogent advice. A teacher must be ever aware: What kind of people am I graduating?

IX

What is the goal of education? Simple human flourishing. Alright, perhaps not so simple. My wife, a philosophy professor, has taught me about natural law theory, which holds that human flourishing is life's highest value. Poetry—that most personal *and* universal of expressions—can play a significant role in this.

I have in mind a certain young man. An early graduate of my poetry seminars who has gone on to Jesuit seminary, among other pursuits, he would most likely be considered a failure by the campus career advisor. He hasn't a penny to his name, does not own a car or house, has no graduate degree nor any Fortune 500 corporation on his resume. Instead, he has spent his time working with the poor in Peru; assisting in literacy programs for children in Kentucky; reading widely; and writing finely crafted poems. A half-hour of conversation with this young man and you will be wowed, in a quiet way. I know, one day, he will do something remarkable.

Promise cannot be measured, nor can creativity. But I can assure you that this young man is the sort who carries the waves inside him. You would know it too, straightaway, could you meet him. Perhaps you know someone like him. For this do we teach.

Poetry   **Gary Soto**

WHAT THE FEDERAL BAILOUT MEANS TO ME

Still the bankers went on with their adding machines
And their three bags full . . .
And at three in the afternoon
We poets with shadowy faces arrived
With stones in our pockets,   5
With lint and unclaimed receipts for madness.

I asked, "Might you help?"
From where I sit at a long table,
I can see through the glass partition small sandwiches,
Crackers like poker chips,   10
Olives on toothpicks, carrots like oars,
Cheese that smelled of stinky dollar bills.
A woman sipped water,
Runoff of some successful company.

De Medici, I name dropped,   15
Carnegie, Rockefeller and Mr. Bill Gates.
I rolled a pencil between my palms for the friction
Of friendship. It didn't help.
We were eraser markings
On the literary landscape, outdated carbon copies,   20
Faxed recipes for poverty soup.
Our eyes? Infinite zeros from too much coffee.

The banker spoke with his mouth open—
An ugly merging of crackers on the back molars.
He wasn't pleased. We had interrupted the feast   25
In the glass room. He rolled his tongue
Over his teeth and said, "My son drew a house
On fire, right on the kitchen wall. What does that mean?"

It means foreclosures, I thought,
Whole families standing on the street   30
With embers in their eyes. It means a father will juggle
Three olives for his family's supper.

This is nice, all of it is nice . . .
But I'm afraid, the banker said, we deal in numbers, not words.

35   We were led out the door and to an elevator—
        Three musicians with their instruments were getting off.
        I told them with my eyes, "Don't even try."

        Bankers: we give them our money.
        When we ask for some of it back,
40   They allow us to peer into their ugly mouths
        Where it all went.

Poetry　**Leon Stokesbury**

UNSENT MESSAGE TO MY BROTHER IN HIS PAIN

Please do not die now. Listen.
Yesterday, storm clouds rolled
out of the west like thick muscles.
Lightning bloomed. Such a sideshow
of colors. You should have seen it.   5
A woman watched with me, then we slept.
Then, when I woke first, I saw
in her face that rest is possible.
The sky, it suddenly seems
important to tell you, the sky   10
was pink as a shell. Listen
to me. People orbit the moon now.
They must look like flies around
Fatty Arbuckle's head, that new
and that strange. My fellow American,   15
I bought a French cookbook. In it
are hundreds and hundreds of recipes.
If you come to see me, I shit you not,
we will cook with wine. Listen
to me. Listen to me, my brother,   20
please don't go. Take a later flight,
a later train. Another look around.

Poetry **Adrienne Su**

FOUR SONNETS ABOUT FOOD

1

Words can't do
what bird bones
can: stew
to the stony
5   essence
of one
small soul, the spent
sacrifice boiled down
to the hard white
10   matter that nourishes
the mighty
predator, who flourishes
on the slaughtered
animal and water.

2

15   Who feeds
another is like bones
to him who eats
(I say "him" only
because it is a man
20   in my house
who eats and a woman
who goes about
the matter of sustenance),
food being always
25   a matter of life and
death and each day's
dining
another small dying.

3

Scallops seared
30   in hot iron
with grated ginger,
rice wine,

and a little oil
of sesame, served
with boiled   35
jasmine rice, cures
the malaise
of long, fluorescent
weekdays
spent   40
in the city
for money.

4

I am afraid
I can't always be
here when you need   45
a warm body
or words; someday
I'll slip
into the red clay
I started with   50
and forget
who you are,
but
for now, here's
my offering: baked red   55
fish, clear soup, bread.

Drama   **Bara Swain**

CRITICAL CARE

Characters

CAROL: Forties or fifties.
THERESA: Twenties or thirties, Carol's daughter.

Setting

Twenty-four-hour diner.

Time

Winter, graveyard shift, 1:30 A.M.

At rise: CAROL and her daughter, THERESA, are sitting at a table for four in an empty coffee shop. THERESA is wearing jeans and red high heels. CAROL is carelessly dressed. Their winter coats are hung over the back of a chair. The downstage chair is empty. On the table are menus, two cups of coffee, milk and sugar. In the background, the sound of a siren is heard over the softly playing music. Lights up on CAROL, who empties several sugar packets into her coffee.

CAROL: So I ran down the Coleman West corridor and up four flights of stairs to the Coronary Care Unit. And there's your Aunt Evelyn in front of the nurse's station crying, "Help! Help! I was just swallowed whole by a hungry red fox!"

THERESA: She wore her new fur coat to the hospital?

CAROL: Bingo! With a red fox handbag that cost more than your college education, Theresa. So I'm trying to catch my breath, and Evelyn plants her hands on those childbearing hips of hers, and she says to me, "Carol, did you read Walter's Discharge Plan!?" And I unbuttoned my designer coat from K-Mart, and I said to my sister, "What are you talking about, Evelyn? Walter never left the hospital! He's back in critical care, for God's sake!" *(Raising the pitcher of milk.)* Do you want some milk?

THERESA: I'll drink it black, Mom.

CAROL: And then I said—in my very best "inside" voice, I said, "It's the middle of the night, Evelyn. I'm missing my favorite rerun of *Everybody Loves Raymond* just to be with you, Evelyn. What else do you want?"

THERESA: That's a loaded question.

CAROL: Yeah, well your aunt tosses her head back and looks down her aquiline nose at me like I stole her prom date or something.

THERESA: You did, Mom.

CAROL: What?

THERESA: You stole Aunt Evelyn's prom date. Everyone knows that.

CAROL: Oh, that's water under the dam.

THERESA: I think it's a bridge, Mom.

CAROL: Water under the damn bridge, then. God, this coffee is hot. Hot
and strong—*(She adds some more milk.)*—like Evelyn's first husband.

THERESA: Mother!

CAROL: What?

THERESA: Poor Aunt Evelyn.

CAROL: Yeah, right. So then your poor Aunt Evelyn—not!—says to me
for the second time in thirty seconds, "Carol," she says, "did you or
did you not read Walter's discharge plan!?" And her hips are wiggling
and her nose is flaring, and I'm thinking to myself: Is this a trick
question? And—why do nostrils flare in instead of out? And then—
just then, I remembered something else, Theresa. I remembered a
piece of paper lying next to your Uncle Walter's dinner tray yesterday.
And so I said to my sister, "What are you talking about, Evelyn? Are
you talking about that piece of colored paper?" *(To Theresa.)* Honestly,
Theresa, it wasn't even lined! It was just a plain, stupid sheet of
light . . . a sort of light purple-colored paper.

THERESA: Lavender?

CAROL: More like a bruise.

THERESA: Mauve?

CAROL: Bingo! The color of that awful bridesmaid dress I wore to
Evelyn's second wedding.

(THERESA laughs.)

CAROL: Zip it up, Theresa. That will never, ever be a laughing matter to
me. I mean it!

THERESA: It was twenty-five years ago, Mom.

CAROL: Well, it seems just like yesterday. Are you ready to order?

THERESA: No, I want to know what Aunt Evelyn said.

CAROL: Oh, she just turned redder than your Fuck-Me pumps—

(THERESA laughs again.)

THERESA: They were on sale, Mom!!!

CAROL: Uh-huh. And I said to her, "Evelyn, for the last time, it was just
a loose sheet of goddamned paper lying next to Walter's chicken
breast and string beans with blanched almonds, and it said things
with bullets. You know, like: Bullet. Make sure you get your blood
work done when you leave the hospital, and . . . Bullet. Don't forget to
make a follow-up appointment with your doctor. And —"

(Whispering.) Oh my God, Theresa! Don't look now, but there's a drop-dead handsome busboy wiping down the counter.

THERESA: Mother . . . ! "Bullet."

CAROL: Right. "Bullet: Get a medical alert. Ask your son, Evelyn," I said. "He was there."

THERESA: I thought Jimmy went to the orthodontist yesterday.

CAROL: He did. We met afterwards, and I took him over to the hospital to visit his dad. I thought it would be a nice surprise, right?

THERESA: Right.

CAROL: So then your Aunt Evelyn says to me—excuse me—she roars at me. Wait—did I say "roar"? I meant, she bellows at me: "Are you saying that you read Walter's discharge plan in front of our son!!?" And I was dumbstruck, you know? Really, I felt . . . struck dumb or something, and I said, "Jimmy is fifteen years old, Evelyn. He knows algorithms, for crying out loud. He can conjugate verbs, for God's sake! He tried pot!"

THERESA: He did?

CAROL: I don't know. He looks like a pothead.

THERESA: Did you say that to her, Mom?

CAROL: No, I didn't say that to her. I said, "Yes, Evelyn, yes. I read it in front of Jimmy."

THERESA: Did you beat your chest, too?

CAROL: No, I did not beat my chest. I said, "I had no choice, Evelyn, because your husband kept crossing his legs." "Walter," I said, "you just had a triple bypass. You should keep your legs elevated and un-crossed." And so your uncle uncrossed his legs, speared another green bean, and then he did it again!

THERESA: I don't get it.

CAROL: His legs. He crossed them again. Like this.

(CAROL pushes out the empty chair and lifts her legs up. She raises her right leg up high and crosses it over the left.)

THERESA: Sorry, Mom.

CAROL: I'll do it again. Observe, Theresa. *(She raises her leg up higher this time and holds it in the air. Then she crosses her raised leg over the other. She looks at THERESA for her reaction.)* Oh, for God's sake. Do I have to spell everything out for you, too? "Evelyn," I said, "every time Walter crossed his bandy little legs, I got a ringside view of the family jewels." *(THERESA laughs.)*

CAROL: Jimmy must've seen his father's whang-bone, too, but he didn't say a word. And, of course, I didn't say anything.

THERESA: Of course.

CAROL: I just . . . averted my eyes and picked up some reading material. At least, I thought it looked like reading material and so I read it. Aloud.

THERESA: You read Uncle Walter's discharge plan?

CAROL: Yeah. NO! It was a piece of goddamned mauve paper!

THERESA: Uh-huh.

CAROL: OK, so shoot me. Yeah, I did it! And you know what else I felt like saying to your precious aunt?

THERESA: Don't hold back, Mom.

CAROL: Honest to God, I wanted to say to her, "Evelyn, I looked in your closet last week, too, and I counted eleven winter coats." That's right, Theresa, plus three lined raincoats, cross my heart and hope to live long enough to use my new George Eastman Grill.

(THERESA laughs.)

CAROL: What's so funny now?

(CAROL grabs THERESA's menu, leans forward, and smacks her on top of her knuckles. CAROL keeps poking her with the menu while THERESA laughs.)

CAROL: Let's see who laughs last when I master Chicken la Poive with Baby Asparagus—

(CAROL smacks the menu on top of THERESA's head several times. THERESA laughs hysterically.)

THERESA: Stop it, Mom!

CAROL:—or Caribbean Tuna with Mango Salsa and a side of sliced Portabello Mushrooms!

THERESA: Cut it out, Mom! I can't breathe!

CAROL: Go tell your Uncle Walter. I don't think he'll be too sympathetic, either.

THERESA: Mother!

CAROL: What?

THERESA: He's in critical care!

CAROL: Bingo! He's like eighty years old, Theresa!

(CAROL prepares to give THERESA another wallop. THERESA cowers, protecting her head.)

THERESA: And . . .! you're making a scene, Mom.

(CAROL thinks about it. She drops her arm. Then she slides the menu toward THERESA.)

CAROL: I concede.

THERESA: Thank you.

CAROL: Even though there's no one else in this place except for you and me and a well-hung busboy. *(Quickly.)* Sorry.

THERESA: Apology accepted.

(THERESA opens her menu and studies the selections carefully. Silence. CAROL studies her daughter. Another siren moans in the background.)

CAROL: I feel terrible about your Uncle Walter. You know that, don't you?

THERESA: Of course you do, Mom. We all do. *(She looks up from the menu.)* So what do you think about splitting a BLT? Or do you want to just order a couple of appetizers?

CAROL: I want you to promise me something.

THERESA: OK, here's the deal. If we order Jumbo Shrimp Cocktail and Potato Skins with Bacon and Cheese, I promise that you can have four of the shrimp and all of the sour cream, and I'll have two shrimp and all of the bacon. How's that?

(THERESA smiles at her mother. CAROL leans forward.)

CAROL: Honey, pay attention. I need you to give me your word on something. It's important to me.

THERESA: Go for it, Mom.

CAROL: If I ever get like Uncle Walter . . .?

THERESA: Uh-huh.

CAROL: . . . just roll me in front of a car, OK?

THERESA: Mother!

CAROL: Or push me off the roof. That should do it.

THERESA: You're out of your mind! Where do you come up with these things?

CAROL: I just don't ever want to be that kind of burden to you, Theresa. Or to your husband.

THERESA: Mother, I'm not married! And I'm not getting married! Not even close.

CAROL: But you will some day.

THERESA: Nuts! You're absolutely nuts!

CAROL: *(Ignoring her.)* Now listen to me carefully, Theresa. If you aren't able to do it yourself, then ask your aunt Evelyn. She can be a little squeamish, but I don't think she'd mind putting a plastic bag over my head while I'm sleeping. Can you do that for me?

THERESA: Aunt Evelyn won't do it either, Mom!

CAROL: Of course, she will. Just make sure my hair has a little bounce to it. I don't want Evelyn criticizing my thin hair.

THERESA: This is ridiculous!

CAROL: This is funny—not! . . . but your Aunt Evelyn has always been very, very . . . exceptionally critical of me over the years and—

THERESA: Don't, Mom.

CAROL: And I know that's no surprise to you, Honey. But Evelyn is my sister and I love her—

THERESA: It's not worth it, Mom.

CAROL:—even though she takes more pride in her goddamned Burberry raincoat than me. And better care of it, too.

THERESA: Mom. Forget about it. Let's not get into it. Let's just order. *(THERESA calls out.)* WAITRESS!

CAROL: I'd do anything for her. You know that, Theresa, don't you?

THERESA: Yes, Mom. What do you want to eat?

CAROL: I love her. And all I ever really wanted was for my sister to—

THERESA: Shh, Mom. Please, let's order. Now what do you want?

CAROL: What do I want?

(She stares at THERESA. Then CAROL picks up the menu. She stares at it.)

THERESA: *(Gently.)* What do you want, Mom?

(CAROL looks up. She appears grief stricken.)

CAROL: *(Whispers.)* It's not on the menu. *(Silence. CAROL raises her voice.)* It's not on the menu. *(CAROL rises, holds onto the table and cries out in anguish.)* WAITRESS! IT'S NOT ON THE MENU!!!

(Lights dim to black.)

END OF PLAY

Graphic Narrative   **Craig Thompson**

EXCERPT FROM *CARNET DE VOYAGE*

20 AVRIL 04 Left Lyon for Toulouse, worn thin with sickness again. On the way to the train station, Laëtitia suggested that illness is a way the body closes in and shelters itself from chaos.

In Toulouse, another friend, whom I first met at that same signing in Boston, greeted me at the Station— Sebastien

Then he took me to meet his friend Blutch — who happens to be one of my most favorite cartoonists in the world.

For a moment, I was a bit shy & fan-boyish, but his life is as mundane as mine, with his Son ill in bed and the phone constantly ringing and water leaking in the kitchen.

20 avril

22 avril 04

Woke to rain and thunder magnified on the tile roof of Marion & Sebastien's attic apartment. Rained all day -- Perfect time to spend at Blutch's — drawing together...

...along with his cartoonist buddy Jake Raynal,

For Lunch, we joined up with Marion and then Blutch's ex-girlfriend.

She was instantly recognizable from his drawings, and I said as much, before realizing it might be inappropriate. But it was overwhelming how familiar every nuance of her movement was through my knowledge of Blutch's work.

After she left, I asked him if she was his muse. Of course, She still is. We debated if one can ever abandon their muse, even after the end of a relationship.

ARE YOU SEARCHING FOR A NEW MUSE?

NOW THE BIRDS & THE TREES & THE MOROCCAN KITTIES ARE MY MUSE.

JAKE'S ATYPICAL CARTOONIST BUILD

Back at his place, I perused hundreds of Blutch's drawings of his ex -- All beautiful, all unpublished --

DRAWINGS ARE MY PRIVATE LIFE.

Poetry **Amber West**

PIRATE'S ADMONITION

Sand dollars and jellyfish corpses litter
her shores. The Pacific, she's an angry blue—
heed this warning: cross her and she'll swallow you.
She does not distinguish: pirates and surfers,
5   boys and girls, size is no lifeboat, my pearls,
you're the skin of a nut not worth her time to chew,
but if she's hungry she'll toss you in her stew.
You'll tumble in the eye of her salt seltzer
hurricane 'til you're coughed up like the whales
10   she leaves leathering in coves for—God knows—
the wind keeps no time, no secrets
as it tows death's rot-stink like a wrecked vessel.
So beware the poisonous white foam
snakes spilled on the sand each wave she breaks.

Poetry   **William Carlos Williams**

YOUNG SYCAMORE

I must tell you
this young tree
whose round and firm trunk
between the wet

pavement and the gutter   5
(where water
is trickling) rises
bodily

into the air with
one undulant   10
thrust half its height—
and then

dividing and waning
sending out
young branches on   15
all sides—

hung with cocoons
it thins
till nothing is left of it
but two   20

eccentric knotted
twigs
bending forward
hornlike at the top

Poetry **Al Young**

A LITTLE MORE TRAVELING MUSIC

    A country kid in Mississippi I drew water
       from the well
    & watched our sun set itself down behind
       the thickets,
5   hurried from galvanized baths to hear music
    over the radio—Colored music, rhythmic & electrifying,
    more Black in fact than politics & flit guns.

    Mama had a knack for snapping juicy fruit gum
    & for keeping track of the generation of chilrens
10   she had raised, reared & no doubt forwarded,
    rising thankfully every half past daybreak
    to administer duties the poor must look after
    if theyre to see their way another day, to eat, to live.

    I lived & upnorth in cities sweltered & froze,
15   got jammed up & trafficked
    in everybody's sun going down but took up with the
       moon
    as I lit about getting it all down up there
    where couldnt nobody knock it out.

20   Picking up slowly on the gists of melodies, most noises
       softened.
    I went on to school & to college too, woke up cold
    & went my way finally, classless, reading all poems,
       some books & listening to heartbeats.

25   Well on my way to committing to memory the ABC
       reality,
    I still couldnt forget all that motherly music,
    those unwatered songs of my babe-in-the-wood days
    until, committed to the power of the human voice,
30   I turned to poetry & to singing by choice,
    reading everyone always & listening, listening for a
       silence deep enough
    to make out the sound of my own background music.

Poetry **Al Zolynas**

LOVE IN THE CLASSROOM

—for my students

Afternoon. Across the garden, in Green Hall,
someone begins playing the old piano—
a spontaneous piece, amateurish and alive,
full of a simple, joyful melody.
The music floats among us in the classroom.   5

I stand in front of my students
telling them about sentence fragments.
I ask them to find the ten fragments
in the twenty-one-sentence paragraph on page forty-five.
They've come from all parts   10
of the world—Iran, Micronesia, Africa,
Japan, China, even Los Angeles—and they're still
eager to please me. It's less than half
way through the quarter.

They bend over their books and begin.   15
Hamid's lips move as he follows
the tortuous labyrinth of English syntax.
Yoshie sits erect, perfect in her pale make-up,
legs crossed, quick pulse minutely
jerking her right foot. Tony,   20
from an island in the South Pacific,
sprawls limp and relaxed in his desk.

The melody floats around and through us
in the room, broken here and there, fragmented,
re-started. It feels mideastern, but   25
it could be jazz, or the blues—it could be
anything from anywhere.
I sit down on my desk to wait,
and it hits me from nowhere—a sudden
sweet, almost painful love for my students.   30

"Never mind," I want to cry out.
"It doesn't matter about fragments.
Finding them or not. Everything's

a fragment and everything's not a fragment.
35   Listen to the music, how fragmented,
     how whole, how we can't separate the music
     from the sun falling on its knees on all the greenness,
     from this moment, how this moment
     contains all the fragments of yesterday
40   and everything we'll ever know of tomorrow!"

     Instead, I keep a coward's silence.
     The music stops abruptly;
     they finish their work,
     and we go through the right answers,
45   which is to say
     we separate the fragments from the whole.

Appendix A:
A Guide to Manuscript Formats

Following, you will find pages made to look like manuscripts in the form of poetry, prose, and plays. The following examples are minimized to fit the book's pages, but full-size versions are available for viewing or downloading at www .oup.com/us/roney. There are, of course, many variations on the way that people format manuscripts for different purposes, but these should give you good basic guidelines for use in your Creative Writing classes and, later on, for submitting your work to journals and contests.

POETRY

Your Name   60 lines
1000 Street Address
City, State Zip (and Country if sending outside USA)
phone number
email address

POEMS ARE DIFFERENT

As with prose pieces, you may either use all
caps or caps and lowercase for the title.
You may either put the title flush left,
as I have done here,
or you may center it as you would with prose.
The latter looks a little funny if
your lines are short.

And please don't think that it's necessary
to center every line of your poem.
That usually just makes it harder
to read
because your eye has to jump
around.

In almost all cases, your poetry for
submissions should be single-spaced and the poem itself
should be flush left. There are many exceptions,
of course. Sometimes
the jumpiness
is part of the point,
as with Becker and Emanuel.

Skip a line between stanzas.

If your poem contains a very long line that runs over from one physical line to the next, you can
        indicate that by indenting it.
The large width of an 8 ½ x 11 piece of paper, fortunately,
means you won't have to do that often,
but be prepared for editors to use that technique
because the widths of journals is often half that of a page.

Once a poem has been "finalized" and you are ready
to submit,

Your Name
[POEMS ARE DIFFERENT, Page 2, continue stanza]

you'll have to go in and indicate
whether or not
the end of the page
also represents
a stanza break.
My "[POEMS ARE DIFFERENT, Page 2, continue stanza]"
means that the stanza
continues.
If it didn't,
I would say "[POEMS ARE DIFFERENT, Page 2, new stanza]."

There are various ways of doing this.
Some writers
indicate [break] or [no break] at the bottom
of the first page. Because strategies
differ, it's best to check
submission guidelines (or ask
your teacher)
what's preferred in a given instance.

You may also want to use your course number and
teacher's name when you're in classes rather
than your personal address, phone number, etc.

Remember that your line count
does not include these extra lines or the run-over long lines.

Another thing to watch for
is that tricky old
word processing programs
like to automatically
capitalize at the beginning of every doggone line,
which you may or may not want to do.
Change your automatic formatting settings
to make your life
as a poet easier.

PROSE

Your Name   973 words
1000 Street Address   fiction/nonfiction
City, State Zip (and Country if sending outside USA)
phone number
email address

TITLE IN CAPS IF YOU LIKE
But Not Necessary

by

Your Name

The first paragraph should be indented, just like all the rest of them. After the single-

spaced address (or class information—see below), center the text and space down about half-way

on the page, then type in your title. Some people use caps, boldface, or a slightly larger type size

for the title, but it's not necessary. Then space out your byline as shown above. When you have

spaced down for the first paragraph, remember to switch to left justification again, and reset the

line spacing for double-spaced text (not 1 or 1.15). You should set your margins to a standard

one inch all around.

Your second paragraph should not have any extra spaces between it and the previous

paragraph. Simply hit "enter" and then "tab" if need be. I'll give some specific instructions here

for Microsoft Word because it is the most common word processing software, but you can adapt

LISA RONEY/TITLE OR ABBREVIATED TITLE   2

these tips for any software that you use, including Open Office. Depending on your settings,

Microsoft Word will eventually start inserting the tab automatically, so you have to be careful

not to get paragraphs indented too far. To delete the extra spacing between paragraphs that newer

versions of Word have begun to insert automatically, go to Page Layout, Spacing, and set both

Before and After to 0. Set your font to Times New Roman 12 pt. It's best to do both of these

steps to your Normal template so that all future documents will be set correctly.

You will also want to add page numbers, at least by going into Insert, then choosing "Top

of Page" and unchecking "Show Number on First Page" or checking "Different First Page." This

depends on which version of Word you have. (You do not need a number on the first page

because its different formatting clearly shows it's the first page.) You will go to the View drop-

down menu and, first select Page View, then select Header and Footer. You must be in Page

View to see the Header with your page numbers in it. Simply click in the page number box, and

type in your name and the title or, if it's a long title, an abbreviated one, flush left in the Header

box. Hit Save at this point, and you should be set in terms of formatting your prose manuscripts.

One more note about your first page, though. On a manuscript for submission to a literary

magazine, you would include the address and other personal contact information I've shown

here. However, for classes, we usually ask that you instead include the course title and

professor's name. There is no need to violate your own privacy by sharing your personal

information with the entire class, and this is a convenient place to note your course number and

professor so you can keep your work straight. Remember that all the identifying information

should be single-spaced.

* * *

If you want a section break without a subhead, use centered asterisks to indicate where that break should be. This is especially important if your section break falls at the end of a page because otherwise it might be hard to tell there's an extra line space.

* * *

Dialogue can be a challenge to format and punctuate. First, remember that each change in speaker usually gets a new paragraph. This helps readers keep track of who is saying what and allows us to see visually something about the pace of the conversation.

Generally, use a comma before or after a quoted statement connected to a tag line that identifies the speaker: **"Hi, there, Mirabelle," Sybil shouted from across the room.** (I am using bold so can compare the punctuation; dialogue in your manuscripts should not be in bold.)

If the dialogue continues with a new sentence after the tag line, end the tag with a period and start a new sentence. **"I'm sleepy," said Derrick. "I don't know how I'm going to stay awake for that test."** However, if a tag line interrupts one complete sentence, put commas on both sides of it. **"After the test, though," continued Derrick, "I'll be pumped for the party."**

If a bit of dialogue ends with an exclamation point (which we should use sparingly) or a question mark, then that punctuation takes place of the usual comma. However, the tag line is still considered part of the same sentence and should not be capitalized.

"You're a nut!" my aunt said.

But not: **"You're a nut!" My aunt said.**

This can be confusing in two main ways. Dialogue can sometimes stand alone without a tag line when it's already clear who the speaker is, and sometimes a separate sentence can look like a tag line. Take the following example.

"Honey, you're up a little too high in the tree," my mother called up to me as I climbed. I ignored her and climbed further. "Get down from there!" My mother yelled at me from what seemed like a great distance. I could hardly hear her.

The last three sentences could easily have been instead: **"Get down from there!" my mother yelled. She seemed so far away that I could hardly hear her.**

Sentences within dialogue should be punctuated just like regular sentences unless in dialect or unless you are making a point about someone's sloppy or unconventional speech. So, NOT: **"What's your problem it's not a big deal," he said to his friend.** But like so: **"What's your problem? It's not a big deal," he said to his friend.** You might want to avoid colons and semi-colons within dialogue, as they don't reflect the usual casual way people speak. However, you can always start a new sentence or use a dash within dialogue to keep the sentences correct.

I also recommend that any student of writing have a good grammar and punctuation book or bookmark favorite good sites on the web. It's your job as a writer to write correctly as well as imaginatively.

PLAYS

Because play formats are designed for maximum readability, they tend to use more space than poetry or prose, and for that reason, here I will give a few guidelines for the separate pages required for title, character list, setting and time, and optional for a list of scenes, that will be useful if your play changes locations or times. I will only give a sample page from one scene. However, don't forget the front matter in your play—it's vital to introduce the action.

Please also note that the format given here is different from how you will see plays and screenplays formatted in most books, including this one. Publishers must be aware of space limitations and use a more condensed style of formatting than used for working scripts where margin space is often used for comments and revisions and where practicing actors need to be able to read at a glance. When you are turning in work for your class or submitting to a contest or other possible performance venue, you should use a format that is focused on readability. You may also want to obtain one of the many scriptwriting software packages such as Final Draft, Adobe Story, or ScriptBuddy. Some of these are available free of charge.

Overall Tips

- Play and screen scripts are both usually formatted in the typeface Courier at the 12-point size. Courier is based on old typewriter fonts, and it is spaced in a more predictable way than any other font. What this means is that anyone assessing a play can tell much more precisely how much time it would take up on stage or screen than if a variety of fonts and sizes were used.
- The rule of thumb is that one page equals one minute of performance. Therefore, for instance, a ten-minute play should be precisely ten pages long. A standard feature film script should be ninety pages long.
- The left margin on plays and screenplays is sometimes wider than the right margin because they are often bound together with binder clips, which can eat into the page. An extra left margin is given to make the pages *look* as though they have even margins. Probably for the short plays you will write for class, using standard one-inch margins is fine.

Front Pages

- Plays use separate title, cast-of-characters, and setting/time pages, which are not given page numbers.
- The title page should contain, centered: the title, how many acts are included, and a byline. Usually flush left, it should also include a copyright designation, address, phone number, and e-mail address for the author.

- The characters page should be given a centered title, then a flush left list of all characters in the order in which they appear in the play, and a brief description of each one.
- The settings/time page should also use centered titles, and flush left under each one a brief clarification of the opening location and time frame for the play. If there are multiple times and locations in different scenes, a following page listing those can be useful.

Main Action of the Play

- Dialogue pages begin with the designation of act and scene, though, of course, if you are writing a one-act, one-scene play, this is not needed. If your one-act play is divided into more than one scene, you should label those with centered capitalized text.
- Usually, opening scene directions are also centered on the page, or they begin in the center of the page. Note, however, that using the centering function in your word processing program won't work well here. You should tab to the center instead, so that you have a centered block of text that is itself flush left.
- Characters' names begin at the center of the page and extend to the right. (See above about using tabs to align.) They look centered, but actually they are aligned to a significant left indent throughout the play.
- Each act and scene begins on a new page. Starting with the first page of Act I, Scene 1, and in page number headers, three numbers are used. The first indicates the act and is given in Roman numeral form; the second number is the scene number, given in Arabic form; and, also in Arabic form, the third number indicates the actual page number. These are continuous throughout the entire manuscript. In a one-act play in one scene, you only use regular Arabic page numbers. These should always be in the upper right-hand corner, never centered or at the bottom of the page.

1

> (Opening stage directions may or may
> not be given in parenthesis, but in any
> case are single spaced starting in the
> center of the page. You might describe
> a bit more about the setting or actions
> that the characters take even before
> they speak.)

DAISY

When I speak, my name will also begin in the center of the page
and flow to the right. If I have a short name, it may look
absolutely centered, but it's not really.

SNOWFLAKE OBSIDIAN

This becomes clear with a longer name. The reason for this has
to do with how the eye works. Lines of dialogue themselves
should be easiest to find (for actors practicing their lines and
those analyzing the dialogue for effectiveness). Characters'
names are vital but repetitive.

DAISY

> (twitching with indignation)

You would think we would be the most important thing, but
somehow they think it's what we say that's crucial. What we do
also comes to the center of the page in embedded stage
directions. But at least they are set off with parentheses for
clarity.

> (Snowflake Obsidian walks back and
> forth behind Daisy.)

SNOWFLAKE OBSIDIAN

Well, you wouldn't want them to confuse what we say and what we
do, now would you?

> (Beat. Snowflake Obsidian stands very
> still, staring out over the audience,
> waiting.)

PLAY TITLE by Author Name

2

SNOWFLAKE OBSIDIAN

If I have to speak again, I guess it's worth saying that the script has to make it clear that it's me, and that you're not answering.

DAISY

Right. Correct. Absolutely perfect! Don't forget that the dialogue and stage directions should be single-spaced with extra spaces between each speaker and direction. Don't forget these details make for ease of reading!

SNOWFLAKE OBSIDIAN

As with all manuscript format issues, various people and places have various preferences, and it's always good to check on specifics. Sometimes, for instance, stage directions and actors' names are lined up on different margins, with the dialogue still furthest left, but then the stage directions, and after that the actor designations. And don't forget that more details about formatting longer plays—with multiple scenes and acts—can be found online.

DAISY

(sniffling)

You talk a lot!

END OF PLAY

PLAY TITLE by Author Name

Appendix B: Verse Forms

Because of the number of forms and types of formal poems that exist, this appendix cannot be complete or comprehensive, but it outlines some terminology and some verse forms that you may want to try, whether assigned by your teacher to do so or because you individually choose the challenge. Remember, the first time you try writing a sonnet or pantoum or one of the other complicated forms discussed here, it probably won't be a masterpiece. Doing so may feel more like a mathematical puzzle than art. It takes a long time to achieve enough familiarity with these forms to make them work for you instead of the other way around. Yet, your familiarity has to start somewhere, and these strictures may eventually force you to hone your words to new levels of clarity and insight. As comedian, actor, and poet Stephen Fry puts it in *The Ode Less Travelled*, "a mastery of . . . techniques . . . allow[s] us a confidence and touch that the uninformed reading and writing of verse could never bestow."

A variety of aspects may be considered under the umbrella of "formal" poetry. For instance, the sonnet form requires a certain number of *lines*, a certain number of *feet per line*, and the *predominance of one kind of foot*, the iambic foot, so that there will also be the same number of syllables per line. Other forms, such as the sestina, villanelle, and pantoum, don't require the dominance of one type of foot, but focus instead on *repetitions of words, rhymes, or entire lines*. The sestina and villanelle consist of *particular numbers of lines*, whereas the pantoum may be any length as long as the stanzas consist of four lines with a certain pattern of repeated lines.

In other words, each of these forms has a distinct "personality" as well as strictures that are more or less suited to particular subject matters. All of them also can be adapted and varied. You will find that, especially in contemporary formal verse, the exact conventions become a source of play and revision themselves. As you read more poetry, you will also learn to recognize each of these forms and elements of them in free verse poems that borrow from them.

Couplets refer to units of two lines. A **heroic couplet** is simply a pair of lines written in iambic pentameter. The term "couplet" doesn't only apply to a poem written all in two-line stanzas; any two-line stanza may be called a couplet, especially when at the end of a poem.

Examples of couplets in the book:

- first two stanzas of Pablo Neruda's "Your Feet" (p. 446)
- Tony Hoagland's "America" (p. 385)
- Michael Palmer's "The Cord" (p. 472)
- second section of Terrance Hayes's "The Golden Shovel" (p. 383)

The **quatrain** is any four-line stanza, the commonest stanza form in English. There are many variations on the quatrain—with different rhyme schemes, some with particular meters, some without set meter. Quatrains are often combined into longer forms, such as the **ballad**, which consists of stanzas with four lines, each one in iambic tetrameter (four iambs, eight syllables) with a rhyme scheme of *abab*. Ballads usually tell a story, and the form has no set length so that the four-line stanzas are akin to chapters in a novel and go on until the conclusion of the particular story. Many ballads vary considerably from the precise form—for instance using different numbers of lines per stanza or changing up the meter—and sometimes the term *ballad* is used simply to refer to long, multiple-stanza poems that tell tales, such as "The Raven" by Edgar Allan Poe.

Examples of quatrains in the book:

- Robin Becker's "The Children's Concert" (p. 291)
- Harryette Mullen's "Tree" (p. 445)
- Alicia Suskin Ostriker's "The Orange Cat" (p. 471)

Perhaps the best known poetic form is, of course, the **sonnet**, which is discussed in Chapter 4. Sonnets are known for compressing difficult emotions and providing a framework for exploring them. Though they originated as a form most common for love poetry, they now cover a wide range of usually personal subject matter focusing on emotions, even reactions to societal events such as war. Both of the most common forms are written in iambic pentameter and named after their earliest prolific practitioners. There are many other variations on the sonnet as well.

The **Petrarchan (or Italian) sonnet** is divided into an octave (eight lines) with a rhyme scheme of *abbaabba* and a sestet (six lines) with a variable combination of rhymes, though final couplet rhymes are avoided. Common sestet rhyming patterns are *cdcdcd* or *cdecde*. In this form of the sonnet, the divide between the first eight lines and the last six often represents what is called the **turn** (or **volta** in Italian), in other words, a shift in the poem's direction, mood, or tone. Often what comes after the turn forms a sort of resolution to the issues raised in the first part of the poem. Elizabeth Barrett Browning's "How Do I Love Thee?" is a classic of the form.

Example in the book:

- Amber West's "Pirate's Admonition" (with variations, but retaining the location of the volta) (p. 532)

The **Shakespearean (or English) sonnet** follows a more consistent rhyme scheme: *abab, cdcd, efef, gg*. In Shakespearean sonnets, as mentioned in Chapter 4, the **turn** usually occurs in the final couplet, often giving it a punchy, surprising, epigrammatic ending.

Examples in the book:

- Richard Frost's "For a Brother" in Chapter 4 (with variations) (p. 69)
- Mary Block's "Moving Song" (p. 292)

Blank verse (not to be confused with free verse) consists of lines written in iambic pentameter, but that don't rhyme. These can be comprised of fourteen lines and create a type of "blank verse sonnet," but blank verse may be used in any length of poem. Amber West's "Pirate's Admonition," for instance, uses blank verse in the last sestet. Many Shakespeare plays or segments of the plays are written in blank verse. Below is a snippet from *Romeo and Juliet*. Notice that Shakespeare here counts on some elision of syllables in "Juliet" and "envious" in order to keep the ten-syllable rhythm per line.

> But soft! What light through yonder window breaks?
> It is the East and Juliet is the sun!
> Arise fair sun and kill the envious moon,
> Who is already sick and pale with grief,
> That thou her maid art far more fair than she.

One of the oldest and most challenging poetic forms is the **sestina**, comprised of six six-line stanzas and a three-line **envoy** (a short concluding stanza). Although there is no determined line length, one thing to note about the sestina is that it will produce a fairly long poem of a total of 39 lines with an intricate pattern of word repetition. A sestina requires that you repeat at intervals in the poem six particular line-end words. So in this typical rhyme scheme, the same letters represent not only rhyming words, but the very same words. A typical pattern:

Stanza 1: *a b c d e f*
Stanza 2: *f a e b d c*
Stanza 3: *c f d a b e*
Stanza 4: *e c b f a d*
Stanza 5: *d e a c f b*
Stanza 6: *b d f e c a*
Stanza 7/Envoy: The envoy uses all six of the end-words, but, of course, only three can be at the ends; the other three usually appear in the middle of the three lines in a pattern like so: *b e, d c, f a* or *a b, c d, e f.* While these are typical orders of arranging the repetition, many poets devise their own patterns of repetition that contribute to their particular purposes. The meaning of the rhyming words often shifts gradually or takes on new layers as the poem progresses, and the form often provides a relentless, even obsessive tone where readers are forced to reconsider their initial impressions.

Example in the book:

- James Byrne's "Sestina for R" (p. 301)

Another popular form is the **villanelle**, which is a nineteen-line poem, consisting of five **tercets** (three-line stanzas) followed by a quatrain and having only two rhymes. It repeats the entire first line (*A1*) and the entire third line (*A2*), but often with variations, according to the following scheme:

Stanza 1: *A1 b A2*
Stanza 2: *a b A1*
Stanza 3: *a b A2*
Stanza 4: *a b A1*
Stanza 5: *a b A2*
Stanza 6: *a b A1 A2*

The repeated lines are usually varied slightly to fit the context and to shift the meaning, similar to the way the words shift meaning in a sestina.

Example in the book:

- Sherine Gilmour's "Little Boys" (p. 372)

Another type you might want to try is the **pantoum**, which emerged out of Malaysia. This uses four-line stanzas (quatrains), in which lines 2 and 4 are carried over, more or less whole, as the next stanza's lines 1 and 3. You write new lines 2 and 4 that are then carried over as lines 1 and 3. The poem can be any length, but the final lines 2 and 4 are in fact lines 3 and 1 of the first stanza, creating a circular feeling. Often this creates a sense of haunting or mystery.

Example in the book:

- Stuart Dischell's "She Put on Her Lipstick in the Dark" (p. 336)

One form that has spread from the Arabic world is the **ghazal**. Written as a series of a minimum of five couplets, but sometimes going up to as many as ten or fifteen, the ghazal is an elusive form that attempts to create subconscious or underground associations through rhyme rather than strict sense or logic. Each couplet ostensibly can stand on its own as a separate poem and often the connection between the couplets is not obvious, though it should be discernible with thought. The lines should all be of the same length, and a word or phrase is repeated at the end of both the lines of the first couplet and in the second line of each subsequent couplet. Sometimes, one or more words before this refrain word or phrase will rhyme or nearly rhyme as well, so that the sounds play throughout the poem, but today most poets writing in this form focus on the repeated refrain.

Example in the book:

- Agha Shahid Ali's "Stars" (p. 282)

We discussed **syllabic** and **strong-stress** (**accentual**) poems in Chapter 4 with James Tate's "Miss Cho Composes in the Cafeteria" (p. 66) as an example of the former and *Beowulf* as the latter. These are often easier types of formal poems to begin trying out, as there are fewer and simpler restrictions. These forms are flexible and easily adapted to however long a poem you want to write and to however long you want your lines to be. Both demonstrate the benefits of consistency, but allow for a playfulness that can help alleviate the challenge of writing in form.

There are many other particular poetic traditional forms—ballade (which is different by more than just one e from the ballad), ottava rima, rondeau, rondel, *rubaiyat*, cinquain, rhyme royal, terza rima, triolet, kyrielle, haiku, tanka, *rengu*, *luc bat*, *pathya vat*, *rajaz*, and many varieties of the sonnet. You can find examples of these and other forms at **www.poetryfoundation.org**, the Poetry Foundation website, and many other online sites. These traditions come from across the globe and across the centuries, and their survival and constant transformation indicate an ongoing desire for pattern and rhythm in poetry and in our use of language more generally. They all point out to us the beauty and intricacy of language, and they evolve just the same way language itself does. Remember that forms are always arising and changing. For instance, the **reverse** or **palindrome poem**, taken literally, means that every exact letter, word, or line must be repeated in reverse, and therefore such poems usually show a simplistic duality and deal with black-and-white opposites. However, even such a gimmicky form can evolve into something much more subtle and nuanced, as in this poem where the reversal is imagistic and emotional rather than rigid.

Example in the book:

- Christopher Shannon's "Apollo (at) Eleven" (p. 509)

If you become fascinated with meter and other formal aspects of poetry, you will inevitably become a contributor to the continued evolution of ancient forms and perhaps to the development of new ones or the transformation of existing ones.

Credits

Agee, James. "Knoxville: Summer 1915," from *A Death in the Family* by James Agee, copyright © 1957 by The James Agee Trust, renewed © 1985 by Mia Agee. Used by permission of Grosset & Dunlap, Inc., a division of Penguin Group (USA) Inc.

Quote from Albee, Edward, interviewed by Bruce J. Mann, "Interview with Edward Albee" in *Edward Albee: A Casebook*. Ed. Bruce J. Mann. New York: Routledge, 2003.

Alexie, Sherman. "Superman and Me," from THE MOST WONDERFUL BOOKS, editors Dorris and Buchwald, Milkweed Editions. Copyright © 1997 Sherman Alexie. All rights reserved. Used by permission of Nancy Stauffer Associates.

Ali, Agha Shahid. "Stars," from *Call Me Ishmael Tonight: A Book of Ghazals* by Agha Shahid Ali. Copyright © 2003 by Agha Shahid Ali Literary Trust. Used by permission of W. W. Norton & Company, Inc.

Quote from Allende, Isabel, *The House of the Spirits*. New York: Alfred A. Knopf, 1984.

Alvarez, Lynne. "On Sundays" © Lynne Alvarez. Reprinted by permission of The Susan Gurman Agency, LLC. In *Plays in One Act*, ed. Daniel Halpern. New York: Ecco Press, 1991.

Armantrout, Rae. "Home Federal" from *Veil: New and Selected Poems* © 2001 by Rae Armantrout. Reprinted by permission of Wesleyan University Press. www.wesleyan.edu/wespress

Quote from Baldwin, James, "James Baldwin Recalls His Childhood," *New York Times* 31 May 1964. Transcript from "Hubert Humphrey's South Dakota and James Baldwin's Harlem," *My Childhood*. WNEW. Prod. Arthur Barron. Dir. Don Horan. 1 June 1964. Television.

Quote from Banks, Russell, "Notes on Literature and Engagement" in *Burn This: PEN Writers Speak Out on the Power of the Word*. Ed. Toni Morrison. New York: HarperCollins, 2009.

Quote from Banville, John, "The Personae of Summer" in *Irish Writers and Their Creative Process*. Ed. Jacqueline Genet and Wynne Hellegouarc'h. Gerrards Cross, UK: Colin Smythe, 1996.

Quote from Barnes, Julian, *Nothing to Be Frightened Of*. New York, Knopf, 2008.

Quote from Barrington, Judith, *Writing the Memoir: From Truth to Art*, second edition. Portland, OR: Eighth Mountain Press, 2002.

Becker, Robin. "The Children's Concert" 25 lines by Robin Becker from *Giacometti's Dog*, by Robin Becker, © 1990. Reprinted by permission of the University of Pittsburgh Press.

Quote from *Beowulf*. Translated by Francis B. Gummere, 1886. *Project Gutenberg*. Web 21 January 2013.

Quote from Blais, Marie-Claire, *Deaf to the City*. Tr. Carol Dunlop. New York and Woodstock: Overlook, 1987. Originally published in French in 1979.

Quote from Blake, William, "Song: I love the jocund dance," in *The Poetical Works*. 1908. *Bartleby.com*. Web 21 January 2013.

Block, Mary. "Moving Song" © Mary Block. Used by permission of the author.

Blumenthal, Michael. "On Not Bringing Your Mother to Creative Writing Class," *Writer's Chronicle* 30.6 (May/Summer 1998). Reprinted by permission of the author.

Borden, William. "The Blues Street Jazz Club Rehearses." Copyright © 1993 by William V. Borden. Reprinted by permission of Nancy Lee-Borden, Executor. For performance rights, contact Nancy Lee-Borden, nancyLB@hughes.net. In *2009: The Best 10-Minute Plays for 2 or More Actors*, ed. Lawrence Harbison. Hanover, NH: Smith and Kraus, 2009.

Quote from Borges, Jorge Luis, "The Garden of Forking Paths" in *Labyrinths*. Translated by David Yates. New York: New Directions, reprint edition, 2007. Previously published as *El jardín de senderos que se bifurcan* in *Ficciones*. Editorial Sur, 1944.

Quote from Boswell, Robert, *The Half-Known World: On Writing Fiction*. Minneapolis: Graywolf Press, 2008.

Quote from Boyce, Frank Cottrell, "How to Write a Movie." *The Guardian* 29 June 2008. Web 2 September 2013.

Byrne, James. "Sestina for R" from *Blood/Sugar*, published by Arc Publications (2009, UK).

Quote from Byron, Lord George Gordon, in letter to Annabella Milbanke, 29 November 1813, in *Lord Byron: Selected Letters and Journals*. Ed. Leslie A. Marchand. Cambridge, MA: Belknap Press, 1982.

Quote about Lord Byron from Lamb, Lady Caroline, journal 1812, quoted in *Lady Morgan's Memoirs: Autobiography, Diaries, and Correspondence*. Vol. 2. Morgan, Lady Sydney Owenson. Second edition. London: William H. Allen, 1863.

Calvino, Italo. "All at One Point" from *Cosmicomics* by Italo Calvino, translated by William Weaver. Copyright © 1965 by Giulio Einaudi editore s.p.a. English translation copyright © 1968, and renewed 1996 by Houghton Mifflin Harcourt Publishing Company and Jonathan Cape Limited. Reprinted by permission Houghton Mifflin Harcourt Publishing Company. All rights reserved.

Quote (Chapter 10) from Capote, Truman, *In Cold Blood*. 1965/1966. New York: Random House, 2002.

Quote (Chapter 14) from Capote, Truman, remark to Judy Green. Quoted in "Unanswered Prayers, Part II: The Magical Drape." Julie Baumgold, *New York* 26 November 1984.

Quote from Carruth, Hayden, "The State of Letters" in *Sewannee Review* 107.2 (Spring 1999).

Quote from Michael Chabon, interviewed by Jane Henderson, "Don't Call Chabon's Genre Explorations 'Hack' Writing." *St. Louis Post-Dispatch* 27 April 2008.

Quote from Chekhov, Anton, letter to Lidya Alexyevna 19 March 1892, in *Letters of Anton Chekhov to His Family and Friends*. Tr. by Constance Garnett. New York: Macmillan, 1920. *Google Books*. Web 27 June 2014.

Quote from Coetzee, J. M. *Foe*. New York: Viking Press, 1986.

Cofer, Judith Ortiz. "The Changeling." Reprinted from *Prairie Schooner* 66.3 (Fall 1992) by permission of the University of Nebraska Press. Copyright 1992 by the University of Nebraska Press.

Quote from Cohen, Ethan, and Joel Cohen, *Barton Fink* in *Collected Screenplays 1: Blood Simple, Raising Arizona, Miller's Crossing, Barton Fink*. London: Faber & Faber, 2002.

Quote from Coleridge, Samuel Taylor. "The Rime of the Ancient Mariner" in *Lyrical Ballads 1798 and 1802* by William Wordsworth and Samuel Taylor Coleridge. Ed. Fiona Stafford. Oxford, UK: Oxford University Press, 2013. Originally published 1798.

Cortázar, Julio. "Letter to a Young Woman" from *End of the Game and Other Stories* by Julio Cortázar, copyright © 1963, 1967 by Random House, Inc. Used by permission of Pantheon Books, an imprint of the Knopf Doubleday Publishing Group, a division of Random House LLC. All rights reserved. Any third party use of this material, outside of this publication, is prohibited. Interested parties must apply directly to Random House LLC for permission. [Retitled "Letter to a Young Lady in Paris" in *Blow-up and Other Stories* by Julio Cortázar, 1985 by Pantheon Books.]

Quote from Descartes, René, "Of the Principles of Human Knowledge" in *The Meditations, and Selections from the Principles of Philosophy*. Trans. John Veitch. Chicago: Open Court Publishing and London: Kegan Paul, Trench, Trübner & Co., 1901. Originally published in Latin 1644.

Díaz, Junot. "Edison, New Jersey," from *Drown* by Junot Díaz, copyright © 1996 by Junot Díaz. Used by permission of Riverhead Books, an imprint of Penguin Group (USA) Inc.

Quote from Dickens, Charles. *A Tale of Two Cities*. 1859. Oxford, UK: Oxford University Press, 2008.

Dillard, Annie. "Total Eclipse" (pp. 84–103) from *Teaching a Stone to Talk: Expeditions and Encounters* by Annie Dillard. Copyright © 1982 by Annie Dillard. Reprinted by permission of HarperCollins Publishers.

Dischell, Stuart. "She Put on Her Lipstick in the Dark," from *Backwards Days* by Stuart Dischell, copyright © 2007 by Stuart Dischell. Used by permission of Penguin, a division of Penguin Group (USA) LLC.

Doctorow, E. L. Excerpt from *World's Fair: A Novel* by E. L. Doctorow, copyright © 1985 by E. L. Doctorow. Used by permission of Random House, an imprint of The Random House Publishing Group, a division of Random House LLC. All rights reserved. Any third party use of this material, outside of this publication, is prohibited. Interested parties must apply directly to Random House LLC for permission.

Dubus, Andre III. "Tracks and Ties" © Andre Dubus III. Reprinted by permission of Philip G. Spitzer Literary Agency. In *Contemporary Creative Nonfiction: The Art of Truth*, ed. Bill Roorbach. New York: Oxford University Press, 2001. Originally published in *Parnassus: The Literary Arts Magazine of Northern Essex Community College*, 2009.

Quote (Chapter 11) from Eliot, T. S., "Hamlet." 1919. Reprinted in *Selected Essays*. London: Faber & Faber, 1932.

Quote (Chapter 16) from Eliot, T. S., letter to his father 18 April 1917, in *The Letters of T. S. Eliot Vol 1: 1898–1922*, revised edition. New Haven: Yale University Press, 2011.

Emanuel, Lynn. "The Out-of-Body Experience," from *The Dig and Hotel Fiesta*. Copyright 1984, 1992, 1995 by Lynn Emanuel. Used with permission of the poet and the University of Illinois Press.

Erdrich, Louise. "Saint Marie" from the book *Love Medicine: New and Expanded Version* by Louise Erdrich. Copyright © 1984, 1993 by Louise Erdrich. Used by permission of Henry Holt and Company, LLC. All rights reserved.

Quote from Faulkner, William, "Faulkner at West Point." Interviewed by Joseph L. Fant, III, and Robert Ashley, in *Conversations with William Faulkner*. Ed. M. Thomas Inge. Jackson, MS: University Press of Mississippi, 1999.

Fill, Simon. "Night Visits." Caution Notice: Copyright © 2000 by Simon Fill. All Rights Reserved. Used with the permission of the author. Professionals and amateurs are hereby warned that this play is subject to a royalty. It is fully protected under the copyright laws of the United States of America, the British Commonwealth, including Canada, and all other countries of the Copyright Union. All rights, including professional, amateur, motion picture, recitation, lecturing, public reading, radio and television broadcasting, Internet and electronic rights, and the rights of translation into foreign languages are strictly reserved. These rights are controlled exclusively by Susan Schulman, A Literary Agency, 454 West 44th St., New York, N.Y. 10036 E: Schulman@AOL.com and royalty arrangements and licenses must be secured in advance of presentation and/or use.

Quote from Forster, E. M., *Aspects of the Novel*. New York: Harcourt, 1927. Copyright renewed 1955.

Fowler, Connie May. "Connie May Is Going to Win the Lottery This Week." In *Don't Quit Your Day Job: Acclaimed Authors and the Day Jobs They Quit*, ed. Sonny Brewer. MP Publishing, 2011. Reprinted by permission of The Joy Harris Literary Agency.

Concept of Freytag's pyramid from Freytag, Gustave in *Freytag's Technique of the Drama: An Exposition of Dramatic Composition and Art*. Tr. from the sixth edition by Elias J. MacEwan. Third edition. Chicago: Scott Foresman and Co., 1900.

Frost, Richard. "For a Brother" from *Neighbor Blood*. Copyright © 1996 by Richard Frost. Reprinted with the permission of The Permissions Company, Inc., on behalf of Sarabande Books, www.sarabandebooks.org

Quote from Fry, Stephen, *The Ode Less Traveled: Unlocking the Poet Within*. New York: Gotham Books/Penguin, 2005.

Quote from Gabriele, Lisa, "The Guide to Being a Groupie" in *Nerve* 29 October 2003. Web 4 March 2013.

Gallagher, Tess. "Ode to My Father" (excerpt from "My Father's Love Letters"), *American Poetry Review* (May/June 1981). Revised and expanded in *A Concert of Tenses: Essays on Poetry* by Tess Gallagher (Ann Arbor: University of Michigan Press, 1986). Copyright © by the University of Michigan Press 1986. Reprinted by permission of University of Michigan Press.

Gallagher, Tess. "3 A.M. Kitchen: My Father Talking" from *Midnight Lantern: New and Selected Poems*. Copyright © 1984, 2011 by Tess Gallagher. Reprinted with the permission of The Permissions Company, Inc. on behalf of Graywolf Press, Minneapolis, Minnesota, www.graywolfpress.org

Quotes and Pathway 8.10 adapted from Gardner, John, *The Art of Fiction*. New York: Vintage, 1991.

Gilmour, Sherine. "Little Boys" © Sherine Gilmour. Used by permission of the author.

Quote from Gladwell, Malcolm, *Outliers: The Story of Success*. New York: Back Bay Books, 2011.

Pathway 7.4 adapted from Goldberg, Natalie, *Wild Mind*. New York: Bantam, 1990.

Quote from Golding, William, *Lord of the Flies*. 1954. New York: Penguin, 1960.

Quote from Gornick, Vivian, *The Situation and the Story: The Art of Personal Narrative*. New York: Farrar, Straus and Giroux, 2002.

Quote from Gottlieb, Adam. "Poet, Breathe Now" in *Louder Than a Bomb*. Dir. Kevin Coval and Jon Siskel. Siskel/Jacobs Productions, 2010. Film.

Quote from Graves, Robert, "The Cost of Letters." *Horizon* September 1946. Quoted in J. C. Kaufman and J. D. Sexton, "Why Doesn't the Writing Cure Work for Poets?" *Review of General Psychology* 10.3 (2006).

Quote from Greene, Graham, in *Quotations for Speakers and Writers*. Ed. Allen Andrews. London, New York: Newnes, 1969.

Quote from Gross, Philip, "Small Worlds: What Works in Workshops If and When They Do?" in *Does the Writing Workshop Still Work?* Ed. Dianne Donnelly. Multilingual Matters: Bristol, UK, 2010.

Gutkind, Lee. "Teeth." Reprinted from *Forever Fat: Essays by the Godfather* by Lee Gutkind by permission of the University of Nebraska Press.

Hadas, Rachel. "Mnemonic" from *Literary Imagination*, vol. 10, no. 3 (2008): 302. © 2008 Association of Literary Scholars, Critics and Writers. By permission of Oxford University Press.

Haines, John. "On the Mountain" from *News from the Glacier: Selected Poems 1960–1980* © 1982 by John Haines. Reprinted by permission of Wesleyan University Press. www.wesleyan.edu/wespress

Quote from Hampl, Patricia, interviewed by Laura Wexler, "An Interview with Patricia Hampl." *The Writer's Chronicle* March/April 1998.

Quote from Hanish, Carol, "The Personal Is Political" in *Notes from the Second Year: Women's Liberation*. Eds. Shulamith Firestone and Anne Koedt. New York: Radical Feminism, 1970. Entire text now available on the Web at carolhanish.org/CHwritings/PIP.html.

Quote from Hauge, Michael, "Revealing Back Story Through Dialogue." *Michael Hauge's Story Mastery*. http://www.storymastery.com/qaa/45-revealing-back-story-through-dialogue. Web 8 August 2013.

Hayes, Terrance. "The Golden Shovel," from *Lighthead* by Terrance Hayes, copyright © 2010 by Terrance Hayes. Used by permission of Penguin, a division of Penguin Group (USA) Inc.

Hemingway, Ernest. "Hills Like White Elephants." Reprinted with the permission of Scribner Publishing Group from *The Short Stories of Ernest Hemingway* by Ernest Hemingway. Copyright © 1927 by Charles Scribner's Sons. Copyright renewed © 1955 by Ernest Hemingway. All rights reserved.

Quote from Henry, O., "Gift of the Magi" in *The Gift of the Magi and Other Short Stories*. Mineola, NY: 1992. Originally published in *The New York Sunday World* 10 December 1905.

Hoagland, Tony. "America" from *What Narcissism Means to Me*. Copyright © 2003 by Tony Hoagland. Reprinted with the permission of The Permissions Company, Inc., on behalf of Graywolf Press, www.graywolfpress.org

Hodgman, Ann. "No Wonder They Call Me a Bitch," *Spy* (1989). Reprinted by permission of the author.

Quote from Hood, Thomas, "The Death-bed," in *The Oxford Book of English Verse: 1250-1900*. Ed. Arthur Quiller-Couch. Oxford: Oxford UP, 1919. Previously published in *The Poetical Works of Thomas Hood*. Vol. I. Boston: Little, Brown and Co., 1857.

Quote from Hurston, Zora Neale, *Dust Tracks on a Road*. Philadelphia: J. P. Lippincott, 1942. Reprint New York: Harper Perennial, 2006.

Quote from Jayaram, Santosh, in "How to Avoid a Bonfire of the Humanities," by Michael S. Malone. *The Wall Street Journal* 24 October 2012. Web 15 January 2012.

Joudah, Fady. "Sleeping Trees" from *The Earth in the Attic* by Fady Joudah. Copyright © 2008 by Fady Joudah. Reprinted by permission of Yale University Press.

Quote from Kincaid, Jamaica, *A Small Place*. New York: Farrar, Straus and Giroux, 2000.

Komunyakaa, Yusef. "Salt" from *Pleasure Dome: New and Collected Poems* © 2001 by Yusef Komunyakaa. Reprinted by permission of Wesleyan University Press. www.wesleyan .edu/wespress

Kuusisto, Stephen. "Letter from Venice," from *Eavesdropping: A Life by Ear* by Stephen Kuusisto. Copyright © 2006 by Stephen Kuusisto. Used by permission of W. W. Norton & Company, Inc.

Quote from Lesser, Ellen, "The Girl I Was, The Woman I Have Become: Fiction's Reminiscent Narrators" in *Words Overflown by Stars: Creative Writing Instruction and Insight from the Vermont College of Fine Arts MFA Program.* Ed. David Jauss. Cincinnati, OH: F+W Media, 2009.

Levis, Larry. "At the Grave of My Guardian Angel: St. Louis Cemetery, New Orleans" from *The Selected Levis,* by Larry Levis, selected by David St. John, © 2000. Reprinted by permission of the University of Pittsburgh Press.

Quote from Lewis, C. S., "Sometimes Fairy Stories May Say Best What's To Be Said," in *Of Other Worlds.* 1966. Reprint edition. New York: Mariner Books, 2002.

Li, Yiyun. "Son" from *A Thousand Years of Good Prayers: Stories* by Yiyun Li, copyright © 2005 by Yiyun Li. Used by permission of Random House, an imprint of The Random House Publishing Group, a division of Random House LLC. All rights reserved. Any third party use of this material, outside of this publication, is prohibited. Interested parties must apply directly to Random House LLC for permission.

Quote from Lincoln, Abraham, "The Gettysburg Address." 1863. "What Lincoln Said" in Garry Wills, *Lincoln at Gettysburg: The Words that Remade America.* New York: Simon and Schuster, 2006.

Quote from Mamet, David, *One Directing Film.* New York: Penguin, 1992.

Quote from Malcolm X (and Alex Haley), *The Autobiography of Malcolm X.* 1965. New York: Ballantine Books, 1990. Also in "Twenty Million Black People in a Political, Economic, and Mental Prison," *Malcolm X: The Last Speeches.* Ed. Bruce Perry. New York: Pathfinder, 1989.

Markarian, Michele. "Phoning It In" from *35 in 10: Thirty-Five Ten-Minute Plays,* ed. Kent R. Brown. Woodstock, IL: Dramatic Publishing, 2005. © 2003 Michele Markarian. Reprinted by permission of the author. The amateur and stock acting rights to this work are controlled exclusively by The Dramatic Publishing Company without whose permission in writing no performance of it may be given. Royalty must be paid every time a play is performed whether or not it is presented for profit and whether or not admission is charged. A play is performed any time it is acted before an audience. Current royalty rates, applications and restrictions may be found at our Web site: www .dramaticpublishing.com. or we may be contacted by mail at: Dramatic Publishing, 311 Washington Street, Woodstock, IL 60098.

Quote from Martin, George R. R., interviewed by Adrià Guxens 7 October 2012. *Adria's News* http://www.adriasnews.com/2012/10/george-r-r-martin-interview.html

Quote from Marvell, Andrew, "The Garden." In *Miscellaneous Poems.* London: Nonesuch Press, 1923. Originally published 1681.

McPherson, Sandra. "To a Penny Postcard, © 1911" from *A Visit to Civilization* © 2002 by Sandra McPherson. Reprinted by permission of Wesleyan University Press. www .wesleyan.edu/wespress

Quote from Means, David, in Introduction to Raymond Carver's "Why Don't You Dance" in *Object Lessons: The Paris Review Presents the Art of the Short Story.* Ed. Lorin Stein and Sadie Stein. Picador, 2012.

Minot, Susan. "Hiding," from *Monkeys* by Susan Minot, copyright © 1986 by Susan Minot. Used by permission of Dutton, a division of Penguin Group (USA) Inc.

Moore, Dinty. "Son of Mr. Green Jeans: A Meditation on Missing Fathers." Reprinted from *Between Panic and Desire* by Dinty Moore by permission of the University of Nebraska Press.

Quote from Moore, Honor, *The Bishop's Daughter: A Memoir*. New York: W. W. Norton, 2008.

Morrison, Toni. "Peril." Reprinted by permission of International Creative Management, Inc. Copyright © 2009 by Toni Morrison. In *Burn This Book: PEN Writers Speak Out on the Power of the Word*, ed. Toni Morrison. New York: HarperStudio, 2009, pp. 1–4.

Moses, Itamar. "Men's Intuition" © 2003 by Itamar Moses. Reprinted by permission of Mark Christian Subias, United Talent Agency, on behalf of Itamar Moses. In *Take Ten II: More Ten-Minute Plays*, ed. Eric Lane and Nina Shengold. New York: Vintage, 2003.

Mueller, Lisel. "Spell for a Traveler" from *The Private Life: Poems* by Lisel Mueller. Copyright © 1976 by Lisel Mueller. Reprinted by permission of Louisiana State University Press.

Mullen, Harryette. "Tree" from *Blues Baby: Early Poems* by Harryette Mullen. Lewisburg, PA: Bucknell University Press, 2002, © Harryette Mullen. Reprinted by permission of the author.

Quote from Nabokov, Vladimir, *Speak, Memory*. 1951. New York: Vintage, reissue edition, 1989.

Quote from Nairn, Rob, *What Is Meditation? Buddhism for Everyone*. Boston: Shambhala, reprint edition, 2000.

Neruda, Pablo. "Your Feet" from *The Captain's Verses*, copyright © 1972 by Pablo Neruda and Donald D. Walsh. Reprinted by permission of New Directions Publishing Corp.

Quote from Novakovich, Josip, *The Fiction Writer's Workshop*. Story Press, 1995. Second edition Cincinnati, OH: F+W Writer's Digest Books, 2008.

Pathway 8.4 adapted from Oates, Joyce Carol, "Joyce Carol Oates: *The Gravedigger's Daughter*" at Book Passage, Corte Madera, CA, 7 June 2007. Reading and address. *ForaTV*. http://fora.tv/2007/06/07/Joyce_Carol_Oates_Gravedigger_s_Daughter

O'Brien, Tim. "How to Tell a True War Story" from *The Things They Carried* by Tim O'Brien. Copyright © 1990 by Tim O'Brien. Reprinted by permission of Houghton Mifflin Harcourt Publishing Company. All rights reserved.

Quotes from Flannery O'Connor, "The Nature and Aim of Fiction" in *Mystery and Manners: Occasional Prose*. Ed. Sally and Robert Fitzgerald. New York: Farrar, Straus & Giroux, 1962.

Offutt, Chris. "Out of the Woods." Reprinted with the permission of Simon & Schuster Publishing Group from *Out of the Woods* by Chris Offutt. Copyright © 1999 by Chris Offutt. All rights reserved.

Ortega, Julio. "Las Papas," translated by Regina Harrison. In *Sudden Fiction International: Sixty Short-Short Stories*, ed. Robert Shapard and James Thomas. New York: W. W. Norton, 1989. First published by *The Magazine of the Boston Globe*, as part of the PEN Syndicated Fiction Project. © Julio Ortega. Reprinted by permission of the author.

Ostriker, Alicia Suskin. "The Orange Cat" from *The Crack in Everything*, by Alicia Suskin Ostriker, © 1996. Reprinted by permission of the University of Pittsburgh Press.

Quote from Paley, Grace, "Conversation with My Father" from *The Collected Stories*. New York: Farrar, Straus and Giroux, 1994.

Palmer, Michael. "The Cord" from *Thread*, copyright © 2005, 2006, 2008, 2009, 2010, 2011 by Michael Palmer. Reprinted by permission of New Directions Publishing Corp.

Panning, Anne. "Remembering, I Was Not There" © 1999 by Anne Panning. Reprinted by permission of the author. In *In Brief: Short Takes on the Personal*, ed. Judith Kitchen and Mary Paumier Jones. New York: W. W. Norton, 1999.

Quote from Pink, Daniel, *A Whole New Mind: Why Right-Brainers Will Rule the Future*. New York: Riverhead Books, 2005.

Quote (Chapter 5) from Pinter, Harold, *Old Times*. London: Eyre Methuen, 1972.

Quote (Chapter 12) from Pinter, Harold, interviewed by Larry Bensky, "The Art of Theater No. 3," *The Paris Review* 39 (Fall 1966).

Quote from Poe, Edgar Allan, "The Fall of the House of Usher" in *The Collected Tales and Poems of Edgar Allan Poe*. New York: Modern Library, 1992. Originally published in 1839.

Poissant, David James. "The History of Flight" by David James Poissant, copyright © 2013. First appeared in *The Pinch*, the lit mag of the University of Memphis, Fall 2013. Used by permission of Brandt & Hochman Literary Agents, Inc. All rights reserved.

Quote from Pound, Ezra, *Make It New*. London: Faber, 1934; New Haven: Yale University Press, 1935.

Quote from Prose, Francine, *Reading Like a Writer: A Guide for People Who Love Books and for Those Who Want to Write Them*. New York: HarperCollins, 2006.

Quote from Proust, Marcel, *Swann's Way*, vol. 1 of *Remembrance of Things Past*. Tr. C. K. Moncrieff and Terence Kilmartin. New York: Random House, 1981. Originally published in the French, Paris: Grasset, 1913.

Description of *Psycho*. Dir. Alfred Hitchcock. Screenplay by Joseph Stefano. Paramount Pictures/Universal Pictures, 1960. Film.

Description of *Pulp Fiction*. Dir. Quentin Tarantino. Screenplay by Quentin Tarantino and Roger Avary. Miramax Films, 1994.

Purpura, Lia. "On Looking Away: A Panoramic" from *On Looking: Essays*. Copyright © 2006 by Lia Purpura. Reprinted with the permission of The Permissions Company, Inc., on behalf of Sarabande Books, www.sarabandebooks.org

Quote (Chapter 2) from Rushdie, Salman. *The Satanic Verses*. New York: Viking Penguin, 1989.

Quote (Chapter 15) from Rushdie, Salman, "Rushdie on Calvino's Absurd, Charming Masterpiece." *NPR Books* 19 September 2008. Web 3 March 2012.

Russell, Karen. "St. Lucy's Home for Girls Raised by Wolves" from *St. Lucy's Home for Girls Raised by Wolves: Stories* by Karen Russell, copyright © 2006 by Karen Russell. Used by permission of Alfred A. Knopf, an imprint of the Knopf Doubleday Publishing Group, a division of Random House LLC. All rights reserved. Any third party use of this material, outside of this publication, is prohibited. Interested parties must apply directly to Random House LLC for permission.

Quote from Sanders, Scott Russell, *Staying Put: Making a Home in a Restless World*. Boston: Beacon Press, 1993.

Sedaris, David. "The Drama Bug" from *Naked* by David Sedaris. Copyright © 1997 by David Sedaris. By permission of Little, Brown and Company. All rights reserved.

Quote from Shakespeare, William, *Romeo and Juliet*. Ed. Horace Howard Furness. Philadelphia: J. B. Lippincott & Co., 1871. *Google Books*. Web 27 June 2014.

Quote from Shange, Ntozake, interviewed by David Savran, in *The Playwright's Voice: American Dramatists on Memory, Writing and the Politics of Culture*. New York: Theatre Communications Group, 1999.

Shannon, Christopher. "Apollo (at) Eleven" © Christopher Shannon. Reprinted by permission of the author. Poem originally appeared in *32 Poems*, vol. 8.1, Spring 2010.

Quote from Shields, David, *Reality Hunger: A Manifesto*. New York: Vintage, 2011.

Pathway 3.11 adapted from Simmerman, Jim, "Twenty Little Projects" in *The Practice of Poetry: Writing Exercises from Poets Who Teach*. Ed. Robin Behn and Chase Twichell. New York: HarperCollins, 2001.

Smock, Frederick. "A Poet's Education," *Writer's Chronicle* 43.2 (October/November 2010), pp. 76–79. © 2010 by Frederick Smock. Reprinted by permission of the author. His recent book of poems is *The Bounteous World* (Broadstone Books).

Quote from Solotaroff, Ted, "Writing in the Cold." *Granta* 15 (Spring 1985). Reprinted in *A Few Good Voices in My Head: Occasional Pieces on Writing, Editing, and Reading My Contemporaries*. New York: Harper & Row, 1987.

Quote from Sondheim, Stephen, anonymous interview, "Master of the Musical." *Academy of Achievement* 5 July 2005. Web 26 August 2013.

Soto, Gary. "What the Federal Bailout Means to Me" from *Human Nature: Poems* by Gary Soto. Copyright © 2010 by Gary Soto. Reprinted by permission of Tupelo Press.

Quote from Spencer, Stuart, *The Playwright's Guidebook*. London: Faber & Faber, 2002.

Quote from Spiegelman, Art, *Maus I: A Survivor's Tale: My Father Bleeds History*. New York: Pantheon, 1991.

Quote from Stern, Jerome, *Making Shapely Fiction*. New York: W. W. Norton, 1991.

Stokesbury, Leon. "Unsent Message to My Brother in His Pain" from *Autumn Rhythm: New and Selected Poems*. Copyright © 1986 by Leon Stokesbury. Reprinted with the permission of The Permissions Company, Inc., on behalf of the University of Arkansas Press, www.uapress.com

Su, Adrienne. "Four Sonnets about Food" from *Middle Kingdom*. Copyright © 1997 by Adrienne Su. Reprinted with the permission of The Permissions Company, Inc., on behalf of Alice James Books, www.alicejamesbooks.org

Swain, Bara. "Critical Care" © 2008 by Bara Swain. Reprinted by permission of Bara Swain. For performance rights, contact author: BCSwain4@aol.com. In *2009: The Best 10-Minute Plays for 2 or More Actors*, ed. Lawrence Harbison. Hanover, NH: Smith and Kraus, 2009.

Quote from Swinburne, Algernon Charles, "Itylus" in *Poems and Ballads*, 1866. Reprinted in *Poems and Ballads and Atalanta in Calydon*. Ed. Kenneth Haynes. New York: Penguin, 2001.

Tate, James. "Miss Cho Composes in the Cafeteria" from *The Lost Pilot* by James Tate. Copyright © 1978 by James Tate. Reprinted by permission of HarperCollins Publishers.

Thompson, Craig. *Carnet de Voyage*. Top Shelf, 2004, pp. 148–149, 153–154, © Craig Thompson. Reprinted by permission of Top Shelf Productions.

Quote from Tolstoy, Leo, *Anna Karenina*. New York: Modern Library, 2000. Originally published in Russian in 1877.

Quote from Vonnegut, Kurt, interviewed by David Hayman, David Michaelis, George Plimpton, and Richard Rhodes, "The Art of Fiction No. 64." *Paris Review* 69 (Spring 1977).

Quote from Welty, Eudora, *One Writer's Beginnings*. Cambridge, MA: Harvard University Press, 1984.

West, Amber. "Pirate's Admonition" © Amber West. Used by permission of the author.

Williams, William Carlos. "Young Sycamore" from *The Collected Poems: Volume I, 1909–1939*, copyright © 1938 by New Directions Publishing Corp. Reprinted by permission of New Directions Publishing Corp.

Wojahn, David. "Gold Glow: Icehouses" from *Icehouse Lights* by David Wojahn. Copyright © 1982 by David Wojahn. Reprinted by permission of Yale University Press.

Quote from Wright, Michael, *Playwriting in Process*, 2nd edition. Newburyport, MA: Focus Publishing/R. Pullins, 2009.

Young, Al. "A Little More Traveling Music" from *The Blues Don't Change: New and Selected Poems* by Al Young. Copyright © 1982 by Al Young. Reprinted by permission of Louisiana State University Press.

Quote from Young, Dean, *The Art of Recklessness: Poetry as Assertive Force and Contradiction*. Minneapolis: Graywolf Press, 2010.

Study by Wadhwa, Vivek, reported in his article, "The Leaders of Silicon Valley" in *The New York Times* 3 August 2011. Web 30 June 2014.

Zolynas, Al. "Love in the Classroom" © Al Zolynas. Reprinted by permission of the author. In *A Book of Luminous Things: An International Anthology of Poetry*, ed. Czeslaw Milosz. New York: Harcourt Brace, 1996.

Index